West's
Criminal Justice Series

WEST PUBLISHING COMPANY

St. Paul, Minnesota 55102

February 1980

CONSTITUTIONAL LAW

Cases and Comments on Constitutional Law 2nd Edition by James L. Maddex, Professor of Criminal Justice, Georgia State University, 486 pages, 1979.

CORRECTIONS

Corrections—Organization and Administration by Henry Burns, Jr., Professor of Criminal Justice, University of Missouri–St. Louis, 578 pages, 1975.

Legal Rights of the Convicted by Hazel B. Kerper, Late Professor of Sociology and Criminal Law, Sam Houston State University and Janeen Kerper, Attorney, San Diego, Calif., 677 pages, 1974.

Selected Readings on Corrections in the Community 2nd Edition by George G. Killinger, Member, Board of Pardons and Paroles, Texas and Paul F. Cromwell, Jr., Director of Juvenile Services, Tarrant County, Texas, 357 pages, 1978.

Readings on Penology—The Evolution of Corrections in America 2nd Edition by George G. Killinger, Paul F. Cromwell, Jr., and Jerry M. Wood, 350 pages, 1979.

Selected Readings on Introduction to Corrections by George G. Killinger and Paul F. Cromwell, Jr., 417 pages, 1978.

Selected Readings on Issues in Corrections and Administration by George G. Killinger, Paul F. Cromwell, Jr., and Bonnie J. Cromwell, San Antonio College, 644 pages, 1976.

Probation and Parole in the Criminal Justice System by George G. Killinger, Hazel B. Kerper and Paul F. Cromwell, Jr., 374 pages, 1976.

Introduction to Probation and Parole 2nd Edition by Alexander B. Smith, Professor of Sociology, John Jay College of Criminal Justice and Louis Berlin, Formerly Chief of Training Branch, New York City Dept. of Probation, 270 pages, 1979.

CRIMINAL JUSTICE SYSTEM

Fundamentals of Law Enforcement by V. A. Leonard, 350 pages, 1980.

Administration of Justice: Principles and Procedures by Garrith D. Perrine, Professor of Administration of Justice, Shasta College, Redding, California, 300 pages, 1980.

Introduction to the Criminal Justice System 2nd Edition by Hazel B. Kerper as revised by Jerold H. Israel, 520 pages, 1979.

Introduction to Criminal Justice by Joseph J. Senna and Larry J. Siegel, both Professors of Criminal Justice, Northeastern University, 540 pages, 1978.

CRIMINAL JUSTICE SYSTEM—Continued

Study Guide to accompany Senna and Siegel's Introduction to Criminal Justice by Roy R. Roberg, Professor of Criminal Justice, University of Nebraska–Lincoln, 187 pages, 1978.

Introduction to Law Enforcement and Criminal Justice by Henry M. Wrobleski and Karen M. Hess, both Professors at Normandale Community College, Bloomington, Minnesota, 525 pages, 1979.

CRIMINAL LAW

California Law Manual for the Administration of Justice by Joel Greenfield, Sacramento City College and Rodney Blonien, Executive Director, California State Peace Officers' Association, 800 pages, 1979.

Basic Criminal Law: Cases and Materials 2nd Edition by George E. Dix, Professor of Law, University of Texas, and M. Michael Sharlot, Professor of Law, University of Texas, 600 pages, 1980.

Readings, on Concepts of Criminal Law by Robert W. Ferguson, Administration of Justice Dept. Director, Saddleback College, 560 pages, 1975.

Criminal Law 2nd Edition by Thomas J. Gardner, Professor of Criminal Justice, Milwaukee Area Technical College and Victor Manian, Milwaukee County Judge, about 600 pages, 1980.

Principles of Criminal Law by Wayne R. LaFave, Professor of Law, University of Illinois, 650 pages, 1978.

CRIMINAL PROCEDURE

Teaching Materials on Criminal Procedure by Jerry L. Dowling, Professor of Criminal Justice, Sam Houston State University, 544 pages, 1976.

Criminal Procedure for the Law Enforcement Officer 2nd Edition by John N. Ferdico, Assistant Attorney General, State of Maine, 409 pages, 1979.

Cases, Materials and Text on the Elements of Criminal Due Process by Phillip E. Johnson, Professor of Law, University of California, Berkeley, 324 pages, 1975.

Cases, Comments and Questions on Basic Criminal Procedure 4th Edition by Yale Kamisar, Professor of Law, University of Michigan, Wayne R. LaFave, Professor of Law, University of Illinois and Jerold H. Israel, Professor of Law, University of Michigan, 790 pages, 1974. Supplement Annually.

EVIDENCE

Criminal Evidence by Thomas J. Gardner, Professor of Criminal Justice, Milwaukee Area Technical College, 694 pages, 1978.

Criminal Evidence by Edward J. Imwinkelried, Professor of Law, University of San Diego; Paul C. Giannelli, Associate Professor, Case Western Reserve University; Francis A. Gilligan, Adjunct Professor, Jacksonville State University; Fredric I. Lederer, Associate Professor, Judge Advocate General's School, U.S. Army, 425 pages, 1979.

Law of Evidence for Police 2nd Edition by Irving J. Klein, Professor of Law and Police Science, John Jay College of Criminal Justice, 632 pages, 1978.

Criminal Investigation and Presentation of Evidence by Arnold Markle, The State's Attorney, New Haven County, Connecticut, 344 pages, 1976.

INTRODUCTION TO LAW ENFORCEMENT

The American Police—Text and Readings by Harry W. More, Jr., Professor of Administration of Justice, California State University of San Jose, 278 pages, 1976.

INTRODUCTION TO LAW ENFORCEMENT—Continued

Police Tactics in Hazardous Situations by the San Diego, California Police Department, 228 pages, 1976.

Law Enforcement Handbook for Police by Louis B. Schwartz, Professor of Law, University of Pennsylvania and Stephen R. Goldstein, Professor of Law, University of Pennsylvania, 333 pages, 1970.

Police Operations—Tactical Approaches to Crimes in Progress by Inspector Andrew Sutor, Philadelphia, Pennsylvania Police Department, 329 pages, 1976.

Introduction to Law Enforcement and Criminal Justice by Henry Wrobleski and Karen M. Hess, both Professors at Normandale Community College, Bloomington, Minnesota, 525 pages, 1979.

JUVENILE JUSTICE

Text and Selected Readings on Introduction to Juvenile Delinquency by Paul F. Cromwell, Jr., George G. Killinger, Rosemary C. Sarri, Professor, School of Social Work, The University of Michigan and H. N. Solomon, Professor of Criminal Justice, Nova University, 502 pages, 1978.

Juvenile Justice Philosophy: Readings, Cases and Comments 2nd Edition by Frederic L. Faust, Professor of Criminology, Florida State University and Paul J. Brantingham, Department of Criminology, Simon Fraser University, 467 pages, 1979.

Introduction to the Juvenile Justice System by Thomas A. Johnson, Professor of Criminal Justice, Washington State University, 492 pages, 1975.

Cases and Comments on Juvenile Law by Joseph J. Senna, Professor of Criminal Justice, Northeastern, University and Larry J. Siegel, Professor of Criminal Justice, Northeastern University, 543 pages, 1976.

MANAGEMENT AND SUPERVISION

Selected Readings on Managing the Police Organization by Larry K. Gaines and Truett A. Ricks, both Professors of Criminal Justice, Eastern Kentucky University, 527 pages, 1978.

Criminal Justice Management: Text and Readings by Harry W. More, Jr., 377 pages, 1977.

Effective Police Administration: A Behavioral Approach 2nd Edition by Harry W. More, Jr., Professor, San Jose State University, 360 pages, 1979.

Police Management and Organizational Behavior: A Contingency Approach by Roy R. Roberg, Professor of Criminal Justice, University of Nebraska at Omaha, 350 pages, 1979.

Police Administration and Management by Sam S. Souryal, Professor of Criminal Justice, Sam Houston State University, 462 pages, 1977.

Law Enforcement Supervision—A Case Study Approach by Robert C. Wadman, Rio Hondo Community College, Monroe J. Paxman, Brigham Young University and Marion T. Bentley, Utah State University, 224 pages, 1975.

POLICE—COMMUNITY RELATIONS

Readings on Police—Community Relations 2nd Edition by Paul F. Cromwell, Jr., and George Keefer, Professor of Criminal Justice, Southwest Texas State University, 506 pages, 1978.

PSYCHOLOGY

Interpersonal Psychology for Law Enforcement and Corrections by L. Craig Parker, Jr., Criminal Justice Dept. Director, University of New Haven and Robert D. Meier, Professor of Criminal Justice, University of New Haven, 290 pages, 1975.

VICE CONTROL

The Nature of Vice Control in the Administration of Justice by Robert W. Ferguson, 509 pages, 1974.

Cases, Text and Materials on Drug Abuse Law by Gerald F. Uelman, Professor of Law, Loyola University, Los Angeles and Victor G. Haddox, Professor of Criminology, California State University at Long Beach and Clinical Professor of Psychiatry, Law and Behavioral Sciences, University of Southern California School of Medicine, 564 pages, 1974.

BASIC CRIMINAL LAW

CASES AND MATERIALS

SECOND EDITION

By

GEORGE E. DIX
Professor of Law, University of Texas

M. MICHAEL SHARLOT
Wright C. Morrow Professor of Criminal Law,
University of Texas

CRIMINAL JUSTICE SERIES

ST. PAUL • NEW YORK • LOS ANGELES • SAN FRANCISCO
WEST PUBLISHING CO.
1980

50 West Kellogg Boulevard
P.O.Box 3526
St. Paul, Minnesota 55165

Printed in the United States of America

Library of Congress Cataloging in Publication Data

Dix, George E
Basic criminal law.
Includes bibliographical references and index.

1. Criminal law—United States—Cases. I. Sharlot, M. Michael, joint author. II. Title.

KF9218.D5 1980 345.73 80-449

ISBN 0-8299-0318-6

1st Reprint—1981

PREFACE TO THE SECOND EDITION

Substantive criminal law deserves careful attention for several reasons. It is, of course, important because it affects the decision to intrude into the lives of numerous persons in an exceptionally significant way—by convicting them of a criminal offense. But in addition, it is a unique vehicle for examination of the great questions of the relationship of the individual to the state. The goals of the criminal law and the unending debate over how they may best be achieved and at what cost to the values of our society should be part of the intellectual life of every thinking citizen. Thus something more than an inquiry into the law of crimes is essential to any meaningful criminal law course.

This volume is designed to facilitate the presentation of a course that serves two purposes. The materials contained in it provide the opportunity to address the traditional problems presented by the definition and application of substantive crimes and defenses to criminal liability as well as more modern statutory offenses and defenses. But, in addition, it permits inquiry into the broader issues involved in the decision to employ the state's ultimate sanction to coerce conduct. In our view, a meaningful criminal law course must consider both of these purposes.

Chapter 1, the introductory portion, deals with the general framework of the criminal law. It contains coverage of the procedure for processing a criminal case, the basic presumption of innocence, and penalty structures. Chapter 2 presents textual readings on the nature of criminal liability and functions of and justifications for criminal punishment. In addition, it contains material relating to three basic legal limitations upon criminalization. These two chapters are designed to enrich the students' understanding of the broader issues which underlie the materials dealing with the general principles and the specific offenses of the criminal law.

Chapters 3 through 8 present the substantive criminal law. Chapter 3 addresses general principles of criminal liability; this is of special importance, given the extent to which modern criminal codes create "new" crimes and define their elements in a statutory framework significantly different from the traditional common law criminal law. The chapter emphasizes the general requirement of an "act" for liability and the need to carefully define the "intent" or state of mind required by each crime. Several "defenses" that actually consist of challenging the adequacy of proof of intent—mistake, ignorance, and intoxication—are also presented here; some teachers may conclude that these are best covered in connection with the other "defenses" in Chapter 8. Complicity—the modern equivalent of the law of "parties"—liability of organizations, and vicarious liability are also presented in this chapter, as are questions of "causation." Since causation issues arise most frequently in homicide situations, some teachers may want to postpone discussion of this material until after coverage of the homicide crimes.

Chapter 4 covers the inchoate (or "preparatory") crimes of attempt, solicitation, and conspiracy, as well as "defenses" which are unique to these forms of liability. Sections 5 through 7 deal with specific offenses. We have, often in introductory or textual notes, attempted to make clear the traditional "black letter" rules, and to highlight the major issues presented by the materials in the particular section. These should prove of aid to the student. The cases have been selected with a view towards illustrating, in interesting factual situations, contemporary application of the crimes and the modern definitions of those offenses.

Chapter 8 deals with "defenses" in the strict sense, i.e., matters that consist not of a challenge to the adequacy of proof of elements of the offense charged but rather of offered justification or excuse.

We hope that we have provided a vehicle that will be attractive to those who wish to offer a treatment of the law of crimes without sacrificing coverage of the broad general issues of substantive criminal law of criminalization as a societal response to deviance. We express our appreciation to the numerous authors and publishers who have given us permission to reproduce their materials in this volume. A special note of gratitude must go to the American Law Institute, which kindly granted permission to reprint extensive portions of the copyrighted Model Penal Code and its various tentative drafts. In editing the material, we have left out citations and footnotes without any specific indications of such omissions. Footnotes retained from the original material are indicated by numbers; we have not renumbered retained footnotes. Footnotes indicated by letters are those we have inserted.

Students who wish guidance as to outside reading that may enrich or clarify sections of the book would be well advised to refer to the hornbook, Handbook on Criminal Law, published in 1972 by Professor Wayne R. LaFave and the late Professor Austin W. Scott, Jr. Professor George P. Fletcher's provocative book, Rethinking Criminal Law, published in 1978, is quite useful as well. Also of significant aid are the two volumes of Working Papers of the National Commission on Reform of the Federal Criminal Laws, published in 1970. Somewhat older but more elaborate and by no means outdated is the commentary contained in the tentative drafts of the American Law Institute's Model Penal Code. The best single source of information about the actual operation of the criminal justice system and recommendations for its improvement is The Challenge of Crime in a Free Society, A Report by the President's Commission on Law Enforcement and Administration of Justice, published in 1967, and the many Task Force Reports produced by the Commission. Finally, no finer overview of the problems of the criminal law exists than the late professor Herbert Packer's short volume, The Limits of the Criminal Sanction, published in 1968.

G.E.D.
M.M.S.

Austin, Texas
September, 1979

*

SUMMARY OF CONTENTS

SUMMARY OF CONTENTS

SUMMARY OF CONTENTS

TABLE OF CONTENTS

TABLE OF CONTENTS

*

TABLE OF CASES

The principal cases are in italic type. Cases cited or discussed are in roman type. References are to Pages.

TABLE OF CASES

TABLE OF CASES

TABLE OF CASES

*

REFERENCES TO THE PROPOSED FEDERAL CRIMINAL CODE

*

REFERENCES TO THE MODEL PENAL CODE

REFERENCES TO THE MODEL PENAL CODE

BASIC CRIMINAL LAW

CASES AND MATERIALS

I. INTRODUCTION

A. LAW, CRIMINAL LITIGATION, AND CASE SELECTION

Some students using this book are probably about to experience their first contact with legal materials. Preliminary explanations concerning the sources of law in general and the specific materials—especially appellate court opinions—included in this book might therefore be useful in enabling students to derive maximum benefit from the book and courses taught with it.

Sources of Law

There are three different sources of law that our secular legal system draws upon, and consequently three different "kinds" of law. Substantive criminal law draws from all three sources and therefore embodies all three kinds of law.

The first source of law consists of constitutions, both the United States Constitution and the constitutions of the individual states. These constitutions, of course, by their nature are supreme over the other kinds of law, and in the event of a conflict, constitutional rules must dominate over others. Similarly, the federal Constitution is dominant over state law as well as over nonconstitutional federal law. If a rule of federal constitutional law conflicts with a rule of state law—whether that state rule is of constitutional dimensions or not—the federal constitutional rule must be followed.

The second source of law is the "common law." Common law is the law developed by courts through the process of resolving particular cases. As more and more cases are decided, underlying rationales or rules appear and these rules constitute the common law. In some strict usages, common law means court-made rules in effect as of a specific time, such as the date of the adoption of the federal Constitution. But for most purposes, common law is best regarded as "judge-made" law.

The third source consists of legislatures. Law from this source is, of course, embodied in statutes. For the substantive criminal law, this type of law is often most important, because all American jurisdictions have extensive statutes dealing with crimes and criminal law. Not infrequently, however, these statutes are intended to merely restate the definition of crimes or defenses developed in judge-made law and consequently the full meaning of the statutes can only be discerned by study of the cases in light of which the statutes were passed.

This tripartite division often breaks down in practice, and the three types of law become interrelated. Although crimes are almost always defined by statute, for example, these statutes quite frequently contain ambiguities that must be resolved through litigation. In many states, moreover, legislation covering substantive criminal law contains gaps, especially regarding defenses to crimes. These gaps are often filled by judicial decisions, sometimes creating or recognizing defenses not provided for in the jurisdiction's statutes.

Constitutional law affects substantive criminal law in several ways. Sometimes it is reasonably clear that a certain interpretation of a statute defining a crime would make the statute unconstitutional. In such cases, courts will frequently assume that the legislature did not intend to enact an unconstitutional statute and will reject the interpretation of the statute that would render it invalid. Sometimes, of course, unconstitutionality cannot be avoided by a judicial interpretation of a statute relating to substantive criminal law and a statute must be held unconstitutional. Since constitutional considerations render such statutes invalid and thus of no effect, constitutional law can be said to sometimes have a very direct effect upon substantive criminal law. In Papachristou v. Jacksonville (page 117), for example, the United States Supreme Court held that the Jacksonville vagrancy ordinance was unconstitutionally vague and therefore could not be enforced. In other situations, the courts will stop short of holding a statute entirely unconstitutional but will hold that particular defendants cannot constitutionally be convicted under it because to do so would violate their constitutional rights. In Ravin v. State (page 87), the Alaska Supreme Court held that while the state statute prohibiting possession of marijuana was not unconstitutional, Ravin's right of privacy prevented him from being convicted under the statute on the basis of possession of marijuana, for personal use, in his home.

Model Penal Code

Throughout these materials, provisions of the Model Penal Code have been included. This document was drafted by a committee of the American Law Institute, an organization composed of leading legal scholars that formulates proposed legislation dealing with a variety of subjects. A number of preliminary—or "tentative"—drafts were prepared and the positions taken in these drafts were supported by extensive commentary. These were then discussed by the Institute and, in some cases, modified. The final document, from which most of the material in this book is taken, is the Proposed Official Draft (abbreviated P.O.D.), the culmination of the Institute's efforts, which was finished in 1962. Sometimes reference back to the earlier drafts is useful, however, especially for purposes of examining the explanations and commentary. The section of this book on insanity, for example, includes the version of the insanity defense offensc offered in the fourth tentative draft of the Code and some of the explanatory comment to that proposal (page 610); it also includes the section of the Proposed Official Draft dealing with the same subject (page 613).

The provisions of the Model Penal Code are included in this book for several related reasons. First, in some areas the Institute decided to merely embody existing present law in the Code. Provisions reflecting this approach are often useful as skillful restatements of what is—or was as of 1962—the "majority approach" of the law to various areas. Second, the positions taken in the Code sometimes reflect the views of a respected institution advised by excellent scholars concerning what should be the law in a number of areas covered by this book. Consequently, the "Model Penal Code approach" deserves consideration as a potentially desirable approach when it does not reflect existing law. The Code's formulation of the defense of duress (see page 518), for example, is substantially broader than the traditional common law defense of duress. The section of this book on duress includes a discussion of a New Jersey case, State v. Toscano (see page 517), in which the court finds the approach suggested by the Model Penal Code more desirable than the traditional one and adopts the Model Penal Code approach as the law of New Jersey in regard to duress. Third, the Code has been very influential in the numerous statutory revisions that have taken place in the criminal law since 1962. Consequently, the Model Penal Code often is consistent with modern statutory law and therefore illustrates positions frequently taken in state legislation, especially where that legislation has changed the law.

Selecting Cases for Inclusion in the Materials

This book is designed for teaching by means of the "case method." While techniques used by teachers differ significantly, most instructors using the case method organize class discussion around the principal cases in the teaching materials. Discussion often involves identifying the issue or issues in the case, understanding the resolution of them by the court that authored the opinion, and perhaps consideration of other ways in which the issues might have been resolved. Principal cases are not selected for inclusion in the book because they necessarily state the only, best, or even majority view of the law or because they apply the law correctly or well to the facts. Rather, they are selected because they will serve effectively as the basis for discussion. This may be because the court's discussion is unusually informative, because the facts present a unique or otherwise interesting opportunity to discuss how the law should be applied to them, or even because the case arguably was wrongly decided so that discussion would be useful.

If the members of the court were divided on how to decide the case, the opinions of the dissenting judges (who would have resolved the case differently than the majority of the members of the court voted to do) are sometimes included. It is important to understand the arguments both ways on the issues presented, and consideration of such dissenting opinions is often helpful in this regard. Sometimes an opinion is included in the materials even though the case was appealed further and the opinion printed is therefore not the final disposition of the case. The opinion in People v. Ball (page 596), in the section of the defense of "domestic authority," was written by the intermediate Illinois appellate court. (The distinction between "intermediate" and other appellate courts is explained later in this note.) As the note following the case indicates, the case was appealed further to the Illinois Supreme Court, where the decision printed in the materials was reversed. The intermediate appellate court's opinion (and that of the judge who dissented in that court) was included, however, because it appears to present the most effective discussion of the issues. In preparing for class, students would generally be well advised to read the materials—and especially the principal cases—keeping in mind the reasons for their inclusion in the book.

Substantive Criminal Law and the Processing of a Criminal Case

Because of the extensive use of cases in this book, it is helpful for students to have an understanding of the way in which substantive criminal law issues arise in litigation and how these issues become embodied in written opinions of the sort used in these materials. In a criminal case, the substantive criminal law is important at several points. The charge (the indictment, information, or complaint), of course, must allege conduct that constitutes a crime under the law of the jurisdiction. A defendant might challenge an indictment on the ground that under the applicable law, the actions charged in the indictment do not constitute a criminal offense. In a burglary case, for example, an indictment which fails to allege that the person charged entered the structure with the intent of committing a crime in it might be challenged on the ground that it fails to allege what under the applicable substantive criminal law is one element of the crime of burglary.

Once a case goes to trial, the admissibility of evidence may be affected by the substantive criminal law. If, for example, the defense offers evidence that it believes might persuade a jury to acquit the defendant, the prosecution might object on the ground that the evidence is not, under the applicable law, relevant. The judge should admit the evidence only if, given the definition of the crime charged, the evidence tends to show that one element of the crime has not been proven (for example, in a burglary case that the defendant did not have the intent to commit a crime when he entered the premises) or if it tends to establish a defense that the substantive criminal law makes available to defendants in the jurisdiction (for example, that the defendant committed the burglary while insane). In State v. Sikora, contained in the section on diminished capacity (page 640) the question addressed by the court is whether, given the meaning of the diminished capacity rule in New Jersey, the trial judge was required to let the defendant ask a specific defense psychiatrist whether in his opinion the defendant was capable of premeditating a murder.

Arguments made by the lawyers to the jury are generally limited to those matters addressed by the substantive law applicable to the case. So the substantive law may affect the arguments that can be made. In United States v. Berrigan, contained in the section ignorance or mistake of law as a "defense" (page 195), the issue presented to the trial judge was whether defense counsel should be permitted to argue to the jury that the defendants should be acquitted of crimes committed in antiwar activities because the Vietnamese conflict was immoral and illegal. The court's decision on this issue turned upon whether, given the applicable law, the illegality or immorality of the war was a defense to the crimes charged.

Perhaps most important, the substantive law is relevant to the trial judge's instructions to the jury. The judge must correctly define the crime with which the defendant is charged and must accurately describe any defenses which might be available to the defendant, given the evidence produced at trial and the substantive law in the jurisdiction. In a burglary case, for example, the judge must not only tell the jury what the elements of the crime of burglary are but he must also define them. "Entry" may require lengthy explanatory instructions. Of course, these same substantive law matters are important when the jury—or the judge, if the defendant waives trial by jury and the case is tried without a jury—considers whether the evidence proves the defendant guilty and, if so, whether it also establishes any defense to the crime. Trial judges only infrequently write opinions explaining their decisions and even those written are generally not published. These materials contain several trial judges' opinions, however. State v. Brown (page 589), in the section on the possible defense of "consent," was written by a trial judge explaining his decision to hold the defendant guilty of assault and battery despite evidence that the victim consented to the defendant's actions. United State v. Pollard, in the section on insanity (page 613), was written by a trial judge to explain why, despite defense evidence that the defendant was mentally ill at the time of the crime, he nevertheless rejected the insanity defense and found the defendant guilty.

Three aspects of trial practice deserve special mention. A trial judge is not required to instruct a jury concerning all matters—such as possible defenses—that are theoretically available to a defendant. Rather, instructions regarding such matters are necessary only if the evidence produced at trial creates a possibility that the jury might find some reasonable basis for considering the matter. This applies not only to possible defenses but also to other offenses, less serious than the crime charged, of which the defendant might be convicted at trial. This rule is sometimes stated as one which requires a trial judge to instruct the jury only on those matters "raised by the evidence." An example of the application of this rule would arise in a murder case in which the defendant asks the judge to instruct the jury on the defense of self defense and the definition of voluntary manslaughter. In deciding whether to give such instructions, the judge should not attempt to decide for himself whether the defendant is guilty of only manslaughter; such a conviction would be appropriate if the evidence shows that the defendant killed the victim but also that the killing was caused by "adequate provocation"; see pages 492, 499. Nor should he decide for himself whether the defendant should be acquitted because of self defense. On the other hand, the judge need not give the jury such instructions simply because some murder defendants are guilty of only involuntary manslaughter or are acquitted because of self defense. His proper function is to examine the evidence produced in the case before him and determine whether there is sufficient evidence from which it is conceivable that a conscientious jury might find adequate provocation or self defense. If such evidence exists—if either matter is "raised by the evidence"—he should instruct the jury regarding the matter.

Another important aspect of trial practice concerns a defendant's most basic trial motion, the motion for a directed verdict of acquittal. (Various other names are used for this motion in some jurisdictions, such as motions for "nonsuit," but the function is the same whatever the label.) This is a request that the trial judge find that the evidence against a defendant is so weak that it is unnecessary to have the jury even consider it. A judge who grants such a motion in effect is saying that no reasonable jury could conceivably convict the defendant on the evidence produced, so there is no need to go through the process of having the jury consider the matter. If the trial judge grants such a motion, the defendant is acquitted and under double jeopardy principles can never be tried for the offense again. Consequently, there is widespread agreement that motions for directed verdicts should be only sparingly granted. If there is any reasonable possibility that a jury could properly find the defendant guilty, the trial judge should deny a defense motion for a directed verdict and let the jury resolve the question of the defendant's guilt or innocence.

Related to this are procedural opportunities available to defendants after juries have convicted them. In virtually all jurisdictions, a convicted defendant is entitled to make a motion for new trial on the ground that the evidence introduced at trial is not sufficient to support the jury's determination that he is guilty. If such a motion is granted, of course, the defendant is not acquitted but is rather entitled to another opportunity, in a new trial, to convince a jury that the prosecution's evidence is not sufficient for conviction.

All of these procedural matters involve consideration of the substantive criminal law. In deciding whether a matter is raised by the evidence and therefore requires a jury instruction, whether the evidence is so inadequate that a reasonable jury could not convict, and whether a jury verdict should be overturned after it has been returned, the trial judge must determine the applicable substantive law and apply that law to the evidence produced by the parties to the lawsuit.

Most of the opinions in this book are appellate court opinions. This means that they were written by judges sitting on a court that does not hear the trial of cases but rather reviews trials to determine whether any serious errors were made in them. The substantive criminal law is relevant to the task of these appellate courts as well, but the issues which they confront are somewhat different from those posed to trial courts. Appellate courts do not decide whether defendants are guilty of the crimes charged. Rather, they review specific decisions and rulings by the trial judge. If a trial judge has excluded evidence offered by the defense, for example, the appellate court has to decide whether the ruling was correct; this often requires the court to determine what the applicable substantive criminal law is and whether the offered evidence was relevant to any issues presented by the law. A defendant may argue on appeal that the trial judge erred in instructing the jury; to resolve such an issue, the appellate court must decide what the applicable law is and, when this has been determined, whether the instructions accurately and fully told the jury about this law. Many of the cases in these materials involve appeals by defendants who claim that in their trials the juries were not adequately informed of the law applicable to the case.

Appellate courts are often asked to decide whether the evidence produced at trial supports defendants' convictions. Procedurally, this may be done by several methods. One is for a defendant to urge that the trial judge erred in refusing to grant the defense motion for a directed verdict of acquittal. In State v. Roberts, contained in the section on assault (page 413), for example, the error which the defendant claimed was committed by the trial judge was the refusal to grant the defense motion for "nonsuit;" as was discussed above, a motion for nonsuit is the same as a motion for a directed verdict of acquittal. Another method is to assert that the trial judge committed error by refusing to grant the defense motions (made after the jury verdict) for a new trial. In Thacker v. Commonwealth, in the section on attempts (page 291), for example, the defendant's appeal is based upon an alleged error by the trial judge in refusing to "set aside the verdict [of conviction] as contrary to the law and the evidence." Whatever the procedural route, the underlying defense argument is that the evidence produced at trial failed to prove guilt beyond a reasonable doubt.

In addressing these matters, the appellate court does not put itself in the position of the jurors and consider whether it would have convicted the defendant had it been the jury. Rather, it considers whether there is substantial evidence to support a conviction, and reverses the conviction for insufficient evidence only if it finds no substantial evidence supporting the trial court's decision that the defendant is guilty. An appellate court may well find that there is sufficient evidence to support a conviction even though the judges on that court would each have voted for acquittal had they been jurors in the case.

There are several procedural aspects of appellate review of the sufficiency of evidence in criminal cases that appear in a number of the cases used in these materials. If the evidence is conflicting, the appellate court will usually not consider which version of the facts should be believed; this rule is often stated as requiring the appellate court to leave the credibility of the witnesses or the evidence to the trial jury or judge. Another way courts often express the same approach is to apply a rule that the evidence produced at trial will be considered by the appellate court in the light most favorable to the prosecution. In other words, the appellate court will first assume that the jury resolved all of the conflicts in the evidence in favor of the prosecution; then, assuming that all of the prosecution's evidence—even where contradicted by defense evidence—should be believed, the appellate court considers whether this evidence proves the defendant's guilt beyond a reasonable doubt.

Another important aspect of appellate review is the rule that trial judges have a great deal of discretion in deciding whether to grant directed verdicts or new trials on the ground of insufficient evidence. Under this rule, a defendant who appeals on the ground that the trial judge erred in refusing to direct a verdict or grant a new trial has a very heavy burden. It is not enough that the defendant convinces the judges on the appellate court that they would have ruled for the defense if they had been the trial judge. Rather, the appellate court must be convinced that the trial judge's decision to rule against the defense was so wrong that it was unreasonable; the trial judge's action must, in the language of the courts, have been so incorrect as to constitute an abuse of discretion.

Some jurisdictions have two levels of appellate courts, and consequently the process by which a conviction is reviewed on appeal may become quite complex. In such jurisdictions, the first appellate court to which a convicted defendant must appeal is regarded as the "intermediate" appellate court, although the specific title of the court varies among states. The second appellate court, which often is authorized to consider an appeal only if it wants to do so, is the highest appellate court in the jurisdiction. Usually, this court is the state

Supreme Court; the most notable exception is New York, in which the trial court is called the Supreme Court, the intermediate court is called the Supreme Court, Appellate Division, and the highest appellate court is called the Court of Appeals. North Carolina is one such jurisdiction whose two-tier appellate process is demonstrated in the cases used in this book. State v. Carswell, contained in the section of materials on larceny (page 360), for example, involved a defendant convicted in a North Carolina trial court. On appeal, the North Carolina Court of Appeals, the intermediate appellate court, reversed the conviction. But the case was then appealed to the highest state appellate court, the North Carolina Supreme Court. The decision of the state Supreme Court, which is contained in these materials, reversed the decision of the intermediate appellate court; this had the effect of reinstating the decision of the trial judge to let the defendant's conviction by the jury stand.

It is important in reading the cases contained in this book to remember that appellate courts' tasks are often more restricted ones than those performed by trial courts. These tasks still require the appellate court to determine the substantive law defining the offense of which the defendant was convicted and any defenses raised by the evidence, and to apply that law to the facts of the case. While both trial and appellate courts address issues relevant to substantive law, however, the primary task of deciding whether the evidence shows the defendant guilty or not lies with the trial jury or trial judge, and written explanations of these decisions are seldom available.

B. ASCERTAINMENT OF GUILT: THE INSTITUTIONAL FRAMEWORK

PRESIDENT'S COMMISSION ON LAW ENFORCEMENT AND ADMINISTRATION OF JUSTICE, THE CHALLENGE OF CRIME IN A FREE SOCIETY

7–12 (1967).

AMERICA'S SYSTEM OF CRIMINAL JUSTICE

* * *

The criminal justice system has three separately organized parts—the police, the courts, and corrections—and each has distinct tasks. However, these parts are by no means independent of each other. What each one does and how it does it has a direct effect on the work of the others. The courts must deal, and can only deal, with those whom the police arrest; the business of corrections is with those delivered to it by the courts. How successfully corrections reforms convicts determines whether they will once again become police business and influences the sentences the judges pass; police activities are subject to court scrutiny and are often determined by court decisions.

And so reforming or reorganizing any part or procedure of the system changes other parts or procedures. Furthermore, the criminal process, the method by which the system deals with individual cases, is not a hodgepodge of random actions. It is rather a continuum—an orderly progression of events—some of which, like arrest and trial, are highly visible and some of which, though of great importance, occur out of public view. A study of the system must begin by examining it as a whole.

The chart below sets forth in simplified form the process of criminal administration and shows the many decision points along its

A general view of The Criminal Justice System

This chart seeks to present a simple yet comprehensive view of the movement of cases through the criminal justice system. Procedures in individual jurisdictions may vary from the pattern shown here. The differing weights of line indicate the relative volumes of cases disposed of at various points in the system, but this is only suggestive since no nationwide data of this sort exists.

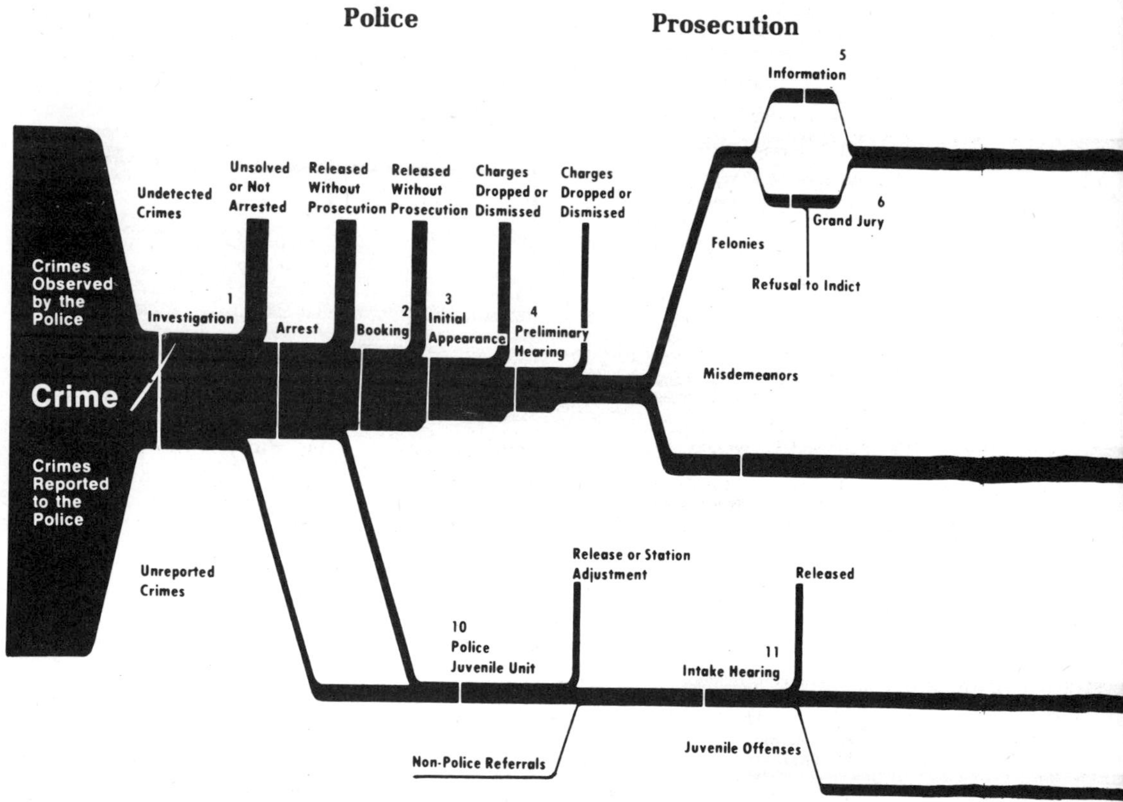

1. May continue until trial.

2. Administrative record of arrest. First step at which temporary release on bail may be available.

3. Before magistrate, commissioner, or justice of peace. Formal notice of charge, advice of rights. Bail set. Summary trials for petty offenses usually conducted here without further processing.

4. Preliminary testing of evidence against defendant. Charge may be reduced. No separate preliminary hearing for misdemeanors in some systems.

5. Charge filed by prosecutor on basis of information submitted by police or citizens. Alternative to grand jury indictment.

6. Reviews whether Government evidence sufficient to justify trial. Some States have no grand jury system; others seldom use it.

[C1147]

course. Since felonies, misdemeanors, petty offenses, and juvenile cases generally follow quite different paths, they are shown separately.

The popular, or even the lawbook, theory of everyday criminal process oversimplifies in some respects and overcomplicates in others what usually happens. That theory is that when an infraction of the law occurs, a policeman finds, if he can, the probable offender, arrests him and brings him promptly before a magistrate. If the offense is minor, the magistrate disposes of it forthwith; if it is serious, he holds the defendant for further action and admits him to bail. The case then is turned over to a prosecuting attorney, who charges the defendant with a specific statutory crime. This charge is subject to review by a judge at a preliminary hearing of the evidence and in many places if the offense charged is a felony, by a grand jury that can dismiss the charge, or affirm it by delivering it to a judge in the form of an indictment. If the defendant pleads "not guilty" to the charge he comes to trial; the facts of his case are marshaled by prosecuting and defense attorneys and presented, under the supervision of

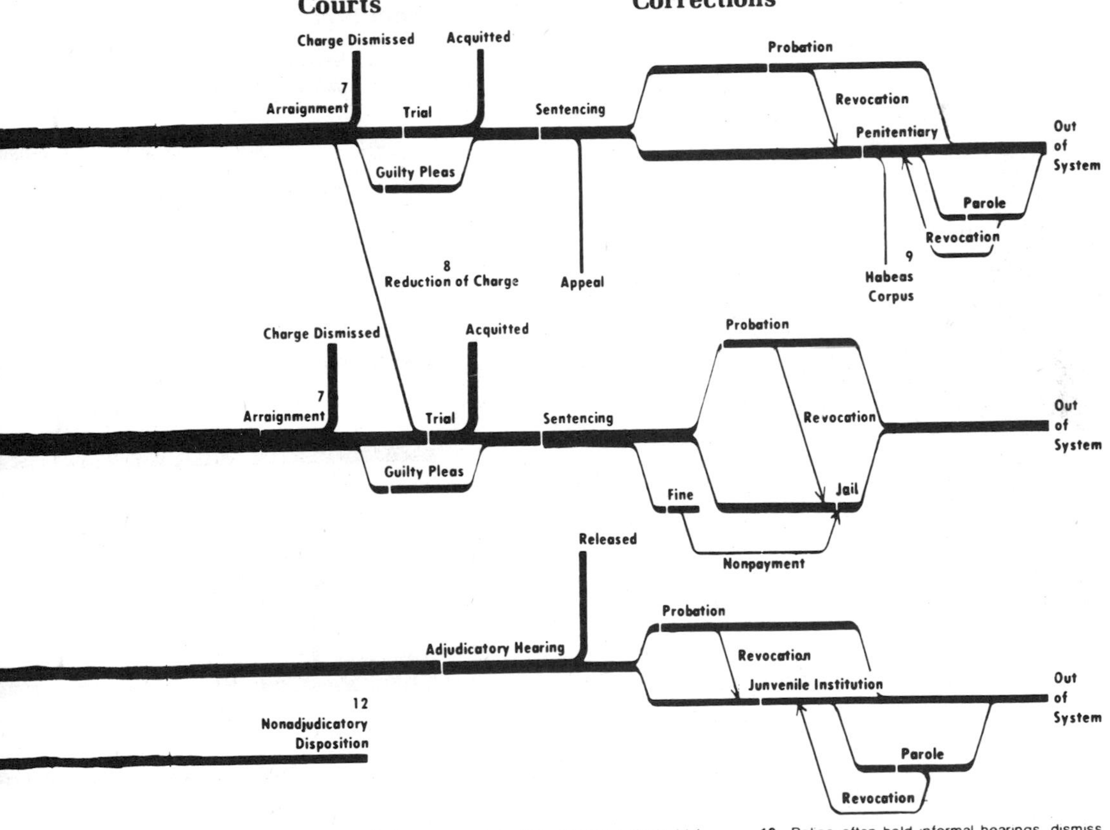

7. Appearance for plea; defendant elects trial by judge or jury (if available).

8. Charge may be reduced at any time prior to trial in return for plea of guilty or for other reasons.

9. Challenge on constitutional grounds to legality of detention. May be sought at any point in process.

10. Police often hold informal hearings, dismiss or adjust many cases without further processing.

11. Probation officer decides desirability of further court action.

12. Welfare agency, social services, counseling, medical care, etc., for cases where adjudicatory handling not needed.

[C1148]

a judge, through witnesses, to a jury. If the jury finds the defendant guilty, he is sentenced by the judge to a term in prison, where a systematic attempt to convert him into a law-abiding citizen is made, or to a term of probation, under which he is permitted to live in the community as long as he behaves himself.

Some cases do proceed much like that, especially those involving offenses that are generally considered "major": serious acts of violence or thefts of large amounts of property. However, not all major cases follow this course, and, in any event, the bulk of the daily business of the criminal justice system consists of offenses that are not major—of breaches of the peace, crimes of vice, petty thefts, assaults arising from domestic or street-corner or barroom disputes. These and most other cases are disposed of in much less formal and much less deliberate ways.

What has evidently happened is that the transformation of America from a relatively relaxed rural society into a tumultuous urban one has presented the criminal justice system in the cities with a volume of cases too large to handle by traditional methods. One result of heavy caseloads is highly visible in city courts, which process many cases with excessive haste and many others with excessive slowness. In the interest both of effectiveness and of fairness to individuals, justice should be swift and certain; too often in city courts today it is, instead, hasty or faltering. Invisibly, the pressure of numbers has effected a series of adventitious changes in the criminal process. Informal shortcuts have been used. The decision making process has often become routinized. Throughout the system the importance of individual judgment and discretion, as distinguished from stated rules and procedures, has increased. In effect, much decision making is being done on an administrative rather than on a judicial basis. Thus, an examination of how the criminal justice system works and a consideration of the changes needed to make it more effective and fair must focus on the extent to which invisible, administrative procedures depart from visible, traditional ones, and on the desirability of that departure.

THE POLICE

At the very beginning of the process—or, more properly, before the process begins at all—something happens that is scarcely discussed in lawbooks and is seldom recognized by the public: law enforcement policy is made by the policeman. For policemen cannot and do not arrest all the offenders they encounter. It is doubtful that they arrest most of them. A criminal code, in practice, is not a set of specific instructions to policemen but a more or less rough map of the territory in which policemen work. How an individual policeman moves around that territory depends largely on his personal discretion.

That a policeman's duties compel him to exercise personal discretion many times every day is evident. Crime does not look the same on the street as it does in a legislative chamber. How much noise or profanity makes conduct "disorderly" within the meaning of the law? When must a quarrel be treated as a criminal assault: at the first threat or at the first shove or at the first blow, or after blood is drawn, or when a serious injury is inflicted? How suspicious must conduct be before there is "probable cause," the constitutional basis for an arrest? Every policeman, however complete or sketchy his education, is an interpreter of the law.

Every policeman, too, is an arbiter of social values, for he meets situation after situation in which invoking criminal sanctions is a questionable line of action. It is obvious that a boy throwing rocks at a school's windows is committing the statutory offense of vandalism, but it is often not at all obvious whether a policeman will better serve the interests of the community and of the boy by taking the boy home to his parents or by arresting him. Who are the boy's parents? Can they control him? Is he a frequent offender who has responded badly to leniency? Is vandalism so epidemic in the neighborhood that he should be made a cautionary example? With juveniles especially, the police exercise great discretion.

Finally, the manner in which a policeman works is influenced by practical matters: the legal strength of the available evidence, the willingness of victims to press charges and of witnesses to testify, the temper of the community, the time and information at the policeman's disposal. Much is at stake in how the policeman exercises this discretion. If he judges conduct not suspicious enough to justify intervention, the chance to prevent a robbery, rape, or murder may be lost. If he overestimates the seriousness of a situation or his actions are controlled by panic or prejudice, he may hurt or kill someone unnecessarily. His actions may even touch off a riot.

THE MAGISTRATE

In direct contrast to the policeman, the magistrate before whom a suspect is first brought usually exercises less discretion than the law allows him. He is entitled to inquire into the facts of the case, into whether there are grounds for holding the accused. He seldom does. He seldom can. The more promptly an arrested suspect is brought into magistrate's court, the less likelihood there is that much information about the arrest other than the arresting officer's statement will be available to the magistrate. Moreover many magistrates, especially in big cities, have such congested calendars that it is almost impossible for them to subject any case but an extraordinary one to prolonged scrutiny.

In practice the most important things, by far, that a magistrate does are to set the amount of a defendant's bail and in some jurisdictions to appoint counsel. Too seldom does either action get the careful attention it deserves. In many cases the magistrate accepts a waiver of counsel without insuring that the suspect knows the significance of legal representation.

Bail is a device to free an untried defendant and at the same time make sure he appears for trial. That is the sole stated legal purpose in America. The Eighth Amendment to the Constitution declares that it must not be "excessive." Appellate courts have declared that not just the seriousness of the charge against the defendant, but the suspect's personal, family, and employment situation, as they bear on the likelihood of his appearance, must be weighed before the amount of his bail is fixed. Yet more magistrates than not set bail according to standard rates: so and so many dollars for such and such an offense.

The persistence of money bail can best be explained not by its stated purpose but by the belief of police, prosecutors, and courts that the best way to keep a defendant from committing more crimes before trial is to set bail so high that he cannot obtain his release.

THE PROSECUTOR

The key administrative officer in the processing of cases is the prosecutor. Theoretically the examination of the evidence against a defendant by a judge at a preliminary hearing, and its reexamination by a grand jury, are important parts of the process. Practically they seldom are because a prosecutor seldom has any difficulty in making a prima facie case against a defendant. In fact most defendants waive their rights to preliminary hearings and much more often than not grand juries indict precisely as prosecutors ask them to. The prosecutor wields almost undisputed sway over the pretrial progress of most cases. He decides whether to press a case or drop it. He determines the specific charge against a defendant. When the charge is reduced, as it is in as many as two-thirds of all cases in some cities, the prosecutor is usually the official who reduces it.

* * *

THE PLEA AND THE SENTENCE

When a prosecutor reduces a charge it is ordinarily because there has been "plea bargaining" between him and a defense attorney. The issue at stake is how much the prosecutor will reduce his original charge or how lenient a sentence he will recommend, in return for a plea of guilty. There is no way of judging how many bargains reflect the prosecutor's belief that a lesser charge or sentence is justified and how many result from the fact that there may be in the system at any one time ten times as many cases as there are prosecutors or judges or courtrooms to handle them, should every one come to trial. In form, a plea bargain can be anything from a series of careful conferences to a hurried consultation in a courthouse corridor. In content it can be anything from a conscientious exploration of the facts and dispositional alternatives available and appropriate to a defendant, to a perfunctory deal. If the interests of a defendant are to be properly protected while his fate is being thus invisibly determined, he obviously needs just as good legal representation as the kind he needs at a public trial. Whether or not plea bargaining is a fair and effective method of disposing of criminal cases depends heavily on whether or not defendants are provided early with competent and conscientious counsel.

Plea bargaining is not only an invisible procedure but, in some jurisdictions, a theoretically unsanctioned one. In order to satisfy the court record, a defendant, his attorney, and the prosecutor will at the time of sentencing often ritually state to a judge that no bargain has been made. Plea bargaining may be a useful procedure, especially in congested urban jurisdictions, but neither the dignity of the law, nor the quality of justice, nor the protection of society from dangerous criminals is enhanced by its being conducted covertly.

* * *

An enormously consequential kind of decision is the sentencing decision of a judge. The law recognizes the importance of fitting sentences to individual defendants by giving judges, in most instances, considerable latitude. For example the recently adopted New York Penal Code, which went into effect in autumn of 1967, empowers a judge to impose upon a man convicted of armed robbery any sentence between a 5-year term of probation and a 25-year term in prison. Even when a judge has presided over a trial during which the facts of a case have been carefully set forth and has been given a probation report that carefully discusses a defendant's character, background, and problems, he cannot find it easy to choose a sentence. In perhaps nine-tenths of all cases there is no trial; the defendants are self-confessedly guilty.

In the lower or misdemeanor courts, the courts that process most criminal cases, probation reports are a rarity. Under such circumstances judges have little to go on and many sentences are bound to be based on conjecture or intuition. When a sentence is part of a plea bargain, which an overworked judge ratifies perfunctorily, it may not even be his conjecture or intuition on which the sentence is based, but a prosecutor's or a defense counsel's. But perhaps the greatest lack judges suffer from when they pass sentence is not time or information, but correctional alternatives. Some lower courts do not have any probation officers, and in almost every court the caseloads of probation officers are so heavy that a sentence of probation means, in fact, releasing an offender into the community with almost no supervision. Few States have a sufficient variety of correctional institutions or treatment programs to inspire judges with the confidence that sentences will lead to rehabilitation.

CORRECTIONS

The correctional apparatus to which guilty defendants are delivered is in every respect the most isolated part of the criminal justice system. Much of it is physically isolated; its institutions usually have thick walls and locked doors, and often they are situated in rural areas, remote from the courts where the institutions' inmates were tried and from the communities where they lived. The correctional apparatus is isolated in the sense that its officials do not have everyday working relationships with officials from the system's other branches, like those that commonly exist between policemen and prosecutors, or prosecutors and judges. It is isolated in the sense that what it does with, to, or for the people under its supervision is seldom governed by any but the most broadly written statutes, and is almost never scrutinized by appellate courts. Finally, it is isolated from the public partly by its invisibility and physical remoteness; partly by the inherent lack of drama in most of its activities, but perhaps most importantly by the fact that the correctional apparatus is often used—or misused—by both the criminal justice system and the public as a rug under which disturbing problems and people can be swept.

The most striking fact about the correctional apparatus today is that, although the rehabilitation of criminals is presumably its major purpose, the custody of criminals is actually its major task. On any given day there are well over a million people being "corrected" in America, two-thirds of them on probation or parole and one-third of them in prisons or jails. However, prisons and jails are where four-fifths of correctional money is spent and where nine-tenths of correctional employees work. Furthermore, fewer than one-fifth of the people who work in State prisons and local jails have jobs that are not essentially either custodial or administrative in character. Many jails have nothing but custodial and administrative personnel. Of course many jails are crowded with defendants who have not been able to furnish bail and who are not considered by the law to be appropriate objects of rehabilitation because it has not yet been determined that they are criminals who need it.

What this emphasis on custody means in practice is that the enormous potential of the correctional apparatus for making creative decisions about its treatment of convicts is largely unfulfilled. This is true not only of offenders in custody but of offenders on probation and parole. Most authorities agree that while probationers and parolees need varying degrees and kinds of supervision, an average of no more than 35 cases per officer is necessary for effective attention; 97 percent of all officers handling adults have larger caseloads than that. In the juvenile correctional system the situation is somewhat better. Juvenile institutions, which typically are training schools, have a higher proportion of treatment personnel and juvenile probation and parole officers generally have lighter caseloads. However, these comparatively rich resources are very far from being sufficiently rich.

Except for sentencing, no decision in the criminal process has more impact on the convicted offender than the parole decision, which determines how much of his maximum sentence a prisoner must serve. This again is an invisible administrative decision that is seldom open to attack or subject to review. It is made by parole board members who are often political appointees. Many are skilled and conscientious, but they generally are able to spend no more than a few minutes on a case. Parole decisions that are made in haste and on the basis of insufficient information, in the absence of parole machinery that can provide good supervision, are necessarily imperfect decisions. And since there is virtually no appeal from them, they can be made arbitrarily or discriminatorily. Just as carefully formulated and clearly stated law enforcement policies would help policemen, charge policies would help prosecutors and sentencing policies would help judges, so parole policies would help parole boards perform their delicate and important duties.

C. ASCERTAINMENT OF GUILT: THE PROSECUTION'S BURDEN OF PROOF BEYOND A REASONABLE DOUBT

One of the most important issues in the legal adjudication of issues, whether criminal or civil, is the allocation of the burden of proof. Often it will be determinative of the outcome of the litigation. The phrase "burden of proof" actually subsumes two distinct concepts: the burden of production or the burden of going forward, and the burden of persuasion. The first identifies the party who must initially produce evidence on a particular proposition or risk dismissal. The second refers to the level of proof which the party bearing the burden must achieve. In criminal cases, it is understood, as a general matter, that the prosecution bears the burden of production of evidence as to all elements of the crime charged, and must persuade the trier of fact of their existence by proof beyond a reasonable doubt. That is, the defendant may stand mute without risk of a directed verdict of guilty. Yet, simultaneously, the defendant has traditionally been thought to bear the burden of production as to certain "defensive" issues, the nature of which vary among jurisdictions, and, as to certain of these, the burden of persuasion, although seldom by more than a preponderance of the evidence. That is, for example, a defendant who wishes to raise the defense of insanity at the time of the offense may be required to produce evidence of this before the prosecution need address this question in its pleadings or proof. If the defendant bears only the burden of production and satisfies it by making a prima facie case, then the burden of production returns to the prosecution which must prove sanity beyond a reasonable doubt. However, if the jurisdiction also places the burden of persuasion as to insanity on the defendant—sometimes terming it an "affirmative defense"—then the burden would not shift back to the prosecution and the defendant would bear the risk of nonpersuasion on this issue.

In recent years, the allocation of these burdens and the use of certain procedural devices called "presumptions" which aid the prosecution in meeting its burden of proof, have been subjected to increased scrutiny for their consistency with perceived constitutional mandates.

An unquestioned premise of American law has been that the prosecution must prove the guilt of a criminal defendant beyond a reasonable doubt. Perhaps because this burden of persuasion had been so uniformly applied, it was not until 1970, that the Supreme Court addressed the question of whether it was constitutionally required. In In re Winship, 397 U.S. 358, 90 S.Ct. 1068, 25 L.Ed.2d 368 (1970),[a] the Court announced that the Due Process Clause of the Fourteenth Amendment required that this standard be applied to the adjudication of serious juvenile delinquency cases. In his opinion for the Court, Mr. Justice Brennan undertook to explain the function served by this burden:

> The requirement of proof beyond a reasonable doubt has this vital role in our criminal procedure for cogent reasons. The accused during a criminal prosecution has at stake interest of immense importance, both because of the possibility that he may lose his liberty upon conviction and because of the certainty that he would be stigmatized by the conviction. Accordingly, a society that values the good name and freedom of every individual should not condemn a man for commission of a crime when there is reasonable doubt about his guilt. As we said in Speiser v. Randall, [357 U.S. 513, 525–526, 78 S.Ct. 1332, 1342 (1958)]: "There is always in litigation a margin of error, representing error in factfinding, which both parties must take into account. Where one party has at stake an interest of transcending value—as a criminal defendant his liberty—this margin of error is reduced as to him by the process of placing on the other party the burden of * * * persuading the fact-

a. The citations following the name of the case are in customary legal form. "U.S." stands for "United States Supreme Court Reports", the official reporting system for decision of the United States Supreme Court. The citation here indicates that the decision in the Winship case can be found in volume 397 of the United States Reports at page 358. "S.Ct." stands for "Supreme Court Reporter", and "L.Ed.2d" for Lawyers Edition, United States Supreme Court Reports, Second Series"; both of these are commercial reporting systems for the decisions of the United States Supreme Court.

> finder at the conclusion of the trial of his guilt beyond a reasonable doubt. Due process commands that no man shall lose his liberty unless the Government has borne the burden of * * * convincing the factfinder of his guilt." To this end, the reasonable-doubt standard is indispensable, for it "impresses on the trier of fact the necessity of reaching a subjective state of certitude on the facts in issue." Dorsen & Rezneck, In re Gault and the Future of Juvenile Law, 1 Family Law Quarterly, No. 4, at 26 (1967).
>
> Moreover, use of the reasonable-doubt standard is indispensable to command the respect and confidence of the community in applications of the criminal law. It is critical that the moral force of the criminal law not be diluted by a standard of proof which leaves people in doubt whether innocent men are being condemned. It is also important in our free society that every individual going about his ordinary affairs have confidence that his government cannot adjudge him guilty of a criminal offense without convincing a proper factfinder of his guilt with utmost certainty.
>
> Lest there remain any doubt about the constitutional stature of the reasonable-doubt standard, we explicitly hold that the Due Process Clause protects the accused against conviction except upon proof beyond a reasonable doubt of every fact necessary to constitute the crime with which he is charged.

397 U.S. at 363–64, 90 S.Ct. at 1072–73, 25 L.Ed.2d at 375.

The last paragraph quoted above, which was far broader than required by the question presented to the Court, was seized upon in Mullaney v. Wilbur, 421 U.S. 684, 95 S.Ct. 1881, 44 L.Ed.2d 508 (1975), a decision which seemed to promise a revolution in the substantive criminal law of this country. Mr. Wilbur had been convicted of murder under the laws of Maine which provided for two kinds of homicide, murder and manslaughter. Both required proof beyond a reasonable doubt that the killing was unlawful—neither justifiable nor excusable—and intentional. The difference between them was that "malice aforethought" was an element of murder. The jury was instructed that if the prosecution proved that the homicide was both unlawful and intentional "malice aforethought was to be conclusively implied unless the defendant proved by a fair preponderance of the evidence that he acted in the heat of passion on sudden provocation".

Mr. Justice Powell, for a unanimous Court, held that placing this burden on the defendant violated due process. He first reviewed the history of the law of homicide and reached two conclusions.

> First, the fact at issue here—the presence or absence of the heat of passion on sudden provocation—has been, almost

> from the inception of the common law of homicide, the single most important factor in determining the degree of culpability attaching to an unlawful homicide. And, second, the clear trend has been toward requiring the prosecution to bear the ultimate burden of proving this fact.

421 U.S. at 696, 95 S.Ct. at 1888, 44 L.Ed.2d at 518.

He then rejected the argument that Winship was distinguishable because the fact on which Wilbur bore the burden of persuasion went merely to mitigation of punishment rather than guilt or innocence. He pointed out that in terms of both stigma and sentence, distinctions as to the degree of an offense may be as or even more important to defendants in some cases than the decision as to guilt or innocence in others. Moreover, if the principle of *Winship* were limited to the facts specifically defined by state law as constituting the crime, the state could, merely by redefining murder as an unlawful killing, impose a life sentence on the proof of such unless the defendant could prove that his act was neither intentional nor reckless. In terms of society's interest in accurate fact finding the Maine procedure posed a greater threat than that involved in *Winship* since there the burden of persuasion, although reduced, remained on the state whereas here the defendant was required to convince the jury of the existence of a critical fact thereby increasing the likelihood of error. Justice Powell rejected the argument that the difficulty of negating the fact that the homicide was committed in the heat of passion was so great or distinctive as to justify the shifting of the burden; indeed, Maine required that when a defendant raised the issue of self-defense the state must prove its absence beyond a reasonable doubt. He concluded that "it is far worse to sentence one guilty only of manslaughter as a murderer than to sentence a murderer for the lesser crime of manslaughter", and that the Maine procedure violated the Due Process Clause of the Constitution.

The *Mullaney* case seems to have been the high-water mark for those who believe that all procedural devices easing the prosecution's burden, such as affirmative defenses and presumptions, are unconstitutional. In Patterson v. New York, 432 U.S. 197, 97 S.Ct. 2319, 53 L.Ed.2d 281 (1977), the Court upheld a state statute requiring a murder defendant, in order to be found guilty of manslaughter, to prove by a preponderance of the evidence that he killed "under the influence of extreme emotional disturbance for which there was a reasonable explanation or excuse. Although the question seemed to be the same as that in *Mullaney,* a crucial distinction was said to be that the New York murder statute did not include the absence of such disturbance as part of its definition of murder which required only that the state prove that the defendant intentionally caused the death. Mr. Justice White for the majority of five (Justice Rehnquist did not participate) stressed that the New York penal code contained some twenty-five affirmative defenses. These, in effect, were expressions of compassion by the state and not required by the Constitution. That is, New York could, if it wished, punish all those who intentionally cause another's death as murderers without recognizing mitigating factors such as extreme emotional disturbance. If this is so, according to Justice White, recognition of such a factor does not require the State to prove its non-existence if "in its judgment this would be too cumbersome, too expensive and too inaccurate". For the three dissenters, the opinion in *Patterson* drew a distinction without a difference and seriously threatened the meaning of the presumption of innocence. For them, this meant that the prosecutor must bear the burden of persuasion on any factor which had historically been recognized as making a substantial difference in the determination of guilt or innocence or of the severity of punishment and stigma.

More recently, a similar problem was addressed in Ulster County Court v. Allen, — U.S. —, 99 S.Ct. 2213, 60 L.Ed.2d 777 (1979). At issue there was the constitutionality of a New York law providing that the presence of a firearm in an automobile is presumptive evidence of its possession by all persons in the car. In a trial of three adults and a 16 year old girl for possession of two handguns found in the girl's open handbag next to where she was sitting in the car the jury was instructed, pursuant to this law, that they might infer that each of the defendants possessed the weapons. All were convicted. Their convictions were affirmed by the highest state court, but reversed by the United States Court of Appeals on the grounds that the presumption was unconstitutional because it was irrational. That is, that it could not be said that the presumed fact (possession by the occupants) is more likely than not to follow from the proven fact (presence of the gun in the car). Allen v. County Court, 568 F.2d 998 (2nd Cir. 1978).[b] Here again, a procedural device that eased the state's burden was at issue and again the Supreme Court upheld the state. For the majority the presumption was rational on the facts of the case since it was highly improbable that the 16 year old was the

b. The abbreviation "F.2d" stands for Federal Reporter, Second Series. The Federal Reporter is where the decisions of the eleven United States Courts of Appeals are reported (there are ten numbered circuits and one for the District of Columbia which is abbreviated "D.C.Cir."). (Decisions of federal trial courts are reported in the Federal Supplement (F.Supp.)). "2nd" indicates that the decision in Allen was rendered by the Court of Appeals for the Second Circuit. The ten numbered circuits are responsible for appeals from decisions of the United States District Courts (trial courts) located within particular geographical areas. The Second Circuit, for example, covers the states of Connecticut, New York and Vermont. The name Allen came first in the Circuit Court because Allen was the petitioner—the party seeking relief (here relief was sought through a writ of habeas corpus, the most common means by which a person convicted in a state court seeks review of his conviction in a federal court). In the Supreme Court the names were reversed because it was the state which sought to have the decision of the Circuit Court reversed.

sole custodian. Rather, it was as though the guns were lying on the floor in which case one might reasonably infer that each passenger knew of their presence and had both ability and intent to exercise control over them. The majority stressed that this was a permissive and not a mandatory presumption. The jury might but need not infer possession. For the four dissenters not only was the presumption irrational but it was improper to evaluate it in light of the other evidence in the case inasmuch as the jury was instructed that it could find possession merely on the basis of the presumption and might have done so.

In contrast, the Court was unanimous in reversing a murder conviction where the jury was instructed that "The law presumes that a person intends the ordinary consequences of his voluntary acts." Sandstrom v. Montana, —— U.S. ——, 99 S.Ct. 2450, 61 L.Ed.2d 39 (1979) (see page 159 infra). In *Sandstrom*, the defendant acknowledged killing the elderly victim but contended that he did not do so purposely or knowingly as required by the statute defining the crime. The Court held that the jury may have understood the instruction either as a direction to find purpose or knowledge on proof of the defendant's voluntary acts—as a mandatory presumption—or to so find unless the defendant proved the contrary. The first would violate the *Winship* requirement that the state prove every element of the crime beyond a reasonable doubt. The second would impermissibly shift to the defendant the burden of persuasion on an element of the offense: a result prohibited by *Mullaney*.

In summary, then, it is clear that the prosecution must prove beyond a reasonable doubt all factors which are part of the definition of a crime. It is also clear that the state may place on the defendant the burden of producing evidence with respect to certain defensive or mitigating factors. The defendant may also be required to bear the burden of persuasion as to such factors if they are not deemed part of the crime. Finally, presumptions which aid the state in meeting its burden of persuasion are constitutional if they are rational as applied to the facts of a case and permit but do not compel the trier of fact to draw the inference which is thought to more likely than not follow from the fact proven.

D. ASCERTAINMENT OF GUILT: THE DECISIONMAKERS AND THEIR RESPECTIVE ROLES

In our legal system the right to a jury trial is thought so important that it is provided for in two sections of our Constitution. Clause 3 of Article III provides as to federal trials: "The trial of all crimes, except in cases of impeachment, shall be by jury", and the Sixth Amendment to the Constitution offers similar guarantees as to state cases: "In all criminal prosecutions, the accused shall enjoy the right to a speedy and public trial, by an impartial jury". The jury has been thought to be an expression of community values and a bulwark against governmental oppression. Not surprisingly, issues have arisen as to the scope of the jury's authority as well as that of the judge who presides at the trial. As our society has become more urban, more heterogeneous, and more complex so have our laws. The result has been to enhance the judge's authority, as the impartial interpreter of the law, at the expense of that of the jury. The following materials examine the tension between the abstract principles of law and the forces of public sentiment.

UNITED STATES v. MOYLAN

United States Court of Appeals, Fourth Circuit, 1969.
417 F.2d 1002, cert. denied [c] 397 U.S. 910, 90 S.Ct. 908, 25 L.Ed.2d 91.

SOBELOFF, Circuit Judge. The defendants appeal their conviction in the United States District Court for the District of Maryland for violation of three federal statutes proscribing the mutilation of Government records, destruction of Government property and interference with the administration of the Selective Service System. The facts are uncontroverted. At 12:50 P.M. on May 17, 1968, the appellants entered the office of Local Board No. 33 in Catonsville, Maryland and removed approximately 378 I–A, I–Y and II–A files to an adjacent parking lot where they burned the files with homemade napalm. The appellants, men and women with sincere and strong commitments, readily admit the commission of these acts as a protest against the war in Vietnam.

* * *

II

Appellants' second contention is that the trial judge should have informed the jury, as requested, that it had the power to acquit even if appellants were clearly guilty of the charged offenses. They maintain that the judge should have told the jury this or permitted their counsel to argue it to the jury in the face of the judge's instruction on the law. Appellants reason that since the jury has "the power to bring in a verdict in the teeth of both law and facts," then the jury should be told that it has this power. Furthermore, the argument runs, the jury's power to acquit where the law may dictate otherwise is a fundamental necessity of a democratic system. Only in this way,

c. The abbreviation "cert." stands for certiorari, and "cert. denied" means that the party which lost in the Court of Appeals has failed in its efforts to have the Supreme Court review the decision. The decision to grant certiorari is totally within the discretion of the Justices of the Supreme Court—there is no right to have such a case reviewed—and a decision to deny does not mean that the Supreme Court approves or disapproves of the lower court's decision.

it is said, can a man's actions be judged fairly by society speaking through the jury, or a law which is considered too harsh be mitigated.

In the early history of the American Colonies and for a time after the Revolution juries were nearly always recognized as having the power to judge both law and fact. * * *

In criminal cases juries remained the judges of both law and fact for approximately fifty years after the Revolution. However, the judges in America, just as in England after the Revolution of 1688, gradually asserted themselves increasingly through their instructions on the law.

We recognize, as appellants urge, the undisputed power of the jury to acquit, even if its verdict is contrary to the law as given by the judge and contrary to the evidence. This is a power that must exist as long as we adhere to the general verdict in criminal cases, for the courts cannot search the minds of the jurors to find the basis upon which they judge. If the jury feels that the law under which the defendant is accused is unjust, or that exigent circumstances justified the actions of the accused, or for any reason which appeals to their logic or passion, the jury has the power to acquit, and the courts must abide by that decision.

Concededly, this power of the jury is not always contrary to the interests of justice. For example, freedom of the press was immeasurably strengthened by the jury's acquittal of John Peter Zenger of seditious libel, a violation of which, under the law as it then existed and the facts, he was clearly guilty. In that case Andrew Hamilton was allowed to urge the jury, in the face of the judge's charge, "to see with their own eyes, to hear with their own ears, and to make use of their consciences and understanding in judging of the lives, liberties, or estates of their fellow subjects."

No less an authority than Dean Pound has expressed the opinion that "Jury lawlessness is the great corrective of law in its actual administration." However, this is not to say that the jury should be encouraged in their "lawlessness," and by clearly stating to the jury that they may disregard the law, telling them that they may decide according to their prejudices or consciences (for there is no check to insure that the judgment is based upon conscience rather than prejudice), we would indeed be negating the rule of law in favor of the rule of lawlessness. This should not be allowed.

* * *

The judgment below is

Affirmed.

NOTE

As is indicated in *Moylan*, there was a period in our history when it was commonly held that the jury was the judge of the law as well as the facts of the case. This view had been almost universally abandoned when the pressures of cases such as *Moylan* and others involving conscientious protesters against widely perceived societal wrongs awakened interest in its revival. See, e. g., Christie, "Lawful Departures From Legal Rules: 'Jury Nullification' a Legitimated Disobedience", 62 Cal.L.Rev. 1289 (1974) and Scheflin, "Jury Nullification: The Right to Say No", 45 S.Cal.L.Rev. 168 (1972). Obviously, giving such power to a jury also creates additional opportunities for discriminatory enforcement of the law although the practice has withstood constitutional challenge based on this ground. Wyley v. Warden, 372 F.2d 742 (4th Cir. 1967) cert. denied 389 U.S. 863, 88 S.Ct. 121, 19 L.Ed.2d 131. It is interesting that although our practice is to restrict the jury's discretion to questions of fact, its discretion with respect to the facts is unlimited. That is, a jury can reject the testimony of ten eye-witnesses plus scientific evidence all pointing to the defendant's guilt. Moreover, the jury's ability to do this is made easier by the practice of the general verdict. Unlike some civil cases where the jury is given a series of specific questions concerning disputed issues, the answers to which must be consistent with its ultimate judgment as to the liability of the parties, a criminal jury is to answer only "guilty" or "not guilty". See United States v. Spock, 416 F.2d 165, 180–83 (1st Cir. 1969). For a brief but valuable historical review and analysis of these problems see Simson, "Jury Nullification in the American System: A Skeptical View", 54 Tex.L.Rev. 488 (1976).

E. PENALTY PROVISIONS AND GRADING OF CRIMINAL OFFENSES

1. THE TASK OF ASSIGNING PENALTIES

TASK FORCE ON ADMINISTRATION OF JUSTICE, THE PRESIDENT'S COMMISSION ON LAW ENFORCEMENT AND ADMINISTRATION OF JUSTICE, TASK FORCE REPORT: THE COURTS

15 (1967).

The penal codes of most jurisdictions are the products of piecemeal construction, as successive legislatures have fixed punishment for new crimes and adjusted penalties for existing offenses through separate sentencing provisions for each offense. As a result the sentencing distinctions among offenses are in excess of those which could rationally be drawn on the basis of relative harmfulness of conduct or the probable dangerousness of the offenders. In Wisconsin, for example, there are 16 variations in the statutory maximum terms of imprisonment for felonies upon a first conviction: 2, 3, 4, 5, 6, 7, 8, 10, 14, 20, 25, 35, and 40 years and life imprisonment. A study of the Oregon penal code revealed that the 1,413 criminal statutes contained a total of 466 different types and lengths of sentences.

The absence of legislative attention to the whole range of penalties may also be demonstrated by comparisons between certain offenses. A recent study of the Colorado statutes disclosed that a person convicted of first degree murder must serve 10 years before becoming eligible for parole, while a person convicted of a lesser degree of the same offense must serve at least 15 years; destruction of a house with fire is punishable by a maximum of 20 years' imprisonment, but destruction of a house with explosives carries a 10-year maximum. In California an offender who breaks into an automobile to steal the contents of the glove compartment is subject to a 15-year maximum sentence, but if he stole the car itself, he would face a maximum 10-year term.

Although each offense must be defined in a separate statutory provision, the number and variety of sentencing distinctions which result when legislatures prescribe a separate penalty for each offense are among "the main causes of the anarchy in sentencing that is so widely deplored."

WECHSLER AND MICHAEL, A RATIONALE FOR THE LAW OF HOMICIDE

37 Columbia Law Review 701, 1261, 1268–1270 (1937).

[S]ome one, legislator or administrator, must face the problem of ordering the severity of penalties within the limits of popular tolerance so that the welfare of individual offenders shall be sacrificed for the sake of deterrence only in those instances in which the sacrifice is most necessary and serves the most desirable ends. We must, therefore, address ourselves to an analysis of that problem. If we are right in believing that the core of the popular demand is for some gradation of the severity of punitive treatment in accordance with the actual or probable results of crimes of various sorts and the characters of criminals of various sorts, the major criteria for an ordered mitigation of punishment are, it will be observed, inherent in popular sentiment itself.

I. There are several reasons why the severity of penalties should be correlated with the relative undesirability of the behavior for which they are imposed. The more undesirable any kind of criminal behavior is, the less expedient it is to relax our efforts to prevent it, the more important it is that we make the incentive to avoid it, which the threat of punishment provides, as strong as it can be made. Moreover, such a correlation serves, as we have said, as an inducement to potential offenders to pursue their ends by the least undesirable criminal means; it also serves as an object lesson in relative evil which is not without some value as general moral education.

II. There are equally valid reasons why the severity of penalties should be correlated with the characters of individual offenders. The more numerous a potential offender's motives to refrain from criminal behavior apart from that of avoiding a threatened penalty, the more he is moved by them habitually, the greater his capacity to guide his conduct by such motives, the less need there is for a vigorous threat to counteract whatever desires to engage in criminal behavior he may have from time to time. Moreover, for the most part, the more severe a penalty, the greater is its incapacitative effect and the more likely it is to harm and the less likely to reform the actual offenders subjected to it. Obviously, the more dangerous men are, the more desirable it is that they be thoroughly incapacitated; the better the lives men can lead, the less desirable it is to debase them; the more likely it is that men are corrigible, the more tragic it is not to attempt to reform them.

Though these are, in our judgment, the major criteria for ordering the severity of punishment, they are not exhaustive. Two subordinate principles merit consideration. They are:

III. The severity of penalties should be correlated with the strength of the desires which motivate men to engage in criminal behavior of different sorts under different circumstances. The stronger the desire, the more need there is for severity in the threatened penalty in order to counteract it.

IV. The severity of penalties should also be correlated with the presence or absence of a discernible relation between the criminal act and some injustice done to the actor by another individual or even by society as a whole. Where such a relationship can be perceived, a mitigation of the penalty on that ground serves, as T. H. Green has pointed out,[25] to direct attention to and strengthen the popular awareness of the original injustice, a result that may be of value in preventing or remedying such injustices in the future. The greater the injustice, the less vigorous the efforts that are being made to deal with it, the more confidently the criminal act can be attributed to it as a cause, the stronger the case for mitigation for that reason becomes.

To the extent that these principles can be developed and employed, the severity of punishment should be susceptible of a rough ordering which is rationally adapted both to its primary deterrent purpose and to the other ends which even the punitive treatment of offenders should as far as possible serve.

25. Lectures on the Principles of Political Obligation (1927) 193–4.

R. DAWSON, SENTENCING REFORM: THE CURRENT ROUND

88 Yale L.J. 440 (1978).[d]

[Professor Dawson reviews P. O'Donnell, M. Churgin, and D. Curtis, *Towards A Just and Efficient Sentencing System: Agenda for Legislative Reform* (1977), which he describes as "a product of, and a contributor to, our national debate on whether to shift from a system of indeterminate sentencing to one of determinate sentencing and whether to change from a system of broad judicial sentencing discretion to one in which that discretion is much more restricted."] Such a shift has already occurred in California and Maine, and similar federal legislation is pending. Although it is unclear what discretion-limited determinate sentencing will accomplish and at what costs, a momentum to change in that direction clearly exists.

* * *

Until recently, the single most important reform in criminal sentencing in the United States was acceptance of the notion that criminal punishments should be individualized to fit the circumstances of each offense and the background of each offender. Only then, it was reasoned, could the criminal sanction hope to attain its goals of deterrence of future criminality, rehabilitation of the offender, at least temporary protection of the public by the offender's incarceration, appropriate restitution to the victim, and proper allocation of community condemnation. Aside from these particularized aims of the criminal process, the individualized sentence was also thought to deter the community generally (or at least identifiable segments of it) from the commission of criminal offenses or, at least, of similar offenses. There were always limits to the ideal of sentence individualization. For example, the legislature and, perhaps, the Constitution would not permit punishing a petty thief with the same severity as a convicted murderer. Nonetheless, the limits were conceived to be just that, upper and sometimes lower limits on the ability of the system to mete out the just punishment postulated to exist for each instance of criminality.

The legislative limits, then, had to be sufficiently broad to permit sentences to take account of the myriad of aggravating and mitigating circumstances that mark each criminal act and to reflect major differences in offender backgrounds. The upper legislative limits tended to be quite high because legislatures have used a "worst case" mentality in setting them. They have, however, relied upon prosecu-

d. Reprinted by permission of the Yale Law Journal Company and Fred B. Rothmen & Company from The Yale Law Journal, Vol. 88, p. 440ff.

tors, trial judges and parole boards to mitigate the severity of punishment in the great majority of cases.

Individualization of sentencing also required the maximum possible information about the offense and the offender. According to this ideal, no information about either was too trivial to be brought to the attention of the sentencing authority since the goal was to choose the one "correct" disposition under all the circumstances. The system had come more and more to rely, not upon the presentation of that information in an adversarial hearing, but upon its presentation in a report prepared by a "disinterested" and "professional" probation officer. The report typically contained a professional "diagnosis" of the case and a recommended disposition.

If a sentence of incarceration was imposed, it was thought to be most precise and sensible to wait until sometime during the process of serving that sentence before selecting the exact release date and to give an agency the authority to select that date for each individual case. This was essential if a major objective in determining the length of incarceration was to maximize the rehabilitative effects of the prison experience for the offender. The response of offenders to prison rehabilitation programs, it was argued, is highly individual and cannot be predicted by the sentencing judge. Through individualized treatment, the progress of the individual in rehabilitation could be gauged accurately and the appropriate time of release could be selected.

Thus, our present system of criminal sanctions in felony cases arose. Legislative limits were set to allow substantial individualization of the sentence to fit offense and offender; complete information was provided to the trial judge who sentenced the offender; timing of the release from incarceration was based in part upon the inmate's response to institutional rehabilitation programs. The premises of this system of individualization are splendid and the system itself is an elegant one that would give maximum justice if it worked.

But it has not. The evidence that it has not is substantial. Study after study has shown that institutional (and other) rehabilitative programs do not make a measurable difference in the likelihood that the person treated will refrain from breaking the law in the future. Studies have demonstrated that two trial judges are much more likely to disagree than to agree upon the appropriate sentence in the same case. Sentences often reflect the race, sex, or class prejudices of the judge. Sentencing has become a numbers game in which a sentence does not mean what it appears to mean because of "good time" and parole laws.[14] Sentence individualization and inde-

14. * * * For example, a trial court, accompanied by great publicity, may sentence a convicted offender to 10 years' imprisonment. By routinized operation of prison goodtime rules, however, the 10-year sentence is likely to be reduced to about six years. If parole eligibility laws permit release after one-third of the sentence less good time, a common provi-

terminacy mean that long periods of time in prison are sometimes served to permit fanciful rehabilitation programs to take effect. The existence of sentence indeterminacy means not that prison inmates are motivated to rehabilitate themselves in order to win early release, but that they are motivated to persuade the parole board they have rehabilitated themselves. In addition, indeterminacy means that inmates regard themselves as being subject to the capricious whim of bureaucrats from whose decisions there are few, if any, avenues of review.

II

A response to these criticisms might be to eliminate the discretion to individualize. We could decide, for example, that all bank robbers should be treated exactly the same because they have engaged in the same misconduct. We could abandon all efforts to adjust the system's punishments to take account of the infinite number of gradations in the seriousness of offenses. We could even say that we will not take account of the background of the offender—first or repeat, deprived or privileged—because it is the law infraction and only the law infraction that should be of concern. I doubt we are willing to go anywhere near that far in our response to the inequities of the present system. Yet, if we are prepared to acknowledge that certain aggravating and mitigating circumstances and certain offender background characteristics should be reflected in sentences, then we must provide a mechanism that gives effect to those distinctions with some degree of accuracy. Otherwise, we have created a new sentencing disparity by not making distinctions between offenders that we agree can and should be made.

A second approach is the new California system. California had been extreme in its adherence to the notions of broad sentencing discretion and sentence indeterminacy. Once the trial court ruled out probation in a case and decided that a prison sentence was necessary, the length of the sentence and the date of actual release from incarceration were determined, within broad legislative limits, by the California Adult Authority. Neither judge nor prosecutor nor defense attorney had much to do with determining the actual length of incarceration. Under such a system there was little or no sentence disparity at the judicial level (with respect to sentence length) because no decision as to length was made there. The decisions of the Adult Authority, however, were subjected to much of the same criticism leveled against judicial sentencing elsewhere.

sion, the inmate will be eligible for release on parole after serving only two years of his sentence. The inmate's parole release, if it comes at the end of two or three years, is not accompanied by the same publicity that accompanied the "tough" sentence imposed initially. This system may accomplish the maximum general deterrence of criminality with the least cost to the individual offender, but it also may simply fool the public into believing that the system is dealing harshly with crime.

California then radically changed its sentencing policy. Instead of employing broad discretion and maximum indeterminacy, California adopted the posture of legislatively restricted discretion and virtually maximum determinacy. For each felony offense category, the legislature authorized only three sentences. The judge is required to select the middle sentence unless upon proof of aggravating or mitigating circumstances he chooses the higher or lower sentence, giving a statement of reasons for the selection. The selection must be based upon guidelines promulgated by the California Judicial Council. The sentence can be increased if certain specific aggravating circumstances or "enhancements" are pleaded and proved.

Under the California scheme, the sentence imposed by the court approximates the sentence actually served. Parole is abolished, except as a period of supervised release added to each sentence. The California legislature apparently attempted to select sentence levels that conformed to the actual time served under the practices of the Adult Authority. The effect of the legislation is to eliminate the extremes of time served under Adult Authority practice and to permit the inmate and others to know how much time must be served when the sentence is imposed.

Toward a Just and Effective Sentencing System takes a third approach to the problem of criminal sentencing. It does not seek to eliminate sentencing discretion or to legislate tight restrictions on its exercise. Rather, it attempts to mandate the development of guidelines by an agency of the federal judiciary. The principal element of the proposal is a Commission on Sentencing and Corrections that would set sentencing guidelines for federal district judges. A judge would select a sentence and give a statement of reasons, showing he has applied the sentence guidelines to the individual case. The defendant could appeal the length of the sentence to the Court of Appeals, and the government, in some circumstances, could also appeal. The appellate court could reverse the sentence and remand for a new sentence or impose a different sentence itself. The sentence selected would be the sentence served. There would be no parole. The Bureau of Prisons would be required to release the inmate when he has served ninety percent of the sentence unless he has violated prison rules. With that exception, however, the inmate would know when he would be released at the time he entered the institution, assuming he or the government does not appeal the sentence. He would not be required to feign rehabilitation or religious conversion in order to win release. Sentencing uniformity would be enhanced by the Commission guidelines and by appellate review. The fiction that release from prison is a function of institutional rehabilitation would be abandoned in favor of a notion that the individualized sentence set at the beginning of the correctional process will be the sentence served, absent extraordinary circumstances.

NOTES AND QUESTIONS

1. Accepting the traditional assumption that the law should provide for both individualized sentencing (in which the trial judge has substantial discretion concerning the sentence to be imposed) and indeterminate sentencing (in which a parole authority has substantial discretion concerning the amount of time an offender actually serves), several important issues are presented. First, should there be a minimum sentence, i. e., a time set before which the defendant cannot be released by the parole authority? If so, should this minimum be set by the legislature, (i. e., be a "mandatory" one) or should the trial judge have the authority—perhaps within legislatively determined limits—to decide whether a minimum sentence should be imposed and, if so, what its length should be? Among the arguments for a mandatory minimum are those that stress the deterrent value of an assurance that all offenders sentenced to imprisonment will serve a certain minimum and others that urge that a correctional program stands a reasonable chance of rehabilitating an offender only if the program will have the offender for a minimum period of time. Opponents of a mandatory minimum urge that this deprives the system of the ability to distinguish offenders from whom society does not need the protection of prolonged incarceration.

The other issue concerns a maximum sentence, at the expiration of which the parole authority must release the offender. Should there be a maximum or, in the alternative, should the parole authority be permitted to retain the offender until he dies in prison? If a maximum should be provided, should this be set by the legislature (i. e., should it be a "mandatory" maximum) or should the sentencing judge have authority—within legislatively defined limits—to determine maximum sentences for particular cases? Among the relevant policy considerations, of course, are the deterrent values of a sentencing scheme which advertises that all offenders sentenced to imprisonment will be subject to a potentially long period of incarceration, the difficulty of a trial judge making at the time of sentence a reliable determination of the duration of confinement necessary for protection of society, and the need to impose some external limits upon the impact which parole decisionmaking can have upon offenders. These issues concerning the structuring of a traditional system for individualized and indeterminate sentencing are explored in great length in American Bar Association Project on Minimum Standards for Criminal Justice, Standards Related to Sentencing Alternatives and Procedures (Approved Draft 1968).

2. Alschuler, "Sentencing Reform and Prosecutorial Power: A Critique of Recent Proposals for 'Fixed' and 'Presumptive' Sentencing," 126 U.Pa.L.Rev. 550, 563–76 (1978) argues that sentencing schemes such as the California "maximum determinacy" one will not result in eliminating discretion but rather will substitute prosecutorial discretion for judicial discretion. The practice of plea bargaining—in which defendants are granted concessions in return for entry of a plea of guilty—will continue, Alschuler reasons. Under the new proposals, prosecutors will not be able to bargain with sentence recommendations, since sentencing judges will be in no position to act on such recommendations. Prosecutors will, however, be able to reduce charges against defendants who are willing to plead guilty and will in fact do this in order to encourage such pleas. As a result, he concludes, sentencing under these new schemes will still be influenced heavily by discretionary decisions. But it will be the prosecutors' decisions made during

the plea bargaining process rather than the trial judges' discretionary sentencing decisions that will come into greater prominence. Is Alschuler correct? Is there any way to avoid the situation he predicts? If not, does this amount to a conclusive argument against the new proposals?

3. Dix, Judicial Review of Sentences: Implications for Individual Disposition, 1969 Law & The Social Order 369, 413–15:

> The proposition that emphasis on individualization causes longer actual incarceration as well as longer potential incarceration finds some support in a comparison of definite and indeterminate sentencing practices. * * * In those jurisdictions using both types of sentences, the indeterminate sentence meant longer potential incarceration—sometimes three times as long. In addition, maximum sentences in those jurisdictions imposing primarily indeterminate sentences were almost always longer than sentences imposed in jurisdictions imposing primarily definite sentences.
>
> [A comparison of] * * * median time actually served by offenders released during 1960, suggests that the exercise of parole discretion under the indeterminate sentences reduced this disparity but did not eliminate it. In some jurisdictions using both types of sentences, the parole authority was so exercised that those sentenced to indeterminate terms served less time than their counterparts serving definite terms; this was not always true, however. Most important, those states adopting a general policy of indeterminate sentencing generally required their offenders to serve significantly longer periods. Indeterminate sentencing, therefore, almost certainly means longer potential incarceration and—especially if the jurisdiction has adopted a general policy of near-exclusive use of indeterminate sentences—it also means longer actual incarceration. Although definite sentences may involve the exercise of significant trial court individualization, it is probably true that indeterminate sentencing represents greater individualization. The opportunity for the exercise of discretionary individualization extends over a longer period of time (during the entire period of parole eligibility) and—although this is more questionable—correctional authorities are probably more likely than trial court judges to view their role as appropriately one of individualization at the expense of other factors such as uniformity and respect for upper limits on incarceration determined by the seriousness of the act for which liability was initially imposed. The general statistical inference is that the greater the opportunity for individualization, the longer the potential and actual incarceration is likely to be. This merely emphasizes that the acceptance of the propriety of individualization increases willingness to incarcerate longer, thus underlining the necessity of examining realistically the basis on which the ability to reliably individualize is accepted.

See, also Rubin, The Concept of Treatment in the Criminal Law, 21 S.C.L. Rev. 3, 5 (1968): "[T]his 'treatment' idea, indeterminate sentences, has had its principal effect increasing terms of imprisonment."

4. What impact is an increase in the severity of sentences imposed likely to have upon sentences actually served? Consider the following (See

chart, infra) from U.S. Department of Justice, Federal Prison System Statistical Report, Fiscal Year 1975 (Washington, D.C.; Federal Prison System, 1977), p. 15: How might this be explained? If it is viewed as undesirable, how might it be changed?

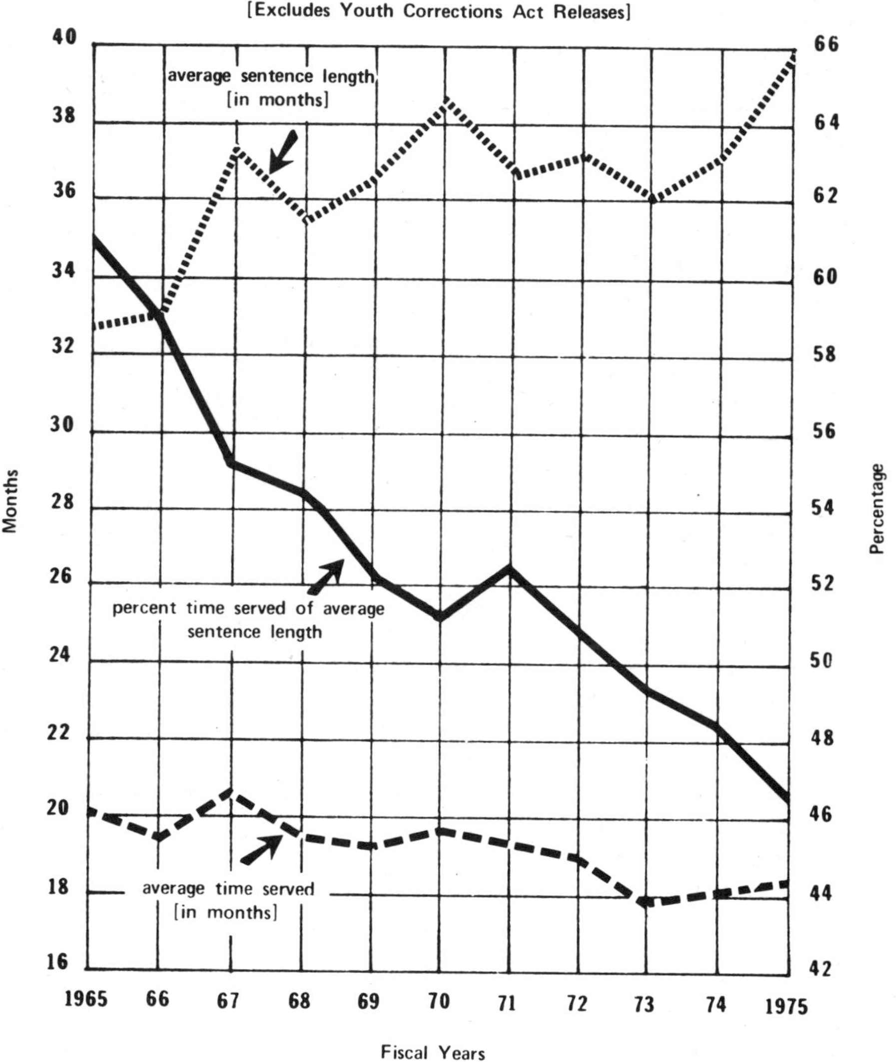

5. Should the imposition of fines be treated differently than the imposition of other penalties? Consider the following provision of the New York Penal Law:

§ 80.00 Fine for felony

1. Criterion for fine. The court may impose a fine for a felony if the defendant has gained money or property through the commission of the crime.

2. Amount of fine. A sentence to pay a fine for a felony shall be a sentence to pay an amount, fixed by the court, not exceeding double the amount of the defendant's gain from the commission of the crime.

3. Determination of amount. As used in this section the term "gain" means the amount of money or the value of property derived from the commission of the crime, less the amount of money or the value of property returned to the victim of the crime or seized by or surrendered to lawful authority prior to the time sentence is imposed.

When the court imposes a fine for a felony the court shall make a finding as to the amount of the defendant's gain from the crime. If the record does not contain sufficient evidence to support such a finding the court may conduct a hearing upon the issue.

If this approach is proper when the offense is a felony, why should it not also be applied to the imposition of a fine for less serious offenses?

2. SPECIFIC PENALTIES

This section addresses three major issues concerning the punishment of those convicted of a criminal offense. Each involves special concern with the severity of the penalty. Two different responses are illustrated. One is to hold that the penalty, at least on particular facts, is unconstitutionally harsh. The other is to focus upon the procedure by which defendants are picked for the penalty and to insist upon special care in the selection process. In regard to the death penalty covered in the first subsection, the United States Supreme Court has limited the offenses which can be punished by death. As to those that can be so punished, it has required that especially careful procedures be used to determine whether a particular defendant is appropriately subjected to the ultimate penalty. The second subsection deals with prison terms imposed under regular sentencing procedures and the argument that these are sometimes so severe as to be unconstitutionally excessive. While the courts are split, a significant number of them are reluctant to review particular sentences to determine whether they are so harsh as to violate constitutional mandates. Finally, the third subsection deals with procedures for identifying psychologically abnormal offenders and subjecting them to special sentencing procedures involving indeterminate sentences, i. e., sentences without an upper limit. Most of these are so-called "sex psychopath" statutes, limited to persons regarded as sexually dangerous. But the discussion covers others as well. Although courts have been unwilling to hold penalties imposed under such programs inherently invalid, at least some courts have imposed rather stringent procedural requirements upon the sentencing process involved in such programs and upon the continued retention of defendants found to be within their terms.

a. THE DEATH PENALTY

The principal case in this subsection deals with the substantive limits on the death penalty, i. e., when it would be unconstitutionally harsh. Most of the recent United States Supreme Court cases dealing with the penalty of death, however, address the related but distinguishable question regarding the procedures that must be used to choose which defendants should be marked for punishment by death. Both the substantive and procedural limits upon the death penalty have their genesis in Furman v. Georgia, 408 U.S. 238, 92 S.Ct. 2726, 33 L.Ed.2d 346 (1972), in which the Court, for the first time, held that the imposition and carrying out of the death penalty, under the circumstances presented there, violated the Cruel and Unusual Punishment Clause of the Eighth Amendment. In nine separate opinions covering 131 pages the Justices sought to explain their varied reasons for concurring in and dissenting from this dramatic judgment.

Mr. Justice Brennan undertook in *Furman* a lengthy analysis of the history of Eighth Amendment jurisprudence. He concluded that the "Cruel and Unusual Punishments Clause prohibits the infliction of uncivilized and inhuman punishments. The State even as it punishes, must treat its members with respect for their intrinsic worth as human beings. A punishment is 'cruel and unusual' therefore, if it does not comport with human dignity." He then found four principles recognized in the cases and "inherent in the Clause" whereby one might determine whether a particular penalty "comports with human dignity". According to Justice Brennan "the primary principle is that a punishment must not be so severe as to be degrading to the dignity of human beings." Physical pain might be an index of severity but the true significance of our hostility to tortuous punishment "is that they treat members of the human race as non-humans, as objects to be toyed with and discarded. They are thus inconsistent with the fundamental premise of the Clause that even the vilest criminal remains a human being possessed of common human dignity."

His second, third, and fourth principles are that a severe penalty not be inflicted arbitrarily, not be unacceptable to contemporary society, and not be excessive.

> A punishment is excessive under this [last] principle if it is unnecessary: The infliction of a severe punishment by the State cannot comport with human dignity when it is nothing more than the pointless infliction of suffering. If there is a

> significantly less severe punishment adequate to achieve the purposes for which the punishment is inflicted the punishment inflicted is unnecessary and therefore excessive.

408 U.S. at 279, 92 S.Ct. at 2747, 33 L.Ed.2d at 372 (Brennan, J., concurring). Applying those principles, Mr. Justice Brennan found death to be a cruel and unusual punishment in violation of the Constitution.

Mr. Justice Marshall's opinion in *Furman* gave special emphasis to three factors. First, the evidence that the penalty is imposed with disproportionate frequency on members of minority groups. Second, the alleged absence of evidence that it is a more effective deterrent than lesser penalties. Third, his belief that capital punishment had generally been rejected by our society.

For Justice Stewart, the nub of the problem was that the legal system permitted "this unique penalty to be so wantonly and so freakishly imposed". Justices Douglas and White also concurred on the basis of the manner in which the statutes were administered. The Chief Justice and Justices Blackmun, Powell and Rehnquist dissented.

In 1976, the Court decided five cases involving statutes which had been enacted in response to *Furman.* Mr. Justice Stewart for himself and Justices Powell and Stevens, focused on whether or not the discretion of those empowered to impose the death penalty was adequately guided so as to minimize the risk that "it would be inflicted in an arbitrary and capricious manner." They were satisfied that a carefully drafted statute could so do and proceeded to uphold three (those of Georgia, Florida and Texas) of the five challenged statutes. Rejected were arguments that the potential for the arbitrary exercise of discretion remained in that prosecutors continued to be totally free to decide, without control, whether or not to charge a capital offense, and in that the standards for exercising sentencing discretion remained so broad as to permit arbitrary action. These justices, and the four others who concurred in the judgment, disassociated themselves from the broader arguments presented by Mr. Justice Brennan in *Furman.* Mr. Justice Stewart wrote:

> Therefore, in assessing a punishment selected by a democratically elected legislature against the constitutional measure, we presume its validity. We may not require the legislature to select the least severe penalty possible so long as the penalty selected is not cruelly inhumane or disproportionate to the crime involved. And a heavy burden rests on those who would attack the judgment of the representatives of the people.

Gregg v. Georgia, 428 U.S. 153, 175, 96 S.Ct. 2909, 2926, 49 L.Ed.2d 859, 876 (1976) (opinion of Stewart, Powell, and Stevens, JJ., announcing the judgment of the Court). He went on to note that those who would argue evolving standards of decency had to face the fact that, as of that time, at least 35 states and the Congress had, since *Furman*, enacted death penalty provisions, and that, as of March 1976, more than 460 persons were subject to sentences of death. Moreover, while punishment cannot be gratuitous, retribution is not "a forbidden objective nor one inconsistent with our respect for the dignity of men." Thus, in the absence of better evidence of its lack of utility, he could not conclude that the death penalty is unconstitutionally severe. Nevertheless, the North Carolina and Louisiana statutes were held to fail the constitutional standard of adequately guided discretion because they provided for mandatory death sentences in certain cases. The Chief Justice and Justices Blackmun, White and Rehnquist dissented from these judgments and concurred in those upholding the validity of the other challenged statutes.

This insistence that the decision-maker must be adequately guided and that both untrammelled discretion and discretionless mandatory sentencing be avoided was further developed in Lockett v. Ohio, 438 U.S. 586, 98 S.Ct. 2954, 57 L.Ed.2d 973 (1978). The petitioner had been convicted of murder and sentenced to death because of her participation in an armed robbery during which another participant killed the merchant. The Court addressed only one of petitioner's claims as to the unconstitutionality of the Ohio statute under which she was condemned. This was that the statute did not permit the sentencing judge to consider mitigating factors such as her character, her prior record, age, lack of specific intent to cause death, and her relatively minor part in the crime. The Court agreed with her with Mr. Chief Justice Burger writing:

> * * * We * * * conclude that the Eighth and Fourteenth Amendments require that the sentencer, in all but the rarest kind of capital case,[11] not be precluded from considering *as a mitigating factor,* any aspect of a defendant's character or record and any of the circumstances of the offense that the defendant proffers as a basis for a sentence less than death. We recognize that, in noncapital cases, the established practice of individualized sentences rests not on constitutional commands but public policy enacted into statutes. The considerations that account for the wide acceptance of individualization of sentences in noncapital cases surely cannot be thought less important in capital cases. Given that the imposition of death by public authority is so profoundly

11. We express no opinion as to whether the need to deter certain kinds of homicide would justify a mandatory death sentence as, for example, when a prisoner—or escapee—under a life sentence is found guilty of murder, See Roberts (Harry) v. Louisiana, 431 U.S. 633, 637 n. 5, 97 S.Ct. 1993, 1996, 52 L.Ed.2d 637 (1977).

> different from all other penalties, we cannot avoid the conclusion that an individualized decision is essential in capital cases. The need for treating each defendant in a capital case with that degree of respect due the uniqueness of the individual is far more important than in noncapital cases. A variety of flexible techniques—probation, parole, work furloughs, to name a few—and various post conviction remedies, may be available to modify an initial sentence of confinement in noncapital cases. The nonavailability of corrective or modifying mechanisms with respect to an executed capital sentence underscores the need for individualized consideration as a constitutional requirement in imposing the death sentence.[13] * * *

Mr. Justice Rehnquist who dissented, in part, pointed out that the Court appeared to be backtracking from its position in *Furman* in that an insistence that any and all evidence be admissible in mitigation would seem to encourage rather than eliminate arbitrariness in sentencing.

COKER v. GEORGIA

Supreme Court of the United States, 1977.
433 U.S. 584, 97 S.Ct. 2861, 53 L.Ed.2d 982.

Mr. Justice WHITE announced the judgment of the Court and filed an opinion in which Mr. Justice STEWART, Mr. Justice BLACKMUN, and Mr. Justice STEVENS, joined.

Georgia Code Ann. § 26–2001 (1972) provides that "[a] person convicted of rape shall be punished by death or by imprisonment for life, or by imprisonment for not less than 20 years." Punishment is determined by a jury in a separate sentencing proceeding in which at least one of the statutory aggravating circumstances must be found before the death penalty may be imposed.[e] Petitioner Coker was convicted of rape and sentenced to death. Both conviction and sen-

13. Sentencing in noncapital cases presents no comparable problems. We emphasize that in dealing with standards for imposition of the death sentence we intimate no view regarding the authority of a State or of the Congress to fix mandatory, minimum sentences for noncapital crimes.

e. Under the Georgia death penalty procedure, one convicted of a capital offense receives death only if the jury so recommends and, except for cases of treason and aircraft highjacking, has found at least one of the statutorily prescribed aggravating conditions to be present. These conditions include factors such as: that the defendant had previously been convicted of a capital felony or has a substantial history of serious assaultive criminal convictions; that the offense was committed during the commission of another specified felony; that in a case of murder, it was done so as to endanger more than one life, or for pay, or was of certain officials such as peace officers; or "was outrageously or wantonly vile, horrible or inhuman in that it involved torture, depravity of mind, or an aggravated battery to the victim.

tence were affirmed by the Georgia Supreme Court. Coker was granted a writ of certiorari, limited to the single claim, rejected by the Georgia court, that the punishment of death for rape violates the Eighth Amendment, which proscribes "cruel and unusual punishments" and which must be observed by the States as well as the Federal Government.

I

While serving various sentences for murder, rape, kidnapping, and aggravated assault, petitioner escaped from the Ware Correctional Institution near Waycross, Ga., on September 2, 1974. At approximately 11 p. m. that night, petitioner entered the house of Allen and Elnita Carver through an unlocked kitchen door. Threatening the couple with a "board," he tied up Mr. Carver in the bathroom, obtained a knife from the kitchen, and took Mr. Carver's money and the keys to the family car. Brandishing the knife and saying "you know what's going to happen to you if you try anything, don't you," Coker then raped Mrs. Carver. Soon thereafter, petitioner drove away in the Carver car, taking Mrs. Carver with him. Mr. Carver, freeing himself, notified the police; and not long thereafter petitioner was apprehended. Mrs. Carver was unharmed.

Petitioner was charged with escape, armed robbery, motor vehicle theft, kidnapping, and rape. Counsel was appointed to represent him. Having been found competent to stand trial, he was tried. The jury returned a verdict of guilty, rejecting his general plea of insanity. A sentencing hearing was then conducted in accordance with the procedures dealt with at length in Gregg v. Georgia, 428 U.S. 153, 96 S.Ct. 2909, 49 L.Ed.2d 859 (1976), where this Court sustained the death penalty for murder when imposed pursuant to the statutory procedures. The jury was instructed that it could consider as aggravating circumstances whether the rape had been committed by a person with a prior record of conviction for a capital felony and whether the rape had been committed in the course of committing another capital felony, namely, the armed robbery of Allen Carver. The court also instructed, pursuant to statute, that even if aggravating circumstances were present, the death penalty need not be imposed if the jury found they were outweighed by mitigating circumstances, that is, circumstances not constituting justification or excuse for the offense in question, "but which, in fairness and mercy, may be considered as extenuating or reducing the degree" of moral culpability or punishment. The jury's verdict on the rape count was death by electrocution. Both aggravating circumstances on which the court instructed were found to be present by the jury.

II

Furman v. Georgia, 408 U.S. 238, 92 S.Ct. 2726, 33 L.Ed.2d 346 (1972), and the Court's decisions last Term, * * * make unnecessary the recanvassing of certain critical aspects of the controversy about the constitutionality of capital punishment. It is now settled that the death penalty is not invariably cruel and unusual punishment within the meaning of the Eighth Amendment; it is not inherently barbaric or an unacceptable mode of punishment for crime; neither is it always disproportionate to the crime for which it is imposed. It is also established that imposing capital punishment, at least for murder, in accordance with the procedures provided under the Georgia statutes saves the sentence from the infirmities which led the Court to invalidate the prior Georgia capital punishment statute in Furman v. Georgia, supra.

In sustaining the imposition of the death penalty in *Gregg*, however, the Court firmly embraced the holdings and dicta from prior cases, to the effect that the Eighth Amendment bars not only those punishments that are "barbaric" but also those that are "excessive" in relation to the crime committed. Under *Gregg*, a punishment is "excessive" and unconstitutional if it (1) makes no measurable contribution to acceptable goals of punishment and hence is nothing more than the purposeless and needless imposition of pain and suffering; or (2) is grossly out of proportion to the severity of the crime. A punishment might fail the test on either ground. Furthermore, these Eighth Amendment judgments should not be, or appear to be, merely the subjective views of individual Justices; judgment should be informed by objective factors to the maximum possible extent. To this end, attention must be given to the public attitudes concerning a particular sentence—history and precedent, legislative attitudes, and the response of juries reflected in their sentencing decisions are to be consulted. In *Gregg*, after giving due regard to such sources, the Court's judgment was that the death penalty for deliberate murder was neither the purposeless imposition of severe punishment nor a punishment grossly disproportionate to the crime. But the Court reserved the question of the constitutionality of the death penalty when imposed for other crimes.

III

That question, with respect to rape of an adult woman is now before us. We have concluded that a sentence of death is grossly disproportionate and excessive punishment for the crime of rape and is therefore forbidden by the Eighth Amendment as cruel and unusual punishment.

A

As advised by recent cases, we seek guidance in history and from the objective evidence of the country's present judgment concerning the acceptability of death as a penalty for rape of an adult woman. At no time in the last 50 years has a majority of the States authorized death as a punishment for rape. * * *

* * *

[The opinion then reviews how, following the invalidation of most capital punishment statutes by Furman, thirty-five states responded by enacting new statutes to satisfy the objections voiced in that decision but that only three included the rape of an adult woman as a capital offense as compared with sixteen which had done so just prior to Furman. Two of these states—Louisiana and North Carolina—had had their new statutes overturned in 1976, because the death penalty was mandatory and when they again revised their laws rape was omitted. Thus, at the time Coker was before the Court, only Georgia authorized death for the rape of an adult woman although Florida and Mississippi did so for the rape of a child by an adult.]

The current judgment with respect to the death penalty for rape is not wholly unanimous among state legislatures, but it obviously weighs very heavily on the side of rejecting capital punishment as a suitable penalty for raping an adult woman.[10]

B

It was also observed in *Gregg* that "[t]he jury * * * is a significant and reliable index of contemporary values because it is so directly involved." 428 U.S., at 181, 96 S.Ct., at 2929, and that it is thus important to look to the sentencing decisions that juries have made in the course of assessing whether capital punishment is an appropriate penalty for the crime being tried. * * *

According to the factual submissions in this Court, out of all rape convictions in Georgia since 1973—and that total number has not been tendered—63 cases had been reviewed by the Georgia Supreme Court as of the time of oral argument; and of these, six involved a death sentence, one of which was set aside, leaving five convicted rapists now under sentence of death in the State of Georgia. Georgia juries have thus sentenced rapists to death six times since 1973. This obviously is not a negligible number; and the State argues that as a practical matter juries simply reserve the extreme sanction for extreme cases of rape and that recent experience surely does not prove that jurors consider the death penalty to be a disproportionate punishment for every conceivable instance of rape, no matter how aggravated. Nevertheless, it is true that in the vast majority of cases, at least nine out of 10, juries have not imposed the death sentence.

IV

These recent events evidencing the attitude of state legislatures and sentencing juries do not wholly determine this controversy, for

10. In Trop v. Dulles, 356 U.S. 86, 102, 78 S.Ct. 590, 598, 2 L.Ed.2d 630 (1958), the Court took pains to note the climate of international opinion concerning the acceptability of a particular punishment. It is thus not irrelevant here that out of 60 major nations in the world surveyed in 1965, only three retained the death penalty for rape where death did not ensue. United Nations, Department of Economic and Social Affairs, Capital Punishment 40, 86 (1968).

the Constitution contemplates that in the end our own judgment will be brought to bear on the question of the acceptability of the death penalty under the Eighth Amendment. Nevertheless, the legislative rejection of capital punishment for rape strongly confirms our own judgment, which is that death is indeed a disproportionate penalty for the crime of raping an adult woman.

We do not discount the seriousness of rape as a crime. It is highly reprehensible, both in a moral sense and in its almost total contempt for the personal integrity and autonomy of the female victim and for the latter's privilege of choosing those with whom intimate relationships are to be established. Short of homicide, it is the "ultimate violation of self." It is also a violent crime because it normally involves force, or the threat of force or intimidation, to overcome the will and the capacity of the victim to resist. Rape is very often accompanied by physical injury to the female and can also inflict mental and psychological damage. Because it undermines the community's sense of security, there is public injury as well.

Rape is without doubt deserving of serious punishment; but in terms of moral depravity and of the injury to the person and to the public, it does not compare with murder, which does involve the unjustified taking of human life. Although it may be accompanied by another crime, rape by definition does not include the death or even the serious injury to another person. The murderer kills; the rapist, if no more than that, does not. Life is over for the victim of the murderers; for the rape victim, life may not be nearly so happy as it was, but it is not over and normally is not beyond repair. We have the abiding conviction that the death penalty, which "is unique in its severity and revocability," 428 U.S. 187, 96 S.Ct., at 2931, is an excessive penalty for the rapist who, as such, does not take human life.

This does not end the matter; for under Georgia law, death may not be imposed for any capital offense, including rape, unless the jury or judge finds one of the statutory aggravating circumstances and then elects to impose that sentence. For the rapist to be executed in Georgia, it must therefore be found not only that he committed rape but also that one or more of the * * * aggravating circumstances were present * * *. Here, * * * two of these aggravating circumstances were alleged and found by the jury.

Neither of these circumstances, nor both of them together, change our conclusion that the death sentence imposed on Coker is a disproportionate punishment for rape. Coker had prior convictions for capital felonies—rape, murder and kidnapping—but these prior convictions do not change the fact that the instant crime being punished is a rape not involving the taking of life.

It is also true that the present rape occurred while Coker was committing armed robbery, a felony for which the Georgia statutes authorize the death penalty.[15] But Coker was tried for the robbery offense as well as for rape and received a separate life sentence for this crime; the jury did not deem the robbery itself deserving of the death penalty, even though accompanied by the aggravating circumstance, which was stipulated, that Coker had been convicted of a prior capital crime.

We note finally that in Georgia a person commits murder when he unlawfully and with malice aforethought, either express or implied, causes the death of another human being. He also commits that crime when in the commission of a felony he causes the death of another human being, irrespective of malice. But even where the killing is deliberate, it is not punishable by death absent proof of aggravating circumstances, It is difficult to accept the notion, and we do not, that the rape, with or without aggravating circumstances, should be punished more heavily than the deliberate killer as long as the rapist does not himself take the life of his victim. The judgment of the Georgia Supreme Court upholding the death sentence is reversed and the case is remanded to that court for further proceedings not inconsistent with this opinion.

So ordered.

[Mr. Justice Brennan and Mr. Justice Marshall concurred on the grounds that they believe that any use of the death penalty is barred by the Eighth Amendment's prohibition of cruel and unusual punishments.]

[Mr. Justice Powell concurred in the judgment insofar as there was no indication that the rape here was committed with excessive brutality or that the victim sustained serious or lasting injury. He dissented, however, from the holding that capital punishment for rape is always disproportionate to the crime.]

[Mr. Chief Justice Burger, in a lengthy dissent joined by Mr. Justice Rehnquist, stressed the heinousness of Coker's record. In December 1971, he raped and stabbed to death a young woman. Eight months later he twice raped a 16-year-old, severely beat her with a club, and left her for dead. He had received three life terms, two 20-year terms, and one 8-year term for offenses arising from these incidents. The rape in question occurred in September 1974. These facts, according to the Chief Justice, indicated that, at least in this case, the Constitution unquestionably permitted Georgia to employ capital punishment. This was so because Coker had demonstrated himself to be a continuing threat to the safety of women, and additional terms

15. In Gregg v. Georgia, the Georgia Supreme Court refused to sustain a death sentence for armed robbery because, for one reason, death had been so seldom imposed for this crime in other cases that such a sentence was excessive and could not be sustained under the statute. As it did in this case, however, the Georgia Supreme Court apparently continues to recognize armed robbery as a capital offence for the purpose of applying the aggravating circumstances provisions of the Georgia Code.

of imprisonment could not affect him. Moreover, rape by any defendant, according to the dissent, could be a capital offense given the Georgia procedure with its requirement of an aggravating circumstance. The plurality's stress on the abandonment of rape as a capital crime was unpersuasive given the short period of time involved and the confusion created by the Court's various and uncertain rulings as to the constitutionality of death penalty statutes. More significant, for the dissenters, was the prior history of the country during which such treatment of rape was common, and the idea that under our federal system states may, subject to some limitations, experiment with different crime control techniques so that they might learn from each other's experience. The dissenters also rejected the conclusion that death for rape was disproportionate simply because the victim was not killed. "It is * * * not irrational—nor constitutionally impermissible—for a legislature to make the penalty more severe than the criminal act it punishes in the hope it would deter wrongdoing." For example, wrote the Chief Justice, few thieves would be deterred if the only punishment on conviction were the return of the stolen property. The decisions on such questions are for the legislatures and not for the judiciary.]

b. IMPRISONMENT AND PROPORTIONALITY

To what extent, if any, should sentences of imprisonment which are within legislatively prescribed limits be subject to constitutional attack on grounds of "excessiveness"? What standards should be used to resolve such attacks? One of the first opinions to engage in an elaborate analysis of these questions is that of the California Supreme Court in In re Lynch, 8 Cal.3d 410, 105 Cal.Rptr. 217, 503 P.2d 921 (1972). Lynch attacked his life sentence for a second indecent exposure conviction on the ground that it violated the state's constitutional prohibition against cruel or unusual punishment. In examining this contention the court formulated the following standards:

> We conclude that in California a punishment may violate article I, section 6, of the Constitution if, although not cruel or unusual in its method, it is so disproportionate to the crime for which it is inflicted that it shocks the conscience and offends fundamental notions of human dignity.
>
> To aid in administering this rule, we point to certain techniques used in the decisions discussed herein. First, a number of courts have examined the nature of the offense and/or the offender, with particular regard to the degree of danger both present to society. * * *
>
> Also relevant to the question of proportionality is the nonviolent nature of the offense. * * *
>
> Nor, finally, is nonviolence or absence of a victim a prerequisite to a finding of disproportionality. In appropriate

> cases the courts have nevertheless held the punishment excessive on the ground that no aggravating circumstances were shown. * * *
>
> The second technique used by the courts is to compare the challenged penalty with the punishments prescribed in the *same jurisdiction* for *different offenses* which, by the same test, must be deemed more serious. The underlying but unstated assumption appears to be that although isolated excessive penalties may occasionally be enacted, e. g., through "honest zeal" generated in response to transitory public emotion, the Legislature may be depended upon to act with due and deliberate regard for constitutional restraints in prescribing the vast majority of punishments set forth in our statutes. The latter may therefore be deemed illustrative of constitutionally permissible degrees of severity; and if among them are found more serious crimes punished less severely than the offense in question, the challenged penalty is to that extent suspect.
>
> * * *
>
> Closely related to the foregoing is the third technique used in this inquiry, i. e., a comparison of the challenged penalty with the punishments prescribed for the *same offense* in *other jurisdictions* having an identical or similar constitutional provision. Here the assumption is that the vast majority of those jurisdictions will have prescribed punishments for this offense that are within the constitutional limit of severity; and if the challenged penalty is found to exceed the punishments decreed for the offense in a significant number of those jurisdictions, the disparity is a further measure of its excessiveness.

8 Cal.3d at 424–27, 105 Cal.Rptr. at 226–28, 503 P.2d at 930–32.

Does the analysis proposed by this court include anything it should not? Does it omit any relevant considerations? What result would you reach under it on the facts of Lynch?

Two recent cases may serve to illustrate the difficulty of these issues. In Carmona v. Ward, 576 F.2d 405 (2nd Cir. 1978), cert. denied 439 U.S. 1091, 99 S.Ct. 874, 59 L.Ed.2d 58 (1979), the statute challenged was the 1973 New York Drug Law which provided for mandatory life sentences for all class A drug felonies. One of the appellees had received a sentence of six years to life for possession of one ounce of cocaine, the other, four years to life for sale of $20 worth (.00455 ounce) of cocaine. After reviewing much of the authority on the question of excessiveness as cruel and unusual punishment, the majority reversed the District Court's decision that the statute was unconstitutional. The Court of Appeals concluded that society could punish conduct on the basis of its potential for harm as well as for the harm caused directly and that drug trafficking could reasonably be viewed as posing grave dangers of disastrous consequences. Rehabilitative approaches to the drug problem had been tried at great expense in New York and had failed. It was neither arbitrary nor irrational for the legislature to conclude that penalties harsher than those employed elsewhere and harsher than applied in New York to crimes other than first and second degree murder, first degree arson and first degree kidnapping—the other offenses carrying a mandatory life sentence—were required. Coker was distinguished because, among other reasons, it involved death which is a unique penalty.

Rummel v. Estelle, the second case posing this problem, is now pending before the United States Supreme Court. In the decision below, 568 F.2d 1193 (5th Cir. 1978), the court, en banc,[f] considered petitioner's request for habeas corpus relief on the grounds of disproportionality. Rummel had been found guilty of the felony offense of obtaining $120.75, by false pretenses. This conviction, together with two prior convictions (one, nine years earlier, involving use of a credit card with intent to defraud of $80.00; another, four years earlier, for passing a forged instrument with a face value of $28.36) resulted under the applicable Texas habitual offender statute, in a mandatory life sentence. The statute, as construed by the Texas courts, required for the imposition of the enhanced penalty, that the state prove that the defendant has been convicted of a felony and sent to prison and that subsequent thereto had been convicted of a second felony and again sent to prison, and finally, that he had committed a third felony subsequent to the commission of and conviction for the preceding two felonies. A split panel of the court had earlier granted Rummel relief on the grounds that the life sentence for these three crimes "is so grossly disproportionate to the offenses as to constitute cruel and unusual punishment in violation of the eighth amendment." 568 F.2d 1193 (5th Cir. 1978). The en banc court, by a vote of 8 to 6, rejected this view. The majority accepted the proposition that a severe sentence for a minor offense could, solely because of its length, be cruel and unusual punishment. However, it held that the petitioner must establish that there is no rational basis for the legislative scheme and not merely that more rational systems might be or have been devised. Moreover, for the majority, the sentence must be viewed not as a fixed term of life but rather as a maximum of life with the possibility of release on parole after serving, due to the Texas system of good time credit, as little as ten years. It concluded:

> After three felony convictions and two ineffectual prison terms, the State of Texas has chosen to place the burden on

f. Appeals to courts of appeals are normally heard and decided by three judges. In cases of exceptional importance the entire court of appeals will rehear and decide it. This is the meaning of the term "en banc."

> the offender to prove his entitlement to a place in society. This is not an irrational choice, and to many, one that is not particularly callous. We do not think that Texas has adopted a system that is cruel and unusual in violation of the eighth amendment, even as applied to William Rummel.

Obviously, a major question is whether the United States Supreme Court's decisions dealing with the death penalty will be expanded to cover other penalties. Perhaps only penalties of death (and perhaps life imprisonment) will be scrutinized to determine whether they are so harsh as to constitute cruel and unusual punishment. On the other hand, as is argued In re Lynch, it is possible that the Court will require that any term of years of imprisonment be reviewed to determine whether it is excessive in relationship to the offense and the offender. The Court may hold that the prohibition against cruel and unusual punishment prohibits mandatory sentencing only in death penalty situations. But it may also expand its holdings and require, at least where unusually severe penalties are at issue, that the judge or jury imposing sentence have substantial discretion to consider potentially mitigating considerations.

The uncertainty of the current law is illustrated by recent litigation concerning a claim that a sentence of 40 years' imprisonment and a $20,000 fine for possession of less than nine ounces of marijuana with intent to distribute and distribution thereof violated the Constitution. A United States District Court struck down such a penalty as arbitrary and irrational, as applied to the particular defendant involved, in Davis v. Zahradnick, 432 F.Supp. 444 (W.D.Va.1977). A panel of the Court of Appeals reversed, stressing the defendant's record as a drug dealer, including a prior conviction for sale of LSD, and the fact that the defendant knew the drugs were to be supplied to prison inmates. Davis v. Davis, 585 F.2d 1226 (4th Cir. 1978). This decision was, in turn, superceded and the District Court upheld by the Court of Appeals sitting en banc. 601 F.2d 152 (4th Cir. 1979). It can be argued that if courts are permitted to review the alleged unconstitutionality of such penalties, their decisions will inevitably turn on the judges' personal values rather than upon "the law," and that this is inappropriate. It can also be argued that democratically elected legislatures are the proper bodies within our system of government to decide on maximum potential sentences, and that the judges before whom defendants are convicted are uniquely qualified to determine the appropriate length of a prison sentence within the legislatively-set limits. Review such as that in the *Davis* case involves, in effect, resentencing by a court with far less competence to make the difficult decision on length of imprisonment.

c. EXPANDED TERMS FOR "ABNORMAL" OFFENDERS

Certain offenders, most notably those who have committed sex-related crimes, have often been regarded as unusually dangerous because their criminal activity is perceived as stemming, in part at least, from some psychological disturbance which, although insufficient to allow for a defense of insanity, is unlikely to be corrected by normal conditions of incarceration. One legislative response, encouraged by the development of the "rehabilitative ideal" in corrections, has been to create special programs whereby these psychologically-abnormal and dangerous offenders may be identified and subjected to special "treatment" which would ensure the elimination of their special dangerousness prior to their release into society. A recent survey found 27 states with so-called "sex psychopath" statutes, which cover persons thought to pose unusual dangers of sexually-related crimes because of their abnormality. L. Sleffel, The Law and the Dangerous Criminal 58 (1977). Other provisions are not limited to the sexually-dangerous. The Model Penal Code sentencing proposals would permit imposition of an extended term of imprisonment upon a defendant who, after conviction, is found to be "a dangerous, mentally abnormal person whose commitment for an extended term is necessary for the protection of the public." Model Penal Code § 7.03 (P.O.D.1962). Sleffel found five statutes following this pattern in effect at the time of her survey. Id. at 21.

A number of legal problems have arisen incident to programs of this sort. The most "substantive" limitation upon these programs was imposed by the California Supreme Court in People v. Feagley,[g] 14 Cal.3d 338, 121 Cal.Rptr. 509, 535 P.2d 373 (1975), which held that the State Constitution, as interpreted in In re Lynch (discussed at page 45, infra) prohibited the indefinite confinement of a "mentally disordered sex offender" in an institutional unit located on prison grounds. The defendant had a history of "molesting" girls and young women allegedly due to his compulsive need to caress or comb feminine hair. Although he never used force he sometimes snipped a lock of hair with scissors. Because of this conduct he had spent 19 years in various mental hospitals and prisons. Following his guilty plea to the misdemeanor charge of battery, the judge empanelled a jury which determined by a preponderance of the evidence and on a vote of 9–3 that he was a mentally disordered sex offender, and the judge found on the basis of expert testimony that there was no known treatment

g. The citation indicates that the opinion is by the Supreme Court of California—since it can be found in "Cal. 3d"—and that it can be found in three different law reporter series. For most state court decisions there will be only two reporting systems; one official and designated by an abbreviation of the state's name, the other, an "unofficial" regional reporter which includes the decisions of the higher courts of a number of states. In this case the regional reporter is "Pacific" which reports the decisions of fifteen western states.

that would cure or even help his condition. On the basis of these findings, Feagley was indefinitely committed to the Department of Mental Hygiene which placed him in a special unit at a prison where, the State Supreme Court found, he was part of the general prison population and held there without treatment. This, said the Court, constituted cruel and unusual punishment. The justification for such indefinite commitments must, in the absence of a showing of dangerousness, be predicated on the provision of treatment. If the defendant was unamenable to treatment he must be processed as a criminal and his confinement limited to that period prescribed by the statute for the violation of which he was convicted.

NOTES AND QUESTIONS

1. In a companion case to *Feagley*, People v. Burnick, 14 Cal.3d 306, 121 Cal.Rptr. 488, 535 P.2d 352 (1975), the court held that the state had to establish that the appellant was a mentally disordered sex offender by the beyond a reasonable doubt standard despite the state's contention that this was a civil proceeding since—as in criminal cases—the subject was threatened with loss of liberty and stigmatization. The court rejected the argument that a lesser standard of persuasion was appropriate because the question posed was predictive in nature, i. e., whether the defendant is predisposed to commit sex crimes in the future. As is indicated by the following excerpts, this, for the court, was a further reason to require the state to bear the heavier burden inasmuch as the extraordinary difficulty of the task posed a high risk of erroneously labeling harmless persons as harmful:

> In the light of recent studies it is no longer heresy to question the reliability of psychiatric predictions. Psychiatrists themselves would be the first to admit that however desirable an infallible crystal ball might be, it is not among the tools of their profession. It must be conceded that psychiatrists still experience considerable difficulty in confidently and accurately *diagnosing* mental illness. Yet those difficulties are multiplied manyfold when psychiatrists venture from diagnosis to prognosis and undertake to predict the consequences of such illness: " 'A diagnosis of mental illness tells us nothing about whether the person so diagnosed is or is not dangerous. Some mental patients are dangerous, some are not. Perhaps the psychiatrist is an expert at deciding whether a person is mentally ill, but is he an expert at predicting which of the persons so diagnosed are dangerous? Sane people, too, are dangerous, and it may legitimately be inquired whether there is anything in the education, training or experience of psychiatrists which renders them particularly adept at predicting dangerous behavior. Predictions of dangerous behavior, no matter who makes them, are incredibly inaccurate, and there is a growing consensus that psychiatrists are not uniquely qualified to predict dangerous behavior and are, in fact, less accurate in their predictions than other professionals.' " (Murel v. Baltimore City Criminal Court (1972) 407 U.S. 355, 364–365, fn. 2, 92 S.Ct. 2091, 2096, 32 L.Ed.2d 791 (Douglas, J., dissenting from dismissal of certiorari).)

2. If one believes that there are mentally ill sex offenders who pose a continuing danger to society but for whom modern psychiatry offers little or no effective treatment, must the protection of the community be limited to that afforded by the penalties provided for misdemeanors? Is it preferable for courts to insist as did the three dissenting Justices in *Burnick* and *Feagley* that courts act to ensure the provision of treatment rather than "erect procedural barriers (such as impractical proof standards) which deprive both the public and the defendant himself of the benefits of the MDSO program"? Is such action by courts feasible? Consider the response of Judge Friendly to a *Burnick*-type attack on a New York statute permitting an indefinite sentence of one day to life for a convicted sex offender "* * * if the record indicated some basis for a finding that the defendant is a danger to society or is capable of being benefited by the confinement envisaged under the statutory scheme."

> To require proof of such elements beyond a reasonable doubt would either prevent the application of such statutes except in the most extreme cases or invite hypocrisy on the part of judges or juries. As Judge Sobeloff said in Tippett v. State of Maryland, 436 F.2d 1153, 1165 (4th Cir. 1971), cert. dismissed 407 U.S. 355, 92 S.Ct. 2091, 32 L.Ed.2d 791 (1972), with respect to the Maryland Defective Delinquents Act:
>
>> It must be recognized, however, that as to the ultimate issue of the inmate's dangerousness, the beyond a reasonable doubt standard may in practical operation be too onerous. After all, the ultimate issue is not as in a criminal case whether an alleged act was committed or event occurred, but the much more subjective issue of the individual's mental and emotional character. Such a subjective judgment cannot ordinarily attain the same "state of certitude" demanded in criminal cases.
>
> On the other hand, we are convinced, as Judge Sobeloff suggested in *Tippett* that even if the beyond a reasonable doubt standard does not fit the kind of determination here required, the "some basis" standard is insufficient. The State was bound to make out its case that Hollis was "a danger to society or [was] capable of being benefited by the confinement envisaged under the statutory scheme" by "clear, unequivocal, and convincing evidence."

Hollis v. Smith, 571 F.2d 685, 695 (2nd Cir. 1978).

3. The major American experiment with programs similar to the sex offender program but not limited to those believed to pose a high risk of illicit sexual activity was the Maryland Defective Delinquency Program. The Program grew out of several studies conducted for the Maryland legislature, stimulated by what was perceived to be the need to deal specifically with certain dangerous repeat offenders. Protection of society was clearly the primary purpose of the program; it was designed to identify offenders who would commit crimes if released at the end of fixed sentences and to incarcerate them until and if it became safe to release them. In addition, the program was designed to attempt to provide treatment to the offenders being detained and to create an opportunity for observation and study of these offenders so that more effective treatment methods might be devised.

Committee on Medico-Legal Procedure, Research Report Number 29. A facility was constructed at Jessup, Maryland, to house the program; this is Patuxent Institution.

The legal framework for the program was contained in Article 31–B of the Maryland Code. Under certain circumstances, persons convicted of an offense could be subjected to examination to determine whether they were defective delinquents. The statute provided:

> [A] defective delinquent [is] an individual who, by the demonstration of persistent aggravated antisocial criminal behavior, evidences a propensity towards criminal activity, and who is found to have either such intellectual deficiency or emotional unbalance, or both, as to clearly demonstrate an actual danger to society so as to require such confinement and treatment, when appropriate, as may make it reasonably safe for society to terminate the confinement and treatment.

Md. Code, Art. 31–B § 5 (repealed in 1977). Patuxent staff personnel conducted the examination. If the staff report recommended that an offender be found a defective delinquent, a hearing on this matter was conducted by the court in which the defendant was convicted. Various procedural rights were accorded the defendant at this hearing, including the right to counsel and to a jury trial. If the court determined that the defendant was in fact a defective delinquent, he was sentenced to an indeterminate period at Patuxent. Each defective delinquent was reexamined annually by an Institutional Board of Review, which made a recommendation concerning the prisoner's future status and treatment. The Program could release a defendant to supervised living in the community, i. e., parole, and could recommend that the sentencing court unconditionally discharge him from the program. Until such discharge, however, the Program had the right to return prisoners on parole to the institution. Prisoners could also petition the court for a redetermination of their status; if they were found to no longer be defective delinquents, they were released unconditionally by the court.

Patuxent Institution opened January 1, 1955, and soon became a major source of controversy. Opponents of the program claimed that it was arbitrary in the manner of selecting offenders for inclusion in the program, that it detained far more offenders than were in fact "dangerous," and that despite appearances it did not in fact provide meaningful treatment. Proponents argued that it used the most effective treatment and predictive methods available and that evidence showed that it was in fact protecting the community from numerous persons who would otherwise commit serious antisocial acts. Compare, e. g., Schreiber, Indeterminate Therapeutic Incarceration of Dangerous Criminals: Perspectives and Problems, 56 Va.L.Rev. 602 (1970) with Hodges, Crime Prevention by the Indeterminate Sentence Law, 128 Am.J. Psychiatry 291 (1971). Despite numerous legal challenges to the program and the procedures used in implementing it, Maryland state courts and lower federal courts upheld it. See Tippett v. Maryland, 436 F. 2d 1153 (4th Cir. 1971); Sas v. Maryland, 334 F.2d 506 (4th Cir. 1964); Director v. Daniels, 243 Md. 16, 221 A.2d 397, cert. den. 385 U.S. 940, 87 S. Ct. 307, 17 L.Ed.2d 219 (1966). The Supreme Court specifically refused to rule on the broader attacks that were leveled against the program. In Murel v. Baltimore City Criminal Court, 407 U.S. 355, 92 S.Ct. 2091, 32 L.Ed.

2d 791 (1972), the Court dismissed certiorari as improvidently granted to Tippett v. Maryland, supra.

During the 1976 legislative session, the Maryland House of Delegates voted to repeal Article 31–B. The Senate, however, voted to defer action pending the results of a thorough reexamination of the program to be commissioned by the Department of Public Safety and Correctional Services. This study was undertaken by Contract Research Corporation, which submitted a final report in February, 1977. Contract Research Corporation, The Evaluation of Patuxent Institution, Final Report (1977) (hereinafter cited as Final Report).

After considering the fairness and effectiveness of decision making in the program, the Final Report concluded:

> Decision making was found to be effective to the extent that those committed to Patuxent did in fact meet the statutory definition of defective delinquent. On the other hand, as a crime control measure the process is seen to be one of dubious effectiveness, since it requires the commitment of far more persons than are actually dangerous in order to ensure that those few who are dangerous are removed from society. In spite of court decisions that the statute * * * was not so vague as to violate due process, the study found it not to be even-handedly applied, there being a wide variation in number of commitments made within different counties and by different judges, and therefore essentially unfair in its effect.

Final Report, at iv. The Report then turned to the effectiveness of the treatment program and concluded:

> The psychotherapy offered at Patuxent was found to be vitiated by the essentially custodial nature of the Institution; that is, the goal of unquestioning obedience to authority characteristic of a custodial institution is in conflict with the goals of self-reliance and personal autonomy which psychotherapy attempts to foster. As for behavior therapy, the Graded Tier System, under which inmates are supposed to progress from minimal privileges and responsibilities to a readiness for the Pre-release Center and the responsibilities of the outside world, was found only moderately effective because inmates received no clear or consistent set of behavior guidelines by which they could advance. These findings, interpreted in conjunction with the conclusions from the literature review, would indicate that psychotherapy at Patuxent is and can be no more successful than previous psychotherapeutic programs, which have never demonstrated consistent effectiveness in changing patient outlook or altering behavior.

Final Report, at v.

To determine the effectiveness of the program in reducing recidivism, the study conducted three-year followups of inmates released from Patuxent and several comparison groups. Since it was found that many Patuxent parolees were returned to the institution following arrest but without formal conviction for a subsequent crime, the study concluded that arrests as well as convictions should be considered. Final Report, at 123. The following table presents the results of a comparison of the program's parolees, persons released from the program by courts despite the staff's position that they were still dangerous (the "partially treated" group), offenders found by the staff to be defective delinquents but not found to be within the statute by the courts (the "not certified" group) and a comparison group of offenders simply sentenced to imprisonment under regular procedures.

	% arrested	% convicted
1. Patuxent Parolees	60.4	23.6
2. Partially Treated Patuxent Releasees	74.3	54.3
3. Offenders Not Certified DD by Courts	67.4	32.6
4. Comparison Group— "Regular" Prisoners	63.5	35.1

Final Report, at 124. This and other information collected prompted the Report to conclude that Patuxent inmates "do about the same or slightly better on all indicators of recidivism [than the comparison groups]." Final Report, at v.

A cost-benefit study team analyzed the costs of keeping offenders in Patuxent and those involved in other Maryland correctional facilities and compared this with the benefits apparently derived by using the program rather than standard correctional programs. The team conclusions were described as follows:

> [Q]uite clearly * * * Patuxent is not cost-effective. When costs are defined as direct state expenditures, Patuxent is considerably more expensive than its alternative. In particular, the direct cost to the state of committing a typical offender to Patuxent is nearly twice the cost of sending him to the Division of Corrections * * *. It is projected that during the nearly ten-year analysis period offenders who had spent time in Patuxent would have a 69 percent chance of being reincarcerated. This would be compared with the 72 percent chance experienced by offenders sent to the Division of Corrections. In short, there are very modest benefits resulting from the substantially higher costs of Patuxent. Since these benefits are very small relative to the large differential costs, the study team concluded that the benefits of Patuxent do not justify its costs.

Final Report at v.

The Final Report recommended that the program as then constituted be abolished. Instead, it urged continuation of a somewhat similar program in which offenders would participate only if both the offender and the program staff consented to the participation. Offenders would be sentenced under regular sentencing provisions. But those with substantial amounts of time on their sentence could request an evaluation and an opportunity to enter the program. The incentive to do this would be the possibility of shortening the time actually served by participating in a well-designed rehabilitation program. Final Report, at vi-vii. The Final Report is discussed in a series of articles in Symposium, 5 Bulletin of the Am. Academy of Psychiatry and the Law 116 (1977). See especially, Gordon, A Critique of the Evaluation of Patuxent Institution, With Particular Attention to the Issues of Dangerousness and Recidivism, 5 Bulletin of the Am. Academy of Psychiatry and the Law 210 (1977).

In 1977, legislation was passed which abolished the existing Defective Delinquency Program and implemented many of the Report's suggestions. Md. Laws, 1977, ch. 678. The term "defective delinquent" was abandoned, and a new program aimed at "eligible persons" was created. An eligible person is

> a person who (1) has been convicted of a crime and is serving a sentence of imprisonment with at least three years remaining on it, (2) has an intellectual deficiency or emotional imbalance, (3) is likely to respond favorably to the programs and services provided at Patuxent Institution, and (4) can be better rehabilitated through those programs and services than by other incarceration.

Md.Ann.Code, Art. 31–B, § 1(g). A convicted person may be transferred by the Commissioner of Corrections to Patuxent for an evaluation upon recommendation of the sentencing court, the prosecutor, the offender himself, or the staff of the institution in which the offender is incarcerated. Md. Ann.Code, Art. 31–B, § 8. If the Patuxent staff finds that the offender is an eligible person, he is to remain at Patuxent. Md.Ann.Code, Art. 31–B, § 9(b). He *may* be released on parole by Patuxent's Institutional Board of Review, but *must* be released upon expiration of his original sentence. Md. Ann.Code, Art. 31–B, § 11. This legislation also provided for a new term of imprisonment for twenty-five years upon a third conviction for a crime of violence, if the defendant has previously served at least one term of imprisonment for a crime of violence. Persons sentenced under this provision may only be paroled by Patuxent's Institutional Board of Review. Md. Ann.Code, Art. 27, § 643B. Apparently, defendants sentenced under this section can hope for parole only if they are accepted in the Patuxent program.

Given the nature of the underlying problem, was the dismantling of the Defective Delinquency Program a sound action? Insofar as there were valid objections to the program, might steps short of abolition (or those taken in the 1977 legislation) have met these objections?

3. A PROPOSED CLASSIFICATION SCHEME

PROPOSED FEDERAL CRIMINAL CODE

(S. 1437, 95th Cong., 2d Sess. (1978).

§ 2001. Authorized Sentences

* * *

(b) Individuals. An individual found guilty of an offense shall be sentenced, in accordance with the provisions of section 2003, to:

(1) probation as authorized by chapter 21;

(2) a fine as authorized by chapter 22; or

(3) a term of imprisonment as authorized by chapter 23.

A sentence to pay a fine may be imposed in addition to any other sentence. * * *.

(c) Organizations. An organization found guilty of an offense shall be sentenced, in accordance with the provisions of section 2003, to:

(1) probation as authorized by chapter 21; or

(2) a fine as authorized by chapter 22.

A sentence to pay a fine may be imposed in addition to a sentence to probation. * * *.

* * *

§ 2003. Imposition of a Sentence

(a) Factors To Be Considered in Imposing a Sentence. (1) The court, in determining the particular sentence to be imposed, shall consider:

(A) the nature and circumstances of the offense and the history and characteristics of the defendant;

(B) the need for the sentence imposed:

(i) to afford adequate deterrence to criminal conduct;

(ii) to protect the public from further crimes of the defendant;

(iii) to reflect the seriousness of the offense, to promote respect for law, and to provide just punishment for the offense; and

(iv) to provide the defendant with needed educational or vocational training, medical care, or other correctional treatment in the most effective manner;

(C) the kinds of sentences available;

(D) the kinds of sentence and the sentencing range established for the applicable category of offense committed by the applicable category of defendant as set forth in the guidelines that are issued by the Sentencing Commission [d] * * *;

(E) any pertinent policy statement issued by the Sentencing Commission * * *; and

(F) the need to avoid unwarranted sentence disparities among defendants with similar records who have been found guilty of similar criminal conduct.

* * *

§ 2004. Order of Criminal Forfeiture

(a) Forfeiture. The court, in imposing a sentence on a defendant who has been found guilty of an offense described in section 1801 (Operating a Racketeering Syndicate), 1802 (Racketeering), or 1803 (Washing Racketeering Proceeds), shall order, in addition to the sentence that is imposed pursuant to the provisions of section 2001, that the defendant forfeit to the United States any property constituting his interest in the racketeering syndicate or enterprise involved.

* * *

§ 2006. Order of Restitution

The court, in imposing a sentence on a defendant who has been found guilty of an offense causing bodily injury or property damage or other loss, may order, in addition to the sentence that is imposed pursuant to the provisions of section 2001, that the defendant make restitution to a victim of the offense in an amount and manner set by the court. * * *

* * *

§ 2101. Sentence of Probation

"(a) *In General.* A defendant who has been found guilty of an offense may be sentenced to a term of probation unless:

(1) the offense is a Class A felony;

(2) the offense is an offense for which probation has been expressly precluded; or

(3) the defendant is sentenced at the same time to a term of imprisonment for the same or a different offense.

d. Chapter 58 of the Act would create a United States Sentencing Commission within the judicial branch. At least three of its seven presidentially-appointed members would be federal judges. The Commission would be charged with establishing sentencing policies and practices for the guidance of the federal courts, and with developing means of measuring the efficacy of sentencing, penal and correctional practices.

(b) *Authorized Terms.* The authorized terms of probation are:

(1) for a felony, not less than one nor more than five years;

(2) for a misdemeanor, not more than two years;

(3) for an infraction, not more than one year.

* * *

§ 2103. Conditions of Probation

(a) *Mandatory Condition.* The court shall provide, as an explicit condition of a sentence of probation, that the defendant not commit another federal, state, or local crime during the term of probation.

(b) *Discretionary Conditions.* The court may provide, as further conditions of a sentence to probation * * * that the defendant:

(1) support his dependents and meet other family responsibilities;

(2) pay a fine imposed pursuant to the provisions of chapter 22;

(3) make restitution to a victim of the offense pursuant to the provisions of section 2006;

(4) give to the victims of the offense the notice ordered pursuant to the provisions of section 2005;

(5) work conscientiously at suitable employment or pursue conscientiously a course of study or of vocational training that will equip him for suitable employment;

(6) refrain from engaging in a specified occupation, business, or profession bearing a reasonable relationship to the offense, or engage in such a specified occupation, business, or profession only under stated circumstances;

(7) refrain from frequenting specified kinds of places or from associating unnecessarily with specified persons;

(8) refrain from excessive use of alcohol, or any use of a narcotic drug or other controlled substance * * * without a prescription by a licensed medical practitioner;

(9) refrain from possessing a firearm, destructive device, or other dangerous weapon;

(10) undergo available medical or psychiatric treatment, including treatment for drug or alcohol dependency, as specified, by the court and remain in a specified institution if required for that purpose;

(11) remain in the custody of the Bureau of Prisons for any time or intervals of time, totaling no more than the lesser of one year or the term of imprisonment authorized

for the offense in section 2301(b), during the first year of the term of probation;

(12) reside at, or participate in the program of, a community treatment facility for all or part of the term of probation;

(13) work in community service as directed by the court;

(14) reside in a specified place or area, or refrain from residing in a specified place or area;

(15) remain within the jurisdiction of the court, unless granted permission to leave by the court or a probation officer;

(16) report to a probation officer as directed by the court or the probation officer;

(17) permit a probation officer to visit him at his home or elsewhere as specified by the court;

(18) answer inquiries by a probation officer and notify the probation officer promptly of any change in address or employment;

(19) notify the probation officer promptly if arrested or questioned by a law enforcement officer; or

(20) satisfy such other conditions as the court may impose.

* * *

§ 2201. Sentence of Fine

(a) *In General.* * * * a defendant who has been found guilty of an offense may be sentenced to pay a fine.

(b) *Authorized Fines.* Except as otherwise provided in subsection (c) or any other provision of law, the authorized fines are:

(1) if the defendant is an individual:

(A) for a felony, not more than $100,000;

(B) for a misdemeanor, not more than $10,000;

(C) for an infraction, not more than $1,000;

(2) if the defendant is an organization:

(A) for a felony, not more than $500,000;

(B) for a misdemeanor, not more than $100,000;

(C) for an infraction, not more than $10,000.

(c) *Alternative Authorized Fine.* In lieu of a fine authorized by subsection (b) or any other provision of law, a defendant who has been found guilty of an offense through which pecuniary gain was directly or indirectly derived, or by which bodily injury or property damage or other loss was caused, may be sentenced to pay a fine that does not exceed twice the gross gain derived or twice the gross loss caused, whichever is the greater.

* * *

§ 2301. Sentence of Imprisonment

(a) *In General.* A defendant who has been found guilty of an offense may be sentenced to a term of imprisonment.

(b) *Authorized Terms.* The authorized terms of imprisonment are:

(1) for a Class A felony, the duration of the defendant's life or any period of time;

(2) for a Class B felony, not more than twenty years;

(3) for a Class C felony, not more than ten years;

(4) for a Class D felony, not more than five years;

(5) for a Class E felony, not more than two years;

(6) for a Class A misdemeanor, not more than one year;

(7) for a Class B misdemeanor, not more than six months;

(8) for a Class C misdemeanor, not more than thirty days;

(9) for an infraction, not more than five days.

(c) *Eligibility for Early Release.* A term of imprisonment in excess of one year may be imposed to be served in full or may be imposed to be served subject to the defendant's eligibility for early release during any portion of the term * * *. A term of imprisonment of one year or less shall be imposed to be served in full * * *.

§ 2303. Parole Term * * * Included in a Sentence of Imprisonment

A sentence to a term of imprisonment in excess of one year automatically includes, in addition to the specified term of imprisonment, a separate:

(a) term of parole * * *.

* * *

§ 3841. Release Subject to Parole

A prisoner who is released from imprisonment after having been sentenced to a term of imprisonment in excess of one year shall be released on parole, whether granted early release * * * or whether released on the expiration of his term of imprisonment.

* * *

§ 3843. Term and Conditions of Parole

* * *

(b) *Authorized Terms of Parole.* The authorized terms of parole, are:

(1) for a Class A or Class B felony, not more than five years;

(2) for a Class C felony, not more than three years;

(3) for a Class D felony, not more than two years;

(4) for a Class E felony, not more than one year; and

(5) for two or more misdemeanors, not more than six months.

(c) *Conditions of Parole.* The Parole Commission shall provide, as an explicit condition of parole, that the parolee not commit another federal, state, or local crime during the term of parole. The Commission may provide, as further conditions of parole * * * any conditions set forth as discretionary conditions of probation in section 2103(b)(1) through (b)(10) and (b)(12) through (b)(19), and any other conditions it considers to be appropriate. * * *

II. THE CRIMINALIZATION DECISION

There is little doubt as to the wisdom of criminalizing certain kinds of conduct, such as serious assaultive activity. But reasonable questions can be raised concerning the propriety of imposing criminal sanctions upon other sorts of behavior. Questions are most frequently raised concerning the so-called victimless crimes: prostitution, public intoxication, possession or sale of "dangerous" substances, and similar matters. This chapter deals with the decision to prohibit such activities by imposing criminal sanctions upon persons who engage in them.

This chapter addresses three matters. First, it explores the nature of criminal legal liability. This obviously will have some impact upon the decision as to which behavior renders the person engaging in it subject to criminal sanctions. Second, it considers justifications for and the function of criminal punishment. What might reasonably be expected to result from criminalizing conduct and punishing persons who engage in it? How might this be expected to occur? The primary concern, of course, is whether criminal punishment might prevent persons from engaging in certain conduct in the future. Also of concern is the possibility that criminal punishment might be justified on grounds not directly related to the value of criminal penalties in preventing antisocial conduct; the fact, if it is true, that the conduct prohibited is morally reprehensible may justify punishing those who engage in it.

Finally, the chapter turns to legal limitations upon the ability of legislatures to create crimes. As might be expected, the cases in this subsection deal with possession or use of controlled substances, behavior while intoxicated, suspicious conduct in the streets, and similar activities. The cases deal only with the legal question of whether legislatures may constitutionally make the conduct at issue a crime. But consider also the underlying policy question of whether it is wise to make the conduct criminal. Many of the same considerations that bear upon the constitutionality of criminalizing certain conduct are also relevant to the legislative decision as to the wisdom of prohibiting the conduct by means of a criminal statute.

A. THE NATURE OF CRIMINAL LIABILITY

There are various forms of legal liability. Something may be "illegal" in the sense that a court will, if asked, order that a person not do it. Or, it may be illegal in the traditional tort sense; thus if a person engages in the behavior, any individual injured by it may recover civil damages from the person who engaged in the behavior. Finally, conduct may be illegal in the sense that it constitutes a crime. It is by no means clear that the fact that conduct is properly made illegal in one sense also justifies making it illegal in all senses. Specifically, it can be argued that even if there are good and adequate reasons for making conduct illegal in one of the first two senses described above, there still may not be sufficient reasons for imposing criminal sanctions. Making conduct criminal, in other words, may appropriately be regarded as only a last resort, given the serious impact which conviction of a crime may have upon a defendant. The extent to which criminalization should be regarded as a last resort depends in part upon the nature of criminal liability; this is addressed in this section. The selection that follows is a portion of a major essay in which the author attempts to identify what about criminal liability makes it different from other forms of legal liability.

HENRY M. HART, JR., THE AIMS OF THE CRIMINAL LAW

23 Law and Contemporary Problems 401, 402–06 (1958).

What do we mean by "crime" and "criminal"? * * *

A great deal of intellectual energy has been misspent in an effort to develop a concept of crime as "a natural and social phenomenon" abstracted from the functioning system of institutions which make use of the concept and give it impact and meaning. But the criminal law, like all law, is concerned with the pursuit of human purposes through the forms and modes of social organization, and it needs always to be thought about in that context as a method or process of doing something.

What then are the characteristics of this method?

1. The method operates by means of a series of directions, or commands, formulated in general terms, telling people what they must or must not do. Mostly, the commands of the criminal law are "mustnots," or prohibitions, which can be satisfied by inaction. "Do not murder, rape, or rob." But some of them are "musts," or affirmative requirements, which can be satisfied only by taking a specifically, or relatively specifically, described kind of action. "Support your wife and children," and "File your income tax return."

2. The commands are taken as valid and binding upon all those who fall within their terms when the time comes for complying with them, whether or not they have been formulated in advance in a single authoritative set of words. They speak to members of the community, in other words, in the community's behalf, with all the power and prestige of the community behind them.

3. The commands are subject to one or more sanctions for disobedience which the community is prepared to enforce.

Thus far, it will be noticed, nothing has been said about the criminal law which is not true also of a large part of the noncriminal, or civil, law. The law of torts, the law of contracts, and almost every other branch of private law that can be mentioned operate, too, with general directions prohibiting or requiring described types of conduct, and the community's tribunals enforce these commands. What, then, is distinctive about the method of the criminal law?

Can crimes be distinguished from civil wrongs on the ground that they constitute injuries to society generally which society is interested in preventing? The difficulty is that society is interested also in the due fulfillment of contracts and the avoidance of traffic accidents and most of the other stuff of civil litigation. The civil law is framed and interpreted and enforced with a constant eye to these social interests. Does the distinction lie in the fact that proceedings to enforce the criminal law are instituted by public officials rather than private complainants? The difficulty is that public officers may also bring many kinds of "civil" enforcement actions—for an injunction, for the recovery of a "civil" penalty, or even for the detention of the defendant by public authority. Is the distinction, then, in the peculiar character of what is done to people who are adjudged to be criminals? The difficulty is that, with the possible exception of death, exactly the same kinds of unpleasant consequences, objectively considered, can be and are visited upon unsuccessful defendants in civil proceedings.

If one were to judge from the notions apparently underlying many judicial opinions, and the overt language even of some of them, the solution of the puzzle is simply that a crime is anything which is *called* a crime, and a criminal penalty is simply the penalty provided for doing anything which has been given that name. So vacant a concept is a betrayal of intellectual bankruptcy. Certainly, it poses no intelligible issue for a constitution-maker concerned to decide whether to make use of "the method of the criminal law." Moreover, it is false to popular understanding, and false also to the understanding embodied in existing constitutions. By implicit assumptions that are more impressive than any explicit assertions, these constitutions proclaim that a conviction for crime is a distinctive and serious matter—a something, and not a nothing. What is that something?

4. What distinguishes a criminal from a civil sanction and all that distinguishes it, it is ventured, is the judgment of community condemnation which accompanies and justifies its imposition. As Professor Gardner wrote not long ago, in a distinct but cognate connection:

> The essence of punishment for moral delinquency lies in the criminal conviction itself. One may lose more money on the stock market than in a court-room; a prisoner of war camp may well provide a harsher environment than a state prison; death on the field of battle has the same physical characteristics as death by sentence of law. It is the expression of the community's hatred, fear, or contempt for the convict which alone characterizes physical hardship as punishment.

If this is what a "criminal" penalty is, then we can say readily enough what a "crime" is. It is not simply anything which a legislature chooses to call a "crime." It is not simply antisocial conduct which public officers are given a responsibility to suppress. It is not simply any conduct to which a legislature chooses to attach a "criminal" penalty. It is conduct which, if duly shown to have taken place, will incur a formal and solemn pronouncement of the moral condemnation of the community.

5. The method of the criminal law, of course, involves something more than the threat (and, on due occasion, the expression) of community condemnation of antisocial conduct. It involves, in addition, the threat (and, on due occasion, the imposition) of unpleasant physical consequences, commonly called punishment. But if Professor Gardner is right, these added consequences take their character as punishment from the condemnation which precedes them and serves as the warrant for their infliction. Indeed, the condemnation plus the added consequences may well be considered, compendiously, as constituting the punishment. Otherwise, it would be necessary to think of a convicted criminal as going unpunished if the imposition or execution of his sentence is suspended.

In traditional thought and speech, the ideas of crime and punishment have been inseparable; the consequences of conviction for crime has been described as a matter of course as "punishment." The Constitution of the United States and its amendments, for example, use this word or its verb form in relation to criminal offenses no less than six times. Today, "treatment" has become a fashionable euphemism for the older, ugly word. This bowdlerizing of the Constitution and of conventional speech may serve a useful purpose in discouraging unduly harsh sentences and emphasizing that punishment is not an end in itself. But to the extent that it dissociates the treatment of criminals from the social condemnation of their conduct which is implicit in their conviction, there is danger that it will confuse thought and do a disservice.

At least under existing law, there is a vital difference between the situation of a patient who has been committed to a mental hospital and the situation of an inmate of a state penitentiary. The core of the difference is precisely that the patient has not incurred the moral condemnation of his community, whereas the convict has.

B. JUSTIFICATION AND FUNCTIONS OF CRIMINALIZATION

The justifications for criminalizing conduct are obviously relevant to the basic policy question of what conduct to make criminal. Given the nature of criminal liability, it seems beyond reasonable question that conduct should not be made subject to the criminal sanction in the absence of good reason for this action. The materials in this section raise a variety of justifications that might be relied upon in criminalizing conduct. Distinguish the different justifications and consider the extent to which each has been demonstrated sufficiently (if it is capable of demonstration) to justify relying upon it in deciding whether to criminalize certain conduct. These materials may also have an important bearing upon other related questions, of course. For example, they may provide some guidance on the question of the severity of punishment that is appropriate for persons who are convicted of crime. What is sought to be accomplished by criminalizing conduct and imposing criminal sanctions upon individuals who engage in that conduct may determine whether specific offenders should in fact be punished and—if so—how severely they should be penalized.

H. L. A. HART, MURDER AND THE PRINCIPLES OF PUNISHMENT: ENGLAND AND THE UNITED STATES

52 Nw.U.L.Rev. 433, 448–49 (1957).[a]

[W]e must distinguish two questions commonly confused. They are, first "Why do men in fact punish?" * * * The second question * * * is "What justifies men in punishing? Why is it morally good or morally permissible for them to punish?" It is clear that no demonstration that in fact men have punished or do punish for certain reasons can amount *per se* to a justification for this practice unless we subscribe to what is itself a most implausible moral position, namely, that whatever is generally done is justified or morally right * * *.

When this simple point is made clear and the two questions * * * are forced apart, very often the objector to the utilitarian position will turn out to be a utilitarian of a wider and perhaps more imaginative sort. He will perhaps say that what justifies punishment is that it satisfies a popular demand (perhaps even for revenge) and explain that it is good that it satisfies this demand because if it did not there would be disorder in society, disrespect for the law, or even lynching. Such a point of view, of course, raises disputable questions of fact * * *. Nevertheless, this objection itself turns out to be a utilitarian position, emphasizing that the good to be secured by punishment must not be narrowly conceived as simply protecting society from the harm represented by the particular type of crime punished but also as a protection from a wider set of injuries to society.

a. Reprinted by special permission of the Northwestern University Law Review (Northwestern University School of Law), Copyright © 1958, Vol. 52, No. 4.

1. RETRIBUTION

To what extent is criminal law properly a reflection of moral values? To put the matter in terms of a justification for criminalization, to what—if any—extent is the law justified in making conduct criminal *because* that conduct is viewed as immoral? The materials in this section address this question.

A number of subissues may arise. For example, Mill seems to suggest that the immoral nature of conduct should not, in the absence of an adverse impact from the conduct on persons other than the actor, be regarded as justifying the criminalization of that conduct. But is it possible to draw an acceptable line between conduct that is simply immoral and that which is—in addition, perhaps, to being immoral—injurious to persons other than the actor? It may also be relevant to consider what might be accomplished in utilitarian terms by criminalizing conduct because it is viewed as immoral. Devlin urges that certain concrete effects will flow from causing the criminal law to reflect moral values; Hart, on the other hand, questions this. But reconsider the basic question: Even if we cannot reasonably expect specific beneficial effects to flow from the criminalization of immoral conduct, can it be argued that the mere fact that the conduct is immoral justifies its criminalization?

P. BRETT, AN INQUIRY INTO CRIMINAL GUILT

51 (1963).

The retributive theory of punishment can be formulated in a number of ways. Its distinguishing feature is that it asks for no further justification of the right to punish than that the offender has committed a wrong. "Judicial punishment * * * can never serve merely as a means to further *another* good, whether for the offender himself or of society, but must always be inflicted on him for the sole reason that he *has committed a crime.* * * * The law of punishment is a categorical imperative, and woe to him who crawls through the serpentine windings of the happiness theory seeking to discover something which in virtue of the benefit it promises will release him from the duty of punishment or even from a fraction of its full severity." Thus Kant expounded the theory, and he based it upon his view that man must always be treated as an end in himself and never as a means of achieving some other end. Kant's position here is an intuitive one, with which one can only either agree or disagree in the light of one's own intuitions. Other formulations of the retributive theory are likewise intuitive, and occasionally they take on a somewhat mystical tinge, as with Hegel's view that crime is a negation and punishment a negation of that negation.

NOTE AND QUESTION

Insofar as retributive notions provide the justification for criminal punishment, do they also suggest a limitation upon those who may be punished? Consider the following:

> The aim of criminal legislation is to prevent the perpetration of acts classified as criminal (because they are regarded as being socially damaging). * * * I can subscribe fully to this premise, and would only add the rider that, if by putting it forward it is sought to suggest, as does Barbara Wooton, that the purpose of penal legislation is *not* retribution for guilt, then the point rests on a misunderstanding. For this is something no one has even claimed. The so-called retributivist theories are not concerned with the *purpose* of penal law (its intended effects) but with the moral basis for sentencing a particular person and for the kind and extent of the punishment imposed. The substance of the retributivist's case is that the guilt requirement sets a moral limitation upon the state's right to pursue its preventive aims.

Ross, The Campaign Against Punishment, 14 Scandinavian Studies in Law 109, 124–25 (1970).

2. MORALITY

P. DEVLIN, THE ENFORCEMENT OF MORALS

9 (1965).

I think it is clear that the criminal law as we know it is based upon moral principle. In a number of crimes its function is simply to enforce a moral principle and nothing else.

J. MILL, UTILITARIANISM: LIBERTY AND REPRESENTATIVE GOVERNMENT 73 [b]

The sole end for which mankind is warranted, individually or collectively, in interfering with the liberty of action of any of their number is self-protection. That the only purpose for which power can be rightfully exercised over any member of a civilized community, against his will, is to prevent harm to others. His own good, whether physical or moral, is not a sufficient warrant. He cannot rightfully be compelled to do or forbear because it will be better for him to do so, because it will make him happier, because, in the opinion of others, to do so would be wise, or even right. These are good

b. From the book Utilitarianism: Liberty and Representative Government by John Stuart Mill. Everyman's Library Edition. Published by E. P. Dutton & Co., Inc. and used with their permission.

reasons for remonstrating with him, or reasoning with him or persuading him, or entreating him but not for compelling him, or visiting him with any evil in case he do otherwise. To justify that, the conduct from which it is desired to deter him must be calculated to produce evil to some one else. The only part of the conduct of any one, for which he is amenable to society, is that which concerns others. In the part which merely concerns himself, his independence is, of right, absolute.

NOTE AND QUESTION

If Mill's statement set out above is accepted, does this provide a practical method of determining which actions are properly made criminal? What conduct of a person—to adopt Mill's own terms—"merely concerns himself" and what conduct "concerns others?" Nagel, The Enforcement of Morals, The Humanist, May/June 1968, 21 suggests that relatively few if any human actions have no impact upon persons other than the actor. As a result, Nagel argues, Mill's standard can only be applied if there is "a fairly detailed moral philosophy" that permits the identification of those impacts upon others that justify regarding conduct as concerning others. Nagel also argues that even if such a moral philosophy does exist, applying it requires more than appeal to "uncriticized custom" or consideration of conduct in isolation from "the enormously complex field of human relations" in which conduct is frequently embedded. Empirical study of the actual consequences of conduct is essential. Is Nagel correct? If so, does Mill's essay contribute much to the question of what conduct to criminalize?

P. DEVLIN, THE ENFORCEMENT OF MORALS

9–10 (1965).[c]

What makes a society of any sort is community of ideas, not only political ideas but also ideas about the way its members should behave and govern their lives; these latter ideas are its morals. Every society has a moral structure as well as a political one: or rather, since that might suggest two independent systems, I should say that the structure of every society is made up both of politics and morals. Take, for example, the institution of marriage. Whether a man should be allowed to take more than one wife is something about which every society has to make up its mind one way or the other. In England we believe in the Christian idea of marriage and therefore adopt monogamy as a moral principle. Consequently the Christian institution of marriage has become the basis of family life and so part of the structure of our society. It is there not because it is Christian. It has got there because it is Christian, but it remains there because it is built into the house in which we live and could not be removed without bringing it down. The great majority of those who live in this country accept it because it is the Christian idea of

c. From Morals and the Criminal Law included in The Enforcement of Morals by Lord Devlin, published by Oxford University Press.

marriage and for them the only true one. But a non-Christian is bound by it, not because it is part of Christianity but because, rightly or wrongly, it has been adopted by the society in which he lives. It would be useless for him to stage a debate designed to prove that polygamy was theologically more correct and socially preferable; if he wants to live in the house, he must accept it as built in the way in which it is.

We see this more clearly if we think of ideas or institutions that are purely political. Society cannot tolerate rebellion; it will not allow argument about the rightness of the cause. Historians a century later may say that the rebels were right and the Government was wrong and a percipient and conscientious subject of the State may think so at the time. But it is not a matter which can be left to individual judgement.

The institution of marriage is a good example for my purpose because it bridges the division, if there is one, between politics and morals. Marriage is part of the structure of our society and it is also the basis of a moral code which condemns fornication and adultery. The institution of marriage would be gravely threatened if individual judgements were permitted about the morality of adultery; on these points there must be a public morality. But public morality is not to be confined to those moral principles which support institutions such as marriage. People do not think of monogamy as something which has to be supported because our society has chosen to organize itself upon it; they think of it as something that is good in itself and offering a good way of life and that it is for that reason that our society has adopted it. I return to the statement that I have already made, that society means a community of ideas; without shared ideas on politics, morals, and ethics no society can exist. Each one of us has ideas about what is good and what is evil; they cannot be kept private from the society in which we live. If men and women try to create a society in which there is no fundamental agreement about good and evil they will fail; if, having based it on common agreement, the agreement goes, the society will disintegrate. For society is not something that is kept together physically; it is held by the invisible bonds of common thought. If the bonds were too far relaxed the members would drift apart. A common morality is part of the bondage. The bondage is part of the price of society; and mankind, which needs society, must pay its price.

Common lawyers used to say that Christianity was part of the law of the land. That was never more than a piece of rhetoric * * * [.] What lay behind it was the notion which I have been seeking to expound, namely that morals—and up till a century or so ago no one thought it worth distinguishing between religion and morals—were necessary to the temporal order.

H. L. A. HART, SOCIAL SOLIDARITY AND THE ENFORCEMENT OF MORALITY

35 U.Chi.L.Rev. 1, 8–13 (1967).

If we ask in relation to theories such as Lord Devlin's * * * precisely what empirical claim they make concerning the connection between the maintenance of a common morality and the existence of society, some further disentangling of knots has to be done.

It seems a very natural objection to such theories that if they are to be taken seriously * * * the justification which they attempt to give for the enforcement of social morality is far too general. It is surely both possible and good sense to discriminate between those parts of a society's moral code (assuming it has a single moral code) which are essential for the existence of a society and those which are not. Prima facie, at least, the need for such a discrimination seems obvious even if we assume that the moral code is only to be enforced where it is supported by "sentiments which are strong and precise" * * * or by "intolerance, indignation and disgust" * * *. For the decay of all moral restraint on the free use of violence or deception would not only cause individual harm but would jeopardise the existence of a society since it would remove the main conditions which make it possible and worthwhile for men to live together in close proximity to each other. On the other hand the decay of moral restraint on, say, extramarital intercourse, or a general change of sexual morality in a permissive direction seems to be quite another matter and not obviously to entail any such consequences as "disintegration" or "men drifting apart."

It seems, therefore, worthwhile pausing to consider two possible ways of discriminating within a social morality the parts which are to be considered essential.

(i) The first possibility is that the common morality which is essential to society, and which is to be preserved by legal enforcement, is that part of its social morality which contains only those restraints and prohibitions that are essential to the existence of any society of human beings whatever. Hobbes and Hume have supplied us with general characterisations of this moral minimum essential for social life: they include rules restraining the free use of violence and minimal forms of rules regarding honesty, promise keeping, fair dealing, and property. It is, however, quite clear that * * * Devlin * * * [does not mean] that only those elements, which are to be found in common morality, are to be enforced by law * * *. Quite clearly the argument * * * concerns moral rules which may differ from society to society * * *

(ii) The second possibility is this: the morality to be enforced, while not coextensive with every jot and tittle of an existent moral code, includes not only the restraints and prohibitions such as those relating to the use of violence or deception which are necessary to any society whatever, but also what is essential for a particular society. The guiding thought here is that for any society there is to be found, among the provisions of its code of morality, a central core of rules or principles which constitutes its pervasive and distinctive style of life. Lord Devlin frequently speaks in this way of what he calls monogamy adopted "as a moral principle," and of course this does deeply pervade our society in two principal ways. First, marriage is a *legal* institution and the recognition of monogamy as the sole legal form of marriage carries implications for the law related to wide areas of conduct: the custody and education of children, the rules relating to inheritance and distribution of property, etc. Second, the principle of monogamy is also morally pervasive: monogamous marriage is at the heart of our conception of family life, and with the aid of the law has become part of the structure of society. Its disappearance would carry with it vast changes throughout society so that without exaggeration we might say that it had changed its character.

On this view the morality which is necessary to the existence of society is neither the moral minimum required in all societies (Lord Devlin himself says that polygamous marriage in a polygamous society may be an equally cohesive force as monogamy is in ours), nor is it every jot and tittle of a society's moral code. What is essential and is to be preserved is the central core. On this footing it would be an open and empirical question whether any particular moral rule or veto, e. g., on homosexuality, adultery, or fornication, is so organically connected with the central core that its maintenance and preservation is required as a vital outwork or bastion. There are perhaps traces of some of these ideas in Lord Devlin * * *. But even if we take this to be the position, we are still not really confronted with an empirical claim concerning the connection of the maintenance of a common morality and the prevention of disintegration or "drifting apart." Apart from the point about whether a particular rule is a vital outwork or bastion of the central core, we may still be confronted only with the unexciting tautology depending now on the identification of society, not with the whole of its morality but only with its central core or "character" and this is not the disintegration thesis.

* * *

What is required to convert the last mentioned position into the disintegration thesis? It must be the theory that the maintenance of the core elements in a particular society's moral life is in fact necessary to prevent disintegration, because the withering or malignant decay of the central morality is a disintegrating factor. But even if we have got thus far in identifying an empirical claim, there would of course be very many questions to be settled before anything empirically testable could be formulated. What are the criteria in a complex society for determining the existence of a single recognised morality or its central core? What is "disintegration" and "drifting apart" under modern conditions? I shall not investigate these difficulties but I shall attempt to describe in outline the types of evidence that might conceivably be relevant to the issue if and when these difficulties are settled. They seem to be the following:

(a) Crude historical evidence in which societies—not individuals—are the units. The suggestion is that we should examine societies which have disintegrated and enquire whether their disintegration was preceded by a malignant change in their common morality. This done, we should then have to address ourselves to the possibility of a causal connection between decay of a common morality and disintegration. But of course all the familiar difficulties involved in macroscopic generalisations about society would meet us at this point, and anyone who has attempted to extract generalisations from what is called the decline and fall of the Roman Empire would know that they are formidable. To take only one such difficulty: suppose that all our evidence was drawn from simple tribal societies or closely knit agrarian societies * * * We should not, I take it, have much confidence in applying any conclusions drawn from these to modern industrial societies. Or, if we had, it would be because we had some well developed and well evidenced theory to show us that the differences between simple societies and our own were irrelevant to these issues as the differences in the size of a laboratory can safely be ignored as irrelevant to the scope of the generalisations tested by laboratory experiments. * * *

(b) The alternative type of evidence must be drawn presumably from social psychology and must break down into at least two subforms according to the way in which we receive the alternatives to the maintenance of a common morality. One alternative is general uniform *permissiveness* in the area of conduct previously covered by the common morality. The lapse, for example, of the conception that the choices between two wives or one, heterosexuality or homosexuality, are more than matters of personal taste. This (the alternative of permissiveness) is what Lord Devlin seems to envisage or to fear when he says: "The enemy of society is not error but indifference," and "Whether the new belief is better or worse than the old, it is the interregnum of disbelief that is perilous." On the other hand the alternative may not be permissiveness but moral *pluralism* involving divergent submoralities in relation to the same area of conduct.

To get off the ground with the investigation of the questions that either of these two alternatives opens up, it would be reasonable to abandon any general criteria for the disintegration of society in favour of something sufficiently close to satisfy the general spirit of the disintegration thesis. It would be no doubt sufficient if our evidence were to show that malignant change in a common morality led to a general increase in such forms of antisocial behaviour as would infringe what seem the minimum essentials: the prohibitions and restraints of violence, disrespect for property, and dishonesty. We should then require some account of the conceivable psychological mechanisms supposed to connect the malignant decay of a social morality with the increase in such forms of behavior. Here there would no doubt be signal differences between the alternatives of permissiveness and moral pluralism. On the permissiveness alternative, the theory to be tested would presumably be that in the "interregnum conditions," without the discipline involved in the submission of one area of life, e. g., the sexual, to the requirements of a common morality, there would necessarily be a weakening of the general capacity of individuals for self control. So, with permissiveness in the area formally covered by restrictive sexual morality, there would come increases in violence and dishonesty and a general lapse of those restraints which are essential for any form of social life. This is the view that the morality of the individual constitutes a seamless web. There is a hint that this, in the last resort, is Lord Devlin's view of the way in which the "interregnum" constitutes a danger to the existence of society: for he replied to my charge that he had assumed without evidence that morality was a seamless web by saying that though "[s]eamlessness presses the simile rather hard," "most men take their morality as a whole." But surely this assumption cannot be regarded as obviously true. The contrary view seems at least equally plausible: permissiveness in certain areas of life (even if it has come about through the disregard of a previously firmly established social morality) might make it easier for men to submit to restraints on violence which are essential for social life.

If we conceive the successor to the "common morality" to be not permissiveness but moral pluralism in some area of conduct once covered by a sexual morality which has decayed through the flouting of its restrictions, the thesis to be tested would presumably be that where moral pluralism develops in this way quarrels over the differences generated by divergent moralities must eventually destroy the minimal forms of restraints necessary for social cohesion. The counter-thesis would be that plural moralities in the conditions of modern large scale societies might perfectly well be mutually tolerant. To many indeed it might seem that the counter-thesis is the more cogent of the two, and that over wide areas of modern life, sometimes hiding behind lip service to an older common morality, there actually are divergent moralities living in peace.

3. PREVENTION: DETERRENCE, MORALIZATION AND THE LIKE

Whether—or to what extent—criminalizing conduct will prevent persons from engaging in that conduct is perhaps the most difficult empirical question posed by criminal jurisprudence. The material in this section suggests the need to distinguish among a number of different means by which criminalization might have a preventive effect. Some of the empirical evidence concerning the preventive effect of criminalization and punishment is also discussed and reviewed in this section. To what extent may the law rely upon the demonstrated or suggested preventive effect of criminal punishment in deciding whether or not to criminalize certain conduct?

ANDENAES, THE GENERAL PREVENTIVE EFFECTS OF PUNISHMENT

114 U.Pa.L.Rev. 949–51 (1966).[d]

In continental theories of criminal law, a basic distinction is made between the effects of punishment on the man being punished —individual prevention or special prevention—and the effects of punishment upon the members of society in general—general prevention. The characteristics of special prevention are termed "deterrence," "reformation" and "incapacitation," and these terms have meanings similar to their meanings in the English speaking world. General prevention, on the other hand, may be described as the *restraining influences emanating from the criminal law and the legal machinery.*

By means of the criminal law, and by means of specific applications of this law, "messages" are sent to members of a society. The criminal law lists those actions which are liable to prosecution, and it specifies the penalties involved. The decisions of the courts and actions by the police and prison officials transmit knowledge about the law, underlining the fact that criminal laws are not mere empty threats, and providing detailed information as to what kind of penalty might be expected for violations of specific laws. To the extent that these stimuli restrain citizens from socially undesired actions which they might otherwise have committed, a general preventive effect is secured. While the effects of special prevention depend upon how the law is implemented in each individual case, general prevention occurs as a result of an interplay between the provisions of the law and its enforcement in specific cases. In former times, emphasis was often placed on the physical exhibition of punishment as a deterrent influence, for example, by performing executions in public. Today it is customary to emphasize the *threat* of punishment as such. From this point of view the significance of the individual sentence and the execution of it lies in the support that these actions give to the law. It may be that some people are not particularly sensitive to an abstract threat of penalty, and that these persons can be motivated toward conformity only if the penalties can be demonstrated in concrete sentences which they feel relevant to their own life situations.

The effect of the criminal law and its enforcement may be *mere deterrence.* Because of the hazards involved, a person who contemplates a punishable offense might not act. But it is not correct to regard general prevention and deterrence as one and the same thing. The concept of general prevention also includes the *moral* or *sociopedagogical* influence of punishment. The "messages" sent by law and the legal processes contain factual information about what would be risked by disobedience, but they also contain proclamations specifying that it is *wrong* to disobey. * * *

The moral influence of the criminal law may take various forms. It seems to be quite generally accepted among the members of society that the law should be obeyed even though one is dissatisfied with it and wants it changed. If this is true, we may conclude that the law as an institution itself to some extent creates conformity. But more important than this formal respect for the law is respect for the values which the law seeks to protect. It may be said that from law and the legal machinery there emanates a flow of propaganda which favors such respect. Punishment is a means of expressing social disapproval. In this way the criminal law and its enforcement supplement and enhance the moral influence acquired through education and other nonlegal processes. Stated negatively, the penalty neutralizes the demoralizing consequences that arise when people witness crimes being perpetrated.

Deterrence and moral influence may both operate on the conscious level. The potential criminal may deliberate about the hazards involved, or he may be influenced by a conscious desire to behave lawfully. However, with fear or moral influence as an intermediate link, it is possible to create unconscious inhibitions against crime, and perhaps to establish a condition of habitual lawfulness. In this case, illegal actions will not present themselves consciously as real alternatives to conformity, even in situations where the potential criminal would run no risk whatsoever of being caught.

General preventive effects do not occur only among those who have been informed about penal provisions and their applications. Through a process of learning and social imitation, norms and taboos may be transmitted to persons who have no idea about their origins —in much the way that innovations in Parisian fashions appear in the clothing of country girls who have never heard of Dior or Lanvin.

Making a distinction between special prevention and general prevention is a useful way of calling attention to the importance of legal punishment in the lives of members of the general public, but the distinction is also to some extent an artificial one. The distinction is simple when one discusses the reformative and incapacitative effects of punishment on the individual criminal. But when one discusses the deterrent effects of punishment the distinction becomes less clear. Suppose a driver is fined ten dollars for disregarding the speed limit. He may be neither reformed or incapacitated but he might, perhaps, drive more slowly in the future. His motivation in subsequent situations in which he is tempted to drive too rapidly will not differ fundamentally from that of a driver who has not been fined; in other words a general preventive effect will operate. But for the driver who has been fined, this motive has, perhaps, been strengthened by the recollection of his former unpleasant experience. We may say that a general preventive feature and special preventive feature here act together.

NOTES AND QUESTIONS

1. Andenaes mentions the possibility that deterrence and moral influence may operate on an unconscious level. Under psychoanalytic theory (or at least under some versions of it), law-abiding persons have an unconscious need to have those who transgress laws punished. The personality's ability to restrain instinctual urges to engage in aggressive and antisocial behavior will remain effective only if it is periodically reinforced by punishment of those who engage in such behavior. Probably the leading presentation of this view is F. Alexander and H. Staub, The Criminal, The Judge, and The Public (1931). This theory explains the "urge to punish": law-abiding persons are unconsciously motivated to demand punishment of offenders because failure to punish the offenders is likely to weaken the self-control of the law-abiding persons and to lead to the commission of conduct which the law-abiding person will find deeply offensive to values he has unconsciously developed. If accepted, this theory also presents a utilitarian justification for punishment: punishment serves to reinforce the mechanism that keeps most persons from engaging in antisocial behavior.

2. Can the law justifiably rely upon an expectation that criminal punishment will have a general preventive effect? Consider the following from Andenaes, The Morality of Deterrence, 37 U.Chi.L.Rev. 649, 663–64 (1970):

> [I]t is often asserted that there is no scientific proof for the general preventive effects of punishment, and it may be argued that it is morally unjustifiable to inflict punishment on the basis of a belief which is not corroborated by scientific evidence. The burden of proof, it is sometimes said, is on those who would invoke punishment. Others may answer that the burden of proof is on those who would experiment at the risk of society by removing or weakening the protection which the criminal law now provides.
>
> Two points should be made. First, our lack of knowledge of general prevention may be exaggerated. In some areas of criminal law we have experiences which come as close to scientific proof as could be expected in human affairs. In many other areas it seems reasonably safe to evaluate the general preventive effects of punishment on a common sense basis. Modern psychology has shown that the pleasure-pain principle is not as universally valid as is as-

sumed, for instance, in Bentham's penal philosophy. Nevertheless, it is still a fundamental fact of social life that the risk of unpleasant consequences is a very strong motivational factor for most people in most situations.

Second, even in questions of social and economic policy we rarely are able to base our decisions on anything which comes close to strict scientific proof. Generally we must act on the basis of our best judgment. In this respect, the problems of penal policy are the same as problems of education, housing, foreign trade policy, and so on. The development of social science gradually provides a better factual foundation for decisions of social policy, but there is a long way to go. Besides, research always lags behind the rapid change of social conditions.

However, it is undeniable that punishment—the intentional infliction of suffering—is a special category among social policies. It contrasts sharply with the social welfare measures which characterize our modern state. This calls for caution and moderation in its application. I do not think the legal concept of "burden of proof" is very useful in this context. The balance that should be struck between defense of society and humaneness towards the offender can hardly be expressed in a simple formula. The solution of the conflict will depend on individual attitudes. Some people identify more with the values threatened by criminal behavior; others identify more with the lawbreaker. But certainly punishment should not be imposed precipitously. History provides a multitude of examples of shocking cruelty based on ideas of deterrence, often in combination with ideas of just retribution.

3. Sociological researchers have provided some material bearing on this issue, but it is difficult to evaluate because of complex methodological differences and difficulties. Gibbs, Crime, Punishment, and Deterrence, 48 Southwestern Social Science Quarterly 515 (1968) compared certainty of punishment for homicide (the number of prison admissions related to homicides known to police), severity of punishment for homicide (median number of months served by those imprisoned), and homicide rates. He found a distinct inverse association between both certainty and severity of punishment and the homicide rate in various jurisdictions. The degree of association was much greater for certainty than severity, although Gibbs believed that the statistics "caution[ed] against entirely rejecting the possibility that severity in some way operates as a deterrent." Id. at 525. He concluded that the overall results of the study "question[ed] the common assertion that no evidence exists of a relationship between legal reactions to crime and the crime rate". Id. at 529–30. Similar results were reached by Gray and Martin, Punishment and Deterrence: Another Analysis of Gibbs' Data, 50 Social Science Quarterly 389 (1969), using other methods of statistical analysis. Their methodology, however, did not substantiate Gibbs' conclusion that certainty was more important than severity.

Tittle, Crime Rate and Legal Sanctions, 16 Social Problems 409 (1969) compared certainty and severity of punishment with the rates of the F.B.I.'s "index crimes"—homicide, rape, assault, larceny, robbery, burglary, and auto theft. In each category, he found a negative association between certainty and crime rate. This was much stronger in more highly urbanized areas. Variations among the offenses is clear from the following list of associations:

All Felonies	–.45
Sex Offenses	–.57
Assault	–.46
Larceny	–.37
Robbery	–.36
Burglary	–.31
Homicide	–.17
Auto Theft	–.08

Tittle notes that there is an almost perfect negative rank order correlation between this list and one ranking offenses by offense rate. What might account for the variations? Tittle suggests that the likelihood of being punished at all for auto theft is so small that changes in this factor are unlikely to affect offenders. He also suggests that the likelihood of being punished for homicide is so high that variations in certainty are similarly unlikely to have any effect.

Tittle also found—for all offenses except homicide—a positive correlation between severity and crime rate. Controlling for urbanization in regard to nonhomicide crimes, however, eliminated any association whatsoever. This led him to the conclusion that "severity alone is simply irrelevant to the control of deviance." Id. at 416.

Chiricos and Waldo, Punishment and Crime: An Examination of Some Empirical Evidence, 18 Social Problems 200 (1970) reached similar results, although they concluded that the evidence was not strong enough to justify reliance upon deterrence as a matter of policy. Their attempts to find a relationship between changes in certainty or severity of punishment and crime rate led to data with no discernible pattern.

Recent years have seen an increase in the amount of investigation into the possible deterrent impact of criminal punishment. Cook, Punishment and Crime: A Critique of Current Findings Concerning the Preventive Effects of Punishment, 41 Law and Contemporary Problems 164 (1977) summarizes recent efforts and notes that many report evidence that "the probability and (less consistently) the severity of punishment have the expected inhibiting influence on crime rates." Id. at 194. But given the conceptual and statistical problems of the studies, he concludes that "they have produced little persuasive evidence concerning the size or even the existence of the deterrence mechanism." Id. See also, e. g., J. Gibbs, Crime, Punishment, and Deterrence (1975); Nagin, General Deterrence: A Review of the Empirical Evidence, in Deterrence and Incapacitation: Estimating the Effects of Criminal Sanctions on Crime Rates 95 (1978).

One interesting development has been the use of economic theory and methods in attempting to evaluate the effect of punishment on criminal behavior. See generally Palmer, Economic Analyses of the Deterrent Effect of Punishment: A Review, 14 J. Research in Crime and Delinquency 4 (1977). She concludes that "the deterrent hypothesis is supported by many but certainly not all of the Economic studies." Id. at 15. Ehrlich, Participation in Illegitimate Activities: A Theoretical and Empirical Investigation, 81 J. Political Economy 521 (1973), for example, studied seven index crime felonies and their variations among 1940, 1950, and 1960. He concludes:

> The rate of specific crime categories, with virtually no exception, varies inversely with estimates of the probability of apprehension and punishment by imprisonment * * * and with the average length of time served in state prisons.

Id. at 545. It is important to note, however, that this is not the only conclusion of such studies. Ehrlich, for example, also notes:

> Our empirical investigation also indicates that the rates of all felonies, particularly crimes against property, are positively related to the degree of a community's income inequality, and this suggests a social incentive for equalizing training and earning opportunities.

Id. at 561.

An important recent project involved a group—established in 1975—called the Panel on Research on Deterrent and Incapacitative Effects. The project was approved by the Governing Board of the National Research Counsel, whose members are drawn from the Councils of the National Academy of Science, the National Academy of Engineering, and the Institute of Medicine. The report of the Panel was published as Deterrence and Incapacitation: Estimating the Effects of Criminal Sanctions on Crime Rates (1978). The objective of the group is stated as providing "an objective technical assessment of the studies of deterrent and incapacitative effects of sanctions on crime rates." Id. at 16. The group's conclusion regarding the evidence related to deterrence is as follows:

> [W]e cannot yet assert that the evidence warrants an affirmative conclusion regarding deterrence. We believe scientific caution must be exercised in interpreting the limited validity of the available evidence and the number of competing explanations for the results. Our reluctance to draw stronger conclusions does not imply support for a position that deterrence does not exist, since the evidence certainly favors a proposition supporting deterrence more than it favors one asserting that deterrence is absent.

Id. at 7.

4. Social scientists are turning some attention to measurement of the "incapacitative" effect of punishment, i. e., that effect accomplished simply by keeping offenders imprisoned so that their opportunity to commit crimes is at least minimized. But the available work suggests that the incapacitative effect may be less than is generally assumed. Greenberg, The Incapacitative Effect of Imprisonment: Some Estimates, 9 Law & Society Review 540 (1975) concludes that the amount of index crime prevented by the physical detention of offenders amounted to no more than 8% of the total index crime. Increasing the present average length of sentence from two years to three years, he suggests, could be expected to increase this effect by about 4%. Van Dine, Dinitz, and Conrad, The Incapacitation of the Dangerous Offender: A Statistical Experiment, 14 J. Research in Crime and Delinquency 22 (1977) studied all persons charged with violent crimes in an Ohio

county during 1973 and attempted to determine the effect that would have resulted had the county adopted a policy of imposing a five year net mandatory prison term upon all persons convicted of any felony. Thus it was assumed that any person charged with a crime in 1973 who had a felony conviction in any of the preceding five years would have been imprisoned and would not have been able to commit the 1973 offense or offenses. Had such a mandatory sentencing policy been in effect, the authors conclude, only 4% of the 2,982 crimes of violence reported in the county during 1973 would have been prevented. "[I]ncapacitation," they comment, "makes only a small and modest impact upon the violent crime rate." Id. at 31. In explanation they note that since the proposed policy dealt only with adults, it did not affect the numerous crimes by juveniles. Moreover, more than ⅔ of the persons studied were first-time offenders whose crimes could not have been prevented by incapacitation on a prior conviction. But they also note that the typical offender studied committed—or at least was arrested for—violent crime quite infrequently. Id. at 31–32. Are these studies of much value in deciding the preventive confinement value of punishment? See generally Cohen, The Incapacitative Effect of Imprisonment: A Critical Review of the Literature, in Deterrence and Incapacitation: Estimating the Effects of Criminal Sanctions on Crime Rates 187 (1978).

The Panel on Research on Deterrent and Incapacitative Effects (see note 3 on page 80, supra) concludes that because of the limits on models available and problems in obtaining accurate data, the present studies "cannot be relied upon for exact numerical calculations of incapacitative effects." Deterrence and Incapacitation: Estimating the Effects of Criminal Sanctions on Crime Rates 10 (1978). It does note, however, that the lower the existing crime rate and the rate of imprisonment per crime, the greater a percentage increase in prison population is necessary to achieve a given percentage reduction in crime. Since high crime rate jurisdictions that are most likely to look to incapacitation as a means of reducing crime are also likely to have a relatively low rate of time served per person imprisoned, these jurisdictions must expect to pay a high cost in terms of percentage increase in the prison population to achieve a given percentage reduction in the crime rate. Id.

5. Whether the death penalty has a deterrent effect is often regarded as posing a separable issue. The classic case for the proposition that no deterrent effect exists is presented in Sellin, the Death Penalty 23–24 (1959). Selling compared homicide rates during 1920–1955 in states that he believes differed significantly only in the penalties imposed for murder. He concluded that there was no relationship between the murder rate and whether the death penalty is used or not or whether executions are frequent or not. This position was recently questioned by a scholar using economic theory to analyze murder rates in American states from 1935 to 1969. Ehrlich, The Deterrent Effect of Capital Punishment: A Question of Life and Death, 65 Am. Economic Review 397 (1975). He found that the murder rate is inversely related to the risk of execution. His results suggest, in Ehrlich's language, that "an additional execution per year over the period in question may have resulted, on average, in 7 or 8 fewer murders," although he acknowledged that his estimate as to the magnitude of the effect "may be

subject to relatively large predictive errors" because of data problems. Id. at 414. He concluded:

> These observations do not imply that the empirical investigation has proved the existence of the deterrent * * * effect of capital punishment * * *. [But] in view of the new evidence presented here, one cannot reject the hypothesis that law enforcement activities in general and executions in particular do exert a deterrent effect on acts of murder. Strong inferences to the contrary drawn from earlier investigations appear to have been premature.

Id. at 416. Ehrlich's work has given rise to a great deal of discussion, some of it critical of his theories and techniques. See, e. g., Symposium, Statistical Evidence on the Deterrent Effect of Capital Punishment, 85 Yale L.J. 164 (1975); Peck, The Deterrent Effect of Capital Punishment: Ehrlich and His Critics, 85 Yale L.J. 359 (1976); Passell, The Deterrent Effect of the Death Penalty: A Statistical Test, 28 Stanford L.Rev. 61 (1975). Forst, The Deterrent Effect of Capital Punishment: A Cross-State Analysis of the 1960's, 61 Minn.L.Rev. 743 (1977) analyzed homicide data from 1960 to 1970, focusing in part upon changes across states. He concluded:

> The findings do not support the hypothesis that capital punishment deters homicides. The 53 percent increase in the homicide rate in the United States from 1960 to 1970 appears to be the product of factors other than the elimination of capital punishment. Foremost among these are a decline in the rate at which homicide offenses resulted in imprisonment * * * and increasing affluence during the 1960's.

Id. at 762. The Panel on Research on Deterrent and Incapacitative Effects (see note 3 at page 80, supra) concluded that "the available studies provide no useful evidence on the deterrent effect of capital punishment." Deterrence and Incapacitation: Estimating the Effects of Criminal Sanctions on Crime Rates 9 (1978).

4. PREVENTION: TREATMENT OF OFFENDERS

It is arguable that criminalizing conduct might prevent conduct of the sort involved by creating the opportunity to "treat" those who engage in the conduct and who would, in the absence of such treatment, engage in it in the future. To what extent is this treatment rationale an adequate justification for criminalizing conduct? This may depend in part, of course, upon whether "treatment" is available —or, indeed, feasible—in the correctional programs into which some criminal defendants are channeled following conviction. This section presents divergent views concerning the extent to which the law might reasonably rely upon the promise of treatment following conviction.

K. MENNINGER, THE CRIME OF PUNISHMENT

253, 257–61 (1968).[e]

The medical use of the word *treatment* implies a program of presumably beneficial action prescribed for and administered to one who seeks it. The purpose of treatment is to relieve pain, correct disability, or combat an illness. Treatment may be painful or disagreeable but, if so, these qualities are incidental, not purposive.

* * *

When the community begins to look upon the expression of aggressive violence as the symptom of an illness or as indicative of illness, it will be because it believes doctors can do something to correct such a condition. At present, some better-informed individuals do believe and expect this. However angry at or sorry for the offender, they want him "treated" in an effective way so that he will cease to be a danger to them. And they know that the traditional punishment, "treatment-punishment," will not effect this.

What *will*? What effective treatment is there for such violence? It will surely have to begin with motivating or stimulating or arousing in a cornered individual the wish and hope and intention to change his methods of dealing with the realities of life. Can this be done by education, medication, counseling, training? I would answer *yes*. It can be done successfully in a majority of cases, if undertaken in time.

The present penal system and the existing legal philosophy do not stimulate or even expect such a change to take place in the criminal. Yet change is what medical science always aims for. The prisoner, like the doctor's other patients, should emerge from his treatment experience a different person, differently equipped, differently functioning, and headed in a different direction from when he began the treatment.

It is natural for the public to doubt that this can be accomplished with criminals. But remember that the public used to doubt that change could be effected in the mentally ill. * * * The average length of time required for restoring a mentally ill patient to health in [one particular] hospital has been reduced from years, to months, to weeks. Four-fifths of the patients living there today will be back in their homes by the end of the year. There are many empty beds, and the daily census is continually dropping.

What Is This Effective Treatment?

If these "incurable" patients are now being turned to their homes and their work in such numbers and with such celerity, why

e. From the Crime of Punishment by Karl Menninger, M.D. Copyright © 1966, 1968 by Jeannette Lyle Menninger. Reprinted by permission of The Viking Press, Inc.

not something similar for offenders? Just what are the treatments used to effect these rapid changes? Are they available for use with offenders?

The forms and techniques of psychiatric treatment used today number in the hundreds. Psychoanalysis; electroshock therapy; psychotherapy; occupational and industrial therapy; family group therapy; milieu therapy; the use of music, art, and horticultural activities; and various drug therapies—these are some of the techniques and modalities of treatment used to stimulate or assist the restoration of a vital balance of impulse control and life satisfaction. No one patient requires or receives all forms, but each patient is studied with respect to his particular needs, his basic assets, his interests, and his special difficulties. In addition to the treatment modalities mentioned, there are many facilitations and events which contribute to total treatment effect: a new job opportunity (perhaps located by a social worker) or a vacation trip, a course of reducing exercises, a cosmetic surgical operation or a herniotomy, some night school courses, a wedding in the family (even one for the patient!), an inspiring sermon. Some of these require merely prescription or suggestion; others require guidance, tutelage, or assistance by trained therapists or by willing volunteers. A therapeutic team may embrace a dozen workers—as in a hospital setting—or it may narrow down to the doctor and the spouse. Clergymen, teachers, relatives, friends, and even fellow patients often participate informally but helpfully in the process of readaptation.

All of the participants in this effort to bring about a favorable change in the patient, i. e., in his vital balance and life program, are imbued with what we may call a *therapeutic attitude.* This is one in direct antithesis to attitudes of avoidance, ridicule, scorn, or punitiveness. Hostile feelings toward the subject, however justified by his unpleasant and even destructive behavior, are not in the curriculum of therapy or in the therapist. This does not mean that therapists approve of the offensive and obnoxious behavior of the patient; they distinctly disapprove of it. But they recognize it as symptomatic of continued imbalance and disorganization, which is what they are seeking to change. * * * A patient may cough in the doctor's face or may vomit on the office rug; a patient may curse or scream or even struggle in the extremity of his pain. But these acts are not "punished." Doctors and nurses have no time or thought for inflicting unnecessary pain even upon patients who may be difficult, disagreeable, provocative, and even dangerous. It is their duty to care for them, to try to make them well, and to prevent them from doing themselves or others harm. This requires love, not hate.

This is the deepest meaning of the therapeutic attitude. Every doctor knows this; every worker in a hospital or clinic knows it (or should). * * *

"But you were talking about the mentally ill," readers may interject, "those poor, confused, bereft, frightened individuals who yearn for help from you doctors and nurses. Do you mean to imply that willfully perverse individuals, our criminals, can be similarly reached and rehabilitated? Do you really believe that effective treatment of the sort you visualize can be applied to people *who do not want any help*, who are so willfully vicious, so well aware of the wrongs they are doing, so lacking in penitence or even common decency that punishment seems to be the only thing left?"

Do I believe there is effective treatment for offenders, and that they *can* be changed? *Most certainly and definitely I do.* Not all cases, to be sure; there are also some physical afflictions which we cannot cure at the moment. Some provision has to be made for incurables—pending new knowledge—and these will include some offenders. But I believe the majority of them would prove to be curable. The willfulness and the viciousness of offenders are part of the thing for which they have to be treated. These must not thwart the therapeutic attitude.

NOTE

The optimism expressed by Dr. Menninger in the selection above has been challenged by a number of recent commentators. Perhaps the most widely quoted is Martinson, What Works? Questions and Answers About Prison Reform, 35 Public Interest 22 (1974). The review article presents the results of a study of research reports on correctional programs published from 1945 through 1967; the material is presented in greater detail in D. Lipton, R. Martinson, and J. Wilks, The Effectiveness of Correctional Treatment (1975). Martinson's "rather bald" summary of the researchers' findings is:

> *With few and isolated exceptions, the rehabilitative efforts that have been reported so far have had no appreciable effect on recidivism.* Studies that have been done since our survey was completed do not represent any major ground for altering that original conclusion.

Martinson, supra, at 25 (emphasis in original). Later, he does acknowledge having found instances of success or partial success, but he describes them as having "been isolated, producing no clear pattern to indicate the efficacy of any particular method of treatment." Id. at 49. The Martinson article was criticized severly in Palmer, Martinson Revisited, 12 J.Research in Crime and Delinquency 133 (1975), which indicated that 48% of the 82 individual studies examined by Martinson reported positive or partly positive results. Id. at 142. Because of Martinson's criteria, Palmer argued, methods of treatment that were proven successful for some offenders but not others were improperly classified as unsuccessful. Id. at 150. Martinson defended his original results in Martinson, California Research at the Crossroads, 22 Crime & Delinquency 180 (1976). In this piece, Martinson summarizes the implications of his earlier essay as follows: "the *addition* of isolated 'treatment' elements to a system (probation, imprisonment, parole) in which a given flow of offenders has generated a gross rate of recidivism has very little effect (and, in most cases, no effect) in making this rate of recidivism better or worse." Id. at 190 (emphasis in original).

At a recent workshop, however, Martinson is said to have engaged in a "blistering critique" of his earlier work. Subsequent work in the area, he is reported to have said, has convinced him that in his earlier efforts he needlessly rejected significant pieces of research because of methodological flaws. "Martinson Attacks His Own Earlier Work," Criminal Justice Newsletter, Vol. 9, No. 24, p. 4 (Dec. 4, 1978).

C. LEGAL LIMITATIONS UPON CRIMINALIZATION

The unique nature of criminal liability gives rise to some limitations upon what can be made a crime. This section deals with three constitutional limitations upon making behavior criminal. The first two—the right of privacy and the Eighth Amendment prohibition against cruel and unusual punishment—address what conduct or conditions can be made a crime. The third—the requirement of precision or the vice of vagueness—addresses a related but distinguishable matter, the way in which the statute defining the crime must be drafted.

It is necessary to keep in mind that these are constitutional doctrines. As a general matter, it is sound policy for constitutional doctrines to give substantial leeway to state legislatures, especially where the questions involved concern unresolved matters of social policy. In other words, the constitutional rule should only define the outer boundaries beyond which there is general agreement that the law should not go. Within those boundaries, there should be enough room for legislatures to take any of a number of different positions, depending upon how each legislature resolves the underlying questions of social policy. In examining the decisions in this section, consider whether the courts are giving state legislatures sufficient flexibility (or are perhaps giving them too much flexibility) in deciding what should be criminal and in drafting criminal statutes to implement these decisions.

Applying the doctrines discussed in this section requires consideration of a variety of policy considerations. In regard to each of the cases, consider two different issues: (1) Is there—or should there be—a constitutional rule that forbids making this conduct a crime?; and (2) If the conduct may constitutionally be made a crime, is it sound policy for a legislature to do so? Many of the policy considerations that suggest it may be unconstitutional to make conduct a crime also suggest that it may be unwise to criminalize the conduct. Even if the policy considerations are not so clearly one-sided as to justify a constitutional rule that prohibits making the conduct criminal, these considerations may nevertheless make a convincing case for the position that it is unwise—even if permissible—to make the behavior at issue a criminal offense.

1. PRIVACY

One of the limitations upon what conduct may be made criminal is the developing right of privacy. As the principal case in this section makes clear, privacy is to some extent protected by the federal constitution and by some state constitutions. If behavior is protected by these constitutional rights of privacy, any law making such conduct criminal cannot constitutionally be enforced. As the principal case also demonstrates, the precise meaning of "privacy" in this constitutional context is not well settled. Privacy is a developing constitutional doctrine. In reading the principal case, consider whether the federal and state constitutions should be read as embodying a right of privacy that cannot be invaded by laws making conduct a crime. If constitutional privacy doctrine prohibits convicting a person of a crime consisting of possession (or use) of marijuana in the privacy of his or her home, should this same doctrine permit conviction for possession or use of the substance in a public park? For providing another adult person with marijuana for that person's individual use?

RAVIN v. STATE

Supreme Court of Alaska, 1975.
537 P.2d 494.

RABINOWITZ, Chief Justice.

The constitutionality of Alaska's statute prohibiting possession of marijuana is put in issue in this case. Petitioner Ravin was arrested on December 11, 1972 and charged with violating AS 17.12.010.[1] Before trial Ravin attacked the constitutionality of AS 17.12.010 by a motion to dismiss in which he asserted that the State had violated his right of privacy under both the federal and Alaska constitutions, and further violated the equal protection provisions of the state and federal constitutions. Lengthy hearings on the questions were held before District Court Judge Dorothy D. Tyner, at which testimony from several expert witnesses was received. Ravin's motion to dismiss was denied by Judge Tyner. The superior court then granted review and after affirmance by the superior court, we, in turn, granted Ravin's petition for review from the superior court's affirmance.

* * *

1. AS 17.12.010 provides:

Except as otherwise provided in this chapter, it is unlawful for a person to manufacture, compound, counterfeit, possess, have under his control, sell, prescribe, administer, dispense, give, barter, supply or distribute in any manner, a depressant, hallucinogenic or stimulant drug.

AS 17.12.150 defines "depressant, hallucinogenic, or stimulant drug" to include all parts of the plant *Cannabis Sativa L.*

We have previously stated the tests to be applied when a claim is made that state action encroaches upon an individual's constitutional rights. In Breese v. Smith, 501 P.2d 159 (Alaska 1972), we had before us a school hairlength regulation which encroached on what we determined to be the individual's fundamental right to determine his own personal appearance. There we stated:

> Once a fundamental right under the constitution of Alaska has been shown to be involved and it has been further shown that this constitutionally protected right has been impaired by governmental action, then the government must come forward and meet its substantial burden of establishing that the abridgement in question was justified by a compelling governmental interest.

This standard is familiar federal law as well. As stated by the United States Supreme Court:

> Where there is a significant encroachment upon personal liberty, the State may prevail only upon showing a subordinating interest which is compelling.[4] The law must be shown "necessary, and not merely rationally related, to the accomplishment of a permissible state policy."

When, on the other hand, governmental action interferes with an individual's freedom in an area which is not characterized as fundamental, a less stringent test is ordinarily applied. In such cases our task is to determine whether the legislative enactment has a reasonable relationship to a legitimate governmental purpose. Under this latter test, which is sometimes referred to as the "rational basis" test, the State need only demonstrate the existence of facts which can serve as a rational basis for belief that the measure would properly serve the public interest.

In our recent opinion in Lynden Transport, Inc. v. State, 532 P. 2d 700 (Alaska 1975), we recognized the existence of considerable dissatisfaction with the fundamental right-compelling state interest test. There we said:

> * * * We are in agreement with the view that the Supreme Court's recent equal protection decisions have shown a tendency towards less speculative, less deferential, more intensified means-to-end inquiry when it is applying the traditional rational basis test and we approve of this development. * * *

4. Bates v. Little Rock, 361 U.S. 516, 524, 80 S.Ct. 412, 417, 4 L.Ed.2d 480, 486 (1960). See Roe v. Wade, 410 U.S. 113, 155, 93 S.Ct. 705, 35 L.Ed.2d 147, 178 (1973).

This court has previously applied a test different from the rigid two-tier formulation to state regulations. In State v. Wylie,[7] we tested durational residency requirements for state employment by both the compelling state interest test and a test which examined whether the means chosen suitably furthered an appropriate governmental interest. It is appropriate in this case to resolve Ravin's privacy claims by determining whether there is a proper governmental interest in imposing restrictions on marijuana use and whether the means chosen bear a substantial relationship to the legislative purpose. If governmental restrictions interfere with the individual's right to privacy, we will require that the relationship between means and ends be not merely reasonable but close and substantial.

Thus, our undertaking is two-fold: we must first determine the nature of Ravin's rights, if any abridged by AS 17.12.010, and, if any rights have been infringed upon, then resolve the further question as to whether the statutory impingement is justified.

As we have mentioned, Ravin's argument that he has a fundamental right to possess marijuana for personal use rests on both federal and state law, and centers on what may broadly be called the right to privacy. This "right" is increasingly the subject of litigation and commentary and is still a developing legal concept.

In Ravin's view, the right to privacy involved here is an autonomous right which gains special significance when its situs is found in a specially protected area, such as the home. Ravin begins his privacy argument by citation of and reliance upon Griswold v. Connecticut,[10] in which the Supreme Court of the United States struck down as unconstitutional a state statute effectively barring the dispensation of birth control information to married persons. Writing for five members of the Court, Mr. Justice Douglas noted that rights protected by the Constitution are not limited to those specifically enumerated in the Constitution. In order to secure the enumerated rights, certain peripheral rights must be recognized. In other words, the "specific guarantees in the Bill of Rights have penumbras, formed by emanations from those guarantees that help give them life and substance." Certain of these penumbral rights create "zones of privacy", for example, First Amendment rights of association, Third and Fourth Amendment rights pertaining to the security of the home, and the Fifth Amendment right against self-incrimination. The Supreme Court of the United States then proceeded to find a right to privacy in marriage which antedates the Bill of Rights and yet lies within the zone of privacy created by several fundamental constitutional guarantees. It was left unclear whether this particular right to privacy exists independently, or comes into being only because of its connection with fundamental enumerated rights.

7. 516 P.2d 142 (Alaska 1973).

10. 381 U.S. 479, 85 S.Ct. 1678, 14 L.Ed.2d 510 (1965).

The next important Supreme Court opinion regarding privacy is Stanley v. Georgia,[12] in which a state conviction for possession of obscene matter was overturned as violative of the First and Fourteenth Amendments. The Supreme Court had previously held that obscenity is not protected by the First Amendment. But in *Stanley* the Court made a distinction between commercial distribution of obscene matter and the private enjoyment of it at home. The Constitution, it said, protects the fundamental right to receive information and ideas, regardless of their worth. Moreover, the Supreme Court said,

> * * * in the context of this case—a prosecution for mere possession of printed or filmed matter in the privacy of a person's own home—that right takes on an added dimension. For also fundamental is the right to be free, except in very limited circumstances, from unwanted governmental intrusions into one's privacy.

The Supreme Court concluded that the First Amendment means a state has no business telling a man, sitting alone in his own home, what books he may read or what films he may watch. The Court took care to limit its holding to mere possession of obscene materials by the individual in his own home. It noted that it did not intend to restrict the power of the state or federal government to make illegal the possession of items such as narcotics, firearms, or stolen goods.

The Stanley holding was subsequently refined by a series of cases handed down in 1973. In Paris Adult Theatre I v. Slaton,[15] the Supreme Court rejected the claim of a theater owner that his showing of allegedly obscene films was protected by *Stanley* because his films were shown only to consenting adults. The Court explicitly rejected the comparison of a theater to a home and found a legitimate state interest in regulating the use of obscene matter in local commerce and places of public accommodation. It apparently found no fundamental right involved in viewing obscene matter under these conditions, for it noted that the right to privacy guaranteed by the Fourteenth Amendment extends only to fundamental rights. The protection offered by *Stanley*, the Supreme Court stated, was restricted to the home, and it explicity refused to say that all activities occurring between consenting adults were beyond the reach of the government.[16]

12. 394 U.S. 557, 89 S.Ct. 1243, 22 L.Ed.2d 542 (1969).

15. 413 U.S. 49, 93 S.Ct. 2628, 37 L.Ed.2d 446 (1973).

16. In a companion case, United States v. Orito, 413 U.S. 139, 93 S.Ct. 2674, 37 L.Ed.2d 513 (1973), the Supreme Court observed that the *Stanley* right to possess obscene matter in the home is limited to the home and does not create a right to transport, receive, or distribute the matter. The Supreme Court further said that it is not true that a zone of constitutionally protected privacy follows such materials when they are moved outside the home. See United States v. 12 200-Ft. Reels, 413 U.S. 123, 93 S.Ct. 2665, 37 L.Ed.2d 500 (1973).

These Supreme Court cases indicate to us that the federal right to privacy arises only in connection with other fundamental rights, such as the grouping of rights which involve the home. And even in connection with the penumbra of home-related rights, the right of privacy in the sense of immunity from prosecution is absolute only when the private activity will not endanger or harm the general public.

The view is confirmed by the Supreme Court's abortion decision, Roe v. Wade.[17] There appellant claimed that her right to decide for herself concerning abortion fell within the ambit of a right to privacy flowing from the federal Bill of Rights. The Court's decision in her favor makes clear that only personal rights which can be deemed "fundamental" or "implicit in the concept of ordered liberty" are protected by the right to privacy. The Supreme Court found this right "broad enough to encompass a woman's decision whether or not to terminate her pregnancy," but it rejected the idea that a woman's right to decide is absolute. At some point, the state's interest in safeguarding health, maintaining medical standards, and protecting potential life becomes sufficiently compelling to sustain regulations. One does not, the Supreme Court said, have an unlimited right to do with one's body as one pleases.

The right to privacy which the Court found in *Roe* is closely akin to that in *Griswold*; in both cases the zone of privacy involves the area of the family and procreation, more particularly, a right of personal autonomy in relation to choices affecting an individual's personal life.

In Alaska this court has dealt with the concept of privacy on only a few occasions. One of the most significant decisions in this area is Breese v. Smith,[19] where we considered the applicability of the guarantee of "life, liberty, the pursuit of happiness" found in the Alaska Constitution,[20] to a school hairlength regulation. Noting that hairstyles are a highly personal matter in which the individual is traditionally autonomous, we concluded that governmental control of personal appearance would be antithetical to the concept of personal liberty under Alaska's constitution. Since the student would be forced to choose between controlling his own personal appearance and asserting his right to an education if the regulations were upheld, we concluded that the constitutional language quoted above embodied an affirmative grant of liberty to public school students to choose their own hairstyles, for "at the core of [the concept of liberty] is the notion of total personal immunity from government control: the right 'to be let alone.' " That right is not absolute, however; we also noted

17. 410 U.S. 113, 93 S.Ct. 705, 35 L.Ed. 2d 147 (1973).

19. 501 P.2d 159 (Alaska 1972).

20. Alaska Const. Art. I, § 1.

that this "liberty" must yield where it "intrude[s] upon the freedom of others."

Subsequent to our decision in *Breese*, a right to privacy amendment was added to the Alaska Constitution. Article I, section 22 reads:

> The right of the people to privacy is recognized and shall not be infringed. The legislature shall implement this section.

The effect of this amendment is to place privacy among the specifically enumerated rights in Alaska's constitution. But this fact alone does not, in and of itself, yield answers concerning what scope should be accorded to this right of privacy. * * *

* * *

Generally * * * privacy as a constitutional defense in marijuana cases has not met with much favor. It was rejected, for instance, by the Massachusetts Supreme Judicial Court in Commonwealth v. Leis,[32] where the court held that there was no constitutional right to smoke marijuana, that smoking marijuana was not fundamental to the American scheme of justice or necessary to a regime of ordered liberty, and that smoking marijuana was not locatable in any "zone of privacy". Furthermore, the court said, there is no constitutional right to become intoxicated.

Assuming this court were to continue to utilize the fundamental right-compelling state interest test in resolving privacy issues under article I, section 22 of Alaska's constitution, we would conclude that there is not a fundamental constitutional right to possess or ingest marijuana in Alaska. For in our view, the right to privacy amendment to the Alaska Constitution cannot be read so as to make the possession or ingestion of marijuana itself a fundamental right. * * *

The foregoing does not complete our analysis of the right to privacy issues. For in Gray [v. State, 525 P.2d 524 (Alaska 1974)] we stated that the right of privacy amendment in the Alaska Constitution "clearly it shields the ingestion of food, beverages or other substances", but that this right may be held to be subordinate to public health and welfare measures. Thus, Ravin's right to privacy contentions are not susceptible to disposition solely in terms of answering the question whether there is a general fundamental constitutional right to possess or smoke marijuana. This leads us to a more detailed examination of the right to privacy and the relevancy of where the right is exercised. At one end of the scale of the scope of the right to privacy is possession or ingestion in the individual's home. If

32. 243 N.E.2d 898 (Mass.1969).

there is any area of human activity to which a right to privacy pertains more than any other, it is the home. * * *

* * *

The home * * * carries with it associations and meanings which make it particularly important as the situs of privacy. Privacy in the home is a fundamental right, under both the federal and Alaska constitutions. We do not mean by this that a person may do anything at anytime as long as the activity takes place within a person's home. There are two important limitations on this facet of the right to privacy. First, we agree with the Supreme Court of the United States, which has strictly limited the *Stanley* guarantee to possession for purely private, noncommercial use in the home. And secondly, we think this right must yield when it interferes in a serious manner with the health, safety, rights and privileges of others or with the public welfare. No one has an absolute right to do things in the privacy of his own home which will affect himself or others adversely. Indeed, one aspect of a private matter is that it *is* private, that is, that it does not adversely affect persons beyond the actor, and hence is none of their business. When a matter does affect the public, directly or indirectly, it loses its wholly private character, and can be made to yield when an appropriate public need is demonstrated.

Thus, we conclude that citizens of the State of Alaska have a basic right to privacy in their homes under Alaska's constitution. This right to privacy would encompass the possession and ingestion of substances such as marijuana in a purely personal, non-commercial context in the home unless the state can meet its substantial burden and show that proscription of possession of marijuana in the home is supportable by achievement of a legitimate state interest.

This leads us to the second facet of our inquiry, namely, whether the State has demonstrated sufficient justification for the prohibition of possession of marijuana in general in the interest of public welfare; and further, whether the State has met the greater burden of showing a close and substantial relationship between the public welfare and control of ingestion or possession of marijuana in the home for personal use.

The evidence which was presented at the hearing before the district court consisted primarily of several expert witnesses familiar with various medical and social aspects of marijuana use. Numerous written reports and books were also introduced into evidence.

* * *

Scientific testimony on the physiological and psychological effects of marijuana on humans generally stresses the variability of effects upon different individuals and on any one individual at different times. * * *

The short-term physiological effects are relatively undisputed. An immediate slight increase in the pulse, decrease in salivation, and a slight reddening of the eyes are usually noted. There is also impairment of psychomotor control. These affects generally end within two to three hours of the end of smoking.

Long-term physiological effects raise more controversy among the experts. The National Commission on Marihuana and Drug Abuse reported that among users "no significant physical, biochemical, or mental abnormalities could be attributed solely to their marijuana smoking."[47] Certain researchers have pointed to possible deleterious effects on the body's immune defenses, on the chromosomal structures of users, and on testosterone levels in the body. The methodology of certain of these studies has been extensively criticized by other qualified medical scientists, however. These studies cannot be ignored. It should be noted that most of the damage suggested by these studies comes in the context of intensive use of concentrated forms of THC. It appears that the use of marijuana, as it is presently used in the United States today, does not constitute a public health problem of any significant dimensions. It is, for instance, far more innocuous in terms of physiological and social damage than alcohol or tabacco. But the studies suggesting dangers in intensive cannabis use do raise valid doubts which cannot be dismissed or discounted.

The immediate psychological effects of marijuana are typically a mild euphoria and a relaxed feeling of well-being. The user may feel a heightened sensitivity to taste and to visual and aural sensations, and his perception of time intervals may be distorted. A desire to become high can lead to a greater high; fear of becoming high or general nervousness can cause the user to fail to experience any high at all. In rare cases, excessive nervousness or fear of the drug can even precipitate a panic reaction. Occasionally a user will experience a negative reaction such as anxiety or depression, particularly when he takes in more of the substance than needed to achieve the desired high. However, in smoking marijuana, the usual method of taking it in this country, the user can self-titrate, or control the amount taken in, since the effect builds up gradually.

Additional short-term effects are an impairment of immediate-past-memory facility and impairment in performing psychomotor tasks. Experienced users seem less impaired in this regard than naive users.

In extremely rare instances, use of marijuana has been known to precipitate psychotic episodes; however, the consensus of the experts seems to be that the potential for precipitating psychotic episodes exists only for a limited number of prepsychotic persons who could be

47. Marihuana: A Signal of Misunderstanding, First Report of the National Commission on Marihuana and Drug Abuse (March 1972), p. 61.

pushed into psychosis by any number of drug or nondrug-related influences.

There is considerable debate as to the long-term effects of marijuana on mental functioning. Certain researchers cite evidence of an "amotivational syndrome" among long-term heavy cannabis users. However, the main examples of this effect are users in societies where large segments of the population exhibit such traits as social withdrawal and passivity even without drug use. The National Commission concludes that long-time heavy users do not deviate significantly from their social peers in terms of mental functioning, at least to any extent attributable to marijuana use.[51]

The experts generally agree that the early widely-held belief that marijuana use directly causes criminal behavior, and particularly violent, aggressive behavior, has no validity. On the contrary, the National Commission found indications that marijuana inhibits "the expression of agressive impulses by pacifying the user, interfering with muscle coordination, reducing psychomotor activities and generally producing states of drowsiness, lethargy, timidity and passivity." Moreover, the Commission and most other authorities agree that there is little validity to the theory that marijuana use leads to use of more potent and dangerous drugs. Although it has been stated that the more heavily a user smokes marijuana, the greater the probability that he has used or will use other drugs, "it has been suggested that such use is related to 'drug use proneness' and involvement in drug subcultures rather than to the characteristics of cannabis, *per se*."[53]

The most serious risk to the public health discerned by the National Commission is the possibility of an increase in the number of heavy users, who now constitute about 2% (500,000) of those who have used the drug. Within this group certain emotional changes have been observed among "predisposed individuals" as a result of prolonged heavy use. This group seems to carry the highest risk, particularly in view of the risk of retarding social adjustment among adolescents if heavy use should grow.

* * *

The National Commission rejected the notion that marijuana is physically addicting. It also rejected the notion that marijuana as used in the United States today presents a significant risk of causing psychological dependency in the user. Rather, the experimental or intermittent user develops little or no psychological dependence. Lengthy use on a regular basis does present a risk of such dependence and of subsequent heavier use, and strong psychological depend-

51. Marihuana: A Signal of Misunderstanding, the First Report of the National Commission on Marihuana and Drug Abuse (March 1972), 63. * * *

53. Marihuana and Health, Fourth Report to the United States Congress from the Secretary of Health, Education, and Welfare (1974) at 6.

ence is characteristic of heavy users in other countries. This pattern of use is rare in the United States today, however.

* * *

The number of persons arrested for marijuana possession has climbed steeply in recent years. In 1973, over 400,000 marijuana arrests occurred, a 43% rise over the previous year. It should also be noted that 81% of persons arrested for marijuana-related crimes have never been convicted of any crime in the past, and 91% have never been convicted of a drug-related crime.[55]

The justifications offered by the State to uphold AS 17.12.010 are generally that marijuana is a psychoactive drug; that it is not a harmless substance; that heavy use has concomitant risk; that it is capable of precipitating a psychotic reaction in at least individuals who are predisposed towards such reaction; and that its use adversely affects the user's ability to operate an automobile. The State relies upon a number of medical researchers who have raised questions as to the substance's effect on the body's immune system, on chromosomal structure, and on the functioning of the brain. On the other hand, in almost every instance of reports of potential danger arising from marijuana use, reports can be found reaching contradictory results. It appears that there is no firm evidence that marijuana, as presently used in this country, is generally a danger to the user or to others. But neither is there conclusive evidence to the effect that it is harmless. The one significant risk in use of marijuana which we do find established to a reasonable degree of certainty is the effect of marijuana intoxication on driving. We shall return to this aspect of the problem later in this opinion.

Possibly implicit in the State's catalogue of possible dangers of marijuana use is the assumption that the State has the authority to protect the individual from his own folly, that is, that the State can control activities which present no harm to anyone except those enjoying them. Although some courts have found the "public interest" to be broad enough to justify protecting the individual against himself, most have found inherent limitations on the police power of the state. An apposite example is the litigation regarding the constitutionality of laws requiring motorcyclists to wear helmets. Most of the courts addressing the issue, including this one, have resolved it by finding a connection between the helmet requirement and the safety of other motorists,[58] but a significant number of courts have explicitly rejected such restrictive measures as beyond the police power of the state because they do not benefit the public.[59] * * *

55. Marihuana: A Signal of Misunderstanding, Appendix II, at 622.

58. E. g., Kingery v. Chappel, 504 P.2d 831 (Alaska 1972); People v. Bielmeyer, 54 Misc.2d 466, 282 N.Y.S.2d 797 (1967); State v. Mele, 103 N.J.Super. 353, 247 A.2d 176 (1968).

59. E. g., American Motorcycle Ass'n v. Davids, 11 Mich.App. 351, 158 N.W.2d 72 (1968); People v. Fries, 42 Ill.2d

We glean from these cases the general proposition that the authority of the state to exert control over the individual extends only to activities of the individual which affect others or the public at large as it relates to matters of public health or safety, or to provide for the general welfare. * * *

* * * It appears that effects of marijuana on the individual are not serious enough to justify widespread concern, at least as compared with the far more dangerous effects of alcohol, barbiturates and amphetamines. Moreover, the current patterns of use in the United States are not such as would warrant concern that in the future consumption patterns are likely to change.

* * *

But one way in which use of marijuana most clearly does affect the general public is in regard to its effect on driving. All of which brings us to the opposite (from the home) end of the scale of the right to privacy in the context of ingestion or possession of marijuana, namely, when the individual is operating a motor vehicle. Recent research has produced increasing evidence of significant impairment of the driving ability of persons under the influence of cannabis. Distortion of time perception, impairment of psychomotor function, and increased selectivity in attentiveness to surroundings apparently can combine to lower driver ability. * * *

In view of the foregoing, we believe that at present, the need for control of drivers under the influence of marijuana and the existing doubts as to the safety of marijuana, demonstrate a sufficient justification for the prohibition found in AS 17.12.010 as an exercise of the state's police power for the public welfare. Given the evidence of the effect of marijuana on driving an individual's right to possess or ingest marijuana while driving would be subject to the prohibition provided for in AS 17.12.010. However, given the relative insignificance of marijuana consumption as a health problem in our society at present, we do not believe that the potential harm generated by drivers under the influence of marijuana, standing alone, creates a close and substantial relationship between the public welfare and control of ingestion of marijuana or possession of it in the home for personal use. Thus we conclude that no adequate justification for the state's intrusion into the citizen's right to privacy by its prohibition of possession of marijuana by an adult for personal consumption in the home has been shown. * * *

The state has a legitimate concern with avoiding the spread of marijuana use to adolescents who may not be equipped with the maturity to handle the experience prudently, as well as a legitimate con-

446, 250 N.E.2d 149 (1969). See Everhardt v. New Orleans, 208 So.2d 423 (La.App.1968), rev'd, 217 So.2d 400 (1969); People v. Carmichael, 53 Misc.2d 584, 279 N.Y.S.2d 272 (1967), rev'd, 56 Misc.2d 388, 288 N.Y.S.2d 931 (1968).

cern with the problem of driving under the influence of marijuana. Yet these interests are insufficient to justify intrusions into the rights of adults in the privacy of their own homes. Further, neither the federal or Alaska constitution affords protection for the buying or selling of marijuana, nor absolute protection for its use or possession in public. Possession at home of amounts of marijuana indicative of intent to sell rather than possession for personal use is likewise unprotected.

* * *

The record does not disclose any facts as to the situs of Ravin's arrest and his alleged possession of marijuana. In view of these circumstances, we hold that the matter must be remanded to the district court for the purpose of developing the facts concerning Ravin's arrest and circumstances of his possession of marijuana. Once this is accomplished, the district court is to consider Ravin's motion to dismiss in conformity with this opinion.

Remanded for further proceedings consistent with this opinion.

NOTES AND QUESTIONS

1. If the result in *Ravin* is accepted as correct, should the same position be taken in regard to possession of cocaine? The Alaska Supreme Court has rejected the argument that possession of cocaine in the home is protected. State v. Erickson, 574 P.2d 1 (Alaska 1978).

2. Other courts considering the issue litigated in *Ravin* have uniformly held that possession in the home is not constitutionally protected. See, e. g., State v. Murphy, 117 Ariz. 57, 570 P.2d 1070 (1977); Laird v. State, 342 So.2d 962 (Fla.1977) (over dissent); Marcoux v. Attorney General, 78 Mass.Adv.Sh. 1011, 375 N.E.2d 688 (1978); State v. Kells, 199 Neb. 374, 259 N.W.2d 19 (1977); State v. Anderson, 16 Wash.App. 553, 558 P.2d 307 (1976).

3. In Doe v. Commonwealth's Attorney for City of Richmond, 403 F. Supp. 1199 (E.D.Va.1975), male plaintiffs sought a declaration that Virginia's statute making sodomy a crime was unconstitutional when applied to active and regular homosexual relationships among adult males, in private, and on a consensual basis. An injunction against enforcement of the statute in such situations was also requested. The three judge district court, over the dissent of one judge, denied relief. Responding to the plaintiffs' reliance upon the privacy caselaw discussed in *Ravin*, the majority characterized the decisions as condemning only legislation "that trespasses upon the privacy of the incidents of marriage, upon the sanctity of the home, or upon the nurture of family life." 403 F.Supp. at 1200. Homosexuality, the majority continued, "is obviously no portion of marriage, home or family life." Id. at 1202. It concluded:

> If a State determines that punishment [for homosexuality], even when committed in the home, is appropriate in the promotion of morality and decency, it is not for the courts to say that the State is not free to do so.

Id. The majority also, however, cited Lovisi v. Slayton, 363 F.Supp. 620 (E.D.Va.1973) [later affirmed 539 F.2d 349 (4th Cir. 1974), cert. den. 429 U.S. 977, 97 S.Ct. 485, 50 L.Ed.2d 585 (1976)] as supporting the proposition that the State legislature could have concluded that the conduct prohibited by the sodomy statute is likely to end in a contribution to moral delinquency. In *Lovisi,* a married couple was convicted for participating in acts of fellatio with a third male person; one version of the testimony was to the effect that the wife's daughters, age 11 and 13, witnessed the activity. Judge Merhige, dissenting, reasoned:

> A mature individual's choice of an adult sexual partner, in the privacy of his or her own home, would appear to me to be a decision of the utmost private and intimate concern. Private consensual sex acts between adults are matters, absent evidence that they are harmful, in which the state has no legitimate interest.

403 F.Supp. at 1203. Finding no basis in the record for supporting the statutory prohibition other than "what the majority refers to as the promotion of morality and decency," Judge Merhige concluded that this did not justify intrusion by the State into the privacy of its citizens. Id. at 1205. On direct appeal, the United States Supreme Court affirmed the district court. 425 U.S. 901, 96 S.Ct. 1489, 47 L.Ed.2d 751 (1976).

2. PROHIBITION AGAINST CRUEL AND UNUSUAL PUNISHMENT

The Eighth Amendment's prohibition against cruel and unusual punishment, binding on the states through the Fourteenth Amendment's guarantee of due process of law, is one of the other few constitutional limitations upon what may be made a crime. The limitations upon capital punishment imposed by the Eighth Amendment are discussed on pages 36–45. For purposes of this section, the most important question is whether the Eighth Amendment does—or should—prohibit convicting a person on the basis of behavior that was in some sense "involuntary." The first case in this section, Robinson v. California, suggests the possibility that convicting a narcotics addict for the addiction itself or for use of narcotics would be unconstitutional because the addiction is an "illness." But in the second case, Powell v. Texas, the Supreme Court seems to refuse to read the Eighth Amendment as prohibiting the conviction of a chronic alcoholic for public intoxication. After *Powell,* it does seem clear that it is constitutionally impermissible to make it a crime to have a certain "status," i. e., to "be a narcotics addict," or to "be a prostitute." It appears, however, that there is no prohibition against convicting a person of a crime which is an involuntary result of an illness or status, i. e., of "using" narcotics, or of engaging in acts of prostitution. Consider whether this is desirable. If the Supreme Court had held in *Powell* that a chronic alcoholic could not be convicted of public intoxication, would it be possible to convict a person of any crime committed while the person was intoxicated or mentally ill? One argument against reading the Eighth Amendment as containing a prohibition against convicting a person for an involuntary act is that there is no feasible way of limiting such a rule and consequently any such constitutional rule would be far too broad. "Too broad", in this argument, assumes that states should be free to adopt different positions on the extent to which a defendant should be able to escape conviction on the basis of intoxication, insanity, or related matters. These "defenses" are discussed later in this book; see pages 184 and 514. At present, consider only whether the Supreme Court was correct in refusing to develop a constitutional rule prohibiting states from making at least some involuntary behavior criminal.

ROBINSON v. CALIFORNIA

Supreme Court of the United States, 1962.
370 U.S. 660, 82 S.Ct. 1417, 8 L.Ed.2d 758, reh. den.
371 U.S. 905, 83 S.Ct. 202, 9 L.Ed.2d 166.

Mr. Justice STEWART delivered the opinion of the Court.

A California statute makes it a criminal offense for a person to "be addicted to the use of narcotics." This appeal draws into question the constitutionality of that provision of the state law, as construed by the California courts in the present case.

The appellant was convicted after a jury trial in the Municipal Court of Los Angeles. The evidence against him was given by two Los Angeles police officers. Officer Brown testified that he had had occasion to examine the appellant's arms one evening on a street in Los Angeles some four months before the trial. The officer testified that at that time he had observed "scar tissue and discoloration on the inside" of the appellant's right arm, and "what appeared to be numerous needle marks and a scab which was approximately three inches below the crook of the elbow" on the appellant's left arm. The officer also testified that the appellant under questioning had admitted to the occasional use of narcotics.

Officer Lindquist testified that he had examined the appellant the following morning in the Central Jail in Los Angeles. The officer stated that at that time he had observed discolorations and scabs on the appellant's arms, and he identified photographs which had been taken of the appellant's arms shortly after his arrest the night before. Based upon more than ten years of experience as a member of the Narcotic Division of the Los Angeles Police Department, the witness gave his opinion that "these marks and the discoloration were the result of the injection of hypodermic needles into the tissue into the vein that was not sterile." He stated that the scabs were several days old at the time of his examination, and that the appellant was neither under the influence of narcotics nor suffering withdrawal symptoms at the time he saw him. This witness also testified that the appellant had admitted using narcotics in the past.

The appellant testified in his own behalf, denying the alleged conversations wtih the police officers and denying that he had ever used narcotics or been addicted to their use. He explained the marks on his arms as resulting from an allergic condition contracted during his military service. His testimony was corroborated by two witnesses.

The trial judge instructed the jury that the statute made it a misdemeanor for a person "either to use narcotics, or to be addicted to the use of narcotics * * *. That portion of the statute referring to the 'use' of narcotics is based upon the 'act' of using. That portion of the statute referring to 'addicted to the use' of narcotics is based upon a condition or status. They are not identical. * * * To be addicted to the use of narcotics is said to be a status or condition and not an act. It is a continuing offense and differs from most other offenses in the fact that [it] is chronic rather than acute; that it continues after it is complete and subjects the offender to arrest at any time before he reforms. The existence of such a chronic condition may be ascertained from a single examination, if the characteristic reactions of that condition be found present."

The judge further instructed the jury that the appellant could be convicted under a general verdict if the jury agreed *either* that he was of the "status" *or* had committed the "act" denounced by the statute. "All that the People must show is either that the defendant did use a narcotic in Los Angeles County, or that while in the City of Los Angeles he was addicted to the use of narcotics * * *."

Under these instructions the jury returned a verdict finding the appellant "guilty of the offense charged."

* * *

Such regulation, it can be assumed, could take a variety of valid forms. A State might impose criminal sanctions, for example, against the unauthorized manufacture, prescription, sale, purchase, or possession of narcotics within its borders. In the interest of discouraging the violation of such laws, or in the interest of the general health or welfare of its inhabitants, a State might establish a program of compulsory treatment for those addicted to narcotics. Such a program of treatment might require periods of involuntary confinement. And penal sanctions might be imposed for failure to comply with established compulsory treatment procedures. Or a State might choose to attack the evils of narcotics traffic on broader fronts also —through public health education, for example, or by efforts to ameliorate the economic and social conditions under which those evils might be thought to flourish. In short, the range of valid choice which a State might make in this area is undoubtedly a wide one, and the wisdom of any particular choice within the allowable spectrum is not for us to decide. Upon that premise we turn to the California law in issue here.

It would be possible to construe the statute under which the appellant was convicted as one which is operative only upon proof of the actual use of narcotics within the State's jurisdiction. But the California courts have not so construed this law. Although there was evidence in the present case that the appellant had used narcotics in Los Angeles, the jury were instructed that they could convict him even if they disbelieved that evidence. The appellant could be convicted, they were told, if they found simply that the appellant's "status" or "chronic condition" was that of being "addicted to the use of narcotics." And it is impossible to know from the jury's verdict that the defendant was not convicted upon precisely such a finding.

* * *

This statute, therefore, is not one which punishes a person for the use of narcotics, for their purchase, sale or possession, or for antisocial or disorderly behavior resulting from their administration. It is not a law which even purports to provide or require medical treatment. Rather, we deal with a statute which makes the "status" of narcotic addiction a criminal offense, for which the offender may be prosecuted "at any time before he reforms." California has said that a person can be continuously guilty of this offense, whether or not he has ever used or possessed any narcotics within the State, and whether or not he has been guilty of any antisocial behavior there.

It is unlikely that any State at this moment in history would attempt to make it a criminal offense for a person to be mentally ill, or a leper, or to be afflicted with a venereal disease. A State might determine that the general health and welfare require that the victims of these and other human afflictions be dealt with by compulsory treatment, involving quarantine, confinement, or sequestration. But, in the light of contemporary human knowledge, a law which made a criminal offense of such a disease would doubtless be universally thought to be an infliction of cruel and unusual punishment in violation of the Eighth and Fourteenth Amendments. * * *

We cannot but consider the statute before us as of the same category. In this Court counsel for the State recognized that narcotic addiction is an illness.[8] Indeed, it is apparently an illness which may be contracted innocently or involuntarily.[9] We hold that a state law which imprisons a person thus afflicted as a criminal, even though he has never touched any narcotic drug within the State or been guilty

8. In its brief the appellee stated: "Of course it is generally conceded that a narcotic addict, particularly one addicted to the use of heroin, is in a state of mental and physical illness. So is an alcoholic." Thirty-seven years ago this Court recognized that persons addicted to narcotics "are diseased and proper subjects for [medical] treatment." Linder v. United States, 268 U.S. 5, 18, 45 S.Ct. 446, 449, 69 L.Ed. 819.

9. Not only may addiction innocently result from the use of medically prescribed narcotics, but a person may even be a narcotics addict from the moment of his birth. * * *

of any irregular behavior there, inflicts a cruel and unusual punishment in violation of the Fourteenth Amendment. To be sure, imprisonment for ninety days is not, in the abstract, a punishment which is either cruel or unusual. But the question cannot be considered in the abstract. Even one day in prison would be a cruel and unusual punishment for the "crime" of having a common cold.

We are not unmindful that the vicious evils of the narcotics traffic have occasioned the grave concern of government. There are, as we have said, countless fronts on which those evils may be legitimately attacked. We deal in this case only with an individual provision of a particularized local law as it has so far been interpreted by the California courts.

Reversed.

Mr. Justice DOUGLAS, concurring.

While I join the Court's opinion, I wish to make more explicit the reasons why I think it is "cruel and unusual" punishment in the sense of the Eighth Amendment to treat as a criminal a person who is a drug addict. * * * [T]he principle that would deny power to exact capital punishment for a petty crime would also deny power to punish a person by fine or imprisonment for being sick. * * *

Mr. Justice HARLAN, concurring.

I am not prepared to hold that on the present state of medical knowledge it is completely irrational and hence unconstitutional for a State to conclude that narcotics addiction is something other than an illness nor that it amounts to cruel and unusual punishment for the State to subject narcotics addicts to its criminal law. * * * Since addiction alone cannot reasonably be thought to amount to more than a compelling propensity to use narcotics, the effect of [the] instruction was to authorize criminal punishment for a bare desire to commit a criminal act.

If the California statute reaches this type of conduct, * * * it is an arbitrary imposition which exceeds the power that a State may exercise in enacting its criminal law. Accordingly, I agree that the application of the California statute was unconstitutional in this case and join the judgment of reversal.

Mr. Justice CLARK, dissenting.

* * *

[T]he majority admits that "a State might establish a program of compulsory treatment for those addicted to narcotics" which "might require periods of involuntary confinement." I submit that California has done exactly that. The majority's error is in instructing the California Legislature that hospitalization is the *only treatment* for narcotics addiction—that anything less is a punishment denying due process. California has found otherwise after a study which I suggest was more extensive than that conducted by the Court. Even in California's program for hospital commitment of nonvolitional narcotic addicts—which the majority approves—it is recognized that some addicts will not respond to or do not need hospital treatment. As to these persons its provisions are identical to those of § 11721—confinement for a period of not less than 90 days. Section 11721 provides this confinement as treatment for the volitional addicts to whom its provisions apply, in addition to parole with frequent tests to detect and prevent further use of drugs. The fact that § 11721 might be labeled "criminal" seems irrelevant,* not only to the majority's own "treatment" test but to the "concept of ordered liberty" to which the States must attain under the Fourteenth Amendment. The test is the overall purpose and effect of a State's act, and I submit that California's program relative to narcotic addicts—including both the "criminal" and "civil" provisions—is inherently one of treatment and lies well within the power of a State.

* * *

Mr. Justice WHITE, dissenting.

If appellant's conviction rested upon sheer status, condition or illness or if he was convicted for being an addict who had lost his power of self-control, I would have other thoughts about this case. But this record presents neither situation. * * * [T]here was no evidence at all that appellant had lost the power to control his acts. * * * He was an incipient addict, a redeemable user, and the State chose to send him to jail for 90 days rather than to attempt to confine him by civil proceedings under another statute which requires a finding that the addict has lost the power of self-control. In my opinion, on this record, it was within the power of the State of California to confine him by criminal proceedings for the use of narcotics or for regular use amounting to habitual use.

* * *

POWELL v. TEXAS

Supreme Court of the United States, 1968.
392 U.S. 514, 88 S.Ct. 2145, 20 L.Ed.2d 1254.

Mr. Justice MARSHALL announced the judgment of the Court and delivered an opinion in which THE CHIEF JUSTICE, Mr. Justice BLACK, and Mr. Justice HARLAN join.

In late December 1966, appellant was arrested and charged with being found in a state of intoxication in a public place, in violation of

* Any reliance upon the "stigma" of a misdemeanor conviction in this context is misplaced as it would hardly be different from the stigma of a civil commitment for narcotics addiction.

Vernon's Ann.Texas Penal Code, Art. 477 (1952), which reads as follows:

> "Whoever shall get drunk or be found in a state of intoxication in any public place, or at any private house except his own, shall be fined not exceeding one hundred dollars."

Appellant was tried in the Corporation Court of Austin, Texas, found guilty, and fined $20. He appealed to the County Court at Law No. 1 of Travis County, Texas, where a trial *de novo* was held. His counsel urged that appellant was "afflicted with the disease of chronic alcoholism," that "his appearance in public [while drunk was] * * * not of his own volition," and therefore that to punish him criminally for that conduct would be cruel and unusual, in violation of the Eighth and Fourteenth Amendments to the United States Constitution.

The trial judge in the county court, sitting without a jury, made certain findings of fact, * * * but ruled as a matter of law that chronic alcoholism was not a defense to the charge. He found appellant guilty, and fined him $50. There being no further right to appeal within the Texas judicial system, appellant appealed to this Court * * *.

I.

The principal testimony was that of Dr. David Wade, a Fellow of the American Medical Association, duly certificated in psychiatry. His testimony consumed a total of 17 pages in the trial transcript. Five of those pages were taken up with a recitation of Dr. Wade's qualifications. In the next 12 pages Dr. Wade was examined by appellant's counsel, cross-examined by the State, and re-examined by the defense, and those 12 pages contain virtually all the material developed at trial which is relevant to the constitutional issue we face here. Dr. Wade sketched the outlines of the "disease" concept of alcoholism; noted that there is no generally accepted definition of "alcoholism"; alluded to the ongoing debate within the medical profession over whether alcohol is actually physically "addicting" or merely psychologically "habituating"; and concluded that in either case a "chronic alcoholic" is an "involuntary drinker," who is "powerless not to drink," and who "loses his self-control over his drinking." He testified that he had examined appellant, and that appellant is a "chronic alcoholic," who "by the time he has reached [the state of intoxication] * * * is not able to control his behavior, and [who] * * * has reached this point because he has an uncontrollable compulsion to drink." Dr. Wade also responded in the negative to the the question whether appellant has "the willpower to resist the constant excessive consumption of alcohol." He added that in his opinion jailing appellant without medical attention would operate neither to rehabilitate him nor to lessen his desire for alcohol.

On cross-examination, Dr. Wade admitted that when appellant was sober he knew the difference between right and wrong, and he responded affirmatively to the question whether appellant's act in taking the first drink in any given instance when he was sober was a "voluntary exercise of his will." Qualifying his answer, Dr. Wade stated that "these individuals have a compulsion, and this compulsion, while not completely overpowering, is a very strong influence, an exceedingly strong influence, and this compulsion coupled with the firm belief in their mind that they are going to be able to handle it from now on causes their judgment to be somewhat clouded."

Appellant testified concerning the history of his drinking problem. He reviewed his many arrests for drunkenness; testified that he was unable to stop drinking; stated that when he was intoxicated he had no control over his actions and could not remember them later, but that he did not become violent; and admitted that he did not remember his arrest on the occasion for which he was being tried. On cross-examination, appellant admitted that he had had one drink on the morning of the trial and had been able to discontinue drinking.

* * *

Following this abbreviated exposition of the problem before it, the trial court indicated its intention to disallow appellant's claimed defense of "chronic alcoholism." Thereupon defense counsel submitted, and the trial court entered, the following "findings of fact":

> "(1) That chronic alcoholism is a disease which destroys the afflicted person's will power to resist the constant, excessive consumption of alcohol.
>
> "(2) That a chronic alcoholic does not appear in public by his own volition but under a compulsion symptomatic of the disease of chronic alcoholism.
>
> "(3) That Leroy Powell, defendant herein, is a chronic alcoholic who is afflicted with the disease of chronic alcoholism."

Whatever else may be said of them, those are not "findings of fact" in any recognizable, traditional sense in which that term has been used in a court of law; they are the premises of a syllogism transparently designed to bring this case within the scope of this Court's opinion in Robinson v. State of California, 370 U.S. 660, 82 S. Ct. 1417, 8 L.Ed.2d 758 (1962). Nonetheless, the dissent would have us adopt these "findings" without critical examination; it would use them as the basis for a constitutional holding that "a person may not be punished if the condition essential to constitute the defined crime is part of the pattern of his disease and is occasioned by a compulsion symptomatic of the disease." * * *

The difficulty with that position * * * is that it goes much too far on the basis of too little knowledge. In the first place, the record in this case is utterly inadequate to permit the sort of informed and responsible adjudication which alone can support the announcement of an important and wide-ranging new constitutional principle. We know very little about the circumstances surrounding the drinking bout which resulted in this conviction, or about Leroy Powell's drinking problem, or indeed about alcoholism itself. The trial hardly reflects the sharp legal and evidentiary clash between fully prepared adversary litigants which is traditionally expected in major constitutional cases. The State put on only one witness, the arresting officer. The defense put on three—a policeman who testified to appellant's long history of arrests for public drunkenness, the psychiatrist, and appellant himself.

Furthermore, the inescapable fact is that there is no agreement among members of the medical profession about what it means to say that "alcoholism" is a "disease." * * *

Nor is there any substantial consensus as to the "manifestations of alcoholism." * * *

The trial court's "finding" that Powell "is afflicted with the disease of chronic alcoholism," which "destroys the afflicted person's will power to resist the constant, excessive consumption of alcohol" covers a multitude of sins. Dr. Wade's testimony that appellant suffered from a compulsion which was an "exceedingly strong influence," but which was "not completely overpowering" is at least more carefully stated, if no less mystifying. * * *

Dr. Wade did testify that once appellant began drinking he appeared to have no control over the amount of alcohol he finally ingested. Appellant's own testimony concerning his drinking on the day of the trial would certainly appear, however, to cast doubt upon the conclusion that he was without control over his consumption of alcohol when he had sufficiently important reasons to exercise such control. However that may be, there are more serious factual and conceptual difficulties with reading this record to show that appellant was unable to abstain from drinking. Dr. Wade testified that when appellant was sober, the act of taking the first drink was a "voluntary exercise of his will," but that this exercise of will was undertaken under the "exceedingly strong influence" of a "compulsion" which was "not completely overpowering." Such concepts, when juxtaposed in this fashion, have little meaning.

* * *

It is one thing to say that if a man is deprived of alcohol his hands will begin to shake, he will suffer agonizing pains and ultimately he will have hallucinations; it is quite another to say that a man has a "compulsion" to take a drink, but that he also retains a certain amount of "free will" with which to resist. It is simply impossible, in the present state of our knowledge, to ascribe a useful meaning to the latter statement. This definitional confusion reflects, of course, not merely the undeveloped state of the psychiatric art but also the conceptual difficulties inevitably attendant upon the importation of scientific and medical models into a legal system generally predicated upon a different set of assumptions.

II.

Despite the comparatively primitive state of our knowledge on the subject, it cannot be denied that the destructive use of alcoholic beverages is one of our principal social and public health problems. The lowest current informed estimate places the number of "alcoholics" in America (definitional problems aside) at 4,000,000, and most authorities are inclined to put the figure considerably higher. The problem is compounded by the fact that a very large percentage of the alcoholics in this country are "invisible"—they possess the means to keep their drinking problems secret, and the traditionally uncharitable attitude of our society toward alcoholics causes many of them to refrain from seeking treatment from any source. Nor can it be gainsaid that the legislative response to this enormous problem has in general been inadequate.

There is as yet no known generally effective method for treating the vast number of alcoholics in our society. Some individual alcoholics have responded to particular forms of therapy with remissions of their symptomatic dependence upon the drug. But just as there is no agreement among doctors and social workers with respect to the causes of alcoholism, there is no consensus as to why particular treatments have been effective in particular cases and there is no generally agreed-upon approach to the problem of treatment on a large scale. Most psychiatrists are apparently of the opinion that alcoholism is far more difficult to treat than other forms of behavioral disorders, and some believe it is impossible to cure by means of psychotherapy; indeed, the medical profession as a whole, and psychiatrists in particular, have been severely criticised for the prevailing reluctance to undertake the treatment of drinking problems. Thus it is entirely possible that, even were the manpower and facilities available for a full-scale attack upon chronic alcoholism, we would find ourselves unable to help the vast bulk of our "visible"—let alone our "invisible"—alcoholic population.

However, facilities for the attempted treatment of indigent alcoholics are woefully lacking throughout the country. It would be tragic to return large numbers of helpless, sometimes dangerous and frequently unsanitary inebriates to the streets of our cities without even the opportunity to sober up adequately which a brief jail term provides. Presumably no State or city will tolerate such a state of affairs. Yet the medical profession cannot, and does not, tell us with any assurance that, even if the buildings, equipment and trained personnel were made available, it could provide anything more than slightly higher-class jails for our indigent habitual inebriates. Thus we run the grave risk that nothing will be accomplished beyond the hanging of a new sign—reading "hospital"—over one wing of the jailhouse.

One virtue of the criminal process is, at least, that the duration of penal incarceration typically has some outside statutory limit; this is universally true in the case of petty offenses, such as public drunkenness, where jail terms are quite short on the whole. "Therapeutic civil commitment" lacks this feature; one is typically committed until one is "cured." Thus, to do otherwise than affirm might subject indigent alcoholics to the risk that they may be locked up for an indefinite period of time under the same conditions as before, with no more hope than before of receiving effective treatment and no prospect of periodic "freedom."

Faced with this unpleasant reality, we are unable to assert that the use of the criminal process as a means of dealing with the public aspects of problem drinking can never be defended as rational. The picture of the penniless drunk propelled aimlessly and endlessly through the law's "revolving door" of arrest, incarceration, release and re-arrest is not a pretty one. But before we condemn the present practice across-the-board, perhaps we ought to be able to point to some clear promise of a better world for these unfortunate people. Unfortunately, no such promise has yet been forthcoming. If, in addition to the absence of a coherent approach to the problem of treatment, we consider the almost complete absence of facilities and manpower for the implementation of a rehabilitation program, it is difficult to say in the present context that the criminal process is utterly lacking in social value. This Court has never held that anything in the Constitution requires that penal sanctions be designed solely to achieve therapeutic or rehabilitative effects, and it can hardly be said with assurance that incarceration serves such purposes any better for the general run of criminals than it does for public drunks.

Ignorance likewise impedes our assessment of the deterrent effect of criminal sanctions for public drunkenness. The fact that a high percentage of American alcoholics conceal their drinking problems, not merely by avoiding public displays of intoxication but also by shunning all forms of treatment, is indicative that some powerful deterrent operates to inhibit the public revelation of the existence of alcoholism. Quite probably this deterrent effect can be largely attributed to the harsh moral attitude which our society has traditionally taken toward intoxication and the shame which we have associated with alcoholism. Criminal conviction represents the degrading public revelation of what Anglo-American society has long condemned as a moral defect, and the existence of criminal sanctions may serve to reinforce this cultural taboo, just as we presume it serves to reinforce other, stronger feelings against murder, rape, theft, and other forms of antisocial conduct.

Obviously, chronic alcoholics have not been deterred from drinking to excess by the existence of criminal sanctions against public drunkenness. But all those who violate penal laws of any kind are by definition undeterred. The long-standing and still raging debate over the validity of the deterrence justification for penal sanctions has not reached any sufficiently clear conclusions to permit it to be said that such sanctions are ineffective in any particular context or for any particular group of people who are able to appreciate the consequences of their acts. Certainly no effort was made at the trial of this case, beyond a monosyllabic answer to a perfunctory one-line question, to determine the effectiveness of penal sanctions in deterring Leroy Powell in particular or chronic alcoholics in general from drinking at all or from getting drunk in particular places or at particular times.

III.

Appellant claims that his conviction on the facts of this case would violate the Cruel and Unusual Punishment Clause of the Eighth Amendment as applied to the States through the Fourteenth Amendment. The primary purpose of that clause has always been considered, and properly so, to be directed at the method or kind of punishment imposed for the violation of criminal statutes; the nature of the conduct made criminal is ordinarily relevant only to the fitness of the punishment imposed.

* * *

Appellant, however, seeks to come within the application of the Cruel and Unusual Punishment Clause announced in Robinson v. State of California, 370 U.S. 660, 82 S.Ct. 1417, 8 L.Ed.2d 758 (1962), which involved a state statute making it a crime to "be addicted to the use of narcotics." This Court held there that "a state law which imprisons a person thus afflicted [with narcotic addiction] as a criminal, even though he has never touched any narcotic drug within the State or been guilty of an irregular behavior there, inflicts a cruel and unusual punishment * * *." Id., at 667, 82 S.Ct., at 1420–1421.

On its face the present case does not fall within that holding, since appellant was convicted, not for being a chronic alcoholic, but for being in public while drunk on a particular occasion. The State of Texas thus has not sought to punish a mere status, as California did in *Robinson*; nor has it attempted to regulate appellant's behavior in the privacy of his own home. Rather, it has imposed upon appellant a criminal sanction for public behavior which may create substantial health and safety hazards, both for appellant and for members of the general public, and which offends the moral and esthetic sensibilities of a large segment of the community. This seems a far cry from convicting one for being an addict, being a chronic alcoholic, being "mentally ill, or a leper * * *." Id., at 666, 82 S.Ct., at 1420.

Robinson so viewed brings this Court but a very small way into the substantive criminal law. And unless *Robinson* is so viewed it is difficult to see any limiting principle that would serve to prevent this Court from becoming, under the aegis of the Cruel and Unusual Punishment Clause, the ultimate arbiter of the standards of criminal responsibility, in diverse areas of the criminal law, throughout the country.

It is suggested in dissent that *Robinson* stands for the "simple" but "subtle" principle that "[c]riminal penalties may not be inflicted upon a person for being in a condition he is powerless to change." Post, at 2171. In that view, appellant's "condition" of public intoxication was "occasioned by a compulsion symptomatic of the disease" of chronic alcoholism, and thus, apparently, his behavior lacked the critical element of *mens rea.* Whatever may be the merits of such a doctrine of criminal responsibility, it surely cannot be said to follow from *Robinson.* The entire thrust of *Robinson's* interpretation of the Cruel and Unusual Punishment Clause is that criminal penalties may be inflicted only if the accused has committed some act, has engaged in some behavior, which society has an interest in preventing, or perhaps in historical common law terms, has committed some *actus reus.* It thus does not deal with the question of whether certain conduct cannot constitutionally be punished because it is, in some sense, "involuntary" or "occasioned by a compulsion."

* * *

Ultimately, then, the most troubling aspects of this case, were *Robinson* to be extended to meet it, would be the scope and content of what could only be a constitutional doctrine of criminal responsibility. In dissent it is urged that the decision could be limited to conduct which is "a characteristic and involuntary part of the pattern of the disease as it afflicts" the particular individual, and that "[i]t is not foreseeable" that it would be applied "in the case of offenses such as driving a car while intoxicated, assault, theft, or robbery." That is limitation by fiat. In the first place, nothing in the logic of the dissent would limit its application to chronic alcoholics. If Leroy Powell cannot be convicted of public intoxication, it is difficult to see how a State can convict an individual for murder, if that individual, while exhibiting normal behavior in all other respects, suffers from a "compulsion" to kill, which is an "exceedingly strong influence," but "not completely overpowering." Even if we limit our consideration to chronic alcoholics, it would seem impossible to confine the principle within the arbitrary bounds which the dissent seems to envision.

It is not difficult to imagine a case involving psychiatric testimony to the effect that an individual suffers from some aggressive neurosis which he is able to control when sober; that very little alcohol suffices to remove the inhibitions which normally contain these aggressions, with the result that the individual engages in assaultive behavior without becoming actually intoxicated; and that the individual suffers from a very strong desire to drink, which is an "exceedingly strong influence" but "not completely overpowering." Without being untrue to the rationale of this case, should the principles advanced in dissent be accepted here, the Court could not avoid holding such an individual constitutionally unaccountable for his assaultive behavior.

Traditional common-law concepts of personal accountability and essential considerations of federalism lead us to disagree with appellant. We are unable to conclude, on the state of this record or on the current state of medical knowledge, that chronic alcoholics in general, and Leroy Powell in particular, suffer from such an irresistible compulsion to drink and to get drunk in public that they are utterly unable to control their performance of either or both of these acts and thus cannot be deterred at all from public intoxication. * * *

* * *

Affirmed.

Mr. Justice BLACK, whom Mr. Justice HARLAN joins, concurring.

While I agree that the grounds set forth in Mr. Justice MARSHALL's opinion are sufficient to require affirmance of the judgment here, I wish to amplify my reasons for concurring.

* * *

The rule of constitutional law urged by appellant is not required by Robinson v. State of California, 370 U.S. 660, 82 S.Ct. 1417, 8 L.Ed.2d 758 (1962). In that case we held that a person could not be punished for the mere status of being a narcotics addict. We explicitly limited our holding to the situation where no conduct of any kind is involved * * * [.] The argument is made that appellant comes within the terms of our holding in *Robinson* because being drunk in public is a mere status or "condition." Despite this many-faceted use of the concept of "condition," this argument would require converting *Robinson* into a case protecting actual behavior, a step we explicitly refused to take in that decision.

A different question, I admit, is whether our attempt in *Robinson* to limit our holding to pure status crimes, involving no conduct whatever, was a sound one. I believe it was. Although some of our objections to the statute in *Robinson* are equally applicable to statutes that punish conduct "symptomatic" of a disease, any attempt to explain *Robinson* as based solely on the lack of voluntariness encounters a number of logical difficulties. Other problems raised by status crimes are in no way involved when the State attempts to punish for conduct, and these other problems were, in my view, the controlling aspects of our decision.

Punishment for a status is particularly obnoxious, and in many instances can reasonably be called cruel and unusual, because it involves punishment for a mere propensity, a desire to commit an offense; the mental element is not simply one part of the crime but may constitute all of it. This is a situation universally sought to be avoided in our criminal law; the fundamental requirement that some action be proved is solidly established even for offenses most heavily based on propensity, such as attempt, conspiracy, and recidivist crimes. * * *

The reasons for this refusal to permit conviction without proof of an act are difficult to spell out, but they are nonetheless perceived and universally expressed in our criminal law. Evidence of propensity can be considered relatively unreliable and more difficult for a defendant to rebut; the requirement of a specific act thus provides some protection against false charges. See 4 Blackstone, Commentaries 21. Perhaps more fundamental is the difficulty of distinguishing, in the absence of any conduct, between desires of the day-dream variety and fixed intentions that may pose a real threat to society; extending the criminal law to cover both types of desire would be unthinkable, since "[t]here can hardly be anyone who has never thought evil. When a desire is inhibited it may find expression in fantasy; but it would be absurd to condemn this natural psychological mechanism as illegal."

In contrast, crimes that require the State to prove that the defendant actually committed some proscribed act involve none of these special problems. * * *

Mr. Justice WHITE, concurring in the result.

If it cannot be a crime to have an irresistible compulsion to use narcotics, Robinson v. State of California, 370 U.S. 660, 82 S.Ct. 1417, 8 L.Ed.2d 758, rehearing denied 371 U.S. 905, 83 S.Ct. 202, 9 L.Ed.2d 166 (1962), I do not see how it can constitutionally be a crime to yield to such a compulsion. Punishing an addict for using drugs convicts for addiction under a different name. Distinguishing between the two crimes is like forbidding criminal conviction for being sick with flu or epilepsy but permitting punishment for running a fever or having a convulsion. Unless *Robinson* is to be abandoned, the use of narcotics by an addict must be beyond the reach of the criminal law. Similarly, the chronic alcoholic with an irresistible urge to consume alcohol should not be punishable for drinking or for being drunk.

Powell's conviction was for the different crime of being drunk in a public place. Thus even if Powell was compelled to drink, and so could not constitutionally be convicted for drinking, his conviction in this case can be invalidated only if there is a constitutional basis for saying that he may not be punished for being in public while drunk. * * *

The trial court said that Powell was a chronic alcoholic with a compulsion not only to drink to excess but also to frequent public places when intoxicated. Nothing in the record before the trial court supports the latter conclusion which is contrary to common sense and to common knowledge. The sober chronic alcoholic has no compulsion to be on the public streets; many chronic alcoholics drink at home and are never seen drunk in public. Before and after taking the first drink, and until he becomes so drunk that he loses the power to know where he is or to direct his movements, the chronic alcoholic with a home or financial resources is as capable as the nonchronic drinker of doing his drinking in private, of removing himself from public places and, since he knows or ought to know that he will become intoxicated, of making plans to avoid his being found drunk in public. For these reasons, I cannot say that the chronic alcoholic who proves his disease and a compulsion to drink is shielded from conviction when he has knowingly failed to take feasible precautions against committing a criminal act, here the act of going to or remaining in a public place. On such facts the alcoholic is like a person with smallpox, who could be convicted for being on the street but not for being ill, or, like the epileptic, who would be punished for driving a car but not for his disease.

* * *

It is unnecessary to pursue at this point the further definition of the circumstances or the state of intoxication which might bar conviction of a chronic alcoholic for being drunk in a public place. For the purposes of this case, it is necessary to say only that Powell showed nothing more than that he was to some degree compelled to drink and that he was drunk at the time of his arrest. He made no showing that he was unable to stay off the streets on the night in question.

Because Powell did not show that his conviction offended the Constitution, I concur in the judgment affirming the Travis County court.

Mr. Justice FORTAS, with whom Mr. Justice DOUGLAS, Mr. Justice BRENNAN, and Mr. Justice STEWART join, dissenting.

* * *

I.

The issue posed in this case is a narrow one. There is no challenge here to the validity of public intoxication statutes in general or to the Texas public intoxication statute in particular. * * *

* * * Nor does [this case] concern the responsibility of an alcoholic for criminal *acts*. We deal here with the mere *condition* of being intoxicated in public.[2]

* * * The questions for this Court are not settled by reference to medicine or penology. Our task is to determine whether the principles embodied in the Constitution of the United States place any limitations upon the circumstances under which punishment may be inflicted, and, if so, whether, in the case now before us, those principles preclude the imposition of such punishment.

It is settled that the Federal Constitution places some substantive limitation upon the power of state legislatures to define crimes for which the imposition of punishment is ordered. In Robinson v. State of California, 370 U.S. 660, 82 S.Ct. 1417, 8 L.Ed.2d 758 (1962), the Court considered a conviction under a California statute making it a criminal offense for a person "[t]o be addicted to the use of narcotics." * * *

This Court reversed Robinson's conviction on the ground that punishment under the law in question was cruel and unusual, in violation of the Eighth Amendment of the Constitution as applied to the States through the Fourteenth Amendment. * * *

Robinson stands upon a principle which, despite its subtlety, must be simply stated and respectfully applied because it is the foundation of individual liberty and the cornerstone of the relations between a civilized state and its citizens: Criminal penalties may not be inflicted upon a person for being in a condition he is powerless to change. In all probability, Robinson at some time before his conviction elected to take narcotics. But the crime as defined did not punish this conduct. The statute imposed a penalty for the offense of "addiction"—a condition which Robinson could not control. Once Robinson had become an addict, he was utterly powerless to avoid criminal guilt. He was powerless to choose not to violate the law.

In the present case, appellant is charged with a crime composed of two elements—being intoxicated and being found in a public place while in that condition. The crime, so defined, differs from that in *Robinson*. The statute covers more than a mere status. But the essential constitutional defect here is the same as in *Robinson*, for in both cases the particular defendant was accused of being in a condi-

2. It is not foreseeable that findings such as those which are decisive here—namely that the appellant's being intoxicated in public was a part of the pattern of his disease and due to a compulsion symptomatic of that disease—could or would be made in the case of offenses such as driving a car while intoxicated, assault, theft, or robbery. Such offenses require independent acts or conduct and do not typically flow from and are not part of the syndrome of the disease of chronic alcoholism. If an alcoholic should be convicted for criminal conduct which is not a characteristic and involuntary part of the pattern of the disease as it afflicts him, nothing herein would prevent his punishment.

tion which he had no capacity to change or avoid. The trial judge sitting as trier of fact found upon the medical and other relevant testimony, that Powell is a "chronic alcoholic." He defined appellant's "chronic alcoholism" as "a disease which destroys the afflicted person's will power to resist the constant, excessive consumption of alcohol." He also found that "a chronic alcoholic does not appear in public by his own volition but under a compulsion symptomatic of the disease of chronic alcoholism." I read these findings to mean that appellant was powerless to avoid drinking; that having taken his first drink, he had "an uncontrollable compulsion to drink" to the point of intoxication; and that, once intoxicated, he could not prevent himself from appearing in public places.

Article 477 of the Texas Penal Code is specifically directed to the accused's presence while in a state of intoxication, "in any public place, or at any private house except his own." This is the essence of the crime. Ordinarily when the State proves such presence in a state of intoxication, this will be sufficient for conviction, and the punishment prescribed by the State may, of course, be validly imposed. But here the findings of the trial judge call into play the principle that a person may not be punished if the condition essential to constitute the defined crime is part of the pattern of his disease and is occasioned by a compulsion symptomatic of the disease. This principle, narrow in scope and applicability, is implemented by the Eighth Amendment's prohibition of "cruel and unusual punishment," as we construed that command in *Robinson.* It is true that the command of the Eighth Amendment and its antecedent provision in the Bill of Rights of 1689 were initially directed to the type and degree of punishment inflicted. But in *Robinson* we recognized that "the principle that would deny power to exact capital punishment for a petty crime would also deny power to punish a person by fine or imprisonment for being sick." 370 U.S., at 676, 82 S.Ct., at 1425 (Mr. Justice DOUGLAS, concurring).

* * *

I would reverse the judgment below.

3. REQUIREMENT OF PRECISION

Robinson v. California and Powell v. Texas deal with the basic policy decision of what to make criminal. But the task of the law is not only to make such a decision but to embody it in a "rule." As with the decision to make given activity criminal, the decision as to how to express the result can best be initially approached by examining constitutional limitations upon possible solutions. In the case of expressing the result, the basic constitutional limitation is the due process requirement of precision or, in negative terms, the defect of vagueness.

PAPACHRISTOU v. JACKSONVILLE

Supreme Court of the United States, 1972.
405 U.S. 156, 92 S.Ct. 839, 31 L.Ed.2d 110.

Vagrancy

Mr. Justice DOUGLAS delivered the opinion of the Court.

This case involves eight defendants who were convicted in a Florida municipal court of violating a Jacksonville, Florida, vagrancy ordinance.[1] * * * For reasons which will appear, we reverse.

At issue are five consolidated cases. Margaret Papachristou, Betty Calloway, Eugene Eddie Melton, and Leonard Johnson were all arrested early on a Sunday morning, and charged with vagrancy—"prowling by auto."

Jimmy Lee Smith and Milton Henry were charged with vagrancy—"vagabonds."

Henry Edward Heath and a co-defendant were arrested for vagrancy—"loitering" and "common thief."

Thomas Owen Campbell was charged with vagrancy—"common thief."

Hugh Brown was charged with vagrancy—"disorderly loitering on street" and "disorderly conduct—resisting arrest with violence."

The facts are stipulated. Papachristou and Calloway are white females. Melton and Johnson are black males. Papachristou was enrolled in a job-training program sponsored by the State Employment Service at Florida Junior College in Jacksonville. Calloway was a typing and shorthand teacher at a state mental institution located near Jacksonville. She was the owner of the automobile in which the four defendants were arrested. Melton was a Vietnam war veteran

1. Jacksonville Ordinance Code § 26–57 provided at the time of these arrests and convictions as follows:

"Rogues and vagabonds, or dissolute persons who go about begging, common gamblers, persons who use juggling or unlawful games or plays, common drunkards, common night walkers, thieves, pilferers or pickpockets, traders in stolen property, lewd, wanton and lascivious persons, keepers of gambling places, common railers and brawlers, persons wandering or strolling around from place to place without any lawful purpose or object, habitual loafers, disorderly persons, persons neglecting all lawful business and habitually spending their time by frequenting houses of ill fame, gaming houses, or places where alcoholic beverages are sold or served, persons able to work but habitually living upon the earnings of their wives or minor children shall be deemed vagrants and, upon conviction in the Municipal Court shall be punished as provided for Class D offenses."

Class D offenses as the time of these arrests and convictions were punishable by 90 days imprisonment, $500 fine, or both. Jacksonville Ordinance Code § 1–8 (1965). The maximum punishment has since been reduced to 75 days or $450. § 304.101 (1971). We are advised that that downward revision was made to avoid federal right-to-counsel decisions. The Fifth Circuit case extending right to counsel in misdemeanors where a fine of $500 or 90-days imprisonment could be imposed is Harvey v. Mississippi, 340 F. 2d 263 (CA 5 1965).

who had been released from the Navy after nine months in a veterans' hospital. On the date of his arrest he was a part-time computer helper while attending college as a full-time student in Jacksonville. Johnson was a tow-motor operator in a grocery chain warehouse and was a lifelong resident of Jacksonville.

At the time of their arrest the four of them were riding in Calloway's car on the main thoroughfare in Jacksonville. They had left a restaurant owned by Johnson's uncle where they had eaten and were on their way to a night club. The arresting officers denied that the racial mixture in the car played any part in the decision to make the arrest. The arrest, they said, was made because the defendants had stopped near a used-car lot which had been broken into several times. There was, however, no evidence of any breaking and entering on the night in question.

Of these four charged with "prowling by auto" none had been previously arrested except Papachristou who had once been convicted of a municipal offense.

[The details of the arrests in the other cases are omitted.]

Jacksonville's ordinance and Florida's statute were "derived from early English law," * * * and employ "archaic language" in their definitions of vagrants. The history is an often-told tale. The breakup of feudal estates in England led to labor shortages which in turn resulted in the Statutes of Laborers, designed to stabilize the labor force by prohibiting increases in wages and prohibiting the movement of workers from their home areas in search of improved conditions. Later vagrancy laws became criminal aspects of the poor laws. The series of laws passed in England on the subject became increasingly severe. But "the theory of the Elizabethan poor laws no longer fits the facts," Edwards v. California, 314 U.S. 160, 174, 62 S.Ct. 164, 167, 86 L.Ed. 119. The conditions which spawned these laws may be gone, but the archaic classifications remain.

This ordinance is void-for-vagueness, both in the sense that it "fails to give a person of ordinary intelligence fair notice that his contemplated conduct is forbidden by the statute," United States v. Harriss, 347 U.S. 612, 617, 74 S.Ct. 808, 812, 98 L.Ed. 989, and because it encourages arbitrary and erratic arrests and convictions. * * *

Living under a rule of law entails various suppositions, one of which is that "All [persons] are entitled to be informed as to what the State commands or forbids." Lanzetta v. New Jersey, 306 U.S. 451, 453, 59 S.Ct. 618, 619, 83 L.Ed. 888.

Lanzetta is one of a well-recognized group of cases insisting that the law give fair notice of the offending conduct. * * * In the field of regulatory statutes governing business activities, where the acts limited are in a narrow category, greater leeway is allowed. * * *

The poor among us, the minorities, the average householder are not in business and not alerted to the regulatory schemes of vagrancy laws; and we assume they would have no understanding of their meaning and impact if they read them. Nor are they protected from being caught in the vagrancy net by the necessity of having a specific intent to commit an unlawful act. * * *

The Jacksonville ordinance makes criminal activities which by modern standards are normally innocent. "Nightwalking" is one. Florida construes the ordinance not to make criminal one night's wandering, Johnson v. State, [Fla., 202 So.2d 852, 855,] only the "habitual" wanderer or as the ordinance describes it "common night walkers." We know, however, from experience that sleepless people often walk at night, perhaps hopeful that sleep-inducing relaxation will result.

"Persons able to work but habitually living on the earnings of their wives or minor children"—like habitually living "without visible means of support"—might implicate unemployed pillars of the community who have married rich wives.

"Persons able to work but habitually living on the earnings of their wives or minor children" may also embrace unemployed people out of the labor market, by reason of a recession or disemployed by reason of technological or so-called structural displacements.

Persons "wandering or strolling" from place to place have been extolled by Walt Whitman and Vachel Lindsay. The qualification "without any lawful purpose or object" may be a trap for innocent acts. Persons "neglecting all lawful business and habitually spending their time by frequenting * * * places where alcoholic beverages are sold or served" would literally embrace many members of golf clubs and city clubs.

Walkers and strollers and wanderers may be going to or coming from a burglary. Loafers or loiterers may be "casing" a place for a holdup. Letting one's wife support him is an intra-family matter, and normally of no concern to the police. Yet it may, of course, be the setting for numerous crimes.

The difficulty is that these activities are historically part of the amenities of life as we have known it. They are not mentioned in the Constitution or in the Bill of Rights. These unwritten amenities have been in part responsible for giving our people the feeling of independence and self-confidence, the feeling of creativity. These amenities have dignified the right of dissent and have honored the right to be nonconformists and the right to defy submissiveness. They have encouraged lives of high spirits rather than hushed, suffocating silence.

This aspect of the vagrancy ordinance before us is suggested by what this Court said in 1875 about a broad criminal statute enacted by Congress: "It would certainly be dangerous if the legislature could set a net large enough to catch all possible offenders, and leave it to the courts to step inside and say who could be rightfully detained, and who should be set at large." United States v. Reese, 92 U.S. 214, 221, 23 L.Ed. 563.

While that was a federal case, the due process implications are equally applicable to the States and to this vagrancy ordinance. Here the net cast is large, not to give the courts the power to pick and choose but to increase the arsenal of the police. * * *

Where the list of crimes is so all-inclusive and generalized as that one in this ordinance, those convicted may be punished for no more than vindicating affronts to police authority:

> "The common ground which brings such a motley assortment of human troubles before the magistrates in vagrancy-type proceedings is the procedural laxity which permits 'conviction' for almost any kind of conduct and the existence of the House of Correction as an easy and convenient dumping-ground for problems that appear to have no other immediate solution." Foote, Vagrancy Type Law and Its Administration, 104 U.Pa.L.Rev. 603, 631.

Another aspect of the ordinance's vagueness appears when we focus, not on the lack of notice given a potential offender, but on the effect of the unfettered discretion it places in the hands of the Jacksonville police. Caleb Foote, an early student of this subject, has called the vagrancy-type law as offering "punishment by analogy." Id., at 609. Such crimes, though long common in Russia, are not compatible with our constitutional system. We allow our police to make arrests only on "probable cause," a Fourth and Fourteenth Amendment standard applicable to the States as well as to the Federal Government. Arresting a person on suspicion, like arresting a person for investigation, is foreign to our system, even when the arrest is for past criminality. Future criminality, however, is the common justification for the presence of vagrancy statutes. See Foote, op. cit. supra, at 625. Florida has indeed construed her vagrancy statute "as necessary regulations," *inter alia,* "to deter vagabondage and prevent crimes." Johnson v. State, Fla., 202 So.2d 852; Smith v. State, Fla., 239 So.2d 250, 251.

A direction by a legislature to the police to arrest all "suspicious" persons would not pass constitutional muster. A vagrancy prosecution may be merely the cloak for a conviction which could not be obtained on the real but undisclosed grounds for the arrest. People v. Moss, 309 N.Y. 429, 131 N.E.2d 717. But as Chief Justice Hewart said in Frederick Dean, 18 Cr.App.Rep. 133, 134 (1924):

"It would be in the highest degree unfortunate if in any part of the country those who are responsible for setting in motion the criminal law should entertain, connive at or coquette with the idea that in a case where there is not enough evidence to charge the prisoner with an attempt to commit a crime, the prosecution may, nevertheless, on such insufficient evidence, succeed in obtaining and upholding a conviction under the Vagrancy Act, 1824."

Those generally implicated by the imprecise terms of the ordinance—poor people, nonconformists, dissenters, idlers—may be required to comport themselves according to the life-style deemed appropriate by the Jacksonville police and the courts. Where, as here, there are no standards governing the exercise of the discretion granted by the ordinance, the scheme permits and encourages an arbitrary and discriminatory enforcement of the law. It furnishes a convenient tool for "harsh and discriminatory enforcement by prosecuting officials, against particular groups deemed to merit their displeasure." Thornhill v. Alabama, 310 U.S. 88, 97–98, 60 S.Ct. 736, 742, 84 L.Ed. 1093. It results in a regime in which the poor and the unpopular are permitted to "stand on a public sidewalk * * * only at the whim of any police officer." * * *

The implicit presumption in these generalized vagrancy standards—that crime is being nipped in the bud—is too extravagant to deserve extended treatment. Of course, vagrancy statutes are useful to the police. Of course they are nets making easy the roundup of so-called undesirables. But the rule of law implies equality and justice in its application. Vagrancy laws of the Jacksonville type teach that the scales of justice are so tipped that even-handed administration of the law is not possible. The rule of law, evenly applied to minorities as well as majorities, to the poor as well as the rich, is the great mucilage that holds society together.

The Jacksonville ordinance cannot be squared with our constitutional standards and is plainly unconstitutional.

Reversed.

Mr. Justice POWELL and Mr. Justice REHNQUIST took no part in the consideration or decision of this case.

NOTE

In Rose v. Locke, 423 U.S. 48, 96 S.Ct. 243, 46 L.Ed.2d 185 (1975), petitioner Locke had been convicted under a Tennessee statute which provided:

> Crimes against nature, either with mankind or any beast, are punishable by imprisonment in the penitentiary not less than five (5) nor more than fifteen (15) years.

Facts produced at his trial showed that Locke had forced his victim to submit to cunnilingus. Locke urged before the Supreme Court that the statute under which he was convicted was unconstitutionally vague because jurisdictions differ as to whether the phrase, "crime against nature," includes only the common law offense of sodomy or whether it encompasses additional forms of sexual behavior. Since the Tennessee courts had not determined whether the phrase as used in the Tennessee statutes covered cunnilingus, he argued, the statute defining the crime was impermissibly vague. The Supreme Court held that the statute, as construed by the state courts, was sufficiently precise. It noted that in 1955 the Tennessee Supreme Court had held that the statute covered fellatio, Fisher v. State, 197 Tenn. 594, 277 S.W.2d 340 (1955), and it reaffirmed that view four years later, quoting with approval language in a Maine decision that "the prohibition brings all unnatural copulation with mankind or beast, including sodomy, within its scope." Sherrill v. State, 204 Tenn. 427, 429, 321 S.W.2d 811, 812 (1959), quoting from State v. CYR, 135 Me. 513, 198 A. 742 (1938). It also observed that before the Tennessee decisions the Maine court had held its statute covered cunnilingus, State v. Townsend, 145 Me. 384, 71 A.2d 517 (1950). "[W]e think," the Supreme Court concluded, "the Tennessee Supreme Court had given sufficiently clear notice that [the statute] would be applied to acts such as those committed here when such a case arose." 423 U.S. at 52, 96 S.Ct. at 245, 46 L.Ed.2d at 190. Justice Brennan, dissenting, stressed that the Tennessee Supreme Court never cited State v. Townsend and that some state courts have held similar statutory language to include fellatio but not cunnilingus. Is the Court's analysis a reasonable one? If due process requires that the law give citizens an adequate opportunity to find out in advance whether anticipated conduct is criminal, is this accomplished by a series of appellate cases apparently looking with favor upon the approach taken by the courts of another state towards that state's statute?

III. PRINCIPLES OF CRIMINAL LIABILITY

Crimes are generally—and perhaps constitutionally must be—statutory. Nevertheless, it is often difficult or impossible to evaluate the liability of defendants from the face of the offenses with which they are charged. With the possible exception of some of the recently revised statutory criminal codes, most statutory schemes were initially written as codifications of the common law of crimes and have received only piecemeal revision. Thus many statutory definitions of crimes must be read in light of the common law of crimes to determine the elements of the offense, and recourse must often be had to general defenses which may or may not be codified in the statutory scheme.

The material in Part III makes almost no attempt to deal directly with the definition of particular common law offenses. Rather, it proposes a scheme of analysis which is designed to provide the facility and background necessary to deal with a body of law that is essentially statutory. Basically the task is to define the elements of liability, given the statute and general principles of substantive and constitutional law, and to ascertain the defenses to liability in light of the same factors.

The analysis proposed here is a three-step one. The first step is the ascertainment of the elements of the offense, those matters as to which the prosecution must introduce sufficient evidence to avoid a directed verdict of not guilty. For the sake of convenience and clarity, it is valuable to consider elements of offenses in terms of four categories. A particular crime may not contain an element in each category, although to some extent constitutional considerations may require that a crime require proof of some element in each of the first two categories:

1. The "Act". Although the latin phrase "actus reus" has a much broader meaning, it is valuable to think of the act required for liability in terms of what physical activity must be shown on the part of the accused. The statutory definition may rather specifically describe the type of physical activity, as, for example, requiring that the defendant have been "driving". Or, it may make no attempt to describe the required physical activity, in which case any action or failure to act that meets general requirements will suffice.
2. The State of Mind. For policy reasons, the criminal law is concerned with the accused's conscious state of mind at the time of the offense. Probably all offenses require that the trier of fact be convinced beyond a reasonable doubt that the accused was, at the time he performed

the physical act required for liability, aware of something, but the state of mind required differs drastically among offenses.

3. Circumstances. Some offenses require a showing of the existence of particular circumstances. These differ from results (see the fourth category) in that there is no necessity of a causal relationship between the accused's actions and circumstances, while such a relationship must be shown between his actions and results. Circumstances may serve an important policy purpose, or they may be of relatively minor importance. Federal crimes, for example, often require the showing of circumstances for the purpose of establishing federal jurisdiction over the offense.

4. Results. A number of offenses require that a particular result be shown to have occurred. It is important to differentiate between circumstances and results because the complex problems of causation arise only in regard to the latter.

The second step of the analysis involves the ascertainment of any so-called "defenses" which are really means of disproving one of the elements of the offense. Most often this amounts to disproving the state of mind required for the crime. Proof of a defendant's mistake as to the facts at the time of his acts, for example, may well serve simply to raise in the jury's mind a reasonable doubt as to whether he entertained the requisite state of mind.

The final step involves consideration of defenses in the true sense. These are matters which, if established to the satisfaction of the trier of fact, prevent (or reduce) liability despite proof of all elements of the offense. One who kills to preserve his own life, for example, may have entertained an awareness that his action would cause the death of the victim that suffices (under most statutes) for second degree murder; yet if the elements of self defense are established he is relieved of liability.

While one should not pretend that the substantive criminal law may be analyzed "scientifically" it may be helpful to visualize the basic framework of analysis through the following formula:

$$\text{Act} + \text{State of Mind} \xrightarrow{\text{Causation}} \text{Results} = \text{Liability}.$$

In considering the material which follows periodically pause to place it within the framework of the above formula. See whether a reduction in the importance of any particular element in the definition of an offense is accompanied by a compensatory increase in the emphasis given another element on the left of the equation or a reduction to the right of it, and, if so, reflect on why this is the case.

During the course of the examination of substantive criminal law in the following material, it might occasionally be worthwhile to refer to the following statutes, using the material as a guide to interpreting more precisely the elements of the crimes created by the statutes. In some cases, reference to analogous common law crimes might be helpful. In others, the only assistance will be provided by general principles of criminal liability.

A. THE "ACT"

1. GENERAL REQUIREMENT OF AN ACT

Conceptually, it is possible to include within the "act" required for criminal liability not only the physical activity which the accused must be shown to have performed but also the circumstances under which it was performed and the consequences of it. It is more satisfactory, however, to differentiate "circumstances" and "results" from the act required, as this forces a more thorough examination of the proof necessary for liability. As to the constitutional necessity that a crime require proof of some act on the part of the accused, review Robinson v. California, supra, as interpreted by Mr. Justice Marshall in Powell v. Texas, supra. Aside from any possible constitutional imperative, the act requirement places an obvious restriction on the authority of the state to employ the criminal sanction. Given that it marks an extreme outer limit on the exercise of governmental power, the student should consider whether the requirement is desirable, and why. Consider also whether it is of any practical importance: For purposes of determining whether the state may employ the criminal sanction; for purposes of determining the severity of the sanction which may be employed?

Several of the most basic questions regarding the requirement of an "act" are raised in this section. What is the significance, if any, of the requirement that the "act" be "willed" or "voluntary"? In particular, after becoming familiar with the "state of mind" requirement, Section III. B, infra, the student should reconsider the *Mercer* case, infra, to decide whether the issues involved there could not have been as effectively analyzed and resolved without any reference whatever to the "act" requirement.

In this regard consider the view of Professor Perkins:

It is sometimes said that no crime has been committed unless the harmful result was brought about by a "voluntary act." Analysis of such a statement will disclose, however, that as so used the phrase "voluntary act" means no more than the mere word "act." An act must be a willed movement or the omission of a possible and legally-required performance. This is essential to the *actus reus* rather than to the *mens rea.* "A spasm is not an act."

* * * A positive act (willed movement) always has a voluntary element and hence the phrase "voluntary act" is merely tautological as so applied. A negative act may be either a forbearance or an unintentional omission of a legally-required performance. The former is voluntary, the latter is not. If a watchman charged with the duty of lowering the gates at a crossing whenever a train is approaching fails to do so on a particular occasion, with fatal consequences to a motorist, the death is due to his (negative) act. But it would be absurd to speak of this act as "voluntary" if he was inattentive and did not know the train was approaching. As his legal duty required him to be attentive in this regard his want of knowledge of the need for immediate action will not excuse him, but it leaves his failure wholly unintentional. Hence the assertion that there is no crime without a "voluntary act" is redundant as to positive action and incorrect as to negative action.

Furthermore, such an assertion invites confusion in two directions—first because the modifier may be improperly extended to the legally-recognized consequences of the act, and second because it may raise a false issue as to the meaning of the word "voluntary." As to the first, assume the unintentional, but fatal, discharge of a weapon which had been pointed unlawfully at the deceased with no thought other than to intimidate him. The intentional pointing of the weapon was an act and the resulting death is imputable to the pointer. It is not improper to hold the slayer guilty of criminal homicide in certain cases of this nature, but to speak of the "shooting" or the "killing" as voluntary or intentional is merely confusion of words. * * * the notion of a "voluntary act" as requisite to criminal guilt may result in the jury's being confused by argument of counsel to the effect that defendant's act was committed under the stress and strain of difficult circumstances and hence was not "voluntary." If the harm was caused by a willed movement of the defendant it was caused by his "act" no matter how much "pressure" he may have been under at the moment. Perkins, Criminal Law 749–50 (1969).

18 U.S.C.A. § 1792 provides, in pertinent part: "Whoever conveys * * * from place to place [within a Federal penal institution] any * * * weapon * * * designed to kill, injure or disable any officer, agent, employee or inmate thereof * * *. Shall be imprisoned not more than ten years." Does a prisoner violate this provision if, while carrying a knife under his clothing, he walks from his cell pursuant to a guard's order? What if he is running a knife across a sander in the prison workshop and, on the approach of his foreman, he drops it to the floor? Which of the following factors would control your interpretation: the meaning of the verb "convey"; the "voluntariness" of the conduct; or the purpose of the statute given the fact that mere possession of a knife by an inmate is not

criminal? Compare United States v. Meador, 456 F.2d 197 (10th Cir. 1972) with United States v. Bedwell, 456 F.2d 448 (10th Cir. 1972).

To what extent is a failure to act sufficient for liability? To what extent may a defendant be held liable if the acts relied upon are performed by someone other than himself, i. e., to what extent may "vicarious liability" be imposed?

MODEL PENAL CODE *

(Proposed Official Draft, 1962).

Section 2.01. Requirement of Voluntary Act; Omission as Basis of Liability; Possession as an Act

(1) A person is not guilty of an offense unless his liability is based on conduct which includes a voluntary act or the omission to perform an act of which he is physically capable.

(2) The following are not voluntary acts within the meaning of this Section:

(a) a reflex or convulsion;

(b) a bodily movement during unconsciousness or sleep;

(c) conduct during hypnosis or resulting from hypnotic suggestion;

(d) a bodily movement that otherwise is not a product of the effort or determination of the actor, either conscious or habitual.

(3) Liability for the commission of an offense may not be based on an omission unaccompanied by action unless:

(a) the omission is expressly made sufficient by the law defining the offense; or

(b) a duty to perform the omitted act is otherwise imposed by law.

(4) Possession is an act, within the meaning of this Section, if the possessor knowingly procured or received the thing possessed or was aware of his control thereof for a sufficient period to have been able to terminate his possession.

STATE v. MERCER

Supreme Court of North Carolina, 1969.
275 N.C. 108, 165 S.E.2d 328.

Separate indictments charged defendant with the first degree murder on September 14, 1967, of (1) Myrtle R. Mercer, defendant's wife, (2) Ida Mae Dunn, and (3) Jeffrey Lane Dunn, Ida's five-year-old son. * * *

There was evidence tending to show the facts narrated below.

Defendant, a member of the United States Army for 19½ years, was stationed at Fort Benning, Georgia, at the time of the trial.

Defendant and Myrtle Mercer were married in Fayetteville, N. C., in April, 1965. Thereafter, he was stationed at duty posts in and out of the United States. Myrtle Mercer, Ida Mae Dunn, and Jeffrey Lane Dunn, Ida's five-year-old boy, lived together in Wilson, N. C. Defendant visited Myrtle in Wilson from time to time when on leaves. He was thirty-nine; Myrtle was twenty-three.

Marital difficulties developed. Defendant had heard that Myrtle was having affairs with other men. He thought Myrtle's relationship with Ida involved more than normal affection. As time passed, defendant's strong affection for Myrtle was not reciprocated.

On July 6, 1967, defendant received a letter from Myrtle, referred to in the evidence as a "Dear John" letter, in which she told him she was tired of being tied down and wanted to come and go as she pleased. In a letter mailed August 10th from Kentucky (where he was then stationed), defendant wrote Myrtle: "Please don't make me do something that will send both of us to our graves." Also: "I could never see you with another man, and I would die and go to hell before I would see you with some other man, and take myself with you."

In September, 1967, defendant obtained a ten-day leave "to come home and see if he could get straightened out with his wife. * * *" Defendant told his first sergeant that "if he did not get straightened out he would not be back."

On September 13, 1967, defendant visited the house in Wilson where Myrtle, Ida, and Jeffrey lived. He talked with Myrtle. However, she would not discuss their marital problems and did not want him to stay at that house.

Defendant stayed at the home of his cousin, Mrs. Mable Owens, in Tarboro. He left there on the morning of September 14, 1967, and arrived at Myrtle's around noon. She would not talk with him. (Note: Defendant testified Myrtle at that time gave him some clothes, a camera and a paper bag containing a pistol he had given to her for her protection.) At the conclusion of this visit, he returned to the home of Mrs. Owens. Sometime during the day defendant bought a pint of vodka and had two drinks from it.

About 8:30 p. m., Mrs. Owens, at the request of defendant, drove defendant to Myrtle's house in Wilson. The two children of Mrs. Owens accompanied them. Defendant knocked. There was no response. The house was unlighted and apparently no one was there. They left and visited defendant's brother (in Wilson) for some twenty-five or thirty-five minutes. While there, defendant telephoned Myrtle's house. The line was busy. They went back to Myrtle's house. Defendant asked Mrs. Owens if she and her children would go into the house with him. She replied that they would wait in the car.

Defendant went to the front door and knocked several times. There was no answer. Defendant shot at the door twice, pushed it open with his foot and went inside. At that time, a light came on in the front bedroom. Someone said, "Ervin, don't do that." Defendant fired three or four shots killing Myrtle instantly and fatally wounding Ida and Jeffrey. He then left the house. A neighbor called the police.

* * *

Defendant was arrested at the home of his brother in Wilson, a few hours after the fatal shots were fired. He accompanied the officers to a lot behind Myrtle's house where the gun which inflicted the fatal injuries was hidden.

Testimony of defendant, in addition to that referred to above, is set out in the opinion. It tended to show he was completely unconscious of what transpired when Myrtle, Ida and Jeffrey were shot.

In each case, the jury returned a verdict of guilty of murder in the second degree. * * *

BOBBITT, Judge.

* * *

The court's final instructions were as follows: "(T)he Court instructs you that the evidence in regard and surrounding the alleged loss of memory by the defendant will be considered by you *on the question of premeditation and deliberation in the charge of murder in the first degree.* * * * if you find from the evidence, not by the greater weight, nor by the preponderance, but if the defendant has satisfied you—merely satisfied you—that he lost consciousness, sufficient consciousness, to the extent that he did not have sufficient time to *premeditate or deliberate*, that is, if he did not have sufficient time to form in his mind the intent to kill, under the definition of *premeditation* and *deliberation*, then it would be your duty to return a verdict of not guilty of murder in the first degree, because the Court has instructed you if the State has failed to satisfy you of the element of *premeditation* or *deliberation*, or if there arises in your minds a reasonable doubt in regard to those two elements or either one of those two elements, it would be your duty to return a verdict of not guilty. And further in regard, when you come to consider those elements of *premeditation* and *deliberation*, if the defendant has satisfied you, not beyond a reasonable doubt, not by the greater weight of the evidence, but has merely satisfied you that he lost consciousness to such an extent that he was unable to *premeditate*, and was unable to *deliberate*, according to the definition of those terms that the law has given you, then he could not be guilty of murder in the first degree, and it would be your duty to return a verdict of not guilty as to murder in the first degree, under those circumstances. Now, *the Court feels that those are the only two elements in the case in which this evidence in regard to his loss of consciousness applies*, and the Court has ruled that there is no element of legal insanity in the evidence." (Our italics.)

Defendant's assignment of error, based on his exception to the foregoing portion of the charge, must be sustained. Defendant testified he was completely unconscious of what transpired when Myrtle, Ida and Jeffrey were shot. The court instructed the jury that this evidence was for consideration *only* in respect of the elements of premeditation and deliberation in first degree murder. This restriction of the legal significance of the evidence as to defendant's unconsciousness was erroneous.

* * *

"If a person is in fact unconscious at the time he commits an act which would otherwise be criminal, he is not responsible therefor. The absence of consciousness not only precludes the existence of any specific mental state, but also excludes the possibility of a voluntary act without which there can be no criminal liability." 1 Wharton's Criminal Law and Procedure (Anderson), § 50, p. 116.

"Unconsciousness is a complete, not a partial, defense to a criminal charge." 21 Am.Jur.2d, Criminal Law § 29, p. 115.

"*Unconsciousness*. A person cannot be held criminally responsible for acts committed while he is unconscious. Some statutes broadly exempt from responsibility persons who commit offenses without being conscious thereof. Such statutes, when construed in connection with other statutes relating to criminal capacity of the insane and voluntarily intoxicated, do not include within their protection either insane or voluntarily intoxicated persons, and are restricted in their contemplation to persons of sound mind suffering from some other agency rendering them unconscious of their acts * * *." 22 C.J.S. Criminal Law § 55, p. 194.

Defendant contends he had no knowledge of and did not consciously commit the act charged in the indictments. He does not contend he was insane. Unconsciousness and insanity are separate grounds of exemption from criminal responsibility.

* * *

There was no evidence defendant was a somnambulist or an epileptic. Nor was there evidence he was under the influence of intoxicants or narcotics. Under cross-examination, defendant testified his only previous "blackout" experience, which was of brief duration, occurred when he received and read the "Dear John" letter.

Upon the present record, defendant was entitled to an instruction to the effect the jury should return verdicts of not guilty if in fact defendant was *completely* unconscious of what transpired when Myrtle, Ida and Jeffrey were shot.

* * *

It should be understood that unconsciousness, although always a factor of legal significance, is not a complete defense under all circumstances. Without undertaking to mark the limits of the legal principles applicable to varied factual situations that will arise from time to time, but solely by way of illustration, attention is called to the following: In California, "unconsciousness produced by voluntary intoxication does not render a defendant incapable of committing a crime." People v. Cox, 67 Cal.App.2d 166, 153 P.2d 362, and cases cited. In Colorado, a person who precipitates a fracas and as a result is hit on the head and rendered semi-conscious or unconscious cannot maintain that he is not criminally responsible for any degree of homicide above involuntary manslaughter, or that he is not criminally responsible at all. Watkins v. People, 158 Colo. 485, 408 P.2d 425. In Oklahoma, a motorist is guilty of manslaughter if he drives an automobile with knowledge that he is subject to frequent blackouts, when his continued operation of the automobile is in reckless disregard to the safety of others and constitutes culpable or criminal negligence. Carter v. State [376 P.2d 351 (Okl.Cr.1962)]; Smith v. Commonwealth [268 S.W.2d 937 (Ky.1954)]. As to somnambulism, see Fain v. Commonwealth [78 Ky. 183 (1879)], and Lewis v. State, 196 Ga. 755, 27 S.E.2d 659.

POWELL v. TEXAS

United States Supreme Court, 1968.
392 U.S. 514, 88 S.Ct. 2145, 20 L.Ed.2d 1254.

[The opinion of Mr. Justice MARSHALL for the Court, from which this excerpt is taken, is more fully reprinted at page 168].

Appellant * * * seeks to come within the application of the Cruel and Unusual Punishment Clause announced in Robinson v. California, 370 U.S. 660 (1962), which involved a state statute making it a crime to "be addicted to the use of narcotics." This Court held there that "a state law which imprisons a person thus afflicted [with narcotic addiction] as a criminal, even though he has never touched any narcotic drug within the State or been guilty of any irregular behavior there, inflicts a cruel and unusual punishment * * *." Id., at 667.

On its face the present case does not fall within that holding, since appellant was convicted, not for being a chronic alcoholic, but for being in public while drunk on a particular occasion. The State of Texas thus has not sought to punish a mere status, as California did in *Robinson*; nor has it attempted to regulate appellant's behavior in the privacy of his own home. Rather, it has imposed upon appellant a criminal sanction for public behavior which may create substantial health and safety hazards, both for appellant and for members of the general public and which offends the moral and esthetic sensibilities of a large segment of the community. This seems a far cry from convicting one for being an addict, being a chronic alcoholic, being "mentally ill, or a leper * * *." Id., at 666.

Robinson so viewed brings this Court but a very small way into the substantive criminal law. And unless *Robinson* is so viewed it is difficult to see any limiting principle that would serve to prevent this Court from becoming, under the aegis of the Cruel and Unusual Punishment Clause, the ultimate arbiter of the standards of criminal responsibility, in diverse areas of the criminal law, throughout the country.

It is suggested in dissent that *Robinson* stands for the "simple" but "subtle" principle that "[c]riminal penalties may not be inflicted upon a person for being in a condition he is powerless to change." *Post*, at 567. In that view, appellant's "condition" of public intoxication was "occasioned by a compulsion symptomatic of the disease" of chronic alcoholism, and thus, apparently, his behavior lacked the critical element of *mens rea*. Whatever may be the merits of such a doctrine of criminal responsibility, it surely cannot be said to follow from *Robinson*. The entire thrust of *Robinson's* interpretation of the Cruel and Unusual Punishment Clause is that criminal penalties may be inflicted only if the accused has committed some act, has engaged in some behavior, which society has an interest in preventing or perhaps in historical common law terms, has committed some *actus reus*. It thus does not deal with the question of whether certain conduct cannot constitutionally be punished because it is, in some sense, "involuntary" or "occasioned by a compulsion."

Mr. Justice BLACK, whom Mr. Justice HARLAN joins, concurring.

Punishment for a status is particularly obnoxious, and in many instances can reasonably be called cruel and unusual, because it involves punishment for a mere propensity, a desire to commit an offense; the mental element is not simply one part of the crime but may constitute all of it. This is a situation universally sought to be avoided in our criminal law; the fundamental requirement that some action be proved is solidly established even for offenses most heavily based on propensity, such as attempt, conspiracy, and recidivist crimes.[4] In fact, one eminent authority has found only one isolated

4. As Glanville Williams puts it, "[t]hat crime requires an act is *invariably* true if the proposition be read as meaning that a private thought is not sufficient to found responsibility." Williams, Criminal Law—the General Part 1 (1961). (Emphasis added.) For the requirement of some act as an ele-

instance, in all of Anglo-American jurisprudence in which criminal responsibility was imposed in the absence of any act at all.[5]

The reasons for this refusal to permit conviction without proof of an act are difficult to spell out, but they are nonetheless perceived and universally expressed in our criminal law. Evidence of propensity can be considered relatively unreliable and more difficult for a defendant to rebut; the requirement of a specific act thus provides some protection against false charges. See 4 Blackstone, Commentaries 21. Perhaps more fundamental is the difficulty of distinguishing, in the absence of any conduct, between desires of the day-dream variety and fixed intentions that may pose a real threat to society; extending the criminal law to cover both types of desire would be unthinkable, since "[t]here can hardly be anyone who has never thought evil. When a desire is inhibited it may find expression in fantasy; but it would be absurd to condemn this natural psychological mechanism as illegal."

In contrast, crimes that require the State to prove that the defendant actually committed some proscribed act involve none of these special problems. In addition, the question whether an act is "involuntary" is, as I have already indicated, an inherently elusive question, and one which the State may, for good reasons, wish to regard as irrelevant. In light of all these considerations, our limitation of our *Robinson* holding to pure status crimes seems to me entirely proper.

NOTES AND QUESTIONS

1. As Mr. Justice Marshall makes clear there must be "some act * * * some behavior" before criminal penalties may be imposed. The Court in *Robinson* explicitly included "possession of narcotics" in its recitation of acts which might properly be criminalized. Is possession an "act" or "behavior"? See Section 2.01 of the Model Penal Code, reprinted at page 127, supra.

2. As is suggested by the definition of possession cited in note 1 supra, the contraband need not be actually possessed in the sense of being on the person of the possessor. The ambit of possession statutes is significantly broadened by the doctrine of "constructive possession" which extends culpability to situations where the defendant may be found to have been "in a position to exercise dominion or control" over the contraband. United States v. Holland, 445 F.2d 701, 703 (D.C.Cir.1971). See Annotation, 91 A. L.R.2d 810. An especially common problem in this area arises where the alleged possession is not only constructive but joint; as where the contraband is found in a car or room occupied by more than one person. See Folk v. State, 11 Md.App. 508, 275 A.2d 184 (1971).

3. As is indicated by the following case, joint, constructive possession of the prohibited drug has not been the minimum "behavior" on which the use of the criminal sanction has been predicated.

ment of conspiracy and attempt, see id., at 631, 663, 668; R. Perkins, Criminal Law 482, 531–532 (1957).

5. Williams, supra, n. 4, at 11.

CRAWFORD v. UNITED STATES

District of Columbia Court of Appeals, 1971.
278 A.2d 125.

Before GALLAGHER, REILLY and YEAGLEY, Associate Judges.

GALLAGHER, Associate Judge. Appellant was charged with carrying a pistol without a license and possession of implements of a crime—narcotics paraphernalia. A jury found him not guilty of carrying a pistol without a license and rendered a special verdict finding him guilty of possession of one hypodermic needle and one hypodermic syringe found under the front seat of the car he was driving. He was found not guilty of possession of implements of a crime as to other narcotics paraphernalia found in the rear seat. Appellant was sentenced to serve 180 days in jail.

At the close of the Government's case in chief and again upon final submission of the case, appellant moved for judgment of acquittal contending the Government's evidence was insufficient to support a finding that he was in possession of the narcotics paraphernalia. The trial judge denied the motions and appellant now contends this was reversible error.

The Government's evidence consisted of the following: Officer Richardson testified that he stopped appellant's car for speeding and while waiting for appellant (who had alighted from the car) to produce his license he noticed a syringe at the foot of one of the occupants in the rear seat.[3] Upon the arrival of other officers he had called by radio, the occupants were removed from the car. He then recovered two pieces of tinfoil, a spoon, two syringes and one needle from the rear seat and one syringe and needle protruding from beneath the front seat on the driver's side where appellant had been sitting. A pistol was also recovered from the rear seat. A Detective Dotson testified that he examined appellant at the precinct on the day of the arrest and found ten to twenty "individual needle marks—small punctures on the arm." The Government chemist testified that neither the spoon nor the aluminum foil recovered contained any narcotics. He could not testify each syringe positively contained heroin because the sample he tested was a composite from all three syringes; and consequently, he could not testify specifically that there was heroin in the syringe found under appellant's seat.[a]

3. There were three youths in the rear seat and one in the front passenger seat in addition to appellant.

a. Is there any point to requiring that the drug paraphernalia contain at least a trace of the prohibited drugs? In a jurisdiction which permits conviction of possession of less than a usable amount?

"A motion for acquittal must be granted when the evidence, viewed in the light most favorable to the Government, is such that a reasonable juror must have a reasonable doubt as to the existence of any of the essential elements of the crime." * * * If, on the other hand the evidence is such that a reasonable man might or might not have a reasonable doubt as to the defendant's guilt, the case should go to the jury. We think the motions were properly denied under this standard.

Possession in this instance could have been either actual or constructive, i. e., the exercise of, or right to exercise, dominion and control over the narcotics paraphernalia under appellant's seat. See Hill v. District of Columbia, D.C.App., 264 A.2d 145, 146 (1970); cf. Garza v. United States, 385 F.2d 899, 901 (5th Cir. 1967). There is no question but that appellant did not have actual possession of the needle and syringe at the time of his arrest. But appellant had been present in the automobile immediately before the officer noticed the paraphernalia protruding from under the seat where appellant had just been seated. He had been driving the car immediately prior to the time the articles were recovered in plain view from beneath that seat. He was the owner of the vehicle. The single needle and syringe were certainly within his reach. Additionally, puncture marks were found on his arm which indicated he was a user of drugs. Garza v. United States, supra, 385 F.2d at 900. From these facts it was reasonable to infer that appellant had dominion and control over the needle and syringe under his seat. Viewing the evidence in the light most favorable to the Government, as we must, we conclude it was adequate to support the jury's finding that appellant had possession of that needle and syringe.

Appellant also contends that possession of a single hypodermic needle and syringe alone will not support a conviction under the statute[5] without proof of specific intent to use the instruments to commit a crime since they do not in themselves raise "sinister" implications. See McKoy v. United States, D.C.App., 263 A.2d 649, 651 (1970). He raises this point for the first time on appeal. "[O]ur power to notice errors raised for the first time on appeal is discretionary, and will be exercised only where the error alleged is 'plain error' and clearly prejudicial to the appellant." Bunter v. United States, D.C.App., 245 A.2d 839, 842 (1968). Our review of the record in this case reveals no such plain error. We conclude upon the record before us that there existed sufficient independent circumstantial evidence of appellant's intent above and beyond his mere possession

5. D.C.Code 1967, § 22–3601 provides in part:

No person shall have in his possession in the District any instrument, tool, or other implement for picking locks or pockets, or that is usually employed, or reasonably may be employed in the commission of any crime, if he is unable satisfactorily to account for the possession of the implement. * * *

of a single needle and syringe to support his conviction of possession of implements of a crime. Therefore, we are not met with the issue posed by appellant that possession of the needle and syringe, standing alone, would not violate the statute.

This court has recognized the use of surrounding circumstances to evidence the requisite criminal intent under the statute. McKoy v. United States, supra. In the present case appellant possessed a hypodermic needle and syringe but, in addition, two other syringes and one other needle, with two pieces of foil and a spoon, were found in the rear seat of the automobile driven by appellant. While it is true that the jury found that appellant did not possess these items in the rear seat, this is not to say that he did not know of their presence. And their presence would indicate an apparent intention to administer narcotics illegally, if this had not already been done. These materials constituted a narcotics "kit" and thus appellant was in the immediate company of others who had this "kit." There was evidence that at least one of the syringes contained heroin, though which one could not be determined due to the nature of the chemist's test. Further, ten to twenty puncture marks were observed on appellant's left forearm by Detective Dotson indicating appellant was a drug user.

We believe that these circumstances taken together, and when viewed in a light most favorable to the Government, were sufficient for the jury to conclude that appellant possessed the hypodermic needle and syringe with the intent to use them for a criminal purpose.

For these reasons, the judgment of the trial court is

Affirmed.

STATE v. BUGGER

Supreme Court of Utah, 1971.
25 Utah 2d 404, 483 P.2d 442.

TUCKETT, Justice. The defendant was found guilty of a violation of Section 41–6–44, U.C.A.1953, and from that conviction he has appealed to this court.

During the night of July 28, 1969, the defendant was asleep in his automobile which was parked upon the shoulder of a road known as Tippet's Lane in Davis County. The automobile was completely off the traveled portion of the highway and the motor was not running. An officer of the Highway Patrol stopped at the scene and discovered the defendant was asleep. With some effort the officer succeeded in awakening the defendant, at which time the officer detected the smell of alcohol and arrested the defendant for being in actual physical control of the vehicle while under the influence of intoxicating liquor.

The complaint charges the defendant with the violation of the statute above referred to which provides as follows:

> It is unlawful and punishable as provided in subsection (d) of this section for any person who is under the influence of intoxicating liquor to drive or be in actual physical control of any vehicle within this state.

The defendant is here challenging the validity of the statute on the grounds of vagueness. However, we need not decide the case upon that ground. That part of the statute which states: "be in actual physical control of any vehicle" has been before the courts of other jurisdictions which have statutes with similar wordings. The word "actual" has been defined as meaning "existing in act or reality; * * * in action or existence at the time being; present; * * *." The word "physical" is defined as "bodily," and "control" is defined as "to exercise restraining or directing influence over; to dominate; regulate; hence, to hold from actions; to curb." The term in "actual physical control" in its ordinary sense means "existing" or "present bodily restraint, directing influence, domination or regulation." It is clear that in the record before us the facts do not bring the case within the wording of the statute. The defendant at the time of his arrest was *not* controlling the vehicle, nor was he exercising any dominion over it. It is noted that the cases cited by the plaintiff in support of its position in this matter deal with entirely different fact situations, such as the case where the driver was seated in his vehicle on the traveled portion of the highway; or where the motor of the vehicle was operating; or where the driver was attempting to steer the automobile while it was in motion; or where he was attempting to brake the vehicle to arrest its motion.

We are of the opinion that the facts in this case do not make out a violation of the statute and the defendant's conviction is reversed. We do not consider it necessary to discuss the other claimed errors raised by the defendant.

CALLISTER, C. J., and HENRIOD and CROCKETT, JJ., concur.

ELLETT, Justice (dissenting).

I dissent.

The statute formerly made it unlawful for a person under the influence of intoxicating liquor to drive any vehicle upon any highway within this state. The amendment added a provision making it unlawful to be in actual physical control of a vehicle while under the influence of intoxicating liquor. It removed the need to be upon a highway before the crime was made out and did away with the necessity of driving before a crime was committed.

The reason for the change is obvious. It is better to prevent an intoxicated person in charge of an automobile from getting on the highway than it is to punish him after he gets on it. The amended statute gives officers a right to arrest a drunk person in the control of an automobile and thus prevent him from wreaking havoc a minute later by getting in traffic, or from injuring himself by his erratic driving.

It does not matter whether the motor is running or is idle nor whether the drunk is in the front seat or in the back seat. His potentiality for harm is lessened but not obviated by a silent motor or a backseat position—provided, of course, that he is the one in control of the car. It only takes a flick of the wrist to start the motor or to engage the gears, and it requires only a moment of time to get under the wheel from the back seat. A drunk in control of a motor vehicle has such a propensity to cause harm that the statute intended to make it criminal for him to be in a position to do so.

Restraining the movement of a vehicle is controlling it as much as moving it is. A person finding a drunk in the back seat of a car parked in one's driveway is likely to learn who is in control of that car if he should attempt to move it. A drunk may maliciously block one's exit, and in doing so he is in control of his own vehicle.

I think the defendant in this case was in control of his truck within the meaning of the statute even though he may have been asleep. He had the key and was the only one who could drive it. The fact that he chose to park it is no reason to say he was not in control thereof.

I, therefore, think that we should consider the question which he raises in his brief as to the validity of the statute.

Cases wherein an attack was made on statutes like ours have been decided in a number of jurisdictions. They hold the statute good.

In the case of State v. Webb, 78 Ariz. 8, 274 P.2d 338 (1954), the defendant was intoxicated and asleep in a truck parked next to some barricades in a lane of traffic. An officer passed by and observed no one in the car. Later he returned and found the defendant "passed out." The statute made it a crime to be in actual physical control of a car while under the influence of intoxicating liquor. The defendant contended that the wording of the statute was not meant to apply to a situation where the car was parked and that it was only concerned with the driving of an automobile and other acts and conduct of a positive nature. In holding that the statute was applicable to the conduct of the defendant, the court said:

> An intoxicated person seated behind the steering wheel of a motor vehicle is a threat to the safety and welfare of the public. The danger is less than that involved when the vehicle is actually moving, but it does exist.

In the case of Parker v. State, 424 P.2d 997 (Okl.Cr.App.1967), the appellant challenged the constitutionality of a statute making it unlawful for "any person who is under the influence of intoxicating liquor to drive, operate, or be in actual physical control of any motor vehicle within this state." There the defendant (appellant) claimed that the statute was unconstitutional in that it was so vague and indefinite that a person charged thereunder would be deprived of due process of law. The court held that the statute did not violate any of appellant's constitutional rights.

Under a similar statute the Montana Supreme Court in State v. Ruona, 133 Mont. 243, 321 P.2d 615 (1958), held that the statute was not void for vagueness, and in doing so said:

> * * * Thus one could have "actual physical control" while merely parking or standing still so long as one was keeping the car in restraint or in position to regulate its movements. Preventing a car from moving is as much control and dominion as actually putting the car in motion on the highway. Could one exercise any more regulation over a thing, while bodily present, than prevention of movement or curbing movement. As long as one were physically or bodily able to assert dominion, in the sense of movement, then he has as much control over an object as he would if he were actually driving the vehicle.
>
> * * * [I]t is quite evident that the statute in the instant case is neither vague nor uncertain. * * *

The appellant here claims some federally protected rights in that he says he was improperly arrested. It is difficult for me to see where that has anything to do with guilt or innocence. If he were improperly arrested, he would have an action against the officer for false arrest, but surely our courts have not lost contact with reality to the extent that we turn a guilty man free simply "because the constable may have blundered".

From what has been said above, there is absolutely no merit to this claim. By being in control of an automobile while under the influence of intoxicating liquor, the defendant was guilty of a misdemeanor which was in the presence of the officer, and the officer had a right and a duty to arrest him.

The defendant was found guilty in the court below of being in actual physical control of his truck while he was under the influence of intoxicating liquor. He does not dispute that he was drunk. If the statute is good, we should not attempt to overrule the trier of the facts and find that the defendant was not the one actually controlling his truck.

I would affirm the judgment of the trial court.

2. LIABILITY BASED ON FAILURE TO ACT

Although in the vast majority of criminal cases the defendant's conduct which is alleged to have caused the prohibited harm will have involved action on his part, this is not necessary as a matter of theory or logic. Some crimes are even defined in terms of inaction as with a failure to file an income tax return or a failure to yield the right of way. In these situations it is clear why defendant, assuming proof of his conduct and of the required mental state, should be found guilty; a clear duty was properly imposed which he failed to meet. The difficulty arises in situations where it is clear that a harm has resulted, in part at least due to the defendant's inaction, but we are uncertain as to the nature and source of the duty, if any, which the defendant had to prevent the harm. For reasons that will be examined in the following material, Anglo-American law has been quite reluctant to find culpability in these situations.

POPE v. STATE

Court of Appeals of Maryland, 1979.
284 Md. 309, 396 A.2d 1054.

ORTH, Judge.

Joyce Lillian Pope was found guilty by the court in the Circuit Court for Montgomery County under the 3rd and 5th counts of a nine count indictment, no. 18666. The 3rd count charged child abuse, presenting that "on or about April 11, 1976, * * * while having the temporary care, custody and responsibility for the supervision of Demiko Lee Norris, a minor child under the age of eighteen years [she] did unlawfully and feloniously cause abuse to said minor child in violation of Article 27, Section 35A of the Annotated Code of Maryland. * * *" The 5th count charged misprision of felony under the common law, alleging that on the same date she "did unlawfully and wilfully conceal and fail to disclose a felony to wit: the murder of Demiko Lee Norris committed by Melissa Vera Norris on April 11, 1976, having actual knowledge of the commission of the felony and the identity of the felon, with the intent to obstruct and hinder the due course of justice and to cause the felon to escape unpunished. * * *"

On direct appeal the Court of Special Appeals reversed the judgment entered on the child abuse conviction and affirmed the judgment entered on the misprision of felony conviction.[2] Pope v. State, 38

2. The trial court sentenced Pope to the Department of Corrections for a period of seven years on each of the convictions under the 3rd and 5th counts, the sentences to run concurrently. It suspended all but eighteen months of the sentence and recommended that it be served in the Montgomery County Detention Center. Upon release, Pope was to be placed on supervised probation for two years upon condition that she "seek and take psychiatric or psychological assistance."

Md.App. 520, 382 A.2d 880 (1978). We granted Pope's petition and the State's cross-petition for a writ of certiorari. We affirm the judgment of the Court of Special Appeals with respect to the 3rd count, child abuse. We reverse the judgment of the Court of Special Appeals with respect to the 5th count, misprision of felony. We remand to that court with direction to remand to the Circuit Court for Montgomery County for the entry of a judgment of acquittal on the third count and dismissal of the fifth count.

ISSUES FOR DECISION

I. The sufficiency of the evidence to sustain the conviction of Pope of the crime of child abuse as (1) a principal in the first degree, or (2) a principal in the second degree.

II. The status in Maryland of the crime of misprision of felony.

THE EVIDENCE

The evidence adduced at the trial established that Demiko Lee Norris, three months old, died as a result of physical injuries inflicted by his mother, Melissa Vera Norris.[4] The abuse by the mother occurred over a period of several hours on a Sunday morning at Pope's home and in Pope's presence. Pope's involvement in the events leading to the child's abuse and death began on the preceding Friday evening when she and Melissa, with the child, were driven home by Pope's sister, Angela Lancaster, from a service held at the Christian Tabernacle Church. When they arrived at Melissa's grandparents' home, where Melissa was living, Melissa refused to enter the house, claiming that it was on fire, although in fact it was not. During the evening, Melissa had sporadically indicated mental distress. "She would at times seem caught up in a religious frenzy with a wild look about her, trying to preach and declaring that she was God. She would as quickly resume her normal self without ever seeming to notice her personality transitions." *Pope,* 38 Md.App. at 531, 382 A.2d at 886. Pope agreed to take Melissa and the child into her home for the night because she did not want to put them "out on the street," and Angela would not let them stay in her home. Melissa had no money and Pope and Angela bought food and diapers for the baby. That evening Pope cleaned and dried the baby and inquired of Melissa about a bad rash he had. Melissa slept in Pope's bedroom. Pope kept the baby with her in the living room, telling Melissa: "[Y]ou can go to sleep * * * I'll be up, I'll just stay up, I'll watch the baby. * * *"

4. The mother, charged and tried separately from Pope, was found to be not responsible for her criminal conduct at the time of the commission of the offense, and, therefore, not guilty by reason of insanity. [According to the Court of Special Appeals, the mother had since been released as sane and had given birth to another child. 38 Md.App. 520, 382 A.2d 880, 892 n. 6.]

She explained in her testimony: "And I don't know why it was just, just a funny feeling that I had, you know, and ever since the baby was there I just kept it close to me for some reason." Pope fed the baby and fixed a bed for it in a dresser drawer. She stayed with the baby to care for him during the night because he was spitting up. She could not sleep while Melissa was there.

The next morning, awakened by the crying of the child, Pope fed him. Throughout the day Melissa "changed back and forth." When Melissa was "herself" she took care of her child. When Melissa thought she was God, Pope undertook the maternal duties. Pope watched the child "like it was my own," because "I felt maybe [Melissa] could [hurt the child] when she confessed she was God. * * * I felt close to the baby, maybe because, you know, I felt I haven't had a baby for so long, you know, I enjoyed taking care of the baby and watching it." At a baby shower Saturday evening at the home of Pope's mother, Melissa again reverted to being God, looking wild, speaking loudly, preaching and giving orders. Melissa and the baby returned to Pope's home. Melissa put the child in bed with her, but Pope thought it better that the child not remain there. She was afraid Melissa would roll over and "smother it to death." She told Melissa: "I'll just take the baby in [the living room] * * * I'll watch it, I'll get up and feed it * * * I don't mind." The next morning, Sunday, at about 4:30 o'clock, Pope prepared the baby's bottle and fed him. When Melissa got up, Pope suggested that she go back to bed. Melissa behaved normally for awhile. Then her "episodes of 'changing to God' became more pronounced. She stomped and gestured as she strode back and forth, putting crosses on doors and demanding the departure of the evil which she claimed to see. She kicked and banged at the door of [Pope's] son, and fearful that by breaking in Melissa would frighten him, [Pope] unfastened the door to permit entry. Loudly exhorting Satan to leave the premises, Melissa 'annointed' [Pope's] son with oil, placing some of the oil in the child's mouth. She subsequently repeated the process with [Pope's] daughter. When dressed, [Pope's] children left the house expeditiously, lingering only long enough to embrace their mother." *Pope*, 38 Md.App. at 531, 382 A.2d at 887.

During a lucid period, Melissa prepared to go to church. She got a tub of water to bathe the baby. What next occurred is graphically described in the opinion of the Court of Special Appeals:

> "Then, from her suddenly changed voice and appearance, [Pope] knew Melissa had changed again to 'God.' Calling out that Satan had hidden in the body of her son, Melissa began to verbally exorcise that spirit and physically abuse the child by punching and poking him repeatedly about the stomach, chest and privates. After she undressed the child, that which ensued was hardly describable. In her religious

> frenzy of apparent exorcism, Melissa poked the child's vitals and beat the child about the head. She reached her fingers down its throat, wiping mucus and blood on diapers at hand, and even lifted the child by inserting her hands in its mouth, and shook him like a rag." Id.

Continuing to talk and stomp, Melissa began to squeeze the baby. Then, holding the child by the neck with one hand, she took him into the bathroom, acting like she did not know that Pope was present. When she first started this abuse, Melissa, in her "God voice," called Pope and asked her: "Didn't I give you eyes to see?" Pope noticed that Melissa's finger nails were "real long," and she said to Melissa: "[H]ow do you handle a baby with such long nails," but Pope did nothing. She admitted that she knew at some point that Melissa was hurting the baby and was "fearful, amazed and shocked at the 'unbelievable' and 'horrible' thing that was happening."

Melissa's frenzy diminished. Angela came to the house to take them to church. Pope did not tell Angela what happened—"I could not get it out." Angela asked her what was wrong, and Pope said: "[I]t's Melissa, the baby. * * *" She locked the door at Angela's direction so Angela's children would stay in the yard with Pope's children. Angela wrapped the child in a towel, raised him over her head and prayed.

Pope, Melissa and Angela left with the child to go to the church. At Melissa's request they stopped by her grandfather's house, arriving about 2:00 p. m. Pope told him the child was dead, but he did not believe her because all three were acting so strangely. He refused to take or look at the baby. The three women with the child then went to Bel Pre Health Center, picked up another member of the Christian Tabernacle congregation, telling her that "God has a job for you to do," and proceeded to the church. En route, they passed several hospitals, police stations and rescue squads. At the church, the child was given to, or taken by the Reverend Leon Hart, who handed him to Mother Dorothy King for her prayers. She discovered that the baby's body was cool and sent for ambulance assistance. Police and rescue personnel arrived and determined that the child was dead. There was expert medical testimony that the child had died sometime during the period of fifteen minutes to several hours after it was injured. The medical expert expressed no opinion as to whether the child could have been successfully treated if the injury had been reported sooner.

The police questioned Melissa in Pope's presence. Pope did not contradict Melissa's denial of abusing the child. In fact, Pope, in response to inquiry by the police, said that the baby did not fall, and told them that she had not seen Melissa strike the baby. She explained this untruth in subsequent statements to the police: "[I]t was her body in the flesh, but it wasn't her, because it was something else."

Pope, Melissa and Angela attended the evening service at the church. Melissa reverted to God during the service and Reverend Hart restrained her and attempted to convince her that she was not Jesus Christ. Melissa refused to go to her grandfather's home and returned home with Pope. The next morning Pope was again interviewed at the police station and wrote a full explanation of what had happened. She later made an oral statement which was recorded.

I

THE CRIME OF CHILD ABUSE

* * *

* * * We pointed out in State v. Fabritz, 276 Md. 416, 348 A.2d 275 (1975), cert. denied, 425 U.S. 942, 96 S.Ct. 1680, 48 L.Ed.2d 185 (1976), that * * * "[in] making it an offense for a person having custody of a minor child to 'cause' the child to suffer a 'physical injury,' the Legislature did not require that the injury result from a physical assault upon the child or from any physical force initially applied by the accused individual; it provided instead, in a more encompassing manner, that the offense was committed if physical injury to the child resulted either from a course of conduct constituting 'cruel or inhumane treatment' or by 'malicious act or acts.'" Id. at 424, 348 A.2d at 280.

We found that the failure of the mother to seek or obtain any medical assistance for her child, although the need therefor was obviously compelling and urgent, caused the child to sustain bodily injury additional to and beyond that inflicted upon the child by reason of the original assault by another. The act of omission by the mother "constituted a cause of the further progression and worsening of the injuries which led to [the child's] death; and that in these circumstances [the mother's] treatment of [the child] was 'cruel or inhumane' within the meaning of the statute and as those terms are commonly understood." Id. at 425–426, 348 A.2d at 281. * * *

Responsibility for Abuse of a Child

In *Fabritz* we went no farther than to determine that the Legislature intended that the "cause" of an injury may include an act of omission so as to constitute cruel or inhumane treatment, in that case the failure of the mother to seek or obtain medical assistance for her child who had been abused by another. *Fabritz* did not go to the class of persons to whom the statutory proscription applies, as the accused there was a "parent," the victim's mother, expressly designated in the statute.

* * *

In Bowers v. State, 283 Md. 115, 389 A.2d 341 (1978), we discussed the class of persons to whom § 35A applies, in rejecting the contention that the statute was vague and therefore constitutionally defective for the reason that it failed to define adequately that class. Bowers urged that the statute was too indefinite to inform a person who is not a parent or adoptive parent of a child whether he comes within the ambit of the statute. He argued that no one in such position is capable of ascertaining whether the statute is aimed only at persons who have been awarded custody by judicial decree or includes also those who may simply be caring for a child in place of the parent. We were of the view that the General Assembly intended that the statute apply to persons who stand in loco parentis to a child. We said: "Had the Legislature wished to narrow application of the child abuse law to those who had been awarded custody or control by court order, it could readily have done so in explicit language to that end." Id., at 130, 389 A.2d at 350. We observed that Bowers' "own testimony amply established that he had assumed 'the care or custody or responsibility for the supervision' of his stepdaughter, and thus stood in loco parentis with respect to her." Id.

* * *

> "The term 'in loco parentis,' according to its generally accepted common law meaning, refers to a person who has put himself in the situation of a lawful parent by assuming the obligations incident to the parental relation without going through the formalities necessary to legal adoption. It embodies the two ideas of assuming the parental status and discharging the parental duties. Niewiadomski v. United States, 159 F.2d 683, 686 (6th Cir.), cert. denied, 331 U.S. 850, 67 S.Ct. 1730, 91 L.Ed. 1859 (1947).
>
> "This relationship involves more than a duty to aid and assist, more than a feeling of kindness, affection or generosity. It arises only when one is willing to assume all the obligations and to receive all the benefits associated with one standing as a natural parent to a child." Fuller v. Fuller, 247 A.2d 767 (D.C.1968), appeal denied, 135 U.S.App.D.C. 353, 418 F.2d 1189 (1969).

* * * Absent a court order or award by some appropriate proceeding pursuant to statutory authority, we think it to be self-evident that responsibility for supervision of a minor child may be obtained only upon the mutual consent, expressed or implied, by the one legally charged with the care of the child and by the one assuming the responsibility. In other words, a parent may not impose responsibility for the supervision of his or her minor child on a third person unless that person accepts the responsibility, and a third person may not assume such responsibility unless the parent grants it. So it is that a baby sitter temporarily has responsibility for the supervision of a child; the parents grant the responsibility for the period they are not at home, and the sitter accepts it. And it is by mutual consent that a school teacher has responsibility for the supervision of children in

connection with his academic duties. On the other hand, once responsibility for the supervision of a minor child has been placed in a third person, it may be terminated unilaterally by a parent by resuming responsibility, expressly or by conduct. The consent of the third party in such circumstances is not required; he may not prevent return of responsibility to the parent. But, of course, the third person in whom responsibility has been placed is not free to relinquish that responsibility without the knowledge of the parent. For example, a sitter may not simply walk away in the absence of the parents and leave the children to their own devices.

Under the present state of our law, a person has no legal obligation to care for or look after the welfare of a stranger, adult or child.

> "Generally one has no legal duty to aid another person in peril, even when that aid can be rendered without danger or inconvenience to himself. * * * A moral duty to take affirmative action is not enough to impose a legal duty to do so." W. LaFave & A. Scott, Criminal Law 183 (1972).

* * * Ordinarily, a person may stand by with impunity and watch another being murdered, raped, robbed, assaulted or otherwise unlawfully harmed. "He need not shout a warning to a blind man headed for a precipice or to an absentminded one walking into a gunpowder room with a lighted candle in hand. He need not pull a neighbor's baby out of a pool of water or rescue an unconscious person stretched across the railroad tracks, though the baby is drowning, or the whistle of an approaching train is heard in the distance." LeFave & Scott at 183. The General Assembly has enacted two "Good Samaritan" statutes which afford protection to one who assists another in certain circumstances. Those statutes, however, impose no requirement that assistance be rendered.[12]

In the face of this status of the law we cannot reasonably conclude that the Legislature, in bringing a person responsible for the supervision of a child within the ambit of the child abuse law, intended that such responsibility attach without the consent criteria we have set out. Were it otherwise, the consequences would go far beyond the legislative intent. For example, a person taking a lost child into his home to attempt to find its parents could be said to be responsible for that child's supervision. Or a person who allows his neighbor's children to play in his yard, keeping a watchful eye on their activities

12. Maryland Code (1957, 1976 Repl. Vol.) Art. 27, § 12A provides:

> "Any person witnessing a violent assault upon the person of another may lawfully aid the person being assaulted by assisting in that person's defense. The force exerted upon the attacker or attackers by the person witnessing the assault may be that degree of force which the assaulted person is allowed to assert in defending himself."

Code (1957, 1971 Repl.Vol., 1978 Cum. Supp.) Art. 43, § 132 grants immunity from liability from civil damages to physicians and certain other persons rendering aid under emergency conditions.

to prevent them from falling into harm, could be held responsible for the children's supervision. Or a person performing functions of a maternal nature from concern for the welfare, comfort or health of a child, or protecting it from danger because of a sense of moral obligation, may come within the reach of the act. In none of these situations would there be an intent to grant or assume the responsibility contemplated by the child abuse statute, and it would be incongruous indeed to subject such persons to possible criminal prosecution.

The Sufficiency of the Evidence

* * *

* * * Under the teaching of *Fabritz,* Pope's lack of any attempt to prevent the numerous acts of abuse committed by the mother over a relatively protracted period and her failure to seek medical assistance for the child, although the need therefor was obviously compelling and urgent, could constitute a cause for the further progression and worsening of the injuries which led to the child's death. In such circumstances, Pope's omissions constituted in themselves cruel and inhumane treatment within the meaning of the statute. It follows that Pope would be guilty of child abuse *if her status brought her within the class of persons specified by the statute.* It being clear that she was neither the child's parent nor adoptive parent, and there being no evidence sufficient to support a finding that she had "the permanent or temporary care or custody" of the child as that status was construed in Bowers v. State, supra, so as to be in loco parentis to the child, the sole question is whether she had "responsibility for the supervision of" the child in the circumstances. If she had such responsibility the evidence was legally sufficient to find her guilty of child abuse * * *.

The State would have us translate compassion and concern, acts of kindness and care, performance of maternal functions, and general help and aid with respect to the child into responsibility for the supervision of the child. The crux of its argument is that although Pope was not under any obligation to assume responsibility for the supervision of the child at the outset, "once she undertook to house, feed, and care for [the mother and child], she did accept the responsibility and came within the coverage of the statute." But the mother was always present. Pope had no right to usurp the role of the mother even to the extent of responsibility for the child's supervision. We are in full accord with the view of the Court of Special Appeals that it could not "in good conscience hold that a person who has taken in a parent and child is given the responsibility for the child's supervision and protection even while the child is in the very arms of its mother." *Pope,* 38 Md.App. at 538, 382 A.2d at 890. It would be most incongruous that acts of hospitality and kindness, made out of common decency and prompted by sincere concern for the well-being of a mother and her child, subjected the Good Samaritan to criminal prosecution for abusing the very child he sought to look after. And it would be especially ironic were such criminal prosecution to be predicated upon an obligation to take affirmative action with regard to abuse of the child by its mother, when such obligation arises solely from those acts of hospitality and kindness.

The evidence does not show why Pope did not intervene when the mother abused the child or why she did not, at least, timely seek medical assistance, when it was obvious that the child was seriously injured. * * * But Pope's conduct, during and after the acts of abuse, must be evaluated with regard for the rule that although she may have had a strong moral obligation to help the child, she was under no legal obligation to do so unless she then had responsibility for the supervision of the child as contemplated by the child abuse statute. She may not be punished as a felon under our system of justice for failing to fulfill a moral obligation, and the short of it is that she was under no legal obligation. In the circumstances, the mother's acquiescence in Pope's conduct was not a grant of responsibility to Pope for the supervision of the child, nor was Pope's conduct an acceptance of such responsibility. "[Pope's] concern for the child [did] not convert to legal responsibility nor parental prerogatives." *Pope*, 38 Md.App. at 538, 382 A.2d at 890. We hold that the evidence was not sufficient in law to prove that Pope fell within that class of persons to whom the child abuse statute applies. Thus it is that the judgment of the trial court that she was * * * [guilty] of child abuse was clearly erroneous and must be set aside.

The mental or emotional state of the mother, whereby at times she held herself out as God, does not change the result. We see no basis in the statute for an interpretation that a person "has" responsibility for the supervision of a child, if that person believes or may have reason to believe that a parent is not capable of caring for the child. There is no right to make such a subjective judgment in order to divest parents of their rights and obligations with respect to their minor children, and therefore, no obligation to do so.

* * *

* * * The evidence certainly showed that Pope "witnessed a terrible event" and that she "stood by" while the mother killed the child. But the culpability for her conduct during the abuse of the child must be determined strictly within the law or else the basic tenets of our system of justice are prostituted. There is an understandable feeling of outrage at what occurred, intensified by the fact that the mother, who actually beat the child to death, was held to be not responsible for her criminal acts. But it is the law, not indignation, which governs. The law requires that Pope's conviction of the felony of child abuse be set aside as clearly erroneous due to evidentiary insufficiency.

[The court's discussion of the misprision of felony charge is reprinted at page 186, infra.

NOTES AND QUESTIONS

1. The following statute is proposed for your jurisdiction. Would you support it or not? What if any changes would you recommend?

> *Liability for Omission.* A person shall be criminally responsible for a result if he fails to take action to prevent that result, but for his failure to take action the result would not have occurred, and the failure to take action constitutes a substantial deviation from common decency. In determining whether a failure to act constitutes a substantial deviation from common decency the following factors shall be taken into account:
>
> 1. the seriousness of the result,
> 2. the likelihood that the result would occur without action,
> 3. any burden or risk which taking action would have required the person to assume, and
> 4. any responsibility of the person for creating the need for action.

Compare this proposal with the following provision of the Texas Penal Code.

> **Sec. 6.01** (c) A person who omits to perform an act does not commit an offense unless a statute provides that the omission is an offense or otherwise provides that he has a duty to perform the act.

Statutes quite similar to the first proposal are found in European Codes. Feldbrugge, "Good and Bad Samaritans," 14 Am.J.Comp.L. 630 (1966). The Texas statute is typical of the Anglo-American approach to this issue except that its use of "a statute" as the source of the duty is somewhat narrower than the more common reference to duties imposed "by law". Why do you think European Codes are different? Which approach is preferable in dealing with the following problems?

a. A, from the safety of his home, sees a young woman being assaulted by a man on a deserted street in the early hours of the morning. She cries for aid, screaming: "Oh my God, he stabbed me! Please help me!" A shouts at the assailant who stops momentarily but then pursues the victim. A takes no further action and the victim is again struck. The police, responding to a call from B who passes by after the assault has ended, arrive within two minutes after being notified. The victim dies on the way to the hospital.

b. A, a physician who has stopped at a rural restaurant while on vacation, hears a distraught young man announce that his wife is in very painful labor in a car outside. He asks if there is a doctor there or nearby. A does not respond but gets in his car and drives away. For want of proper assistance the woman and child perish.

c. Assume that the young man in "b." is rushing his wife to the hospital when he is involved in a minor accident with A who is at least partly to blame. The young man's car is disabled but A, fearing loss of his license because of prior violations and possible criminal penalties if his involvement is discovered by the police, flees the scene. Because the woman can't be taken to the hospital in time she and the child perish.

d. A, a school-crossing guard, leaves her post to obtain a cup of coffee on a bitterly cold winter day. A first-grader, slightly late for school, dashes across the street and is struck and killed by a car.

e. A group of air traffic controllers call in sick in a wage dispute knowing that there are insufficient replacements. In the course of diverting planes from that area, a mistake is made by an inexperienced substitute and a crash ensues killing all aboard.

2. Can one be convicted of a criminal omission in the absence of knowledge of the duty to act? See Lambert v. California, 355 U.S. 225, 78 S.Ct. 240, 2 L.Ed.2d 228 (1957) reprinted at page 165.

B. THE STATE OF MIND

COWAN, TOWARDS AN EXPERIMENTAL DEFINITION OF CRIMINAL MIND, IN PHILOSOPHICAL ESSAYS IN HONOR OF EDGAR ARTHUR SINGER, JR.

163 (F. Clarke and M. Nahm eds. 1942).

In the 17th year of the reign of Edward IV, Brian pronounced his celebrated dictum that a man is responsible only for his words and deeds and not for his thoughts, because "the devil himself knoweth not the mind of man." What the learned judge apparently took to be an axiomatic rule of evidence has become a part of the substantive law of contracts in the form of the doctrine of objective intent. Contract law is now taken to be concerned only with intent as outwardly manifested by the conduct of the parties.

Similarly, the law of torts is almost exclusively occupied with the external behavior of the parties. Only in the case of intentional wrongs does it purport to refer to states of mind as qualifying responsibility. The great body of non-intentional torts applies what are called "objective standards." In determining negligence, for instance, the law does not inquire whether the harmful act was accompanied by a culpable state of mind. On the contrary, it merely decides whether the defendant failed to conform to external standards of reasonably expectable conduct. His state of mind is immaterial. Anglo-American *civil* law, therefore, has from the earliest times indicated that, with certain few exceptions, objective intent is the only kind of intent with which it is prepared to deal.

The theory of the *criminal* law is different. Here it is still felt necessary to investigate a man's secret thought, or absence of thought, whenever intention, or malice, or even negligence is an element of the crime in question.

NOTES

1. The so-called subjective theory of criminal liability assumes that state of mind and therefore "mind" itself as ascertainable. This underlying assumption has been called into question on both practical and theoretical grounds.

The practical ground is based upon difficulty of proof. If there is such a "thing" as state of mind, it is nevertheless so subjective and difficult of proof that it is unrealistic to believe that an individual's state of mind at a past time can generally be reliably determined. Thus, it is argued, the criminal law should not attempt to make criminal liability turn on state of mind.

The theoretical ground is more basic. This view holds that "mind" is a mere abstraction and therefore it is artificial to treat states of mind as if they actually existed. Rather than waste time attempting to infer an offender's state of mind from his behavior, this view holds that the law would better serve its purposes if it regarded the so-called mind as the criminal behavior itself rather than using the behavior as evidence from which to infer "mind". See T. Cowan, Towards an Experimental Definition of Criminal Mind, in Philosophical Essays in Honor of Edgar Arthur Singer, Jr. (F. Clarke and M. Nahm eds. 1942); Cowan, A Critique of the Moralistic Conception of Criminal Law, 97 U.Pa.L.Rev. 502, 510 (1949). In fact, Cowan represents, the law in fact does this by procedural devices such as the presumption that a person "intends" the natural consequences of his act. Inserting the concept of "state of mind", he concludes, merely serves to confuse analysis.

2. The historical development of the criminal law's emphasis upon an alleged offender's state of mind (the mens rea requirement) is traced in the following portions of Sayre, Mens Rea, 45 Harv.L.Rev. 974, 981–83, 988–89, 993–94 (1932): [b]

[S]tudy of the early law seems to show that up to the twelfth century the conception of *mens rea* in anything like its present sense was nonexistent. In certain cases at least criminal liability might attach irrespective of the actor's state of mind. But because the old records fail to set forth a *mens rea* as a general requisite of criminality one must not reach the conclusion that even in very early times the mental element was entirely disregarded. The very nature of the majority of the early offenses rendered them impossible of commission without a criminal intent. Waylaying and robbery are impossible without it; so is rape; and the same is roughly true of housebreaking. * * *

Furthermore, the intent of the defendant seems to have been a material factor, even from the very earliest times, in determining the extent of punishment.

By the end of the twelfth century two influences were making themselves strongly felt. One was the Roman law[;] * * * the Roman law

b. Reprinted from 45 Harvard Law Review 974 (1932).

conceptions of *dolus* and *culpa* required careful consideration of the mental element in crime.

A second influence, even more powerful, was the canon law, whose insistence upon moral guilt emphasized still further the mental element in crime. * * * Henceforth, the criminal law of England, developing in the general direction of moral blameworthiness, begins to insist upon a *mens rea* as an essential element of criminality. * * *

We can trace the changed attitude in the new generalizations concerning the necessity of an evil intent which are found scattered through the Year Books in the remarks of judges and counsel * * *. We sense it in the growing insistence upon more and more sharply defined mental requisites as essentials of the common-law felonies. We find it fermenting in the form of new defenses which show the absence of an evil mind and therefore of criminal liability-defenses such as infancy or insanity or cumpulsion.

* * *

By the second half of the seventeenth century, it was universally accepted law that an evil intent was as necessary for felony as the act itself. * * *

At the outset when the *mens rea* necessary for criminality was based on general moral blameworthiness, the conception was an exceedingly vague one. As a result of the slow judicial process of discriminating one case from another and "talking of diversities," much sharper and more precise lines gradually came to be drawn as to the exact mental requisites for various crimes. Since each felony involved different social and public interests, the mental requisites for one almost inevitably came to differ from those of another.

1. TYPES OF STATES OF MIND

One common characteristic of most modern criminal codes is an effort to define with specificity the states of mind required for the various offenses. This is done by distinguishing several different kinds of state of mind and then using these in the substantive definitions of crimes. Most codes follow the pattern of Section 2.02 of the Model Penal Code reprinted in this subsection. Some use the label "intentionally" where the Model Penal Code uses "purposely." But all distinguish this from the other three possible requirements, i. e., that the defendant have acted "knowingly," "recklessly," or "negligently." Note that Section 2.02 and similar provisions deal only with definition of terms and do not attempt to determine what states of mind are required by various offenses. This is done in the definitions of the offenses themselves, which define the state of mind required by using the terms defined in Section 2.02 or its equivalent.

MODEL PENAL CODE *

(Proposed Official Draft, 1962).

Section 2.02. General Requirements of Culpability

* * *

(2) *Kinds of Culpability Defined.*

(a) *Purposely.*

A person acts purposely with respect to a material element of an offense when:

(i) if the element involves the nature of his conduct or a result thereof, it is his conscious object to engage in conduct of that nature or to cause such a result; and

(ii) if the element involves the attendant circumstances, he is aware of the existence of such circumstances or he believes or hopes that they exist.

(b) *Knowingly.*

A person acts knowingly with respect to a material element of an offense when:

(i) if the element involves the nature of his conduct or the attendant circumstances, he is aware that his conduct is of that nature or that such circumstances exist; and

(ii) if the element involves a result of his conduct, he is aware that it is practically certain that his conduct will cause such a result.

(c) *Recklessly.*

A person acts recklessly with respect to a material element of an offense when he consciously disregards a substantial and unjustifiable risk that the material element exists or will result from his conduct. The risk must be of such a nature and degree that, considering the nature and purpose of the actor's conduct and the circumstances known to him, its disregard involves a gross deviation from the standard of conduct that a law-abiding person would observe in the actor's situation.

(d) *Negligently.*

A person acts negligently with respect to a material element of an offense when he should be aware of a substantial and unjustifiable risk that the material element exists or will result from his conduct. The risk must be of such a nature and degree that the actor's failure to perceive it, considering the nature and purpose of his conduct and the circumstances known to him, involves a gross deviation from the standard of care that a reasonable person would observe in the actor's situation.

2. THE STANDARD STATE OF MIND REQUIREMENT FOR CRIMINAL LIABILITY: "GENERAL INTENT"

In the absence of a generally-applicable statute defining a legislatively directed analysis of the states of mind required by various crimes, there is often a great deal of confusion in the statutes and the caselaw on the issue of "intent." Section 2.02 of the Model Penal Code (reprinted at page 155, infra) and some modern statutes patterned after it provide a requirement of at least recklessness concerning all things that are elements of the crime, unless there is a clear indication of a contrary legislative intent. Consider the extent to which in the absence of such a statute the law does—or should—impose a similar or identical requirement. Such a generally-applicable requirement of a state of mind in regard to all elements of the offense is usefully regarded as a requirement of "general intent."

REGINA v. PEMBLITON

Court of Criminal Appeal, 1874.
12 Cox Crim. Cases 607.

LORD COLERIDGE, C. J.—I am of opinion that this conviction must be quashed. The facts of the case are these. The prisoner and some other persons who had been drinking in a public house were turned out of it at about 11 p. m. for being disorderly, and they then began to fight in the street near the prosecutor's window. The prisoner separated himself from the others, and went to the other side of the street, and picked up a stone, and threw it at the persons he had been fighting with. The stone passed over their heads, and broke a large plate glass window in the prosecutor's house, doing damage to an amount exceeding 5*l*. The jury found that the prisoner threw the stone at the people he had been fighting with, intending to strike one or more of them with it, but not intending to break the window. The question is whether under an indictment for unlawfully and maliciously committing an injury to the window in the house of the prosecutor the proof of these facts alone, coupled with the finding of the jury, will do? Now I think that is not enough. The indictment is framed under the 24 & 25 Vict. c. 97, s. 51. The Act is an Act relating to malicious injuries to property, and sect. 51 enacts that whosoever shall unlawfully and maliciously commit any damage, &c., to or upon any real or personal property whatsoever of a public or a private nature, for which the punishment is hereinbefore provided, to an amount exceeding 5*l* shall be guilty of a misdemeanor. There is also the 58th section which deserves attention. "Every punishment and forfeiture by this Act imposed on any person maliciously committing any offence, whether the same be punishable upon indictment or upon summary conviction, shall equally apply and be enforced whether the offence shall be committed from malice conceived against the owner of the property in respect of which it shall be committed, or otherwise." It seems to me on both these sections that what was intended to be provided against by the Act is the wilfully doing an unlawful Act, and that the Act must be wilfully and intentionally done on the part of the person doing it, to render him liable to be convicted. Without saying that, upon these facts, if the jury had found that the prisoner had been guilty of throwing the stone recklessly, knowing that there was a window near which it might probably hit, I should have been disposed to interfere with the conviction, yet as they have found that he threw the stone at the people he had been fighting with intending to strike them and not intending to break the window, I think the conviction must be quashed. I do not intend to throw any doubt on the cases which have been cited and which show what is sufficient to constitute malice in the case of murder. They rest upon the principles of the common law, and have no application to a statutory offence created by an Act in which the words are carefully studied.

MODEL PENAL CODE *

(Proposed Official Draft, 1962).

Section 2.02. General Requirements of Culpability

(1) *Minimum Requirements of Culpability.* Except as provided in Section 2.05, a person is not guilty of an offense unless he acted purposely, knowingly, recklessly or negligently, as the law may require, with respect to each material element of the offense.

* * *

(3) *Culpability Required Unless Otherwise Provided.* When the culpability sufficient to establish a material element of an offense is not prescribed by law, such element is established if a person acts purposely, knowingly or recklessly with respect thereto.

(4) *Prescribed Culpability Requirement Applies to All Material Elements.* When the law defining an offense prescribes the kind of culpability that is sufficient for the commission of an offense, without distinguishing among the material elements thereof, such provision shall apply to all the material elements of the offense, unless a contrary purpose plainly appears.

(5) *Substitutes for Negligence, Recklessness and Knowledge.* When the law provides that negligence suffices to establish an element of an offense, such element also is established if a person acts pur-

posely, knowingly or recklessly. When recklessness suffices to establish an element, such element also is established if a person acts purposely or knowingly. When acting knowingly suffices to establish an element, such element also is established if a person acts purposely.

(6) *Requirement of Purpose Satisfied if Purpose Is Conditional.* When a particular purpose is an element of an offense, the element is established although such purpose is conditional, unless the condition negatives the harm or evil sought to be prevented by the law defining the offense.

(7) *Requirement of Knowledge Satisfied by Knowledge of High Probability.* When knowledge of the existence of a particular fact is an element of an offense, such knowledge is established if a person is aware of a high probability of its existence, unless he actually believes that it does not exist.

(8) *Requirement of Wilfulness Satisfied by Acting Knowingly.* A requirement that an offense be committed wilfully is satisfied if a person acts knowingly with respect to the material elements of the offense, unless a purpose to impose further requirements appears.

(9) *Culpability as to Illegality of Conduct.* Neither knowledge nor recklessness or negligence as to whether conduct constitutes an offense or as to the existence, meaning or application of the law determining the elements of an offense is an element of such offense, unless the definition of the offense or the Code so provides.

(10) *Culpability as Determinant of Grade of Offense.* When the grade or degree of an offense depends on whether the offense is committed purposely, knowingly, recklessly or negligently, its grade or degree shall be the lowest for which the determinative kind of culpability is established with respect to any material element of the offense.

NOTES

The position of the Model Penal Code—that in the absence of a specific indication to the contrary "wilfullness" would be required—was defended by the draftsmen of the Model Penal Code as representing "what is usually regarded as the common law position." Model Penal Code, Comments to § 2.02, 127 (Tent.Draft No. 4, 1955). It also, according to the comments, "represents the most convenient norm for drafting purposes, since when purpose or knowledge is to be required, it is normal to so state; and negligence ought to be viewed as an exceptional basis of liability." Id.

Why should negligence be regarded as "an exceptional basis of liability," to be used only where the legislative intent to impose it is extremely clear? Consider the following:

> Since negligence involves no *mens rea*, the question is raised as to the advisability of punishing negligent conduct with criminal sanctions. Professor Edwin Keedy responded to this question as follows: "If the defendant, being mistaken as to the material

facts, is to be punished because his mistake is one an average man would not make, punishment will sometimes be inflicted *when the criminal mind does not exist*. Such a result is contrary to fundamental principles, and is plainly unjust, for a man should not be held criminal because of lack of intelligence."[10] This argument is persuasive, especially when considered in conjunction with the traditional concepts and goals of criminal punishment.

The concept of criminal punishment is based on one, or a combination, of four theories: deterrence, retribution, rehabilitation and incapacitation.

The deterrence theory of criminal law is based on the hypotheses that the prospective offender knows that he will be punished for any criminal activity, and, therefore, will adjust his behavior to avoid committing a criminal act. This theory rests on the idea of "rational utility," i. e., prospective offenders will weigh the evil of the sanction against the gain of the contemplated crime. However, punishment of a negligent offender in no way implements this theory, since the negligent harm-doer is, by definition, unaware of the risk he imposes on society. It is questionable whether holding an individual criminally liable for acts the risks of which he has failed to perceive will deter him from failing to perceive in the future.

The often-criticized retributive theory of criminal law presupposes a "moral guilt," which justifies society in seeking its revenge against the offender. This "moral guilt" is ascribed to those forms of conduct which society deems threatening to its very existence, such as murder and larceny. However, the negligent harm-doer has not actually committed this type of morally reprehensible act, but has merely made an error in judgment. This type of error is an everyday occurrence, although it may deviate from a normal standard of care. Nevertheless, such conduct does not approach the moral turpitude against which the criminal law should seek revenge. It is difficult to comprehend how retribution requires such mistakes to be criminally punished.

It is also doubtful whether the negligent offender can be rehabilitated in any way by criminal punishment. Rehabilitation presupposes a "warped sense of values" which can be corrected. Since inadvertence, and not a deficient sense of values, has caused the "crime," there appears to be nothing to rehabilitate.

The underlying goal of the incapacitation theory is to protect society by isolating an individual so as to prevent him from perpetrating a similar crime in the future. However, this approach is only justifiable if less stringent methods will not further the same goal of protecting society. For example, an insane individual would not be criminally incarcerated, if the less stringent means of medical treatment would afford the same societal protection. Like-

10. Keedy, Ignorance and Mistake in the Criminal Law, 22 Harv.L.Rev. 75, 84 (1908) (Emphasis added.)

wise, with a criminally negligent individual, the appropriate remedy is not incarceration, but "to exclude him from the activity in which he is a danger."

The conclusion drawn from this analysis is that there appears to be no reasonable justification for punishing negligence as a criminal act under any of these four theories. It does not further the purposes of deterrence, retribution, rehabilitation or incapacitation; hence, there is no rational basis for the imposition of criminal liability on negligent conduct.

This view, favoring exclusion of negligence from the criminal law, is not without support. The chief exponent of this position is Professor Jerome Hall, who maintains that there are persuasive historical, ethical and scientific reasons to support the exclusionary argument.[16]

Hall's historical ground rests upon a continuing trend toward restricting criminal negligence in many Anglo-American legal systems. In addition, the same trend can be noted in civil law systems, where negligence is not criminally punishable absent a specific provision to that effect. Such provisions are very few. While Hall recognizes that history is often a dubious ground upon which to support a thesis, he argues that a long and sustained movement, such as that limiting the applicability of criminal negligence, places the burden of retention upon the proponents of penalization. This burden, Hall maintains, has not been carried.

Professor Hall's ethical argument is based on the premise that, throughout the long history of ethics, the essence of fault has been voluntary harm-doing. He maintains that this requirement of voluntary action becomes even more persuasive in the penal law, because no one should be criminally punished unless he has clearly acted immorally, by voluntarily harming someone. Negligence, of course, cannot be classified as voluntary harm-doing. Therefore, no fault is involved and accordingly no punishment is justified.

In addition, Hall suggests scientific arguments for the exclusion of negligence from penal liability. One contention is that the incorporation of negligence into the penal law imposes an impossible function on judges, namely, to determine whether a person, about whom very little is known, had the competence and sensitivity to appreciate certain dangers in a particular situation when the facts plainly indicate that he did not exhibit that competence. Also, Hall maintains that "the inclusion of negligence bars the discovery of a scientific theory of penal law, i. e., a system of propositions interrelating variables that have a realistic foundation in fact and values."

Comment, Is Criminal Negligence A Defensible Basis for Penal Liability?, 16 Buffalo L.Rev. 749, 750–52 (1967).[c] See also Fletcher, The Theory of

16. Hall, Negligent Behavior Should be Excluded from Penal Liability, 63 Colum.L.Rev. 632 (1963).

Criminal Negligence: A Comparative Analysis, 119 U.Pa.L.Rev. 401 (1971); Note, Negligence and the General Problem of Criminal Liability, 81 Yale L.J. 949 (1972).

SANDSTROM v. MONTANA

Supreme Court of the United States, 1979.
— U.S. —, 99 S.Ct. 2450, 61 L.Ed.2d 39.

Mr. Justice BRENNAN delivered the opinion of the Court.

The question presented is whether, in a case in which intent is an element of the crime charged, the jury instruction, "the law presumes that a person intends the ordinary consequences of his voluntary acts," violates the Fourteenth Amendment's requirement that the State prove every element of a criminal offense beyond a reasonable doubt.

I

On November 22, 1976, 18-year-old David Sandstrom confessed to the slaying of Annie Jessen. Based upon the confession and corroborating evidence, petitioner was charged on December 2nd with "deliberate homicide," 1947 Mont.Rev.Codes § 94–5–102 (Crim.Code of 1973), in that he "purposely or knowingly caused the death of Annie Jessen." At trial, Sandstrom's attorney informed the jury that, although his client admitted killing Jessen, he did not do so "purposely or knowingly," and was therefore not guilty of "deliberate homicide" but of a lesser crime. The basic support for this contention was the testimony of two court-appointed mental health experts, each of whom described for the jury petitioner's mental state at the time of the incident. Sandstrom's attorney argued that this testimony demonstrated that petitioner, due to a personality disorder aggravated by alcohol consumption, did not kill Annie Jessen "purposely or knowingly."

The prosecution requested the trial judge to instruct the jury that "[t]he law presumes that a person intends the ordinary consequences of his voluntary acts." Petitioner's counsel objected, arguing that "the instruction has the effect of shifting the burden of proof on the issue of" purpose or knowledge to the defense, and that "that is impermissible under the Federal Constitution, due process of law." He offered to provide a number of federal decisions in support of the objection, including this Court's holding in Mullaney v. Wilbur, 421 U.S. 684, 95 S.Ct. 1881, 44 L.Ed.2d 508 (1975), but was told by the judge: "You can give those to the Supreme Court. The objection is overruled." The instruction was delivered, the jury found petitioner guilty of deliberate homicide, and petitioner was sentenced to 100 years in prison.

Sandstrom appealed to the Supreme Court of Montana, again contending that the instruction shifted to the defendant the burden of disproving an element of the crime charged, in violation of Mullaney v. Wilbur, supra, In re Winship, 397 U.S. 358, 90 S.Ct. 1068, 25 L.Ed.2d 368 (1970), and Patterson v. New York, 432 U.S. 197, 97 S.Ct. 2319, 53 L.Ed.2d 281 (1977). The Montana Court conceded that these cases did prohibit shifting the burden of proof to the defendant by means of a presumption, but held that the cases "do not prohibit allocation of *some* burden of proof to a defendant under certain circumstances." 580 P.2d 106, 109 (1978). Since in the Court's view, "[d]efendant's sole burden under instruction No. 5 was to produce *some* evidence that he did not intend the ordinary consequences of his voluntary acts, not to disprove that he acted 'purposely' or 'knowingly,' * * * the instruction does not violate due process standards as defined by the United States or Montana Constitution * * *." Ibid. (emphasis added).

* * * We granted certiorari to decide the important question of the instruction's constitutionality. We reverse.

II

The threshold inquiry in ascertaining the constitutional analysis applicable to this kind of jury instruction is to determine the nature of the presumption it describes. * * *

* * * [E]ven respondent admits that "it's possible" that the jury believed they were required to apply the presumption. Sandstrom's jurors were told that "the law presumes that a person intends the ordinary consequences of his voluntary acts." They were not told that they had a choice, or that they might infer that conclusion; they were told only that the law presumed it. It is clear that a reasonable juror could easily have viewed such an instruction as mandatory.

In the alternative, respondent urges that even if viewed as a mandatory presumption rather than as a permissive inference, the presumption did not conclusively establish intent but rather could be rebutted. * * * [A]ccording to the State, all the defendant had to do to rebut the presumption was produce "some" contrary evidence; he did not have to "prove" that he lacked the required mental state. Thus, "[a]t most, it placed a *burden of production* on the petitioner," but "did not shift to petitioner the *burden of persuasion* with respect to any element of the offense. * * *"

* * *

* * * Petitioner's jury was told that "*the law presumes* that a person intends the ordinary consequences of his voluntary acts." They were not told that the presumption could be rebutted, as the Montana Supreme Court held, by the defendant's simple presentation of "some" evidence; nor even that it could be rebutted at all. Given the common definition of "presume" as "to suppose to be true without

proof," Webster's New Collegiate Dictionary 911 (1974), and given the lack of qualifying instructions as to the legal effect of the presumption, we cannot discount the possibility that the jury may have interpreted the instruction in either of two more stringent ways.

First, a reasonable jury could well have interpreted the presumption as "conclusive," that is, not technically as a presumption at all, but rather as an irrebuttable direction by the court to find intent once convinced of the facts triggering the presumption. Alternatively, the jury may have interpreted the instruction as a direction to find intent upon proof of the defendant's voluntary actions (and their "ordinary" consequences), unless *the defendant* proved the contrary by some quantum of proof which may well have been considerably greater than "some" evidence—thus effectively shifting the burden of persuasion on the element of intent.

* * *

* * * It is clear that under Montana law, whether the crime was committed purposely or knowingly is a fact necessary to constitute the crime of deliberate homicide. Indeed, it was the lone element of the offense at issue in Sandstrom's trial, as he confessed to causing the death of the victim, told the jury that knowledge and purpose were the only questions he was controverting, and introduced evidence solely on those points. Moreover, it is conceded that proof of defendant's "intent" would be sufficient to establish this element. Thus, the question before this Court is whether the challenged jury instruction had the effect of relieving the State of the burden of proof enunciated in *Winship* on the critical question of petitioner's state of mind. We conclude that under either of the two possible interpretations of the instruction set out above, precisely that effect would result, and that the instruction therefore represents constitutional error.

We consider first the validity of a conclusive presumption. This Court has considered such a presumption on at least two prior occasions. In Morissette v. United States, 342 U.S. 246, 72 S.Ct. 240, 96 L.Ed. 288 (1952), the defendant was charged with willful and knowing theft of government property. Although his attorney argued that for his client to be found guilty, " 'the taking must have been with felonious intent'," the trial judge ruled that " '[t]hat is presumed by his own act.' " Id., at 249, 72 S.Ct. at 243. After first concluding that intent was in fact an element of the crime charged, and after declaring that "[w]here intent of the accused is an ingredient of the crime charged, its existence is a * * * jury issue," *Morissette* held:

> "*It follows that the trial court may not withdraw or prejudge the issue by instruction that the law raises a presumption of intent from an act.* It often is tempting to cast in terms of a 'presumption' a conclusion which a court

thinks probable from given facts. * * * [But] [w]e think presumptive intent has no place in this case. *A conclusive presumption which testimony could not overthrow would effectively eliminate intent as an ingredient of the offense.* A presumption which would permit but not require the jury to assume intent from an isolated fact would prejudge a conclusion which the jury should reach of its own volition. A presumption which would permit the jury to make an assumption which all the evidence considered together does not logically establish would give to a proven fact an artificial and fictional effect. In either case, *this presumption would conflict with the overriding presumption of innocence with which the law endows the accused and which extends to every element of the crime.*" 342 U.S., at 274–275, 72 S.Ct. at 255–256. (Emphasis added.)

Just last Term, in United States v. United States Gypsum, 438 U.S. 422, 98 S.Ct. 2864, 57 L.Ed.2d 854 (1978), we reaffirmed the holding of *Morissette.* In that case defendants, who were charged with criminal violations of the Sherman Act, challenged the following jury instruction:

> "The law presumes that a person intends the necessary and natural consequences of his acts. Therefore, if the effect of the exchanges of pricing information was to raise, fix, maintain and stabilize prices, then the parties to them are presumed, as a matter of law, to have intended that result." Id., at 430, 98 S.Ct. at 2869.

After again determining that the offense included the element of intent, we held

> "[A] defendant's state of mind or *intent is an element of a criminal antitrust offense which * * * cannot be taken from the trier of fact through reliance on a legal presumption* of wrongful intent from proof of effect on prices. Cf. Morissette v. United States * * *.
>
> * * *
>
> "Although an effect on prices may well support an inference that the defendant had knowledge of the probability of such a consequence at the time he acted, the jury must remain free to consider additional evidence before accepting or rejecting the inference. * * * [U]ltimately the decision on the issue of intent must be left to the trier of fact alone. The instruction given invaded this factfinding function." 438 U.S., at 435, 446, 98 S.Ct. at 2872, 2878 (emphasis added).

As in *Morissette* and *United States Gypsum,* a conclusive presumption in this case would "conflict with the overriding presumption of innocence with which the law endows the accused and which extends to every element of the crime," and would "invade [the] factfinding function" which in a criminal case the law assigns solely to the jury. The instruction announced to David Sandstrom's jury may well have had exactly these consequences. Upon finding proof of one element of the crime (causing death), and of facts insufficient to establish the second (the voluntariness and "ordinary consequences" of defendant's action), Sandstrom's jurors could reasonably have concluded that they were directed to find against defendant on the element of intent. The State was thus not forced to prove "beyond a reasonable doubt * * * every fact necessary to constitute the crime * * * charged," 397 U.S., at 364, 90 S.Ct. at 1073, and defendant was deprived of his constitutional rights as explicated in *Winship*.

A presumption which, although not conclusive, had the effect of shifting the burden of persuasion to the defendant, would have suffered from similar infirmities. If Sandstrom's jury interpreted the presumption in that manner, it could have concluded that upon proof by the State of the slaying, and of additional facts not themselves establishing the element of intent, the burden was shifted to the defendant to prove that he lacked the requisite mental state. Such a presumption was found constitutionally deficient in Mullaney v. Wilbur * * *.

Because David Sandstrom's jury may have interpreted the judge's instruction as constituting either a burden-shifting presumption like that in *Mullaney,* or a conclusive presumption like those in *Morissette* and *United States Gypsum,* and because either interpretation would have deprived defendant of his right to the due process of law, we hold the instruction given in this case unconstitutional.

* * *

* * * Accordingly, the judgment of the Supreme Court of Montana is reversed and remanded for further proceedings not inconsistent with this opinion.

It is so ordered.

[The separate concurring opinion of Mr. Justice Rehnquist, joined by the Chief Justice, is omitted.]

3. STATES OF MIND BEYOND "GENERAL INTENT"

It is clear that a number of crimes require proof of a state of mind that goes beyond what was described in the preceding subsection as "general intent." This may be a more rigorous requirement relating to some element of the offense, such as a requirement of knowledge rather than recklessness in rape regarding the absence of consent by the victim. Or, it may be a state of mind concerning some action, result, or circumstance that need not itself be shown to prove the defendant guilty of the offense. The case law often speaks of at least some such requirements as ones of "specific intent." But the phrase "specific intent" is used inconsistently in judicial and scholarly discussions. Consider the following uses of the terminology:

> [S]pecific intent is present when from the circumstances the offender must have subjectively desired the prohibited result; whereas general intent exists when from the circumstances the prohibited result may reasonably be expected to follow from the offender's voluntary act, irrespective of any subjective desire to have accomplished such result."

State v. Daniels, 236 La. 998, 1007, 109 So.2d 896, 899 (1958).

> Crimes are either mala in se or mala prohibita, and intent is a necessary element. In crimes which are mala in se, a specific intent, a wrongful intent, to commit the crime must be established, but in crimes that are mala prohibita the only intent requisite to a conviction is the intent or purpose to do the prohibited act.

State v. Binders, 24 Conn.Sup. 214, 1 Conn.Cir. 506, 216, 189 A.2d 408, 409 (1962).

> Some crimes require a specified intention in addition to the intentional doing of the *actus reus* itself * * *. The physical part of the crime of larceny, for example is the trespassory taking and carrying away of the personal goods of another, but this may be done intentionally, deliberately, and with full knowledge of all the facts and complete understanding of the wrongfulness of the act, without constituting larceny. If this wilful misuse of another's property is done with the intention of returning it * * * the special mens rea requirement of larceny is lacking * * *. This additional requirement is a 'specific intent,' an additional intent specifically required for guilt of the particular offense.

R. Perkins, Criminal Law 762 (2nd ed. 1969).

Many of the traditional specific intents—such as the intent to steal required by larceny and other property crimes—are covered in the later chapters of the material. The principal cases in this subsection deal with the possibility that in some exceptional situations, due process of law may require that the defendant be proved to have been aware of some relevant law. In Lambert v. California, the Supreme Court appears to hold that Lambert could not be convicted of remaining in Los Angeles without registering as a convicted felon in the absence of proof that she was or reasonably should have been aware of her legal duty to register. In United States v. International Minerals & Chemical Corp., on the other hand, the same Court holds that the defendant corporation need not be shown to have been aware of the regulations violated by its prohibited shipment of certain acid in interstate commerce. Perhaps the difference lies in the nature of the defendants and the situations in which they operated. The corporate defendant in *International Minerals & Chemical Corp.* was heavily involved in the regulated business of interstate shipping and might be expected, in the exercise of reasonable care, to be aware of the regulations involved. On the other hand, the individual defendant in *Lambert* might not, under the circumstances, be likely to find out about the ordinance requiring registration of convicted felons even if she exercised reasonable prudence in her affairs. Due process may require awareness of the applicable law where, but only where, it is quite unlikely that defendants who exercise reasonable care will learn of that law.

LAMBERT v. CALIFORNIA

Supreme Court of the United States, 1957.
355 U.S. 225, 78 S.Ct. 240, 2 L.Ed.2d 228.

Mr. Justice DOUGLAS delivered the opinion of the Court.

Section 52.38(a) of the Los Angeles Municipal Code defines "convicted person" as follows:

> "Any person who, subsequent to January 1, 1921, has been or hereafter is convicted of an offense punishable as a felony in the State of California, or who has been or who is hereafter convicted of any offense in any place other than the State of California, which offense, if committed in the State of California, would have been punishable as a felony."

Section 52.39 provides that it shall be unlawful for "any convicted person" to be or remain in Los Angeles for a period of more than five days without registering; it requires any person having a place of abode outside the city to register if he comes into the city on five occasions or more during a 30-day period; and it prescribes the information to be furnished the Chief of Police on registering.

Section 52.43(b) makes the failure to register a continuing offense, each day's failure constituting a separate offense.

Appellant, arrested on suspicion of another offense, was charged with a violation of this registration law. The evidence showed that she had been at the time of her arrest a resident of Los Angeles for over seven years. Within that period she had been convicted in Los Angeles of the crime of forgery, an offense which California punishes as a felony. Though convicted of a crime punishable as a felony, she had not at the time of her arrest registered under the Municipal Code.

At the trial, appellant asserted that § 52.39 of the Code denies her due process of law and other rights under the Federal Constitution, unnecessary to enumerate. The trial court denied this objection. The case was tried to a jury which found appellant guilty. The court fined her $250 and placed her on probation for three years. Appellant, renewing her constitutional objection, moved for arrest of judgment and a new trial. This motion was denied. On appeal the constitutionality of the Code was again challenged. The Appellate Department of the Superior Court affirmed the judgment, holding there was no merit to the claim that the ordinance was unconstitutional. The case is here on appeal. * * * The case having been argued and reargued, we now hold that the registration provisions of the Code as sought to be applied here violate the Due Process requirement of the Fourteenth Amendment.

The registration provision, carrying criminal penalties, applies if a person has been convicted "of an offense punishable as a felony in the State of California" or, in case he has been convicted in another State, if the offense "would have been punishable as a felony" had it been committed in California. No element of willfulness is by terms included in the ordinance nor read into it by the California court as a condition necessary for a conviction.

We must assume that appellant had no actual knowledge of the requirement that she register under this ordinance, as she offered proof of this defense which was refused. The question is whether a registration act of this character violates due process where it is applied to a person who has no actual knowledge of his duty to register, and where no showing is made of the probability of such knowledge.

We do not go with Blackstone in saying that "a vicious will" is necessary to constitute a crime, 4 Bl.Comm. 21, for conduct alone without regard to the intent of the doer is often sufficient. There is wide latitude in the lawmakers to declare an offense and to exclude elements of knowledge and diligence from its definition. * * * But we deal here with conduct that is wholly passive—mere failure to register. It is unlike the commission of acts, or the failure to act under circumstances that should alert the doer to the consequences of his deed. * * * The rule that "ignorance of the law will not excuse" is deep in our law, as is the principle that of all the powers of local government, the police power is "one of the least limitable." District of Columbia v. Brooke, 214 U.S. 138, 149, 29 S.Ct. 560, 563, 53 L.Ed. 941. On the other hand, due process places some limits on its exercise. Engrained in our concept of due process is the requirement of notice. Notice is sometimes essential so that the citizen has the chance to defend charges. Notice is required before property interests are disturbed, before assessments are made, before penalties are assessed. Notice is required in a myriad of situations where a penalty or forfeiture might be suffered for mere failure to act. [citations omitted] These cases involved only property interests in civil litigation. But the principle is equally appropriate where a person, wholly passive and unaware of any wrongdoing, is brought to the bar of justice for condemnation in a criminal case.

Registration laws are common and their range is wide. * * * Many such laws are akin to licensing statutes in that they pertain to the regulation of business activities. But the present ordinance is entirely different. Violation of its provisions is unaccompanied by any activity whatever, mere presence in the city being the test. Moreover, circumstances which might move one to inquire as to the necessity of registration are completely lacking. At most the ordinance is but a law enforcement technique designed for the convenience of law enforcement agencies through which a list of the names and addresses of felons then residing in a given community is compiled. The disclosure is merely a compilation of former convictions already publicly recorded in the jurisdiction where obtained. Nevertheless, this appellant on first becoming aware of her duty to register was given no opportunity to comply with the law and avoid its penalty, even though her default was entirely innocent. She could but suffer the consequences of the ordinance, namely, conviction with the imposition of heavy criminal penalties thereunder. We believe that actual knowledge of the duty to register or proof of the probability of such knowledge and subsequent failure to comply are necessary before a conviction under the ordinance can stand. As Holmes wrote in The Common Law, "A law which punished conduct which would not be blameworthy in the average member of the community would be too severe for that community to bear." Id., at 50. Its severity lies in the absence of an opportunity either to avoid the consequences of the law or to defend any prosecution brought under it. Where a person did not know of the duty to register and where there was no proof of the probability of such knowledge, he may not be convicted consistently with due process. Were it otherwise, the evil would be as great as it is when the law is written in print too fine to read or in a language foreign to the community.

Mr. Justice BURTON, dissents because he believes that, as applied to this appellant, the ordinance does not violate her constitutional rights.

Mr. Justice FRANKFURTER, whom Mr. Justice HARLAN and Mr. Justice WHITTAKER join, dissenting.

The present laws of the United States and of the forty-eight States are thick with provisions that command that some things not be done and others be done, although persons convicted under such provisions may have had no awareness of what the law required or that what they did was wrongdoing. The body of decisions sustaining such legislation, including innumerable registration laws, is almost as voluminous as the legislation itself. The matter is summarized in United States v. Balint, 258 U.S. 250, 252, 42 S.Ct. 301, 302, 66 L.Ed. 604: "Many instances of this are to be found in regulatory measures in the exercise of what is called the police power where the emphasis of the statute is evidently upon achievement of some social betterment rather than the punishment of the crimes as in cases of *mala in se.*"

Surely there can hardly be a difference as a matter of fairness, of hardship, or of justice, if one may invoke it, between the case of a person wholly innocent of wrongdoing, in the sense that he was not remotely conscious of violating any law, who is imprisoned for five years for conduct relating to narcotics, and the case of another person who is placed on probation for three years on condition that she pay $250, for failure, as a local resident, convicted under local law of a felony, to register under a law passed as an exercise of the State's "police power." Considerations of hardship often lead courts, naturally enough, to attribute to a statute the requirement of a certain mental element—some consciousness of wrongdoing and knowledge of the law's command—as a matter of statutory construction. Then, too, a cruelly disproportionate relation between what the law requires and the sanction for its disobedience may constitute a violation of the Eighth Amendment as a cruel and unusual punishment, and, in respect to the States, even offend the Due Process Clause of the Fourteenth Amendment.

But what the Court here does is to draw a constitutional line between a State's requirement of doing and not doing. What is this but a return to Year Book distinctions between feasance and nonfeasance—a distinction that may have significance in the evolution of common-law notions of liability, but is inadmissible as a line between constitutionality and unconstitutionality. * * *

If the generalization that underlies, and alone can justify, this decision were to be given its relevant scope, a whole volume of the United States Reports would be required to document in detail the legislation in this country that would fall or be impaired. I abstain from entering upon a consideration of such legislation, and adjudications upon it, because I feel confident that the present decision will turn out to be an isolated deviation from the strong current of precedents—a derelict on the waters of the law. Accordingly, I content myself with dissenting.

NOTE

The response of the California courts to the United States Supreme Court's decision was to grant a new trial. Mrs. Lambert sought a writ of prohibition enjoining such retrial, primarily on the ground that the Supreme Court decision held that the ordinance was invalid. The trial court refused to issue the writ and this was first reversed by the District Court of Appeal. Lambert v. Municipal Court, 334 P.2d 605 (Cal.App.1959).

Upon rehearing, however, the District Court of Appeal vacated its initial opinion and order and affirmed. Lambert v. Municipal Court, 343 P.2d 81 (Cal.App.1959). In the second opinion the court noted that the prosecution's brief asserted that the records established that Mrs. Lambert was advised by a deputy probation officer to register with the Los Angeles Police Department in accordance with the city's regulation. On appeal to the California Supreme Court, the judgment of the District Court of Appeal was reversed and the trial court was ordered to issue the writ on the authority of another case holding such municipal ordinances void as encroaching upon an area preempted by state legislation. Lambert v. Municipal Court, 53 Cal.2d 690, 349 P.2d 984, 3 Cal.Rptr. 168 (1960).

UNITED STATES v. INTERNATIONAL MINERALS & CHEMICAL CORP.

Supreme Court of the United States, 1971.
402 U.S. 558, 91 S.Ct. 1697, 29 L.Ed.2d 178.

Mr. Justice DOUGLAS delivered the opinion of the Court.

The information charged that appellee shipped sulfuric acid and hydrofluosilicic acid in interstate commerce and "did knowingly fail to show on the shipping papers the required classification of said property, to wit, Corrosive Liquid, in violation of 49 CFR 173.427."

18 U.S.C.A. § 834(a) gives the Interstate Commerce Commission power to "formulate regulations for the safe transportation" of "corrosive liquids" and 18 U.S.C.A. § 834(f) states that whoever "knowingly violates any such regulation" shall be fined or imprisoned.

Pursuant to the power granted by § 834(a) the regulatory agency promulgated the regulation already cited which reads in part:

> "Each shipper offering for transportation any hazardous material subject to the regulations in this chapter, shall describe that article on the shipping paper by the shipping name prescribed in § 172.5 of this chapter, and by the classification prescribed in § 172.4 of this chapter, and may add a further description not inconsistent therewith. Abbreviations must not be used." 49 CFR 173.427.

The District Court * * * ruled that the information did not charge a "knowing violation" of the regulation and accordingly dismissed the information, 318 F.Supp. 1335.

Here as in United States v. Freed, 401 U.S. 601, 91 S.Ct. 1112, 28 L.Ed.2d 356, which dealt with the possession of hand grenades, strict or absolute liability is not imposed; knowledge of the shipment of the dangerous materials is required. The sole and narrow question is whether "knowledge" of the regulation is also required. It is in that narrow zone that the issue of "*mens rea*" is raised; and appellee bears down hard on the provision in 18 U.S.C.A. § 834(f) that whoever "knowingly violates any such regulation" shall be fined, etc.

Boyce Motor Lines, Inc. v. United States, 342 U.S. 337, 72 S.Ct. 329, on which the District Court relied is not dispositive of the issue. It involved a regulation governing transporting explosive, inflammable liquid, and the like and required drivers to "avoid, so far as practicable, and, where feasible, by prearrangement of routes, driving into or through congested thoroughfares, places where crowds are assembled, streetcar tracks, tunnels, viaducts, and dangerous crossings." The statute punished whoever "knowingly" violated the regulation. Id., at 339, 72 S.Ct. at 330. The issue of "*mens rea*" was not raised below, the sole question turning on whether the standard of guilt was unconstitutionally vague. Id., at 340, 72 S.Ct. 330–331. In holding the statute was not void for vagueness we said:

> "The statute punishes only those who knowingly violate the Regulation. This requirement of the presence of culpable intent as a necessary element of the offense does much to destroy any force in the argument that application of the Regulation would be so unfair that it must be held invalid. That is evident from a consideration of the effect of the requirement in this case. To sustain a conviction, the Government not only must prove that petitioner could have taken another route which was both commercially practicable and appreciably safer (in its avoidance of crowded thoroughfares, etc.) than the one it did follow. It must also be shown that petitioner knew that there was such a practicable, safer route and yet deliberately took the more dangerous route through the tunnel, or that petitioner willfully neglected to exercise its duty under the Regulation to inquire into the availability of such an alternative route.
>
> * * *
>
> "In an effort to give point to its argument, petitioner asserts that there was no practicable route its trucks might have followed which did not pass through places they were required to avoid. If it is true that in the congestion surrounding the lower Hudson there was no practicable way of crossing the River which would have avoided such points of danger to a substantially greater extent than the route taken, then petitioner has not violated the Regulation. But that is plainly a matter for proof at the trial. We are not so conversant with all the routes in that area that we may, with no facts in the record before us, assume the allegations of the indictment to be false. We will not thus distort the judicial notice concept to strike down a regulation adopted only after much consultation with those affected and penalizing only those who knowingly violate its prohibition." Id., at 342–343, 72 S.Ct. at 331–332.

The "*mens rea*" that emerged in the foregoing discussion was not knowledge of the regulation but knowledge of the more safe and the less safe routes within the meaning of the regulation. * * *

We * * * see no reason why the word "regulations" should not be construed as a shorthand designation for specific acts or omissions which violate the Act. The Act, so viewed, does not signal an exception to the rule that ignorance of the law is no excuse and is wholly consistent with the legislative history.

The principle that ignorance of the law is no defense applies whether the law be a statute or a duly promulgated and published regulation. In the context of these 1960 amendments we decline to attribute to Congress the inaccurate view that that Act requires proof of knowledge of the law, as well as the facts, and intended to endorse that interpretation by retaining the word "knowingly." We conclude that the meager legislative history of the 1960 amendments makes unwarranted the conclusion that Congress abandoned the general rule and required knowledge of both the facts and the pertinent law before a criminal conviction could be sustained under this Act.

So far as possession, say, of sulfuric acid is concerned the requirement of "*mens rea*" has been made a requirement of the Act as evidenced by the use of the word "knowingly." A person thinking in good faith that he was shipping distilled water when in fact he was shipping some dangerous acid would not be covered. * * *

There is leeway for the exercise of congressional discretion in applying the reach of "*mens rea*." United States v. Balint, 258 U.S. 250, 42 S.Ct. 301, 66 L.Ed. 604. United States v. Murdock, 290 U.S. 389, 54 S.Ct. 223, 78 L.Ed. 381, closely confined the word "wilfully" in the income tax law to include a purpose to bring about the forbidden result * * *.

In *Balint* the Court was dealing with drugs, in *Freed* with hand grenades, in this case with sulfuric and other dangerous acids. Pencils, dental floss, paper clips may also be regulated. But they may be the type of products which might raise substantial due process questions if Congress did not require, as in *Murdock*, "*mens rea*" as to each ingredient of the offense. But where, as here and as in *Balint* and *Freed*, dangerous or deleterious devices or products or obnoxious waste materials are involved, the probability of regulation is so great that anyone who is aware that he is in possession of them or dealing with them must be presumed to be aware of the regulation.

Reversed.

Mr. Justice STEWART, with whom Mr. Justice HARLAN and Mr. Justice BRENNAN join, dissenting.

This case stirs large questions—questions that go to the moral foundations of the criminal law. Whether postulated as a problem of "*mens rea*," of "willfulness," of "criminal responsibility," or of "*scienter*," the infliction of criminal punishment upon the unaware has long troubled the fair administration of justice. * * * But there is no occasion here for involvement with this root problem of criminal jurisprudence, for it is evident to me that Congress made punishable only knowing violations of the regulation in question. That is what the law quite clearly says, what the federal courts have held, and what the legislative history confirms.

The statutory language is hardly complex. Section 834(a) of Title 18, U.S.C.A., gives the regulatory agency power to "formulate regulations for the safe transportation" of, among other things, "corrosive liquids." Section 834(f) provides that "[w]hoever knowingly violates any such regulation shall be fined not more than $1,000 or imprisoned not more than one year, or both." In dismissing the information in this case because it did not charge the appellee shipper with knowing violation of the applicable labeling regulation, District Judge Porter did no more than give effect to the ordinary meaning of the English language.

* * *

The Court today * * * grants to the Executive Branch what Congress explicitly refused to grant * * *. It effectively deletes the word "knowingly" from the law. I cannot join the Court in this exercise, requiring as it does such a total disregard of plain statutory language, established judicial precedent, and explicit legislative history.

A final word is in order. Today's decision will have little practical impact upon the prosecution of interstate motor carriers or institutional shippers. For interstate motor carriers are members of a regulated industry and their officers, agents, and employees are required by law to be conversant with the regulations in question. As a practical matter, therefore, they are under a species of absolute liability for violation of the regulations despite the "knowingly" requirement. This, no doubt, is as Congress intended it to be. Cf. United States v. Dotterweich, 320 U.S. 277, 64 S.Ct. 134, 88 L.Ed. 48; United States v. Balint, 258 U.S. 250, 42 S.Ct. 301, 66 L.Ed. 604. Likewise, prosecution of regular shippers for violations of the regulations could hardly be impeded by the "knowingly" requirement, for triers of fact would have no difficulty whatever in inferring knowledge on the part of those whose business it is to know, despite their protestations to the contrary. The only real impact of this decision will be upon the casual shipper, who might be any man, woman, or child in the Nation. A person who had never heard of the regulation might make a single shipment of an article covered by it in the course of a lifetime. It would be wholly natural for him to assume that he could deliver the article to the common carrier and depend upon the carrier to see that it was properly labeled and that the shipping papers were in order. Yet today's decision holds that a person who does just that is guilty of a criminal offense punishable by a year in prison. This seems to me a perversion of the purpose of criminal law.

I respectfully dissent from the opinion and judgment of the Court.

4. STATES OF MIND LESS THAN "GENERAL INTENT": THE "STRICT LIABILITY" OFFENSES

While some crimes require proof of more than "general intent," others require less. These are the so-called "strict liability" crimes. In covering the material in this subsection, consider in regard to each case whether the issue is whether any state of mind is required for guilt of the offense at issue, or rather whether there is no state of mind required concerning one or more but less than all elements of the crime. When, as a matter of policy, should legislatures dispense with the state of mind requirement, at least concerning some elements of a crime? If legislative intent is not clear, when should courts interpret a crime as imposing liability without a showing of a culpable state of mind? To what extent does the Federal Constitution preclude the imposition of such "strict liability?"

MORISSETTE v. UNITED STATES

Supreme Court of the United States, 1952.
342 U.S. 246, 72 S.Ct. 240, 96 L.Ed. 288.

Mr. Justice JACKSON delivered the opinion of the Court.

This would have remained a profoundly insignificant case to all except its immediate parties had it not been so tried and submitted to the jury as to raise questions both fundamental and far-reaching in federal criminal law, for which reason we granted certiorari.

On a large tract of uninhabited and untilled land in a wooded and sparsely populated area of Michigan, the Government established a practice bombing range over which the Air Force dropped simulated bombs at ground targets. * * * At various places about the range signs read "Danger—Keep Out—Bombing Range." Nevertheless, the range was known as good deer country and was extensively hunted.

Spent bomb casings were cleared from the targets and thrown into piles "so that they will be out of the way." They were not stacked or piled in any order but were dumped in heaps, some of which had been accumulating for four years or upwards, were exposed to the weather and rusting away.

Morissette, in December of 1948, went hunting in this area but did not get a deer. He thought to meet expenses of the trip by salvaging some of these casings. He loaded three tons of them on his truck and took them to a nearby farm, where they were flattened by driving a tractor over them. After expending this labor and trucking them to market in Flint, he realized $84.

Morissette, by occupation, is a fruit stand operator in summer and a trucker and scrap iron collector in winter. An honorably discharged veteran of World War II, he enjoys a good name among his neighbors and has had no blemish on his record more disreputable than a conviction for reckless driving.

The loading, crushing and transporting of these casings were all in broad daylight, in full view of passers-by, without the slightest effort at concealment When an investigation was started, Morissette voluntarily, promptly and candidly told the whole story to the authorities, saying that he had no intention of stealing but thought the property was abandoned, unwanted and considered of no value to the Government. He was indicted, however, on the charge that he "did unlawfully, wilfully and knowingly steal and convert" property of the United States of the value of $84, in violation of 18 U.S.C. § 641, 18 U.S.C.A. § 641, which provides that "whoever embezzles, steals, purloins, or knowingly converts" government property is punishable by fine and imprisonment. Morissette was convicted and sentenced to imprisonment for two months or to pay a fine of $200. The Court of Appeals affirmed, one judge dissenting.

On his trial, Morissette, as he had at all times told investigating officers, testified that from appearances he believed the casings were cast-off and abandoned, that he did not intend to steal the property, and took it with no wrongful or criminal intent. * * * The court stated: "I will not permit you to show this man thought it was abandoned. * * * I hold in this case that there is no question of abandoned property." The court refused to submit or to allow counsel to argue to the jury whether Morissette acted with innocent intention. It charged: "* * * That if this young man took this property (and he says he did), without any permission (he says he did), that was on the property of the United States Government (he says it was), that it was of the value of one cent or more (and evidently it was), that he is guilty of the offense charged here. If you believe the government, he is guilty. * * * The question on intent is whether or not he intended to take the property. He says he did. Therefore, if you believe either side, he is guilty." Petitioner's counsel contended "But the taking must have been with a felonious intent." The court ruled, however: "That is presumed by his own act."

The Court of Appeals * * * ruled that this particular offense requires no element of criminal intent. This conclusion was thought to be required by the failure of Congress to express such a requisite and this Court's decisions in United States v. Behrman, 258 U.S. 280, 42 S.Ct. 303, 66 L.Ed. 619, and United States v. Balint, 258 U.S. 250, 42 S.Ct. 301, 66 L.Ed. 604.

I.

In those cases this Court did construe mere omission from a criminal enactment of any mention of criminal intent as dispensing with it. If they be deemed precedents for principles of construction generally applicable to federal penal statutes, they authorize this conviction. Indeed, such adoption of the literal reasoning announced in those cases would do this and more—it would sweep out of all federal crimes, except when expressly preserved, the ancient requirement of a culpable state of mind. We think a résumé of their historical background is convincing that an effect has been ascribed to them more comprehensive than was contemplated and one inconsistent with our philosophy of criminal law.

The contention that an injury can amount to a crime only when inflicted by intention is no provincial or transient notion. It is as universal and persistent in mature systems of law as belief in freedom of the human will and a consequent ability and duty of the normal individual to choose between good and evil. A relation between some mental element and punishment for a harmful act is almost as instinctive as the child's familiar exculpatory "But I didn't mean to," and has afforded the rational basis for a tardy and unfinished substitution of deterrence and reformation in place of retaliation and vengeance as the motivation for public prosecution. Unqualified acceptance of this doctrine by English common law in the Eighteenth Century was indicated by Blackstone's sweeping statement that to constitute any crime there must first be a "vicious will." * * *

Crime, as a compound concept, generally constituted only from concurrence of an evil-meaning mind with an evil-doing hand, was congenial to an intense individualism and took deep and early root in American soil. As the states codified the common law of crimes, even if their enactments were silent on the subject, their courts assumed that the omission did not signify disapproval of the principle but merely recognized that intent was so inherent in the idea of the offense that it required no statutory affirmation. Courts, with little hesitation or division, found an implication of the requirement as to offenses that were taken over from the common law. The unanimity with which they have adhered to the central thought that wrongdoing must be conscious to be criminal is emphasized by the variety, disparity and confusion of their definitions of the requisite but elusive mental element. However, courts of various jurisdictions, and for the purposes of different offenses, have devised working formulae, if not scientific ones, for the instruction of juries around such terms as "felonious intent," "criminal intent," "malice aforethought," "guilty knowledge," "fraudulent intent," "wilfulness," *"scienter,"* to denote guilty knowledge, or *"mens rea,"* to signify an evil purpose or mental culpability. By use or combination of these various tokens, they have sought to protect those who were not blameworthy in mind from conviction of infamous common-law crimes.

However, the Balint and Behrman offenses belong to a category of another character, with very different antecedents and origins. The crimes there involved depend on no mental element but consist only of forbidden acts or omissions. This, while not expressed by the Court, is made clear from examination of a century-old but accelerating tendency, discernible both here and in England, to call into existence new duties and crimes which disregard any ingredient of intent. The industrial revolution multiplied the number of workmen exposed to injury from increasingly powerful and complex mechanisms, driven by freshly discovered sources of energy, requiring higher precautions by employers. Traffic of velocities, volumes and varieties unheard of came to subject the wayfarer to intolerable casualty risks if owners and drivers were not to observe new cares and uniformities of conduct. Congestion of cities and crowding of quarters called for health and welfare regulations undreamed of in simpler times. Wide distribution of goods became an instrument of wide distribution of harm when those who dispersed food, drink, drugs, and even securities, did not comply with reasonable standards of quality, integrity, disclosure and care. Such dangers have engendered increasingly numerous and detailed regulations which heighten the duties of those in control of particular industries, trades, properties or activities that affect public health, safety or welfare.

While many of these duties are sanctioned by a more strict civil liability,[13] lawmakers, whether wisely or not,[14] have sought to make

13. The development of strict criminal liability regardless of intent has been roughly paralleled by an evolution of a strict civil liability for consequences regardless of fault in certain relationships, as shown by Workmen's Compensation Acts, and by vicarious liability for fault of others as evidenced by various Motor Vehicle Acts.

14. Consequences of a general abolition of intent as an ingredient of serious crimes have aroused the concern of responsible and disinterested students of penology. Of course, they would not justify judicial disregard of a clear command to that effect from Congress, but they do admonish us to caution in assuming that Congress, without clear expression, intends in any instance to do so.

Radin, Intent, Criminal, 8 Encyc.Soc.Sci. 126, 130, says, "* * * as long as in popular belief intention and the freedom of the will are taken as axiomatic, no penal system that negates the mental element can find general acceptance. It is vital to retain public support of methods of dealing with crime." * * *

Sayre, Public Welfare Offenses, 33 Col. L.Rev. 55, 56, says: "To inflict substantial punishment upon one who is morally entirely innocent, who caused injury through reasonable mistake or pure accident, would so outrage the feelings of the community as to nullify its own enforcement."

Hall, Prolegomena to a Science of Criminal Law, 89 U. of Pa.L.Rev. 549, 569, appears somewhat less disturbed by the trend, if properly limited, but, as to so-called public welfare crimes, suggests that "There is no reason to continue to believe that the present mode of dealing with these offenses is the best solution obtainable, or that we must be content with this sacrifice of established principles. *The raising of a presumption of knowledge might be an improvement.*" (Italics added.)

* * *

such regulations more effective by invoking criminal sanctions to be applied by the familiar technique of criminal prosecutions and convictions. This has confronted the courts with a multitude of prosecutions, based on statutes or administrative regulations, for what have been aptly called "public welfare offenses." These cases do not fit neatly into any of such accepted classifications of common-law offenses, such as those against the state, the person, property, or public morals. Many of these offenses are not in the nature of positive aggressions or invasions, with which the common law so often dealt, but are in the nature of neglect where the law requires care, or inaction where it imposes a duty. Many violations of such regulations result in no direct or immediate injury to person or property but merely create the danger or probability of it which the law seeks to minimize. While such offenses do not threaten the security of the state in the manner of treason, they may be regarded as offenses against its authority, for their occurrence impairs the efficiency of controls deemed essential to the social order as presently constituted. In this respect, whatever the intent of the violator, the injury is the same, and the consequences are injurious or not according to fortuity. Hence, legislation applicable to such offenses, as a matter of policy, does not specify intent as a necessary element. The accused, if he does not will the violation, usually is in a position to prevent it with no more care than society might reasonably expect and no more exertion than it might reasonably exact from one who assumed his responsibilities. Also, penalties commonly are relatively small, and conviction does no grave damage to an offender's reputation. Under such considerations, courts have turned to construing statutes and regulations which make no mention of intent as dispensing with it and holding that the guilty act alone makes out the crime. This has not, however, been without expressions of misgiving.

* * *

After the turn of the Century, a new use for crimes without intent appeared when New York enacted numerous and novel regulations of tenement houses, sanctioned by money penalties. Landlords contended that a guilty intent was essential to establish a violation. Judge Cardozo wrote the answer: "The defendant asks us to test the meaning of this statute by standards applicable to statutes that govern infamous crimes. The analogy, however, is deceptive. The element of conscious wrongdoing, the guilty mind accompanying the guilty act, is associated with the concept of crimes that are punished as infamous. * * * Even there it is not an invariable element. * * * But in the prosecution of minor offenses there is a wider range of practice and of power. Prosecutions for petty penalties have always constituted in our law a class by themselves. * * * That is true, though the prosecution is criminal in form." Tenement House Department of City of New York v. McDevitt, 1915, 215 N.Y. 160, 168, 109 N.E. 88, 90.

Soon, employers advanced the same contention as to violations of regulations prescribed by a new labor law. Judge Cardozo, again for the court, pointed out, as a basis for penalizing violations whether intentional or not, that they were punishable only by fine "moderate in amount", but cautiously added that in sustaining the power so to fine unintended violations "we are not to be understood as sustaining to a like length the power to imprison. We leave that question open." People ex rel. Price v. Sheffield Farms-Slawson-Decker Co., 1918, 225 N.Y. 25, 32–33, 121 N.E. 474, 476, 477.

* * *

Before long, similar questions growing out of federal legislation reached this Court. Its judgments were in harmony with this consensus of state judicial opinion, the existence of which may have led the Court to overlook the need for full exposition of their rationale in the context of federal law. In overruling a contention that there can be no conviction on an indictment which makes no charge of criminal intent but alleges only making of a sale of a narcotic forbidden by law, Chief Justice Taft, wrote: "While the general rule at common law was that the *scienter* was a necessary element in the indictment and proof of every crime, and this was followed in regard to statutory crimes even where the statutory definition did not in terms include it * * *, there has been a modification of this view in respect to prosecutions under statutes the purpose of which would be obstructed by such a requirement. It is a question of legislative intent to be construed by the court. * * *" United States v. Balint, supra, 258 U.S. 251–252, 42 S.Ct. 302.

* * *

Of course, the purpose of every statute would be "obstructed" by requiring a finding of intent, if we assume that it had a purpose to convict without it. Therefore, the obstruction rationale does not help us to learn the purpose of the omission by Congress. * * *

* * *

Neither this Court nor, so far as we are aware, any other has undertaken to delineate a precise line or set forth comprehensive criteria for distinguishing between crimes that require a mental element and crimes that do not. We attempt no closed definition, for the law on the subject is neither settled nor static. The conclusion reached in the Balint and Behrman cases has our approval and adherence for the circumstances to which it was there applied. A quite different question here is whether we will expand the doctrine of crimes without intent to include those charged here.

Stealing, larceny, and its variants and equivalents, were among the earliest offenses known to the law that existed before legislation; they are invasions of rights of property which stir a sense of insecurity in the whole community and arouse public demand for retribution, the penalty is high and, when a sufficient amount is involved, the infamy is that of a felony, which, says Maitland, is "* * * as bad a word as you can give to man or thing." State courts of last resort, on whom fall the heaviest burden of interpreting criminal law in this country, have consistently retained the requirement of intent in larceny-type offenses. If any state has deviated, the exception has neither been called to our attention nor disclosed by our research.

Congress, therefore, omitted any express prescription of criminal intent from the enactment before us in the light of an unbroken course of judicial decision in all constituent states of the Union holding intent inherent in this class of offense, even when not expressed in a statute. Congressional silence as to mental elements in an Act merely adopting into federal statutory law a concept of crime already so well defined in common law and statutory interpretation by the states may warrant quite contrary inferences than the same silence in creating an offense new to general law, for whose definition the courts have no guidance except the Act. Because the offenses before this Court in the Balint and Behrman cases were of this latter class, we cannot accept them as authority for eliminating intent from offenses incorporated from the common law. * * *

The Government asks us by a feat of construction radically to change the weights and balances in the scales of justice. The purpose and obvious effect of doing away with the requirement of a guilty intent is to ease the prosecution's path to conviction, to strip the defendant of such benefit as he derived at common law from innocence of evil purpose, and to circumscribe the freedom heretofore allowed juries. Such a manifest impairment of the immunities of the individual should not be extended to common-law crimes on judicial initiative.

The spirit of the doctrine which denies to the federal judiciary power to create crimes forthrightly admonishes that we should not enlarge the reach of enacted crimes by constituting them from anything less than the incriminating components contemplated by the words used in the statute. And where Congress borrows terms of art in which are accumulated the legal tradition and meaning of centuries of practice, it presumably knows and adopts the cluster of ideas that were attached to each borrowed word in the body of learning from which it was taken and the meaning its use will convey to the judicial mind unless otherwise instructed. In such case, absence of contrary direction may be taken as satisfaction with widely accepted definitions, not as a departure from them.

We hold that mere omission from § 641 of any mention of intent will not be construed as eliminating that element from the crimes denounced.

* * *

III.

As we read the record, this case was tried on the theory that even if criminal intent were essential its presence (a) should be decided by the court (b) as a presumption of law, apparently conclusive, (c) predicated upon the isolated act of taking rather than upon all of the circumstances. In each of these respects we believe the trial court was in error.

NOTES AND QUESTIONS

1. The Supreme Court has addressed itself to the question of the necessity for the state of mind element on a number of occasions since *Morissette*. Three are of particular interest.

In United States v. Park, 421 U.S. 658, 95 S.Ct. 1903, 44 L.Ed.2d 489 (1975), the defendant, president of a major supermarket chain, was charged with violating the Federal Food, Drug and Cosmetic Act because the firm's warehouse contained rats which resulted in the introduction into interstate commerce of contaminated food. He was convicted by a jury which, over defendant's objection, was instructed, in effect, that it was to find him guilty if he "had a responsible relation to the situation, even though he may not have participated personally * * * [and] did not consciously do wrong" and "by virtue of his position * * * had * * * authority and responsibility to deal with the situation." Defendant was fined $50 on each of five counts.

Relying on the nature and purpose of the statute, the Supreme Court held, 6–3, that this did not offend the Constitution. The only defense permitted such a defendant, said the Court, was to produce evidence that he was powerless to prevent or correct the violation.

Mr. Park was faced with minor penalties in the context of a business in which he was a knowledgeable and responsible actor. However, in United States v. Freed, 401 U.S. 601, 91 S.Ct. 1112, 28 L.Ed.2d 356 (1971) the defendants were subject to penalties of a $10,000 fine and imprisonment for ten years for possessing hand grenades not registered under the National Firearms Act. The issue was whether there was a *mens rea* requirement with respect to the fact of registration. Mr. Justice Douglas, for the Court, wrote that there was a continuum of statutes posing this issue, from the larceny provision in *Morissette* with its common law history of *mens rea* to that in *Lambert* where there was nothing about the defendant's conduct which would have given notice of a duty to act. The Firearms Act was said to pose neither difficulty to the imposition of strict liability. It was a regulatory measure, akin to the statute in *Balint*, and "premised on the theory that one would hardly be surprised to learn that possession of hand grenades is not an innocent act." Should it matter whether Freed was a gun dealer or a one-time purchaser?

The conviction in *Freed* required proof beyond a reasonable doubt of a mental element with respect to the fact of possession and the item possessed. Moreover, the statute, despite its substantial penalties, closely resembled other regulatory or public welfare offenses. This was arguably not the case in United States v. Feola, 420 U.S. 671, 95 S.Ct. 1255, 43 L.Ed.2d 541 (1975), where the defendants had agreed to sell heroin to their victims but intended to substitute a form of sugar for the drug. If the ruse failed, they intended to simply rob the buyer of the purchase money. During the transaction, a fight broke out and the victims—who turned out to be undercover agents of the Bureau of Narcotics and Dangerous Drugs—arrested the defendants. The defendants were charged with assault upon federal officers, under 18 U.S.C.A. § 111. At trial, the trial court instructed the jury that in order to convict the defendants, it was not necessary to find that at the time of the assault the defendants were aware that the victims were federal officers. In considering the propriety of this interpretation of the statute, the Supreme Court saw the issue as related to the purpose of the crime:

> If the primary purpose is to protect federal law enforcement personnel, that purpose could well be frustrated by the imposition of a strict scienter requirement. On the other hand, if § 111 is seen primarily as an anti-obstruction statute [intended to prevent hinderance to the execution of federal duties and to protect federal officers only as incidental to that aim] it is likely that Congress intended criminal liability to be imposed only when a person acted with the specific intent to impede enforcement activities.

420 U.S. at 678, 95 S.Ct. at 1261, 43 L.Ed.2d at 549. After reviewing the legislative history of the statute, the Court concluded that Congress intended the statute to serve both purposes. It then reasoned that the Congressional purpose of giving federal officers maximum protection by making prosecutions for assault upon such officers cognizable in federal courts precluded an interpretation of the statute that would require awareness that the victim of the assault was a federal officer. "A contrary conclusion," the Court explained, "would give insufficient protection to the agent enforcing an unpopular law, and none to the agent acting under cover." 420 U.S. at 684, 95 S.Ct. at 1264, 43 L.Ed.2d at 553. Defending this result on policy grounds, the Court continued:

> This interpretation poses no risk of unfairness to defendants. It is no snare for the unsuspecting. Although the perpetrator of a narcotics 'rip-off', such as the one involved here, may be surprised to find that his intended victim is a federal officer in civilian apparel, he nonetheless knows from the very outset that his planned course of conduct is wrongful. The situation is not one where legitimate conduct becomes unlawful solely because of the identity of the individual or agency affected. In a case of this kind the offender takes the victim as he finds him. The concept of criminal intent does not extend so far as to require that the actor understand not only the nature of his act but also its consequences for the choice of a judicial forum.

420 U.S. at 685, 95 S.Ct. at 1264, 43 L.Ed.2d at 553. The defendants were also convicted of conspiracy to assault federal officers; the Supreme Court's treatment of the state of mind required for the conspiracy charge was to reject any requirement of knowledge of the victims' status as officers.

2. Is "strict liability" appropriate or defensible in regard to those "regulatory offenses" as to which it has traditionally been imposed? Con-

sider the following comments from Mueller, Mens Rea and the Law Without It, 58 W.Va.L.Rev. 34, 37–38, 50, 59–60 (1955):

> The reasons for * * * [imposing strict liability in regard to such offenses] have been variously stated: If "mens rea" were required, (1) the enforcement of the statute would be impeded; or (2) the courts would be overburdened; or (3) justice would be hampered; or (4) fraudulent defenses could be fabricated, etc. Prima facie such claims can be just as easily made as refuted. The often stated reason here listed under (1), for instance, seems to be nothing more than a * * * "because", and proves no more.
>
> (2) supra, is a little more specific. It is certainly true that there is hardly any aspect of human activity which has escaped control by the law. When we eat, the (pure food and drug) law eats with us; when we walk, the (traffic) law walks with us; and even the health and soundness of our sleep is regulated by law. To litigate every one of the regulated problems of daily life would surely hamper the administration of justice. But what good will it do to punish indiscriminately, regardless of guilt or innocence, merely to save the time it would take to determine the validity of a defense? And what of the deterrent effect of such a frustrating law? Would it not ease the burden on the court and reduce the length of the court calendar much more if, for instance, in January we would prosecute only blond culprits, in February only bald ones, in March brunettes, etc.? That would at least deter some of the culprits some of the time, whereas absolute criminal liability is totally without deterrent effect. * * *
>
> *Ad* (3) it might be answered that absolute criminal liability surely is not the vehicle to unhamper criminal justice. If anything, it does away with justice altogether by distributing penalties indiscriminately. *Ad* (4) it will suffice to ask: what crime is there which is not subject to the interposition of fraudulent defenses? Surely the temptation for tricking one's way out of a jam is much greater in crimes threatening serious consequences than it is in petty offenses.
>
> * * *
>
> [It has been feared that the enforcement of the regulatory schemes would bog down if strict liability were not imposed.]
>
> Now then, how can a law deter anybody which inflicts punishment for the mere doing of the outward act? Is it not manifest that a law which punishes without caring about the factual and moral blamelessness of a defendant thereby frustrates him and the community at large? Why should the citizen bother to use care if the courts do not bother whether or not he used care, inflicting punishment in any event? Punishment which befalls the innocent and the guilty alike, like hay fever, hail or hurricane, can have no good effect at all, except perhaps for insurance companies, for whom it creates a new insurable interest.
>
> * * *

[It has also been argued that unless strict liability were imposed, "many unscrupulous persons would not hesitate to fabricate such facts as would be needful to accomplish" the assertion of a defense of mistake of fact.]

The ease of manufacturing surreptitious or fraudulent defenses is, as any lawyer knows, not confined to such cases. * * * Since the temptation to fabricate defenses is even greater in prosecutions in which the stakes are higher, for instance in murder prosecutions, why then not dispense with "mens rea" altogether and make every act, e. g., the killing of a human being, conclusive evidence of a criminal intent to do the act, e. g., killing a human being conclusive evidence of a criminal intent, thus murder?

* * * All other arguments in favor of absolute criminal liability failing, it has sometimes been reasoned that the raising of issues in defense of regulatory violations would require dealing with collateral and irrelevant issues. Hence, too much time, in proportion to the slightness of the offense, would have to be devoted to the matter if the defendant were permitted to present an elaborate defense, or, indeed, any defense. It has been said that courts would never be able to clear their calendars if in this vast mass of petty offenses a judge, or a jury, were to try all defensive facts. Speediness of "justice" is said to be the compelling reason for absolute criminal liability.

If this were truly the only, or major, reason for resort to absolute criminal liability, then it would be sheer folly to dispense with the "mens rea" and nevertheless to consider all defensive arguments for the purpose of possibly mitigating the punishment * * *. Of course, this only goes to show that the "speediness of justice" argument is absurd. The choice does not lie between speedy justice and slow justice, but between speedy injustice and justice of whatever celerity we can achieve by whatever court reform may be necessary. Justice ought to be speedy, but absolute criminal liability is not apt to achieve it.

* * *

[It has also been argued in support of strict liability that "as the penalty is slight, no great injustice is perpetrated by enforcing this type of statute regardless of knowledge".]

Are we compelled to prefer small injustice over justice? I do not think that the writer regarded this point as a major reason for the imposition of absolute criminal liability. But even as collateral support it fails miserably. Such reasoning may be appropriate in a country where absolutism and dictatorial utility sacrifice life, liberty and property to the Moloch state, but not here.

For a very different view see the excellent student Note, Criminal Liability Without Fault: A Philosophical Perspective, 75 Columb.L.Rev. 1517 (1975).

3. Despite judicial hostility towards "strict" liability for other than "public welfare" offenses one area in which the absence of mens rea has long been accepted is that of morals offenses such as bigamy and statutory

rape. For example, intercourse with a female below the age of consent has been defined as criminal without regard to the reasonableness of the defendant's belief that his willing partner was of age. Thus, we may say that statutory rape is a "strict" liability offense insofar as no state of mind need be shown by the prosecution on the element of the female's age, nor can the defendant offer evidence on that point. This view has come under challenge in recent years and was rejected in State v. Guest, 583 P.2d 836 (Alaska 1978) which is reprinted at page 443, infra. A more complete discussion of this issue is found in *Guest* and the note which follows it.

4. As mentioned in note 3 above, bigamy has often been regarded as imposing strict liability in regard to that element requiring proof of the existence of a prior spouse. But see the California Supreme Court's decision to the contrary in People v. Vogel, 46 Cal.2d 798, 299 P.2d 850 (1956). The Supreme Court seems to have approved, or at least not disapproved. See Williams v. North Carolina, 325 U.S. 226, 238, 65 S.Ct. 1092, 1099, 89 L.Ed. 1577 (1945). However, many bigamy statutes provide for a defense consisting of proof that the prior spouse had been absent for a specified number of years during which time the defendant had no knowledge that the spouse was alive.

5. For discussions of "strict" liability offenses, see Starrs, The Regulatory Offense in Historical Perspective, in Essays in Criminal Science (G. Mueller ed. 1961); Packer, Mens Rea and the Supreme Court, 1962 Sup.Ct.Rev. 107; Moore, Bigamy, A Crime Though Unwittingly Committed, 30 U.Cinn.L.Rev. 35 (1961); Borre, Public Welfare Offenses: A New Approach, 52 J.Crim.L.C. & P.S. 418 (1961); Sayre, Public Welfare Offenses, 33 Colum.L.Rev. 55 (1933); Wasserstrom, Strict Liability in the Criminal Law, 12 Stan.L.Rev. 731 (1960); Comment, Liability Without Fault: Logic and Potential of a Developing Concept, 1970 Wis.L.Rev. 1201.

5. "DEFENSES" CONSISTING OF "DISPROOF" OF STATE OF MIND

Perhaps the major importance of the state of mind requirements is not the burden they impose upon the prosecution in making out the basic case against defendants but rather the opportunity they provide for defendants to persuade judges and juries that the required states of mind were in fact lacking. As Lord Hailsham notes in *Morgan* (see page 186, infra), matters such as this are not "defenses" in the normal sense of that word, because the burden remains on the prosecution to establish the existence of the required state of mind. But consider the possibility that as a practical matter, the burden is on the defense to persuade the trier of fact that the defendant did not have the state of mind that a reasonable person would have had under the circumstances.

This subsection deals with three matters: ignorance or mistake concerning matters of "fact," ignorance or mistake concerning "law," and intoxication. Given the general requirement that crimes require a culpable state of mind and in the absence of any specific doctrine applicable to mistake, ignorance or intoxication, a defendant can obviously challenge the sufficiency of the prosecution's evidence on the basis that the facts considered as a whole, including any proof tending to show ignorance, mistake, or intoxication, does not prove beyond a reasonable doubt that the defendant acted with the requisite state of mind. This approach to some extent limits defendants' ability to use these "defenses" to escape liability. For example, ignorance or mistake of law are in theory, unavailing with respect to a strict liability crime inasmuch as there is no mental state to be negated. Should they be? Is this treatment consistent with the requirements of due process?

Current law sometimes imposes additional limits upon the ability of defendants to use the opportunities provided by this approach. Intoxication is sometimes excluded from consideration entirely, although more commonly its use is limited to "specific intent" crimes. A mistake of fact may be given effect only if it is reasonable. Consider the desirability of these limits. Should defendants be convicted if the prosecution's proof fails to establish the state of mind required for the crime, if it is clear that the reason the defendant lacked the requisite state of mind was because of an unreasonable mistake of fact or voluntary intoxication?

Might it be desirable to create opportunities for a defendant to use mistake or intoxication defensively even if there is no question that the prosecution can prove that the necessary state of mind existed? For example, should a defendant be entitled to acquittal because he mistakenly believed that his actions were not in violation of the criminal law, if he establishes that this mistake was based upon what appears to be an extraordinarily reasonable basis? The query is answered affirmatively by section 2.04(3) of the Model Penal Code, reprinted at page 251, infra.]

a. IGNORANCE OR MISTAKE OF FACT

MODEL PENAL CODE *

(Proposed Official Draft, 1962).

Section 2.04. Ignorance or Mistake

(1) Ignorance or mistake as to a matter of fact or law is a defense if:

(a) the ignorance or mistake negatives the purpose, knowledge, belief, recklessness or negligence required to establish a material element of the offense; or

(b) the law provides that the state of mind established by such ignorance or mistake constitutes a defense.

(2) Although ignorance or mistake would otherwise afford a defense to the offense charged, the defense is not available if the defendant would be guilty of another offense had the situation been as he supposed. In such case, however, the ignorance or mistake of the defendant shall reduce the grade and degree of the offense of which he may be convicted to those of the offense of which he would be guilty had the situation been as he supposed.

(3) A belief that conduct does not legally constitute an offense is a defense to a prosecution for that offense based upon such conduct when:

(a) the statute or other enactment defining the offense is not known to the actor and has not been published or otherwise reasonably made available prior to the conduct alleged; or

(b) he acts in reasonable reliance upon an official statement of the law, afterward determined to be invalid or erroneous, contained in (i) a statute or other enactment; (ii) a judicial decision, opinion or judgment; (iii) an administrative order or grant of permission; or (iv) an official interpretation of the public officer or body charged by law with responsibility for the interpretation, administration or enforcement of the law defining the offense.

(4) The defendant must prove a defense arising under Subsection (3) of this Section by a preponderance of evidence.

DIRECTOR OF PUBLIC PROSECUTIONS v. MORGAN

House of Lords, 1975.
2 All ER 347.

LORD HAILSHAM OF ST MARYLEBONE. * * * This appeal is concerned with the mental element in rape. It involves two questions at vastly different levels of importance but each strangely illustrative of the other, which were argued before us. The first is a question of great academic importance in the theory of English criminal law, certified for this House by the Court of Appeal, which also gave leave to appeal. The second, which arises only if the first is answered favourably to the appellants, is whether the House can be satisfied that no miscarriage of justice has taken place so as to compel them to apply the proviso to s 2(1) of the Criminal Appeal Act 1968. As I propose to answer these two questions, as to the first favourably, and as the second, unfavourably to the appellants, and thus dismiss the appeals, I will begin this opinion with the facts.

The four appellants were all convicted at the Stafford Crown Court of various offences connected with alleged rapes on the person of Daphne Ethel Morgan of whom the first appellant is, or at the material time was, the husband. The second, third and fourth appellants were convicted each of a principal offence against Mrs. Morgan, and each of aiding and abetting the principal offences alleged to have been committed by each of the other two. The appellant Morgan, who also had connection with his wife allegedly without her consent as part of the same series of events, was not charged with rape, the prosecution evidently accepting and applying the ancient common law doctrine that a husband cannot be guilty of raping his own wife. Morgan was therefore charged with and convicted of aiding and abetting the rapes alleged to have been committed by the other three.

* * * The question certified * * * is:

> "Whether, in rape, the defendant can properly be convicted notwithstanding that he in fact believed that the woman consented if such belief was not based on reasonable grounds."

The question arises in the following way. The appellant Morgan and his three coappellants, who were all members of the RAF, spent the evening of 15th August 1973 in one another's company. The appellant Morgan was significantly older than the other three, and considerably senior to them in rank. He was, as I have said, married to the alleged victim, but not, it seems, at the time habitually sleeping in the same bed. At this time, Mrs. Morgan occupied a single bed in the same room as her younger son aged about 11 years, and by the time the appellants arrived at Morgan's house, Mrs. Morgan was already in bed and asleep, until she was awoken by their presence.

According to the version of the facts which she gave in evidence, and which was evidently accepted by the jury, she was aroused from her sleep, frog-marched into another room where there was a double bed, held by each of her limbs, arms and legs apart, by the four appellants, while each of the three young appellants in turn had intercourse with her in the presence of the others, during which time the other two committed various lewd acts on various parts of her body. When each had finished and had left the room, the appellant Morgan completed the series of incidents by having intercourse with her himself.

According to Mrs. Morgan she consented to none of this and made her opposition to what was being done very plain indeed. In her evidence to the court, she said that her husband was the first to seize her and pull her out of bed. She then "yelled" to the little boy who was sleeping with her to call the police, and later, when the elder boy came out on the landing, she called to him also to get the police, and "screamed". Her assailants, however, covered her face and pinched her nose, until she begged them to let her breathe. She was held, wrists and feet, "dragged" to the neighbouring room, put on the bed where the various incidents occurred. At this stage she was overcome by fear of "being hit". There was never a time when her body was free from being held. When it was all over she grabbed her coat, ran out of the house, drove straight to the hospital and immediately complained to the staff of having been raped. This last fact was fully borne out by evidence from the hospital.

In their evidence in court, the appellants made various damaging admissions which certainly amounted to some corroboration of all this. They admitted that some degree of struggle took place in the bedroom, that Mrs. Morgan made some noise which was forcibly suppressed, and that she was carried out forcibly into the other bedroom, and that her arms and legs were separately held. In addition to this, Mrs. Morgan's evidence was far more fully corroborated by a number of statements (each, of course, admissible only against the maker) which virtually repeated Mrs. Morgan's own story but in far greater and more lurid detail. Of course, the appellants repudiated their statements in the witness box, saying that the words were put into their mouths by the police, even though at least one was written out in the hand of the maker of the statement. * * * I mention all these details simply to show, that if, as I think plain, the jury accepted Mrs. Morgan's statement *in substance* there was no possibility whatever of any of the appellants holding any belief whatever, reasonable or otherwise, in their victim's consent to what was being done.

The primary "defence" was consent. I use the word "defence" in inverted commas, because, of course, in establishing the crime of rape, the prosecution must exclude consent in order to establish the essential ingredients of the crime. There is no burden at the outset on the accused to raise the issue. Nevertheless, at the close of the prosecution case the appellants had a formidable case to answer, and they answered by going into the witness box and swearing to facts which, if accepted, would have meant, not merely that they reasonably believed that Mrs. Morgan had consented, but that, after she entered the bedroom where the acts of intercourse took place, she not merely consented but took an active and enthusiastic part in a sexual orgy which might have excited unfavourable comment in the courts of Caligula or Nero.

All four appellants explained in the witness box that they had spent the evening together in Wolverhampton, and by the time of the alleged offences had had a good deal to drink. Their original intention had been to find some women in the town but, when this failed, Morgan made the surprising suggestion to the others that they should all return to his home and have sexual intercourse with his wife. According to the three younger appellants (but not according to Morgan who described this part of their story as "lying") Morgan told them that they must not be surprised if his wife struggled a bit, since she was "kinky" and this was the only way in which she could get "turned on". However this may be, it is clear that Morgan did invite his three companions home in order that they might have sexual intercourse with his wife and, no doubt, he may well have led them in one way or another to believe that she would consent to their doing so. This, however, would only be matter predisposing them to believe that Mrs. Morgan consented, and would not in any way establish that, at the time, they believed she did consent whilst they were having intercourse.

I need not enter into the details of what the appellants said happened after they had arrived at the house. As I have said they admitted that some degree of struggle took place in the wife's bedroom. But all asserted that after she got into the double bedroom she not merely consented to but actively co-operated with and enjoyed what was being done. * * *

* * * The learned judge said:

> "* * * The crime of rape consists in having unlawful sexual intercourse with a woman without her consent and by force. By force. Those words mean exactly what they say. It does not mean there has to be a fight or blows have to be inflicted. It means that there has to be some violence used against the woman to overbear her will or that there has to be a threat of violence as a result of which her will is overborne. * * * Further, the prosecution have to prove that each defendant intended to have sexual intercourse with this woman without her consent. * * * Therefore if the defendant believed or may have believed that Mrs. Morgan consented to him having sexual intercourse with her, then there would be no such intent in his mind and he would be not guilty of the offence of rape, but such a belief must be honestly held by the defendant in the first place. He must really believe that. And, secondly, his belief must be a reasonable belief; such a belief as a reasonable man would entertain if he applied his mind and thought about the matter. It is not enough for a defendant to rely upon a belief, even though he honestly held it, if it was completely fanciful; contrary to every indication which could be given which would carry some weight with a reasonable man. * * *"

It is on the second proposition about the mental element that the appellants concentrate their criticism. An honest belief in consent, they contend, is enough. It matters not whether it be also reasonable. No doubt a defendant will wish to raise argument or lead evidence to show that this belief was reasonable, since this will support its honesty. No doubt the prosecution will seek to cross-examine or raise arguments or adduce evidence to undermine the contention that the belief is reasonable, because, in the nature of the case, the fact that a belief cannot reasonably be held is a strong ground for saying that it was not in fact held honestly at all. Nonetheless, the appellants contend, the crux of the matter, the factum probandum, or rather the fact to be refuted by the prosecution, is honesty and not honesty plus reasonableness. In making reasonableness as well as honesty an ingredient in this "defence" the judge, say the appellants, was guilty of a misdirection.

My first comment on this direction is that the propositions described "in the first place" and "secondly" in the above direction as to the mental ingredient in rape are wholly irreconcilable. * * * If it be true, as the learned judge says "in the first place", that the prosecution have to prove that "each defendant intended to have sexual intercourse without her consent. Not merely that he intended to have intercourse with her but that he intended to have intercourse without her consent", the defendant must be entitled to an acquittal if the prosecution fail to prove just that. The necessary mental ingredient will be lacking and the only possible verdict is "not guilty". If, on the other hand, as is asserted in the passage beginning "secondly", it is necessary for any belief in the woman's consent to be "a reasonable belief" before the defendant is entitled to an acquittal, it must either be because the mental ingredient in rape is not "to have intercourse and to have it without her consent" but simply "to have intercourse" subject to a special defence of "honest and reasonable belief", or alternatively to have intercourse without a reasonable belief in her consent. * * *

No doubt it would be possible, by statute, to devise a law by which intercourse, voluntarily entered into, was an absolute offence, subject to a "defence" of belief whether honest or honest and reasonable, of which the "evidential" burden is primarily on the defence and the "probative" burden on the prosecution. But in my opinion such is not the crime of rape as it has hitherto been understood. The prohibited act in rape is to have intercourse without the victim's consent. The minimum mens rea or guilty mind in most common law offences, including rape, is the intention to do the prohibited act, and that is correctly stated in the proposition stated "in the first place" of the judge's direction. * * *

The only qualification I would make to the direction of the learned judge's "in the first place" is the refinement for which, as I shall show, there is both Australian and English authority, that if the intention of the accused is to have intercourse nolens volens, that is recklessly and not caring whether the victim be a consenting party or not that is equivalent on ordinary principles to an intent to do the prohibited act without the consent of the victim.

The alternative version of the learned judge's direction would read that the accused must do the prohibited act with the intention of doing it without an honest and reasonable belief in the victim's consent. * * * In principle, however, I find it unacceptable. I believe that "mens rea" means "guilty or criminal mind", and if it be the case, as seems to be accepted here, that mental element in rape is not knowledge but intent, to insist that a belief must be reasonable to excuse it is to insist that either the accused is to be found guilty of intending to do that which in truth he did not intend to do, or that his state of mind though innocent of evil intent, can convict him if it be honest but not rational. * * * This is to insist on an objective element in the definition of intent, and this is a course which I am extremely reluctant to adopt * * *.

Once one has accepted, what seems to me abundantly clear, that the prohibited act in rape is non-consensual sexual intercourse, and that the guilty state of mind is an intention to commit it, it seems to me to follow as a matter of inexorable logic that there is no room either for a "defence" of honest belief or mistake, or of a defence of honest and reasonable belief and mistake. Either the prosecution proves that the accused had the requisite intent, or it does not. In the former case it succeeds, and in the latter it fails. Since honest belief clearly negatives intent, the reasonableness or otherwise of that belief can only be evidence for or against the view that the belief and therefore the intent was actually held, and it matters not whether * * * "the definition of a crime includes no specific element beyond the prohibited act." * * * Any other view, as for insertion of the word "reasonable" can only have the effect of saying that a man intends something which he does not.

[T]he appellants invited us to overrule the bigamy cases from R. v. Tolson [1] onwards and perhaps also R. v. Prince [2] (the abduction case) as wrongly decided at least insofar as they purport to insist that a mistaken belief must be reasonable. * * * I am content to rest my view of the instant case on the crime of rape by saying that it is my opinion that the prohibited act is and always has been intercourse without consent of the victim and the mental element is and always has been the intention to commit that act, or the equivalent intention of having intercourse willy-nilly not caring whether the victim consents or no. A failure to prove this involves an acquittal because the intent, an essential ingredient, is lacking. It matters not why it is lacking if only it is not there, and in particular it matters not that the intention is lacking only because of a belief not based on reasonable grounds. I should add that I myself am inclined to view R. v. Tolson as a narrow decision based on the construction of a statute, which prima facie seemed to make an absolute statutory offence, with a proviso, related to the seven year period of absence, which created a statutory defence. The judges in R. v. Tolson decided that this was not

1. (1889) 23 QBD 168, [1886–90] All ER Rep. 26.

2. (1875) LR 2 CCR 154, [1874–80] All ER Rep. 881.

reasonable, and, on general jurisprudential principles, imported into the statutory offence words which created a special "defence" of honest and reasonable belief of which the "evidential" but not the probative burden lay on the defence. I do not think it is necessary to decide this conclusively in the present case. But if this is the true view there is a complete distinction between R. v. Tolson and the other cases based on statute and the present.

* * *

For the above reasons I would answer the question certified in the negative, but would apply the proviso to s 2(1) of the Criminal Appeal Act 1968 on the ground that no miscarriage of justice has or conceivably could have occurred. In my view, therefore these appeals should be dismissed.

[The other separate opinions are omitted.]

NOTES

1. It should be noted that the view of Lord Hailsham (and of the House of Lords) is a departure from the traditional rule that a mistake must be reasonable as well as honest. See, e. g., United States v. Short, 4 U.S.C.M.A. 437, 16 C.M.R. 11 (1954), in which a divided Court of Military Appeals held that an army private's unreasonable though arguably honest mistake that a Japanese woman had consented to an act of prostitution would not be a defense to a charge of assault with intent to rape. Isn't the position of the House of Lords more consistent with the rule that a defendant must be at least reckless with regard to all of those factors which are necessary to guilt? Can a person who honestly believes a woman has consented be said to have intended to have intercourse without her consent, or even to have been reckless about her consent?

2. Howard, The Reasonableness of Mistake in the Criminal Law, 4 U. Queens L.J. 45 (1961) suggests that the confusion concerning whether a mistake need be reasonable results from a failure to distinguish mistake as a defense to a crime requiring "general intent" and mistake offered as a defense to a crime for which negligence is sufficient. In the former case, he suggests, no reasonableness is necessary; in the latter, only a reasonable mistake prevents liability.

3. For general discussions of both mistakes of fact and of law, see Haddad, The Mental Attitude Requirement in Criminal Law—and Some Exceptions, 59 J.Crim.L., C. & P.S. 4, 11–21 (1968); Hall, Ignorance and Mistake in Criminal Law, 33 Ind.L.J. 1, 2–14 (1957); Hall and Seligman, Mistake of Law and Mens Rea, 8 U.Chi.L.Rev. 641 (1941); Keedy, Ignorance and Mistake in the Criminal Law, 22 Harv.L.Rev. 81–88 (1908); Mueller-Rappard, The Mistake of Law as a Defense, 36 Temple L.Q. 261 (1963); Perkins, Ignorance and Mistake in Criminal Law, 88 U.Pa.L.Rev. 35, 54–65 (1939); Ryu and Silving, Error Juris: A Comparative Study, 24 U.Chi.L. Rev. 421 (1957).

b. IGNORANCE OR MISTAKE OF LAW

In regard to ignorance or mistake as to matters of "law", it is useful to distinguish some subquestions. It is commonly asserted that "ignorance of the law is no excuse" and, as a generalization concerning the criminal law, this is correct. Thus, a defendant charged with possession of wine on May 12, 1926, in violation of a state prohibition statute which took effect on April 28, of that year, could not defend on the grounds that mere possession was not a crime under prior law and that he did not know of the enactment of the new law. In affirming his conviction, the court wrote: "All persons are charged with knowledge of the criminal laws which define crimes". Zakrasek v. State, 197 Ind. 249, 150 N.E. 615 (1926).

Should it make any difference that before engaging in the conduct alleged to be criminal the defendant consulted an attorney and was assured by him of the legality of his proposed action? It has been stated that the decisions "uniformly hold" that there is no bar to conviction in such cases. W. LaFave and A. Scott, Criminal Law 368 (1972). But the discussion of the court in Long v. State, 44 Del. (5 Terry) 262, 65 A.2d 489 (1949) suggests that in some such cases, at least, the defendant has "made a bona fide, deligent effort, adopting a course and resorting to sources and means at least as appropriate as any afforded under our legal system, to ascertain and abide by the law," and consequently should be excused. The Delaware court expressed the view that a defendant might appropriately be excused on the basis of advice of counsel where, but only where:

> he made a full disclosure to the attorney of the relevant circumstances as well as of what he proposed to do, and * * * he had no substantial reason to believe that the advice he received was ill founded, such as circumstances reasonably indicating that the attorney was incompetent to give advice about the matter, or had not given the question sufficient consideration, or that the advice was lacking in candor.

44 Del. at 282, 65 A.2d at 498–99. This view has not been accepted, perhaps because of fears that it would encourage ignorance of the law rather than efforts to ascertain it. Moreover, it might create a substantial danger of collusion between defendants and attorneys, pursuant to which attorneys would falsely testify that they had been consulted and had advised that the contemplated conduct was not criminal.

Even if acting on a lawyer's advice should not be a defense, what of the defendant who relies upon a judicial decision? In State v. V.F.W. Post No. 3722, 215 Kan. 693, 527 P.2d 1020 (1974), the defendant had installed slot machines on its premises in reliance upon a local trial court decision that slot machines were not illegal gambling devices under the state statute. This decision was subsequently overturned by the state supreme court. The defendant relied upon Kan. Stat.Ann. § 21–3203(2):

> A person's reasonable belief that his conduct does not constitute a crime is a defense if:
>
> * * *
>
> (c) He acts in reliance upon an order or opinion of the supreme court of Kansas or a United States appellate court later overruled or reversed;
>
> (d) He acts in reliance upon an official interpretation of the statute, regulation or order defining the crime made by a public officer or agency legally authorized to interpret such statute.

The state supreme court held that a trial judge was not a public officer within the meaning of the statute. The court noted:

> In researching the law in other jurisdictions we find that the defense of reliance upon judicial decision generally is limited to decisions of courts of last resort such as the United States Supreme Court and the state supreme courts.

215 Kan. at 697, 527 P.2d at 1024.

A very different question is whether there should be a difference in treatment when the defendant's ignorance or mistake concerns some aspect of law other than the existence or meaning of the law creating and defining the crime with which he or she is charged.

MODEL PENAL CODE *

(Proposed Official Draft, 1962).

Section 2.04. Ignorance or Mistake

[For text of this section, see page 185, supra.]

(1) IGNORANCE OR MISTAKE AS TO THE LAW PROHIBITING THE CRIMINAL ACT

LAMBERT v. CALIFORNIA

Supreme Court of the United States, 1957.
355 U.S. 225, 78 S.Ct. 240, 2 L.Ed.2d 228.

[The opinion in this case is reprinted at page 165.]

UNITED STATES v. BERRIGAN

United States District Court for Maryland, 1968.
283 F.Supp. 336, convictions aff'd 417 F.2d 1002, 1009 (4th Cir. 1969), cert. den. 397 U.S. 909, 90 S.Ct. 907, 25 L.Ed.2d 90.

NORTHROP, District Judge. The defendants before this court are charged in three counts that they did willfully

1. injure property of the United States;
2. mutilate records filed in a public office of the United States; and
3. hinder the administration of the Military Selective Service Act.

Defendants wish to proffer an opening statement to the jury as to what they would present for their defense. Specifically, they contend that, by virtue of what they have read, heard, and seen, the war in Vietnam is immoral and illegal; and that the United States in carrying on the war in Vietnam, is violating certain precepts of international law, constitutional law, and judgments which were handed down at Nurnberg.

To serve as a foundation and a basis for their beliefs, defendants wish to produce in court, among other evidence, "the outstanding experts" on international law who would testify that the acts of the United States government in Vietnam are illegal. Their conduct, they say, was prompted by their belief that the United States is acting illegally and was intended to prevent criminal acts from being committed. Because this belief prompted their acts, they argue that the necessary *mens rea* is lacking.

Initially, it must be pointed out that in law once the commission of a crime is established—the doing of a prohibited act with the necessary intent—proof of a good motive will not save the accused from conviction. * * * This point is best illustrated and highlighted by those cases where a defendant has been found guilty of murder even though the motive advanced for justification was of the highest and most selfless level. For example, a man drowns his children because he loves them and wants to prevent their suffering in poverty; and a man poisons his wife, at her request, to end her agony from an incurable disease.

Counsel for defendants candidly admits that there is no precedent for the proposition advanced here, namely that any citizen is justified in mutilating and damaging government property and interfering with vital governmental functions—all acts specifically prohibited by penal statutes—if he reasonably believes that the government is acting illegally under international and possibly constitutional law.

* * *

That there is no legal precedent for defendants' proposition is not surprising. No civilized nation can endure where a citizen can select what law he would obey because of his moral or religious belief. It matters not how worthy his motives may be. It is axiomatic that chaos would exist if an individual were permitted to impose his beliefs upon others and invoke justification in a court to excuse his transgression of a duly-enacted law. * * *

[N]o matter how reasonably, sincerely, or deeply these defendants believed that the government was acting illegally does not go to the question whether they sincerely and honestly believed that *their* acts were lawful and thus negate the specific intent necessary for conviction, namely willfulness. Thus, the proposition presented here is to be distinguished from a case where a defendant believed that he was acting within the law, although subsequently it turns out that he was mistaken as to the applicable law.

In essence, the defendants are arguing not that they were legally justified in acting the way they chose to, or that they had a *bona fide* belief that they were legally justified, but that their lofty motives and sincerely-held convictions negate criminal intent.

* * *

Finally, counsel contends that these defendants should be allowed to present to the jury what is popularly known as the "Nurnberg Defense." The trial of the Nazi war criminals at Nurnberg was premised on the generally accepted view that there are, as a part of international law, certain crimes against peace and humanity which are punishable. The Nurnberg Trial, 6 F.R.D. 69 (1946). It is urged here that the belief of these defendants that the United States was waging a war of aggression, and thus committing a crime against peace, justified the acts charged.

It is not clear what standing these defendants have to raise the legality of this country's involvement in Vietnam when they have not been called to serve in the armed forces, are not directly affected by our government's actions in that country, and are not even directly affected by the Selective Service apparatus. As pointed out by Judge Charles E. Wyzanski in an article in the February 1968 issue of the Atlantic Monthly:

> "As the Nuremberg verdicts show, merely to fight in an aggressive war is no crime. What is a crime is *personally* to fight by foul means." [Emphasis supplied.]

The important element in this defense, assuming its applicability in an American court, is the individual responsibility which is necessary before it can be raised. These defendants do not have standing to raise the validity of governmental actions, either under international law or constitutional law, on the grounds that the rights of parties not before this court are violated. * * *

But irrespective of the lack of standing of these defendants to raise the issue of the legality of the government's actions as they relate to the Vietnam situation, the proffered defense suffers from a more fundamental bar. It is clear that there are certain questions of substantive law, that is, "political questions", which are not cognizable in our courts because of the nature of our governmental system which is based upon a separation of functions among different branches of the government. * * *

The activities of these defendants were directed towards the Selective Service System, which system counsel has admitted is not criminal or illegal in and of itself. What is called into question here is the utilization of the armed forces by the executive and legislative branches. It cannot be disputed that the recognition of belligerency abroad, and the measures necessary to meet a crisis to preserve the peace and safety of this country, is uniquely an executive and a legislative responsibility. Whether the actions by the executive and the legislative branches in utilizing our armed forces are in accord with international law is a question which necessarily must be left to the elected representatives of the people and not to the judiciary. This is so even if the government's actions are contrary to valid treaties to which the government is a signatory. * * *

Counsel will govern themselves accordingly, and the court's instructions to the jury will reflect this decision if any transgression makes it necessary.

NOTES AND QUESTIONS

1. Should the substantive criminal law make any attempt to exempt some or any who commit the act because of a commitment to a moral value they hold above the obligation to obey the criminal law? If so, how should this be done?

2. If some provision is made for such exemptions, should it apply to the facts of the following case: The defendant was a physician and member of the armed forces. As chief of dermatology services at a military hospital, he was ordered to provide training for "special service aidmen," who would serve in the Vietnam war. He refused and is charged with disobeying the order. May he assert as a defense the argument that the aidmen would, while in Vietnam, commit acts in violation of international law? Cf. United States v. Levy, 39 Court Martial Reports 672 (1967). The "Nuremberg Defense" aspect of the case is discussed in 9 Harv.Inter.L.J. 169 (1968). For general discussions, see D'Amato, Gould, and Woods, War Crimes and Vietnam: The "Nuremberg Defense" and the Military Service Register, 57 Cal.L.Rev. 1055 (1969); Ferencz, War Crimes Law and the Vietnam War, 17 Am.U.L.Rev. 403 (1968); Woetzel, Comment on the Nuremberg Principles and Conscientious Objection with Special Reference to War Crimes, 16 Cath.Law. 257 (1970).

3. It has been argued that even if such an exemption is not allowed, evidence of motive should be admissible, and that counsel should be per-

mitted to argue to the jury that it should use its inherent power to acquit despite proof of guilt beyond a reasonable doubt? Reconsider United States v. Moylan, above at 23.

(2) IGNORANCE OR MISTAKE REGARDING LAW OTHER THAN THAT PROHIBITING THE CRIMINAL ACT

MODEL PENAL CODE (TENT. DRAFT NO. 4, 1955) *

Comment to § 2.02, p. 131.

[T]he general principle that ignorance or mistake of law is no excuse is usually greatly overstated; it has no application when the circumstances made material by the definition of the offense include a legal element. * * * The law involved is not the law defining the offense; it is some other legal rule that characterizes the attendant circumstances that are material to the offense.

RICHARDSON v. UNITED STATES

United States Court of Appeals for the District of Columbia, 1968.
131 U.S.App.D.C. 168, 403 F.2d 574.

EDGERTON, Senior Circuit Judge. Appellant was charged with robbery (count one), assault with a dangerous weapon (count two), and carrying a dangerous weapon (count three). A jury found him guilty as charged on count one, guilty of simple assault on count two and not guilty on count three.

The complaining witness Snowden testified that appellant and another held him up at gunpoint and took $98 from his wallet. Appellant testified that Snowden, who had recently been convicted of a gambling offense, owed him a $270 gambling debt which he had several times unsuccessfully tried to collect. He admitted reaching into Snowden's wallet and removing $138 without his consent, but denied having a gun. His mother corroborated his story of the gambling debt and testified that Snowden was a known gambler.

The chief ground of this appeal is the trial court's denial of appellant's request for the following standard instruction:

> Evidence has been introduced that the defendant believed that he had a right to take the property he is alleged to have stolen.
>
> If a person takes the property of another, but does so in the good faith belief that he has a right to take the property, the specific intent essential to the crime of robbery is lacking.

> The Government must prove beyond a reasonable doubt that the defendant acted with the specific intent to steal. If you have a reasonable doubt whether or not the defendant acted with a specific intent to steal, you must find him not guilty.

A defendant is not guilty of robbery unless he has a specific intent to take the property of another. Jackson v. United States, 121 U.S.App.D.C. 160, 348 F.2d 772 (1965). Viewing the evidence most favorably to the defendant, as we must where he appeals from the denial of a favorable instruction, he believed in good faith that he was entitled to the money. If so, he did not have that specific intent. We therefore find that the requested instruction should have been given.[2]

The government's position seems to be that no instruction on a claim of right is necessary unless the defendant had a legally enforceable right to the property he took. But specific intent depends upon a state of mind, not upon a legal fact. If the jury finds that the defendant believed himself entitled to the money, it cannot properly find that he had the requisite specific intent for robbery. * * *

The government urges affirmance for policy reasons, claiming that a reversal of this robbery conviction would encourage violent takings and would frustrate the policy of the law that a successful gambler may not recover his winnings from the loser. But "The taking and carrying away of the property of another in the District of Columbia without right to do so" is a misdemeanor. D.C.Code (1967 ed.) § 22–1211. Since this section can be violated without specific intent, it provides a deterrent to self-help by a winning gambler without rejecting the principle that specific intent turns on the actor's state of mind and not upon an objective fact.

* * *

Reversed.

NOTE

Why is *Richardson* properly regarded as a mistake of law case? The defendant's claimed error was in believing that some rule of law gave him the legal right to possession and use of the money in the possession of the victim Snowden. In other words, he believed that the law made that money his because of Snowden's debt to him. Since he believed the money was his, he lacked the state of mind necessary for robbery; he did not intend to take any property *of another* person, nor did he intend to deprive anyone else of *their* property. The rule of law about which Richardson claimed he was mistaken was not the law defining robbery as a crime or even some other part of the criminal law. It was the part of property law that defines rights to personal property (such as money) and deter-

2. Accord: State v. Steele, 150 Wash. 466, 273 P. 742 (1929). The majority rule in cases involving a forceful taking of money under color of a liquidated debt is that the requisite specific intent for robbery is lacking.

mines when, if ever, ownership of property changes because of a debt. Thus *Richardson* is not a traditional mistake of law case in which the defendant claimed that he mistakenly believed the criminal law did not prohibit what he did. Rather, it is one of the unusual cases in which the defendant claimed mistake concerning a collateral (i. e., noncriminal) rule of law and argued that because of this mistake he lacked the state of mind necessary for the crime charged. This issue is also addressed in State v. Lewis, which is reprinted at page 390, infra.

(3) Ignorance or Mistake of Law Based Upon Authority of a Public Official

The extraordinary complexity of the mistake of law defense is throughly examined in United States v. Barker, 514 F.2d 208 (D.C. Cir. 1975), particularly the dissenting opinion of Judge Wilkey. The "foot soldiers" in the famous Watergate break-in sought to withdraw their guilty pleas to burglary and other charges stemming from their ill-fated effort to "bug" and wiretap the offices of the Democratic National Committee at the Watergate office complex in Washington, D.C. One of their arguments was that they lacked the necessary criminal intent because of their honest and reasonable belief that the surrepetitious entry was lawful due to assurances from their leader, Howard Hunt, that the action was authorized by, and on behalf of, the Central Intelligence Agency in connection with an investigation of foreign intelligence operations. Judge Wilkey believed that the defendants should have been given an opportunity to prove this defense which he characterized as a mistake of law. It was not a mistake of fact because, according to the judge, the defendants knew too few facts about the break-in to argue that it would have been legal had the facts been as believed them to be. He analogized their situation to that of the kidnapping defendants in People v. Weiss, 276 N.Y. 384, 12 N.E.2d 514 (1938). The defendants there claimed that they had responded to the request of one whom they believed to be a police officer in arresting and confining an alleged murderer. The New York Court of Appeals in reversing their conviction said that they were entitled to present this defense since if the trier of fact were convinced that they had acted in the good faith belief that they were legally authorized this would negate the statutory requirement that the kidnapping had been "without authority of law". Judge Wilkey recognized that burglary, unlike the kidnapping statute in *Weiss,* does not require that the actor realize the illegality of his conduct so long as it is actually unlawful. That is, it is not part of the prosecution's case to prove that the defendants knew it was against the law to enter another's premises with the intent to commit a crime within. Nevertheless, he argued, even without such an element if one acts in reliance of the mistaken belief that a public official, most particularly a police agent, had whatever authority should be necessary for the action—either a valid warrant or authority to act without a warrant due to the nature of the crime allegedly being investigated—he should be permitted to demonstrate that that belief was honest and reasonable.

Although Judge Wilkey's views did not prevail in the Barker case he was successful in reversing, on these grounds, the convictions of two of the same "foot soldiers for crimes committed in connection with the burglary of the office of the psychiatrist of Daniel Ellsberg, the source of the leak of the famous "Pentagon Papers". United States v. Barker, 546 F.2d 940 (D.C.Cir. 1976).

* * *

c. INTOXICATION

Given the frequently-encountered concidence between consumption of intoxicants and criminal activity, the effect of intoxication upon criminal liability is at least a potentially important issue. Consider the standard applied by the court in the principle case in this subsection—that intoxication can be used only to "prove" the absence of a specific intent if one is required by the crime charged—and alternatives to this approach. Is there any sound reason for not acquitting a defendant who persuades a trier of fact that in view of his or her intoxication at the time of the act constituting the crime, the prosecution has not proven guilt? Is there a need to discourage consumption of intoxicants, especially by those prone to commit crimes, and—if so—is this relevant to the matter? Consider the ethical or moral implications of becoming intoxicated. Is it defensible to take the position that at least to some extent the culpability involved in becoming intoxicated adequately substitutes for the state of mind usually required for the crime charged?

MODEL PENAL CODE *

(Proposed Official Draft, 1962).

Section 2.08. Intoxication

(1) Except as provided in Subsection (4) of this Section, intoxication of the actor is not a defense unless it negatives an element of the offense.

(2) When recklessness establishes an element of the offense, if the actor, due to self-induced intoxication, is unaware of a risk of which he would have been aware had he been sober, such unawareness is immaterial.

(3) Intoxication does not, in itself, constitute mental disease within the meaning of Section 4.01 [providing for the defense of insanity].

(4) Intoxication which (a) is not self-induced or (b) is pathological is an affirmative defense if by reason of such intoxication the actor at the time of his conduct lacks substantial capacity either to appreciate its criminality [wrongfulness] or to conform his conduct to the requirements of law.

(5) *Definitions.* In this Section unless a different meaning plainly is required:

(a) "intoxication" means a disturbance of mental or physical capacities resulting from the introduction of substances into the body;

(b) "self-induced intoxication" means intoxication caused by substances which the actor knowingly introduces into his body, the tendency of which to cause intoxication he knows or ought to know, unless he introduces them pursuant to medical advice or under such circumstances as would afford a defense to a charge of crime;

(c) "pathological intoxication" means intoxication grossly excessive in degree, given the amount of the intoxicant, to which the actor does not know he is susceptible.

UNITED STATES v. WILLIAMS

United States District Court for the District of Maryland, 1971.
332 F.Supp. 1.

Herbert F. MURRAY, District Judge. In this case the defendant was charged in a two-count indictment under Title 18, U.S.C.A. Sections 2113(a) and (b) with robbery of a branch of the Maryland National Bank in Cambridge, Maryland on December 4, 1970. [The relevant portions of the statute were as follows:

§ 2113. Bank robbery and incidental crimes

(a) Whoever, by force and violence, or by intimidation, takes, or attempts to take, from the person or presence of another any property or money or any other thing of value belonging to, or in the care, custody, control, management, or possession of, any bank, credit union, or any savings and loan association * * *

Shall be fined not more than $5,000 or imprisoned not more than twenty years, or both.

(b) Whoever takes and carries away, with intent to steal or purloin, any property or money or any other thing of value exceeding $100 belonging to, or in the care, custody, control, management, or possession of any bank, credit union, or any savings and loan association, shall be fined not more than $5,000 or imprisoned not more than ten years, or both * * *]

The case was tried non-jury on September 13 and 14, 1971.

The basic facts are not in dispute. In a stipulation signed by government counsel, the defendant and his counsel, it was agreed that on the date set out in the indictment, the defendant went into the bank in Cambridge, Maryland and requested a loan from a branch officer of the bank. The officer declined to grant the defendant a loan. Thereafter the defendant walked up to Mrs. Martina Bennett, a teller, and handed to her a note stating "This is a stickup". Mrs. Bennett gave him all her cash, and defendant then left the bank with the money. It was also stipulated that Mrs. Bennett was intimidated by defendant giving her the note and for that reason turned over to defendant the funds in her drawer. An audit made immediately after the robbery showed the defendant had taken $4,727 of the bank's money.

While defendant thus does not contest the fact that a robbery occurred and he committed it, his counsel urges upon the Court that an essential element of the crime is lacking. It is contended that the two sections of the bank robbery statute on which the counts in the indictment are based both require a specific intent to steal, and that at the time of the robbery defendant was so intoxicated from alcohol and drugs that he was incapable of forming such specific intent.

The threshold legal questions thus are whether voluntary intoxication can negative specific intent as an element of crime and, if so, whether the offenses charged in either or both counts of the indictment require proof of specific intent. If specific intent is an element of the offense in either count of the indictment, the factual question then arises as to whether on all the evidence the degree of defendant's intoxication was such as to create a reasonable doubt that defendant had a specific intent to steal when the robbery took place.

It is clear from the cases that while voluntary intoxication is ordinarily no defense to crime, it may have that effect if specific intent is an element of the crime. * * *

The rule has also been adopted by the American Law Institute. Model Penal Code, Tentative Draft No. 9, Section 2–08.

Thus in the area of criminal responsibility as affected by voluntary intoxication, a distinction must be drawn between so-called "general intent" to commit a crime and a "specific intent" to do a particular criminal act.

These terms are often used in the cases but seldom defined. * * *

Did Congress in the several subsections of the bank robbery statute create "general intent" crimes or "specific intent" crimes? Some cases uncritically lump all subsections of the statute under the "specific intent" label. Other cases ascribe more careful draftsmanship to the Congress, and find a specific intent an element of the crime only in those subsections of the statute where the language "with intent" is used.

Thus, in United States v. DeLeo, 422 F.2d 487 (1st Cir. 1970), cert. den. 397 U.S. 1037, 90 S.Ct. 1355, 25 L.Ed.2d 648 (1970), the indictment was under 18 U.S.C.A. Sections 2113(a) and (d). On appeal the defendant contended that the crime was of the common law larceny genus requiring allegation and proof of specific intent. The Court rejected this argument, stating at pages 490–491:

> "Six specific crimes are set out in Section 2113. Felonious intent is specifically incorporated in the definition of two of them: entering a federally insured institution with intent to commit a felony (a—second paragraph), and taking property with intent to steal or purloin (b). However, it is not made part of the crimes of taking by force and violence or by intimidation (a—first paragraph); knowingly receiving stolen property (c); assaulting or putting in jeopardy the life of a person by a dangerous weapon (d); or killing a person, or forcing a person to accompany him, while in the course of committing one of the other offenses or avoiding apprehension or confinement for any of them (e).
>
> "This differentiation shows careful draftsmanship. Entering and taking can be innocent acts, and therefore require felonious intent to constitute crime; receiving stolen property can be innocent, unless done knowingly. However, the other offenses described acts which, when performed, are so unambiguously dangerous to others that the requisite mental element is necessarily implicit in the description. * * *

The Court in the present case concludes as a matter of law * * * that the act of the defendant, which he admits of taking by intimidation from the presence of another money belonging to the bank, constitutes a violation of subsection (a) of the statute as charged in Count I of the indictment. The Court rejects as a defense to the crime charged in Count I of the indictment any voluntary intoxication of the defendant.

As to Count II of the indictment, the Court feels that historically and legally the contention of the defendant is correct, and that a specific intent to steal is an element of the crime. The Court on a review of all the evidence in the case is satisfied beyond a reasonable doubt that defendant when he took and carried away money belonging to the bank exceeding $100 in value did so with the intent to steal or purloin.

The Court in finding as a fact that defendant had the intent to steal is not unmindful of the fact that there was substantial evidence to show that defendant had imbibed significant quantities of alcohol and drugs, but the Court from all the evidence finds beyond a reasonable doubt that he both had the capacity to and did intend to steal when he took the bank's money. The basis for the Court's finding in this regard requires some reference to the evidence of defendant's taking of alcohol and drugs and his condition at the time of the robbery.

In testifying on his own behalf, defendant claimed that as a result of an argument with his wife he started drinking with a companion around 9:00 A.M. on December 3, 1970, the day before the robbery and over the next fourteen hours the two consumed three fifths of whiskey, of which defendant had about half. During this period defendant also took 6 or 7 "yellow jackets" or barbiturate pills. Between midnight on December 3 and the occurrence of the robbery around 1:00 P.M. on December 4, defendant claims that he and a companion drank an additional one or one and a half fifths of whiskey, of which defendant had all but half a pint. In addition, sometime in this latter period defendant took some LSD pills, with the result that he had only "spotty" recollection of events the morning of the robbery. Defendant does recall going into the bank and talking with the branch officer, and leaving the bank stuffing money under his jacket, but disclaims any recollection of confronting the teller, presenting her with a "stickup" note and actually receiving from her over $4,000 in cash.

The witnesses who actually observed the defendant on the day of the robbery indicate he had been drinking but not that he was drunk. A cab driver named Hopkins who drove the defendant at 6:00 A.M. to redeem his watch and then to a drive-in said his eyes were red and he had been drinking. His speech was "heavy" and he did not seem to walk normally.

Mrs. Florence Brannock, a teller in the bank, spoke briefly with defendant when he asked for the loan department and directed him to the branch officer. She felt he smelled strongly of cheap wine or alcohol and that his speech while understandable was not normal—it was a little "slurred" or "thick".

Branch Officer John Bramble testified that the defendant came into his office seeking a $400 loan for Christmas. In their conversation defendant gave his place of employment, said he owned a 1969 Chevrolet and had an account in the Farmer's and Merchant's bank across the street. The witness said he could smell a strong odor of alcohol on the defendant's breath and felt he was under the influence of liquor and that he also appeared somewhat nervous. After declining to grant the defendant a loan, the witness watched the defendant walk towards the lobby of the bank and could not remember anything unusual about the defendant's walk.

Mrs. Martina Bennett, a cash teller, recalled that a little after 1:00 P.M. a man approached from the side aisle of the bank. She recalled having seen him previously at Mrs. Brannock's desk. He put a note on her counter and said nothing. At first she thought he might be deaf and read the note. It was printed in pencil on a torn piece of paper and read "This is a stickup". She noticed that he had his right hand in his jacket pocket which was thrust forward pointing at her as though he had a gun. She was terrified and afraid he was going to shoot her. She put all her money on the counter, but she did not see what he did with it, although she believes he dropped some and then picked it up. She noticed nothing unusual about the defendant's appearance and did not smell any alcohol. When he was standing before her he did not appear to waver, but his eyes did appear sleepy. She watched him walk away from her counter and down a flight of four steps leading to the lobby entrance.

A cab driver witness named Wilson Wright testified defendant and two other men approached him around 5:00 P.M. on December 4, 1970 in Salisbury, Maryland. He took the men to two different destinations in Salisbury and then the defendant and one of the men hired him to take them to Hartsville, South Carolina where the other man, "Charles", lived. The witness noticed the defendant had a large sum of money in a bag, which the defendant said was earned in five years of work in Vietnam. The witness said the defendant looked and acted normal while they were in Salisbury, but en route to Virginia the defendant and his companions were drinking from two fifths of whiskey and the defendant fell into a deep sleep about 8:30 P.M. About 4:00 A.M. the witness left the two men off at a house in Hartsville, South Carolina, and that was the last he saw of the defendant.

The testimony as to acts of the defendant closest in time to the robbery was given by the owner of a small store in Cambridge, George Heist. His store is located about two blocks from the bank. He recalled that the defendant came into his store about noon and asked for a piece of paper to figure a bill. The defendant reached for a sales pad but the witness did not want the defendant to use the pad and gave him a piece of paper instead. The defendant turned around with his back to the witness and put the piece of paper on top of some stocking boxes and started to write. Apparently dissatisfied, he balled up the piece of paper and threw it on the floor. Defendant reached again for the witness' sales pad, which the witness again refused to give him, tearing off a piece of old calendar paper instead. Defendant again turned around and wrote some more, and then left the store.

The witness said that the defendant while in his store seemed coherent, didn't stagger, and acted normally except for trying to take his sales pad twice. However, because the defendant "seemed a little high on something" he decided, after the defendant left the store, to read what was on the balled up piece of paper. It read "This is a stick". Although defendant on leaving the store walked away from and not towards the bank, the witness appropriately concluded a robbery might be in prospect and got a policeman to whom he gave a description of the defendant. Later he heard the fire whistle blow about 1:00 P.M., which was a signal that the bank had been robbed.

Dr. Leonard Rothstein, a private psychiatrist called by defendant, had an interview examination with defendant on May 24, 1971 and also talked to defendant's wife. The defendant gave the doctor a history of abusing alcohol since age 19, and told the doctor he was drinking beer all day before the robbery and took some "yellow jackets" in the evening, and some LSD in the morning before the robbery. Dr. Rothstein found no significant evasiveness in the defendant and no discrepancies between defendant's account and his wife's.

On the basis of defendant's account to him and his examination the doctor expressed the opinion that at the time of the offense the defendant had no psychosis or structural alteration in the brain. However, the doctor concluded from what the defendant told him of his ingestion of alcohol and drugs that the higher centers governing the making of judgments, control of behavior and retention of experience in memory had been affected. While the defendant knew what he was doing, his judgment about the appropriateness of his actions and his ability to control them were severely impaired. From the history the doctor concluded the defendant had taken the alcohol and drugs voluntarily and with knowledge from previous experience of their probable effect. In response to a hypothetical question asked on cross examination by counsel for the government, the doctor admitted that if the defendant had not taken alcohol and drugs before the offense, he would at the time have had no psychiatric illness and would have had the capacity to conform his conduct to the requirements of the law.

Dr. William Fitzpatrick, who had examined the defendant on July 15, 1971 at the request of the government, was called as an expert psychiatric witness by the defense. He related a personal history and account of the offense given him by the defendant very similar to that related by defendant's own expert, Dr. Rothstein. He found the defendant of normal intelligence with no evidence of psychosis or structural brain disorder. From the history he judged defendant to be a passive dependent personality of the type more likely to abuse alcohol than the average person. Although from defendant's own account he was an episodic heavy user of alcohol and drugs, he did not find evidence that he was an alcoholic or a drug addict. He felt that because defendant was a passive dependent type he had a condition something short of total mental health. However, had the defendant not taken alcohol and drugs at time of the offense, he would not consider that defendant lacked criminal responsibility or capacity to conform his conduct to the requirements of the law. Although the doctor did not know the quantity of alcohol or drugs defendant consumed before the offense, he assumed the defendant was intoxicated at the time and that his intoxication was self-induced with knowledge on the part of the defendant that he would get drunk if he drank. He admitted that if he assumed a lesser degree of intoxication he would have to alter his opinion, but his opinion that defendant at the time of the offense could not conform his conduct to the requirements of the law was based on assumed intake of large quantities of alcohol. However, the doctor honestly disclaimed any opinion on whether defendant could specifically intend to rob a bank.

In expressing their conclusions, both psychiatrists obviously had in mind the ALI formulation [of the insanity defense] contained in Model Penal Code, Section 4.01, approved in this circuit in United States v. Chandler, 393 F.2d 920 (1968). [Under this formulation, "a person is not responsible for criminal conduct if at the time of such conduct as a result of mental disease or defect he lacks substantial capacity either to appreciate the criminality of his conduct or to conform his conduct to the requirements of law."] However, defense counsel disclaimed any contention that this standard was applicable in determining the issue of the criminal responsibility of this defendant. In this connection it is noted that Section 2.08(3) of the Model Penal Code provides "Intoxication does not, in itself, constitute mental disease within the meaning of Section 4.01."

As then Circuit Judge Burger stated in Heideman v. United States, 104 U.S.App.D.C. 128, 259 F.2d 943, at p. 946 (1958): "Drunkenness, while efficient to reduce or remove *inhibitions,** does not readily negate *intent.** " (* Footnotes omitted)

The Court believes that the defendant had taken alcohol and drugs to the point of being "under the influence" but that he was not so intoxicated as not to understand what he was doing or to not have the intention to steal from the bank. There is a marked difference between the accounts of the persons who observed defendant and defendant's own account as to his condition. It appears from a witness called by the defense that he was able to write a "stickup" note shortly before the robbery, to go into the bank, hold a coherent conversation about a loan, present the note, obtain over $4,000 in cash, none of which has been returned, and make good his escape. The Court concludes beyond a reasonable doubt that defendant had the intent to steal from the bank as required for conviction under Count II, and that he is in any event guilty under Count I of the indictment. If an intent to steal is an element of the offense charged in Count I, the Court finds that intent proved as to Count I also. The Court therefore finds the defendant guilty as charged in both counts of the indictment.

NOTES AND QUESTIONS

1. When a case such as the instant case is submitted to a jury, how are they likely to consider the evidence of the defendant's intoxication? Is it likely that they actually do consider it only as evidence tending to dis-

prove the existence of a specific intent required by the definition of the crime? If not, what (if anything) should the law do?

2. To what extent would the relevance of intoxication to liability for serious criminal acts be simplified by enactment of the following statute:

> Dangerous Intoxication.
>
> A person is guilty of an offense if he takes or permits to be administered to him intoxicating substances while aware of a substantial and unjustifiable risk that he will become intoxicated and, while intoxicated, commit acts that except for his intoxication would be crimes.

What penalty should be assigned to the offense of "dangerous intoxication?" Should the penalty be related to the penalty assigned to the crime which the offender was aware he might commit? Should it be related to the number of crimes the offender was aware he might commit? The number actually committed? For a discussion of a German statute similar to this proposal and suggested English legislation, see Daly, Intoxication and Crime: A Comparative Approach, 27 Inter. & Comp.L.Q. 378 (1978).

3. It is generally held that intoxication from substances other than alcohol have the same effect upon criminal liability as alcohol intoxication. Is this appropriate? Consider the following from Commonwealth v. Campbell, 445 Pa. 388, 284 A.2d 798, 801 (1971):

> Defendant contends that the law with respect to voluntary intoxication is [as it is] because human experience has shown the effects of taking alcohol are predictable, but not predictable with LSD [and therefore LSD intoxication should be permitted to result in complete acquittal]. The expert testimony in this case (if believed * * *) showed * * * that LSD produces widely varying results among different persons and even different results with the same person on different occasions. This distinction of nonpredictability of effect on the human body is devoid of any adequate legal justification based upon legal precedent, or reason, or policy considerations for a radical change and departure from our law of criminal responsibility. The very fact that the effects of a voluntary, nonmedical use of a hallucinogenic drug are predictably unforeseeable should require Courts to decide in the public interest that this is not legally sufficient to completely exculpate a person from murder or any criminal act.

4. What arguments could be made for or against the enactment of the following statute:

> Effect of Intoxication Upon Criminal Liability.
>
> (a) Except under the circumstances described in subsection (b), no person shall be convicted of an offense committed while intoxicated if it is found that [Alternative A: except for such intoxication he would not have committed the offense.] [Alternative B: his intoxication so reduces his culpability that given general community standards of accountability and blameworthiness he should not be held liable.]

(b) If a person, contemplating the commission of an offense, becomes intoxicated as a means of causing or enabling himself to commit the offense, he shall be liable for that offense without regard to subsection (a).

5. Not all American jurisdictions permit evidence of voluntary intoxication to be used to negate even "specific" intents. E. g., Texas Penal Code § 8.04 (evidence of intoxication can be considered only in mitigation of penalty and then only if it reaches point of "temporary insanity"). In Chittum v. Commonwealth, 211 Va. 12, 174 S.E.2d 779 (1970), the court held that the jury need not have been instructed to consider the defendant's voluntary intoxication in determining whether he had been capable of forming the states of mind required for the crimes charged, kidnapping and attempted rape. The defendant later applied for federal habeas corpus relief, arguing that the trial court's refusal to instruct the jury on intoxication rendered his convictions invalid. The federal district court, although acknowledging that the Virginia position may well be the "minority view," found nothing in the Federal Constitution that would require the state to adopt a rule permitting juries to consider intoxication as bearing upon whether defendants had the specific intents required by the crimes with which they were charged. Chittum v. Cunningham, 326 F.Supp. 87 (D.C.Va.1971). Is this correct? Can a state impose a state of mind requirement and then refuse to permit a defendant to show that because of his intoxication the prosecution failed to prove that state of mind?

6. See generally Baumgartner, The Effect of Drugs on Criminal Responsibility, Specific Intent, and Mental Competency, 8 Am.Crim.L.Q. 118 (1970); Paulson, Intoxication as a Defense to Crime, 1961 U.Ill.L.Forum 1; Note, Volitional Fault and the Intoxicated Criminal Offender, 36 U.Cin.L. Rev. 258 (1967); Annot., Modern Status of the Rules as to Voluntary Intoxication as Defense to Criminal Charge, 8 A.L.R.3d 1236 (1966). For a historical analysis, see Singh, History of the Defense of Drunkenness in English Criminal Law, 49 L.Q.Rev. 528 (1933). For comparative purposes, see Bryden, Mens Rea and the Intoxicated Offender, 1968 Juridical Review 48 (Scottish) and Parker and Beck, The Intoxicated Offender—A Problem of Responsibility, 44 Can.B.Rev. 563 (1966) (Canadian). The relationship between the "insanity" defense and the voluntary intoxication "defense," especially in one who exhibits symptoms of mental illness when intoxicated, is discussed in Comment, The Mentally Impaired and Voluntarily Intoxicated Offender, 1972 Wash.U.L.Q. 160.

ROBINSON v. CALIFORNIA

Supreme Court of the United States, 1962.
370 U.S. 660, 82 S.Ct. 1417, 8 L.Ed.2d 758, rehearing den.
371 U.S. 905, 83 S.Ct. 202, 9 L.Ed.2d 166.

[The opinion in this case is reprinted at page 100, supra].

POWELL v. TEXAS

Supreme Court of the United States, 1968.
392 U.S. 514, 88 S.Ct. 2145, 20 L.Ed.2d 1254.

[The opinion in this case is reprinted at page 104, supra].

NOTES

1. Probably the most difficult issue posed by the Model Penal Code as well as by other model statutory formulations relates to the question of whether intoxication should be permitted to "disprove" recklessness when that is sufficient for guilt. Present law is generally stated as in accord with the position of the Model Penal Code. See W. LaFave and A. Scott, Criminal Law 346–47 (1972). The commentary to the Model Penal Code defends this position as follows:

> Those who oppose a special rule [making intoxication unavailable to "disprove" recklessness] draw strength initially from the presumptive disfavor of any special rules of liability. * * * [They] draw further strength from the proposition that it is precisely the awareness of the risk in recklessness that is the essence of its moral culpability—a culpability dependent on the magnitude of the specific risk advertently created. When that risk is greater in degree than that which the actor perceives at the time of getting drunk, as is frequently the case, the result of a special rule is bound to be a liability disproportionate to culpability. * * *
>
> The case thus made is worthy of respect, but there are strong considerations on the other side. We mention first the weight of the prevailing law * * *. Beyond this, there is the fundamental point that awareness of the potential consequences of excessive drinking on the capacity of human beings to gauge the risks incident to their conduct is by now so dispersed in our culture that we believe it fair to postulate a general equivalence between the risks created by the conduct of the drunken actor and the risks created by his conduct in becoming drunk. Becoming so drunk as to destroy temporarily the actor's power of perception and of judgment is conduct which plainly has no affirmative social value to counterbalance the potential danger. The actor's moral culpability lies in engaging in such conduct. Added to this are the impressive difficulties posed in litigating the foresight of any particular actor at the time when he imbibes and the relative rarity of cases where intoxication really does engender unawareness as distinguished from imprudence. These considerations lead us to propose, on balance,

> that the Code declare that unawareness of a risk of which the actor would have been aware had he been sober be declared immaterial.

Model Penal Code § 2.08, comment (Tent.Draft No. 9, 1959).

2. Parker v. State, 7 Md.App. 167, 177, 178, 254 A.2d 381, 387 (1969): Lord Hale, in 1 Pleas of the Crown, Ch. IV, pp. 29–33 (1847) recognized three types of "idiocy, madness and lunacy" under the general name of "dementia". The third type was "dementia affectata, namely drunkenness".

> "This vice doth deprive men of the use of reason, and puts many men into a perfect, but temporary phrenzy; and therefore, according to some Civilians, such a person committing homicide, shall not be punished simply for the crime of homicide, but shall suffer for his drunkenness answerable to the nature of the crime occasioned thereby; so that yet the formal cause of his punishment is rather the drunkenness, than the crime committed in it: but by the laws of England such a person shall have no privilege by this voluntary contracted madness, but shall have the same judgment as if he were in his right senses. But yet there seems to be two allays to be allowed in this case. 1. That if a person by the unskillfulness of his physician, or by the contrivance of his enemies, eat or drink such a thing as causeth such a temporary or permanent phrenzy, as aconitum or nux vomica, this puts him into the same condition, in reference to crimes, as any other phrenzy, and equally excuseth him. 2. That although the simplex phrenzy occasioned immediately by drunkenness excuse not in criminals, yet if by one or more such practices, an habitual or fixed phrenzy be caused, though this madness was contracted by the vice and will of the party, yet this habitual and fixed phrenzy thereby caused puts the man into the same condition in relation to crimes, as if the same were contracted involuntarily at first." pp. 31–33.

Thus Hale, as the law does today, distinguished between temporary insanity caused by voluntary drunkenness and that caused by involuntary drunkenness and he recognized that permanent insanity, even though caused by voluntary drinking, excused the commission of a crime.

The rule of law with respect to responsibility for criminal conduct as affected by voluntary intoxication which has been consistently followed by the majority of courts in the United States is substantially that stated by Lord Hale. Regardless of what test is applicable to determining insanity, the majority distinguish between (1) the mental effect of voluntary intoxication which is the immediate result of a particular alcoholic bout; and (2) an alcoholic psychosis [3] resulting from long continued habits of excessive drinking. The first does not excuse responsibility for a criminal act; the second may. In other words, if a person drinks intoxicating liquor and is sane both prior to drinking and after the influences of the intoxicant has

3. The term "alcoholic psychosis" has been defined as "Insanity due to alcohol", Davidson, Forensic Psychiatry, p. 316 (1952), and as "grave mental disorder found in connection with excessive use of alcohol which was imbibed because of defective personality integration and resulting unsolved conflicts", Cavanaugh & McGoldrick, Fundamental Psychiatry, p. 426 (1958).

worn off, but is insane by the applicable test while under the influence of the intoxicant, he comes under the first category. If he is insane whether or not he is directly under the influence of an intoxicant, even though that insanity was caused by voluntary drinking, he comes under the second category. The cases usually refer to the first category as a "temporary" insanity and the second category as a "permanent", "fixed" or "settled" insanity. These terms may be an oversimplification. What "permanent", "fixed" or "settled" means within the frame of reference is that the insanity not only existed while a person was under the influence of intoxicating spirits as an immediate result of imbibing, but existed independent of such influence, even though the insanity was caused by past imbibing. So if a person while in the throes of delirium tremens which may meet the test for insanity, commits a crime, he is not responsible for his criminal conduct, although such defect, resulting remotely from excessive drinking is only a temporary toxic state. It would seem that the distinction, notwithstanding the language of the cases, is not so much between temporary and permanent insanity as it is one between the direct results of drinking, which are voluntarily sought after, and its remote and undesired consequences. We adopt the majority view.

C. RESULTS AND THE REQUIREMENT OF CAUSATION

A number of crimes, including but by no means restricted to the homicide offenses, require proof of the occurrence of a result and of a causal relationship between the defendant's acts and that result. Other crimes such as perjury and bribery do not require a result as part of their definition. For perjury it is enough that one makes a false statement under oath with intent to deceive and with knowledge of the statement's falsity even though no one is deceived by it. Similarly, bribery involves an intentional or knowing offer of a benefit in consideration for the recipient's official action whether or not the recipient's official behavior is affected. In such cases causation will not, of course, ever be an issue.

As will be seen from the following materials, causation problems will almost always involve homicides and most commonly will pose issues of grading rather than complete exculpation. That is, a decision that the defendant did not legally cause the victim's death will seldom leave the defendant free of all penal liability. For example, a defendant found not to have "caused" a victim's death within the meaning of the law may still be guilty of battery, which, of course, does not require that the victim be shown to have died because of the blow. Or the defendant may be guilty of attemped murder, if the requirements for attempt are met, because no showing that death resulted from the defendant's act is necessary for attempt.

Even though causation problems arise with relative infrequency, enormous effort has been devoted to trying to resolve the issue. This is because commonly the particular result—the death—which has occurred, and which provides the basis for the prosecution carries a significantly higher penalty than the ordinary results of defendant's acts would carry, or because the connection between the result and the defendant's act is so attenuated that there are doubts as to the ethical propriety of imposing the severe penalty attached to the result. The courts and commentators have sought ways to ensure that the defendant is truly deserving of the higher penalty. Also, there is concern over the possibility of jury nullification in situations in which the net of causation is spread too widely. In many ways, the problem of causation is but another technique for adjusting penal sanctions to the subjective blameworthiness of the defendant.

The problem of causation will seldom be one of cause in fact. Cases are most unlikely to be prosecuted where it is not obvious that "but for" the defendant's actions the prohibited harm would not have occurred. Rather, the cases over which courts have struggled are those involving questions of "proximate" or "legal" cause which involve judgments as to the degree to which the result and the manner of its occurrence may be said to have been within the intent or contemplation of the actor. Thus, the cases commonly involve defendants who have intended or been reckless as to harming another but, due to natural events or conditions, or the actions of the victim or of third parties, the person harmed or the degree of harm or the manner of its occurrence is quite different from that intended or contemplated.

It may safely be asserted that these problems present some of the most perplexing matters with which the substantive criminal law must deal.

WEINREB, COMMENT ON BASIS OF CRIMINAL LIABILITY; CULPABILITY; CAUSATION, IN 1 WORKING PAPERS OF THE NATIONAL COMMISSION ON REFORM OF FEDERAL CRIMINAL LAWS

142–43 (1970).

The principles governing attribution of consequences to a person's conduct for purposes of criminal liability are not ordinarily stated collectively as a coherent body of doctrine. Still less often have such principles been codified. * * *

If anything but for which an event would not have occurred is a cause of the event, there are any number of "causes" of every event. The presence of oxygen in the air and the physical properties of paper are as much causes, in that sense, of the burning of a piece of paper as is touching a lit match to the paper. When we select a cause as *the cause*, the selection is based on some principle that reflects our interests. By making the selection, we focus our attention on some aspect of the situation, usually one which we think is under our control, so that we can assure or prevent a repetition of the occurrence.

If someone drops a cup and it breaks, we are more likely to say "You should be more careful," than to say "I wish the floor were not so hard"; but if an infant drops the cup, we are likely to say "We'll have to get him a plastic cup," instead of "He really must not drop things." As a crude and preliminary approximation of ordinary speech and understanding it is fair to say that we distinguish the cause of an event from the (necessary) conditions of an event according to our interests, which usually but not always means that we single out as the "cause" some element of the situation which we can control and describe as "conditions" other necessary elements. Some necessary conditions are taken so much for granted—for example, the presence of oxygen in the air, the physical properties of paper—that unless some curious feature of the situation focuses our attention on them, we do not mention them even as conditions. Without some frame of reference, the question, "What is (are) the cause(s) of *X*?" is as meaningless as the question, "What are all the conditions but for which *X* would not have occurred?" Ordinarily the frame of reference is clear and is supplied by commonsense out of common experience.

The inadequacy of principles of causation in the criminal law reflects uncertainty about the basis of criminal liability in situations where results are important to liability. We are not certain whether the assailant who gives the hemophiliac a light blow that causes a bruise from which the hemophiliac dies should be punished for assault or homicide; or whether all the senators should be punished as Caesar's murderers even though any dozen could have stayed away from the Forum on the fateful day without changing the result.

PEOPLE v. HEBERT

California District Court of Appeal, 1964.
228 Cal.App.2d 514, 39 Cal.Rptr. 539.

SHINN, Presiding Justice. Henry Hebert was charged with the murder of Charles Swallow, pleaded not guilty, and after a trial by jury was convicted of involuntary manslaughter, a lesser included offense. Probation was denied and he was sentenced to the state prison. Defendant was represented by the Public Defender. Appeal is brought from the judgment in propria persona.

Defendant was a patron in a Venice bar, drinking beer but not intoxicated, when the victim entered at about 11 p. m. According to all the witnesses who testified on the subject, Swallow appeared to be either drunk or ill; the barmaid refused him service. He sat on a stool near defendant and an argument arose between them. It was established that defendant, while standing, hit Swallow in the face with his fist while Swallow was sitting on a bar stool, and that the assault was without sufficient provocation. When hit, the victim was knocked to the floor. Defendant testified that Swallow asked him for a quarter, which was refused, and Swallow said "All I done for you niggers, I can't get anything out of you" and defendant said "That is where you are wrong, man." Swallow shoved him, put his hand into his coat pocket and said "I ought to cut your throat"; Swallow did not fall off the bar stool but that after he was hit another patron said "watch that knife," grabbed Swallow around the waist and pulled him off the stool. This other patron did not testify, nor was any knife found. No one actually saw Swallow fall, but several witnesses heard him fall. There was sufficient evidence to prove that the victim was knocked off the bar stool by the force of defendant's blows and that his head hit the wooden barroom floor with what one witness described as a loud "thud."

Officers arrived about ten minutes later. Swallow was lying on the floor on his back, but apparently conscious. Officers assisted him to a sitting position and thought he was not seriously injured, but was intoxicated. They partly carried, partly dragged him to a patrol car and took him to the police station for booking for being intoxicated in a public place. Thelma McCord, the barmaid, testified that the two officers dragged Swallow from the place where he lay on the floor to the sidewalk; one officer lifted Swallow by holding onto his belt in the rear; the other lifted at his head; Swallow's feet were dragging; at the sidewalk the officers dropped him on his face; the drop was 12 to 14 inches; he was perfectly limp. The two officers testified that they partly carried, partly dragged Swallow to the sidewalk, sat him down in a sitting position and then laid him gently on his back; they did not drop him.

The officers arrived at the station with the victim about 35 minutes after the altercation. According to the officers, during the booking procedure and just after Swallow was searched and he was standing with his hands high against a wall, he was observed to fall over backwards with his arms at his sides and "completely rigid as though a plank were falling"; his buttocks hit the floor first and then the back of his head; his head bounced about six inches off the floor and fell back, striking the floor a second time. The floor was concrete with an asphalt tile covering. Immediately after hitting the floor he started bleeding from one ear and within a few seconds from both ears. He was removed to a hospital where he died that morning.

The determinative question on the trial was whether defendant's act of striking decedent and knocking him to the floor was a proximate cause of death.

Dr. Kade, autopsy surgeon for the Los Angeles County Coroner's office, testified that there were three areas of injury to the head, each caused by a separate impact; one to the nasal area, causing a fracture of the nasal bones; one to the left rear of the skull, causing severe hemorrhaging; and a third to the right rear portion of the skull, causing additional fracturing and hemorrhaging. The nasal fracture was apparently due to the direct blows of defendant; the injury to the left rear of the skull was the most serious and the injury was more consistent with the decedent's having struck his head on the wooden barroom floor than with his falling and striking his head on the concrete floor at the police station. In the opinion of the witness, the injury to the left rear of the skull was received as the result of decedent's being knocked off the bar stool. Both these injuries to the brain caused hemorrhaging, and either one, in Dr. Kade's opinion, would have resulted in a loss of consciousness. It was the opinion of Dr. Kade that the injury to the right side of decedent's head was caused at the police station when decedent suddenly lost consciousness and fell backward. The opinion of Dr. Kade was stated on cross-examination as follows: "In my opinion, death was caused by the two blows to the rear of the head. Whether the injury causing the fracture of the nasal bone would have been enough to cause death in and of itself, is difficult for me to establish, since there were these two additional injuries to the back of the head."

The witness was questioned further on cross-examination: "Q You feel at this time, Doctor, that it is difficult for you to say that the damage to the nasal area and the front of the skull there, that that would have been sufficient in and of itself to have brought about death; is that right? A Well, it is difficult to say because it is a conjectural question. It is like saying, if a boat is on fire and there is an explosion on board and the boat sinks would the fire have been enough to destroy the boat by itself had there not been an explosion. It is trying to infer what would have happened or could have happened if something else didn't happen. But the something else did happen and so I would be hesitant to conjecture about what could or might have happened under other circumstances." And when questioned further on cross-examination, he answered as follows: "Q Well, when you stated earlier, Doctor, that you felt it would be speculative or conjectural for you to say that the damage to the front part of the skull was sufficient in itself to be fatal, did you mean that you felt it was conjectural, too conjectural or speculative for you to testify under oath that such damage could cause death in and of itself? A No, I did not. It is my opinion that it easily could have, but I did not wish to state it as an absolute certainty that it would have definitely and unequivocally have caused death as an inevitable result in and of itself. It is my opinion that the greatest likelihood, the greatest medical probability is that it would have been sufficient to cause death. But I hesitate to state it as an absolute certainty."

The statement of the doctor that death resulted from the blows on the rear portions of the skull is clear enough. His opinion with respect to the probable consequences of the blow which fractured the nasal bones was an expression of his belief that the blow "easily could have" and that according "to the greatest medical probability" would have been sufficient to cause death. The force of this opinion was not destroyed by the stated qualification that he was not saying that death would have been the inevitable result of the blow or would have followed as an absolute certainty. The opinions expressed with respect to the probable consequences of the blow to the face, considered with the opinion that the major brain hemorrhage resulted from the fall on the barroom floor left no doubt that the opinion of the doctor was that the injuries in the barroom were probably fatal.

The evidence of the several injuries, the blow to the face, the fall in the barroom, the incident on the sidewalk and the fall in the police station presented the critical question as to the proximate cause of the death.

Upon this issue the primary factual question was whether the injuries received in the barroom would have resulted in death. Defendant was responsible for all the injuries inflicted in the barroom and if the jury had found those injuries to have been so severe as to have resulted in death the fact that other injuries were suffered later would have been immaterial. The only support for a finding of the jury that the injuries in the barroom were fatal would have been the opinion expressed by Dr. Kade. The jury was not required to give full effect to his opinion, and could have doubted that the fatal injuries were suffered in the barroom incident. It is of common knowledge that a blow which causes a broken nose does not ordinarily cause death. The picture of deceased taken at the police station merely showed him lying on his back with his head on the floor. There was evidence that his head bounced after hitting the floor. It was a matter of pure speculation which side of the skull hit the floor first. Moreover, the opinion of the doctor that the most serious fall was the one in the barroom was inconsistent with the fact that it was the fall in the police station that caused immediate bleeding from both ears. If it was doubted that the first injuries would have produced a fatal result and that death would have resulted despite the injuries received in the police station, the question necessarily arose whether defendant was responsible for the consequences of the later fall. It was, therefore, vitally important that the jury be adequately and correctly instructed on the doctrine of proximate cause.

The court instructed that in order to find the defendant guilty of either murder or involuntary manslaughter the jury must find that the injury inflicted by defendant was a proximate cause of the death and that "The proximate cause of an injury is that cause which, in natural and continuous sequence, unbroken by any efficient intervening cause, produces the injury, and without which the result would not have occurred. It is the efficient cause—the one that necessarily sets in operation the factors that accomplish the injury."

The court also instructed as follows: "You are instructed that to be a legal cause of death, a defendant's act must be its proximate cause, not merely its possible cause. A defendant's act may be considered the proximate cause of the death of another though it is not the immediate cause, if it is the ultimate cause. But where there is a supervening cause the defendant's act cannot be considered a proximate cause. The fact, if it be a fact, that the deceased or some other person or persons were guilty of negligence, which was a contributory cause of the death involved in the case, is not deemed to be a supervening cause and is no defense to a criminal charge if the defendant's own conduct was a proximate cause of the death." We are of the opinion that these instructions were wholly inadequate.

It has been the practice for many years to instruct in the language of the first quoted instruction, but we do not believe it was a satisfactory or sufficient instruction to give in the present case where the question of proximate cause was an intricate and difficult one to be resolved by the jury. We do not say the instruction misstates the law, but only that in the present case it was unclear and confusing as a statement of the doctrine of proximate cause. * * *

There have been many attempts to phrase an all-purpose definition of proximate cause, but we think that in ordinary circumstances all the definitions have had their roots in the doctrine of foreseeability. We think the jury should have been instructed in clear and simple language as to the measure of the responsibility of defendant for the acts which caused Swallow's death. He was responsible not only for the injuries inflicted in the barroom, but for any later injuries to Swallow that were reasonably foreseeable, and which he would not have sustained if in a normal condition. The issue here was clearcut and vital and should have been submitted to the jury upon the test of foreseeability. Instead of being submitted in this simple form, the issue was confused by the use in the first instruction of the terms "natural and continuous sequence," "efficient intervening cause" and "necessarily sets in operation the factors that accomplish the result." And in the second quoted instruction, we find "superseding cause" added. The jury was given no definition of "efficient intervening cause" or "supervening cause." These are vague and confusing terms, at best, and the jury should not have been left to guess at their meaning and their application to the facts. What test was the jury to apply in determining their meaning? Do the terms "intervening" and "supervening" mean the same thing, or have they different meanings? What would be an "efficient intervening cause" or "supervening cause" that would break the chain of causation? Would the chain remain unbroken even though the later event was one that was extraordinary and unpredictable? The instructions did not answer these questions.

We cannot doubt that in an effort to understand the full purport of the instructions the minds of the jurors would have been distracted from the question of foreseeability of future injury. They were told to look for an "efficient intervening cause" or a "supervening cause" as if it made no difference whether after-occurring causes were reasonably foreseeable. The fall in the police station, judged from appearances, was extremely serious, as evidenced by the bleeding from both ears. The jury could well have believed that except for that fall death would not have occurred. Of course, the question was not whether that particular event might occur, but whether any serious injury was likely to occur because of Swallow's condition. Defendant had a duty to anticipate the common and ordinary consequences of his act, and these he was responsible for. They could be said to be the direct consequences. But the fall in the police station could have been found to be an extraordinary and abnormal occurrence, not reasonably foreseeable as a result of the first injuries. The failure of the court to instruct that defendant would have been responsible for the consequences of the injuries received after Swallow was taken from the barroom only if further injury was reasonably to be anticipated, and the giving of instructions that enabled the jury to hold him responsible for later injuries even if the same were not reasonably foreseeable was prejudicial and reversible error.

The judgment is reversed.

NOTE

The court suggests that "supervening" and "intervening" were not adequately defined. But R. Perkins, Criminal Law 698 (2nd ed. 1969) has suggested that "superceding cause" be defined as a factor that intervenes between the defendant's act and the result in question in such a way that legally speaking it is "the cause." Thus a superceding cause is simply one that has the legal effect of breaking the chain of proximate causation between the defendant's act and the result of death. Supervening cause, as used by the trial court in this case, could be given the same definition.

McLaughlin, Proximate Cause, 39 Harv.L.Rev. 149, 159–60 (1925) defines "intervening" force as follows:

> An intervening force is a force which is neither operating in the defendant's presence, nor at the place where the defendant's act takes effect at the time of the defendant's act, but comes into effective operation at or before the time of the damage. Thus where a fire is started in a then existing wind, the wind is not an intervening force, but a condition existing at the time of the defendant's act.

An "intervening cause" could be similarly defined. If a "supervening cause" must be an "intervening cause," this only means that it must be something that comes into operation at or before the time of the damage. For example, in the instant case if Swallow was intoxicated at the time he was struck by the defendant, his intoxication was a "condition existing at the time of the defendant's act," not an intervening factor, and therefore it could not break the chain of proximate causation between the defendant's blow and Swallow's death.

MODEL PENAL CODE *

(Tent. Draft No. 4, 1955).

Section 2.03. Causal Relationship Between Conduct and Result; Divergence Between Result Designed or Contemplated and Actual Result or Between Probable and Actual Result

(1) Conduct is the cause of a result when:

(a) it is an antecedent but for which the result in question would not have occurred; and

(b) the relationship between the conduct and result satisfies any additional causal requirements plainly imposed by law.

(2) When purposely or knowingly causing a particular result is a material element of an offense, the element is not established if the actual result is not within the purpose or the contemplation of the actor unless:

(a) the actual result differs from that designed or contemplated, as the case may be, only in the respect that a different person or different property is injured or affected or that the injury or harm designed or contemplated would have been more serious or more extensive than that caused; or

(b) the actual result involves the same kind of injury or harm as that designed or contemplated and is not too accidental in its occurrence to have a just bearing on the actor's liability or on the gravity of his offense. [Alternative: and it occurs in a manner which the actor knows or should know is rendered substantially more probable by his conduct.]

(3) When recklessly or negligently causing a particular result is a material element of an offense, the element is not established if the actual result is not within the risk of which the actor is aware, or in the case of negligence, of which he should be aware unless:

(a) the actual result differs from the probable result only in the respect that a different person or different property is injured or affected or that the probable injury or harm would have been more serious or more extensive than that caused; or

(b) the actual result involves the same kind of injury or harm as the probable result and is not too accidental in its occurrence to have a just bearing on the actor's liability or on the gravity of his offense. [Alternative: and it occurs in a manner which the actor knows or should know is rendered substantially more probable by his conduct.]

Commentary

Section 2.03. Causal relationship between conduct and result; Divergence between result designed or contemplated and actual result or between probable and actual result

1. This section is concerned with offenses that are so defined that causing a particular result is a material element of the offense, as in the case of homicide, theft, etc. It undertakes to define the causality relationship that should generally be required to establish liability for such offenses and to deal with inevitable problems incident to variations between the actual result of conduct and the result sought or contemplated by the actor or probable under the circumstances of the action. These problems are now faced as issues of "proximate causation" and they present enormous difficulty, especially in homicide, because of the vague meaning of that term. Rather than seek to systematize variant and sometimes inconsistent rules in different areas in which the problem has arisen, the section undertakes a fresh approach to what appear to be the central issues.

2. Paragraph 1(a) treats but-for cause as the causality relationship that normally should be regarded as sufficient, in the view that this is the simple, pervasive meaning of causation that is relevant for purposes of penal law. When concepts of "proximate causation" disassociate the actor's conduct and a result of which it was a but-for cause, the reason always inheres in the judgment that the actor's culpability with reference to the result, i. e., his purpose, knowledge, recklessness or negligence, was such that it would be unjust to permit the result to influence his liability or the gravity of the offense of which he is convicted. Since this is so, the draft proceeds upon the view that problems of this kind ought to be faced as problems of the culpability required for conviction and not as problems of "causation."

Paragraph 1(b) contemplates, however, that this general position may prove unacceptable in dealing with particular offenses. In that event, additional causal requirements may be imposed explicitly, such for example, as a temporal limitation with respect to causing death.

3. Paragraphs (2) and (3) are drafted on the theory stated. They assume that liability requires purpose, knowledge, recklessness or negligence with respect to the result which is an element of the of-

fense and deal explicitly with variations between the actual result and that designed, contemplated or threatened, as the case may be, stating when the variation is considered immaterial.

4. Paragraph (2) is addressed to the case where the culpability requirement with respect to the result is purpose or knowledge, i. e. where purposely or knowingly causing a specified result is a material element of the offense. Here if the actual result is not within the purpose or the contemplation of the actor, the culpability requirement is not established, except in the circumstances set forth in sub-paragraphs (a) and (b).

Sub-paragraph (a) deals with the situation where the actual result differed from the result designed or contemplated only in the respect that a different person or different property was injured or affected or that the injury or harm designed or contemplated was more serious or more extensive than that caused. Such variations between purpose or contemplation and result are made immaterial, as almost certainly would be the view under existing law.

Sub-paragraph (b) deals with the situation where the actual result involved the same kind of injury or harm as that designed or contemplated but the precise injury inflicted was different or occurred in a different way. Here the draft makes no attempt to catalogue the possibilities, e. g., to deal with the intervening or concurrent causes, natural or human; unexpected physical conditions; distinctions between the infliction of mortal or non-mortal wounds. It deals only with the ultimate criterion by which the significance of such possibilities ought to be judged, presenting two alternative formulations. The first proposes that the question to be faced is whether the actual result is "too accidental in its occurrence to have a just bearing on the actor's liability or on the gravity of his offense." The alternative proposes that the issue turn on whether the actual result "occurs in a manner which the actor knows or ought to know is rendered substantially more probable by his conduct."

It may be useful in appraising either treatment of the problem to note that what will usually turn on the determination will not be the criminality of a defendant's conduct but rather the gravity of his offense. Since the actor, by hypothesis, has sought to cause a criminal result or has been reckless or negligent with respect to such a result, he will be guilty of some crime under a well-considered penal code even if he is not held for the actual result, i. e. he will be guilty of attempt, assault or some offense involving risk creation, such as reckless driving. Thus the issue in penal law is very different than in torts. Only in form is it, in penal law, a question of the actor's liability. In substance, it is a question of the severity of sentence which the Court is authorized or obliged to impose. Its practical importance thus depends on the disparity in sentence for the various offenses that may be involved, e. g. the sentences for an attempted and completed crime.

How far a Model Code ought to attribute importance in the grading of offenses to the actual result of conduct, as distinguished from results attempted or threatened, presents an issue of some difficulty which is of general importance in the Code. It may be said, however, that distinctions of this order are to some extent essential, at least when the severest sanctions are involved. For juries will not lightly find convictions that will lead to the severest types of sentences unless the resentments caused by the infliction of important injuries have been aroused. Whatever abstract logic may suggest, a prudent legislator cannot disregard these facts of life in the enactment of a penal code.

It may be added that attributing importance to the actual result does not substantially detract from the deterrent efficacy of the law, at least in dealing with cases of purposeful misconduct. One who attempts to kill and thus expects to bring about the result punishable by the gravest penalty, is unlikely to be influenced in his behavior by the treatment that the law provides for those who fail in such attempts; his expectation is that he is going to succeed. See Michael and Wechsler, A Rationale of the Law of Homicide, 37 Columbia L. Rev. 1261, 1294–1298.

Viewed in these terms, it may be said that either the proposed or the alternative formulation should suffice for the exclusion of those situations where the actual result is so remote from the actor's purpose or contemplation that juries can be expected to believe that it should have no bearing on the actor's liability for the graver offense or, stated differently, on the gravity of the offense of which he is convicted. If, for example, the defendant attempted to shoot his wife and missed, with the result that she retired to her parents' country home and then was killed in falling off a horse, no one would think that the defendant should be held guilty of murder, though he did intend her death and his attempt to kill her was a but-for cause of her encounter with the horse. Both court and jury would regard the actual result as "too accidental in its occurrence to have a just bearing on the actor's liability or on the gravity of his offense." Alternatively, they would regard the actual result as one which did not occur in a manner that the actor knew or should have known was rendered substantially more probable by his conduct when he attempted to shoot his wife to death.

It is in closer cases that a difference in result might be expected. Thus, if the defendant in the case supposed had shot his wife and in the hospital she had contracted a disease which was medically unrelated to the wound (though related to her presence in the hospital), her death from the disease may well be thought to have been rendered substantially more probable by the defendant's conduct, as presumably he should have known. Yet juries might regard it as a too unusual result to justify convicting him of murder. The advantage of putting the issue squarely to the jury's sense of justice is that it does not attempt to force a result which the jury may resist. It also leaves the principle flexible for application to the infinite variety of cases likely to arise. The argument for the alternative is, on the other hand, that flexibility will involve inequality of application; that if the actual result was foreseen or foreseeable as a substantial probability, there can be no injustice in holding the actor responsible for its occurrence, nor is there any reason to expect that jury action will nullify such a rule.

In the Reporter's view, either formulation is acceptable. What is important is to free the law from the encrusted precedents on "proximate causation", offering a principle that will permit both courts and juries to begin afresh in facing problems of this kind.

5. Paragraph (3) deals with the case where recklessness or negligence is the required kind of culpability and where the actual result is not within the risk of which the actor was aware, or, in the case of negligence, of which he should have been aware. The principles proposed to govern are the same as in the case where purposely or knowingly causing the specified result is the material element of the crime. If the actual result differed from the probable result only in the respect that a different person or different property was injured or affected, the variation is declared to be inconsequential. In other situations, if the actual result involved the same kind of injury or harm as the probable result, the question asked is whether it was too accidental in its occurrence to have just bearing on the actor's liability or on the gravity of his offense or, if the alternative is preferred, whether the result occurred in a manner which the actor knew or should have known was rendered substantially more probable by his conduct. The governing considerations are the same as in the situation dealt with by paragraph (2).

PEOPLE v. SCOTT

Court of Appeals of Michigan, 1971.
29 Mich.App. 549, 185 N.W.2d 576.

J. H. GILLIS, Presiding Judge. Defendant appeals as of right from a conviction by jury of involuntary manslaughter, M.C.L.A. § 750.321 (Stat.Ann.1954 Rev. § 28.553).

The defendant, after engaging in an exchange of verbal hostilities with the occupants of a police patrol car, attempted to force the vehicle off the road. A chase ensued and a radio alert was relayed to other cars in the vicinity. An unmarked patrol car, in pursuit of defendant, collided at an intersection with a DSR bus, killing one of the officers in the patrol car.

The single issue raised on appeal is whether trial court committed reversible error when it instructed the jury that to find the defendant guilty of involuntary manslaughter it must be established that the defendant's negligence was "a" proximate cause of the police officer's death and whether the court further erred in rejecting the defendant's contention that his negligence must constitute "the" proximate cause.

* * *

Michigan courts have traditionally held that a conviction for involuntary manslaughter, especially when committed with an automobile, may be sustained if the trier of fact is

> "[Able to] determine [that] the defendant was guilty of gross and culpable negligence in the operation of his motor vehicle and that said gross negligence in the operation of such motor vehicle was the proximate cause of the death of the deceased." People v. Layman (1941), 299 Mich. 141, 145, 146, 299 N.W. 840, 841.

* * *

Defendant stipulates, on appeal, that the speed and manner in which he was operating his car was such as could be deemed wilful and wanton disregard for the safety of others. It is the contention of the people that because the defendant readily admits that his driving was grossly negligent, that that erratic driving then becomes the proximate cause of the death of the police officer. They contend that if the defendant's driving had not been in violation of state law, the police would never have given chase and the death would not have occurred. Further, it is their contention that even if there were another independent cause for the officer's death, the jury could still find the defendant guilty of the offense charged if they found that his gross negligence was "a proximate cause" of the death. We find this logic unacceptable.

The trial judge's charge to the jury defined "proximate cause" to be

> "A direct and producing cause of the damage or injury. It doesn't have to be 'the' direct. The reason I say 'a' direct is that there can be more than one proximate cause of the damage or injury complained of * * *. As far as you [the jury] are concerned in this case, it is up to you to determine whether there was a causal connection between the driving of the defendant, if you find there was improper driving, and the end result * * *. There can be more than one proximate cause, as I told you."

* * *

The court, in its definition of "proximate cause," has adopted the civil law definition and applied it to a criminal prosecution.

* * *

If the tort liability concept of proximate cause were applied in criminal homicide prosecutions, the conduct of the decedent would have to be considered. That conduct would be examined not to prove that it was merely an additional proximate cause, but rather to determine whether it amounted to a subsequent wrongful act and thus superseded the original conduct chargeable to defendant. The trial court properly instructed the jury that they could find defendant not guilty if they determined that deceased's conduct was the sole cause of the collision. However, the court did give the instruction that the defendant could be found guilty if it was determined that both defendant and deceased had acted negligently. Such a charge is in opposition to the fundamental principles of criminal responsibility. It is axiomatic that "criminal guilt under our law is personal fault." People v. Sobczak (1955), 344 Mich. 465, 470, 73 N.W.2d 921, 923. "It is the very essence of our deep-rooted notions of criminal liability that guilt be personal and individual." [3] Commentary on Commonwealth v. Redline, 391 Pa. 486, 137 A.2d 472 (1958), reiterates why the tort standard of proximate cause is unacceptable in criminal prosecutions:

> "A closer causal connection between the felony and the killing than the proximate-cause theory normally applicable to tort cases should be required because of the extreme penalty attaching to a conviction for felony murder and the difference between the underlying rationales of criminal and tort law. The former is intended to impose punishment in appropriate cases while the latter is primarily concerned with who shall bear the burden of a loss." [4]

Other states have agreed with the reasoning adopted by Pennsylvania and have compelled their triers of fact, when implementing "proximate causation" in criminal prosecutions, to find that the defendant's act be the proximate cause of the homicide charged. * * *

The people, here, as in People v. Marshall (1961), 362 Mich. 170, 174, 106 N.W.2d 842, actually seek from us an "interpretation of the manslaughter statute which would impose open-ended criminal liability". This we cannot do. It is true as a general rule of law:

> "That a person engaged in the commission of an unlawful act is legally responsible for all of the consequences which may naturally or necessarily flow or result from such unlawful act." People v. Barnes, 182 Mich. 179, 197, 148 N. W. 400, 406 (1914).

3. Sayre, "Criminal Responsibility for the Acts of Another," 43 Harvard Law Review 689, 716 (1930).

4. Note, 71 Harvard Law Review 1565, 1566 (1958).

But before this principle of law can have any application in this case before us, it must first appear that the defendant's act was grossly negligent and that the resulting homicide was "*the* natural or necessary result of *the act* of [the defendant]." *Barnes,* supra, p. 198, 148 N.W. p. 406. (Emphasis supplied.) * * *

While there are no Michigan cases which are factually similar, there are many Michigan cases dealing with involuntary manslaughter,

> "[W]hich make it clear that to sustain a conviction of manslaughter the conduct of the accused must have been the immediate and direct cause of the death." People v. Ogg (1970), 26 Mich.App. 372, 400, 182 N.W.2d 570, 584, dissent by Danhof, J. and cases cited. See also: People v. Beardsley (1907), 150 Mich. 206, 113 N.W. 1128.

Although neither party is able to cite authority which requires that the defendant's criminally negligent act be the only direct and proximate cause of the ensuing homicide, this Court feels that the reasoning proffered by the Pennsylvania court in Commonwealth v. Root, 403 Pa. 571, 170 A.2d 310 (1961), constitutes the better standard. In criminal prosecutions there must be a more direct causal connection between the criminal conduct of the defendant and the homicide charged than is required by the tort liability concept of proximate cause.

Reversed and remanded for new trial not inconsistent herewith.

NOTES AND QUESTIONS

1. If it had been Scott's car, rather than that of the pursuing officer, which had crashed and caused a death would there be any doubt as to his culpability? See Tegethoff v. State, 220 So.2d 399 (Fla.Dist.Ct.App.1969). In *Tegethoff*, the defendant's car struck another vehicle while the defendant was attempting to elude pursuing police officers; the driver of the other vehicle was killed. Tegethoff was convicted of killing another by culpable negligence in the operation of a motor vehicle. Affirming this conviction, the appellate court held that the victim's death had been proved to be the proximate result of the defendant's negligent driving. It can be argued that the same logic applies to *Scott*. The accident involving the pursuing police vehicle seems to have been as foreseeable to the fleeing Scott as the accident in *Tegethoff* was to that defendant. The general "sense of fairness" would be no more offended by Scott's conviction than it was by the conviction of Tegethoff. Perhaps *Scott* was wrongly decided.

2. In Commonwealth v. Feinberg, 433 Pa. 558, 253 A.2d 636 (1969), the defendant owned a small store in the skid-row area of Philadelphia. He commonly sold "Sterno", a jelly-like substance made for use as a fuel and composed primarily of methanol (wood alcohol) and ethanol (grain alcohol) to the local residents knowing that at least some of them would extract the alcohol to drink. The manufacturer changed the formula of the product so that it contained 54% rather than 3.75% of the highly toxic methanol. The

cans containing the new product were the same as the old but, in addition to the previous warnings about use only for fuel and the danger of internal consumption, carried a skull and crossbones on the lid and were marked "Poison". The defendant sold approximately 400 cans of the new Sterno which resulted in the death of thirty-one persons in the area due to methanol poisoning. He was charged with thirty-one counts of involuntary manslaughter and convicted on a number of these counts.

On appeal, Feinberg argued, in part, that the causal connection was broken by the victims' voluntary acts in drinking. He sought to rely on the *Root* case (cited in *Scott*) where the Pennsylvania Supreme Court had held that the defendant could not be held criminally responsible for the death of his drag race competitor who was killed when he passed the defendant on a two lane road and collided with a truck. The *Root* court said that there was not a sufficiently direct causal connection between the defendant's act and the death. The court in *Feinberg* held that *Root* was of no aid to the defendant and that the contributory negligence of the victims could not be a defense where the defendant had been reckless.

In Commonwealth v. Atencio, 345 Mass. 627, 189 N.E.2d 223 (1963), the defendants were convicted of manslaughter based upon the self-inflicted death of a companion in the course of a game of "Russian roulette". Both of the defendants had, prior to the fatal shot, examined the revolver, seen that it contained one cartridge, spun the cylinder, pointed at his own head, and pulled the trigger. The court upheld the conviction despite the victim's voluntary involvement in the "game", and without approving the result in *Root* distinguished it on the basis of the skill involved in drag-racing as contrasted with the luck which controlled in Russian roulette.

Is *Atencio* to be distinguished from *Scott* because the chances of a fatal result in Russian roulette are greater than in high speed auto chases? Because of the comparative lack of social utility of the two activities? Because the driving skills of the pursuing officer in *Scott*, or the lack thereof, are a variable for which the defendant should not be held responsible? Is the *Scott* court's reliance on *Root* well-placed given the voluntary participation of the decedent there? Is *Feinberg* distinguishable from *Root* because of our doubts about the voluntary nature of the acts of those who drink Sterno?

3. In *Jordan*, 40 Crim.App. 158 (Eng.1956), the defendant's conviction of murder (sentence, death) was quashed on the basis of new evidence indicating that the victim died not from the defendant's perforation of his intestine but from pneumonia which resulted from medical treatment which was "palpably wrong" and "not normal." Id. at 157, 158. The court's judgment was based upon the testimony of two medical witnesses who apparently had not been involved in the treatment of the deceased. Following the court's action a medical board of inquiry found that the treatment had been "devoted and exemplary". Williams, Causation in Homicide, [1957] Crim.L.Rev. (Eng.) 429, 430, 510. An interesting critical piece on *Jordan* is Camps & Havard, Causation in Homicide—A Medical View, [1957] Crim.L.Rev. (Eng.) 576 which concludes:

> In future when victims of homicidal assaults survive long enough to receive hospital treatment it may well become a routine of the defense to impeach the medical treatment in order to show that the

> treatment was 'not normal.' There must be a strong body of opinion to agree with the old authorities that the point is legally irrelevant providing a wound has been given which is dangerous to life and the treatment has been adopted bona fide by competent medical attendants. The consequence of this change in the substantive law of homicide may be greater than has been appreciated. In particular, the courts may find themselves involved in protracted, undesirable, and, it is respectfully submitted, unnecessary investigations into the medical treatment of victims of homicidal assaults.

Id. at 585. If Jordan is absolved of murder as a result of the acts of the medical personnel should they be charged with some form of negligent homicide? If not, why?

4. It was, of course, possible to reindict and convict Jordan of some lesser offense. What value or values are served by thus reducing his liability? Are these the same values which would limit his liability if his victim had recovered and then died in an auto mishap?

5. The result in *Jordan* may be consistent with the insistence of the *Scott* court that the tort concept of proximate cause should not be applied to criminal cases but that a more direct causal connection be shown. In the context of medical treatment as an intervening cause does this mean that the care received, due to the defendant's infliction of the injury, must constitute medical malpractice before it can substitute for the defendant as the proximate cause of death? State v. Ulin, 113 Ariz. 141, 548 P.2d 19 (1976). If the victim's death is due to cardiac arrest in the course of an operation prolonged by the surgeon's decision to repair a hernia discovered upon opening the victim's abdomen to treat a stab wound inflicted by the defendant, can the defendant be held responsible for the death? In People v. Stewart, 40 N.Y.2d 692, 389 N.Y.S.2d 804, 358 N.E.2d 487 (1976), the court reversed a jury verdict of guilty when the undisputed evidence showed that the hernia repair was not required by the stabbing and that the cardiac arrest may have been due to the negligence of the anesthesiologist.

Would the malpractice standard preclude conviction for murder where the defendant's shooting of the victim required the amputation of a leg and the transfusion of eleven pints of blood resulting in the victim contracting serum hepatitis from which he died? Expert testimony indicated that the chances of exposure to serum hepatitis was 100% after receipt of six pints and that the incidence of death due to such exposure varied from .01 to three percent. If the victim might have collected damages for the hepatitis infection should that excuse the defendant whose act made it necessary for the victim to undergo this unavoidable risk. The court said "no" in People v. Flenon, 42 Mich.App. 457, 202 N.W.2d 471 (1972).

6. In many American jurisdictions, the common law rule that one may not be convicted of murder unless the victim died within a year and one day from the time the fatal blow was given or the cause of death administered is applied. See, e. g., Louisville E. & St. L. R. Co. v. Clarke, 152 U.S. 230, 239 (1894). In Commonwealth v. Ladd, 402 Pa. 164, 166 A.2d 501 (1966) the Pennsylvania Supreme Court interpreted the requirement as only a common law rule of evidence which the court was empowered to change, and abandoned it. Seeing the purpose of the requirement as preventing prose-

cutions in which the passage of time would make it too difficult to accurately ascertain the cause of death, the court concluded that advances in crime detection and medicine were such that the interest in accuracy would be served by putting no restriction upon the time within which prosecutions might be brought and requiring "proof of causation of conventional quality" at the trial. Musmanno, J. dissented, arguing that despite advances in crime detection and medicine there remains a real danger of unjustified prosecutions if the year and a day requirement was removed. He pointed to specifically the facts of the case—the victim had died of pneumonia thirteen months after being assaulted by the defendant—as demonstrating the difficult issues the rule was designed to withdraw from courts' consideration.

D. COMPLICITY

The law of "parties" is the doctrinal device by which the criminal law defines the outer limits of liability for activity indirectly related to a crime. At common law, participants in—or "parties" to—felonies [c] were categorized as follows:

Principal in the First Degree	One who, with the requisite state of mind, performed the criminal act or directly caused the criminal result, either with his own hand, with an instrument or a non-human agent, or by means of an innocent human agent.
Principal in the Second Degree	One who was actually or constructively present at the scene of the crime and who, with the required state of mind, aided, counseled, commanded, or encouraged the principal in the first degree.
Accessory Before the Fact	One neither actually nor constructively present at the scene of the crime who, with the requisite state of mind, ordered, counseled, encouraged or otherwise aided and abetted the principal in the first degree.
Accessory After the Fact	One who, with knowledge of the commission of an offense by an offender, concealed the offender or gave him some other assistance to prevent his detection, arrest, trial, or punishment.

c. Treason was the sole exception. All participants in treason were regarded as principals.

All participants in misdemeanors were simply principals. Concealment or assistance of a misdemeanant did not give rise to criminal liability at all.

Initially, all participants in a felony were subject to the same penalty without regard to which category they fell into. But it was soon recognized that the involvement of an accessory after the fact rendered him significantly less culpable than other participants. This category was set aside as a separate offense, independent of the felony of the individual aided or concealed, and penalty was assigned to it that was less severe than that assigned to the offense committed by the assisted felon. Although no jurisdiction still retains unmodified the common law of parties, statutory changes have been widely varied. Most, however, retain the basic notion of the common law of parties, that all who aid or abet the commission of a serious offense are subject to the same punishment as the person who actually commits it.

Clearly the law of parties (or its modern statutory progeny) is significant insofar as it defines the liability of those whose activity is only indirectly related to the offense. At common law, however, the law of parties had other implications. Jurisdictional complexities arose because of the common law rule that an accessory was punishable only where his act of accessoryship was committed, not where the final offense was committed. Strict attitudes towards pleading resulting in holdings that a defendant must be charged with the specific form of liability that the proof showed at trial; one charged as a principal in the first degree could not be convicted if the proof at trial showed that he was an accessory before the fact. (This was not expanded, however, to distinguish between the two degrees of principals.) Finally, the liability of an accessory was tied to that of the principal. Thus an accessory could not be tried before the principal and anything which prevented the conviction of the principal also prevented conviction of the accessory. This was even expanded to the point of holding that reversal of the principal's conviction required reversal of the conviction of the accessory.

Many of the procedural implications of the law of parties have been modified by statutes, and other offenses have been created in many jurisdictions to supplement that defining the accessory after the fact as guilty of an offense as a means of dealing with those whose actions impede official investigation of crime. The emphasis on the following material, then, is upon the law of parties as it defines the outer limits of liability for conduct other than that consisting of the criminal act itself or conduct directly causing the criminal result.

1. LIABILITY AS AN AIDER AND ABETTOR OR INCITOR

The most common form of liability for the conduct of another is that of one who assists another in committing a crime (an aider and abettor) or who encourages the other person to commit it (an incitor). In modern statutes, the distinctions among the various participants in a crime are generally eliminated. The following statutes are typical of modern provisions defining liability for participation in a crime other than by directly committing the crime through one's own actions.

18 UNITED STATES CODE

§ 2. Principals

(a) Whoever commits an offense against the United States or aids, abets, counsels, commands, induces or procures its commission, is punishable as a principal.

(b) Whoever willfully causes an act to be done which if directly performed by him or another would be an offense against the United States, is punishable as a principal.

CALIFORNIA PENAL CODE

§ 30. Classification

Classification of Parties to Crime. The parties to crimes are classified as:

1. Principals; and,
2. Accessories.

§ 31. Principals defined

Who are Principals. All persons concerned in the commission of a crime, whether it be felony or misdemeanor, and whether they directly commit the act constituting the offense, or aid and abet in its commission, or, not being present, have advised and encouraged its commission, and all persons counseling, advising, or encouraging children under the age of fourteen years, lunatics or idiots, to commit any crime, or who, by fraud, contrivance, or force, occasion the drunkenness of another for the purpose of causing him to commit any crime, or who, by threats, menaces, command, or coercion, compel another to commit any crime, are principals in any crime so committed.

MODEL PENAL CODE *

(Proposed Official Draft, 1962).

Section 2.06. Liability for Conduct of Another; Complicity

(1) A person is guilty of an offense if it is committed by his own conduct or by the conduct of another person for which he is legally accountable, or both.

(2) A person is legally accountable for the conduct of another person when:

(a) acting with the kind of culpability that is sufficient for the commission of the offense, he causes an innocent or irresponsible person to engage in such conduct; or

(b) he is made accountable for the conduct of such other person by the Code or by the law defining the offense; or

(c) he is an accomplice of such other person in the commission of the offense.

(3) A person is an accomplice of another person in the commission of an offense if:

(a) with the purpose of promoting or facilitating the commission of the offense, he

(i) solicits such other person to commit it; or

(ii) aids or agrees or attempts to aid such other person in planning or committing it; or

(iii) having a legal duty to prevent the commission of the offense, fails to make proper effort so to do; or

(b) his conduct is expressly declared by law to establish his complicity.

(4) When causing a particular result is an element of an offense, an accomplice in the conduct causing such result is an accomplice in the commission of that offense, if he acts with the kind of culpability, if any, with respect to that result that is sufficient for the commission of the offense.

(5) A person who is legally incapable of committing a particular offense himself may be guilty thereof if it is committed by the conduct of another person for which he is legally accountable, unless such liability is inconsistent with the purpose of the provision establishing his incapacity.

(6) Unless otherwise provided by the Code or by the law defining the offense, a person is not an accomplice in an offense committed by another person if:

(a) he is a victim of that offense; or

(b) the offense is so defined that his conduct is inevitably incident to its commission; or

(c) he terminates his complicity prior to the commission of the offense and

(i) wholly deprives it of effectiveness in the commission of the offense; or

(ii) gives timely warning to the law enforcement authorities or otherwise makes proper effort to prevent the commission of the offense.

(7) An accomplice may be convicted on proof of the commission of the offense and of his complicity therein, though the person claimed to have committed the offense has not been prosecuted or convicted or has been convicted of a different offense or degree of offense or has an immunity to prosecution or conviction or has been acquitted.

NOTE

The official draft does not include a provision proposed earlier which would, as part of paragraph 3, have criminalized the knowing facilitation of a crime. This earlier draft provided:

(3) A person is an accomplice of another person in commission of a crime if:

* * *

(b) acting with knowledge that such other person was committing or had the purpose of committing the crime, he knowingly, substantially facilitated its commission; or

[Alternative: (b) acting with knowledge that such other person was committing or had the purpose of committing the crime, he knowingly provided means or opportunity for the commission of the crime, substantially facilitating its commission; or]

Model Penal Code, Section 2.04 (Tent. Draft No. 1, 1953).

a. THE EXTENT OF PARTICIPATION NECESSARY

A major issue raised by existing provisions for the liability of participants in crime is the amount of participation necessary to render one liable. How much assistance or encouragement must one provide? The principal case in this subsection, State v. Spillman raises the issue: What sort of participation in Felix's rape of the victim would the state have to show before Spillman could be convicted of aiding and abetting? It is at least arguable that the court ignores persuasive evidence that Spillman participated in securing the victim's presence and in providing the isolation used by Felix to commit rape. The case also raises the question of whether conviction of an aider and abettor (or an incitor) should be permitted if the person alleged to have directly committed the criminal act has been acquitted. *Spillman* follows the clear modern, although not uniformly accepted, rule that such convictions are permissible, provided that the prosecution as part of its case against the aider and abettor proves the commission of the offense by the person aided or encouraged.

STATE v. SPILLMAN

Supreme Court of Arizona, 1970.
105 Ariz. 523, 468 P.2d 376.

HAYS, Justice. Defendant Erich Spillman was charged by information with two counts of forcible rape of Marguerite Basko. Count II of the complaint alleged that defendant raped Margie Basko * * * and Count I charged that defendant aided and abetted another rape of Miss Basko by one Gilbert Felix * * *. Trial on both charges was held in the Maricopa County Superior Court, at which the jury returned a verdict of guilty to Count I. The jury was unable to reach a verdict on Count II. The trial court sentenced defendant to a term of not less than five nor more than seven years at the Arizona State Prison. Defendant appeals from this conviction and sentence.

The alleged crimes purportedly took place in a downtown Phoenix flower shop around 11:00 p. m. on the night of April 4, 1967. Margie Basko, eighteen and a half years of age and a student at Arizona State University, was living at home with her parents near 40th Street and Thomas Road in East Phoenix. About 9 p. m. that evening, she received a telephone call from her former boyfriend, Bill Dickerson, who related that he had shown her picture to a couple of male acquaintances who wanted to drive over to her house to meet her. Margie agreed to their coming over, and about a half hour later, defendant and Gilbert Felix arrived at the Basko home and identified themselves as Dickerson's friends. Margie had never met either of the young men before, but invited them into the house, conversed with them for a few minutes, and introduced them to her parents. Afterward, the two men asked her to go out with them for a coke. Margie received permission from her mother to go out for a few minutes, and left the Basko home with defendant and Felix in defendant's Jaguar automobile. They drove from her home to a flower shop where defendant worked in downtown Phoenix.

After looking around the flower shop for about five minutes, the three went upstairs to the office of the shop, which was furnished with a couch and desk. While Margie sat on the couch, defendant Spillman showed her a copy of Playboy magazine and a book called "Sexes." Felix went downstairs to fix a drink, and Spillman moved next to Margie on the couch and tried to kiss her. Margie thwarted the gesture by pushing him away, and defendant did not persist. Felix returned with a drink, and defendant immediately proceeded downstairs.

While defendant was downstairs, Felix attempted several times to kiss Margie. Each time she told him to stop and pushed him away. She got up from the couch and started to walk away, but Felix pursued her over to a corner and held her against the wall. At this time the lights went out. Felix somehow got Margie back over to the couch, where he allegedly forcibly raped her. Margie testified at defendant's trial that while Felix was having intercourse with her, defendant Spillman returned upstairs, knelt beside her on the couch, and said "What's the matter." Felix then got off of her and Margie stood up from the couch and pulled up her pants. Defendant forced her back down on the couch and allegedly proceeded to rape her.

Defendant and Felix drove Margie back to her home, and let her off around midnight. Margie went inside and reported the incident to her mother. The police were called shortly thereafter, and defendant was arrested the next day, April 5. Gilbert Felix was not apprehended until several months later.

The information filed against Gilbert Felix was identical to that filed against defendant, that is, Count II of rape and Count I of aiding and abetting a rape. Felix was tried separately from and subsequent to defendant. At the time of Felix' trial, Count I, the aiding and abetting charge was dropped, and the jury subsequently found Felix not guilty of rape. In this appeal, defendant Spillman contends that his conviction of aiding and abetting Felix' rape cannot stand for the reason that Felix, the actual perpetrator of the alleged rape, was acquitted. The argument is made that where, as here, there is no question as to the identity of the party allegedly committing the forcible rape, the acquittal of the principal establishes that no forcible rape took place at all, thus invalidating the conviction for aiding and abetting. We do not agree.

* * *

Aiding and abetting is an independent and distinct substantive offense, and it is not necessary to try and convict the perpetrator of a criminal act before an aider and abettor can be tried. * * * But where a principal has been acquitted of a criminal act, can his accomplice, in a separate trial, be convicted of aiding and abetting that criminal act? We hold that he can.

The State is never required to prove more than the allegations contained in an information in order to sustain the conviction of an aider and abettor. Where, as here, a principal and an aider and abettor are jointly charged in the same information, and the aider and abettor is tried first, there can be no truthful allegation that the principal has been convicted of the crime. What is required at the trial of the aider and abettor is proof, complete and convincing, of the guilt of the principal. Justice demands that the principal crime be fully proved, since the guilt of the aider and abettor depends upon the commission of the principal crime. Thus, whether or not the principal is convicted or acquitted in a separate trial can have no bearing on the trial of the aider and abettor, if the evidence shows the latter guilty. Society is no less injured by the illegal acts of the aider and abettor even though the principal himself escapes conviction. In order to convict an aider and abettor, justice demands no more than the information properly charge and the evidence convincingly show that a crime was committed by the principal. * * * We hold that defendant's conviction * * * was not made invalid by the fact that Gilbert Felix was later acquitted of rape.

Defendant also contends that the evidence introduced at his trial was insufficient to support a conviction of aiding and abetting rape. Specifically, defendant contends that the evidence failed to show that he "assist(ed) in the commission of an act (the rape), either by active participation in it or in some manner advising or encouraging it," State v. Roberts, 85 Ariz. 252, 254, 336 P.2d 151, 152 (1959), or that he "(stood) in the same relation to the crime as the criminal, approach(ed) it from the same angle, touch(ed) it at the same point and possess(ed) criminal intent," State v. Bearden, supra, 99 Ariz. at 3, 405 P.2d at 886. A thorough review of the record, in a light most favorable to the allegations of the State, compels us to agree with defendant's position.

The evidence is clear and undisputed that Margie Basko voluntarily accompanied defendant and Felix to the flower shop where the alleged rapes occurred. She clearly testified that she was not in any fear and in no way felt coerced in either going to the flower shop or in going upstairs to the office of the shop. Margie unequivocally explained to the trial court that the first time she began to feel frightened was after defendant had gone downstairs leaving her alone upstairs with Felix. When Felix grabbed her and assaulted her, defendant was out of the room. Defendant did not return to the upstairs office until after the rape had commenced.

Nowhere does the evidence indicate that defendant assisted in any way, either physically or by advice and encouragement, Felix' alleged rape of Margie Basko. The State makes much of the fact that the lights to the upstairs office went out at the time Felix had Margie pinned against the wall. Margie testified that she did not douse the lights and that she did not see Felix turn off a light switch. Such testimony, however, is insufficient to link defendant with the act of turning out the lights in aid of Felix. The State failed to introduce evidence as to the location of the light switch in the room or building. In addition, testimony was never offered concerning any discussion between Felix and Spillman which would indicate a plot, scheme or agreement to rape Margie Basko.

In Carroll v. State, 90 Ariz. 411, 368 P.2d 649 (1962), we held that the mere presence of a defendant at the scene of a crime is insufficient to establish guilt. The evidence in this case, concerning Gilbert Felix' alleged rape of Margie Basko, indicates nothing more than defendant Erich Spillman being present, somewhere in the building, at the time Felix assaulted Margie. Without evidence indicating defendant Spillman's complicity in the crime, defendant's conviction for aiding and abetting a rape cannot stand.

The judgment of conviction is reversed.

NOTES AND QUESTIONS

1. Compare United States v. Prince, 430 F.2d 1324 (4th Cir. 1970), reversing a conviction for aiding and abetting a hunting companion in taking a rail bird from a boat powered by a motor in violation of federal law on the ground that while the appeal was pending the companion was tried as a principal and acquitted. What arguments can be made for the result in *Prince*? Is the acquittal of the principal logically inconsistent with the guilt of the aider and abettor? Does not the verdict in the principal's trial simply establish that on this occasion the prosecution failed to meet its especially high burden of proof of the principal's guilt, a determination in no way conclusive as to the actual guilt of the principal? What policy would be served by granting an alleged aider and abettor the "windfall" of acquittal?

2. If Spillman had the requisite state of mind, is there any real doubt that he performed sufficient acts to give rise to liability? In view of the victim's potential reluctance to accompany a single man, might not Spillman's actions in accompanying Felix be sufficient? If not, would his furnishing the transportation to the scene of the crime? Even if he did not turn off the lights, is it not arguable that his conduct at the flower shop facilitated the rape?

Is there adequate evidence of the requisite state of mind? Does not the testimony of the apparently coordinated activity of Spillman and Felix together with Spillman's lack of surprise at the time he came upon Felix and the victim permit the inference that he knew Felix intended to accomplish intercourse with the victim, by force if necessary? Would this be enough, or would it be necessary to establish that Spillman believed that such force would in fact be necessary?

3. Is there any helpful way to describe in general terms what nature of activity related to an offense committed by another will give rise to liability for aiding and abetting? Is the matter one of describing the acts of the potential aider and abettor, or is it one of describing the requisite impact (or likely impact) upon the principal? Consider Perkins, Parties to Crime, 89 U.Pa.L.Rev. 581, 598 (1941), who makes the following comment concerning the encouragement necessary for liability as a principal in the second degree: "Guilt or innocence of the abettor * * * is not determined by the quantum of his advice or encouragement. If it is rendered to

induce another to commit the crime and actually has this effect, no more is required." Cf. Commonwealth v. Pierce, 437 Pa. 266, 263 A.2d 350 (1970). Is it accurate to say that there is guilt as an aider and abettor if one, with the requisite state of mind, does any act within the meaning of the general principle that an act is required for criminal liability, or fails to act under circumstances making that failure sufficient for liability under general principles, and there is a resulting significant impact upon the principal in the commission of the crime? Must some impact, (i. e., a "result" factually and proximately caused by the alleged aider and abettor) be proved, or is it sufficient that the accused's act would generally tend to cause such an impact?

Complicity doctrine may pose serious free speech problems when the prosecution is predicated on verbal incitement. In United States v. Buttorff, 572 F.2d 619 (8th Cir., 1978), the defendants had been convicted under 18 U.S.C.A. § 2, quoted on page 233, supra, of aiding and abetting others in the filing of false income tax forms. Defendants were strong opponents of the graduated income tax and spoke concerning its alleged unconstitutionality before large gatherings. A number of those who had filed the false forms testified that they had done so because of the defendants' advice. Some claimed that the defendants had suggested techniques whereby they could eliminate any withholding from their wages. In only one instance was a further affirmative action claimed and that involved the provision of a form already marked with a claim of 20 exemptions. The Court of Appeals, although acknowledging it to be a close question, affirmed the convictions. It found that the

> defendants did go beyond mere advocacy of tax reform. They explained how to avoid withholding and * * * incited several individuals to activity that violated federal law * * *. This speech is not entitled to first amendment protection and * * * was sufficient action to constitute aiding and abetting * * *.

572 F.2d at 624.

b. THE STATE OF MIND NECESSARY

This section considers the state of mind necessary for liability as a participant in a crime. It is clear that as a general rule one is liable as an aider and abettor or incitor only if one has the intent necessary for the crime committed. One who assists another in taking property of a third person, for example, is liable as a participant in larceny or theft only if he has the intent to deprive the third person of the property (or knows that the person assisted or encouraged has such an intent). But, as the notes in this section indicate, one who becomes an aider and abettor to one crime committed by another person will also, under the rule applied by some courts, also be liable for other crimes committed by that other person, if those other crimes were a foreseeable result of the crime originally intended. Under this rule, it is not necessary that the defendant have the intent necessary for the other, foreseeable crimes.

The major problem is presented where the defendant knows that his actions will have the effect of assisting or encouraging its commission, but lacks the purpose to commit the crime. The defendant, in other words, remains indifferent as to whether the person assisted or encouraged is successful in completing the offense. The two principal cases in this section suggest opposite results. Wyatt v. United States indicates that the defendant is guilty of aiding and abetting the sale of illicit whiskey, even if he lacked any affirmative desire to have the sale finalized. But State v. Gladstone suggests that the defendant there is not guilty of aiding and abetting the sale of marijuana because the evidence shows he would not have profited from the sale and therefore apparently lacked any affirmative desire or purpose that it be successfully completed. No general rule can be stated as to which position is "the law." In many jurisdictions, the law is not clear concerning whether such purpose is required. Consider whether, as a matter of policy, a purpose to have the crime committed should be a requirement for conviction as an aider and abettor or incitor.

WYATT v. UNITED STATES

United States Court of Appeals, Tenth Circuit, 1968.
388 F.2d 395.

HILL, Circuit Judge. * * * [A]ppellant [Chester] Chandler attacks the sufficiency of the evidence to sustain his conviction * * * [of] aiding and abetting in the sale of non-tax-paid liquor to Agent Carpenter * * *.

Carpenter, an undercover agent and the Government's witness, testified that on August 14 he went to "Sonny Boy's" place in Guthrie, Oklahoma, and there he contacted Sonny Boy and asked him if he could buy some whiskey. Sonny Boy, not having any whiskey, directed him to go see Quinnon Chandler. Carpenter testified that he did go to the residence of Quinnon Chandler. Further: "When I arrived, I walked up to the front door and knocked and was invited into the house. Inside the house I observed Chester Chandler and Quinnon Chandler, they said they were glad to see me and told me to come out in the garage and see what they had. I walked out into the garage with Quinnon Chandler and Chester Chandler and observed seventeen and one-half gallons of moonshine whiskey inside the garage. After a brief conversation, I agreed to purchase six gallons of whiskey that night. After the agreement was made, Quinnon Chandler took two gallons, Chester Chandler took the four gallons in the case and placed them in the front of my vehicle, which was a Corvair with a trunk in the front. After the six gallons of whiskey was placed in the, in my vehicle, I asked Quinnon Chandler how much I owed him for the six gallons of whiskey, and he replied $36.00. I then paid Quinnon Chandler $36.00 for the six gallons of non-tax-paid whiskey, non-tax paid spirits." To be guilty of the crime of "aiding and abetting" one does not have to have an active stake in the outcome of the crime but merely participate therein. * * * Clearly and without any doubt, appellant Chandler participated here to the extent of helping his brother carry the illegally sold alcohol to the purchaser's car.

* * *

Affirmed.

STATE v. GLADSTONE

Supreme Court of Washington, 1970.
78 Wash.2d 306, 474 P.2d 274.

HALE, Justice. A jury found defendant Bruce Gladstone guilty of aiding and abetting one Robert Kent in the unlawful sale of marijuana. Deferring imposition of sentence, the court placed defendant on probation. He appeals * * * contending that the evidence as a matter of law was insufficient to sustain a verdict of guilty. His point, we think, is well taken.

* * *

Gladstone's guilt as an aider and abettor in this case rests solely on evidence of a conversation between him and one Douglas MacArthur Thompson concerning the possible purchase of marijuana from one Robert Kent. There is no other evidence to connect the accused with Kent who ultimately sold some marijuana to Thompson.

* * *

The conversation between defendant and Thompson occurred at defendant's residence. Douglas MacArthur Thompson, a 25-year-old student at the University of Puget Sound in Tacoma and an employee of the Internal Revenue Service of the United States, had done some investigative work for the government. From time to time, the Tacoma Police Department engaged him to investigate the use, possession and sale of narcotics, principally marijuana, among college students. When working for the Tacoma Police Department, he operated under the control and direction of the department's narcotics detail.

Thompson testified that Lieutenant Seymour and Detective Gallwas of the narcotics detail asked him to attempt a purchase of marijuana from Gladstone. During the evening of April 10, 1967—between 10 and 11 o'clock—the two officers and Thompson drove in a police car to the vicinity of defendant's apartment. Thompson went to Gladstone's door alone, beyond the hearing and out of the sight of the two officers. He knocked at the door and Gladstone responded. Thompson asked Gladstone if he would sell him some marijuana. Describing this incident, Thompson testified as follows:

Well, I asked—at the time Gladstone told me that he was—he did not have enough marijuana on hand to sell me any, but he did know an individual who had quite a sufficient quantity and that was very willing to sell and he named the individual as Robert Kent, or Bob Kent as he put it, and he gave me directions to the residence and he —due to the directions I asked him if, you know, if he could draw me a map and he did.

When Thompson said he asked Gladstone to draw the map for him, he added, "I'm not sure whether he did give me the exact address or not, he told me where the residence was." He said that Gladstone then with pencil and paper sketched the location of Kent's place of residence. Thompson had no prior knowledge of where Kent lived, and did not know if he might have marijuana or that he had ever possessed it.

The two officers then took Thompson to Kent's residence where marijuana was purchased. The actual purchase was made by Thompson directly from Kent while Officer Gallwas and Lieutenant Seymour stayed in the police car. Kent was subsequently arrested and convicted of selling Thompson approximately 8 ounces of marijuana —the very sale which defendant here was convicted of aiding and abetting.

That ended the prosecution's case. Even if it were accorded all favorable inferences, there appears at this point a gap in the evidence which we feel as a matter of law is fatal to the prosecution's cause. Neither on direct examination nor under cross-examination did Thompson testify that he knew of any prior conduct, arrangements or communications between Gladstone and Kent from which it could be even remotely inferred that the defendant had any understanding, agreement, purpose, intention or design to participate or engage in or aid or abet any sale of marijuana by Kent. Other than to obtain a simple map from Gladstone and to say that Gladstone told him Kent might have some marijuana available, Thompson did not even establish that Kent and the defendant were acquainted with each other. Testimony of the brief conversation and Gladstone's very crude drawing consisting of 8 penciled lines indicating where Kent lived constitute the whole proof of the aiding and abetting presented.

* * *

If all reasonable inferences favorable to the state are accorded the evidence, it does not, in our opinion, establish the commission of the crime charged. That vital element—a nexus between the accused and the party whom he is charged with aiding and abetting in the commission of a crime—is missing. The record contains no evidence whatever that Gladstone had any communication by word, gesture or sign, before or after he drew the map, from which it could be inferred that he counseled, encouraged, hired, commanded, induced or procured Kent to sell marijuana to Douglas Thompson as charged, or took any steps to further the commission of the crime charged. He was not charged with aiding and abetting Thompson in the purchase of marijuana, but with Kent's sale of it.

* * *

[E]ven without prior agreement, arrangement or understanding, a bystander to a robbery could be guilty of aiding and abetting its commission if he came to the aid of a robber and knowingly assisted him in perpetrating the crime. But regardless of the modus operandi and with or without a conspiracy or agreement to commit the crime and whether present or away from the scene of it, there is no aiding and abetting unless one " 'in some sort associate himself with the venture, that he participate in it as in something that he wishes to bring about, that he seek by his action to make it succeed.' " Nye & Nissen v. United States, 336 U.S. 613, 619, 69 S.Ct. 766, 769, 93 L.Ed. 919 (1949).

Although an aider and abettor need not be physically present at the commission of the crime to be held guilty as a principal, his conviction depends on proof that he did something in association or connection with the principal to accomplish the crime. Learned Hand, J., we think, hit the nail squarely when, in United States v. Peoni, 100 F.2d 401, 402 (2d Cir. 1938), he wrote that, in order to aid and abet another to commit a crime, it is necessary that a defendant

> in some sort associate himself with the venture, that he participate in it as in something that he wishes to bring about, that he seek by his action to make it succeed. All the words used—even the most colorless, "abet"—carry an implication of purposive attitude towards it.

* * *

Another case—and one nearly identical with the instant case—affirms the foregoing principles. In Morei v. United States, 127 F.2d 827 (6th Cir. 1942), undercover narcotic agents approached the defendant, a physician, and asked him to sell them narcotics. The doctor told the agents he had none, but gave the agents the name of another party and advised the agent to tell the latter that the doctor had sent him. The doctor added that "he will take care of you." The agents did arrange a purchase of illegal narcotics from the person to whom the doctor had referred them, and the doctor was thereupon charged with aiding and abetting in the sale.

After tracing the common-law distinction between a principal in the second degree and an accessory before the fact and pointing out that an aider and abettor must at least procure, counsel or command another to commit the felony actually committed, the court said, at 830:

> It is not necessary that there should be any direct communication between an accessory before the fact and the princi-

> pal felon; it is enough if the accessory direct an intermediate agent to procure another to commit the felony, without naming or knowing of the person to be procured. *A person is not an accessory before the fact, unless there is some sort of active proceeding on his part; he must incite, or procure, or encourage the criminal act, or assist or enable it to be done, or engage or counsel, or command the principal to do it.* Halsbury, supra, § 531. [9 Halsbury, Laws of England § 531 (1909)]. * * *
>
> * * * It is not to be assumed that Congress, in defining as a principal, one who "procures the commission of an offense," and using almost the identical language by which the common law defined aiders, abettors, and accessories, was providing for a new crime theretofore unknown. If the criterion for holding that one is guilty of procuring the commission of an offense, is that the offense would not have been committed except for such a person's conduct or revelation of information, it would open a vast field of offenses that have never been comprehended within the common law by aiding, abetting, inducing or procuring. * * *
>
> * * * [T]he only thing Dr. Platt did was to give Beach the name of Morei as a man from whom he might secure heroin to dose horses in order to stimulate them in racing. This is not the purposive association with the venture that, under the evidence in this case, brings Dr. Platt within the compass of the crime of selling or purchasing narcotics, either as principal, aider and abettor, or accessory before the fact. (Italics ours.)

* * *

It would be a dangerous precedent indeed to hold that mere communications to the effect that another might or probably would commit a criminal offense amount to an aiding and abetting of the offense should it ultimately be committed.

There being no evidence whatever that the defendant ever communicated to Kent the idea that he would in any way aid him in the sale of any marijuana, or said anything to Kent to encourage or induce him or direct him to do so, or counseled Kent in the sale of marijuana, or did anything more than describe Kent to another person as an individual who might sell some marijuana, or would derive any benefit, consideration or reward from such a sale, there was no proof of an aiding and abetting, and the conviction should, therefore, be reversed as a matter of law. Remanded with directions to dismiss.

HAMILTON, Justice (dissenting).

* * *

The statutory language and the overt action it contemplates does * * * give rise to the requirement that the aider or abettor entertain a conscious intent, i. e., knowledge and intent that his action will instigate, induce, procure or encourage perpetration of the primary crime. * * *

The question to be resolved, then, in the instant case is whether the evidence sustains the jury's conclusion that the appellant entertained the requisite intent to render him culpable as an aider or abettor.

* * *

Although the evidence in the case is conflicting, the jury was entitled to believe * * * that prior to the evening of April 10, 1967, when Thompson talked to appellant, *Thompson and the Tacoma Police Department were unaware of Kent or his association with marijuana;* * * * *that Thompson approached Kent and told him "Gladstone had sent me" whereupon Kent invited him to a room and sold him some marijuana for $30* * * *.

Based upon the * * * inferences reasonably derivable therefrom, I am satisfied that the jury was fully warranted in concluding that appellant, when he affirmatively recommended Kent as a source and purveyor of marijuana, entertained the requisite conscious design and intent that his action would instigate, induce, procure or encourage perpetration of Kent's subsequent crime of selling marijuana to Thompson. Furthermore, insofar as an element of preconcert be concerned, certainly the readiness with which the passwords, "Gladstone had sent me," gained a stranger's late evening entree to Kent's domain and produced two illegal sales strongly suggests, if not conclusively establishes, the missing communal nexus which the majority belabors.

NOTES AND QUESTIONS

1. Perkins, Parties to Crime, 89 U.Pa.L.Rev. 581, 603–04 (1941), in discussing the liability as an accessory before the fact of one conducting a lawful business who becomes aware that one purchasing his wares or services intends to use them in the commission of a crime, concludes as follows: "[T]he gravity of the social harm resulting from the unlawful conduct is used to determine whether mere knowledge of the intended use will be sufficient. * * * A seller who completes the sale of goods after correctly divining that the purchaser is buying them as an agent of an armed combination attempting to overthrow the government, thereby 'voluntarily aids the treason' * * *. But the mere knowledge of one party to the transaction that the other intends later to make an unlawful use of the property will not of itself be sufficient * * * if [the offense] is of a relatively minor nature. * * * It is otherwise, even as to such an offense, if the one charged as an inciter has not only had knowledge of the intended offense but has gone out of his way to promote it, as by packing the goods sold in an unusual manner to conceal their identity."

2. A very different problem is posed where the defendant clearly intended to aid the commission of one crime and is charged with responsibility for the commission of another committed by an accomplice in the course of the first crime. For example, in People v. Poplar, 20 Mich.App. 132, 173 N.W.2d 732 (1969), the defendant had allegedly served as a "look out" for a breaking and entering in the course of which the manager of the building was shot. Defendant was charged under complicity theory not only for breaking and entering but also for assault with intent to commit murder. The court held that he could not be held for a crime requiring specific intent unless he, himself, possessed that intent or aided the crime knowing that the actual perpetrator had that intent. However, proof of his knowledge could be established by evidence showing that the crime was within the scope of the original enterprise; that is, that it was reasonably foreseeable. Here, defendant's knowledge that his accomplices had a shotgun would be sufficient to permit a jury to infer that he knew that it might be used to resist the thwarting of their crime or their apprehension. Is defendant's knowledge under these circumstances more like being reckless as to the assault with intent to murder, or like having that intent? Is it improper to hold him for a specific intent crime when he is only reckless as to that?

c. RENUNCIATION OR WITHDRAWAL

If a defendant encourages another to commit a crime or provides some assistance to another for this purpose, may the defendant avoid liability as an aider and abettor or incitor by withdrawing from the venture or in some other way disassociating himself from it before the other person commits the offense? This is addressed in this subsection. Once the offense has been committed, of course, liability is finalized; remorse is not a defense and does not otherwise prevent conviction.

COMMONWEALTH v. HUBER

Court of Quarter Sessions, Montgomery County, Pennsylvania, 1958.
15 D. & C.2d 726.

GROSHENS, J. Defendant was indicted * * * on the charge of accessory before the fact to robbery, and on * * * the charge of accessory after the fact to robbery.

At the trial before the Hon. Harold G. Knight, sitting without a jury, defendant was found guilty of accessory before the fact.

Defendant's motions for a new trial and in arrest of judgment are now before the court for disposition. In support of his motions, defendant contends in his brief: (a) That the Commonwealth failed to prove his guilt beyond a reasonable doubt, and (b) that defendant withdrew from any plan or scheme of robbery so as to make him not guilty as an accessory before the fact.

* * *

The happening of the robbery was not in dispute at the trial, as counsel for defendant admitted in open court that a robbery had taken place. The issue was narrowed down to defendant's connection with the robbery.

To prove defendant's implications the Commonwealth called the two police officers who investigated the case and one of the principals to the robbery. Both police officers testified defendant freely admitted to them three days after the robbery that he had furnished the rifle used in the robbery and the naptha type fluid used on the victim, that he knew a "hold-up" was planned, that he had been asked to accompany the principals which he refused to do, that defendant had gone to the police station on the night of the robbery where he learned that the robbery had taken place and that he went forthwith to the home of one of the principals to get his rifle back.

One of the three principals, Ernest Farr, testified that defendant knew of the plan and that defendant furnished the rifle and naptha (ether).

Defendant took the stand in his own defense and corroborated much of the Commonwealth's evidence. For example defendant testified concerning his rifle and his knowledge of its proposed use in a conversation with John Goodwin, one of the principals:

" 'Sure, you can borrow it,', and I asked him what he was going to do with it, and he said:

" 'I am going to rob somebody.' "

By the Court:

"Q. Going to what?

"A. He said he was going to rob somebody.

"Q. Rob somebody?

"A. That's it."

By Mr. Pearlstine:

"Q. And then what did you say to him about that?

"A. I just laughed right then, and then Landis, Dave Landis came in and I hadn't had a chance to talk to him again till we got down to my place.

"Q. Did Goodwin at that time say anything about you going with him or where they were going or anything like that or what they planned to?

"A. Yes, at that time he asked me to go along.

"Q. What did you say?

"A. I said no I had a date at first; and then he was persistent and it seemed like he wanted me to go and I says: *'No I ain't going to get involved in anything like that'* (Italics supplied)

"Q. Did you or not think he was serious at the time?

"A. No, I did not."

* * *

Certainly, the Commonwealth's evidence of aid given by this defendant, supported as it is by defendant's own testimony, amply supports the finding of guilt. The defense of withdrawal remains but to be considered.

The aid given by defendant to the principals in the perpetration of the robbery was supplying the rifle and the naptha type fluid which were indubitably used by the principals. To "aid" literally means to "help". A rifle, for instance, may be of great help to a robber. A pointed rifle is one of the oldest and most effective methods to cow a person into the quick and docile relinquishment of his wallet. Hence, a person who supplies an avowed robber with a rifle which is shortly thereafter used by the robber in a robbery may be said to have aided the robber.

The fact that this defendant was asked to participate in the robbery as a principal, and that he refused, does not constitute such a withdrawal as would relieve him of criminal liability as an accessory before the fact. Had this defendant demanded and received back his rifle, or had he reported the principals to the police in time to thwart the robbery, then he could be said to have withdrawn successfully. Having placed the rifle in the hands of John Goodwin who, according to defendant's own testimony, told defendant "he was going to rob somebody", defendant committed himself to a sequence of events from which he could only extricate himself by getting his rifle out of the hands of John Goodwin before the robbery, or by thwarting the robbery in some other way. The "aid" in this case was the rifle. Therefore, to effectively withdraw made it incumbent upon defendant to get the rifle out of the hands of John Goodwin, or the equivalent thereof. He did neither of these things. He did, however, go to the police station where he learned of the perpetration of the robbery. He then rushed posthaste to get his rifle, not to withdraw from the crime, but to get incriminating evidence out of the possession of a principal who was then the object of a police investigation.

* * *

[D]efendant's motions for a new trial and in arrest of judgment are dismissed, and defendant is ordered to appear for sentence at miscellaneous court on Friday, March 28, 1958.

NOTE AND QUESTIONS

Suppose Huber had sought Goodwin to get the rifle back, but was unable to find him despite thorough search? Suppose he had retrieved the rifle because he learned of increased police surveillance of prime robbery targets, but the others nevertheless committed the robbery using a knife one of them already had?

Consider the Model Penal Code provision on this issue, Section 2.-06(6)(c) reprinted at page 235, supra. To avoid liability as an accomplice one must undo the assistance previously rendered. Thus, one who has merely offered verbal encouragement may be required only to voice disapproval to the others in sufficient time for them to reconsider their actions. Perkins, Criminal Law 663 (2d Ed., 1969). If the aid was of a more concrete nature, as with Huber, reacquisition of the instruments may be necessary or, should that be impossible, an effort to prevent the crime as by giving timely notice to the police. LaFave and Scott, Criminal Law 519 (1972).

2. LIABILITY FOR CONDUCT AFTER THE COMMISSION OF AN OFFENSE

The previous subsections dealt with liability for an offense based upon involvement in it prior to its commission. This subsection considers liability for conduct related to a crime but taking place after the crime has been completed. At common law, one who assisted or concealed an offender was an accessory after the fact and a party to the crime committed by the person assisted or concealed. This has been universally changed. As the following federal statute illustrates, those jurisdictions that retain the concept of an accessory after the fact make such a person guilty of a separate offense rather than the crime committed by the person assisted and generally provide a penalty less harsh than that attached to the principle crime.

The other traditional form of liability for conduct after the commission of an offense is the crime of misprision, also illustrated by the federal statute. As the principal case in this subsection illustrates, the crime of misprision has fallen into disrepute in American law and is not vigorously construed. The underlying policy question is an interesting one: Why should not a citizen be guilty of a crime if he has information relevant to the apprehension or conviction of a criminal but nevertheless remains silent?

18 UNITED STATES CODE

§ 3. Accessory after the fact

Whoever, knowing that an offense against the United States has been committed, receives, relieves, comforts or assists the offender in order to hinder or prevent his apprehension, trial or punishment, is an accessory after the fact.

Except as otherwise expressly provided by any Act of Congress, an accessory after the fact shall be imprisoned not more than one-half the maximum term of imprisonment or fined not more than one-half the maximum fine prescribed for the punishment of the principal, or both; or if the principal is punishable by death, the accessory shall be imprisoned not more than ten years.

§ 4. Misprision of felony

Whoever, having knowledge of the actual commission of a felony cognizable by a court of the United States, conceals and does not as soon as possible make known the same to some judge or other person in civil or military authority under the United States, shall be fined not more than $500 or imprisoned not more than three years, or both.

POPE v. STATE

Court of Appeals of Maryland, 1979.
284 Md. 309, 396 A.2d 1054.

[The facts of this case are reprinted at page 140].

II

THE CRIME OF MISPRISION OF FELONY

* * *

We assume, *arguendo,* that misprision of felony was a crime under the common law of England, and that it became the law of this State pursuant to Art. 5 of the Declaration of Rights. The question is whether it is to be deemed an indictable offense in Maryland today. In determining the question, we look first to what misprision of felony is. According to Blackstone, the crime at common law consisted merely in the "concealment of a felony which a man knows, but never assented to; for if he assented this makes him either principal or accessory." 4 W. Blackstone, Commentaries *121. * * * Glazebrook, Misprision of Felony—Shadow or Phantom?, 8 Am.J. of Legal History 189 and 283 (1964) cites eminent authority that in England the offense fell "into desuetude." Id. at 300. * * * In any event, if the crime had died, it was resurrected by the House of Lords in H. L. Sykes v. Director of Public Prosecution, [1961] 3 All E.R. 33. Lord Denning stated that "it is plain that there is and always has been an offence of misprision of felony and that it is not obsolete." Id. at 40. *Sykes* acknowledged only two necessary elements, knowledge and concealment. "[M]isprision requires nothing active. The failure or refusal to disclose the felony is enough." Id. at 41. This followed the Blackstone definition.

The "revival" in England of the crime of misprision of felony was not generally welcomed. "Resistance to the crime culminated in the Seventh Report of the Criminal Law Revision Committee which recommended the abolition of the crime of misprision by eliminating all distinctions between felonies and misdemeanors. Misprision was replaced in the report by a new crime of withholding information with regard to certain offenses for a consideration other than restitution. * * * The Criminal Law Act of 1967 [c. 58 §§ 1 and 5] adopted these two recommendations and has been interpreted as eliminating the crime of misprision of felony in England."

The American experience paralleled that of England; the common law offense was simply not used. The status of the crime in the United States was summed up in Glazebrook, How Long, Then, Is The Arm Of The Law To Be?, 25 Mod.L.Rev. 301, 307, n. 51 (1962):

> "No court in the United States has been prepared to adopt the English doctrine in its simplicity, and hold that a mere failure to disclose knowledge of a felony is itself an offence. * * * And in interpreting the Federal statute (1 Stat. 113, s. 6) [18 U.S.C. § 4 (1976)] which provides that 'whoever having knowledge of the actual commission, of a felony cognizable by a court of the United States conceals and does not as soon as possible make known the same to some judge or other person in civil or military authority under the U.S. shall be fined not more than $500 or imprisoned not more than three years or both,' it has been held that there must be some affirmative act of concealment, for instance the suppression of evidence, the harbouring of the criminal or the intimidation of witnesses, as well as the failure to disclose, for otherwise 'the words *conceals and* would be effectively excised from the statute.' This interpretation was necessary to rescue the statute from an 'intolerable oppressiveness,' for while federal statutes were few when it was enacted in 1790, the great increase in their number would make it unenforceable today if any other were adopted: Bratton v. U. S., 73 F.(2d) 795 [10 cir.] (1934). * * *"

Perkins in the second edition (1969) of his Criminal Law states that "there seems to be no such offense as misprision of felony in most of the states." At 516. No such offense is included in the Model Penal Code (U.L.A.).[22] * * *

* * *

Maryland has been in line with the practically universal view of the other states. We find no case prior to the case *sub judice* in which a conviction of misprision of felony has reached an appellate court of this State and, insofar as can be ascertained from appellate dockets, there is only one other in which the crime was charged. It is true, as observed by the trial court in the case at hand, that "[a] dearth of appellate cases is not proof that the crime is not charged at trial level," but in view of the numerous appeals in criminal causes spawned by present day procedures and rights afforded an accused, it is remarkable indeed that, if convictions upon charge of the crime have occurred, the present case was the first in which an appeal was filed.

22. The Model Penal Code (U.L.A.) would make it an offense to volunteer false information to a law enforcement officer, § 242.3(4) and to aid the consummation of crime, § 242.4.

We think that it is a fair inference that the crime has been seldom charged, and, if charged, has resulted in very few, if any convictions.

* * *

In exercising our duty to determine whether a common law crime presently exists in this State, mere non-use is not sufficient, as we have indicated, to conclude that the offense has become obsolete. But nonuse, we believe, is not without significance. When an offense has lain virtually dormant for over two hundred years, it is difficult to argue that the preservation of society and the maintenance of law and order demand recognition of it. * * *

Even more relevant, however, to a consideration of whether a common law crime is applicable as compatible with our local circumstances and situation and our general codes of law and jurisprudence is the nature of the crime. The reason for the failure of common law misprision of felony to survive in the United States was well expressed by Chief Justice Marshall over a hundred and fifty years ago in Marbury v. Brooks, 20 U.S. (7 Wheat.) 556, 575–576, 5 L.Ed. 522 (1822) and thereafter noted by many commentators, text book authors and other authorities:

> "It may be the duty of a citizen to accuse every offender, and to proclaim every offence which comes to his knowledge; but the law which would punish him in every case for not performing this duty is too harsh for man."

* * *

Misprision of felony at common law is an impractically wide crime, a long-standing criticism which remains unanswered in *Sykes*. It has an undesirable and indiscriminating width:

> "The real harshness lies in the fact that the duty to disclose arises when a person acquires knowledge of an offence, and this he may do quite involuntarily. A says to B: 'Did you know that X stole a book from the library last week?' adding appropriate circumstantial details; or X says to B: 'I stole some money yesterday; will you help me to repay it?' B is a friend of X; he wished to know nothing of X's misdeeds; and yet he is to be a criminal if he does not betray him. It is, furthermore, particularly difficult to defend a law which indiscriminately adds to the injuries of the victim of a crime the penalties of the criminal law should he or she wish to forgive and forget." 25 Mod.L.Rev. at 311.

Misprision differs from almost all other common law offenses of omission:

> "[T]he duty to act arises not because of the willing assumption of responsibility, the occupation of an office, or the ownership of property, but because of the mere possession

of certain knowledge—knowledge possessed accidentally and undesired—knowledge which may indeed have been acquired through some malevolent person." Id.

* * *

Under *Sykes,* no active step need be taken to conceal the felony (it is only thus that it remains quite distinct from the crime of accessory after the fact), and the concealment need bring no benefit to the accused. But three fundamental questions remained: when does the duty to reveal a felony arise; how is that duty discharged; and does a relationship with the felon prevent the duty arising?

It seems that the duty arises when "a man knows" of the commission of a felony. When, then, can a man, be said to *know* and *what* is it that he must know? Lord Goddard held that there must be disclosure when the knowledge a man has "is so definite that it ought to be disclosed. A man is neither bound nor would he be wise to disclose rumours or mere gossip, but, if facts are within his knowledge that would materially assist in the detection and arrest of a felon, he must disclose them as it is a duty he owes to the state." *Sykes* at 46. Lord Goddard left the matter to the jury as a question of fact. Glazebrook suggests that "unless the jury is to be entirely uncontrolled, it has to be told how precise and certain the accused's knowledge must have been before he can be convicted." 25 Mod.L.Rev. at 313. Is the duty to be confined to felonies committed in the presence of the accused, and, if not, is hearsay sufficient? Should the felon's own admission, standing alone, be enough? Knowledge of the commission of a crime is an ingredient of the offenses of accessory after the fact and receiving stolen goods, but, unlike misprision, they require a positive act. It is reasonable, in such circumstance, to require a person who has reason to believe something is wrong to inquire further before embarking on some course of conduct, and to hold that he fails to do so at his peril. "If this rule is applied to misprision, two duties are imposed: a duty to disclose knowledge of a felony, and a duty also to make inquiries to resolve a suspicion concerning the commission of a felony." Id. To paraphrase Glazebrook, must the inhabitants of Maryland become detectives as well as informers?

Sykes fails to provide a working rule for *what* the accused must know. * * * That is, on the one hand, it must have been a felony of which the accused knew, but on the other hand, he need not know whether the crime was a felony or a misdemeanor. According to Lord Denning, it would be enough that the accused knew that a *serious* offense had been committed if it turns out to be a felony. * * *

When the duty to disclose has arisen, it is not clear how it is discharged. * * * Lord Denning saw the duty as requiring a citizen "to disclose to proper authority all material facts known to him relative to the offence. * * * If he fails or refuses to perform this duty when there is a reasonable opportunity available to him to do so, then he is guilty of misprision." *Sykes* at 42. This was not sufficient for Lord Goddard. He thought that "facts * * * within his knowledge that would materially assist in the detection and arrest of a felon" must be disclosed as a duty owed to the State. Id. at 46. "Thus if a man disclosed all he knew about the commission of a felony and yet did not disclose the whereabouts of the felon he would be acquitted by Lord Denning and convicted by Lord Goddard." 25 Mod.L.Rev. at 315.

Their lordships agreed that the questions of when the knowledge must be revealed and how much trouble must be taken to reveal it were for the jury. Glazebrook is critical of this as assigning unsuitably vague questions to the trier of fact:

> "If a man is to be punished for not doing something, he ought to know precisely what is expected of him. The standard which he fails at his peril to attain ought not to be left to be fixed after the event by the whim of a particular jury. Formulae that pass muster in determining the liability of one who engages in a dangerous course of conduct are not always suited to crimes of pure omission." Id. at 316.

Only Lord Denning considered relationship with the felon with respect to the duty to disclose:

> "Non-disclosure may be due to a claim of right made in good faith. For instance, if a lawyer is told by his client that he has committed a felony, it would be no misprision in the lawyer not to report it to the police, for he might in good faith claim that he was under a duty to keep it confidential. Likewise with doctor and patient, and clergyman and parishioner. There are other relationships which may give rise to a claim in good faith that it is in the public interest not to disclose it. For instance, if an employer discovers that his servant has been stealing from the till, he might well be justified in giving him another chance rather than reporting him to the police. Likewise with the master of a college and a student. But close family or personal ties will not suffice where the offence is of so serious a character that it ought to be reported." *Sykes* at 42.

Glazebrook finds * * * "the choice of relationship perverse." 25 Mod.L.R. at 317. He explains:

* * *

> "[t]he exclusion in misprision of 'close family or personal ties' is utterly callous and certainly futile: how can the relation between doctor and patient, an employer and his servant, be thought more sacred, more deserving of respect and consideration—even by the law—than that between husband

> and wife, between father and son? By what standard is it unreasonable to expect an employer to report his servant's crimes to the police, and yet proper that a son should betray his father?" Id. at 318.

We observe that common law misprision is not only beset with practical defects but may implicate constitutional privileges. To sustain the Fifth Amendment right against self-incrimination,[30] "it need only be evident from the implications of the question, in the setting in which it is asked, that a responsive answer * * * might be dangerous because injurious disclosure might result." Hoffman v. United States, 341 U.S. 479, 486–487, 71 S.Ct. 814, 818, 95 L.Ed. 1118 (1951). * * * We note also that it has been suggested that the federal misprision statute may involve the right of privacy. In United States v. Worcester, 190 F.Supp. 548, 566 (D.Mass.1961), Judge Wyzanski, discussing the federal statute, said:

> "To suppose that Congress reached every failure to disclose a known federal crime, in this day of myriad federal tax statutes and regulatory laws, would impose a vast and unmeasurable obligation. It would do violence to the unspoken principle of the criminal law that 'as far as possible privacy should be respected.' There is 'a strong reluctance on the part of judges and legislators to sanction invasion of privacy in the detection of crime.' There is 'a general sentiment that the right to privacy is something to be put in balance against the enforcement of the law.' Sir Patrick Devlin, The Enforcement of Morals, p. 19."

We have proceeded on the assumption that the House of Lords was correct in concluding in *Sykes* that "there is and always has been an offense of misprision of felony. * * * " *Sykes* at 40. We are persuaded, finding no sound reason not to be, that their lordships' definition of the offense and the composition of its elements properly reflected the crime as it existed at common law. We are satisfied, considering its origin, the impractical and indiscriminate width of its scope, its other obvious deficiencies, and its long non-use, that it is not now compatible with our local circumstances and situation and our general code of laws and jurisprudence. Maintenance of law and order does not demand its application, and, overall, the welfare of the inhabitants of Maryland and society as enjoyed by us today, would not be served by it. If the Legislature finds it advisable that the people be obligated under peril of criminal penalty to disclose knowledge of criminal acts, it is, of course, free to create an offense to that end, within constitutional limitations, and hopefully, with adequate safeguards. We believe that the common law offense is not acceptable

30. "No person * * * shall be compelled in any criminal case to be a witness against himself * * *." U.S.Const. amend. V.

by today's standards, and we are not free to usurp the power of the General Assembly by attempting to fashion one that would be. We hold that misprision of felony is not a chargeable offense in Maryland.

* * *

NOTES AND QUESTIONS

1. Is the Court of Appeals analysis convincing in the context of the *Pope* case? Is it reasonable to believe Ms. Pope was in doubt as to the felonious nature of the conduct she had witnessed? Is it undesirable for our society to impose a duty to speak on facts such as these? Compare United States v. Hodges, 566 F.2d 674 (9th Cir. 1977) (misprision conviction affirmed on basis of defendant's knowingly making untruthful statements to F.B.I. concerning whereabouts of kidnapper).

2. Goldberg, Misprision of Felony: An Old Concept in a New Context, 52 A.B.A.J. 148, 149–50 (1966):[d]

> Unfortunately, the courts have interpreted "conceals" [in statutes making misprision of felony an offense, such as 18 U.S.C.A. § 4] as requiring a positive act, thus effectively emasculating the statute by merging it into the general accessory provisions of the law. This history of misprision of felony strongly suggests that this interpretation is erroneous. The Supreme Court of Vermont in 1907 defined the offense in its traditional sense:
>
> > Misprision of felony is * * * a criminal neglect either to prevent a felony from being committed or to bring the offender to justice after its commission, but without such previous concert with or subsequent assistance of him as will make the concealer an accessory before or after the fact.[17]
>
> Thus defined, misprision of felony would be a very salutary influence in our distressed society. If limited by its terms to serious crimes, perhaps only serious crimes against the person, few injustices are likely to result. Then Chief Justice Marshall's concern that "It may be the duty of a citizen to accuse every offender, and to proclaim every offense which comes to his knowledge; but the law which would punish him in every case for not performing this duty is too harsh for man"[19] need not deter legislators from passing a much-needed law. In the case which elicited Marshall's compassion, the defendant had advanced money to his son-in-law in an attempt to save him from the consequences of forgery. The law which would punish such behavior and even require a man to report his family's peculations to the police *is* too harsh. Restricting the operation of the law to serious crimes (and perhaps exempting certain degrees of consanguinity) ought to remove this objection.
>
> Exceptions must also be made for conflicting legal duties. A lawyer is legally obliged not to divulge information confidentially

d. Reprinted with permission from American Bar Association Journal.

17. Vermont v. Wilson [67 Atl. 533,] 533 [(1907)].

19. Marbury v. Brooks, 7 Wheat. 556, 575–76 (1822).

revealed to him by his client regarding a committed felony. Nor may a doctor broadcast his patient's confidential communications, nor a clergyman his parishioner's. Misprision of felony statutes must allow for these obligations to be respected without fear of law-breaking.

It may finally be objected that a legal duty to report criminal acts to the authorities would be so novel in most American jurisdictions that even responsible citizens would unavoidably break the law. But all Americans are familiar with their legal duty to report serious traffic accidents to the police. It is about time we consider violent assault on persons as important as automobile crashes.

3. The tendency in recent legislative revision has been to replace accessory-after-the-fact statutes and misprision crimes with offenses defined in terms of interfering with law enforcement activity. Consider the extent to which the following sections of the Model Penal Code (Proposed Official Draft, 1962) adequately serve the purposes which ought to be served:

Section 242.3. Hindering Apprehension or Prosecution

A person commits an offense if, with purpose to hinder the apprehension, prosecution, conviction or punishment of another for crime, he:

(a) harbors or conceals the other; or

(b) provides or aids in providing a weapon, transportation, disguise or other means of avoiding apprehension or effecting escape; or

(c) conceals or destroys evidence of the crime, or tampers with a witness, informant, document or other source of information, regardless of its admissibility in evidence; or

(d) warns the other of impending discovery or apprehension, except that this paragraph does not apply to a warning given in connection with an effort to bring another into compliance with law; or

(e) volunteers false information to a law enforcement officer.

The offense is a felony of the third degree if the conduct which the actor knows has been charged or is liable to be charged against the person aided would constitute a felony of the first or second degree. Otherwise it is a misdemeanor.

Section 242.4. Aiding Consummation of Crime

A person commits an offense if he purposely aids another to accomplish an unlawful object of a crime, as by safeguarding the proceeds thereof or converting the proceeds into negotiable funds. The offense is a felony of the third degree if the principal offense was a felony of the first or second degree. Otherwise it is a misdemeanor.

Section 242.5. Compounding

A person commits a misdemeanor if he accepts or agrees to accept any pecuniary benefit in consideration of refraining from reporting to law enforcement authorities the commission or suspected commission of any offense or information relating to an offense. It is an affirmative defense to prosecution under this Section that the pecuniary benefit did not exceed an amount which the actor believed to be due as restitution or indemnification for harm caused by the offense.

E. OTHER ASPECTS OF LIABILITY FOR THE ACTS OF ANOTHER

Complicity doctrine considered in the preceding subsections is, of course, a means of making one person liable for crimes actually committed by other persons. Several other doctrines have a similar effect; these doctrines are examined in this subsection. The first is so-called "vicarious liability." The second is the criminal liability of a corporation or association. This fits in the present subsection because when a corporation or organization is penalized, part of the financial burden ultimately is imposed upon the shareholders or other members of the organization who did not commit the crime themselves.

1. VICARIOUS LIABILITY

One of the principals limiting the scope of criminal liability which has already been examined is that crimes normally require a mental element; strict liability offenses are rare and viewed unfavorably. Another basic limitation is that one is not to be held liable in the absence of conduct on his part (including a failure to act in the face of a lawfully-imposed duty to do so). This situation is to be distinguished from liability based upon complicity theory since then the defendant will have been shown to have associated himself with the crime through some conduct on his part and the requisite state of mind. Nevertheless, various liability, liability based on another's act without the need to show a specific act or omission by the defendant which contributed to the crime, has entered our law. As the following materials indicate, the concept is usually applied in the context of criminal acts by persons who are employees or agents of the defendant even though the criminal conduct was not authorized by the defendant. As our society has become more complex an ever-growing proportion of economic activity has come to be carried out by groups and legislatures have increased the volume and detail of statutes, civil and penal, aimed at controlling such activity. These two developments have together brought the issue of the legitimacy of vicarious liability to the courts. This section poses the question of whether such liability is consistent with the idea of personal culpability, and, whatever the answer to that, whether our society can afford not to employ this device as a means of social control.

COMMONWEALTH v. KOCZWARA

Supreme Court of Pennsylvania, 1959.
397 Pa. 575, 155 A.2d 825, certiorari denied 363 U.S. 848,
80 S.Ct. 1624, 4 L.Ed.2d 1731.

COHEN, Justice. This is an appeal from the judgment of the Court of Quarter Sessions of Lackawanna County sentencing the defendant to three months in the Lackawanna County Jail, a fine of five hundred dollars and the costs of prosecution, in a case involving violations of the Pennsylvania Liquor Code.

John Koczwara, the defendant, is the licensee and operator of an establishment on Jackson Street in the City of Scranton known as J. K.'s Tavern. At that place he had a restaurant liquor license issued by the Pennsylvania Liquor Control Board. The Lackawanna County Grand Jury indicted the defendant on five counts for violations of the Liquor Code. The first and second counts averred that the defendant permitted minors, unaccompanied by parents, guardians or other supervisors, to frequent the tavern on February 1st and 8th, 1958; the third count charged the defendant with selling beer to minors on February 8th, 1958; the fourth charged the defendant with permitting beer to be sold to minors on February 8th, 1958, and the fifth or final count was an averment of a prior conviction for violations of the Liquor Code.

Prior to trial, the averment of prior convictions was removed from the consideration of the jury upon motion of counsel that submission of the same would deprive the defendant of his fundamental right to exclude evidence of former convictions.

At the conclusion of the Commonwealth's evidence, count three of the indictment, charging the sale by the defendant personally to the minors, was removed from the jury's consideration by the trial judge on the ground that there was no evidence that the defendant had personally participated in the sale or was present in the tavern when sales to the minors took place. Defense counsel then demurred to the evidence as to the other three counts. The demurrer was overruled. Defendant thereupon rested without introducing any evidence and moved for a directed verdict of acquittal. The motion was denied, the case went to the jury and the jury returned a verdict of guilty as to each of the remaining three counts: two counts of permitting minors to frequent the licensed premises without parental or other supervision, and the count of permitting sales to minors.

* * *

Defendant raises two contentions, both of which, in effect, question whether the undisputed facts of this case support the judgment and sentence imposed by the Quarter Sessions Court. Judge Hoban found as fact that "in every instance the purchase [by minors] was made from a bartender, not identified by name, and service to the boys was made by the bartender. There was *no* evidence that the defendant was present on any one of the occasions testified to by these witnesses, nor that he had any personal knowledge of the sales to them or to other persons on the premises." We, therefore, must determine the criminal responsibility of a licensee of the Liquor Control Board for acts committed by his employees upon his premises, without his personal knowledge, participation, or presence, which acts violate a valid regulatory statute passed under the Commonwealth's police power.

While an employer in almost all cases is not criminally responsible for the unlawful acts of his employees, unless he consents to, approves, or participates in such acts, courts all over the nation have struggled for years in applying this rule within the framework of "controlling the sale of intoxicating liquor." See Annotation, 139 A.L.R. 306 (1942). At common law, any attempt to invoke the doctrine of *respondeat superior* in a criminal case would have run afoul of our deeply ingrained notions of criminal jurisprudence that guilt must be personal and individual.[1] In recent decades, however, many states have enacted detailed regulatory provisions in fields which are essentially noncriminal, e. g., pure food and drug acts, speeding ordinances, building regulations, and child labor, minimum wage and maximum hour legislation. Such statutes are generally enforceable by light penalties, and although violations are labelled crimes, the considerations applicable to them are totally different from those applicable to true crimes, which involve moral delinquency and which are punishable by imprisonment or another serious penalty. Such so-called statutory crimes are in reality an attempt to utilize the machinery of criminal administration as an enforcing arm for social regulations of a purely civil nature, with the punishment totally unrelated to questions of moral wrongdoing or guilt. It is here that the social interest in the general well-being and security of the populace has been held to outweigh the individual interest of the particular defendant. The penalty is imposed despite the defendant's lack of a criminal intent or mens rea.

1. The distinction between *respondeat superior* in tort law and its application to the criminal law is obvious. In tort law, the doctrine is employed for the purpose of settling the incidence of loss upon the party who can best bear such loss. But the criminal law is supported by totally different concepts. We impose penal treatment upon those who injure or menace social interests, partly in order to reform, partly to prevent the continuation of the anti-social activity and partly to deter others. If a defendant has personally lived up to the social standards of the criminal law and has not menaced or injured anyone, why impose penal treatment?

Not the least of the legitimate police power areas of the legislature is the control of intoxicating liquor. As Mr. Justice B. R. Jones recently stated in In re Tahiti Bar, Inc., 1959, 395 Pa. 355, 360, 150 A.2d 112, 115, "There is perhaps no other area of permissible state action within which the exercise of the police power of a state is more plenary than in the regulation and control of the use and sale of alcoholic beverages." It is abundantly clear that the conduct of the liquor business is lawful only to the extent and manner permitted by statute. Individuals who embark on such an enterprise do so with knowledge of considerable peril, since their actions are rigidly circumscribed by the Liquor Code.

Because of the peculiar nature of this business, one who applies for and receives permission from the Commonwealth to carry on the liquor trade assumes the highest degree of responsibility to his fellow citizens. As the licensee of the Board, he is under a duty not only to regulate his own personal conduct in a manner consistent with the permit he has received, but also to control the acts and conduct of any employee to whom he entrusts the sale of liquor. Such fealty is the *quid pro quo* which the Commonwealth demands in return for the privilege of entering the highly restricted and, what is more important, the highly *dangerous* business of selling intoxicating liquor.

In the instant case, the defendant has sought to surround himself with all the safeguards provided to those within the pale of criminal sanctions. He has argued that a statute imposing criminal responsibility should be construed strictly, with all doubts resolved in his favor. While the defendant's position is entirely correct, we must remember that we are dealing with a statutory crime within the state's plenary police power. In the field of liquor regulation, the legislature has enacted a comprehensive Code aimed at regulating and controlling the use and sale of alcoholic beverages. The question here raised is whether the legislature *intended* to impose vicarious criminal liability on the licensee-principal for acts committed on his premises without his presence, participation or knowledge.

This Court has stated, as long ago as Commonwealth v. Weiss, 1891, 139 Pa. 247, 251, 21 A. 10, 11 L.R.A. 530, that "whether a criminal intent, or a guilty knowledge, is a necessary ingredient of a statutory offense * * * is a matter of construction. It is for the legislature to determine whether the public injury, threatened in any particular matter, is such, and so great as to justify an absolute and indiscriminate prohibition." * * *[3]

3. This case is not governed by cases [which] hold persons answerable for sales made by *themselves*, and prevent them from pleading ignorance of the nonage or intemporate habits of those to whom they sell. Nor is this case governed by Commonwealth v. Junkin, 1895, 170 Pa. 194, 32 A. 617, 31 L.R.A. 124, which refused to hold a principal criminally liable for the wrongful act of his agent, where the act was in positive disobedience of the principal's instructions. The Junkin case did *not* involve a comprehensive regulatory

In the Liquor Code, Section 493, the legislature has set forth twenty-five specific acts which are condemned as unlawful, and for which penalties are provided in Section 494. Subsections (1) and (14) of Section 493 contain the two offenses charged here. In neither of these subsections is there any language which would require the prohibited acts to have been done either knowingly, wilfully or intentionally, there being a significant absence of such words as "knowingly, wilfully, etc." That the legislature intended such a requirement in other related sections of the same Code is shown by examining Section 492(15), wherein it is made unlawful to *knowingly* sell any malt beverages to a person engaged in the business of illegally selling such beverages. The omission of any such word in the subsections of Section 494 is highly significant. It indicates a legislative intent to eliminate both knowledge and criminal intent as necessary ingredients of such offenses. To bolster this conclusion, we refer back to Section 491 wherein the Code states, "It shall be unlawful (1) For any person, by himself *or by an employe or agent*, to expose or keep for sale, or directly or *indirectly* * * * to sell or offer to sell any liquor within this Commonwealth, except in accordance with the provisions of this act and the regulations of the board." The Superior Court has long placed such an interpretation on the statute.[4]

As the defendant has pointed out, there is a distinction between the requirement of a mens rea and the imposition of vicarious absolute liability for the acts of another. It may be that the courts below, in relying on prior authority, have failed to make such a distinction.[5] In any case, we fully recognize it. Moreover, we find that the intent of the legislature in enacting this Code was not only to eliminate the common law requirement of a mens rea, but also to place a very high degree of responsibility upon the holder of a liquor license to make certain that neither he nor anyone in his employ commit any of the prohibited acts upon the licensed premises. Such a burden of care is imposed upon the licensee in order to protect the public from the potentially noxious effects of an inherently dangerous business. We of course, express no opinion as to the *wisdom* of the legislature's imposing vicarious responsibility under certain sections of the Liquor Code. There may or may not be an economic-sociological justification for such liability on a theory of deterrence. Such de-

scheme which clearly evidenced a legislative purpose to hold a licensee responsible for all illegal acts conducted on the licensed premises. The Liquor Code of Pennsylvania in effect makes the act of the employee the act of the licensee for the purpose of enforcing the rigid restrictions on the sale of liquor.

4. It is established that a liquor license may be legally suspended or revoked for violations of the Code committed by employees of the licensee even though there is no evidence that the licensee knew of such violations.

5. We must also be extremely careful to distinguish the present situation from the question of *corporate* criminal liability * * *. For a penetrating inquiry into this latter subject, see Mens Rea And The Corporation, 19 U.Pitt.L.Rev. 21 (1957).

termination is for the legislature to make, so long as the constitutional requirements are met.

Can the legislature, consistent with the requirements of due process, thus establish absolute criminal liability? Were this the defendant's first violation of the Code, and the penalty solely a minor fine of from $100–$300, we would have no hesitation in upholding such a judgment. Defendant, by accepting a liquor license, must bear this financial risk. Because of a prior conviction for violations of the Code, however, the trial judge felt compelled under the mandatory language of the statute, Section 494(a), to impose not only an increased fine of five hundred dollars, but also a three month sentence of imprisonment. Such sentence of imprisonment in a case where liability is imposed vicariously cannot be sanctioned by this Court consistently with the law of the land clause of Section 9, Article I of the Constitution of the Commonwealth of Pennsylvania., P.S.[7]

The Courts of the Commonwealth have already strained to permit the legislature to carry over the civil doctrine of *respondeat superior* and to apply it as a means of enforcing the regulatory scheme that covers the liquor trade. We have done so on the theory that the Code established petty misdemeanors involving only light monetary fines. It would be unthinkable to impose vicarious criminal responsibility in cases involving true crimes. Although to hold a principal criminally liable might possibly be an effective means of enforcing law and order, it would do violence to our more sophisticated modern-day concepts of justice. Liability for all true crimes, wherein an offense carries with it a jail sentence, must be based exclusively upon personal causation. It can be readily imagined that even a licensee who is meticulously careful in the choice of his employees cannot supervise every single act of the subordinates. A man's liberty cannot rest on so frail a reed as whether his employee will commit a mistake in judgment.

This Court is ever mindful of its duty to maintain and establish the proper safeguards in a criminal trial. To sanction the imposition of imprisonment here would make a serious change in the substantive criminal law of the Commonwealth, one for which we find no justification. We have found *no* case in any jurisdiction which has permitted a *prison term* for a vicarious offense. The Supreme Court of the United States has had occasion only recently to impose due process limitations upon the actions of a state legislature in making unknowing conduct criminal. Lambert v. People of State of California, 1957, 355 U.S. 225, 78 S.Ct. 240, 2 L.Ed.2d 228. Our own courts have stepped in time and again to protect a defendant from being held criminally responsible for acts about which he had no knowledge and

7. Sec. 9. "* * * nor can he be deprived of his life, liberty or property, unless by the judgment of his peers or the law of the land."

over which he had little control. We would be utterly remiss were we not to so act under these facts.

In holding that the punishment of imprisonment deprives the defendant of due process of law under these facts, we are not declaring that Koczwara must be treated as a first offender under the Code. He has clearly violated the law for a second time and must be punished accordingly. Therefore, we are only holding that so much of the judgment as calls for imprisonment is invalid, and we are leaving intact the five hundred dollar fine imposed by Judge Hoban under the subsequent offense section.

* * *

Judgment, as modified, is affirmed.

BELL, MUSMANNO and McBRIDE, JJ., file separate dissenting opinions.

* * *

MUSMANNO, Justice (dissenting).

The Court in this case is doing what it has absolutely no right to do. It is laying aside its judicial robes and officiating as members of the General Assembly. It is declaring a crime which has no existence in the statute books, it is imposing a penalty which is not authorized by the criminal code.

* * *.

The Majority introduces into its discussion a proposition which is shocking to contemplate. It speaks of "vicarious criminal liability". Such a concept is as alien to American soil as the upas tree. There was a time in China when a convicted felon sentenced to death could offer his brother or other close relative in his stead for decapitation. The Chinese law allowed such "vicarious criminal liability". I never thought that Pennsylvania would look with favor on anything approaching so revolting a barbarity.

* * *.

If it is wrong to send a person to jail for acts committed by another, is it not wrong to convict him at all? There are those who value their good names to the extent that they see as much harm in a degrading criminal conviction as in a jail sentence. The laceration of a man's reputation, the blemishing of his good name, the wrecking of his prestige by a criminal court conviction may blast a person's chances for honorable success in life to such an extent that a jail sentence can hardly add much to the ruin already wrought to him by the conviction alone.

* * *

NOTES AND QUESTIONS

1. If Koczwara himself had made the sale would the court have had difficulty in affirming the conviction and sentence? Even if the minors

appeared to be of age and presented apparently valid evidence in proof thereof?

2. Is there any question as to Koczwara's liability if he had known of his agent's practice of selling to minors? Cf. Commonwealth v. Feinberg, 433 Pa. 558, 253 A.2d 636 (1969) (convictions for involuntary manslaughter arising from death of thirty-one skid-row denizens due to drinking industrial Sterno sold, in some cases, by appellant's agent in his absence, upheld given finding that appellant stocked the same for sale knowing that purchasers would ingest it).

3. Does the statute in *Koczwara* require for conviction a finding that the defendant acted with knowledge of wrong-doing? If not, and if Koczwara would have been held responsible if he had made the sale, albeit in good faith reliance on the appearance, assertions and identification of the minor customers, what values are served by limiting his liability where he acts through an agent? To what extent, if any, are legitimate objectives of the criminal law sacrificed by such a limitation? Is the problem here that the liability is vicarious or that it is strict?

2. CRIMINAL LIABILITY OF ORGANIZATIONS AND THEIR AGENTS

Among the problems presented by use of traditional concepts of criminal liability in an increasingly organized society are those concerning the criminal liability of a corporation or other organization and the criminal liability of members of such organizations for crimes involving the organization. These materials raise questions regarding the extent to which criminal liability in this context serves traditional (or other) functions of imposing such liability, and the extent to which imposing it may run counter to traditional limitations upon the imposition of criminal liability.

A corporation or organization cannot, of course, be imprisoned. The only practical penalty to impose upon a corporation or organization is a fine. The burden of such fines rests ultimately upon the shareholders or members of the organization. The major policy question involved here is whether there is justification for imposing a penalty upon persons such as shareholders who have not participated in the commission of the offense. This may be regarded as unfair. On the other hand, it may create an incentive that will cause shareholders and others involved in organizations to prevent the commission of crimes by agents of the organizations.

As a general rule, a corporation may be liable for crimes committed by its agents, although an unincorporated organization (such as a partnership) may not. The major question that arises in the application of this rule is when and under what circumstances the corporation (and indirectly the shareholders) will be held liable for a crime committed by an agent of the corporation.

MODEL PENAL CODE *

(Proposed Official Draft 1962).

Section 2.07. Liability of Corporations, Unincorporated Associations and Persons Acting, or Under a Duty to Act, in Their Behalf

(1) A corporation may be convicted of the commission of an offense if:

(a) the offense is a violation or the offense is defined by a statute other than the Code in which a legislative purpose to impose liability on corporations plainly appears and the conduct is performed by an agent of the corporation acting in behalf of the corporation within the scope of his office or employment, except that if the law defining the offense designates the agents for whose conduct the corporation is accountable or the circumstances under which it is accountable, such provisions shall apply; or

(b) the offense consists of an omission to discharge a specific duty of affirmative performance imposed on corporations by law; or

(c) the commission of the offense was authorized, requested, commanded, performed or recklessly tolerated by the board of directors or by a high managerial agent acting in behalf of the corporation within the scope of his office or employment.

(2) When absolute liability is imposed for the commission of an offense, a legislative purpose to impose liability on a corporation shall be assumed, unless the contrary plainly appears.

(3) An unincorporated association may be convicted of the commission of an offense if:

(a) the offense is defined by a statute other than the Code which expressly provides for the liability of such an association and the conduct is performed by an agent of the association acting in behalf of the association within the scope of his office or employment, except that if the law defining the offense designates the agents for whose conduct the association is accountable or the circumstances under which it is accountable, such provisions shall apply; or

(b) the offense consists of an omission to discharge a specific duty of affirmative performance imposed on associations by law.

(4) As used in this Section:

(a) "corporation" does not include an entity organized as or by a governmental agency for the execution of a governmental program;

(b) "agent" means any director, officer, servant, employee or other person authorized to act in behalf of the corporation or association and, in the case of an unincorporated association, a member of such association;

(c) "high managerial agent" means an officer of a corporation or an unincorporated association, or, in the case of a partnership, a partner, or any other agent of a corporation or association having duties of such responsibility that his conduct may fairly be assumed to represent the policy of the corporation or association.

(5) In any prosecution of a corporation or an unincorporated association for the commission of an offense included within the terms of Subsection (1) (a) or Subsection (3) (a) of this Section, other than an offense for which absolute liability has been imposed, it shall be a defense if the defendant proves by a preponderance of evidence that the high managerial agent having supervisory responsibility over the subject matter of the offense employed due diligence to prevent its commission. This paragraph shall not apply if it is plainly inconsistent with the legislative purpose in defining the particular offense.

STATE v. ADJUSTMENT DEPT. CREDIT BUREAU, INC.

Supreme Court of Idaho, 1971.
94 Idaho 156, 483 P.2d 687.

McFADDEN, Justice.

The defendant, Adjustment Department Credit Bureau, Inc., an Idaho corporation, conducts a bill collection service as a part of its operation. It was charged by an amended information of the crime of extortion alleged to have been committed by and through its agent, Howard Short, in August, 1967. * * *

The case was tried to a jury which returned its verdict of guilty of the crime charged in the information and judgment of conviction was entered and a fine of $1,500.00 imposed against the corporation. The defendant appealed from this judgment.

One of the defendant's customers, a pharmacy, assigned an open account owed to the pharmacy by Rodney Price to the defendant for collection. Howard Short, an agent of the defendant, handled this particular claim for the defendant company. Price had executed a promissory note to the defendant on this claim, and when the note was not paid in accord with its terms, suit was instituted in a justice court in Ada County and default judgment entered in July of 1967.

Short attempted to collect on this judgment against Price, who was out of work at the time. Subsequently, Short accepted a check with the understanding it would be paid in installments. At the time of execution of this check Price told Short that there were no funds in the bank on which the check was written. After other subsequent conversations Short had Price execute another check on a different bank even though Price had told him that he had no account there, and the first check was torn up. This second check was presented for payment to the bank and returned unpaid.

Later in the summer of 1967 Price secured employment away from Boise and Short contacted Mrs. Price concerning the obligation. Price testified that on an occasion when he was in Boise, Short contacted him and advised him that Short would prosecute him for issuance of a bad check unless Price made a payment on the debt. Price then paid $20.00 to Short, which was evidenced by a receipt.

Later Price stated he believed he was going to be prosecuted for the bad check and went to see Mr. Slayton, who was the head of the collection division of the defendant corporation. Price testified "Mr. Slayton told me it was out of his hands, it was between me and Mr. Short." Mr. Slayton testified that he remembered Mr. Price came in to see him one time and was asking questions about the account. Slayton stated "I told him Mr. Short was handling the account."

On this appeal the defendant has made numerous assignments of error. The crucial issue presented by these assignments of error concerns the instruction given by the trial court to the effect that a corporation (which acts only through its agents) can be held criminally liable "for the acts of its agents who are authorized to act for it in the particular matter out of which the unlawful conduct with which it is charged grows or in the business to which it related." It is the defendant's contention that this instruction by the trial court was in error, arguing that the trial court should have instructed that the defendant corporation could have been found guilty only if the agent committed the prohibited acts, and that the agent's acts were authorized, requested or commanded by another corporate agent having responsibility for formation of corporate policy, or by a managerial agent having supervisory responsibility over the subject matter.

It is our conclusion that there is merit in the defendant's position in regard to these instructions. A corporation, being an artificial being, a creature of statute, can only act through its agents and employees. At the early common law, the fact that a corporation had no tangible, physical existence, was regarded as making it impossible for a corporation to commit a crime. 1 Wharton's Criminal Law (Anderson 1957), § 52, p. 117. Under the modern view, however, a corporation may be found guilty of a breach of a duty imposed by law, both for acts of nonfeasance and misfeasance. A corporation is criminally responsible for statutory crimes, such as obtaining money under false pretenses (Joseph L. Sigretto & Sons, Inc. v. State, 127 N.J.L. 578, 24 A.2d 199 (1942)), usury (State v. First Nat'l Bank of Clark, 2 S.D. 568, 51 N.W. 587 (1892)), illegal sale of liquor (Zito v. United States, 64 F.2d 772 (7th Cir.1933), and United States v. Wilson, 59 F.2d 97 (D.C.1932)), unlawful sale of adulterated foods (Golden Guernsey Farms, Inc. v. State, 223 Ind. 606, 63 N.E.2d 699 (1945)).

By reason of the fact that corporations can only act through their agents, the courts have struggled with the problem of holding a corporation criminally liable in those cases involving crimes where a specific intent is required. 19 Am.Jur.2d, Corporations § 1435, p. 829. The question is, how can a corporation, an artificial being, have the necessary *mens rea* to commit those crimes where specific intent is required. The answer is found in the relationship between the corporation and the agent that performed the acts for which the corporation is being criminally charged, and in the nature of the crime with which the corporation is being charged.

There are certain crimes defined by statute for which a corporation is guilty without regard to any unlawful intent. See New York Cent. & Hudson R.R. Co. v. United States, [212 U.S. 481, 29 S.Ct. 304, 53 L.Ed. 613 (1908)], which was a prosecution under the Elkins Act, which made it a misdemeanor for any carrier to knowingly pay or receive a rebate, and which specifically provided that the act of an agent within the scope of his employment "shall in every case be also deemed to be the act, omission or failure of such carrier, as well as of that person." There are numerous other cases involving specific statutes where the violation by an agent is considered as a violation by the corporation. See C.I.T. Corp. v. United States, 150 F.2d 85 (9th Cir.1945); United States v. General Motors Corp., 226 F.2d 745 (3d Cir.1955).

Some students of the problem of corporate criminal responsibility have drawn a distinction between those types of criminal cases where the crime is one created by statute, and where the crime is a codification of a common law offense. 50 Georgetown L.Rev. 547 (1962). The conclusion of the authors in this discussion is that when a statutory offense is involved, the commission of a crime by a corporate agent within the scope of his authority is a crime of the corporation, regardless of knowledge, acquiescence, or ratification by a higher corporate officer. However, when the crime is a statutory codification of a common law crime requiring *mens rea* this reasoning as to corporate criminal liability is insufficient to bind the corporation, and more must be established to justify a conviction under this type of crime than a mere proof of an agency relationship.

* * *

[Under the Idaho statute,] a specific intent to extort money or another thing of value is an essential element of [the] crime.

* * *

2 Corporation Law and Practice, Hornstein, 1959, § 566, p. 47, in our opinion correctly states the rule as to criminal liability as follows:

> "A corporation may be convicted if (a) legislative purpose plainly appears to impose absolute liability on the corporation for the offense; or (b) the offense consists of an omission to perform an act which the corporation is required by law to perform; or (c) the commission of the offense was authorized, requested, commanded or performed (i) by the board of directors, or (ii) by an agent having responsibility for formation of a corporate policy or (iii) by a 'high managerial agent' having supervisory responsibility over the subject matter of the offense and acting within the scope of his employment in behalf of the corporation. * * *."

Thus the instructions given by the trial court to the effect that the corporation could be found guilty if the jury found that the agent was acting within the scope of his authority was not a correct statement of the law under the circumstances of this case; it was not established that Short was in a managerial capacity, and no issue was submitted to the jury as to whether Short's actions were authorized, requested, or commanded by either an agent of the corporation responsible for formation of corporate policy or by a high managerial agent. This error is of a prejudicial nature and the case must be remanded.

* * *

NOTES AND QUESTIONS

1. In determining whether Short's position was such as to render the corporate defendant liable for acts of extortion committed by Short, should emphasis be placed on Short's general position in the corporate hierarchy or on his authority in regard to the particular corporate activity related to the acts of extortion? This was the issue considered in what is probably the most extensive recent consideration of the standards that should be applied to determine corporate criminal liability, Commonwealth v. Beneficial Finance, 360 Mass. 188, 275 N.E.2d 33 (1971), cert. den. 407 U.S. 910, 92 S. Ct. 2433, 32 L.Ed.2d 683 (1972). After reviewing and rejecting the Model Penal Code formulation (reprinted at page 267, supra), the court concluded:

> [W]e are of the opinion that the quantum of proof necessary to sustain the conviction of a corporation for the acts of its agents is sufficiently met if it is shown that the corporation has placed the agent in a position where he has enough authority and responsibility to act for and in behalf of the corporation in handling the *particular* corporate business, operation or project in which he was engaged at the time he committed the criminal act. * * * [T]his

> standard does not depend upon the responsibility or authority which the agent has with respect to the entire corporate business, but only to his position with relation to the particular business in which he was serving the corporation. Some of the factors that the jury [is] entitled to consider in applying the * * * test, although perhaps not in themselves decisive, are the following: (1) the extent of control and authority exercised by the individual over and within the corporation; (2) the extent and manner to which corporate funds were used in the crime; (3) a repeated pattern of criminal conduct tending to indicate corporate toleration or ratification of the agent's acts.

360 Mass. at 280–81, 275 N.E.2d at 86. Explaining its desire to focus upon the authority of the corporate agent in regard to the particular activity involved rather than the agent's powers and responsibility in regard to the entire corporate business (as the court read the Model Penal Code standard as doing), the court explained:

> In a large corporation, with many numerous and distinct departments, a high ranking corporate officer or agent may have no authority or involvement in a particular sphere of corporate activity, whereas a lower ranking corporate executive might have much broader power in dealing with a matter peculiarly within the scope of his authority. Employees who are in the lower echelon of the corporate hierarchy often exercise more responsibility in the *every-day operations* of the corporation than the directors or officers.

360 Mass. at 275, 275 N.E.2d at 83. Is this true? Would use of the *Beneficial Finance* standard result in imposing liability upon corporations more efficiently, i. e., where—but only where—it can be expected to result in the corporation taking preventive actions to preclude similar crimes in the future? Would it result in imposing liability more fairly, i. e., where—but only where—those upon whom the ultimate penalty falls are sufficiently blameworthy to justify imposition of a criminal penalty?

2. Can a corporation ever be criminally liable for acts done by its agents in express disregard of instructions from corporate superiors? In United States v. Hilton Hotels Corp., 467 F.2d 1000 (9th Cir. 1972), cert. den. 409 U.S. 1125, 93 S.Ct. 938, 35 L.Ed.2d 256 (1973) the corporate defendant was charged with a criminal violation of the Sherman Antitrust Act. The indictment alleged that a corporate agent had joined an agreement to give preferential treatment to suppliers who joined a local promotion association in Portland, Oregon. The purchasing manager of the defendant's Portland hotel admitted that he had threatened a supplier with loss of the hotel's business unless he joined the association. But the evidence also showed that the corporation's policy was such that this was contrary to policy, that the purchasing agent had been told on two occasions to take no part in the actions against the suppliers, and that the purchasing agent made the threat because of anger and personal pique towards the individual representing the supplier. Considering the nature of Sherman Act violations, the court concluded that employees are likely to be under great pressure to maximize profits despite Sherman Act limitations, that generalized directions to obey the Act are not likely to be taken seriously, and

when the Act is violated the corporation (and not the individual agent) will benefit. The court then held:

> For these reasons we conclude that as a general rule a corporation is liable under the Sherman Act for the acts of its agents in the scope of their employment, even though contrary to general corporate policy and express instructions to the agent.

467 F.2d at 1007.

When employees knowingly act so as to violate the law without benefit to their corporate employer, can the corporation be held liable? In Standard Oil of Tex. v. United States, 307 F.2d 120 (5th Cir. 1962), defendant's employees entered a scheme with one Thompson, the owner of an oil lease, whereby Thompson would be credited by defendant for oil produced in violation of production limitations imposed by state law and thus "hot oil" within the meaning of the Connolly Act, 15 U.S.C.A. § 715. In some instances, records were falsified so that oil produced by other leases, some owned in part by defendant, was attributed to Thompson's wells. The court held that, although absence of benefit to the corporate employer would not preclude liability, here there was no showing that the employees had the purpose of furthering their master's business and hence their acts could not be equated with those of the corporation.

3. Traditionally, unincorporated associations have not been subject to criminal penalties. But some statutory crimes are specifically defined so as to include them. The Motor Carrier Act of 1935, for example, provides a criminal penalty for any "person" violating the Act; "person" is defined as meaning "any individual, firm, copartnership, corporation, company, association, or joint-stock association." 49 U.S.C.A. §§ 332(a), 303(a). The Supreme Court has held that a partnership may be held liable under the statute. United States v. A. & P. Trucking Co., 358 U.S. 121, 79 S.Ct. 203, 3 L.Ed.2d 165 (1958). Other statutory provisions are broader. The Arizona Criminal Code contains broad provisions for liability of "enterprises." Ariz.Rev.Stat. § 13–305. "Enterprise" is defined as including "any corporation, association, labor union or other legal entity." Ariz.Rev.Stat. § 13–105(10).

The New York statutes provide more flexibility. Crimes are drafted in terms that provide that "a person" is guilty of the offense when certain matters are established. E. g., N.Y. Penal L. § 135.25 (kidnapping). No general provisions concerning liability of partnerships and unincorporated associations exist, but "person" is defined as:

> a human being, and where appropriate, a public or private corporation, an unincorporated association, a partnership, a government or a governmental instrumentality.

N.Y. Penal L. § 10.00(10). In what is apparently the first reported case under the provision, People v. Smithtown General Hospital, 92 Misc.2d 144, 399 N.Y.S.2d 993 (1977), the court considered the liability of a 42 person partnership which operated a hospital. The partnership had been charged with assault and falsifying business records, based on facts tending to show that an unauthorized person had been permitted to participate in a surgical procedure involving a nonconsenting patient and that records were modified to conceal this. Stressing that the public has an important interest in the operation of a hospital, that hospitals are extensively regulated, and that the hospital functions as a practical entity (in providing care and receiving accreditation), the court held it "appropriate" to regard the crimes charged as providing for the liability of the partnership defendant:

> [T]his defendant may be charged * * * as an entity with the commission of crimes related to the discharge of its primary obligations as a general hospital even though there is no showing of culpability on the part of the * * * partners.

92 Misc.2d at 148, 399 N.Y.S.2d at 996.

4. If a corporation or association is liable because of the criminal actions of its agent, does this have any impact upon the agent's personal criminal liability? The answer is clearly not; both the corporation and the agent can be held liable. State v. Louchheim, 36 N.C.App. 271, 244 S.E.2d 195, rev. den. 295 N.C. 263, 245 S.E.2d 779 (1978). As one court explained:

> The existence of the corporate entity does not shield from prosecution the corporate agent who knowingly and intentionally causes the corporation to commit a crime. The corporation obviously acts, and can act, only by and through its human agents, and it is their conduct which the criminal law must deter, and those actors who in fact are culpable.

State v. Placzek, 380 A.2d 1010, 1015 (Me.1977). It is widely accepted, however, that if the crime involved is one that requires intent, the prosecution must show not only that the agent was responsible for the conduct constituting the crime but also that the agent had the intent required for liability. Bourgeois v. Commonwealth, 217 Va. 268, 227 S.E.2d 714 (1976). The Model Penal Code takes a similar position. Model Penal Code § 2.07(6) (P.O.D.1962).

5. What goals of the criminal law are furthered by the imposition of criminal liability on a corporation given the fact that the only possible punishment is a fine which may be passed on to either the stockholders or customers, both of which groups are likely to be innocent of any wrongdoing?

6. If financial penalties are seen as efficacious, why wouldn't civil suits for damages resulting from the "criminal" conduct of the corporation serve the same purpose as well or better than the generally small—relative to the assets of many corporations—fines, which can be imposed?

7. Would not punishment of the responsible individual more effectively achieve legitimate goals of the criminal law without raising the problems incident to vicarious liability? Who would be the appropriate individual in a situation such as that presented in *Smithtown*, note 3, supra?

8. The 1970 Study Draft of the Proposed Federal Criminal Code reflected in section 405 the unusual problems involved in devising effective sanctions for organizations. That section provided, in part:

> (1) Organization. When an organization is convicted of an offense, the court may, in addition to or in lieu of imposing other authorized sanctions, do either or both of the following:
>
> (a) require the organization to give appropriate publicity to the conviction by notice to the class or classes of

persons or sector of the public interested in or affected by the conviction, by advertising in designated areas or by designated media, or otherwise;

(b) direct the Attorney General, United States Attorney, or other attorney designated by the court to institute supplementary proceedings in the case in which the organization was convicted of the offense to determine, collect and distribute damages to persons in the class which the statute was designed to protect who suffered injuries by reason of the offense, if the court finds that the multiplicity of small claims or other circumstances make restitution by individual suit impractical.

The Final Report retreated somewhat from this position. It omitted (1)(b) because of separate congressional consideration of class actions by consumers, and offered (1)(a) only as a bracketed alternative to the following provision:

§ 3007. Special Sanction for Organizations

When an organization is convicted of an offense, the court may require the organization to give notice of its conviction to the persons or class of persons ostensibly harmed by the offense, by mail or by advertising in designated areas or by designated media or otherwise.

The Report comment explained that a "broader sanction envisioning 'publicity,' rather than 'notice,' was rejected as inappropriate with respect either to organizations or to individuals, despite its possible deterrent effect, since it came too close to the adoption of a policy approving social ridicule as a sanction."

IV. THE INCHOATE CRIMES

The offenses of attempt, solicitation, and conspiracy are all "inchoate" in that they consist of incompleted activity related to other acts, usually criminal acts. Part IV deals with these three offenses and defenses to them. Conspiracy raises a number of special problems, largely because in addition to serving as an inchoate offense conspiracy may (when conviction is sought for conspiracy as well as completed offenses) serve as a means of aggravating the actual or potential punishment for other crimes or may be used to attach liability to one individual for crimes committed by others.

MODEL PENAL CODE COMMENT TO ARTICLE 5, 24–26 *

(Tent. Draft No. 10, 1960).

Introduction

This Article undertakes to deal systematically with attempt, solicitation and conspiracy to commit crimes, conduct which has in common that it is designed to culminate in the commission of a substantive offense but either has failed to do so in the discrete case or has not yet achieved its culmination because there is something that the actor or another still must do. The offenses are inchoate in this sense.

These, to be sure, are not the only crimes which are so defined that their commission does not rest on proof of the occurrence of the evil that it is the object of the law to prevent; many specific, substantive offenses also have a large inchoate aspect. This is true not only with respect to crimes of risk-creation, such as reckless driving, or specific crimes of preparation, like those of possession with unlawful purpose. It is also true, at least in part, of crimes like larceny, forgery, kidnaping and even arson, not to speak of burglary, where a purpose to cause greater harm than that which is implicit in the actor's conduct is an element of the offense. It may be thought, indeed, that murder is the only crime which by its definition calls for proof that the full evil that the law endeavors to prevent has come to pass. This reservation notwithstanding, attempt, solicitation and conspiracy have such generality of definition and of application as inchoate crimes that it is useful to bring them together in the Code and to confront the common problems they present.

Since these offenses always presuppose a purpose to commit another crime, it is doubtful that the threat of punishment for their commission can significantly add to the deterrent efficacy of the sanction—which the actor by hypothesis ignores—that is threatened for the crime that is his object. There may be cases where this does occur, as when the actor thinks the chance of apprehension low if he succeeds but high if he should fail in his attempt, or when reflection is promoted at an early stage that otherwise would be postponed until too late, which may be true in some conspiracies. These are, however, special situations. Viewed generally, it seems clear that general deterrence is at most a minor function to be served in fashioning provisions of the penal law addressed to these inchoate crimes; that burden is discharged upon the whole by the law dealing with the substantive offenses.

Other and major functions of the penal law remain, however, to be served. They may be summarized as follows:

First: When a person is seriously dedicated to commission of a crime, there is obviously need for a firm legal basis for the intervention of the agencies of law enforcement to prevent its consummation. In determining that basis, there must be attention to the danger of abuse; equivocal behavior may be misconstrued by an unfriendly eye as preparation to commit a crime. It is no less important, on the other side, that lines should not be drawn so rigidly that the police confront insoluble dilemmas in deciding when to intervene, facing the risk that if they wait the crime may be committed while if they act they may not yet have any valid charge.

Second: Conduct designed to cause or culminate in the commission of a crime obviously yields an indication that the actor is disposed towards such activity, not alone on this occasion but on others. There is a need, therefore, subject again to proper safeguards, for a legal basis upon which the special danger that such individuals present may be assessed and dealt with. They must be made amenable to the corrective process that the law provides.

Third: Finally, and quite apart from these considerations of prevention, when the actor's failure to commit the substantive offense is due to a fortuity, as when the bullet misses in attempted murder or when the expected response to solicitation is withheld, his exculpation on that ground would involve inequality of treatment that would shock the common sense of justice. Such a situation is unthinkable in any mature system, designed to serve the proper goals of penal law.

These are the main considerations in the light of which the draft has been prepared.

A. ATTEMPTS

According to Sayre, Criminal Attempts, 41 Harv.L.Rev. 821 (1928), until quite recently there was no generalized doctrine that attempts to commit crime were, in themselves, criminal. Although some few early convictions for unsuccessful efforts to commit especially heinous crimes are reported, these, according to Professor Sayre, were based on an earlier doctrine that the intention is to be taken for the deed (*voluntas reputabitur pro facto*). The danger of imposing liability upon mere intent was too great to permit resort to this maxim often. Professor Sayre dates the modern doctrine of attempts from Rex v. Scofield, Cald. 397 (1784) where it was declared that "[t]he *intent* may make an act, innocent in itself, criminal; nor is the *completion* of an act, criminal in itself, necessary to constitute criminality." Id. at 400. Many issues vital to the law of attempts seem unsettled and resistant to ready resolution. Perhaps the relative youth of the doctrine explains this; perhaps the difficulties are inherent in efforts to criminalize in the absence of a prohibited result. The draftspersons of the Model Penal Code have addressed the general policy considerations relevant to the issues presented by attempt:

> The literature and decisions dealing with the definition of a criminal attempt reflect ambivalence as to how far the governing criterion should be found in the dangerousness of the actor's conduct, measured by objective standards, and how far in the dangerousness of the actor, as a person manifesting a firm disposition to commit a crime. Both criteria may lead, of course, to the same disposition of a concrete case. When they do not, we think, for reasons stated in the *Introduction*, that the proper focus of attention is the actor's disposition, and the draft is framed with this in mind. Needless to say, we are in full agreement that the law must be concerned with conduct, not with evil thoughts alone. The question is what conduct, when engaged in with a purpose to commit a crime or to advance towards the attainment of a criminal objective, should suffice to constitute a criminal attempt?
>
> In fashioning an answer we must keep in mind that in attempt, as distinct from solicitation and conspiracy, it is not intrinsic to the actor's conduct that he has disclosed his criminal design to someone else; nor is there any natural line that is suggested by the situation—like utterance or agreement. The law must deal with the problem presented by a single individual and must address itself to conduct that may fall anywhere upon a graded scale from early preparation to the final effort to commit the crime.
>
> We think, therefore, that it is useful to begin with any conduct designed to effect or to advance towards the attainment of the criminal objective and to ask when it ought *not* to be regarded as a crime, either because it does not adequately manifest the dangerousness of the actor or on other

overriding grounds of social policy. The formulations in this section are intended as responses to this question.

Model Penal Code, Comment to § 5.01, 26 (Tent. Draft No. 10, 1960).

MODEL PENAL CODE *

(Proposed Official Draft, 1962).

Section 5.01. Criminal Attempt

(1) *Definition of Attempt.* A person is guilty of an attempt to commit a crime if, acting with the kind of culpability otherwise required for commission of the crime, he:

(a) purposely engages in conduct which would constitute the crime if the attendant circumstances were as he believes them to be; or

(b) when causing a particular result is an element of the crime, does or omits to do anything with the purpose of causing or with the belief that it will cause such result without further conduct on his part; or

(c) purposely does or omits to do anything which, under the circumstances as he believes them to be, is an act or omission constituting a substantial step in a course of conduct planned to culminate in his commission of the crime.

(2) *Conduct Which May Be Held Substantial Step Under Subsection (1)(c).* Conduct shall not be held to constitute a substantial step under Subsection (1) (c) of this Section unless it is strongly corroborative of the actor's criminal purpose. Without negativing the sufficiency of other conduct, the following, if strongly corroborative of the actor's criminal purpose, shall not be held insufficient as a matter of law:

(a) lying in wait, searching for or following the contemplated victim of the crime;

(b) enticing or seeking to entice the contemplated victim of the crime to go to the place contemplated for its commission;

(c) reconnoitering the place contemplated for the commission of the crime;

(d) unlawful entry of a structure, vehicle or enclosure in which it is contemplated that the crime will be committed;

(e) possession of materials to be employed in the commission of the crime, which are specially designed for such unlawful use or which can serve no lawful purpose of the actor under the circumstances;

(f) possession, collection or fabrication of materials to be employed in the commission of the crime, at or near the place contemplated for its commission, where such possession, collection or fabrication serves no lawful purpose of the actor under the circumstances;

(g) soliciting an innocent agent to engage in conduct constituting an element of the crime.

(3) *Conduct Designed to Aid Another in Commission of a Crime.* A person who engages in conduct designed to aid another to commit a crime which would establish his complicity under Section 2.06 if the crime were committed by such other person, is guilty of an attempt to commit the crime, although the crime is not committed or attempted by such other person.

(4) *Renunciation of Criminal Purpose.* When the actor's conduct would otherwise constitute an attempt under Subsection (1) (b) or (1) (c) of this Section, it is an affirmative defense that he abandoned his effort to commit the crime or otherwise prevented its commission, under circumstances manifesting a complete and voluntary renunciation of his criminal purpose. The establishment of such defense does not, however, affect the liability of an accomplice who did not join in such abandonment or prevention.

Within the meaning of this Article, renunciation of criminal purpose is not voluntary if it is motivated, in whole or in part, by circumstances, not present or apparent at the inception of the actor's course of conduct, which increase the probability of detection or apprehension or which make more difficult the accomplishment of the criminal purpose. Renunciation is not complete if it is motivated by a decision to postpone the criminal conduct until a more advantageous time or to transfer the criminal effort to another but similar objective or victim.

Section 5.05 Grading of Criminal Attempt * * *; Mitigation in Cases of Lesser Danger; Multiple Convictions Barred

(1) *Grading.* Except as otherwise provided in this Section, attempt [is a crime] of the same grade and degree as the most serious offense which is attempted * * *.

(2) *Mitigation.* If the particular conduct charged to constitute a criminal attempt * * * is so inherently unlikely to result or culminate in the commission of a crime that neither such conduct nor the actor presents a public danger warranting the grading of such offense under this Section, the Court shall exercise its power under Section 6.12 to enter judgment and impose sentence for a crime of lower grade or degree or, in extreme cases, may dismiss the prosecution.

(3) *Multiple Convictions.* A person may not be convicted of more than one offense defined by this Article for conduct designed to commit or to culminate in the commission of the same crime.

1. THE ACT: BEYOND MERE PREPARATION

Probably the most frequent problem encountered in the application of attempt law is whether the defendant has "gone far enough" to complete an attempt. As the discussion in the principal case in this subsection indicates, a variety of standards have been offered for defining how far a defendant must go towards completion of a crime before an attempt is committed. None of the standards are easy to apply in practice. The trend seems to be towards use of a flexible standard such as that proposed by the Model Penal Code and discussed in the principal case below.

UNITED STATES v. JACKSON

United States Court of Appeals, Second Circuit, 1977.
560 F.2d 112, cert. den. 434 U.S. 941, 98 S.Ct. 434, 54 L.Ed. 301.

FREDERICK van PELT BRYAN, Senior District Judge:

* * * [Robert Jackson, William Scott and Martin Allen were convicted of conspiracy to rob the Manufacturers Hanover Trust branch bank and of attempting to rob this bank on June 14 and June 21, 1976. On appeal, appellants do not contest the sufficiency of the evidence on the conspiracy count but they] assert that, as a matter of law, their conduct never crossed the elusive line which separates "mere preparation" from "attempt." This troublesome question was recently examined by this court in United States v. Stallworth, 543 F.2d 1038 (2d Cir. 1976), which set forth the applicable legal principles.

I.

The Government's evidence at trial consisted largely of the testimony of Vanessa Hodges, an unindicted co-conspirator, and of various FBI agents who surveilled the Manufacturers Hanover branch on June 21, 1976. Since the facts are of critical importance in any attempt case, we shall review the Government's proof in considerable detail.

On June 11, 1976, Vanessa Hodges was introduced to appellant Martin Allen by Pia Longhorne, another unindicted co-conspirator. Hodges wanted to meet someone who would help her carry out a plan to rob the Manufacturers Hanover branch located at 210 Flushing Avenue in Brooklyn, and she invited Allen to join her. Hodges proposed that the bank be robbed the next Monday, June 14th, at about 7:30 A.M. She hoped that they could enter with the bank manager at that time, grab the weekend deposits, and leave. Allen agreed to rob the bank with Hodges, and told her he had access to a car, two sawed-off shotguns, and a .38 caliber revolver.

The following Monday, June 14, Allen arrived at Longhorne's house about 7:30 A.M. in a car driven by appellant Robert Jackson. A suitcase in the back seat of the car contained a sawed-off shotgun, shells, materials intended as masks, and handcuffs to bind the bank manager. While Allen picked up Hodges at Longhorne's, Jackson filled the car with gas. The trio then left for the bank.

When they arrived, it was almost 8:00 A.M. It was thus too late to effect the first step of the plan, *viz.*, entering the bank as the manager opened the door. They rode around for a while longer, and then went to a restaurant to get something to eat and discuss their next move. After eating, the trio drove back to the bank. Allen and Hodges left the car and walked over to the bank. The peered in and saw the bulky weekend deposits, but decided it was too risky to rob the bank without an extra man.

Consequently, Jackson, Hodges, and Allen drove to Coney Island in search of another accomplice. In front of a housing project on 33rd Street they found appellant William Scott, who promptly joined the team. Allen added to the arsenal another sawed-off shotgun obtained from one of the buildings in the project, and the group drove back to the bank.

When they arrived again, Allen entered the bank to check the location of any surveillance cameras, while Jackson placed a piece of cardboard with a false license number over the authentic license plate of the car. Allen reported back that a single surveillance camera was over the entrance door. After further discussion, Scott left the car and entered the bank. He came back and informed the group that the tellers were separating the weekend deposits and that a number of patrons were now in the bank. Hodges then suggested that they drop the plans for the robbery that day, and reschedule it for the following Monday, June 21. Accordingly, they left the vicinity of the bank and returned to Coney Island where, before splitting up, they purchased a pair of stockings for Hodges to wear over her head as a disguise and pairs of gloves for Hodges, Scott, and Allen to don before entering the bank.

Hodges was arrested on Friday, June 18, 1976 on an unrelated bank robbery charge, and immediately began cooperating with the Government. After relating the events on June 14, she told FBI agents that a robbery of the Manufacturers branch at 210 Flushing Avenue was now scheduled for the following Monday, June 21. The three black male robbers, according to Hodges, would be heavily armed with hand and shoulder weapons and expected to use a brown four-door sedan equipped with a cardboard license plate as the getaway car. She told the agents that Jackson, who would drive the car, as light-skinned with a moustache and a cut on his lip, and she described Allen as short, dark-skinned with facial hair, and Scott as 5′9″, slim build, with an afro hair style and some sort of defect in his right eye.

At the request of the agents, Hodges called Allen on Saturday, June 19, and asked if he were still planning to do the job. He said that he was ready. On Sunday she called him again. This time Allen said that he was not going to rob the bank that Monday because he had learned that Hodges had been arrested and he feared that federal agents might be watching. Hodges nevertheless advised the agents that she thought the robbery might still take place as planned with the three men proceeding without her.

At about 7:00 A.M. on Monday, June 21, 1976, some ten FBI agents took various surveilling positions in the area of the bank. At about 7:39 A.M. the agents observed a brown four-door Lincoln, with a New York license plate on the front and a cardboard facsimile of a license plate on the rear, moving in an easterly direction on Flushing Avenue past the bank, which was located on the southeast corner of Flushing and Washington Avenues. The front seat of the Lincoln was occupied by a black male driver and a black male passenger with muttonchop sideburns. The Lincoln circled the block and came to a stop at a fire hydrant situated at the side of the bank facing Washington Avenue, a short distance south of the corner of Flushing and Washington.

A third black male, who appeared to have an eye deformity, got out of the passenger side rear door of the Lincoln, walked to the corner of Flushing and Washington, and stood on the sidewalk in the vicinity of the bank's entrance. He then walked south on Washington Avenue, only to return a short time later with a container of coffee in his hand. He stood again on the corner of Washington and Flushing in front of the bank, drinking the coffee and looking around, before returning to the parked Lincoln.

The Lincoln pulled out, made a left turn onto Flushing, and proceeded in a westerly direction for one block to Waverly Avenue. It stopped, made a U-turn, and parked on the south side of Flushing between Waverly and Washington—a spot on the same side of the street as the bank entrance but separated from it by Washington Avenue. After remaining parked in this position for approximately five minutes, it pulled out and cruised east on Flushing past the bank again. The Lincoln then made a right onto Grand Avenue, the third street east of the bank, and headed south. It stopped halfway down the block, midway between Flushing and Park Avenues, and remained there for several minutes. During this time Jackson was seen working in the front of the car, which had its hood up.

The Lincoln was next sighted several minutes later in the same position it had previously occupied on the south side of Flushing Avenue between Waverly and Washington. The front license plate was now missing. The vehicle remained parked there for close to thirty minutes. Finally, it began moving east on Flushing Avenue once more, in the direction of the bank.

At some point near the bank as they passed down Flushing Avenue, the appellants detected the presence of the surveillance agents. The Lincoln accelerated down Flushing Avenue and turned south on Grand Avenue again. It was overtaken by FBI agents who ordered the appellants out of the car and arrested them. The agents then observed a black and red plaid suitcase in the rear of the car. The zipper of the suitcase was partially open and exposed two loaded sawed-off shotguns, a toy nickel-plated revolver, a pair of handcuffs, and masks. A New York license plate was seen lying on the front floor of the car. All of these items were seized.

* * *

In his memorandum of decision, Chief Judge Mishler * * * characterized the question of whether the defendants had attempted a bank robbery as charged in counts two and three or were merely engaged in preparations as "a close one." After canvassing the authorities on what this court one month later called a "perplexing problem," Chief Judge Mishler applied the following two-tiered inquiry formulated in United States v. Mandujano, 499 F.2d 370, 376 (5th Cir. 1974), cert. den. 419 U.S. 1114, 95 S.Ct. 792, 42 L.Ed.2d 812 (1975):

> First, the defendant must have been acting with the kind of culpability otherwise required for the commission of the crime which he is charged with attempting. * * *
>
> Second, the defendant must have engaged in conduct which constitutes a substantial step toward commission of the crime. A substantial step must be conduct strongly corroborative of the firmness of the defendant's criminal intent.

He concluded that on June 14 and again on June 21, the defendants took substantial steps, strongly corroborative of the firmness of their criminal intent, toward commission of the crime of bank robbery and found the defendants guilty on each of the two attempt counts. These appeals followed.

II.

"[T]here is no comprehensive statutory definition of attempt in federal law." United States v. Heng Awkak Roman, 356 F.Supp. 434, 437 (S.D.N.Y.), aff'd 484 F.2d 1271 (2d Cir. 1973), cert. den. 415 U.S. 978, 94 S.Ct. 1565, 39 L.Ed.2d 874 (1974). Fed.R.Crim.P. 31(c), however, provides in pertinent part that a defendant may be found guilty of "an attempt to commit either the offense charged or an offense necessarily included therein if the attempt is an offense." 18 U.S.C.A. § 2113(a) specifically makes attempted bank robbery an offense.

* * *

Chief Judge KAUFMAN, writing for the court [in United States v. Stallworth, supra] selected the two-tiered inquiry of United States v. Mandujano, supra, "properly derived from the writings of many distinguished jurists," as stating the proper test for determining whether the foregoing conduct constituted an attempt. He observed that this analysis "conforms closely to the sensible definition of an attempt proferred by the American Law Institute's Model Penal Code." * * *

The draftsmen of the Model Penal Code recognized the difficulty of arriving at a general standard for distinguishing acts of preparation from acts constituting an attempt. They found general agreement that when an actor committed the "last proximate act," i. e., when he had done all that he believed necessary to effect a particular result which is an element of the offense, he committed an attempt. They also concluded, however, that while the last proximate act is *sufficient* to constitute an attempt, it is not *necessary* to such a finding. The problem then was to devise a standard more inclusive than one requiring the last proximate act before attempt liability would attach, but less inclusive than one which would make every act done with the intent to commit a crime criminal. *See* Model Penal Code § 5.01, Comment at 38–39 (Tent. Draft No. 10, 1960).

The draftsmen considered and rejected the following approaches to distinguishing preparation from attempt, later summarized in *Mandujano*:

> (a) The physical proximity doctrine—the overt act required for an attempt must be proximate to the completed crime, or directly tending toward the completion of the crime, or must amount to the commencement of the consummation.
>
> (b) The dangerous proximity doctrine—a test given impetus by Mr. Justice Holmes whereby the greater the gravity and probability of the offense, and the nearer the act to the crime, the stronger is the case for calling the act an attempt.
>
> (c) The indispensable element test—a variation of the proximity tests which emphasizes any indispensable aspect of the criminal endeavor over which the actor has not yet acquired control.
>
> (d) The probable desistance test—the conduct constitutes an attempt if, in the ordinary and natural course of events, without interruption from an outside source, it will result in the crime intended.
>
> (e) The abnormal step approach—an attempt is a step toward crime which goes beyond the point where the normal citizen would think better of his conduct and desist.

> (f) The res ipsa loquitur or unequivocality test—an attempt is committed when the actor's conduct manifests an intent to commit a crime.

499 F.2d at 373 n. 5.

The formulation upon which the draftsmen ultimately agreed required, in addition to criminal purpose, that an act be a substantial step in a course of conduct designed to accomplish a criminal result, and that it be strongly corroborative of criminal purpose in order for it to constitute such a substantial step. The following differences between this test and previous approaches to the preparation-attempt problem were noted:

> First, this formulation shifts the emphasis from what remains to be done—the chief concern of the proximity tests—to what the actor *has already done.* The fact that further major steps must be taken before the crime can be completed does not preclude a finding that the steps already undertaken are substantial. It is expected, in the normal case, that this approach will broaden the scope of attempt liability.
>
> Second, although it is intended that the requirement of a substantial step will result in the imposition of attempt liability only in those instances in which some firmness of criminal purpose is shown, no finding is required as to whether the actor would probably have desisted prior to completing the crime. Potentially the probable desistance test could reach very early steps toward crime—depending upon how one assesses the probabilities of desistance—but since in practice this test follows closely the proximity approaches, rejection of probable desistance will not narrow the scope of attempt liability.
>
> Finally, the requirement of proving a substantial step generally will prove less of a hurdle for the prosecution than the *res ipsa loquitur* approach, which requires that the actor's conduct must itself manifest the criminal purpose. The difference will be illustrated in connection with the present section's requirement of corroboration. Here it should be noted that, in the present formulation, the two purposes to be served by the *res ipsa loquitur* test are, to a large extent, treated separately. Firmness of criminal purpose is intended to be shown by requiring a substantial step, while problems of proof are dealt with by the requirement of corroboration (although, under the reasoning previously expressed, the latter will also tend to establish firmness of purpose).

Model Penal Code § 5.01, Comment at 47 (Tent. Draft No. 10, 1960).

The draftsmen concluded that, in addition to assuring firmness of criminal design, the requirement of a substantial step would preclude attempt liability, with its accompanying harsh penalties, for relatively remote preparatory acts. At the same time, however, by not requiring a "last proximate act" or one of its various analogues it would permit the apprehension of dangerous persons at an earlier stage than the other approaches without immunizing them from attempt liability. Id. at 47–48.

* * *

In the case at bar, Chief Judge Mishler anticipated the precise analysis which this Court adopted in the * * * *Stallworth* case. He then found that on June 14 the appellants, already agreed upon a robbery plan, drove to the bank with loaded weapons. In order to carry the heavy weekend deposit sacks, they recruited another person. Cardboard was placed over the license, and the bank was entered and reconnoitered. Only then was the plan dropped for the moment and rescheduled for the following Monday. On that day, June 21, the defendants performed essentially the same acts. Since the cameras had already been located there was no need to enter the bank again, and since the appellants had arrived at the bank earlier, conditions were more favorable to their initial robbery plan than they had been on June 14. He concluded that on both occasions these men were seriously dedicated to the commission of a crime, had passed beyond the stage of preparation, and would have assaulted the bank had they not been dissuaded by certain external factors, *viz.*, the breaking up of the weekend deposits and crowd of patrons in the bank on June 14 and the detection of the FBI surveillance on June 21.

We cannot say that these conclusions which Chief Judge Mishler reached as the trier of fact as to what the evidence before him established were erroneous. As in *Stallworth,* the criminal intent of the appellants was beyond dispute. The question remaining then is the substantiality of the steps taken on the dates in question, and how strongly this corroborates the firmness of their obvious criminal intent. This is a matter of degree. See Model Penal Code § 5.01, Comments at 47 (Tent. Draft No. 10, 1960).

On two separate occasions, appellants reconnoitered the place contemplated for the commission of the crime and possessed the paraphernalia to be employed in the commission of the crime—loaded sawed-off shotguns, extra shells, a toy revolver, handcuffs, and masks—which was specially designed for such unlawful use and which could serve no lawful purpose under the circumstances. Under the Model Penal Code formulation, approved by the *Stallworth* court, either type of conduct, standing alone, was sufficient as a matter of law to constitute a "substantial step" if it strongly corroborated their criminal purpose. Here both types of conduct coincided on both June 14 and June 21, along with numerous other elements strongly corroborative of the firmness of appellants' criminal intent.[8] The steps taken toward a successful bank robbery thus were not "insubstantial" as a matter of law, and Chief Judge Mishler found them "substantial" as a matter of fact. We are unwilling to substitute our assessment of the evidence for his, and thus affirm the convictions for attempted bank robbery * * *.

NOTES AND QUESTIONS

1. Consider the following discussion by Judge Learned Hand in United States v. Coplon, 185 F.2d 629 (2nd Cir.1950), cert. den. 342 U.S. 920, 72 S.Ct. 362, 96 L.Ed. 688 (1952):

> "A neat doctrine by which to test when a person, intending to commit a crime which he fails to carry out, has 'attempted' to commit it, would be that he has done all that it is within his power to do, but has been prevented by intervention from outside; in short, that he has passed beyond any *locus poenitentiae*. Apparently that was the original notion * * *; but it is certainly not now generally the law in the United States, for there are many decisions which hold that the accused has passed beyond 'preparation,' although he has been interrupted before he has taken the last of his intended steps."

185 F.2d at 633.

2. The preparation attempt distinction is obviously quite vague and this may permit the imposition of liability for conduct far removed from the harm and, perhaps, from what the legislature sought to make culpable. This concern has led at least one commentator to suggest that, rather than having a single "catch-all" attempt provision, the definition of each offense should include the conduct which should give rise to the liability although it falls short of the completed offense. Glazebrook, Should We Have a Law of Attempted Crime?, 85 L.Q.Rev. 28 (1969). Others have argued that the problem is not susceptible to precise solution and, indeed, such efforts are undesirable. "There is more harm than good in telling people precisely how far they may go without risking punishment in the pursuit of an unlawful object". Stephen, A General View of the Criminal Law of England 83 (1890). Of course, we do have statutes specially designed to penalize conduct that threatens harm without achieving it. Examples are statutes prohibiting possession of burglary tools, or the use, manufacture, or distribution of combustible or explosive substances with intent to burn property. See People v. Davis, 24 Mich.App. 304, 180 N.W.

8. After securing the extra man they needed on June 14, the gang returned to the bank with their weapons ready and the car's license plate disguised for the getaway. Hodges' testimony was that they were ready to rob the bank at that time, but eventually postponed the robbery because conditions did not seem favorable. The fact that they then made further preparations by buying the stockings and gloves, an afterthought according to Hodges, does not undercut the firmness of their criminal intent when they were at the bank on June 14. By only postponing execution of the plan, appellants did not renounce their criminal purpose but reaffirmed it. They reflected further upon the plan and embellished it by acquiring the stockings and gloves.
* * *

2d 285 (1970) where the defendant was held to have been properly convicted because he aided others in making molotov cocktails although he did not participate in their use.[a]

3. It has been suggested that deterrence is of minor or no consequence in the law of attempts inasmuch as the fact of the attempt establishes that the actor was not deterred by the sanction attached to the substantive offense which it was his object to commit. Nevertheless, it seems reasonable to assume that the more frequently criminal conduct is punished the more likely it is that the rest of us will be conscious of the reality of the existence of the sanction and the greater its deterrent effect. If so, is this a reason to spread the net of attempt as widely as possible consistent with other values in the criminal justice system?

2. THE STATE OF MIND REQUIRED

Whether a defendant has acted with the requisite intent is a less frequent issue in attempt cases than whether the required act was performed. But in those infrequent cases in which it arises, the problem of intent is often a difficult one. There seems widespread agreement that the defendant must have any intent or state of mind required for the crime which he is alleged to have attempted. A defendant is not guilty of attempted burglary, for example, if he does not have the intent to commit an offense in the structure which he attempts to enter. The more difficult problem is whether, in addition, the defendant must have the purpose of engaging in the conduct constituting the crime, or causing the result which is the essence of the completed crime. The problem arises most often in attempted homicide cases, such as Thacker v. Commonwealth, the principal case in this subsection. As the subsection on homicide (page 291, infra) makes clear, a defendant may sometimes be guilty of criminal homicide and even of murder even though he did not have the intent or purpose to cause death. It is sufficient for murder, for example, that the defendant has, at the time he causes the death of the victim, the intent to inflict serious bodily injury or that he is aware that his con-

a. Another and rather more dramatic example of penalizing conduct well removed from an actual attempt is 18 U.S.C.A. § 871 (1970) which provides for a fine of $1,000 and/or not more than five years imprisonment for any person who "knowingly and willfully" makes any threat of bodily harm against the President or any officer in the order of succession to the President. Then Judge Burger has written, in the course of affirming a conviction under this statute—the defendant had publically stated that if required to carry a gun (be drafted) "the first person I want in my sights is LBJ"—that its ultimate purpose was to deter the killing or injuring of the President by deterring such threats, and that there is no requirement that the threat be made with intent to execute it. Watts v. United States, 402 F.2d 676 (D.C.Cir.) rev'd on other grounds, per curiam, 394 U.S. 705, 89 S.Ct. 1399, 22 L.Ed.2d 664 (1968). The Supreme Court's reversal was grounded on the view that the statement was mere "political hyperbole". The opinion announces, without discussion, that the statute is facially constitutional, but questions the validity of the Court of Appeals position on the intent required.

duct creates a very high risk of death. But suppose a defendant does not kill but engages in conduct that almost causes death? Can he be guilty of *attempted* murder if the evidence fails to show that he had the purpose of causing the victim's death? This is the basic problem addressed in the present subsection.

MODEL PENAL CODE, COMMENT TO § 5.01, 27–30 *

(Tent. Draft No. 10, 1960).

3. *5.01(1). The Requirement of Purpose.* As previously stated, the proposed definition of attempt follows the conventional pattern of limiting this inchoate crime to purposive conduct. In the language of the courts, there must be "intent in fact" or "specific intent" to commit the crime allegedly attempted. Nonetheless a problem of drafting is presented in endeavoring to explain the nature of the requisite purpose.

This section adopts the view that the actor must have for his purpose to engage in the criminal conduct or accomplish the criminal result which is an element of the substantive crime but that his purpose need not encompass all the surrounding circumstances included in the formal definition of the substantive offense. As to them it is sufficient that he acts with the culpability that is required for commission of the crime. Suppose, for example, that it is a federal offense to kill or injure an FBI agent and that recklessness or even negligence with respect to the identity of the victim as an agent suffices for commission of the crime. There would be an attempt to kill or injure such an agent under the present formulation if the actor with recklessness or negligence as to the official position of the victim attempts to kill or injure him. Under paragraph (b) the killing or injuring would be the required purpose; the fact that the victim is an agent would be only a circumstance as to which the actor had "the kind of culpability otherwise required for commission of the crime."

It is difficult to say what the result would be in this kind of case under prevailing principles of attempt liability. However, the proposed formulation imposes attempt liability in a group of cases where the normal basis of such liability is present—purposive conduct manifesting dangerousness—and allows the policy of the substantive crime, respecting recklessness or negligence as to surrounding circumstances, to be applied to the attempt to commit that crime.

With rare exceptions, the necessity for showing intent has not given rise to many difficulties in applying prevailing attempt principles. * * *

Under paragraph (b), liability for an attempt may be founded upon the actor's belief that his conduct will cause a particular result which is an element of the crime. If, for example, the actor's purpose were to demolish a building and, knowing and believing that persons in the building would be killed by the explosion, the actor nonetheless detonated a bomb, there would be an attempt to kill even though it was no part of the actor's purpose—i. e., he did not consciously desire—that the building's inhabitants should be killed. Again, it is difficult to say what the decision would be under prevailing attempt principles in a case of this kind. It might be held that the actor did not specifically intend to kill the inhabitants of the building; on the other hand, the concept of "intent" has always been an ambiguous one and might be thought to include results which are believed by the actor to be the inevitable consequences of his conduct.

The inclusion of such conduct as a basis for liability under paragraph (b) is based on the conclusion that the manifestation of dangerousness is as great—or very nearly as great—as in the case of purposive conduct. In both instances a deliberate choice is made to bring about the consequence forbidden by the criminal laws, and the actor has done all within his power to cause this result to occur. The absence in one instance of any desire for the forbidden result is not, under these circumstances, a sufficient basis for differentiating between the two types of conduct involved.

It should be emphasized that this extension of paragraph (b) beyond the area of purposive behavior does *not* result in the inclusion of reckless conduct. Indeed, as previously noted, the additional ground of liability may well be within the common law concept of intentional behavior. Certain types of non-causal reckless conduct are encompassed by § 201.11 of the Code, Tentative Draft No. 9 (1959).

THACKER v. COMMONWEALTH

Supreme Court of Appeals of Virginia, 1922.
134 Va. 767, 114 S.E. 504.

WEST, J. This writ of error is to a judgment upon the verdict of a jury finding John Thacker, the accused, guilty of attempting to murder Mrs. J. A. Ratrie, and fixing his punishment at two years in the penitentiary.

The only assignment of error is the refusal of the trial court to set aside the verdict as contrary to the law and the evidence.

The accused, in company with two other young men, Doc Campbell and Paul Kelly, was attending a church festival in Alleghany county, at which all three became intoxicated. They left the church between 10 and 11 o'clock at night, and walked down the county road about 1½ miles, when they came to a sharp curve. Located in this curve was a tent in which the said Mrs. J. A. Ratrie, her husband, four children, and a servant were camping for the summer. The husband, though absent, was expected home that night, and Mrs. Ratrie, upon retiring, had placed a lighted lamp on a trunk by the head of her bed. After 11 o'clock she was awakened by the shots of a pistol and loud talking in the road near by, and heard a man say, "I am going to shoot that God-damned light out;" and another voice said, "Don't shoot the light out." The accused and his friends then appeared at the back of the tent, where the flaps of the tent were open, and said they were from Bath county and had lost their way, and asked Mrs. Ratrie if she could take care of them all night. She informed them she was camping for the summer, and had no room for them. One of the three thanked her, and they turned away, but after passing around the tent the accused used some vulgar language and did some cursing and singing. When they got back in the road, the accused said again he was going to shoot the light out, and fired three shots, two of which went through the tent, one passing through the head of the bed in which Mrs. Ratrie was lying, just missing her head and the head of her baby, who was sleeping with her. The accused did not know Mrs. Ratrie, and had never seen her before. He testified he did not know any of the parties in the tent, and had no ill will against either of them; that he simply shot at the light, without any intent to harm Mrs. Ratrie or any one else; that he would not have shot had he been sober, and regretted his action.

The foregoing are the admitted facts in the case.

An attempt to commit a crime is composed of two elements: (1) The intent to commit it; and (2) a direct, ineffectual act done towards its commission. The act must reach far enough towards the accomplishment of the desired result to amount to the commencement of the consummation.

The law can presume the intention so far as realized in the act, but not an intention beyond what was so realized. The law does not presume, because an assault was made with a weapon likely to produce death, that it was an assault with the intent to murder. And where it takes a particular intent to constitute a crime, that particular intent must be proved either by direct or circumstantial evidence, which would warrant the inference of the intent with which the act was done.

When a statute makes an offense to consist of an act combined with a particular intent, that intent is just as necessary to be proved as the act itself, and must be found as a matter of fact before a conviction can be had; and no intent in law or mere legal presumption, differing from the intent in fact, can be allowed to supply the place of the latter.

In discussing the law of attempts, Mr. Clark in his work on Criminal Law says, at page 111:

> "The act must be done with the specific intent to commit a particular crime. This specific intent at the time the

act is done is essential. To do an act from general malevolence is not an attempt to commit a crime, because there is no specific intent, though the act according to its consequences may amount to a substantive crime. To do an act with intent to commit one crime cannot be an attempt to commit another crime, though it might result in such other crime. To set fire to a house and burn a human being who is in it, but not to the offender's knowledge, would be murder, though the intent was to burn the house only; but to attempt to set fire to the house under such circumstances would be an attempt to commit arson only and not an attempt to murder. A man actuated by general malevolence may commit murder, though there is no actual intention to kill; to be guilty of an attempt to murder there must be a specific intent to kill."

Mr. Bishop, in his Criminal Law, vol. 1 (8th Ed.), at section 729, says:

"When the law makes an act, whether more or less evil in itself, punishable, though done simply from general malevolence, if one takes what, were all accomplished, would be a step towards it, yet if he does not mean to do the whole, no court can justly hold him answerable for more than he does. And when the thing done does not constitute a substantive crime, there is no ground for treating it as an attempt. So that necessarily an act prompted by general malevolence, or by a specific design to do something else, is not an attempt to commit a crime not intended. * * * When we say that a man attempted to do a given wrong, we mean that he intended to do specifically it, and proceeded a certain way in the doing. The intent in the mind covers the thing in full; the act covers it only in part. Thus (section 730) to commit murder, one need not intend to take life, but to be guilty of an attempt to murder, he must so intend. It is not sufficient that his act, had it proved fatal, would have been murder. Section 736. We have seen that the unintended taking of life may be murder, yet there can be no attempt to murder without the specific intent to commit it—a rule the latter branch whereof appears probably in a few of the states to have been interfered with by statutes (citing Texas cases). For example, if one from a housetop recklessly throws down a billet of wood upon the sidewalk where persons are constantly passing, and it falls upon a person passing by and kills him, this would be the common-law murder, but if, instead of killing, it inflicts only a slight injury, the party could not be convicted of an assault with attempt to commit murder, since, in fact, the murder was not intended."

The application of the foregoing principles to the facts of the instant case shows clearly, as we think, that the judgment complained of is erroneous. While it might possibly be said that the firing of the shot into the head of Mrs. Ratrie's bed was an act done towards the commission of the offense charged, the evidence falls far short of proving that it was fired with the intent to murder her.

However averse we may be to disturb the verdict of the jury, our obligation to the law compels us to do so.

The judgment complained of will be reversed, the verdict of the jury set aside, and the case remanded for a new trial therein, if the commonwealth shall be so advised.

Reversed.

NOTES AND QUESTIONS

1. Can one be convicted of an attempt to commit a strict liability offense without proof of intent to commit the offense? Cf. Gardner v. Akeroyd, [1952] 2 Q.B. 743 (although a butcher may be held strictly and vicariously liable for the sale of meat at prices in excess of the regulatory maxima, he cannot be held liable for "any act preparatory to the commission" of that offense (prepared but undelivered parcels of meat were found in the shop with tickets showing overcharges) in the absence of mens rea).

2. Is there any doubt that Thacker had identified himself as a dangerous person and a proper subject for correction? If so, is it desirable to make the assessment of his punishment so dependent upon the fortuity of the result of his conduct? For an argument in favor of permitting verdicts of attempted manslaughter where the defendant has acted recklessly or with gross negligence see Stuart, Mens Rea, Negligence and Attempts [1968] Crim.L.Rev. 647.

3. THE "DEFENSE" OF IMPOSSIBILITY

A fascinating but most troublesome problem in the law of attempts is whether a defendant may avoid conviction on the grounds that it was impossible for him to have achieved his objective. Not surprisingly this defense has been rejected when it is clear that the only reason completion of the crime was impossible was a mistake by the defendant with respect to factors such as whether there was a wallet in the pocket he sought to pick; a bullet in the gun he sought to discharge at his victim; or a person in the bed into which he fired his weapon. These are all deemed matters of factual impossibility and not to be entertained as a defense. The difficulty arises in situations in which the mistake seems to be one of law. Can one be charged with attempting to receive stolen goods when the goods in question had already been recovered by the police and had thus lost their stolen quality? In such a case the law has recognized the defense of "legal impossibility". Booth v. State, 398 P.2d 863 (Okl.Cr. App.1964). As a matter of doctrinal purity there is some attraction to the idea that a person should not be punished for attempting something which could not have been a crime even if he had done all that he wished to do. Nevertheless, many have been troubled by the rule since it is often difficult to distinguish between factual and legal impossibility and, more importantly, because these defendants usually seem, by their conduct and desires, to have identified themselves as dangerous persons who are suitable subjects for the use of the criminal sanction. The case which follows illustrates the intractable nature of the question and the modern impatience with the use of the defense.

PEOPLE v. DLUGASH

Court of Appeals of New York, 1977.
41 N.Y.2d 725, 395 N.Y.S.2d 419, 363 N.E.2d 1155.

JASEN, Judge.

The criminal law is of ancient origin, but criminal liability for attempt to commit a crime is comparatively recent. At the root of the concept of attempt liability are the very aims and purposes of penal law. The ultimate issue is whether an individual's intentions and actions, though failing to achieve a manifest and malevolent criminal purpose, constitute a danger to organized society of sufficient magnitude to warrant the imposition of criminal sanctions. Difficulties in theoretical analysis and concomitant debate over very pragmatic questions of blameworthiness appear dramatically in reference to situations where the criminal attempt failed to achieve its purpose solely because the factual or legal context in which the individual acted was not as the actor supposed them to be. Phrased somewhat differently, the concern centers on whether an individual should be liable for an attempt to commit a crime when, unknown to him, it was impossible to successfully complete the crime attempted. For years, serious studies have been made on the subject in an effort the resolve the continuing controversy when, if at all, the impossibility of successfully completing the criminal act should preclude liability for even making the futile attempt. The 1967 revision of the Penal Law approached the impossibility defense to the inchoate crime of attempt in a novel fashion. The statute provides that, if a person engages in conduct which would otherwise constitute an attempt to commit a crime, "it is no defense to a prosecution for such attempt that the crime charged to have been attempted was, under the attendant circumstances, factually or legally impossible of commission, if such crime could have been committed had the attendant circumstances been as such person believed them to be." (Penal Law, § 110.10.) This appeal presents to us, for the first time, a case involving the application of the modern statute. We hold that, under the proof presented by the People at trial, defendant Melvin Dlugash may be held for attempted murder, though the target of the attempt may have already been slain, by the hand of another, when Dlugash made his felonious attempt.

On December 22, 1973, Michael Geller, 25 years old, was found shot to death in the bedroom of his Brooklyn apartment. The body, which had literally been riddled by bullets, was found lying face up on the floor. An autopsy revealed that the victim had been shot in the face and head no less than seven times. Powder burns on the face indicated that the shots had been fired from within one foot of the victim. Four small caliber bullets were recovered from the victim's skull. The victim had also been critically wounded in the chest. * * *

Detective Joseph Carrasquillo of the New York City Police Department was assigned to investigate the homicide. [On December 27, Detective Carrasquillo contacted the defendant in regard to Geller's death. The defendant stated that he and a friend, Joe Bush, had been on a trip and had only recently learned of Geller's death. Bush was also a suspect in the investigation. During subsequent interrogation, the defendant acknowledged direct information concerning the manner in which Geller had met his fate.] The defendant then proceeded to relate his version of the events which culminated in the death of Geller. Defendant stated that, on the night of December 21, 1973, he, Bush and Geller had been out drinking. Bush had been staying at Geller's apartment and, during the course of the evening, Geller several times demanded that Bush pay $100 towards the rent on the apartment. According to defendant, Bush rejected these demands, telling Geller that "you better shut up or you're going to get a bullet". All three returned to Geller's apartment at approximately midnight, took seats in the bedroom, and continued to drink until sometime between 3:00 and 3:30 in the morning. When Geller again pressed his demand for rent money, Bush drew his .38 caliber pistol, aimed it at Geller and fired three times. Geller fell to the floor. After the passage of a few minutes, perhaps two, perhaps as much as five, defendant walked over to the fallen Geller, drew his .25 caliber pistol, and fired approximately five shots in the victim's head and face. Defendant contended that, by the time he fired the shots, "it looked like Mike Geller was already dead". After the shots were fired, defendant and Bush walked to the apartment of a female acquaintance. Bush removed his shirt, wrapped the two guns and a knife in it, and left the apartment, telling Dlugash that he intended to dispose of the weapons. Bush returned 10 or 15 minutes later and stated that he had thrown the weapons down a sewer two or three blocks away.

After Carrasquillo had taken the bulk of the statement, he asked the defendant why he would do such a thing. According to Carrasquillo, the defendant said, "gee, I really don't know". Carrasquillo repeated the question 10 minutes later, but received the same response. After a while, Carrasquillo asked the question for a third time and defendant replied, "well, gee, I guess it must have been because I was afraid of Joe Bush."

At approximately 9:00 p. m., the defendant repeated the substance of his statement to an Assistant District Attorney. Defendant added that at the time he shot at Geller, Geller was not moving and his eyes were closed. While he did not check for a pulse, defendant stated that Geller had not been doing anything to him at the time he shot because "Mike was dead".

Defendant was indicted by the Grand Jury of Kings County on a single count of murder in that, acting in concert with another person actually present, he intentionally caused the death of Michael Geller. At the trial, there were four principal prosecution witnesses: Detective Carrasquillo, the Assistant District Attorney who took the second admission, and two physicians from the office of the New York City Chief Medical Examiner. For proof of defendant's culpability, the prosecution relied upon defendant's own admissions as related by the detective and the prosecutor. From the physicians, the prosecution sought to establish that Geller was still alive at the time defendant shot at him. Both physicians testified that each of the two chest wounds, for which defendant alleged Bush to be responsible, would have caused death without prompt medical attention. Moreover, the victim would have remained alive until such time as his chest cavity became fully filled with blood. Depending on the circumstances, it might take 5 to 10 minutes for the chest cavity to fill. Neither prosecution witness could state, with medical certainty, that the victim was still alive when, perhaps five minutes after the initial chest wounds were inflicted, the defendant fired at the victim's head.

The defense produced but a single witness, the former Chief Medical Examiner of New York City. This expert stated that, in his view, Geller might have died of the chest wounds "very rapidly" since, in addition to the bleeding, a large bullet going through a lung and the heart would have other adverse medical effects. "Those wounds can be almost immediately or rapidly fatal or they may be delayed in there, in the time it would take for death to occur. But I would say that wounds like that which are described here as having gone through the lungs and the heart would be fatal wounds and in most cases they're rapidly fatal."

The trial court declined to charge the jury, as requested by the prosecution, that defendant could be guilty of murder on the theory that he had aided and abetted the killing of Geller by Bush. Instead, the court submitted only two theories to the jury: that defendant had either intentionally murdered Geller or had attempted to murder Geller.

The jury found the defendant guilty of murder. The defendant then moved to set the verdict aside. He submitted an affidavit in which he contended that he "was absolutely, unequivocally and positively certain that Michael Geller was dead before [he] shot him." Further, the defendant averred that he was in fear for his life when he shot Geller. "This fear stemmed from the fact that Joseph Bush, the admitted killer of Geller, was holding a gun on me and telling me, in no uncertain terms, that if I didn't shoot the dead body I, too, would be killed." This motion was denied.[1]

On appeal, the Appellate Division reversed the judgment of conviction on the law and dismissed the indictment. The court ruled that "the People failed to prove beyond a reasonable doubt that Geller had been alive at the time he was shot by defendant; defendant's conviction of murder thus cannot stand." (51 A.D.2d 974, 975, 380 N.Y.S.2d 315, 317.) Further, the court held that the judgment could not be modified to reflect a conviction for attempted murder because "the uncontradicted evidence is that the defendant, at the time that he fired the five shots into the body of the decedent, believed him to be dead, and * * * there is not a scintilla of evidence to contradict his assertion in that regard".

Preliminarily, we state our agreement with the Appellate Division that the evidence did not establish, beyond a reasonable doubt, that Geller was alive at the time defendant fired into his body. To sustain a homicide conviction, it must be established, beyond a reasonable doubt, that the defendant caused the death of another person. The People were required to establish that the shots fired by defendant Dlugash were a sufficiently direct cause of Geller's death. While the defendant admitted firing five shots at the victim approximately two to five minutes after Bush had fired three times, all three medical expert witnesses testified that they could not, with any degree of medical certainty, state whether the victim had been alive at the time the latter shots were fired by the defendant. Thus, the People failed to prove beyond a reasonable doubt that the victim had been alive at the time he was shot by the defendant. Whatever else it may be, it is not murder to shoot a dead body. Man dies but once.

* * *

[The evidence supports the theory that the defendant intentionally aided Bush in killing Geller. Therefore, the trial court erred in refusing to instruct the jury on the prosecution's aiding and abetting

1. It should be noted that Joe Bush pleaded guilty to a charge of manslaughter in the first degree. At the time he entered his plea, Bush detailed his version of the homicide. According to Bush, defendant Dlugash was a dealer in narcotic drugs and Dlugash claimed that Geller owed him a large sum of money from drug purchases. Bush was in the kitchen alone when Geller entered and threatened him with a shotgun. Bush pulled out his .38 caliber pistol and fired five times at Geller. Geller slumped to the floor. Dlugash then entered, withdrew his .25 caliber pistol and fired five shots into the deceased's face. Bush, however, never testified at Dlugash's trial.

theory. But the prosecution cannot appeal from this error and the judgment must stand or fall on the record.]

The procedural context of this matter, a nonappealable but erroneous dismissal of the issue of accessorial conduct, contributes to the unique nature of the attempt issue presented here. Where two or more persons have combined to murder, proof of the relationship between perpetrators is sufficient to hold all for the same degree of homicide, notwithstanding the absence of proof as to which specific act of which individual was the immediate cause of the victim's death. On the other hand, it is quite unlikely and improbable that two persons, unknown and unconnected to each other, would attempt to kill the same third person at the same time and place. Thus, it is rare for criminal liability for homicide to turn on which of several attempts actually succeeded. In the case of coconspirators, it is not necessary to do so and the case of truly independent actors is unlikely. However, procedural developments make this case the unlikely one and we must now decide whether, under the evidence presented, the defendant may be held for attempted murder, though someone else perhaps succeeded in killing the victim.

* * *

The most intriguing attempt cases are those where the attempt to commit a crime was unsuccessful due to mistakes of fact or law on the part of the would-be criminal. A general rule developed in most American jurisdictions that legal impossibility is a good defense but factual impossibility is not. (See Conspiracy, Attempt-Crime Impossible, Ann., 37 A.L.R.3d 375, 381; see, also, What Constitutes Attempted Murder, Ann., 54 A.L.R.3d 612, 633.) Thus, for example, it was held that defendants who shot at a stuffed deer did not attempt to take a deer out of season, even though they believed the dummy to be a live animal. The court stated that there was no criminal attempt because it was no crime to "take" a stuffed deer, and it is no crime to attempt to do that which is legal. (State v. Guffey, 262 S.W.2d 152 [Mo.App.]; see, also, State v. Taylor, 345 Mo. 325, 133 S.W.2d 336 [no liability for attempt to bribe a juror where person bribed was not, in fact, a juror].) These cases are illustrative of legal impossibility. A further example is Francis Wharton's classic hypothetical involving Lady Eldon and her French lace. Lady Eldon, traveling in Europe, purchased a quantity of French lace at a high price, intending to smuggle it into England without payment of the duty. When discovered in a customs search, the lace turned out to be of English origin, of little value and not subject to duty. The traditional view is that Lady Eldon is not liable for an attempt to smuggle. (1 Wharton, Criminal Law [12th ed.], § 225, p. 304, n. 9; for variations on the hypothetical see Hughes, One Further Footnote on Attempting the Impossible, 42 N.Y.U.L.Rev. 1005.)

On the other hand, factual impossibility was no defense. For example, a man was held liable for attempted murder when he shot into the room in which his target usually slept and, fortuitously, the target was sleeping elsewhere in the house that night. (State v. Mitchell, 170 Mo. 633, 71 S.W. 175.) Although one bullet struck the target's customary pillow, attainment of the criminal objective was factually impossible. State v. Moretti, 52 N.J. 182, 244 A.2d 499, cert. den. 393 U.S. 952, 89 S.Ct. 376, 21 L.Ed.2d 363, presents a similar instance of factual impossibility. The defendant agreed to perform an abortion, then a criminal act, upon a female undercover police investigator who was not, in fact, pregnant. The court sustained the conviction, ruling that "when the consequences sought by a defendant are forbidden by the law as criminal, it is no defense that the defendant could not succeed in reaching his goal because of circumstances unknown to him." (52 N.J., at p. 190, 244 A.2d, at p. 503; see, also, People v. Camodeca, 52 Cal.2d 142, 146–147, 338 P.2d 903.) On the same view, it was held that men who had sexual intercourse with a woman, with the belief that she was alive and did not consent to the intercourse, could be charged for attempted rape when the woman had, in fact, died from an unrelated ailment prior to the acts of intercourse. (United States v. Thomas, 13 U.S.C.M.A. 278.)

The New York cases can be parsed out along similar lines. One of the leading cases on legal impossibility is People v. Jaffe, 185 N.Y. 497, 78 N.E. 169, in which we held that there was no liability for the attempted receipt of stolen property when the property received by the defendant in the belief that it was stolen was, in fact under the control of the true owner. (Accord People v. Rollino, 37 Misc.2d 14, 233 N.Y.S.2d 580; Booth v. State, 398 P.2d 863 [Okl.Cr.]; United States v. Hair, D.C., 356 F.Supp. 339.) Similarly, in People v. Teal, 196 N.Y. 372, 89 N.E. 1086, a conviction for attempted subornation of perjury was overturned on the theory that the testimony attempted to be suborned was irrelevant to the merits of the case. Since it was not subornation of perjury to solicit false, but irrelevant, testimony, "the person through whose procuration the testimony is given cannot be guilty of subornation of perjury and, by the same rule, an unsuccessful attempt to that which is not a crime when effectuated, cannot be held to be an attempt to commit the crime specified." Factual impossibility, however, was no defense. Thus, a man could be held for attempted grand larceny when he picked an empty pocket. (People v. Moran, 123 N.Y. 254, 25 N.E. 412; see, also, People v. Bauer, 32 A.D.2d 463, 468, 305 N.Y.S.2d 42, 47, affd. 26 N.Y.2d 915, 310 N.Y.S.2d 101, 258 N.E.2d 399.)

As can be seen from even this abbreviated discussion, the distinction between "factual" and "legal" impossibility was a nice one indeed and the courts tended to place a greater value on legal form than on any substantive danger the defendant's actions posed for society. The approach of the draftsmen of the Model Penal Code was to eliminate the defense of impossibility in virtually all situations. Under the code provision, to constitute an attempt, it is still necessary that the result intended or desired by the actor constitute a crime. However, the code suggested a fundamental change to shift the locus of analysis to the actor's mental frame of reference and away from undue dependence upon external considerations. The basic premise of the code provision is that what was in the actor's own mind should be the standard for determining his dangerousness to society and, hence, his liability for attempted criminal conduct. (Wechsler, Jones and Korn, Treatment of Inchoate Crimes in Model Penal Code of American Law Institute: Attempt, Solicitation and Conspiracy, 61 Col.L.Rev. 571, 578–585; see, also, American Law Institute, Model Penal Code [Tent. Draft No. 10], Comments to § 5.01—Criminal Attempt, pp. 30–38.)

In the belief that neither of the two branches of the traditional impossibility arguments detracts from the offender's moral culpability, the Legislature substantially carried the code's treatment of impossibility into the 1967 revision of the Penal Law. (See, also, Note, Proposed Penal Law of New York, 64 Col.L.Rev. 1469, 1520–1521.) Thus, a person is guilty of an attempt when, with intent to commit a crime, he engages in conduct which tends to effect the commission of such crime. (Penal Law, § 110.00.) It is no defense that, under the attendant circumstances, the crime was factually or legally impossible of commission, "if such crime could have been committed had the attendant circumstances been as such person believed them to be." (Penal Law, § 110.10.) Thus, if defendant believed the victim to be alive at the time of the shooting, it is no defense to the charge of attempted murder that the victim may have been dead.

Turning to the facts of the case before us, we believe that there is sufficient evidence in the record from which the jury could conclude that the defendant believed Geller to be alive at the time defendant fired shots into Geller's head. Defendant admitted firing five shots at a most vital part of the victim's anatomy from virtually point blank range. Although defendant contended that the victim had already been grievously wounded by another, from the defendant's admitted actions, the jury could conclude that the defendant's purpose and intention was to administer the coup de grace. The jury never learned of defendant's subsequent allegation that Bush had a gun on him and directed defendant to fire at Geller on the pain of his own life. Defendant did not testify and this statement of duress was made only in a postverdict affidavit, which obviously was never placed before the jury. In his admissions that were related to the jury, defendant never made such a claim. Nor did he offer any explanation for his conduct, except for an offhand aside made casually to Detective Carrasquillo. Any remaining doubt as to the question of duress is dispelled by defendant's earlier statement that he and Joe Bush had peacefully spent a few days together on vacation in the country.

Moreover, defendant admitted to freely assisting Bush in disposing of the weapons after the murder and, once the weapons were out of the picture, defendant made no effort at all to flee from Bush. Indeed, not only did defendant not come forward with his story immediately, but when the police arrived at his house, he related a false version designed to conceal his and Bush's complicity in the murder. All of these facts indicate a consciousness of guilt which defendant would not have had if he had truly believed that Geller was dead when he shot him.

Defendant argues that the jury was bound to accept, at face value, the indications in his admissions that he believed Geller dead. * * * However, the jury was not required to automatically credit the exculpatory portions of the admissions. * * * In this case, there is ample other evidence to contradict the defendant's assertion that he believed Geller dead. There were five bullet wounds inflicted with stunning accuracy in a vital part of the victim's anatomy. The medical testimony indicated that Geller may have been alive at the time defendant fired at him. The defendant voluntarily left the jurisdiction immediately after the crime with his coperpetrator. Defendant did not report the crime to the police when left on his own by Bush. Instead, he attempted to conceal his and Bush's involvement with the homicide. In addition, the other portions of defendant's admissions make his contended belief that Geller was dead extremely improbable. Defendant, without a word of instruction from Bush, voluntarily got up from his seat after the passage of just a few minutes and fired five times point blank into the victim's face, snuffing out any remaining chance of life that Geller possessed. Certainly, this alone indicates a callous indifference to the taking of a human life. His admissions are barren of any claim of duress [2] and reflect, instead, an unstinting co-operation in efforts to dispose of vital incriminating evidence. Indeed, defendant maintained a false version of the occurrence until such time as the police informed him that they had evidence that he lately possessed a gun of the same caliber as one of the weapons involved in the shooting. From all of this, the jury was certainly warranted in concluding that the defendant acted in the belief that Geller was yet alive when shot by defendant.

The jury convicted the defendant of murder. Necessarily, they found that defendant intended to kill a live human being. Subsumed within this finding is the conclusion that defendant acted in the belief that Geller was alive. Thus, there is no need for additional fact findings by a jury. Although it was not established beyond a reasonable doubt that Geller was, in fact, alive, such is no defense to attempted

2. Notwithstanding the Appellate Division's implication to the contrary, the record indicates that defendant told the Assistant District Attorney that Bush, after shooting Geller, kept his gun aimed at Geller, and not at Dlugash. As defendant stated, "this was after Joe had his .38 on him, I started shooting on him."

murder since a murder would have been committed "had the attendant circumstances been as [defendant] believed them to be." (Penal Law, § 110.10.) The jury necessarily found that defendant believed Geller to be alive when defendant shot at him.

The Appellate Division erred in not modifying the judgment to reflect a conviction for the lesser included offense of attempted murder. * * *

4. THE "DEFENSE" OF ABANDONMENT

When a person has proceeded "beyond preparation" in an effort to commit an offense and then stops before its achievement, the "defense" of abandonment has sometimes been offered in a prosecution for attempt. Logically, positing the problem as has been done here suggests that the defense should be rejected since the attempt, in theory, has occurred when the actor with the requisite intent has gone "beyond preparation". Yet if the effort is abandoned in a fully voluntary manner can one be satisfied that the intent was present? Moreover, might not the recognition of such a "defense" encourage actors to desist? In reading the following material consider whether the general attempt statutes cast so wide a net of potential liability that devices such as abandonment are desirable techniques to identify those who, although within the net, are not truly dangerous.

PEOPLE v. STAPLES

California Court of Appeal, 1970.
6 Cal.App.3d 61, 85 Cal.Rptr. 589.

REPPY, Associate Justice. Defendant was charged in an information with attempted burglary (Pen.Code, §§ 664, 459). Trial by jury was waived, and the matter submitted on the testimony contained in the transcript of the preliminary hearing together with exhibits. Defendant was found guilty. Proceedings were suspended before pronouncement of sentence, and an order was made granting defendant probation. The appeal is from the order which is deemed a final judgment. (Pen.Code, § 1237.)

In October 1967, while his wife was away on a trip, defendant, a mathematician, under an assumed name, rented an office on the second floor of a building in Hollywood which was over the mezzanine of a bank. Directly below the mezzanine was the vault of the bank. Defendant was aware of the layout of the building, specifically of the relation of the office he rented to the bank vault. Defendant paid rent for the period from October 23 to November 23. The landlord had 10 days before commencement of the rental period within which to finish some interior repairs and painting. During this prerental period defendant brought into the office certain equipment. This included drilling tools, two acetylene gas tanks, a blow torch, a blanket, and a linoleum rug. The landlord observed these items when he came in from time to time to see how the repair work was progressing. Defendant learned from a custodian that no one was in the building on Saturdays. On Saturday, October 14, defendant drilled two groups of holes into the floor of the office above the mezzanine room. He stopped drilling before the holes went through the floor. He came back to the office several times thinking he might slowly drill down, covering the holes with the linoleum rug. At some point in time he installed a hasp lock on a closet, and planned to, or did, place his tools in it. However, he left the closet keys on the premises. Around the end of November, apparently after November 23, the landlord notified the police and turned the tools and equipment over to them. Defendant did not pay any more rent. It is not clear when he last entered the office, but it could have been after November 23, and even after the landlord had removed the equipment. On February 22, 1968, the police arrested defendant. After receiving advice as to his constitutional rights, defendant voluntarily made an oral statement which he reduced to writing.

Among other things which defendant wrote down were these:

> "Saturday, the 14th * * * I drilled some small holes in the floor of the room. Because of tiredness, fear, and the implications of what I was doing, I stopped and went to sleep.
>
> "At this point I think my motives began to change. The actutal [sic] commencement of my plan made me begin to realize that even if I were to succeed a fugitive life of living off of stolen money would not give the enjoyment of the life of a mathematician however humble a job I might have.
>
> "I still had not given up my plan however. I felt I had made a certain investment of time, money, effort and a certain pschological [sic] commitment to the concept.
>
> "I came back several times thinking I might store the tools in the closet and slowly drill down (covering the hole with a rug of linoleum square). As time went on (after two weeks or so). My wife came back and my life as bank robber seemed more and more absurd."

* * *

There was definitely substantial evidence entitling the trial judge to find that defendant's acts had gone beyond the preparation stage.

The instant case provides an out-of-the-ordinary factual situation * * * Usually the actors in cases falling within the category of attempts are intercepted or caught in the act. Here, there was no direct proof of any actual interception. But it was clearly inferable by the trial judge that defendant became aware that the landlord had resumed control over the office and had turned defendant's equipment and tools over to the police. This was the equivalent of interception.

The inference of this nonvoluntary character of defendant's abandonment was a proper one for the trial judge to draw. However, it would seem that the character of the abandonment in situations of this type, whether it be voluntary (prompted by pangs of conscience or a change of heart) or nonvoluntary (established by inference in the instant case), is not controlling. The relevant factor is the determination of whether the acts of the perpetrator have reached such a stage of advancement that they can be classified as an attempt. Once that attempt is found there can be no exculpatory abandonment. "One of the purposes of the criminal law is to protect society from those who intend to injure it. When it is established that the defendant intended to commit a specific crime and that in carrying out his intention he committed an act that caused harm or sufficient danger of harm, it is immaterial that for some collateral reason he could not complete the intended crime." (People v. Camodeca, 52 Cal.2d 142, 147, 338 P.2d 903, 906.)

The order is affirmed.

NOTES AND QUESTIONS

1. The "traditional" position is that abandonment of an attempt after one has proceeded far enough towards completion of the crime to commit criminal attempt does not prevent liability. E. g., Stewart v. State, 85 Nev. 388, 455 P.2d 914 (1969). But consider the following from Model Penal Code,* Comments to § 5.01(4) (reprinted at page 280, supra) 69–74 (Tent. Draft No. 10, 1960):

> *Renunciation of Criminal Purpose.* There is uncertainty under the present law whether abandonment of a criminal effort, after the bounds of preparation have been surpassed, will constitute a defense to a charge of attempt. In passing on this issue it is customary to distinguish between "voluntary" and "involuntary" abandonments.
>
> An "involuntary" abandonment occurs where the actor ceases his criminal endeavor because he fears detection or apprehension, or because he decides he will wait for a better opportunity, or because his powers or instruments are inadequate for completing the crime. There is no doubt that such an abandonment does not exculpate the actor from attempt liability otherwise incurred.
>
> By a "voluntary" abandonment is meant a change in the actor's purpose not influenced by outside circumstances, what may be termed repentance or change of heart. Lack of resolution or timidity may suffice. A reappraisal by the actor of the criminal

sanctions hanging over his conduct would presumably be a motivation of the voluntary type as long as the actor's fear of the law is not related to a particular threat of apprehension or detection. Whether voluntary abandonments constitute a defense to an attempt charge is far from clear, there being few decisions squarely facing the issue.

* * *

The present subsection does not utilize the "voluntary-involuntary" terminology of the prior cases but reaches much the same result by allowing abandonment as a defense only where the circumstances manifest "renunciation of [the actor's] criminal purpose." The requirement of "renunciation" of purpose involves two elements: (1) that the abandonment of the criminal effort originate with the actor and not be forced upon him by some external circumstance such as police intervention; and (2) that the abandonment be permanent and complete rather than temporary or contingent—e. g., a decision by the actor to wait for a better opportunity to commit the crime would not manifest renunciation of criminal purpose.

The basis for allowing the defense involves two related considerations.

First, renunciation of criminal purpose tends to negative dangerousness. As previously indicated, much of the effort devoted to excluding early "preparatory" conduct from criminal attempt liability is based on the desire not to punish where there is an insufficient showing that the actor has a firm purpose to commit the crime contemplated. In cases where the actor has gone beyond the line drawn for preparation, indicating *prima facie* sufficient firmness of purpose, he should be allowed to rebut such a conclusion by showing that he has plainly demonstrated his lack of firm purpose by completely renouncing his purpose to commit the crime.

This line of reasoning, however, may prove unsatisfactory where the actor has proceeded far toward the commission of the contemplated crime, or has perhaps committed the "last proximate act." It may be argued that, whatever the inference to be drawn where the actor's conduct was in the area near the preparation-attempt line, in cases of further progress the inference of dangerousness from such an advanced criminal effort outweighs the countervailing inference arising from abandonment of the effort. However, it is in this latter class of cases that the second of the two policy considerations comes most strongly into play.

A second reason for allowing renunciation of criminal purpose as a defense to an attempt charge is to encourage actors to desist from pressing forward with their criminal designs, thereby diminishing the risk that the substantive crime will be committed. While, under the proposed subsection, such encouragement is held out at all stages of the criminal effort, its significance becomes greatest as the actor nears his criminal objective and the risk that the crime will be completed is correspondingly high. At the very point where abandonment least influences a judgment as to the dangerousness of the actor—where the last proximate act has been committed but the resulting crime can still be avoided—the inducement to desist stemming from the abandonment defense achieves its greatest value.

It is possible, of course, that the defense of renunciation of criminal purpose may add to the incentives to take the *first* steps toward crime. Knowledge that criminal endeavors can be undone with impunity may encourage preliminary steps that would not be undertaken if liability inevitably attached to every abortive criminal undertaking that proceeded beyond preparation. But this is not a serious problem. First, any consolation the actor might draw from the abandonment defense would have to be tempered with the knowledge that the defense would be unavailable if the actor's purposes were frustrated by external forces before he had an opportunity to abandon his effort. Second, the encouragement this defense might lend to the actor taking preliminary steps would be a factor only where the actor was dubious of his plans and where, consequently, the probability of continuance was not great.

On balance, it is concluded that renunciation of criminal purpose should be a defense to a criminal attempt charge because, as to the early stages of an attempt, it significantly negatives dangerousness of character, and, as to later stages, the value of encouraging desistance outweighs the net dangerousness shown by the abandoned criminal effort. And, because of the importance of encouraging desistance in the final stages of the attempt, the defense is allowed even where the last proximate act has occurred but the criminal result can be avoided—e. g., where the fuse has been lit but can still be stamped out. If, however, the actor has gone so far that he has put in motion forces which he is powerless to stop, then the attempt has been completed and cannot be abandoned. In accord with existing law, the actor can gain no immunity for this completed effort (e. g., firing at the intended victim and missing); all he can do is desist from making a second attempt.

* * *

In considering the significance to be attached to abandonment of a criminal attempt, one solution which was rejected was provision for reduction of penalty in the event of such abandonment. Insofar as encouragement of desistance is concerned, reductions in sanction would have to be very great in order to have a substantial impact on those already engrossed in a criminal attempt; indeed it is unlikely that anything short of complete immunity would suffice. And in dealing with the question of dangerousness, it seems that, once liability is established, sanctions should be linked to neutralizing the actor's dangerousness and determined on a broad basis with reference to the requirements of the particular offender. An automatic reduction in the case of abandonment would be inconsistent with this approach.

B. SOLICITATION

If one person solicits another to commit an offense and the person solicited does in fact commit the offense, the solicitor is liable for the crime under principles of complicity. Similarily, if the person solicited begins actions designed to culminate in the offense and goes far enough to complete an attempt, the solicitor is guilty of that attempt. But suppose neither of these situations materializes? Since Rex v. Higgins, 102 Eng.Rep. 269 (1801), solicitation to commit a felony (and apparently at least some misdemeanors) has been recognized as a common law offense. American statutes frequently criminalize solicitation, although the crime is often limited to solicitations to commit extremely serious felonies. E. g., Texas Penal Code § 15.-03(a) (solicitation of capital felonies and felonies of the first degree is itself a crime). Is the crime of solicitation desirable on policy grounds, given the availability of attempt and conspiracy to deal with activity preparatory to the commission of a crime? Under statutes making solicitation an offense, what kind of activity constitutes the crime? How specific and direct must the request or urging be to constitute a criminal solicitation?

MODEL PENAL CODE*

(Proposed Official Draft, 1962).

Section 5.02. Criminal Solicitation

(1) *Definition of Solicitation.* A person is guilty of solicitation to commit a crime if with the purpose of promoting or facilitating its commission he commands, encourages or requests another person to engage in specific conduct which would constitute such crime or an attempt to commit such crime or which would establish his complicity in its commission or attempted commission.

(2) *Uncommunicated Solicitation.* It is immaterial under Subsection (1) of this Section that the actor fails to communicate with the person he solicits to commit a crime if his conduct was designed to effect such communication.

(3) *Renunciation of Criminal Purpose.* It is an affirmative defense that the actor, after soliciting another person to commit a crime persuaded him not to do so or otherwise prevented the commission of the crime, under circumstances manifesting a complete and voluntary renunciation of his criminal purpose.

NOTES AND QUESTIONS

1. Solicitation, like attempt, would be graded by the Model Penal Code the same as the most serious offense solicited. Model Penal Code § 5.05 (P.O.D.1962).

2. If a jurisdiction has no solicitation crime, is it possible that one who solicits another to commit a crime is guilty of an attempt to commit that crime? The general answer given by courts is that a solicitation—as defined by the law of criminal solicitation—is not itself sufficient to constitute an attempt. As the court explained in Gervin v. State, 212 Tenn. 653, 371 S.W.2d 449 (1963):

> To constitute an attempt there must * * * be an act of perpetration. * * * However, solicitation is preparation rather than perpetration. * * * We are reluctant to hold * * * that at the stage of preparation [i. e., solicitation], the attempt will be carried out and that the situation is unequivocal. At this point there are too many contingencies, such as the willingness of the solicitant to carry out the design, to say the [die] is cast. But to hold solicitation an attempt this would be necessary.

212 Tenn. at 658, 371 S.W.2d at 451. But the solicitor who goes beyond the bare minimum required for solicitation—who, for example, provides the person solicited with information and materials related to the commission of the crime—may well have gone far enough to commit attempt. See State v. Mandel, 78 Ariz. 226, 278 P.2d 413 (1954).

STATE v. FURR

Supreme Court of North Carolina, 1977.
292 N.C. 711, 235 S.E.2d 193.

EXUM, Justice.

Defendant was placed on trial for and convicted of murder in the first degree of his wife and twelve counts of solicitation to commit a felony. He was sentenced to death in the murder case and was given three consecutive sentences of 8–10 years each in the solicitation cases. Nine of those cases were consolidated for one judgment by the trial court. Two separate judgments were entered in two others, and in one apparently no judgment was entered upon the verdict.

* * *

The defendant and his wife had been married about 21 years and had four children when they separated in 1973. After the separation, Furr moved his real estate office from their home to a nearby location near the square in Locust, North Carolina. His wife, Earlene, continued to live at the house on Willow Drive and Furr moved into Western Hills Mobile Home Park. The couple's relationship was apparently quite volatile and Furr exhibited increasing hostility towards Earlene after the separation.

In April, 1973, Earlene filed a civil action against defendant resulting in a judgment against him in October, 1973. A year later, on his wife's motion, defendant was adjudged to be in contempt and was committed to jail. While in Stanly County jail, Furr met Raymond Clontz and Donald Owens, and related his marital problems to them, especially his concern over the property dispute. He was released from jail on December 6, 1974, upon payment of $13,623.00. After his release, Furr approached Clontz and Owens, drove them by Earlene's home and explained how to get into the house. He offered Owens $3,000.00 to kill Earlene and offered to give Clontz a lot which the latter wanted to store cars on if Clontz would do the job. Neither man accepted the offer.

In October, 1974, defendant asked "Buck" Baker if he knew a "hit man." At the time Furr was angry because Earlene had disposed of some racing equipment. Furr also approached Donald Eugene Huneycutt on several occasions to ask whether Huneycutt knew a "hit man." In the initial encounters, Furr wanted Johnny Jhue Laney killed because Laney had murdered his own wife, Doris, who was defendant's girl friend. By early 1975, however, Furr's plans extended as well to Earlene and her attorney, Charles Brown. Huneycutt told him killing women and lawyers would create "too much heat," but defendant responded that he could stand the heat and had his mother for an alibi.

Defendant also asked George Arnold Black, Jr., to kill Earlene, and drove him by the house in the fall of 1974. Like the others, Black declined the offer.

Furr was heard to threaten Earlene's life upon several occasions. In February, 1973, Earlene's brother-in-law, David Orrell, went to defendant because Earlene "was literally in terror of her life." Orrell told defendant, "She says that you had threatened to kill her, is that true?" Furr responded that he had, and added, "I can't stand her nagging any more."

In January, 1973, Johnny Jhue Laney called Furr to object to Earlene's telephone calls to Doris Laney accusing Doris of running around with Furr. A month later, Laney called Furr again concerning the same problem. Furr flew into a rage and said "he would kill her, and he would see to it, it wouldn't happen no more * * * that she had caused enough trouble in the community."

In the early part of 1975, during a conversation with Freddie Voncannon, the sister of Ruby Griffin, who was presently defendant's girl friend, Furr suggested Freddie burn Earlene's car.

Just after the 1973 separation, defendant's daughter, Beverly Tucker, overheard her mother begging defendant to come home. Furr responded that "she was ugly and he didn't want her any more, and that he hated her and that he would kill her, but he was going to make her suffer first and that he would grind her up like hamburger meat and feed her to the dogs." Once in 1974, when Beverly was driving her mother's car, defendant warned her to be careful driving that car through his trailer park, that he had told Earlene he would kill her if she came there, and he would hate to hit Beverly instead.

Rick Tallent, who had rented a pasture from Earlene, was embroiled in one of the couple's quarrels when he attempted to repair the fence. He heard defendant tell Earlene he would kill her if she came across the fence. Defendant's son, Chuck, also overheard that threat.

On 3 September 1975 defendant was served with papers in the matter of Frances Earlene H. Furr v. Harold G. Furr, notifying him to appear on 25 September 1975.

Very little evidence was presented of what actually transpired at the time of Earlene's death on 15 September 1975. Chuck Furr, the last to leave home that morning, testified that when he left at about 8:00 his mother was standing in the doorway. At about 2:15 that afternoon, eleven-year-old Todd came home from school and found mother lying on his bed, dressed in a pink nightgown and valuable jewelry, with two gunshot wounds, one in the chin and one in the eye. An SBI chemist testified that Earlene's left-hand palm was either on or near a gun when it was discharged. There was no evidence of forcible entry. The front door was unlocked when Todd came home and the garage door closed. Earlene's watch crystal was broken and the hands stopped at 9:45 or 9:56 or sometime between 10:00 and 12:00 according to the testimony of various state's witnesses. The watch calendar said "15."

Several guns were found both in Earlene's home and in defendant's. None of these was connected to the crime. None of the fingerprints lifted from the scene matched defendant's. Defendant testified that he possessed a remote control device to open the garage door. Raymond Clontz said defendant had shown him the device.

One witness, Cecil Almond, said he saw defendant coming out of the trailer park with a lady in the car who "looked like Earlene" at about 9:30 or 9:40 on 15 September 1975. Nevertheless he testified that he did not actually recognize the lady, and acknowledged the possibility that it might have been Ruby Griffin.

The trip from defendant's trailer to Earlene's home takes about four minutes and forty seconds.

Defendant's alibi evidence tended to show he was in the company of Ruby Griffin almost constantly from between 9:00 and 9:30 that morning, when they left the trailer park together, until late that night. He presented numerous witnesses who had seen him with Ruby Griffin at various times in his office and at work sites between about 10:00 and noon. His testimony and that of his witnesses tends to establish that he and Ruby drove to Salisbury at about noon, were seen on the road, visited a friend there, and returned at about 5:15 to 5:30, when they learned of Earlene's death.

* * *

A few weeks after his wife's death, defendant saw Owens and Clontz. On being asked who had killed his wife, Furr said, "Well, you'all know who did it and I know who did it, but nobody else will ever know but me."

Defendant told Johnny Laney that "that ex-bitch of mine got what she deserved and you're next on the list."

Defendant contends this evidence is insufficient to permit a jury to find him guilty of murder. We agree.

In order to convict the defendant of murder the state must offer evidence from which it can be reasonably inferred that the deceased died by virtue of a criminal act and that the act was committed by the defendant. *State v. Jones,* 280 N.C. 60, 184 S.E.2d 862 (1971); *State v. Palmer,* 230 N.C. 205, 52 S.E.2d 908 (1949).

While the evidence clearly establishes the first of these propositions it falls far short of tending to prove the second. The evidence shows that defendant wanted his wife dead; that he actively sought her death; and that he harbored great hostility toward her. This, however, without more is not enough to permit a jury to find that he killed her.

While the evidence might support a reasonable inference that defendant was responsible for his wife's death and that he procured someone to murder her, these facts alone would not make defendant guilty of murder. Our law of homicide still maintains a careful distinction between principals and accessories. A principal is one who is present at and participates in the crime charged or who procures an *innocent* agent to commit the crime. An accessory before the fact is one who procures, counsels, commands, or encourages the principal to commit it.

The only question before us is whether the evidence is sufficient to convict defendant as a principal. We hold that it is not.

* * *

We next consider defendant's argument that [some] of the solicitation charges should have been nonsuited. * * *

* * *

Solicitation of another to commit a felony is a crime in North Carolina, even though the solicitation is of no effect and the crime solicited is never committed. The offense has been cognizable at common law at least since Rex v. Higgins, 2 East 5, 102 Eng.Rep. 269 (1801) and is still an indictable offense under the common law in this state. G.S. 4–1.

The gravamen of the offense of soliciting lies in counseling, enticing or inducing another to commit a crime. Clark & Marshall, A Treatise on The Law of Crimes, § 4.02 at 220 (7th ed. 1967).

Defendant argues that the evidence shows only that defendant requested that Huneycutt find *someone else* to murder each of the three intended victims, and not that Huneycutt *himself* commit the crime. "Under no authority," says defendant, "is that a criminal offense." Accepting for the moment defendant's argument that defendant solicited Huneycutt *only* to find another "hit man," we hold that such a request constitutes the crime of solicitation to commit a felony in North Carolina. In *W. LaFave and A. Scott,* Criminal Law, § 58 at 419 (1972) it is observed that

> "[i]n the usual solicitation case, it is the solicitor's intention that the criminal result be directly brought about by the person he has solicited; that is, it is his intention that the crime be committed and that the other commit it as a principal in the first degree, as where A asks B to kill C. However, it would seem sufficient that A requested B to get involved in the scheme to kill C in any way which would establish B's complicity in the killing of C were that to occur. Thus it would be criminal for one person to solicit another to in turn solicit a third party, to solicit another to join a conspiracy, or to solicit another to aid and abet the commission of a crime."

See People v. Bloom, 149 App.Div. 295, 133 N.Y.S. 708 (1912); King v. Bentley [1923] 1 K.B. 403 (1922).

In North Carolina, one who procures another to commit murder is an accessory before the fact to murder. G.S. 14–5. Thus if Huneycutt had acceded to defendant's demand and had found someone else to murder defendant's wife or either of the other victims, and that person had in turn committed the murder Huneycutt would have been indictable for a felony under General Statute 14–5. Whether defendant solicited Huneycutt to commit the murder himself or to find another to perpetrate the crime is thus of no consequence; either act is a crime in this state.

* * *

Defendant further contends that there was no evidence to support three indictments alleging solicitation of Raymond Clontz to murder Earlene Furr. There is no merit to these contentions in two of the counts. Indictment Number 76–CR–700 alleges that Clontz was solicited in January to murder Furr's wife. The evidence is that during that month, shortly after both men were released from jail where defendant had been quite talkative about his marital problems, Clontz and Furr met to discuss a lot which Clontz wished to purchase. Furr said he wanted $3,000.00 for the lot and Clontz agreed to take it. Then, as Clontz related at trial Furr told him not to be so hasty, that "he would make some arrangements about the payment for the lot in another way; that he wanted me to do a job for him." Clontz told Furr that he "knew what he was talking about, but that [he] wasn't interested in it * * *." Defendant then told him he had to go to court with his wife in a few weeks and "that he had to have something done before court time or he was going to be in serious trouble. He said his wife was already getting $250.00 a week from him, and she had possession of the house, and had his property tied up and that he had to have something done." In the context, we find no other reasonable interpretation of defendant's words on this occasion than that he was requesting Clontz to kill his wife.

In Indictment Number 76–CR–690, [defendant is charged with again soliciting Clontz to kill defendant's wife, this time in February, 1975. No error exists in regard to this charge and, in any case, the record does not indicate that a judgment of conviction was entered on it.]

In Indictment Number 76–CR–690, a solicitation in May, 1975, is alleged. Clontz's testimony is that "sometime later" (after the February incident) he and Owens were stopped by defendant as they took lumber to Locust. Defendant contends all the evidence points to a solicitation directed only to Owens. Although Clontz testified that Furr asked Owens if "*we* had time to ride with him somewhere," it is apparent that Furr's remarks on this occasion were directed solely to Owens, and in fact, constituted a repetition of his earlier February conversation and ride with Clontz. During the May solicitation, Clontz rode in the back seat. He testified that Furr did not speak to him then, and that he did not make any statements to Clontz because he was talking to Owens. We find, therefore, no evidence except that leading to pure speculation that Furr intended Clontz to hear his suggestion to support the charge of solicitation of Raymond Clontz in May, 1975. Consequently we hold that case Number 76–CR–690 must be nonsuited. We note that, since this case was consolidated for judgment with the other *Clontz* and *Huneycutt* cases, our ruling has no effect on the sentence defendant will serve.

* * *

Defendant's next contention is that the * * * three Clontz solicitation contacts establish only one offense and that the seven Huneycutt contacts likewise establish only one offense. Neither of the two North Carolina cases dealing with solicitation addresses this issue. State v. Hampton, 210 N.C. 283, 186 S.E. 251 (1936); State v. Keen, 25 N.C.App. 567, 214 S.E.2d 242 (1975). In the latter case as defendant correctly points out five contacts were made between the same parties but only one count of solicitation was charged. The distinction between that case and this is that in *Keen* the solicitee never directly refused the defendant's request but "kept him on the string" in order to gather evidence for a conviction.

Defendant analogizes solicitation to conspiracy, and says that only one offense of conspiracy is committed even though there may be multiple discussions and multiple criminal objectives * * * We recognize that, as in *Keen,* a single solicitation may continue over a period of time and involve several contacts where the solicitee gives no definite refusal to the solicitor's request. But a definite refusal on the part of the solicitee plus the lapse of some time may end the transaction so that a new request upon another occasion may constitute a new offense.

If defendant's contentions were correct, he would be entitled to have only one sentence imposed for the Clontz solicitation contacts, and only one for the Huneycutt contacts. In this case, however, the seven Huneycutt indictments and two of the Clontz indictments were consolidated for judgment and one 8–10 year sentence imposed thereon. (No judgment has apparently been entered in the other Clontz indictment.) Since only one sentence was imposed for all of these, no prejudice to defendant could have resulted from error in submitting each contact as a separate count of solicitation.

* * *

NOTES AND QUESTIONS

1. Must the solicitation actually be communicated to the person solicited? W. LaFave and A. Scott, Criminal Law 420 (1972)—citing cases decided between 1873 and 1912—say no, but comment that some courts would require that a noncommunicated solicitation be punished as an attempted solicitation. Compare § 5.02(2) of the Model Penal Code, reprinted at page 308, supra.

2. Is the danger posed by solicitation crimes sufficiently great to justify making such actions criminal? The Comments to § 5.02 of the Model Penal Code, Tent. Draft No. 10 at 82 (1960) acknowledge divergent views on this question, including:

> the view that a solicitation is, if anything, more dangerous than a direct attempt, since it may give rise to that cooperation among criminals that is a special hazard. * * * Moreover, the solicitor, working his will through one or more agents, manifests an approach to crime more intelligent and masterful than that of his hirelings.

But the comment goes on to note that "the imposition of liability for criminal solicitation may be an important means by which the leadership of a movement deemed criminal may be suppressed," citing cases involving prosecution for political and labor "agitation." How great is the danger that solicitation statutes will have the effect of supressing the exercise of First Amendment rights, either by direct application or by an indirect "chilling effect?" Cf. Speiser v. Randall, 357 U.S. 513, 78 S.Ct. 1332, 2 L.Ed.2d 1460 (1958).

3. Does impossibility of any sort prevent liability for solicitation? Should it? In State v. Keen, 25 N.C.App. 567, 214 S.E.2d 242 (1975), the defendant argued that because the persons he solicited to kill his wife were law enforcement officers and would not have accepted the invitation, his conviction for solicitation was not permissible. Upholding the conviction, the court stated, "The crime of solicitation * * * is complete with the solicitation even though there could never have been an acquiescence in the scheme by the one solicited." 25 N.C.App. at 570, 571, 214 S.E.2d at 244.

4. May one who solicits another to commit an offense escape liability by voluntarily renouncing the venture before the crime is committed by the person solicited? The appellate caselaw is inconclusive. See W. LaFave and A. Scott, Criminal Law 421 (1972). In People v. Gordon, 47 Cal.App. 3d 465, 120 Cal.Rptr. 840 (1975), defendant—an attorney acting on behalf of an undisclosed client—solicited a police officer to plant narcotics on another individual. The next day, she called the police officer and told him that she had decided not to be a party to the scheme, as she did not want to take a chance on ruining her political career. The officer made several subsequent contacts with defendant, but she refused to set up a meeting between her client and the officer. Affirming her conviction for solicitation, the court held: "Since the crime was fully committed * * *, it is no defense that the defendant later withdrew or failed to consummate the crime which was the object of the solicitation." 47 Cal.App.3d at 474, 476, 120 Cal.Rptr. at 845. Consider the Model Penal Code proposal, reprinted at page 308, supra. Compare Ariz.Rev.Stat. § 13–1005(B):

> In a prosecution for solicitation, it is a defense that the defendant, under circumstances manifesting a voluntary and complete renunciation of the defendant's criminal intent completed both of the following acts:
>
> 1. Notified the person solicited.
>
> 2. Gave timely warning to law enforcement authorities or otherwise made a reasonable effort to prevent the conduct or result solicited.

Would the defendant in *Gordon* have had a defense under the Arizona statute?

5. The Colorado solicitation statute requires that the solicitation be committed "under circumstances strongly corroborative of [the intent to promote or facilitate the commission of the crime solicited]." Colo.Rev. Stat. § 18–2–301(1). Does the addition of this requirement solve any problems that may be raised by the crime of solicitation? Is the additional requirement imposed by the Colorado statute sufficiently precise? In People v. Latsis, —— Colo. ——, 578 P.2d 1055 (1978), the statute was upheld—by a divided court—over the objection that this language was unconstitutionally vague.

6. Under the California statute, solicitation "must be proved by the testimony of two witnesses, or of one witness and corroborating circumstances." Cal. Penal Code § 653f. Consider the concern expressed by the

New York court regarding its statute, which does not require corroboration:

> "[T]here are types of criminal conduct which might be solicited where there would be a heavy thrust placed on the credibility of a single witness testifying to the conversation. Extraordinary care might be required in deciding whether to prosecute; in determining the truth; and in appellate review of the factual decision.
>
> One example would be the suggestion of one person to another that he commit a sexual offense; another is the suggestion that he commit perjury."

People v. Lubow, 29 N.Y.2d 58, 65, 323 N.Y.S.2d 829, 833, 272 N.E.2d 331, 334 (1971).

7. Another way of limiting the reach of solicitation statutes is that adopted by the Proposed Federal Criminal Code which, in its Final Draft, adds the following clause at the end of § 1003(1)

> "and the person solicited commits an overt act in response to the solicitation."

The Comment explains:

> the solicitee either has not yet agreed (although he has committed an overt act, such as coming back for further discussions) or he has agreed but no overt act has been committed sufficient to make the crime a conspiracy. * * * An overt act is required so that criminality depends on something besides speech.

In what way does the commission by the solicitee of a possibly trivial overt act affect the culpability of the solicitor?

C. CONSPIRACY

Conspiracy serves several functions in criminal law. It is, like attempt and solicitation, a substantive crime for which a defendant may be charged, tried, convicted, and punished. But, in addition, it is sometimes also a vehicle for making one person liable for the crimes of other individuals. The so-called Pinkerton Rule discussed in subsection 3, below, provides that under certain circumstances all conspirators are liable for crimes committed by one member of the conspiracy.

Conspiracy prosecutions often involve complex procedural issues that are beyond the scope of direct concern here. But in part because of these procedural aspects of conspiracy—and in part because of the nature of the crime of conspiracy itself—some have expressed serious misgivings regarding the continued vitality of conspiracy doctrine as a part of substantive criminal law. The numerous issues that must be faced in considering conspiracy law should be evaluated in light of these concerns. They were perhaps most effectively put by Mr. Justice Jackson in his concurring opinion in Krulewitch v.

United States, 336 U.S. 440, 445–454, 69 S.Ct. 716, 719–723, 93 L.Ed. 790, 795–800, (1949):

This case illustrates a present drift in the federal law of conspiracy which warrants some further comment because it is characteristic of the long evolution of that elastic, sprawling and pervasive offense. Its history exemplifies the "tendency of a principle to expand itself to the limit of its logic." The unavailing protest of courts against the growing habit to indict for conspiracy in lieu of prosecuting for the substantive offense itself, or in addition thereto, suggests that loose practice as to this offense constitutes a serious threat to fairness in our administration of justice.

The modern crime of conspiracy is so vague that it almost defies definition. Despite certain elementary and essential elements, it also, chameleon-like takes on a special coloration from each of the many independent offenses on which it may be overlaid. It is always "predominantly mental in composition" because it consists primarily of a meeting of minds and an intent.

The crime comes down to us wrapped in vague but unpleasant connotations. It sounds historical undertones of treachery, secret plotting and violence on a scale that menaces social stability and the security of the state itself. "Privy conspiracy" ranks with sedition and rebellion in the Litany's prayer for deliverance. Conspiratorial movements do indeed lie back of the political assassination, the *coup d'état*, the *putsch*, the revolution, and seizures of power in modern times, as they have in all history.

But the conspiracy concept also is superimposed upon many concerted crimes having no political motivation. It is not intended to question that the basic conspiracy principle has some place in modern criminal law, because to unite, back of a criminal purpose, the strength, opportunities and resources of many is obviously more dangerous and more difficult to police than the efforts of a lone wrongdoer. It also may be trivialized, as [for example] where the conspiracy consists of the concert of a loathsome panderer and a prostitute to go from New York to Florida to ply their trade and it would appear that a simple Mann Act prosecution would vindicate the majesty of federal law. However, even when appropriately invoked, the looseness and pliability of the doctrine present inherent dangers which should be in the background of judicial thought wherever it is sought to extend the doctrine to meet the exigencies of a particular case.

Conspiracy in federal law aggravates the degree of crime over that of unconcerted offending. The act of confederating to commit a misdemeanor, followed by even an innocent overt act in its execution, is a felony and is such even if the misdemeanor is never consummated. The more radical proposition also is well-established that at common law and under some statutes a combination may be a criminal conspiracy even if it contemplates only acts which are not crimes at all when perpetrated by an individual or by many acting severally.

Thus the conspiracy doctrine will incriminate persons on the fringe of offending who would not be guilty of aiding and abetting or of becoming an accessory, for those charges only lie when an act which is a crime has actually been committed.

Attribution of criminality to a confederation which contemplates no act that would be criminal if carried out by any one of the conspirators is a practice peculiar to Anglo-American law. "There can be little doubt that this wide definition of the crime of conspiracy originates in the criminal equity administered in the Star Chamber." In fact, we are advised that "The modern crime of conspiracy is almost entirely the result of the manner in which conspiracy was treated by the court of Star Chamber." The doctrine does not commend itself to jurists of civil-law countries, despite universal recognition that an organized society must have legal weapons for combatting organized criminality. Most other countries have devised what they consider more discriminating principles upon which to prosecute criminal gangs, secret associations and subversive syndicates.

* * *

The interchangeable use of conspiracy doctrine in civil as well as penal proceedings opens it to the danger, absent in the case of many crimes, that a court having in mind only the civil sanctions will approve lax practices which later are imported into criminal proceedings. * * *

Of course, it is for prosecutors rather than courts to determine when to use a scatter-gun to bring down the defendant, but there are procedural advantages from using it which add to the danger of unguarded extension of the concept.

An accused, under the Sixth Amendment, has the right to trial "by an impartial jury of the State and district wherein the crime shall have been committed." The leverage of a conspiracy charge lifts this limitation from the prosecution and reduces its protection to a phantom, for the crime is considered so vagrant as to have been committed in any district where any one of the conspirators did any one of the acts, however innocent, intended to accomplish its object. The Government may, and often does, compel one to defend at a great distance from any place he ever did any act because some accused confederate did some trivial and by itself innocent act in the chosen district. Circumstances may even enable the prosecution to fix the place of trial in Washington, D. C., where a defendant may lawfully be put to trial before a jury partly or even wholly made up of employees of the Government that accuses him. Cf. Frazier v. United States, 335 U.S. 497.

When the trial starts, the accused feels the full impact of the conspiracy strategy. Strictly, the prosecution should first establish *prima facie* the conspiracy and identify the conspirators, after which evidence of acts and declarations of each in the course of its execution are admissible against all. But the order of proof of so sprawling a charge is difficult for a judge to control. As a practical matter, the accused often is confronted with a hodgepodge of acts and statements by others which he may never have authorized or intended or even known about, but which help to persuade the jury of existence of the conspiracy itself. In other words, a conspiracy often is proved by evidence that is admissible only upon assumption that conspiracy existed. The naive assumption that prejudicial effects can be overcome by instructions to the jury, cf. Blumenthal v. United States, 332 U.S. 539, 559, all practicing lawyers know to be unmitigated fiction. See Skidmore v. Baltimore & Ohio R. Co., 167 F.2d 54.

The trial of a conspiracy charge doubtless imposes a heavy burden on the prosecution, but it is an especially difficult situation for the defendant. The hazard from loose application of rules of evidence is aggravated where the Government institutes mass trials. * * *

A co-defendant in a conspiracy trial occupies an uneasy seat. There generally will be evidence of wrongdoing by somebody. It is difficult for the individual to make his own case stand on its own merits in the minds of jurors who are ready to believe that birds of a feather are flocked together. If he is silent, he is taken to admit it and if, as often happens, co-defendants can be prodded into accusing or contradicting each other, they convict each other. There are many practical difficulties in defending against a charge of conspiracy which I will not enumerate.

To the extent that Mr. Justice Jackson's concerns are valid ones, do they justify abolition of the crime of conspiracy? Do they justify modifications of the doctrine so as to favor defendants? Or do they simply suggest that certain procedural rules, such as those governing venue in criminal cases, deserve reevaluation? For an excellent discussion, see Johnson, The Unnecessary Crime of Conspiracy, 61 Calif. L.Rev. 1137 (1973).

1. MODEL STATUTORY FORMULATIONS
MODEL PENAL CODE *

(Proposed Official Draft, 1962).

Section 5.03. Criminal Conspiracy

(1) *Definition of Conspiracy.* A person is guilty of conspiracy with another person or persons to commit a crime if with the purpose of promoting or facilitating its commission he:

(a) agrees with such other person or persons that they or one or more of them will engage in conduct which constitutes such crime or an attempt or solicitation to commit such crime; or

(b) agrees to aid such other person or persons in the planning or commission of such crime or of an attempt or solicitation to commit such crime.

(2) *Scope of Conspiratorial Relationship.* If a person guilty of conspiracy, as defined by Subsection (1) of this Section, knows that a person with whom he conspires to commit a crime has conspired with another person or persons to commit the same crime, he is guilty of conspiring with such other person or persons, whether or not he knows their identity, to commit such crime.

(3) *Conspiracy With Multiple Criminal Objectives.* If a person conspires to commit a number of crimes, he is guilty of only one conspiracy so long as such multiple crimes are the object of the same agreement or continuous conspiratorial relationship.

* * *

(5) *Overt Act.* No person may be convicted of conspiracy to commit a crime, other than a felony of the first or second degree, unless an overt act in pursuance of such consiracy is alleged and proved to have been done by him or by a person with whom he conspired.

(6) *Renunciation of Criminal Purpose.* It is an affirmative defense that the actor, after conspiring to commit a crime, thwarted the success of the conspiracy, under circumstances manifesting a complete and voluntary renunciation of his criminal purpose.

(7) *Duration of Conspiracy.* For purposes of Section 1.06(4):

(a) conspiracy is a continuing course of conduct which terminates when the crime or crimes which are its object are committed or the agreement that they be committed is abandoned by the defendant and by those with whom he conspired; and

(b) such abandonment is presumed if neither the defendant nor anyone with whom he conspired does any overt act in pursuance of the conspiracy during the applicable period of limitation; and

(c) if an individual abandons the agreement, the conspiracy is terminated as to him only if and when he advises those with whom he conspired of his abandonment or he informs the law enforcement authorities of the existence of the conspiracy and of his participation therein.

Section 5.04. Incapacity, Irresponsibility or Immunity of Party to Solicitation or Conspiracy

(1) Except as provided in Subsection (2) of this Section, it is immaterial to the liability of a person who solicits or conspires with another to commit a crime that:

(a) he or the person whom he solicits or with whom he conspires does not occupy a particular position or have a particular characteristic which is an element of such crime, if he believes that one of them does; or

(b) the person whom he solicits or with whom he conspires is irresponsible or has an immunity to prosecution or conviction for the commission of the crime.

(2) It is a defense to a charge of solicitation or conspiracy to commit a crime that if the criminal object were achieved, the actor would not be guilty of a crime under the law defining the offense or as an accomplice under Section 2.06(5) or 2.06(6) (a) or (b).

Section 5.05. Grading of Criminal * * * Conspiracy; Mitigation in Cases of Lessee Danger * * *

(1) *Grading.* Except as otherwise provided in this Section, * * * conspiracy [is a crime of] the same grade and degree as the most serious offense which is * * * an object of the conspiracy. * * *

(2) *Mitigation.* If the particular conduct charged to constitute a criminal * * * conspiracy is so inherently unlikely to result or culminate in the commission of a crime that neither such conduct nor the actor presents a public danger warranting the grading of such offense under this Section, the Court shall exercise its power under Section 6.12 to enter judgment and impose sentence for a crime of lower grade or degree or, in extreme cases, may dismiss the prosecution.

NOTES AND QUESTIONS

1. How should criminal conspiracy be graded for purposes of punishment? Compare the approach of Section 5.05 of the Model Penal Code with that of Section 15.02(d) of the Texas Penal Code, which provides that a criminal conspiracy is graded as one category lower than the most serious offense that is the object of the conspiracy.

2. Traditionally, the crime of conspiracy has included not only agreements to commit felonies and misdemeanors but also combinations to commit "unlawful" acts or lawful acts by "unlawful" means, even if these acts or means were not criminal. It has been said, however, that this has been interpreted to encompass only agreements to engage in conduct that is patently fraudulent, prejudicial to the public welfare, or so oppressive of individuals as to be injurious to the public welfare. Developments in the Law —Criminal Conspiracy, 72 Harv.L.Rev. 922, 942–44 (1959). This approach is still reflected in some state statutes, such as Section 182(5) of the California Penal Code which makes criminal any conspiracy "to commit any act injurious to the public health, to public morals, or to pervert or obstruct justice, or the due administration of the Laws." In Musser v. Utah, 333 U. S. 95, 68 S.Ct. 397, 92 L.Ed. 562 (1948), the Supreme Court indicated that a Utah statute prohibiting conspiracies "to commit any act injurious to the public health, to public morals, or to trade or commerce, or for the perversion or obstruction of justice or the due administration of the laws" might be unconstitutionally vague. In remanding the case to permit the state court to consider this question, the majority stated:

> [The statute] would seem to be warrant for conviction for agreement to do almost any act which a judge and jury might find at the moment contrary to his or its notion of what was good for health, morals, trade, commerce, justice or order.

333 U.S. at 97, 68 S.Ct. at 398, 92 L.Ed. at 565. The state supreme court found the statute unconstitutional. State v. Musser, 118 Utah 537, 223 P.2d 193 (1950). See also State v. Bowling, 5 Ariz.App. 436, 427 P.2d 928 (1967), holding invalid a similar statute. Compare the Model Penal Code formulation of the crime of conspiracy at page 321, supra.

2. ELEMENTS OF THE OFFENSE

The two traditional elements of the crime of conspiracy are the agreement between or among the participants and the "intent" or state of mind required concerning the objective of the agreement. Although an overt act pursuant to the agreement was not an element of the original common law crime of conspiracy, modern statutes impose such a requirement with sufficient frequency that an overt act needs to be considered as a potential additional element in contemporary analysis.

a. AGREEMENT

The essence of conspiracy is the agreement between or among the parties, although as is developed in section IV, C. 2.b, an overt act by one of the parties is sometimes required. The problems raised by the requirement of an agreement are to some extent simply problems of proof—what constitutes sufficient evidence of the agreement required by the crime. In addition, however, traditional law has found "defenses" to charges of conspiracy where the facts are regarded as establishing the logical impossibility of two "guilty" minds having actually met in agreement. This is developed in section IV, C. 2.a.(2).

Before addressing these matters, it is useful to consider the more basic question of what is necessary to establish that an agreement exists and that a specific person is a party to that agreement. Must the person have made a relatively specific commitment to participate in the scheme that is the subject of the discussion? Consider the following language from Cleaver v. United States, 238 F.2d 766, 771 (10th Cir. 1956), addressing the question of whether one Webster was a member of a conspiracy to commit burglary that the court acknowledges was proved by the prosecution:

> Webster * * * did not participate in the planning or the commission of the burglary, although he was present during a number of the conversations among the various conspirators. Mere knowledge, approval of or acquiescence in the object or purpose of the conspiracy, without an intention and agreement to cooperate in the crime is insufficient to constitute one a conspirator.

(1) General Requirement of Agreement

BENDER v. STATE

Supreme Court of Delaware, 1969.
253 A.2d 686.

WOLCOTT, Chief Justice. This is an appeal from a conviction of robbery and conspiracy to commit robbery. William L. Bender, Frank Lightcap and Kenneth Lloyd were jointly indicted, tried and convicted on the two charges. All three appeal. Basically, the question raised is the sufficiency of the State's evidence to support the convictions.

The State's case was as follows:

On June 28, 1967, at about 6:30 p. m., Eli Byler was walking with David Detweiler at Ninth and Shipley Streets in Wilmington. Byler was approached by Lloyd who asked for a cigarette and for money. Byler refused and started to walk away. At this point, Bender and Lightcap came up. Lloyd then threatened Byler with a glass bottle he had in his hand.

Byler began to run and was chased by the three defendants. He was caught from behind by Lightcap and was held from behind by more than one person. His wallet was taken from his pocket and money removed from it by Lloyd. Thereupon, all three defendants, Lightcap, Lloyd and Bender, fled the scene.

Appellants argue that there was insufficient evidence of robbery as to Bender to submit to the jury, and that there was no evidence as to conspiracy to commit robbery as to any of the appellants. Accordingly, they seek a reversal and a remand for new trial as to Lloyd and Lightcap on the robbery charge, and a judgment of acquittal as to Bender on the robbery charge, and as to all three on the conspiracy charge.

We think, however, that under the evidence, the State proved without question that Byler was the victim of a robbery and that all three of the defendants participated in it. No other conclusion seems credible when it is considered that all were present when Byler was threatened by Lloyd. When Byler sought to flee, all three defendants pursued him. At least two of them held him from behind while, presumably, Lloyd removed his wallet. All three defendants then ran off together.

* * *

With respect to the conspiracy charge, the State, of course, produced no evidence of a prior agreement among the defendants to commit this robbery. The State contends that the presence of the three defendants on the scene and their concerted action in committing the crime justify the conclusion that they had agreed among themselves.

A conspiracy is the combination of two or more persons to commit a crime. It is not necessary that there be a formal agreement in advance of the crime. The basic requirement is that there be an unlawful combination, and that the parties have a common design or purpose. If a person understands the unlawful nature of the acts taking place, and nevertheless assists in any manner in the carrying out of the common scheme, he thereupon becomes a conspirator to commit the offense.

We think there is sufficient evidence of the joint participation in this crime of these defendants to warrant the inference that they had the common design or purpose of robbing Byler. The matter was therefore properly submitted to the jury which found them guilty.

The judgments below are affirmed.

NOTES AND QUESTIONS

1. Defendants such as Bender, Lightcap and Lloyd, who complete a conspiracy, are subject to conviction for both the conspiracy and the completed crime and to consecutive penalties for both offenses. The effect of a rule permitting dual conviction and penalties is, of course, that crimes committed by collective action are punishable by a significantly higher penalty than those committed individually. In Callanan v. United States, 364 U.S. 587, 81 S.Ct. 321, 5 L.Ed.2d 312 (1961), the Supreme Court re-

jected an argument that Congress has intended that a defendant who committed conspiracy to obstruct commerce by extorting money and the substantive crime of obstructing commerce by extorting money should be punishable for only one of those offenses created by the Hobbs Anti-Racketeering Act. Explaining the apparent legislative reasoning, the Court stated:

> [C]ollective criminal agreement—partnership in crime—presents a greater potential threat to the public than individual delicts. Concerted action both increases the likelihood that the criminal object will be successfully attained and decreases the probability that the individuals involved will depart from their paths of criminality. Group association for criminal purposes often, if not normally, makes possible the attainment of ends more complex than those which one criminal could accomplish. Nor is the danger of a conspiratorial group limited to the particular end towards which it has embarked. Combination in crime makes more likely the commission of crimes unrelated to the original purpose for which the group was formed. In sum, the danger which a conspiracy generates is not confined to the substantive offense which is the immediate aim of the enterprise.

364 U.S. at 593–94, 81 S.Ct. at 325, 5 L.Ed.2d at 317. The Model Penal Code embraces the "minority" view that conviction for both an offense and conspiracy to commit that offense should not be permitted. See Model Penal Code § 1.07(1)(b) (P.O.D.1962).

2. Conspiracy doctrine permits the state to intervene long before the defendants have taken any action which brings them close to the achievement of their criminal purpose. It permits this intervention on the basis of conduct, other than the agreement, which may be extremely equivocal as an expression of criminal purpose. Therefore, it is clear that the establishment of an agreement is essential to the rationale for conspiracy prosecutions. The existence of the agreement presumably allays any concerns we might have about possible misidentification of the accused. It has been asserted that:

> * * * The act of agreeing with another to commit a crime * * * is concrete and unambiguous; it does not present the infinite degrees and variations possible in the general category of attempts. The danger that truly equivocal behavior may be misinterpreted as preparation to commit a crime is minimized; purpose must be relatively firm before the commitment involved in agreement is assumed.

Wechsler, Jones & Korn, The Treatment of Inchoate Crimes in the Model Penal Code of The American Law Institute: Attempt, Solicitation, and Conspiracy, 61 Colum.L.Rev. 957, 958 (1961). How consistent is this position with that of the Arkansas Supreme Court:

> Appellant seems to take the position that there must be direct evidence of a conspiracy, common design or purpose, and of the intent of the conspirators or joint actors to engage therein. In this he is mistaken. We have long recognized * * * that it is not

> necessary that an unlawful combination, conspiracy or concert of action to commit an unlawful act be shown by direct evidence, and that it may be proved by circumstances. * * * It may be inferred, even though no actual meeting among the parties is proved, if it be shown that two or more persons pursued by their acts the same unlawful object, each doing a part, so that their acts, though apparently independent, were in fact connected.

Griffin v. State, 248 Ark. 1223, 1225, 455 S.W.2d 882, 884 (1970).

Given the obvious difficulties of proving an agreement for criminal purposes isn't it necessary that the state be permitted considerable leeway in how it may establish this element? This view has clearly been expressed in Interstate Circuit v. United States, 306 U.S. 208, 59 S.Ct. 467, 83 L.Ed. 610 (1939). There, defendant motion picture distributors and exhibitors were charged with conspiring, in violation of the Sherman Antitrust Act, to restrain trade by restricting the minimum prices that could be charged by exhibitors. The appellants argued, inter alia, that the finding of conspiracy was not supported by the evidence because all that had been shown was separate agreements between each of the exhibitor defendants and each of the distributor defendants, not acting in concert with any other distributors, to impose restrictions necessary to the protection of their mutual interests in copyright rewards. Mr. Justice Stone, writing for the Court responded.

> As is usual in cases of alleged unlawful agreements to restrain commerce, the Government is without the aid of direct testimony that the distributors entered into any agreement with each other to impose the restrictions upon subsequent-run exhibitors. In order to establish agreement it is compelled to rely on inferences drawn from the course of conduct of the alleged conspirators.
>
> The trial court drew the inference of agreement from the nature of the proposals made on behalf of Interstate and Consolidated; from the manner in which they were made; from the substantial unanimity of action taken upon them by the distributors; and from the fact that appellants did not call as witnesses any of the superior officials who negotiated the contracts with Interstate or any official who, in the normal course of business, would have had knowledge of the existence or non-existence of such an agreement among the distributors. * * *
>
> * * *
>
> While the District Court's finding of an agreement of the distributors among themselves is supported by the evidence, we think that in the circumstances of this case such agreement for the imposition of the restrictions upon subsequent-run exhibitors was not a prerequisite to an unlawful conspiracy. It was enough that, knowing that concerted action was contemplated and invited, the distributors gave their adherence to the scheme and participated in it. Each distributor was advised that the others were asked to participate; each knew that cooperation was essential to successful operation of the plan. They knew that the plan, if carried out, would result in a restraint of commerce, which, we will presently

> point out, was unreasonable within the meaning of the Sherman Act, and knowing it, all participated in the plan. The evidence is persuasive that each distributor early became aware that the others had joined. With that knowledge they renewed the arrangement and carried it into effect for the two successive years.
>
> It is elementary that an unlawful conspiracy may be and often is formed without simultaneous action or agreement on the part of the conspirators. Acceptance by competitors, without previous agreement, of an invitation to participate in a plan, the necessary consequence of which, if carried out, is restraint of interstate commerce, is sufficient to establish an unlawful conspiracy under the Sherman Act.

Is there any reason why these principles should not be equally applicable to conspiracies to commit traditional crimes?

3. As the material in the attempt section, supra, indicates, "legal" but not "factual" impossibility may preclude liability for attempt. Should impossibility ever prevent liability for conspiracy? There is some authority for the proposition that legal or inherent impossibility of success means that no conviction for conspiracy may be had. Ventimiglia v. United States, 242 F.2d 620 (4th Cir. 1957). But most courts hold that impossibility—whether legal or factual as those terms are used in attempt law discussions—has no effect on guilt of conspiracy. E. g., United States v. Rosner, 485 F.2d 1213, 1228–29 (2nd Cir. 1973), cert. den. 417 U.S. 950, 94 S.Ct. 3080, 41 L.Ed.2d 672 (1974); State v. Palumbo, 137 N.J.Super. 13, 347 A.2d 535 (1975). In State v. Moretti, 52 N.J. 182, 244 A.2d 499, cert. den. 393 U.S. 952, 89 S.Ct. 376, 21 L.Ed.2d 363 (1968) the court offered the following explanation for the different treatment accorded impossibility in attempt and conspiracy:

> [A] conspiracy charge focuses primarily on the *intent* of the defendants, while in an attempt case the primary inquiry centers on the defendants' *conduct* tending towards the commission of the substantive crime. The crime of conspiracy is complete once the conspirators, having formed the intent to commit a crime, take any step in preparation; mere preparation, however, is an inadequate basis for an attempt conviction regardless of the intent. Thus, the impossibility that the defendants' conduct will result in the consummation of the contemplated crime is not as pertinent in a conspiracy case as it might be in an attempt prosecution.

52 N.J. at 186–188, 244 A.2d at 502.

4. Should withdrawal be a defense to a charge of conspiring to commit a crime? If so, what should be required for an effective withdrawal? Traditionally, withdrawal has not been a defense. E. g., United States v. Heathington, 545 F.2d 972 (5th Cir. 1977); People v. Hintz, 69 Mich.App. 207, 244 N.W.2d 414 (1976). If, however, a jurisdiction requires an overt act by one of the conspirators before the crime of conspiracy is complete, a withdrawal from the agreement by one of the conspirators before the commission of the overt act would seem to preclude liability. See Developments in the Law—Criminal Conspiracy, 72 Harv.L.Rev. 922, 957 (1959). And consider the wisdom of Section 5.03(6) of the Model Penal Code (reprinted

at page 321, supra), which provides for a defense of renunciation. Some statutory schemes contain such defenses. Texas Penal Code § 15.04, for example, provides:

> It is an affirmative defense to prosecution [for criminal conspiracy] that under circumstances manifesting a voluntary and complete renunciation of his criminal objective the actor * * * withdrew from the conspiracy before commission of the object offense and took further affirmative action that prevented the commission of the object offense.

Withdrawal may, of course, have other effects than raising a defense to the charge of conspiracy itself. When a conspirator withdraws from the conspiracy, the period of limitations as to him begins to run at that time, so withdrawal will affect the time within which a conspirator must be tried. Eldredge v. United States, 62 F.2d 449 (2nd Cir. 1932). While the declarations of one conspirator made during and in furtherance of the conspiracy may be admitted against all the conspirators, a conspirator's withdrawal prevents the use against him of coconspirators' declarations made *after* his withdrawal. United States v. Mardian, 546 F.2d 973, 978 n. 5 (D.C.Cir. 1976). Perhaps more significantly, an effective withdrawal prevents a conspirator from being held liable for substantive crimes committed by other members of the scheme. This matter and other possible formulations of a standard for determining the effectiveness of a withdrawal are discussed in subsection 3., infra.

(2) Defenses Based on the Requirement of an Agreement

The "essence" of conspiracy is agreement. Some courts consider this requirement of a meeting of several guilty minds so important that situations regarded as inconsistent with a union of several "criminal" minds will be held to preclude conviction for conspiracy or even to invalidate a conviction already obtained. Issues arising under this aspect of conspiracy law generally involve the assertion that disposition of actual or potential charges against other members of an alleged conspiracy requires acquittal of the remaining member or members, because the disposition of the charges against the other members is logically inconsistent with the existence of a criminal agreement involving the remaining member or members.

REGLE v. STATE

Court of Special Appeals of Maryland, 1970.
9 Md.App. 346, 264 A.2d 119.

MURPHY, Chief Judge. On September 28, 1968, Sergeant Frank Mazzone, a Maryland State Police officer working under cover, was advised by other police officers that Michael Isele, a police informer, had informed them that he had been invited by the appellant Regle to participate in a robbery. Mazzone immediately contacted Isele, whom he previously knew, and together they went to see the appellant. Isele introduced Mazzone to the appellant as a prospective participant in the planned robbery. After some discussion, the appellant invited Mazzone to participate in the robbery. While appellant did not then specify the place to be robbed, he indicated to Mazzone that Richard Fields had been involved with him in planning the robbery, and that he would also participate in the crime. Appellant, Mazzone, and Isele then met with Fields and the robbery plan was outlined by appellant and Fields. The need for guns was discussed and appellant and Fields spoke of the necessity of killing two employees at O'Donnell's restaurant, the situs of the proposed robbery. The four men then drove in Isele's car to appellant's home where appellant phoned Kent Chamblee for the purpose of purchasing a shotgun. Thereafter, the men drove to Chamblee's home, purchased the gun from him, and tested it in his presence. While Chamblee knew that the shotgun was to be used "for a job," he did not accompany the others when they then drove to the restaurant to perpetrate the robbery. Upon arriving there, Mazzone told appellant that he first wanted to "case" the restaurant. This being agreed, Mazzone and Isele went into the restaurant while appellant and Fields went to a nearby bar to await their return. Once inside the restaurant, Mazzone contacted police headquarters and requested assistance. Thereafter, he and Isele left the restaurant and rejoined appellant and Fields. While several police cars promptly responded to the scene, Mazzone found it necessary, in the interim, to reveal his identity as a police officer and to arrest appellant and Fields at gunpoint. At the same time he also arrested Isele in order "to cover him." After the arrest, appellant made an incriminating statement to the effect that he and Fields had planned the robbery and that he had invited Isele to participate in the crime.

Appellant, Fields, and Chamblee were thereafter jointly indicted for conspiracy to rob with a dangerous and deadly weapon and for carrying a deadly weapon openly with intent to injure. Appellant was separately tried by a jury, found guilty on both counts, and sentenced to twenty years on the conspiracy charge, and two years, concurrent, on the weapons offense.

The docket entries indicate that the conspiracy indictment against Chamblee was *nol prossed* prior to appellant's trial. It also appears that at his trial appellant established through the testimony of a police officer that Fields had been examined by State psychiatrists at the Clifton Perkins State Hospital and found "not guilty by reason of being insane at the time of the alleged crime." The State did not rebut the officer's testimony, although the record indicates that two of the State psychiatrists who had examined Fields were then present in court.

Against this background, appellant contends that since the indictment against Chamblee was *nol prossed,* only he and Fields were charged as conspirators; and that because Fields was found insane at the time of the commission of the crime and thus was not a person legally capable of engaging in a criminal conspiracy, his own conviction cannot stand since one person alone cannot be guilty of the crime of conspiracy.

Conspiracy—a common law misdemeanor in Maryland—is defined as a combination by two or more persons to accomplish a criminal or unlawful act, or to do a lawful act by criminal or unlawful means. Jones v. State, 8 Md.App. 370, 259 A.2d 807. The gist of the offense is the unlawful combination resulting from the agreement, rather than the mere agreement itself, and no overt act is required to constitute the crime. Wilson v. State, 8 Md.App. 653, 262 A.2d 91. In other words, as succinctly stated by the Supreme Court of New Jersey in State v. Carbone, 10 N.J. 329, 91 A.2d 571, 574, the "gist of the offense of conspiracy lies, not in doing the act, nor effecting the purpose for which the conspiracy is formed, nor in attempting to do them, nor in inciting others to do them, but in the forming of the scheme or agreement between the parties." Concert in criminal purpose, it is said, is the salient factor in criminal conspiracy. Criminal conspiracy is a partnership in crime—"It is the coalition of manpower and human minds enhancing possibilities of achievement aimed at the objective that present a greater threat to society than does a lone offender." Clark and Marshall Crimes (6th Edition) Section 9.00. In short, it is *the existence* of the conspiracy which creates the danger. Dennis v. United States, 341 U.S. 494, 511, 71 S.Ct. 857, 95 L. Ed. 1137.

As one person cannot conspire or form a combination with himself, it is essential in proving the existence of a criminal conspiracy to show "the consent of two or more minds," Bloomer v. State, 48 Md. 521, 536, viz., it must be shown that at least two persons had a meeting of the minds—a unity of design and purpose—to have an agreement. Wilson v. State, supra; Jones v. State, supra. A formal agreement need not, however, be established; it is sufficient if the minds of the parties meet understandingly, so as to bring about an intelligent and deliberate agreement to do the acts contemplated. As the crime of conspiracy is one requiring a specific intent, and necessarily involves at the least two guilty parties, the required criminal intent must exist in the minds of two or more parties to the conspiracy.

In view of these principles, it is the well settled general rule that one defendant in a prosecution for conspiracy cannot be convicted where all of his alleged coconspirators, be they one or more, have been acquitted or discharged under circumstances that amount to an acquittal. The validity of the general rule has been consistently recognized by the Court of Appeals. See State v. Buchanan, 5 H & J 317; Bloomer v. State, supra; Hurwitz v. State, 200 Md. 578, 92 A.2d

575. We recognized the rule in Wilson v. State, supra. The rationale underlying the rule appears clear: that it is illogical to acquit all but one of a purported partnership in crime; that acquittal of all persons with whom a defendant is alleged to have conspired is repugnant to the existence of the requisite corrupt agreement; and that regardless of the criminal animus of the one defendant, there must be someone with whom he confected his corrupt agreement, and where all his alleged coconspirators are not guilty, a like finding as to him must be made. See 91 A.L.R.2d, at p. 703. But "It is only where one is convicted and another or others are acquitted, resulting in a repugnancy upon the record, that the convicted conspirator may be discharged." Berry v. State, 202 Ind. 294, 173 N.E. 705 cited with approval in Hurwitz v. State, supra.

Generally speaking, it would appear that so long as the disposition of the case against a coconspirator does not remove the basis for the charge of conspiracy, a single defendant may be prosecuted and convicted of the offense, even though for one reason or another his coconspirator is either not tried or not convicted. See the exhaustive collection of cases at 72 A.L.R. 1180–1192 and 91 A.L.R.2d 700–733. Consistent with this rule, the authorities all agree that the death of one conspirator does not of itself prevent the conviction of the other, where the conspiracy between them is shown by the evidence. In Hurwitz v. State, supra, a case in which all but one of the conspirators were granted immunity from prosecution on a ground not inconsistent with their participation in the conspiracy, the court held that such grant of immunity was not equivalent to acquittal and would not require reversal of the conviction of the one remaining conspirator. The same rule has been applied where one of two conspirators enjoyed diplomatic immunity and therefore could not be prosecuted for the conspiracy. Farnsworth v. Zerbst, 98 F.2d 541 (5th Cir.). In Adams v. State, 202 Md. 455, 97 A.2d 281, it was held that conviction of one defendant in a conspiracy case was proper despite failure to convict of any of the other conspirators where it was alleged and shown that there were persons unknown to the prosecution with whom the convicted defendant had conspired. And while the cases are generally divided on the question whether the entry of a *nolle prosequi* as to one of two alleged conspirators compels an acquittal of the remaining conspirator, the better reasoned view would appear to support the proposition that it does not, at least where the *nolle prosequi* was not entered without the coconspirator's consent after the trial had begun (which then would have amounted to an acquittal and precluded reindictment). See Greathouse v. State, 5 Md.App. 675, 249 A.2d 207. In *Hurwitz*, it was held that the entry of a "stet" to a coconspirator's indictment was not tantamount to an acquittal and did not compel the discharge of the only remaining conspirator.[1]

1. By the Maryland stet procedure, the prosecutor indicates that he does not choose *at that time* to further prosecute the indictment.

Some cases suggest that the rule that acquittal of all save one of the alleged conspirators results in the acquittal of all applies only to acquittals on the merits. See Farnsworth v. Zerbst, supra. Other cases—while recognizing that acquittals are not always tantamount to a declaration of innocence—nevertheless conclude that an acquittal is in effect a judicial determination, binding on the State, that the acquitted defendant was not a participant in a criminal conspiracy. See United States v. Fox, 130 F.2d 56 (3rd Cir.); State v. Smith, 117 Ark. 384, 175 S.W. 392. The State urges that where the acquittal of one of the alleged conspirators is based solely on the fact that he was insane at the time of the crime, the remaining conspirator should nonetheless be held responsible for the offense. The State relies on Jones v. State, 31 Ala.App. 504, 19 So.2d 81, a case in which the defendant, convicted of murder, maintained that the actual killing was done by his brother and that because his brother was insane at the time of the crime, and hence innocent of the offense, he (the defendant) must likewise be exonerated. The court, after characterizing the defendant as "a co-conspirator and an aider and abettor in the homicide," said (p. 83):

> "* * * the insanity [of appellant's brother] would not exculpate the appellant if he conspired with the principal or aided or abetted him in the killing of deceased * * *. If appellant so conspired or aided or abetted in the homicide, the mental irresponsibility of [his brother] could not be invoked to exonerate said appellant. One may or could use an insane person as the agent of destruction—or conspire with such person to accomplish the homicide—just as guilty as with a person of sound mind. The fact, if true, that the coconspirator or principal in the crime is not amenable to justice because of mental irresponsibility does not exempt the other from prosecution. Pruitt v. State, 91 Tex.Cr.R. 189, 237 S.W. 572; People v. Armstrong, 299 Ill. 349, 132 N.E. 547; Conley v. People, 170 Ill. 587, 48 N.E. 911; 22 C.J.S. Criminal Law §§ 85, 101."

We think the cases relied upon by the *Jones* court to support its conclusion stand for the proposition that it is no defense to one who participates either as a principal or aider or abettor in the actual commission of the substantive criminal offense that the principal offender was insane at the time of the crime. The principle would appear similar to the rule that a coconspirator may be convicted of any crime committed by any member of a conspiracy to do an illegal act if the act is done in furtherance of the purpose of the conspiracy. The conspiracy being established, the fact that the member who committed the crime was insane at the time would thus not exonerate the others from complicity in the commisson of the substantive offense. See State v. Alton, 139 Mont. 479, 365 P.2d 527.

We do not find these cases controlling of the primary question before us, namely, whether *under an indictment for conspiracy,* one conspirator may be convicted of the offense where the only other conspirator was shown to be insane at the time the agreement between them was concluded. Conspiracy to commit a crime is a different offense from the crime that is the object of the conspiracy. One necessarily involves joint action; the other does not. By its nature, conspiracy is a joint or group offense requiring a concert of free wills, and the union of the minds of at least two persons is a prerequisite to the commission of the offense. The essence of conspiracy is, therefore, a mental confederation involving at least two persons; the crime is indivisible in the sense that it requires more than one guilty person; and where the joint intent does not exist, the basis of the charge of conspiracy is necessarily swept away. See Feder v. United States, 257 F. 694 (2nd Cir.). In short, the guilt of both persons must concur to constitute that of either. It is upon this premise that the authorities all agree that if two persons are charged as conspirators and one is an entrapper, or merely feigns acquiescence in the criminal intent, there is no punishable conspiracy because there was no agreement on the part of the one to engage in a criminal conspiracy.[2] Delaney v. State, 164 Tenn. 432, 51 S.W.2d 485; Woo Wai v. United States, 223 F. 412 (9th Cir.); State v. Dougherty, 88 N.J.L. 209, 96 A. 56; Solomon v. State, 168 Tenn. 180, 76 S.W.2d 331; Odneal v. State, 117 Tex.Cr.R. 97, 34 S.W.2d 595. For like reasons, we hold that where only two persons are implicated in a conspiracy, and one is shown to have been insane at the time the agreement was concluded, and hence totally incapable of committing any crime, there is no punishable criminal conspiracy, the requisite joint criminal intent being absent.

The evidence in the record before us plainly shows that appellant and Fields planned to commit a robbery at O'Donnell's restaurant. There is some evidence in the record to suggest that Chamblee may also have been a conspirator although the State made little effort at the trial to establish his involvement in the conspiracy. Since an insane person is mentally incapable of forming a criminal intent, Bradford v. State, 234 Md. 505, 514, 200 A.2d 150, it is clear that if Fields was actually insane at the time of the offense, he could not be found guilty of engaging in a criminal conspiracy. It does not appear however, that Fields was ever tried and acquitted of the conspiracy charge. But the only evidence in the record—the testimony of the police officer—is that Fields was found by State psychiatrists upon examination to have been insane at the time of the commission of the offense. While such testimony is hardly the equivalent of the expert medical evidence required to prove insanity, see Millard v. State, 8 Md.App. 119, 261 A.2d 227, the trial judge, in his charge to the jury,

2. This would not be true, however, if after elimination of the alleged entrapper, there are at least two other parties to the conspiracy.

stated as a fact that Fields "was found to be insane." Assuming this to be the true situation, it is unlikely that Fields will ever be brought to trial on the conspiracy charge.

As to Chamblee, the docket entries indicate the entry of a *nolle prosequi* to his conspiracy indictment. We cannot ascertain, therefore, whether, in the circumstances in which it was entered, the *nolle prosequi* operated as an acquittal or not. See Greathouse v. State, supra. It appears, however, from colloquy between counsel and with the court that Chamblee was permitted to plead to a lesser offense than conspiracy, possibly with the understanding that he would not thereafter be charged with that offense.

In his advisory instructions to the jury, the trial judge, after fully defining the crime of conspiracy, stated that under Maryland law where only two parties are involved in the alleged conspiracy, and one is found not guilty, "the other could not be tried because one person cannot conspire except with another to commit a crime." He further advised the jury that there has to be "an outright finding of not guilty" but such was not the case with Fields who was merely found to be insane and for that reason not brought to trial. With reference to Chamblee, the trial judge instructed that he had not been found not guilty of conspiracy; that he did not believe that Chamblee had been prosecuted for that offense.

While appellant made no objection to the court's instructions, on the state of the record before us we think they constituted "plain error * * * material to the rights of the accused" under Maryland Rule 756g. See Parker v. State, 4 Md.App. 62, 241 A.2d 185. We thus deem it essential in the interest of justice that appellant's conspiracy conviction be reversed and that the State be afforded the opportunity to retry the case in light of the principles of law which we consider relevant and controlling. If, upon retrial, the State intends to charge only Fields and appellant as conspirators, and the evidence properly shows that Fields was legally insane at the time the agreement to perpetrate the robbery was concluded, then even though Fields has not been acquitted of the offense of conspiracy by a judicial determination that he was insane, nevertheless the requisite *joint* criminal intent being absent, appellant cannot properly be convicted of engaging with Fields in a criminal conspiracy. If Fields is shown so to be insane, but the facts show that the conspiracy indictment against Chamblee was not *nol prossed* under circumstances amounting to an acquittal (see Greathouse v. State, supra), then the State may undertake to adduce evidence showing that Chamblee was a conspirator, with appellant, in the plan to commit the robbery.

NOTES AND QUESTIONS

1. Does the decision in *Regle* comport with the rationales of the crime of conspiracy? How does the insanity of an alleged co-conspirator lessen the dangers which conspiracy doctrine is designed to avoid?

2. What result would be reached under the Model Penal Code? Consider the following portions of the Comment to Section 5.03(1):

> *Unilateral Approach of the Draft.* The definition of the Draft departs from the traditional view of conspiracy as an entirely bilateral or multilateral relationship, the view inherent in the standard formulation cast in terms of "two or more persons" agreeing or combining to commit a crime. Attention is directed instead to each individual's culpability by framing the definition in terms of the conduct which suffices to establish the liability of any given actor, rather than the conduct of a group of which he is charged to be a part—an approach which in this comment we have designated "unilateral."
>
> One consequence of this approach is to make it immaterial to the guilt of a conspirator whose culpability has been established that the person or all of the persons with whom he conspired have not been or cannot be convicted. Present law frequently holds otherwise, reasoning from the definition of conspiracy as an agreement between two or more persons that there must be at least two guilty conspirators or none.

Model Penal Code, Comment to § 5.03(1), 102 (Tent. Draft No. 10, 1960).

Under the approach of the Model Penal Code, then, Regle would be guilty of criminal conspiracy if he agreed with Fields and Chamblee (or either one of them). The focus is unilateral in the sense that it is only upon Regle and what he did. He could have "agreed" with Fields, Chamblee, or both of them, even if neither of them "agreed" with him. Thus it would be unnecessary, under the Model Penal Code approach, to worry about whether Fields and Chamblee were competent to enter into a criminally culpable "agreement" (whether they were "insane") or whether the charges against them ended in a determination that they are innocent. The only question is whether Regle "agreed" with another person within the meaning of the law of conspiracy. This unilateral approach can be defended on the ground that it permits the conviction of persons who have demonstrated their dangerousness and culpability by engaging in prohibited conduct, i. e., agreeing with others to commit a crime. If, for reasons unknown to a defendant, the other members of the agreement were incapable of entering into a legally-binding agreement or if they are later found not subject to conviction, this does not establish that the defendant is not dangerous or culpable. A true "meeting of the minds," as is required by the court in the principal case, is not necessary to show that a defendant is properly the subject of criminal sanctions. If it can be shown that the defendant "agreed" with others for a criminal purpose, the law is justified in holding the defendant liable.

b. OVERT ACT REQUIREMENT

The common law crime of conspiracy required no more than that the act of agreement have been completed. But a number of American jurisdictions have required that, in addition to the agreement, the prosecution prove the commission of an overt act by one member of the agreement. This is the case under the federal criminal conspiracy statute. 18 U.S.C.A. § 371 (prosecution must prove that "one or more of * * * [the] persons [agreeing did] any act to effect the object of the conspiracy"). Some statutes impose a selective requirement. The Arizona statute, for example, requires proof of an overt act except where the object of the conspiracy is to commit burglary while armed, arson of an occupied structure, or any felony upon the person of another. Ariz.Rev.Stat. § 13–1003. The Supreme Court summarized the basic law applicable to the overt act requirement under the federal statute as follows:

> It is not necessary that an overt act be the substantive crime charged in the indictment as the object of the conspiracy. Nor, indeed, need such act, taken by itself, even be criminal in character. The function of the overt act in a conspiracy prosecution is simply to manifest 'that the conspiracy is at work,' and is neither a project still resting solely in the minds of the conspirators nor a fully completed operation no longer in existence.

Yates v. United States, 354 U.S. 298, 334, 77 S.Ct. 1064, 1084–85, 1 L.Ed.2d 1356, 1384 (1957). There are two major issues posed by this aspect of conspiracy law. The first, of course, is whether sound policy dictates that conspiracy be so defined as to include proof of an overt act as well as an agreement. What does an overt act requirement accomplish? In regard to this inquiry, it may be useful to consider the following comment by a committee proposing that the Illinois conspiracy statute be amended so as to include a requirement of an overt act:

> Heretofore, in Illinois, the agreement alone has constituted sufficient conduct to support a charge of conspiracy * * *. In actuality, however, no case has been found in which some activity pursuant to the agreement has not been present. This leads to the conclusion that prosecutors find proof of the agreement without subsequent activity too difficult, or consider the agreement alone too inconsequential, to warrant criminal prosecution.

Illinois Criminal Code of 1961, Committee Comments to Section 8–2. The second issue is related: What standard should be used to determine whether, under an overt act requirement, specific acts are sufficient? This relates to the rationale for the overt act requirement. What criterion for determining the sufficiency of overt acts best accomplishes the intent of the requirement?

PEOPLE v. TEETER

Supreme Court of New York, Monroe County, 1976.
86 Misc.2d 532, 382 N.Y.S.2d 938, aff'd 62
A.D.2d 1158, 404 N.Y.S.2d 210 (1978).

Robert P. KENNEDY, Justice.

Defendants Teeter and Kropman have been convicted after a jury trial of the crime of Conspiracy * * *. At the close of the People's case and again at the close of proof the defendants moved for trial orders of dismissal of the Conspiracy charge. Decision was reserved both times and the matter was submitted to the jury.

The Conspiracy count of the indictment under which they were tried alleges that the defendants "did agree with one or more persons, to wit, one another and also Ronald Cantaben, Anthony Cotsworth, and others, * * *" to have certain named persons murdered. It further alleges that in furtherance of the conspiracy "one or more of the conspirators did commit overt acts including but not limited to the following * * *". The indictment then sets forth two payments of money to Ronald Cantaben. These are the only alleged overt acts spelled out in the indictment.

One of the major problems, apparent from the above, is that the only overt acts alleged are payments from one coconspirator to another. It is alleged that the first payment was "a down payment for the murder" and the other "to be used as payment for the murder * * *". Case after case has held that, citing only one:

> "Payment of money to a co-conspirator to secure his agreement to the conspiracy is regarded as an act merely cementing the conspiracy and not as an overt act committed in furtherance thereof. (People v. Hines, 284 N.Y. 93, 29 N.E.2d 483.) However, if the money is paid to a co-conspirator to be delivered to another in payment of the services constituting the principal crime, such payment is held to constitute an overt act. (People v. DeCabia, 8 A.D.2d 825, 190 N.Y.S. 2d 142, affd. 7 N.Y.2d 823, 196 N.Y.S.2d 701, 164 N.E.2d 720.)" (People v. Wolff, 24 A.D.2d 828, 264 N.Y.S.2d 40.)

Here, the indictment alleges payment to a co-conspirator, not to be paid to another for services but for the co-conspirator and, therefore, would not constitute an overt act such as is required by law.

People v. DeCabia, 10 Misc.2d 923, 172 N.Y.S.2d 1004, submitted by the prosecution in support of its position is easily distinguishable. In *DeCabia*, money was given to a co-conspirator "to be used by him for the proposed bribe", in other words, to pass on to someone else.

* * *

[But] if Cantaben was not a co-conspirator then the alleged payments to him by one who was would constitute an overt act such as would satisfy the requirements of * * * the Penal Law.

The more perplexing arguments were those presented * * * relating to the role of Cantaben and Cotsworth. Both of these men were undercover police officers. * * *

Defendants' * * * argument on this point is that because the two men are police officers they could not have had the requisite criminal intent to enter into a conspiracy to murder and were, therefore, not co-conspirators * * *. [T]he question as to whether or not the two officers had the requisite criminal intent was for the jury. Unfortunately, there have been incidents where police officers did have such intent.

* * *

I, therefore, find that whether or not Cantaben and Cotsworth were co-conspirators is a question of fact and that if the jury finds that they were not, then the overt acts alleged in the indictment were sufficient. Although nothing which occurred after the motions were made or the verdict was rendered was or could be considered when deciding the motions, the jury was instructed that if they found that Cantaben and Cotsworth were co-conspirators, payment of money to them by another co-conspirator under the circumstances of this case would not constitute an overt act such as is required by the law. Implicit in the verdict of guilty, under such an instruction, was a finding that the two officers were not co-conspirators and that the defendants were.

Defendants' motions * * * to set aside the verdicts are, therefore, in all respects denied.

NOTES AND QUESTIONS

1. If payments by one conspirator to another conspirator "to secure his agreement" do not serve the purpose an overt act is supposed to serve, is this purpose served if the payments were made, as in the instant case, to one mistakenly believed to be entering into the conspiracy? Consider the following discussion of the overt act in People v. Olson, 232 Cal.App.2d 480, 42 Cal.Rptr. 760, 767 (1965):

> But, by definition, the overt act must be one to effect the object of the conspiracy or which, at least, has a tendency to forward the purpose of the conspiracy. In this country, evil thoughts alone cannot constitute a criminal offense; unless and until something objective is done toward the effectuation of the illegal plan, no prosecution is justified; if there is no overt or open act there can be no conviction, and the overt act must be such as furthers the object of the conspiracy.
>
> In United States v. German-American Vocational League, 3 Cir., 153 F.2d 860, 863, it is said:

> "'An overt act is one which manifests the intention of the doer to commit the offense.'"

> It has been reiterated more than once in apposite legal opinions that an overt act must "* * * at least start to carry the conspiracy into effect" (People v. Moran, 166 Cal.App.2d 410, 414, 333 P.2d 243, 245; People v. George, 74 Cal.App. 440, 241 P. 97). Chavez v. United States, 9 Cir., 275 F.2d 813, 817, says:

> > "In criminal law an overt act is an outward act done in pursuance of the crime and in manifestation of an intent or design, looking toward the accomplishment of the crime."

> One reason for requiring the allegation and proof of an overt act in connection with a conspiracy is to allow an opportunity to the conspirators to repent and to terminate the unlawful agreement before any decisive act is done in furtherance of it. The requirement of the allegation and proof of such an overt act "* * * affords a *locus poenitentiae*, so that before the act done either one or all of the parties may abandon their design, and thus avoid the penalty prescribed by the statute." (United States v. Britton, 108 U.S. 199, 2 S.Ct. 531–534, 27 L.Ed. 698.)

2. Suppose in the instant case the prosecution had alleged as the overt act and had proved at trial an incident in which Cantaben was taken by either Teeter or Kropman and shown where the intended victims lived. Would this, without more, have been sufficient to meet the requirement of an overt act? In a portion of the opinion not reprinted here, the court comments that this "might well" have been sufficient. 86 Misc.2d at 534, 382 N.Y.S.2d at 940.

3. To what extent can conversations among members of the conspiracy suffice as overt acts if the applicable law requires an overt act? Perhaps the analysis used in *Teeter* is useful in this context. If the conversations were part of the process of formulating the agreement, they—like the payment of money to secure agreement by others—might not suffice. See People ex rel. Conte v. Flood, 53 Misc.2d 109, 277 N.Y.S.2d 697 (1966). But if, after the agreement has clearly been solidified, there are further conversations among some members of the scheme concerning the implementation of some of the details of the scheme, should not these conversations—like the payment of money by one member of the conspiracy to a second member for ultimate transfer to another person not a member of the scheme—be a sufficient overt act? See United States v. Armone, 363 F.2d 385 (2nd Cir. 1966), cert. den. 385 U.S. 957, 87 S.Ct. 391, 17 L.Ed.2d 303.

4. Even if an overt act is not required for liability as an element of the crime charged, it may have important "procedural" significance. Overt acts are, for example, important in determining whether the period of limitations has run. Generally, a prosecution for conspiracy is permissible if at least one overt act is proven to have been committed within the period required by the applicable period of limitations. See People v. Zamora, 18 Cal.3d 538, 134 Cal.Rptr 784, 557 P.2d 75 (1976).

c. THE STATE OF MIND REQUIRED

The Supreme Court recently noted:

> In a conspiracy, two different types of intent are generally required—the basic intent to agree, which is necessary to establish the existence of the conspiracy, and the more traditional intent to effectuate the object of the conspiracy.

United States v. United States Gypsum Co., 438 U.S. 422, 443 n. 20, 98 S.Ct. 2864, 2876 n. 20, 57 L.Ed.2d 854, 873 n. 20 (1978). The first of the types of intent distinguished by the Court was treated in subsection IV.C.2.a (1), supra. This section deals with the second type of intent, the state of mind regarding effectuation of the object of the agreement. Perhaps the issue can best be identified in terms of a simple hypothetical: A, aware that B and C are manufacturing whiskey, agrees to sell B sugar. This can reasonably be construed as an agreement involving A, B, and C; A has agreed to do something that is part of the scheme, and the production of illicit whiskey is the objective of the scheme. A clearly had that type of "intent" necessary for formulation of the agreement. But what must have been A's state of mind in regard to the object, i. e., the illicit production of whiskey, and did he have it? Must he have desired that whiskey actually be produced? Is it sufficient if he was aware that production of whiskey would result from the scheme? Or might it be sufficient if A was simply aware of a substantial and unjustifiable risk that a result of the venture would be the production of whiskey? Does this end the inquiry? Or might it be necessary to prove that A was aware (or was aware of a risk) that the scheme constituted a *criminal* offense under federal law?

In the *Gypsum* case the defendants were charged with conspiracy to fix the price of gypsum board in violation of the Sherman Act. There was no dispute that the defendants, six major manufacturers and some of their officials, had exchanged price information. The question was the intent with which this was done. The Supreme Court first concluded that the Sherman Act, although an economic regulatory scheme, was not intended to be a strict liability offense, a mental element was needed given, in particular, the vagueness of the Act's prohibitions in the context of complex business dealings any of which might have anticompetitive effects despite the good faith business judgments underlying the actions. The Court's majority then concluded that the level of intent required would be "knowledge" rather than "purpose". To require the government to prove that it was defendants' conscious desire to bring about the anti-competitive effect was thought unduly burdensome. Rather, it would be sufficient to show that they had engaged in the conduct charged with knowledge that the proscribed effects would most likely follow. This decision, it must be noted, involved an interpretation of one specific crime. It does not control the answer to the question addressed in this section with respect to other conspiracies.

PEOPLE v. LAURIA

California Court of Appeal, 1967.
251 Cal.App.2d 471, 59 Cal.Rptr. 628.

FLEMING, Associate Justice. In an investigation of call-girl activity the police focused their attention on three prostitutes actively plying their trade on call, each of whom was using Lauria's telephone answering service, presumably for business purposes.

On January 8, 1965, Stella Weeks, a policewoman, signed up for telephone service with Lauria's answering service. Mrs. Weeks, in the course of her conversation with Lauria's office manager, hinted broadly that she was a prostitute concerned with the secrecy of her activities and their concealment from the police. She was assured that the operation of the service was discreet and "about as safe as you can get." It was arranged that Mrs. Weeks need not leave her address with the answering service, but could pick up her calls and pay her bills in person.

On February 11, Mrs. Weeks talked to Lauria on the telephone and told him her business was modelling and she had been referred to the answering service by Terry, one of the three prostitutes under investigation. She complained that because of the operation of the service she had lost two valuable customers, referred to as tricks. Lauria defended his service and said that her friends had probably lied to her about having left calls for her. But he did not respond to Mrs. Weeks' hints that she needed customers in order to make money, other than to invite her to his house for a personal visit in order to get better acquainted. In the course of his talk he said "his business was taking messages."

On February 15, Mrs. Weeks talked on the telephone to Lauria's office manager and again complained of two lost calls, which she described as a $50 and a $100 trick. On investigation the office manager could find nothing wrong, but she said she would alert the switchboard operators about slip-ups on calls.

On April 1 Lauria and the three prostitutes were arrested. Lauria complained to the police that this attention was undeserved, stating that Hollywood Call Board had 60 to 70 prostitutes on its board while his own service had only 9 or 10, that he kept separate records for known or suspected prostitutes for the convenience of himself and the police. When asked if his records were available to police who might come to the office to investigate call girls, Lauria replied that they were whenever the police had a specific name. However, his service didn't "arbitrarily tell the police about prostitutes on our board. As long as they pay their bills we tolerate them." In a subsequent voluntary appearance before the Grand Jury Lauria testified he had always cooperated with the police. But he admitted he knew some of his customers were prostitutes, and he knew Terry was a prostitute because he had personally used her services, and he knew she was paying for 500 calls a month.

Lauria and the three prostitutes were indicted for conspiracy to commit prostitution, and nine overt acts were specified. Subsequently the trial court set aside the indictment as having been brought without reasonable or probable cause. (Pen.Code, § 995.) The People have appealed, claiming that a sufficient showing of an unlawful agreement to further prostitution was made.

To establish agreement, the People need show no more than a tacit, mutual understanding between coconspirators to accomplish an unlawful act. Here the People attempted to establish a conspiracy by showing that Lauria, well aware that his codefendants were prostitutes who received business calls from customers through his telephone answering service, continued to furnish them with such service. This approach attempts to equate knowledge of another's criminal activity with conspiracy to further such criminal activity, and poses the question of the criminal responsibility of a furnisher of goods or services who knows his product is being used to assist the operation of an illegal business. Under what circumstances does a supplier become a part of a conspiracy to further an illegal enterprise by furnishing goods or services which he knows are to be used by the buyer for criminal purposes?

The two leading cases on this point face in opposite directions. In United States v. Falcone, 311 U.S. 205, 61 S.Ct. 204, 85 L.Ed. 128, the sellers of large quantities of sugar, yeast, and cans were absolved from participation in a moonshining conspiracy among distillers who bought from them, while in Direct Sales Co. v. United States, 319 U. S. 703, 63 S.Ct. 1265, 87 L.Ed. 1674, a wholesaler of drugs was convicted of conspiracy to violate the federal narcotic laws by selling drugs in quantity to a codefendant physician who was supplying them to addicts. The distinction between these two cases appears primarily based on the proposition that distributors of such dangerous products as drugs are required to exercise greater discrimination in the conduct of their business than are distributors of innocuous substances like sugar and yeast.

In the earlier case, *Falcone*, the sellers' knowledge of the illegal use of the goods was insufficient by itself to make the sellers participants in a conspiracy with the distillers who bought from them. Such knowledge fell short of proof of a conspiracy, and evidence on the volume of sales was too vague to support a jury finding that respondents knew of the conspiracy from the size of the sales alone.

In the later case of *Direct Sales*, the conviction of a drug wholesaler for conspiracy to violate federal narcotic laws was affirmed on a showing that it had actively promoted the sale of morphine sulphate in quantity and had sold codefendant physician, who practiced in a small town in South Carolina, more than 300 times his normal requirements of the drug, even though it had been repeatedly warned of the dangers of unrestricted sales of the drug. The court contrasted the restricted goods involved in *Direct Sales* with the articles of free commerce involved in *Falcone*: "All articles of commerce may be put to illegal ends," said the court. "But all do not have inherently the same susceptibility to harmful and illegal use. * * * This difference is important for two purposes. One is for making certain that the seller knows the buyer's intended illegal use. The other is to show that by the sale he intends to further, promote and cooperate in it. This intent, when given effect by overt act, is the gist of conspiracy. While it is not identical with mere knowledge that another purposes unlawful action, it is not unrelated to such knowledge. * * * The step from knowledge to intent and agreement may be taken. There is more than suspicion, more than knowledge, acquiescence, carelessness, indifference, lack of concern. There is informed and interested cooperation, stimulation, instigation. And there is also a 'stake in the venture' which, even if it may not be essential, is not irrelevant to the question of conspiracy." (319 U.S. at 710–713, 63 S. Ct. at 1269–1270.)

While *Falcone* and *Direct Sales* may not be entirely consistent with each other in their full implications, they do provide us with a framework for the criminal liability of a supplier of lawful goods or services put to unlawful use. Both the element of *knowledge* of the illegal use of the goods or services and the element of *intent* to further that use must be present in order to make the supplier a participant in a criminal conspiracy.

Proof of *knowledge* is ordinarily a question of fact and requires no extended discussion in the present case. The knowledge of the supplier was sufficiently established when Lauria admitted he knew some of his customers were prostitutes and admitted he knew that Terry, an active subscriber to his service, was a prostitute. In the face of these admissions he could scarcely claim to have relied on the normal assumption an operator of a business or service is entitled to make, that his customers are behaving themselves in the eyes of the law. Because Lauria knew in fact that some of his customers were prostitutes, it is a legitimate inference he knew they were subscribing to his answering service for illegal business purposes and were using his service to make assignations for prostitution. On this record we think the prosecution is entitled to claim positive knowledge by Lauria of the use of his service to facilitate the business of prostitution.

The more perplexing issue in the case is the sufficiency of proof of *intent* to further the criminal enterprise. The element of intent may be proved either by direct evidence, or by evidence of circumstances from which an intent to further a criminal enterprise by supplying lawful goods or services may be inferred. Direct evidence of participation, such as advice from the supplier of legal goods or services to the user of those goods or services on their use for illegal purposes, such evidence as appeared in a companion case we decide today, People v. Roy, 59 Cal.Rptr. 636, provides the simplest case. When the intent to further and promote the criminal enterprise comes from the lips of the supplier himself, ambiguities of inference from circumstance need not trouble us. But in cases where direct proof of complicity is lacking, intent to further the conspiracy must be derived from the sale itself and its surrounding circumstances in order to establish the supplier's express or tacit agreement to join the conspiracy.

In the case at bench the prosecution argues that since Lauria knew his customers were using his service for illegal purposes but nevertheless continued to furnish it to them, he must have intended to assist them in carrying out their illegal activities. Thus through a union of knowledge and intent he became a participant in a criminal conspiracy. Essentially, the People argue that knowledge alone of the continuing use of his telephone facilities for criminal purposes provided a sufficient basis from which his intent to participate in those criminal activities could be inferred.

In examining precedents in this field we find that sometimes, but not always, the criminal intent of the supplier may be inferred from his knowledge of the unlawful use made of the product he supplies. Some consideration of characteristic patterns may be helpful.

1. Intent may be inferred from knowledge, when the purveyor of legal goods for illegal use has acquired a stake in the venture. (United States v. Falcone, 2 Cir., 109 F.2d 579, 581.) For example, in Regina v. Thomas (1957), 2 All.E.R. 181, 342, a prosecution for living off the earnings of prostitution, the evidence showed that the accused, knowing the woman to be a convicted prostitute, agreed to let her have the use of his room between the hours of 9 p. m. and 2 a. m. for a charge of £3 a night. The Court of Criminal Appeal refused an appeal from the conviction, holding that when the accused rented a room at a grossly inflated rent to a prostitute for the purpose of carrying on her trade, a jury could find he was living on the earnings of prostitution.

In the present case, no proof was offered of inflated charges for the telephone answering services furnished the codefendants.

2. Intent may be inferred from knowledge, when no legitimate use for the goods or services exists. The leading California case is People v. McLaughlin, 111 Cal.App.2d 781, 245 P.2d 1076, in which the court upheld a conviction of the suppliers of horse-racing information by wire for conspiracy to promote bookmaking, when it had been established that wire-service information had no other use than

to supply information needed by bookmakers to conduct illegal gambling operations.

In Rex v. Delaval (1763) 3 Burr. 1434, 97 E.R. 913, the charge was unlawful conspiracy to remove a girl from the control of Bates, a musician to whom she was bound as an apprentice, and place her in the hands of Sir Francis Delaval for the purpose of prostitution. Lord Mansfield not only upheld the charges against Bates and Sir Francis, but also against Fraine, the attorney who drew up the indentures of apprenticeship transferring custody of the girl from Bates to Sir Francis. Fraine, said Lord Mansfield, must have known that Sir Francis had no facilities for teaching music to apprentices so that it was impossible for him to have been ignorant of the real intent of the transaction.

In Shaw v. Director of Public Prosecutions, [1962] A.C. 220, the defendant was convicted of conspiracy to corrupt public morals and of living on the earnings of prostitution when he published a directory consisting almost entirely of advertisements of the names, addresses, and specialized talents of prostitutes. Publication of such a directory, said the court, could have no legitimate use and serve no other purpose than to advertise the professional services of the prostitutes whose advertisements appeared in the directory. The publisher could be deemed a participant in the profits from the business activities of his principal advertisers.

Other services of a comparable nature come to mind: the manufacturer of crooked dice and marked cards who sells his product to gambling casinos; the tipster who furnishes information on the movement of law enforcement officers to known lawbreakers. (Cf. Jackson v. State of Texas, 164 Tex.Cr.R. 276, 298 S.W.2d 837 (1957), where the furnisher of signaling equipment used to warn gamblers of the police was convicted of aiding the equipping of a gambling place.) In such cases the supplier must necessarily have an intent to further the illegal enterprise since there is no known honest use for his goods.

However, there is nothing in the furnishing of telephone answering service which would necessarily imply assistance in the performance of illegal activities. Nor is any inference to be derived from the use of an answering service by women, either in any particular volume of calls, or outside normal working hours. Night-club entertainers, registered nurses, faith healers, public stenographers, photographic models, and free lance substitute employees, provide examples of women in legitimate occupations whose employment might cause them to receive a volume of telephone calls at irregular hours.

3. Intent may be inferred from knowledge, when the volume of business with the buyer is grossly disproportionate to any legitimate demand, or when sales for illegal use amount to a high proportion of the seller's total business. In such cases an intent to participate in

the illegal enterprise may be inferred from the quantity of the business done. For example, in *Direct Sales*, supra, the sale of narcotics to a rural physician in quantities 300 times greater than he would have normal use for provided potent evidence of an intent to further the illegal activity. In the same case the court also found significant the fact that the wholesaler had attracted as customers a disproportionately large group of physicians who had been convicted of violating the Harrison Act. In Shaw v. Director of Public Prosecutions, [1962] A.C. 220, almost the entire business of the directory came from prostitutes.

No evidence of any unusual volume of business with prostitutes was presented by the prosecution against Lauria.

Inflated charges, the sale of goods with no legitimate use, sales in inflated amounts, each may provide a fact of sufficient moment from which the intent of the seller to participate in the criminal enterprise may be inferred. In such instances participation by the supplier of legal goods to the illegal enterprise may be inferred because in one way or another the supplier has acquired a special interest in the operation of the illegal enterprise. His intent to participate in the crime of which he has knowledge may be inferred from the existence of his special interest.

Yet there are cases in which it cannot reasonably be said that the supplier has a stake in the venture or has acquired a special interest in the enterprise, but in which he has been held liable as a participant on the basis of knowledge alone. Some suggestion of this appears in *Direct Sales*, supra, where both the knowledge of the illegal use of the drugs and the intent of the supplier to aid that use were inferred. In Regina v. Bainbridge (1959), 3 W.L.R. 656 (CCA 6), a supplier of oxygen-cutting equipment to one known to intend to use it to break into a bank was convicted as an accessory to the crime. In Sykes v. Director of Public Prosecutions [1962] A.C. 528, one having knowledge of the theft of 100 pistols, 4 submachine guns, and 1960 rounds of ammunition was convicted of misprision of felony for failure to disclose the theft to the public authorities. It seems apparent from these cases that a supplier who furnishes equipment which he *knows* will be used to commit a serious crime may be deemed from that knowledge alone to have intended to produce the result. Such proof may justify an inference that the furnisher intended to aid the execution of the crime and that he thereby became a participant. For instance, we think the operator of a telephone answering service with positive knowledge that his service was being used to facilitate the extortion of ransom, the distribution of heroin, or the passing of counterfeit money who continued to furnish the service with knowledge of its use, might be chargeable on knowledge alone with participation in a scheme to extort money, to distribute narcotics, or to pass counterfeit money. The same result would follow the seller of gasoline who knew the buyer was using his product to make Molotov cocktails for terroristic use.

Logically, the same reasoning could be extended to crimes of every description. Yet we do not believe an inference of intent drawn from knowledge of criminal use properly applies to the less serious crimes classified as misdemeanors. The duty to take positive action to dissociate oneself from activities helpful to violations of the criminal law is far stronger and more compelling for felonies than it is for misdemeanors or petty offenses. In this respect, as in others, the distinction between felonies and misdemeanors, between more serious and less serious crime, retains continuing vitality. In historically the most serious felony, treason, an individual with knowledge of the treason can be prosecuted for concealing and failing to disclose it. (Pen.Code, § 38; 18 U.S.Code, § 2382.) In other felonies, both at common law and under the criminal laws of the United States, an individual knowing of the commission of a felony is criminally liable for concealing it and failing to make it known to proper authority. (4 Blackstone 121; Sykes v. Director of Public Prosecutions [1962] A.C. 528; 18 U.S.Code, § 4.) But this crime, known as misprision of felony, has always been limited to knowledge and concealment of felony and has never extended to misdemeanor. A similar limitation is found in the criminal liability of an accessory, which is restricted to aid in the escape of a principal who has committed or been charged with a *felony*. (Pen.Code, § 32). We believe the distinction between the obligations arising from knowledge of a felony and those arising from knowledge of a misdemeanor continues to reflect basic human feelings about the duties owed by individuals to society. Heinous crime must be stamped out, and its suppression is the responsibility of all. Backun v. United States, 4 Cir., 112 F.2d 635, 636, 637. Venial crime and crime not evil in itself present less of a danger to society, and perhaps the benefits of their suppression through the modern equivalent of the posse, the hue and cry, the informant, and the citizen's arrest, are outweighed by the disruption to everyday life brought about by amateur law enforcement and private officiousness in relatively inconsequential delicts which do not threaten our basic security. The subject has been summarized in an English text on the criminal law: "Failure to reveal a felony to the authorities is now authoritatively determined to be misprision of felony, which is a common-law misdemeanor; misprision of treason is punishable with imprisonment for life. * * * No offence is committed in failing to disclose a misdemeanor. * * *

" 'To require everyone, without distinction, as to the nature and degree of the offence, to become an accuser, would be productive of inconvenience in exposing numbers to penal prosecutions, multiplying criminal charges, and engendering private dissension. It may sometimes be more convenient that offences should be passed over, than that all should indiscriminately be made the subject of prosecution;

and a law would be considered to be harsh and impolitic, if not unjust, which compelled every party injured by a criminal act, and, still more so, to compel everyone who happened to know that another had been so injured, to make a public disclosure of the circumstances. Here, therefore, there is reason for limiting the law against mere misprisions to the concealment of such crimes as are of an aggravated complexion.' " (Criminal Law, Glanville Williams (2d ed.) p. 423.)

With respect to misdemeanors, we conclude that positive knowledge of the supplier that his products or services are being used for criminal purposes does not, without more, establish an intent of the supplier to participate in the misdemeanors. With respect to felonies, we do not decide the converse, viz. that in all cases of felony knowledge of criminal use alone may justify an inference of the supplier's intent to participate in the crime. The implications of *Falcone* make the matter uncertain with respect to those felonies which are merely prohibited wrongs. See also Holman v. Johnson, 98 E.R. 1120, (1775) (sale and delivery of tea at Dunkirk known to be destined for smuggling into England not an illegal contract). But decision on this point is not compelled, and we leave the matter open.

From this analysis of precedent we deduce the following rule: the intent of a supplier who knows of the criminal use to which his supplies are put to participate in the criminal activity connected with the use of his supplies may be established by (1) direct evidence that he intends to participate, or (2) through an inference that he intends to participate based on, (a) his special interest in the activity, or (b) the aggravated nature of the crime itself.

When we review Lauria's activities in the light of this analysis, we find no proof that Lauria took any direct action to further, encourage, or direct the call-girl activities of his codefendants and we find an absence of circumstances from which his special interest in their activities could be inferred. Neither excessive charges for standardized services, or the furnishing of services without a legitimate use, nor any unusual quantity of business with call girls, are present. The offense which he is charged with furthering is a misdemeanor, a category of crime which has never been made a required subject of positive disclosure to public authority. Under these circumstances, although proof of Lauria's knowledge of the criminal activities of his patrons was sufficient to charge him with that fact, there was insufficient evidence that he intended to further their criminal activities, and hence insufficient proof of his participation in a criminal conspiracy with his codefendants to further prostitution. Since the conspiracy centered around the activities of Lauria's telephone answering service, the charges against his codefendants likewise fail for want of proof.

In absolving Lauria of complicity in a criminal conspiracy we do not wish to imply that the public authorities are without remedies to combat modern manifestations of the world's oldest profession. Licensing of telephone answering services under the police power, together with the revocation of licenses for the toleration of prostitution, is a possible civil remedy. The furnishing of telephone answering service in aid of prostitution could be made a crime. (Cf. Pen. Code, § 316, which makes it a misdemeanor to let an apartment with knowledge of its use for prostitution.) Other solutions will doubtless occur to vigilant public authorities if the problem of call-girl activity needs further suppression.

The order is affirmed.

MODEL PENAL CODE, COMMENT TO 5.03, 107–10 *

(Tent. Draft No. 10, 1960).

The Requirement of Purpose. The purpose requirement is crucial to the resolution of the difficult problems presented when a charge of conspiracy is leveled against a person whose relationship to a criminal plan is essentially peripheral. Typical is the case of the person who sells sugar to the producers of illicit whiskey. He may have little interest in the success of the distilling operation and be motivated mainly by the desire to make the normal profit of an otherwise lawful sale. To be criminally liable, of course, he must at least have knowledge of the use to which the materials are being put, but the difficult issue presented is whether knowingly facilitating the commission of a crime ought to be sufficient, absent a true purpose to advance the criminal end. In the case of vendors conflicting interests are also involved: that of the vendors in freedom to engage in gainful and otherwise lawful activities without policing their vendees, and that of the community in preventing behavior that facilitates the commission of crimes. The decisions are in conflict, although many of those requiring purpose properly emphasize that it can be inferred from such circumstances as, for example, quantity sales, the seller's initiative or encouragement, continuity of the relationship, and the contraband nature of the materials sold. The considerations are the same whether the charge be conspiracy or complicity in the substantive crime, and the Institute has resolved them, in the complicity provisions of the Code, in favor of requiring a purpose to advance the criminal end. Under the proposed Draft, the same purpose requirement that governs complicity is essential for conspiracy: the actor must have "the purpose of promoting or facilitating" the commission of the crime.

The requirement of purpose would also play a crucial role in the case where a charge of conspiracy is based on membership in an organization having both lawful and criminal objectives, as in the Communist cases. The defendant's membership and dues may encourage and assist the organization in pursuing all its objects, legal and illegal. He would not be guilty of conspiracy, however, unless he had the purpose of promoting or facilitating the attainment of a criminal objective. Of course, knowledge of that objective and conscious assistance may justify an inference of such purpose, but they would not be independently sufficient to establish liability.

* * *

It is worth noting, further, that as related to those elements of substantive crimes that consist of proscribed conduct or undesirable results of conduct, the Draft requires purposeful behavior for guilt of conspiracy, regardless of the state of mind required by the definition of the substantive crime. If the crime is defined in terms of prohibited conduct, such as the sale of narcotics, the actor's purpose must be to promote or facilitate the engaging in such conduct by himself or another. If it is defined in terms of a result of conduct, such as homicide, his purpose must be to promote or facilitate the production of that result.

Thus, it would not be sufficient, as it is under the attempt draft, if the actor only believed that the result would be produced but did not consciously plan or desire to produce it. For example—to use the same illustration as the comments on attempt—if two persons plan to destroy a building by detonating a bomb, though they know and believe that there are inhabitants in the building who will be killed by the explosion, they are nevertheless guilty only of a conspiracy to destroy the building and not of a conspiracy to kill the inhabitants. While this result may seem unduly restrictive from the viewpont of the completed crime, it is necessitated by the extremely preparatory behavior that may be involved in conspiracy. Had the crime been completed or had the preparation progressed even to the stage of an attempt, the result would be otherwise. As to the attempt, knowledge or belief that the inhabitants would be killed would suffice. As to the completed crime, the complicity draft covers the matter, despite its general requirement of a purpose to promote or facilitate the commission of the crime, by the special provision of Section 2.06(4). This provides that where causing a particular result is an element of a crime, a person is an accomplice in the crime if he was an accomplice in the behavior that caused the result and shared the same purpose or knowledge with respect to the result that is required by the definition of the crime.

A fortiori, where recklessness or negligently suffices for the actor's culpability with respect to a result element of a substantive crime—where, for example, homicide through negligence is made criminal—there could not be a conspiracy to commit that crime. This should be distinguished, however, from a crime defined in terms of conduct that creates a risk of harm, such as reckless driving or driving above a certain speed limit. In this situation the conduct rather than any result it may produce is the element of the crime, and it would suffice for guilt of conspiracy that the actor's purpose is to promote or facilitate such conduct—for example, if he urged the driver of the car to go faster and faster.

3. LIABILITY FOR CRIMES OF CO-CONSPIRATORS

In addition to its function as a substantive crime, conspiracy may also serve as a means for making all members of the venture liable for crimes committed by one of their number. The leading case adopting the doctrine which accomplishes this result (the "Pinkerton Rule") is Pinkerton v. United States, 328 U.S. 640, 66 S.Ct. 1180, 90 L.Ed. 1489 (1946). Walter and Daniel Pinkerton were convicted of criminal conspiracy to violate the United States Internal Revenue Code and of a number of substantive violations of that Code. There was no evidence tending to show that Daniel participated in the commission of the offenses of which he was convicted. The jury had not been instructed on his potential liability as an aider or abettor but rather had been told that he could be found guilty of crimes committed by Walter if at the time of the offenses both were parties to a criminal conspiracy and Walter committed the offenses in furtherance of this conspiracy. Upholding the convictions, the United States Supreme Court explained:

> We have here a continuous conspiracy. There is here no evidence of the affirmative action on the part of Daniel which is necessary to establish his withdrawal from it. Hyde v. United States, 225 U.S. 347, 369, 32 S.Ct. 793, 803, 56 L.Ed. 1114, Ann.Cas.1914A, 614. As stated in that case, "having joined in an unlawful scheme, having constituted agents for its performance, scheme and agency to be continuous until full fruition be secured, until he does some act to disavow or defeat the purpose he is in no situation to claim the delay of the law. As the offense has not been terminated or accomplished, he is still offending. And we think consciously offending,—offending as certainly, as we have said, as at the first moment of his confederation, and consciously, through every moment of its existence." Id., 225 U.S. at page 369, 32 S.Ct. at page 803. And so long as the partnership in crime continues, the partners act for each other in carrying it forward. It is settled that "an overt act of one partner may be the act of all without any new agreement specifically directed to that act." United States v. Kissel, 218 U.S. 601, 608, 31 S.Ct. 124, 126, 54 L.Ed. 1168. Motive or intent

> may be proved by the acts or declarations of some of the conspirators in furtherance of the common objective. Wiborg v. United States, 163 U.S. 632, 657, 658, 16 S.Ct. 1127, 1137, 1197, 46 L.Ed. 289. A scheme to use the mails to defraud, which is joined in by more than one person, is a conspiracy. Yet all members are responsible, though only one did the mailing. The governing principle is the same when the substantive offense is committed by one of the conspirators in furtherance of the unlawful project. The criminal intent to do the act is established by the formation of the conspiracy. Each conspirator instigated the commission of the crime. The unlawful agreement contemplated precisely what was done. It was formed for the purpose. The act done was in execution of the enterprise. The rule which holds responsible one who counsels, procures, or commands another to commit a crime is founded on the same principle. That principle is recognized in the law of conspiracy when the overt act of one partner in crime is attributable to all. An overt act is an essential ingredient of the crime of conspiracy under § 37 of the Criminal Code, 18 U.S.C. § 88, 18 U.S.C.A. § 88. If that can be supplied by the act of one conspirator, we fail to see why the same or other acts in furtherance of the conspiracy are likewise not attributable to the others for the purpose of holding them responsible for the substantive offense.
>
> A different case would arise if the substantive offense committed by one of the conspirators was not in fact done in furtherance of the conspiracy, did not fall within the scope of the unlawful project, or was merely a part of the ramifications of the plan which could not be reasonably foreseen as a necessary or natural consequence of the unlawful agreement. But as we read this record, that is not this case.

328 U.S. at 646–48, 66 S.Ct. at 1183–84, 90 L.Ed. at 1496–97.

The Pinkerton Rule has not been universally accepted. It was rejected by the Supreme Judicial Court of Massachusetts in the following language:

> The rule in this jurisdiction is to the contrary. To be liable for the substantive offense, a conspirator must participate or aid in the commission of it. * * * Long ago this court cautioned that the proof of a conspiracy, without more, did not justify a finding that a conspirator had committed the offense which was the object of the conspiracy. * * * "The fact of the conspiracy being proved against the prisoner is to be weighed as evidence in the case having a tendency to prove that the prisoner aided, but it is not *in*

> *itself* to be taken as a legal presumption of his having aided unless disproved by him."
>
> If the rule were otherwise, the fundamental distinction between a substantive offense and a conspiracy to commit that offense would be ignored. Each is a separate and distinct offense and each may be separately punished * * * Punishment is imposed for entering into the combination. This is not the same thing as participating in the substantive offense which was the object of the conspiracy. While it has been said that a conspiracy is a "partnership in crime" * * *, that metaphor should not be pressed too far. It does not follow that such a partnership is governed by the same principles of vicarious liability as would apply in civil cases. Our criminal law is founded on the principle that guilt, for the more serious offenses, is personal, not vicarious. One is punished for his own blameworthy conduct, not that of others.

Commonwealth v. Stasiun, 349 Mass. 38, 47–48, 206 N.E.2d 672, 678–79 (1965).

STATE v. STEIN

Supreme Court of New Jersey, 1976.
70 N.J. 369, 360 A.2d 347.

CONFORD, P. J. A. D., Temporarily Assigned.

This appeal emanates from a petition for certification by defendant and a cross-petition by the State, both granted by the court to review a judgment of the Appellate Division partly affirming and partly reversing a series of convictions of defendant arising from a number of connected occurrences. * * *

The evidence adduced on the State's case indicates that defendant, a Trenton lawyer, suggested to a certain underworld figure that the house of one Dr. Gordon in Trenton was a likely target for a successful breaking and entering or burglary, as large amounts of cash were kept there. Defendant expected to share in the gains. As a result, there was an armed robbery at that home about a year later. While attempting to evade the police, who had been alerted to the affair, the perpetrators abducted members of the family and injured two policemen. They were caught and arrested. * * *

[Defendant was charged with and convicted of conspiracy to steal currency, armed robbery, assault with an offensive weapon on Edith Gordon, assault with an offensive weapon on Shelly Gordon, kidnapping, kidnapping while armed, and assault on a police officer. He was] sentenced concurrently to terms of imprisonment aggregating 30 years to 30 years and one day.

* * *

On March 17, 1972 Testa and Stasio, impersonating police officers, gained entrance to the Trenton home of Dr. Arnold Gordon. The pair produced pistols and demanded money and jewelry from Gordon. While Testa and Stasio obtained $470 from Gordon and bound him and his wife Edith, a maid telephoned the police. When the police arrived, the robbers took Edith and her 14 year old daughter Shelly from the house at gunpoint as hostages and attempted an escape at high speed in a getaway car. A chase ensued. Ultimately, the getaway car crashed into a police car barrier, seriously injuring two police officers. The police arrested Testa and Stasio and freed Edith and Shelly. * * *

Subsequent investigation aroused the suspicions of the county prosecutor as to the possible involvement of others in the crime. Testa testified before the grand jury as follows: In September 1971 Joe Bradley introduced him to Pontani. Pontani gave Testa particulars about the layout of the Gordon home. Pontani wanted to be sure the children were not in the house at the time of the robbery. Pontani, Testa and Bradley met three times between September and October 18, 1971, the date of Bradley's death. Tassone was present on a few occasions. Testa stated that from the outset it was intended that the crime would be an armed robbery. Although burglary had been initially discussed, it was discarded as an impossibility. After Bradley's death, Pontani spoke to a lawyer who guaranteed the amount of money that would be in the house, the movements of the family and the layout of the telephone system. Pontani had indicated that the lawyer was "Jewish" and a close friend of the Gordons. Testa was present when Pontani telephoned the lawyer. The latter advised Pontani that $200,000 would be found in the house.

* * *

[The investigation led to defendant, who subsequently gave police a statement. In this statement,] Stein gave his age, 46, and stated that he was an attorney who was also engaged in real estate development. He became involved with Pontani as an attorney. Stein was introduced to Pontani by a woman, Wilson Marcello. Stein knew that Pontani was a professional secondstory man who was in financial difficulty. Stein was also in financial straits. It was suggested that if they could locate a home where there was cash, Pontani would burglarize the home. In the course of a casual "almost flippant" conversation on the subject, Stein ventured some names from the area in which he resided, including that of Dr. Gordon. Stein knew that Gordon, a dentist, took cash home. He estimated the amount at less than $10,000 but he did not know where the money was kept. During the course of subsequent conversations over a long period of time, Stein, in response to Pontani's questions, offered such information as the number of people in the Gordon household and where and when the children went to school. Although there was no specific discussion as to Stein's share of the money to be stolen, Stein anticipated that he would participate therein. The attempted robbery occurred anywhere from 9 months to a year after the last conversation on the matter. After two months Stein assumed that no crime would occur. However, he did nothing in the interim to prevent it from happening. After the robbery and other crimes took place, Pontani advised Stein by telephone that the people who had tried to pull off the job had no right to do it, since "they had really in effect stolen information that he had given to another party [Joe Bradley] and that he had abandoned the idea long since." Pontani insisted he had nothing to do with it. Stein had assumed that any attempted larceny would be in the form of breaking and entering while the Gordons were away, not a "personal confrontation." He gave Pontani the information as to when the Gordons were on vacation. * * *

The Appellate Division reversed the convictions of the defendant on the substantive charges of assault with an offensive weapon (against Edith and Shelly Gordon), kidnapping, kidnapping while armed and assaults on a police officer. It sustained that of armed robbery. The former were deemed not within the scope of the original conspiracy * * *. We review this ruling pursuant to our grant of the State's cross-petition for certification.

The question as to the criminal responsibility of a conspirator for the commission by others of substantive offenses having some causal connection with the conspiracy but not in the contemplation of the conspirator has been a matter of considerable debate and controversy. Here there is no question but that Stein did not actually contemplate any criminal consequence of his "tip" to Pontani beyond a burglary and theft of money from the Gordon home. The trial court applied the conventionally stated rule that each conspirator is responsible for "anything done by his confederates which follows incidentally in the execution of the common design as one of its probable and natural consequences, even though it was not intended as part of the original design", citing 15A C.J.S. Conspiracy § 74 at 825; and see Pinkerton v. United States, 328 U.S. 640, 66 S.Ct. 1180, 90 L.Ed. 1489 (1956) * * *.

We regard the rule as just stated to be sound and viable. * * * We hold it represents the law of this State.

It remains to apply the rule to the instant fact situation. Ordinarily the matter of factual application of the rule would be submitted to the jury under appropriate instructions. Here the matter was for the trial judge in the first instance as fact-finder. The Appellate Division found correct the trial ruling that the armed robbery was within the scope of the conspiracy to steal currency from the Gordon home. We are in agreement. The robbery was a "natural" or "probable" consequence of the conspiracy. But the Appellate Division concluded that the assaults with an offensive weapon on the wife and daughter of Dr. Gordon were "not connected with the robbery as such" but "with the preliminary acts of taking the Gordons as hostages and the eventual kidnappings" and therefore "not fairly * * * part of the conspiratorial agreement". The assault convictions were therefore set aside.

We are not in complete agreement with this last determination. The brandishing of handguns by the robbers when they first encountered Dr. and Mrs. Gordon in the house was clearly a foreseeable event in the course of an unlawful invasion of the house for criminal purposes by armed men. * * * Thus the assault conviction as to Mrs. Gordon should not have been set aside as too remote from the conspiracy.

As to the charge of assault with an offensive weapon on Shelly Gordon (daughter of the Gordons), since the evidence indicates that offense occurred only at the time of the attempted escape from the police, its disposition depends on the determination as to the other associated charges, discussed next below.

Liability of the defendant for the kidnapping, kidnapping while armed and assaults on a police officer presents a much closer question. The Appellate Division held that these substantive acts were "offenses committed by the criminals effecting the conspiratorial specific crime after that crime had been committed, as part of a plan to flee when it became evident that they were about to be apprehended" and that defendant could not be charged therefor. On balance, we are satisfied that this is a correct result, particularly in relation to the kidnapping phases of the episode. This holding will also apply to the reversal by the Appellate Division of the conviction for assault with an offensive weapon on Shelly Gordon. However, we rest our concurrence with the Appellate Division not on the ground that the substantive offenses took place subsequent to the commission of the crime conspired or that the offenses were part of a plan to flee, but rather that it would be unreasonable for a fact-finder to find as a fact beyond a reasonable doubt that they were necessary, natural or probable consequences of the conspiracy, having in mind the unique fact-complex presented.

NOTES AND QUESTIONS

1. How does liability for the crimes of coconspirators differ from liability as an aider and abettor or an incitor, discussed in Chapter III.D., supra? Can one be liable for the crimes of a coconspirator even if one has not provided sufficient or direct enough assistance to the coconspirator to be liable as an aider or abettor? if one lacks the state of mind necessary for liability as an aider or abettor? An affirmative answer to these questions is suggested by State v. Trocodaro, 36 Ohio App.2d 1, 65 O.O.2d 1, 301 N.E.2d 898 (1973). Trocodaro and two others agreed to abduct the victim and rob her. Following the robbery, one of the other persons took the victim to a field and killed her. Trocodaro was convicted of the killing. On

appeal, he argued that he could not be convicted in the absence of proof that he had the state of mind necessary for murder or at least that he knew the coconspirator who actually killed the victim had the required state of mind. The court acknowledged that ordinarily an aider or abettor could not be convicted in the absence of such knowledge or intent. But it nevertheless upheld Trocodaro's conviction on the basis of liability for the crimes of coconspirators:

> We hold that where, as here, there has been found to be a criminal conspiracy, it need not be proved that an aider or abettor also possessed those individual elements needed to establish the crime against the perpetrator of the act.

36 Ohio App.2d at 7, 301 N.E.2d at 903.

2. There is general agreement that a conspirator who effectively withdraws from the conspiracy before the commission of a substantive offense by a coconspirator thereby avoids liability for that offense. But what is required for an effective withdrawal?

One authoritative source has stated that "virtually all courts" have demanded for an effective withdrawal that a defendant have committed an affirmative act performed in such manner as would be sufficient to inform a reasonable person of his withdrawal and that such notice be given to all other members of the conspiracy. The authors also state that the withdrawal be made early enough to give the other members of the scheme an opportunity to abandon the venture. See W. LaFave and A. Scott, Criminal Law 486 (1972). But a recent decision by the Supreme Court suggests that this statement may not be entirely correct.

In United States v. United States Gypsum Co., 438 U.S. 422, 98 S.Ct. 2864, 57 L.Ed.2d 854 (1978) defendants were charged with conspiracy to restrain trade in violation of section 1 of the Sherman Act, 15 U.S.C.A. § 1. In light of the five year statute of limitations, no conviction would be possible if the crime terminated before December 27, 1968. During trial, defendant introduced evidence that vigorous price competition existed prior to December 27, 1968, and urged that this established that they had withdrawn from any conspiracy before the critical date. Instructing the jury on defendants' theory, the trial judge told the jurors that withdrawal had to be established by either affirmative notice to each other member of the conspiracy or by disclosure of the illegal enterprise to law enforcement officials. The defendants requested a more expansive instruction which would have specifically permitted the jury to consider resumption of competitive activity, such as intensified price cutting or price wars, as affirmative action showing a withdrawal from the conspiracy; the request was denied. On appeal, the Supreme Court held the instructions on withdrawal to be reversible error:

> The charge, fairly read, limited the jury's consideration to only two circumscribed and arguably impractical methods of demonstrating withdrawal from the conspiracy. [In a footnote the Court commented, "In this case the obligation to notify 'each other member' of the charged conspiracy would be a manageable task; in other situations all 'other' members might not be readily identifiable."] Nothing that we have been able to find in the case law

> suggests, much less commands, that such confining blinders be placed on the jury's freedom to consider evidence regarding the continuing participation of alleged conspirators in the charged conspiracy. Affirmative acts inconsistent with the object of the conspiracy and communicated in a manner reasonably calculated to reach co-conspirators have generally been regarded as sufficient to establish withdrawal or abandonment.

422 U.S. at 464–65, 98 S.Ct. at 2887, 57 L.Ed.2d at 886. Mr. Justice Rehnquist dissented in part, disagreeing with that portion of the Court's opinion that seemed to approve an expansive instruction with respect to withdrawal from a conspiracy. 422 U.S. 471, 98 S.Ct. 2890, 57 L.Ed.2d 890 (1978) (Rehnquist, J., concurring in part and dissenting in part).

Can *United States Gypsum* be relied upon as stating a standard for determining whether withdrawal has become effective so as to preclude liability for the crimes of coconspirators? Withdrawal, of course, is relevant for many purposes other than determining such liability; see the discussion in note 4 at page 328, supra. One commentator has observed that courts have not varied the requirements for an effective withdrawal with the context in which the matter is raised. See Developments in the Law—Criminal Conspiracy, 72 Harv.L.Rev. 922, 959 (1959). The commentator suggests, however, that "a uniform definition does not seem appropriate in all situations." Id. If the standard applied in *United States Gypsum* is appropriate for determining whether a defendant withdrew in sufficient time to being the period of limitations running as to him, does this mean it is also appropriate for determining whether he should no longer be liable for the crime of his former (?) partners?

V. SPECIFIC OFFENSES: CRIMES AGAINST PROPERTY

A. LARCENY

Larceny involves the misappropriation or attempted misappropriation of property without any threat of harm to the person of another. At common law it consisted of the taking and asportation (carrying away) of personal property in the possession of another against the will of the other and by means of a trespass with the intent to permanently deprive the other of his interests in the property. Modern codes generally retain the offense as defined at common law, either as the separate offense of larceny or as one form of theft. The following materials illustrate the meaning commonly given the various elements in the definition of larceny. The third case in the section, State v. Gordon, involves a conviction for robbery rather than larceny. But as the court indicates in the opinion, the intent required for robbery is the same as that demanded by larceny. The case should be read, therefore, as addressing the meaning of "intent to steal" as required by both crimes.

STATE v. CARSWELL

Supreme Court of North Carolina, 1978.
296 N.C. 101, 249 S.E.2d 427.

[Defendant was convicted of felonious larceny.]

The State's evidence tended to show the following:

On the morning of 18 April 1976, Donald Ray Morgan was at the Day's Inn Motel where he was employed as a security guard. With him was Richard Strickland, a helper, and Mrs. Strickland, Richard's mother, who had brought her son some food. The motel was not in use at that time as it was still under construction. Upon inspection of the premises that morning, Mr. Morgan discovered that five or six rooms had been broken into during the night. In one of these, Room 158, the window air conditioner had been pried away from the base on which it rested in the bottom of the window, but it had not been removed.

Mr. Morgan asked Mrs. Strickland to stay at the motel while he called to report the incident to the Sheriff's Department. While he was gone, a pickup truck pulled into the motel with three people in it, one of them being the defendant. They wanted to get into the motel building and claimed that they were sent there by their boss. They left after Mrs. Strickland would not let them in.

Instead of relocking the doors that had been broken into, Mr. Morgan stayed at the motel and guarded the rooms from a point on the balcony of the second level some fifty to seventy-five feet away. Around 10:30 p. m. that night, the defendant and another man walked onto the premises of Day's Inn Motel from some nearby woods and entered Room 158. Through the window running across the entire front of the room, Mr. Morgan saw the two men take the air conditioner off its stand in the window and put it on the floor. The unit was moved approximately four to six inches toward the door.

After setting the air conditioner on the floor, the men left Room 158. Mr. Morgan stopped them as they appeared to be entering another room. The guard sent Mrs. Strickland, who again had come to the motel that night with food for her son, to the nearby Holiday Inn to call the Sheriff's Department.

COPELAND, Justice.

The Court of Appeals held that the movement of the air conditioner in this case was an insufficient taking and asportation to constitute a case of larceny against the defendant. Because we believe that there was enough evidence to send the larceny charge to the jury, we reverse the Court of Appeals on this point and reinstate the judgment of * * * [conviction].

* * *

Larceny has been defined as "a wrongful taking and carrying away of the personal property of another without his consent, * * * with intent to deprive the owner of his property and to appropriate it to the taker's use fraudulently." State v. Griffin, 239 N.C. 41, 45, 79 S.E.2d 230, 232 (1953). "A bare removal from the place in which he found the goods, though the thief does not quite make off with them, is a sufficient asportation, or carrying away." 4 W. Blackstone, Commentaries 231.

In State v. Green, 81 N.C. 560 (1879), the defendant unlocked his employer's safe and completely removed a drawer containing money. He was stopped before any of the money was taken from the drawer. This Court found these actions sufficient to constitute asportation of the money, and we upheld the larceny conviction.

The movement of the air conditioner in this case off its window base and four to six inches toward the door clearly is "a bare removal from the place in which the thief found [it]." The Court of Appeals apparently agreed; however, it correctly recognized that there is a taking element in larceny in addition to the asportation requirement. 4 W. Blackstone, supra at 231. See also State v. Parker, 262 N.C. 679, 138 S.E.2d 496 (1964). The Court of Appeals [noted language in State v. Jackson, 65 N.C. 305, 308 (1871), requiring that the defendant have "for an instant the entire and absolute possession of" the property. It then reasoned:

"We do not believe that moving a heavy air conditioner approximately four to six inches was a sufficient taking and asportation to take this case to the jury on the charge of larceny. Our reading of the cases leads us to the conclusion that, even if only for an instant, there must be a complete severance of the object from the owner's possession, to such an extent that the defendant has absolute possession of it. The cases appear to have, in effect, merged the elements of taking and asportation, but here the problem with the State's case is that the evidence of asportation does not also constitute sufficient evidence of taking. Further, we note that the [cases in which convictions have been upheld] involved the slight movement of small objects * * *. [State v. Jones, 65 N.C. 395 (1871)], on the other hand, dealt with the turning of a barrel of turpentine from a standing position to its side; this was held to be an insufficient asportation, and clearly, we think, an insufficient taking. We do not believe that the result would have been different if the barrel had been moved a few inches while upright."]

This Court has defined "taking" in this context as the "severance of the goods from the possession of the owner." State v. Roper, 14 N.C. 473, 474 (1832). Thus, the accused must not only move the goods, but he must also have them in his possession, or under his control, even if only for an instant. This defendant picked the air conditioner up from its stand and laid it on the floor. This act was sufficient to put the object briefly under the control of the defendant, severed from the owner's possession.

In rare and somewhat comical situations, it is possible to have an asportation of an object without taking it, or gaining possession of it.

> "In a very famous case a rascal walking by a store lifted an overcoat from a dummy and endeavored to walk away with it. He soon discovered that the overcoat was secured by a chain and he did not succeed in breaking the chain. This was held not to be larceny because the rascal did not at any time have possession of the garment. He thought he did until he reached the end of the chain, but he was mistaken." R. Perkins, Criminal Law 222 (1957) (discussing People v. Meyer, 75 Cal. 383, 17 P. 431 (1888)).

The air conditioner in question was not permanently connected to the premises of Day's Inn Motel at the time of the crime. It had previously been pried up from its base; therefore, when defendant and his companion moved it, they had possession of it for that moment. Thus, there was sufficient evidence to take the larceny charge to the jury.

The defendant's and the Court of Appeals' reliance on State v. Jones, 65 N.C. 395 (1871), is misplaced. In that case, the defendant merely turned a large barrel of turpentine, that was standing on its head, over on its side. This Court held that shifting the position of an object without moving it from where it was found is insufficient asportation to support a larceny conviction. The facts of this case show that there was an actual removal of the air conditioner from its base in the window to a point on the floor four to six inches toward the door. Thus, *Jones* is not controlling.

For the reasons stated above * * * the larceny judgment [is] reinstated.

NOTES

1. The essential elements of larceny, the oldest and most important of the acquisition offenses, are that the offender, by trespass, takes and carries away another's personal property with intent to steal it. As *Carswell* makes clear, the taking (caption) and carrying away (asportation) of the property have traditionally been viewed as separate elements. The former refers to the perpetrator's exercise of control over the property, either directly or through an innocent third party, and the latter refers to some movement of the property, however slight, as part of the carrying away process. State v. Jones, discussed in *Carswell,* can be explained (and reconciled with *Carswell*) on the ground that the movement of the barrel in that case was not actually part of the process of carrying it away. The movement was at most part of the process of preparing to begin carrying the barrel from the place where it was located. As *Carswell* demonstrates, even in those jurisdictions which still require both caption and asportation, the distinction is relatively unimportant in practice.

2. The taking of the property must be "trespassory." If it is without the consent of the person from whom the property is taken, it is of course trespassory. But even a taking with permission is trespassory if the permission was obtained by means of misrepresentation. In such cases, there may be a problem as to whether the offense is larceny or false pretenses; see the discussion following *Pollard,* infra.

3. Larceny is a crime against possession. All that is necessary, therefore, is that the offender take the property from one who has a possessory interest superior to that of the offender. Thus it is larceny even to take property from one who has himself obtained the property by larceny. Moreover, one can commit larceny by taking his own property, as if one takes his automobile from the possession of a mechanic who has repaired it and as a result under local law has a lien on it which gives him the right to retain it until he is paid for the repairs.

4. Only personal property with some value and capable of being possessed can be the subject of larceny at common law. Thus land and things attached to it, or services cannot be the subject of larceny. The same is true of intangibles (such as access to the performance of a play) and documents and instruments, which are regarded as "merged" with the land or intangible rights they represented.

VIRGIN ISLANDS v. WILLIAMS

United States Court of Appeals for the Third Circuit, 1970.
424 F.2d 526.

HASTIE, Chief Judge. This case presents the question whether larceny as defined by the Virgin Islands Code can be committed without an intent to deprive the owner permanently of his property.

The five juvenile appellants have been convicted of petit larceny under 14 V.I.C. §§ 1081, 1084. It was stipulated at the beginning of the hearing that the defendants had taken five horses from a pasture in St. Croix, ridden them to another part of the island several miles away, returned them to the general area from which they had been taken and released them. One horse subsequently died of injuries sustained during this unauthorized excursion.

At the close of the prosecution's case and again after all the evidence had been presented, the defendants moved to dismiss the complaint on the basis that there was no proof of an intent to deprive the owners of the horses permanently. The court denied the motion ruling that the Virgin Islands Code does not require proof of such an intent to establish larceny.

Section 1081 of title 14, Virgin Islands Code, defines larceny as "* * * the unlawful taking, stealing, carrying, leading, or driving away the personal property of another." This definition contains no mention of any requisite intent. In these circumstances, the process of interpretation begins with the consideration that the specific intent to deprive the owner permanently of his property is an essential element of the crime of larceny at common law. Absent a clear indication of legislative purpose, we are reluctant to assume that the omission of any mention of intent in the statute which makes "larceny" a crime was intended to eliminate that important and long-accepted element from the crime. * * *

In the tradition of Anglo-American law the crime of larceny is a major felony and as such is not intended to cover the less serious wrong of temporary appropriation of another's property. In the Virgin Islands larceny is deemed such a serious crime that, if the value of the stolen property exceeds $100, the wrongdoer is subject to imprisonment for up to ten years. 14 V.I.C. § 1083. In these circumstances, as had been said at common law, a "momentary loss of possession is not what has been guarded against with such severe penalties. What the law means to prevent is the loss of it wholly and forever * * *." Holmes, The Common Law 71 (1881).

At least one situation of temporary appropriation of property is treated separately by the Virgin Islands Code, and less severe penalties are provided. The unauthorized use of a motor vehicle, however valuable, or bicycle with no intent permanently to deprive the owner of possession is a lesser crime, distinct from larceny. 14 V.I.C. § 1381. One convicted under that section "* * * shall be fined not more than $500 or imprisoned not more than 1 year, or both." We are unable to believe that the Territorial Legislature intended that the "joy-rider" who wrongfully takes even a valuable horse from its pasture for an unauthorized ride should be punishable ten times more severely than one who similarly appropriates an automobile.

If the legislature of the Virgin Islands determines, as it has for motor vehicles and bicycles, that the unauthorized temporary taking of horses is a sufficiently serious wrong, it may properly make such misappropriation criminal. But it has not yet done so.

The judgment will be reversed.

STATE v. GORDON

Supreme Judicial Court of Maine, 1974.
321 A.2d 352.

[Defendant was convicted by a jury of armed robbery and appeals from this conviction.]

One Edwin Strode, and defendant had escaped in Vermont from the custody of the authorities who had been holding them on a misdemeanor charge. In the escape defendant and Strode had acquired two hand guns and also a blue station wagon in which they had fled from Vermont through New Hampshire into Maine. Near Standish, Maine, the station wagon showed signs of engine trouble, and defendant and Strode began to look for another vehicle. They came to the yard of one Franklin Prout. In the yard was Prout's 1966 maroon Chevelle and defendant, who was operating the station wagon, drove it parallel to the Prout Chevelle. Observing that the keys were in the Chevelle, Strode left the station wagon and entered the Chevelle. At this time Prout came out of his house into the yard. Strode pointed a gun at him, and defendant and Strode then told Prout that they needed his automobile, were going to take it but they "would take care of it and see he [Prout] got it back as soon as possible." With defendant operating the station wagon and Strode the Chevelle, defendant and Strode left the yard and proceeded in the direction of Westbrook. Subsequently, the station wagon was abandoned in a sand pit, and defendant and Strode continued their flight in the Chevelle. A spectacular series of events followed—including the alleged assault (with intent to kill) upon Westbrook police officer, Stultz, a shoot-out on Main Street in Westbrook, and a high speed police chase, during which the Chevelle was driven off the road in the vicinity of the Maine Medical Center in Portland where it was abandoned, Strode and defendant having commandeered another automobile to resume their flight. Ultimately, both the defendant and Strode were apprehended, defendant having been arrested on the day following the police chase in the vicinity of the State Police Barracks in Scarborough.

* * * [D]efendant maintains that the evidence clearly established that (1) defendant and Strode had told Prout that they "would take care of * * * [the automobile] and see [that] he [Prout] got it back as soon as possible" and (2) defendant intended only a temporary use of Prout's Chevelle. Defendant argues that the evidence thus fails to warrant a conclusion beyond a reasonable doubt that defendant had the specific intent requisite for "robbery." (Hereinafter, reference to the "specific intent" necessary for "robbery" signifies the "specific intent" incorporated into "robbery" as embracing "larceny.")

Although defendant is correct that robbery is a crime requiring a particular specific intent,[2] defendant wrongly apprehends its substantive content.

A summarizing statement appearing in defendant's brief most clearly exposes his misconception of the law. Acknowledging that on all of the evidence the jury could properly

> "* * * have inferred * * * that [defendant and Strode] * * * intended to get away from the authorities by going to New York or elsewhere *where they would abandon* the car * * *", (emphasis supplied)

defendant concludes that, nevertheless, the State had failed to prove the necessary specific intent because it is

> "* * * entirely irrational to conclude * * * that the
> the car, *to keep the car in their possession for any length of*
> defendant himself intended at the time he and Strode took
> *time*." (emphasis supplied)

Here, defendant reveals that he conceives as an essential element of the specific intent requisite for "robbery" that the wrongdoer must intend: (1) an advantageous relationship between himself and the property wrongfully taken, and (2) that such relationship be permanent rather than temporary.

Defendant's view is erroneous. The law evaluates the "animus furandi" of "robbery" in terms of the detriment projected to the legally protected interests of the owner rather than the benefits intended to accrue to the wrongdoer from his invasion of the rights of the owner.

2. It is generally required that the necessary specific intent exist simultaneously with the wrongful taking of the property. State v. McKeough, supra, (n. 4, 300 A.2d at p. 757) makes clear that, as noted in State v. Boisvert, Me., 236 A.2d 419 (1967):

"Maine is one of the jurisdictions which has recognized as an exception to the simultaneous intent rule the principle that if the property is taken from the owner against his will, by a trespass or fraud, a *subsequently* formed intent * * * [of the requisite content] will constitute larceny."

* * * [M]any of the earlier decisions reveal language disagreements, as well as conflicts as to substance, concerning whether a defendant can be guilty of "robbery" without specifically intending a gain to himself (whether permanent or temporary), so-called "lucri causa." In the more recent cases, there is overwhelming consensus that "lucri causa" is not necessary. * * *

* * *

We now decide, in confirmatory clarification of the law of Maine, that "lucri causa" is not an essential element of the "animus furandi" of "robbery." [T]he specific intent requisite for "robbery" is defined solely in terms of the injury projected to the interests of the property owner:—specific intent "to deprive permanently the owner of his property."

The instant question thus becomes: on the hypothesis, arguendo, that defendant here actually intended to use the Prout automobile "only temporarily" (as he would need it to achieve a successful flight from the authorities), is defendant correct in his fundamental contention that this, *in itself*, negates, *as a matter of law*, specific intent of defendant to deprive permanently the owner of his property? We answer that defendant's claim is erroneous.

Concretely illustrative of the point that a wrongdoer may intend to use wrongfully taken property "only temporarily" and yet, without contradiction, intend that the owner be deprived of his property permanently is the case of a defendant who proposes to use the property only for a short time and then to destroy it. At the opposite pole, and excluding (as a matter of law) specific intent to deprive permanently the owner of his property, is the case of a defendant who intends to make a temporary use of the property and then by his own act to return the property to its owner. Between these two extremes can lie various situations in which the legal characterization of the wrongdoer's intention, as assessed by the criterion of whether it is a specific intent to deprive permanently the owner of his property, will be more or less clear and raise legal problems of varying difficulty.

In these intermediate situations a general guiding principle may be developed through recognition that a "taking" of property is *by definition* "temporary" only if the possession, or control, effected by the taking is relinquished. Hence, measured by the correct criterion of the impact upon the interests of the owner, the wrongdoer's "animus furandi" is fully explored for its true legal significance only if the investigation of the wrongdoer's state of mind extends beyond his anticipated *retention* of possession and includes an inquiry into his contemplated manner of *relinquishing* possession, or control, of the property wrongfully taken.

On this approach, it has been held that when a defendant takes the tools of another person with intent to use them temporarily and then to leave them wherever it may be that he finishes with his work, the fact-finder is justified in the conclusion that defendant had specific intent to deprive the owner permanently of his property. State v. Davis, 38 N.J.L. 176 (1875).

Similarly, it has been decided that a defendant who wrongfully takes the property of another intending to use it for a short time and then to relinquish possession, or control, in a manner leaving to chance whether the owner recovers his property is correctly held specifically to intend that the owner be deprived permanently of his property. State v. Smith, 268 N.C. 167, 150 S.E.2d 194 (1966).

The rationale underlying these decisions is that to negate, as a matter of law, the existence of specific intent to deprive permanently the owner of his property, a wrongful taker of the property of another must have in mind not only that his retention of possession, or control, will be "temporary" but also that when he will relinquish the possession, or control, he will do it in some manner (whatever, particularly, it will be) he regards as having affirmative tendency toward getting the property returned to its owner.[4] In the absence of such thinking by the defendant, his state of mind is fairly characterized as *indifference* should the owner *never* recover his property; and such indifference by a wrongdoer who is the moving force separating an owner from his property is appropriately regarded as his "willingness" that the owner *never* regain his property. In this sense, the wrongdoer may appropriately be held to entertain specific intent that the deprivation to the owner be permanent.

* * *

On this basis, the evidence in the present case clearly presented a jury question as to defendant's specific intent. Although defendant may have stated to the owner, Prout, that defendant

> "would take care of * * * [the automobile] and see [that] * * * [Prout] got it back as soon as possible",

defendant himself testified that

> "[i]n my mind it was just to get out of the area. * * * Just get out of the area and leave the car and get under cover somewhere."

4. Since we are here dealing with specific intent of the wrongdoer, the legal criterion is in subjective terms: whether or not defendant actually has in his mind the thought of relinquishing possession, or control, of the wrongfully taken property in a manner which will, *as defendant thinks of it*, be an affirmative step toward a recovery of the property by its owner. Whether the manner in which defendant *in fact* relinquishes his possession, or control, has, or has not, a reasonable tendency in all the circumstances (objectively) to assist in a recovery of the property by the owner may be *evidence* of defendant's actual state of mind. Evidence, however, must be distinguished from the ultimate fact legally required to be proved by evidence.

This idea to "leave the car" and "get under cover somewhere" existed in defendant's mind as part of an uncertainty about where it would happen. Because defendant was "* * * sort of desperate during the whole day", he had not "really formulated any plans about destination."

Such testimony of defendant, together with other evidence that defendant had already utterly abandoned another vehicle (the station wagon) in desperation, plainly warranted a jury conclusion that defendant's facilely uttered statements to Prout were empty words, and it was defendant's true state of mind to use Prout's Chevelle and abandon it in whatever manner might happen to meet the circumstantial exigencies of defendant's predicament— without defendant's having any thought that the relinquishment of the possession was to be in a manner having some affirmative tendency to help in the owner's recovery of his property. On this finding the jury was warranted in a conclusion that defendant was indifferent should the owner, Prout, *never* have back his automobile and, therefore had specific intent that the owner be deprived permanently of his property.

NOTES

1. Generally, of course, if the person taking property intended at the time of the taking to restore the property to the other, the taking was not larceny. But if he merely intended to pay the owner the value of the property, the taking was larceny unless the other person had placed the property for sale. One who takes property from another openly in the belief that he is entitled to it because of a debt owed by the person from whom the property is taken does not commit larceny; he believes that the other person has no rights in the property and therefore he cannot intend to deprive the "victim" of any such rights.

One who takes property with the intent to return it does not commit larceny simply because he hopes for or expects a reward for the return. But if he intends to return it only upon receipt of a reward, there is sufficient risk that the property will be lost to make the action larceny. Similarly, one who takes property intending to sell it back to the owner or to pledge it commits larceny, because this also involves a high risk of permanent loss of the property.

2. Samuels, Permanently to Deprive, New Law Journal, March 21, 1968, at 281:

> Why should not dishonest borrowing amount to stealing? The reasons given by the Criminal Law Revision Committee are in para. 56 of their report. Borrowing is essentially different from stealing. It would constitute a considerable extension of the criminal law, when there is no existing serious evil. It might have undesirable social consequences. Quarrelling neighbours and families would be able to threaten one another with prosecution. Students and young people sharing accommodation who might be tempted to borrow one another's property in disregard of a prohibition by the owner would be in danger of acquiring a criminal record. It

would be difficult for the police to avoid being involved in wasteful and undesirable investigations into alleged offences which had no social importance. It is difficult to see how the provision could be framed in a way which would satisfactorily exclude trivial cases and meet these objections. * * *

The counter-arguments in favour of making dishonest borrowing a criminal offence are, it is submitted, overwhelming. The reform of the law of theft should be moving towards the concept of dishonest economic deprivation and away from the traditional concept of a physical taking with intent permanently to deprive. The new code should be expressed in terms of simple and comprehensive general principle, and it should not be necessary to have to make special provision for taking and driving away aeroplanes and for removing Goyas, a provision any way rightly recognizing that dishonest borrowing should be criminal. The complete usurpation clause is difficult to construe, complicated, and anyway an admission that the permanently to deprive concept is by itself inadequate. The jury are unlikely to be enlightened by such a clause being put to them in the summing up in every theft case, as presumably it would have to be. My lecture notes in my car are "taken" when my car is criminally taken and driven away. The car and the notes are recovered, after the lecture. Is this complete usurpation? Naturally in order to be criminal the borrowing would have to be dishonest, and the defence of claim of right or subjectively reasonable belief that the owner would have consented if he has been asked would apply. The man in the street readily recognizes "pinching" when he sees it, he does not require or accept the permanently to deprive concept. At the time of taking the thief is not always too sure whether he is going to retain or return the stuff. As for the dishonest student borrowing without authority to the grave inconvenience of a colleague, why should he be protected and privileged? Perhaps an exception should be made for "borrowing" the mascot of a rival college in a student rag, though the student rag is not dishonest. The suggestion that neighbours and families would threaten one another with prosecution is naive. Is knowledge of the subtleties of the criminal law so widespread? And are the police no longer to be trusted to be capable of exercising their discretion not to prosecute in their traditionally responsible manner? It is a crime for a boy of 11 to take an apple from an orchard, but there are few prosecutions. The existence of a civil remedy for the owner against the unauthorized borrower is more of a theoretical than a practical argument. The concept of permanently to deprive is not found in Canada and many other common law jurisdictions.

B. EMBEZZLEMENT

Embezzlement, unlike larceny, was not a crime at common law but was created by an early English statute. It is committed when one who has possession of another's property by virtue of a trust relationship fraudulently appropriates that property to a use inconsistent with the trust. The issues most frequently raised in the application of this crime are whether on particular facts defendants dealt with property in a manner constituting "use inconsistent with the trust" (i. e., whether they "converted" it) and whether they did so fraudulently (i. e., whether they had the intent to defraud). In modern statutes, embezzlement is often renamed but it frequently requires proof of the same elements as the traditional crime. Both of the cases in this section involve application of statutory crimes—theft by conversion and larceny by conversion—that are basically restatements of the traditional crime of embezzlement.

BAKER v. STATE

Court of Appeals of Georgia, 1977.
143 Ga.App. 302, 238 S.E.2d 241.

BANKE, Judge.

J. S. Baker was found guilty by jury of two counts of theft by conversion. He appeals directly from his conviction contending the evidence was insufficient to sustain the verdict. * * *

In January and March 1973 the appellant entered into a written agreement with Brown's Chapel AME Church in Homerville whereby he was to make repairs on the church property, build an annex to the church, and renovate a parsonage. The parties agreed on a fixed sum to cover the cost of the construction. The church also agreed orally to cover the appellant's expenses for materials and labor as the work progressed. The specific charges on which the appellant was convicted involved the construction of a church steeple and the installation of a heating system. When the case came up for trial, all accounts due on both projects had been paid.

1. As defined in Code Ann. § 26–1808, "A person commits theft by conversion when, having lawfully obtained funds * * * of another under an agreement * * * to make a specified application of such funds * * *, he knowingly converts the funds * * * to his own use in violation of such agreement or legal obligation." The state proved that the appellant was given a check for $325 to pay for the cost of building a church steeple. The state also proved that the materials for the steeple cost the appellant only $100.

As held by this court in Baker v. State, 131 Ga.App. 48, 205 S.E. 2d 79 (1974), the terms of the agreement between the parties are decisive in determining whether the defendant has converted funds of another from a directed purpose to his own use. The building committee for the church admitted at trial that the church had given the appellant wide discretion in his use of the funds paid to him. Since the appellant was never told how much of the $325 he was to retain for his own services and since he did in fact pay for all of the materials used in the steeple, the appellant cannot be convicted of criminal conversion simply because the building committee believes his retention of $225 for his own services was excessive. The appellant's conviction on this count is reversed.

2. The second count on which the appellant was convicted charged him with converting to his own use $2,000 given to him to pay for a new heating system. The building committee testified that they gave the appellant this money on April 20, 1973, with specific instructions to use it to pay for the heating system. The committee also testified that he had failed to pay the bill with a previous check for $1,700 given to him for the same purpose. The state then presented evidence showing that the bill for the system was finally paid on May 10, 1973, not with the church's money but with money loaned to the appellant by others.

The crux of this charge is whether the defendant intended to commit a crime by his disposition of the $2,000 in question. It is the presence of a fraudulent intent "* * * that distinguishes theft by conversion from a simple breach of contract." Jackson v. State, 137 Ga.App. 192, 223 S.E.2d 239 (1976).

Two elements of the alleged crime were disputed at trial. The appellant denied that the $2,000 was given to him for any specific purpose or that he knowingly converted the money to his own use. The jury was authorized to believe the committee's testimony that they had in fact given the appellant a second payment for the specific purpose of paying for the heating system. The jury was also authorized to infer, from the evidence that the bill was finally paid with borrowed funds, that the appellant had appropriated the $2,000 payment to his own use. Once the state made out a prima facie case of conversion, the burden shifted to the appellant "* * * to account for the funds received or in some other manner to create a reasonable doubt as to his lack of intent." Baker v. State, 131 Ga.App. 48, 205 S.E.2d 79, 80, supra. The appellant never attempted to do this. Instead, he relied on his assertion that the money was given to him to use wherever it was needed on the project.

The presence of criminal intent is a factual issue for the jury's resolution. The jury may consider the accused's "conduct * * * and all other circumstances connected with the act for which the accused is prosecuted." Code Ann. § 26–605. The evidence before the jury here was that the appellant negotiated two checks given to him by the building committee to pay a particular bill and that he ultimately paid the account with borrowed funds.

The court's duty on review is to construe the evidence most strongly in support of the verdict approved by the trial judge. Under this standard it cannot be said that the jury, upon viewing the evidence collectively, erred in concluding that the appellant intended at the time he cashed the second check for $2,000 to defraud the building committee and to convert the money to his own use. The appellants' conviction on this count is affirmed.

PEOPLE v. SCOTT

Court of Appeals of Michigan, 1976.
72 Mich.App. 16, 248 N.W.2d 693.

BEASLEY, Justice.

The defendant, Earl John Scott, Jr., was convicted by a jury of larceny by conversion and now appeals.

At the time of trial, the defendant and the complaining witness, Erwin Petzel, Jr., had been friends for about ten years and had lived, worked and socialized together on numerous occasions. Sally Petzel, Erwin Petzel's wife, had known the defendant since childhood. The subject matter of the alleged conversion was a 1971 Honda motorcycle owned by Mr. Petzel.

Before the Petzels moved to Florida, the defendant entered into a verbal option agreement with Mr. Petzel in which the parties agreed that the defendant could either purchase the motorcycle for $1,000, in installments of $50 or $60 per month, or, alternatively, that the defendant could sell the motorcycle for a minimum of $1,000 and turn that amount over to Mr. Petzel.

In accordance with this agreement, the defendant took possession of the motorcycle. After making one payment of $60, defendant wrote a letter to the Petzels, who were now in Florida, and informed them that he had decided not to buy the motorcycle, but that he would store it and continue to hold it for sale. The terms of the original agreement remained in effect and, although it appears that Erwin Petzel later decided that he did not want to sell the motorcycle, the defendant was never informed of this fact.

On August 30, 1974, the defendant sold the motorcycle to one Jack Gierman for $500 and issued Mr. Gierman a signed receipt for that amount. Defendant told Mr. Gierman at the time of the sale that the motorcycle belonged to Mr. Petzel and that the defendant had been storing it for a long time and would soon go to Florida to obtain the title from Mr. Petzel.

On the day after the sale, Mr. Petzel returned to Michigan. On that same day, the defendant spotted Mr. Petzel and invited him to the defendant's house. At the defendant's house, the subject of the motorcycle came up. Mr. Petzel testified that the defendant asked him whether he preferred the motorcycle or the money, and that he, Petzel, stated that he wanted the motorcycle back. Following re-cross examination, the court asked Mr. Petzel if he had seen any money offered to him. Mr. Petzel said no. The court then asked whether the defendant had orally offered Petzel any money and Mr. Petzel said yes, in the amount of $500. Mr. Petzel also testified that when he told defendant that he wanted the motorcycle back, the defendant agreed to assist him in recovering it. However, before the defendant could do so, Mr. Petzel contacted Mr. Gierman independently in an attempt to recover the motorcycle.

Fearing that defendant and Mr. Petzel were trying to cheat him, Mr. Gierman immediately contacted the State Police. Mr. Petzel also contacted the State Police at approximately the same time. Subsequently, a warrant was issued and the defendant was arrested for the charged offense.

The foregoing comprised the prosecution's case-in-chief against the defendant. The defendant claims that the trial court erred in denying his motion for directed verdict at the close of plaintiff's proofs. We agree.

* * *

The material elements of larceny by conversion are as follows:

> "(3) First, the property must have some value.
>
> (4) Second, the property of another must be delivered over to the defendant. (It is immaterial whether the property is delivered by legal or illegal means.)
>
> (5) Third, the defendant must have (embezzled the property/money); (converted the property/money to his own use); or (hidden the property/money with the intent to embezzle or fraudulently use such property/money).
>
> (6) Fourth, at the time of the (embezzlement) (conversion) (hiding) the defendant must have intended to defraud or cheat the owner permanently of that property.
>
> (7) Fifth, the (embezzlement) (conversion) (hiding) of the property/money must have been without the consent of the owner." 5 Mich.Proposed Cr.Jury Instructions 1047 (1975).

We find the prosecution's case-in-chief did not present sufficient evidence under the directed verdict test on either element (5) or element (6). The testimony of the plaintiff's witnesses, including Mr. Petzel, does not give rise to an inference that the defendant converted the money to his own use or that he intended to defraud or cheat Mr. Petzel permanently of the money or the motorcycle. On the contrary, the defendant's actions would appear to mandate the opposite conclusion. It was the defendant who initially contacted Mr. Petzel and informed him of the sale. Furthermore, it is uncontroverted that the defendant offered $500 to Mr. Petzel at that time. Mr. Petzel refused this offer because "I just wanted the bike back, feeling to myself that it was worth more than $500". The defendant also offered to help Mr. Petzel recover the motorcycle on the next business day. From these undisputed facts, we cannot perceive how it could be inferred that defendant either converted the property or money to his own use or that he intended to defraud or cheat Mr. Petzel permanently of the property or money. The People's proofs only showed that the defendant sold the property at a price lower than that authorized. While such a showing may subject the defendant to civil liability on a breach of contract claim, it does not subject him to criminal liability under the larceny by conversion statute. The statute would apply to the facts of the present case only if the defendant fraudulently intended to convert the proceeds of the sale to his own use rather than merely holding those proceeds, or a like amount, on Mr. Petzel's behalf. As indicated above, the undisputed facts only show the latter to have occurred here.

Reversed. The defendant is ordered discharged.

NOTES

1. As the instant cases make clear, embezzlement requires conversion of the property. Unlike the caption and asportation necessary for larceny, conversion requires no movement of the property. On the other hand, a mere movement that would suffice for asportation may not, depending on the circumstances, amount to conversion.

2. Embezzlement requires that at the time of conversion, the property be in the rightful possession of the defendant. But a person with some right of access to and control over property may have only "custody" rather than "possession". If he misappropriates the property, the offense is larceny rather than embezzlement. Whether a person has custody or possession of property depends upon how extensive is the authority given him to deal with it. Employees who use their employer's property during the performance of their jobs generally have only custody, unless especially broad power is given to them. A bank teller, for example, has sufficient authority to deal with his employer's money to justify classifying his power over it as possession. Lost property is regarded as "constructively" in the possession of the owner, so one who finds it and misappropriates it is guilty of larceny. Abandoned property, however, is regarded as having no owner.

C. FALSE PRETENSES

As has been seen, larceny involves a misappropriation of another's property against his will and embezzlement the misappropriation of another's property rightfully in the possession of the offender.

But what was to be done where the owner gave ownership (title) and not just possession of the property to the offender due to misplaced reliance on some deed or word of the latter? An easy example would be where the owner sells the property in exchange for counterfeit money. At common law there was an offense of cheating by false tokens which covered such conduct. It did not, however cover the situation where the property is given because of promises by the offender. This gap was largely closed by the statutory development of the crime of false pretenses which involved the fraudulent causing of another to part with ownership of property by means of false representations of fact known to the offender to be false.

POLLARD v. STATE

Supreme Court of Mississippi, 1971.
244 So.2d 729.

ROBERTSON, Justice. The appellant, Norman Pollard, was indicted, tried and convicted in the Circuit Court of Lee County, of the crime of false pretense (giving a bad check), and was sentenced to serve a term of three years in the State Penitentiary and to pay a fine of $250.00.

The appellant assigned as error: the granting of State's Instruction No. 1; the refusal to direct a verdict for the defendant * * *

Appellant had a sideline of buying used cars, repairing and improving them, and then selling them at a profit. He was a young married man with no capital and operated on a shoestring. He had been doing business for some months with Ronald Michael and Charles Baxter, of B & M Motors, Inc., Baldwyn, Mississippi.

On September 5, 1968, Pollard gave B & M Motors a $2,550.00 check for three used cars. September 5th was on Thursday, and Pollard testified that he asked Ronald Michael to hold the check until the following week. The proof showed that the check was held until the following Tuesday, September 10th, when it was deposited to the account of B & M Motors. Michael explained that B & M Motors was charged a flat exchange fee of $5.00 whether he deposited $1,000.00 or $50,000.00, so he usually waited until after the auction sale on Monday to make his deposit. The $2,550.00 check of Pollard was returned because of insufficient funds.

At the November, 1968, term of Circuit Court, Pollard was indicted for the crime of false pretense, (the giving of a bad check for $2,550.00 and receiving value for the check in the form of three used cars). The one indispensable element of this offense is the receiving of value for the check at the very time it is delivered. In other words, the seller parts with something of value on the belief that the check is good at that particular time. * * *

The gravamen of the offense was succinctly stated in Jackson v. State, 251 Miss. 529, 170 So.2d 438 (1965):

> "So an essential element of the offense under section 2153 is the making and delivering of the check to another person for value, *and thereby obtaining from such other person money, goods, or other property of value.*" (Emphasis added). 251 Miss. at 531, 170 So.2d at 439.

It would appear that the transaction between Pollard and B & M Motors was a credit sale, and not an exchange for value based on the belief that Pollard's check was good at that particular moment.

If Pollard is to be believed, he was doing business on a hold-check basis, received the cars on Thursday and his check was deposited the following Tuesday. This would indicate a credit sale.

If Michael is to be believed, he frequently allowed dealers to take cars one day and mail in a check several days later. He testified that he had followed this practice with Pollard on two or three occasions. This also would indicate a credit sale based on Michael's confidence in the purchaser generally. Michael had followed this procedure with Pollard just a week before. Pollard had taken delivery of two used cars on August 24, 1968, and his check to B & M Motors was dated August 27, 1968. Michael's uncertain testimony about this transaction was:

> "A I'm saying it is a possibility that—it's been a long time, Mr. Parker, that he could have bought the cars, come by my place and bought the cars, verbally bought them, and said that when I send after the cars or when somebody brings them to me I'll send the check back or I'll put the check in the mail. There is that possibility, which I do that on numerous occasions.
>
> "Q You have done that for him on numerous occasions, is that right?
>
> "A No, probably a couple of times, but I do that with all of my dealers. *I had no reason to doubt the man wouldn't send me the check.*
>
> "Q In fact you had no reason to doubt that he wouldn't send you the $2550 check?
>
> "A I didn't—
>
> "Q Isn't that a fact?
>
> "A I thought the check was good when he gave it to me, I'll tell that.
>
> "Q You had delivered his cars before that hadn't you?
>
> "A I'm not sure when they delivered the cars on the $2550 check.

"Q That's all my questions.

* * * * * * * * * *

"A I believe he took those cars that day, Mr. McCreary I believe took those cars down there, I'm not sure." (Emphasis added).

This Court said in Grenada Coca Cola Co. et al. v. Davis, 168 Miss. 826, 151 So. 743 (1934):

> "The so-called bad check law does not cover the obtaining of goods where the goods had already been delivered, had passed completely out of the possession of the seller and away from his hands and premises in a previously completed transaction or transactions, *although those transactions may have been at previous hours on the same day. There must be an exchange for the check at the time of delivery.* The bad check law is severe enough without extending it by construction so as to include past deliveries, to say nothing of the question of the constitutional validity of such a statute if it were so construed." (Emphasis added.) 168 Miss. at 832, 151 So. at 744.

In the later case of Broadus v. State, 205 Miss. 147, 38 So.2d 692 (1949), this Court again interpreted the bad check law:

> "In the case at bar, the pressing machinery had been delivered to the agent of Broadus and the agent had completely removed them from the possession and premises of Fowler and had departed from Roses Hill for Escatawpa, and had been gone for some thirty minutes before Broadus came up and delivered the check to Fowler in payment for same. When Fowler let the machinery leave his possession and control without demanding and receiving the purchase price, he extended credit for same, Broadus did not obtain the machinery with the check, for he had already, before that time, obtained the machinery. He obtained nothing with the check. The check was given in discharge of a pre-existing debt. The bad check law has no application here." 205 Miss. at 150–151, 38 So.2d at 693.

The court should have directed a verdict for the Defendant Pollard.

* * *

Judgment reversed and defendant discharged.

GILLESPIE, P. J., and RODGERS, JONES and INZER, JJ., concur.

NOTES

1. Although the English statute creating the crime of false pretenses was limited to obtaining "money, goods, wares, or merchandises," modern

statutes are often broader and cover things which are not the subject of larceny. Thus it may be false pretenses to acquire written instruments and documents relating to land or legal rights, title to real property, board and lodging, labor, or services.

2. A major problem, created by the haphazard historical development of the property acquisition offenses, is distinguishing "larceny by trick" from false pretenses. The traditional distinction turns upon what the victim passes to the offender. If the victim transfers mere possession to the offender in response to the misrepresentation, the offense is larceny by trick. If, on the other hand, title as well as possession is passed, the offense is false pretenses. Whether title or mere possession is passed depends upon the intent of the victim.

3. The misrepresentation must be of "present or past fact." Thus it is not false pretenses to obtain money by a promise to do something in the future, even if that promise is not kept. It is not even the offense of false pretenses if, at the time the promise is made, the promisor does not intend to keep it, although arguably he is misrepresenting his state of mind, a "present fact."

4. The misrepresentation must be the cause of the victim's transferring title to the offender. Thus the offense is not committed if the victim is not in fact deceived but rather transfers the property for some other reason. Nor is it committed if the victim is deceived but this false impression does not play a significant role in his decision to give the property to the other.

5. It should be noted in connection with *Pollard* that "bad check" laws were enacted because of difficulties encountered in fitting this activity within the traditional requirement that in obtaining property by false pretenses there must be reliance by the victim on a false representation with respect to a past or present fact. Cf. Chaplin v. United States, 157 F.2d 697 (D.C.Cir. 1946). Unlike the statute in *Pollard* most such laws do not require that property be obtained as a result of the check. It is sufficient that the check be given with the requisite state of mind; usually knowledge of insufficient funds and an intent to defraud.

D. THEFT

Theft is a crime unknown to the common law. Dissatisfaction with the complexities of the various traditional property crimes and the distinctions among them has led many legislatures to consolidate those offenses as a single new statutory crime, entitled Theft. This section contains the Model Penal Code provisions defining theft, which are reasonably typical of modern statutes defining the crime. The case contained in the section illustrates the reduced difficulties which prosecutors often experience under the theft statutes as contrasted with the old common law offenses.

MODEL PENAL CODE *

(Proposed Official Draft, 1962).

ARTICLE 223. THEFT AND RELATED OFFENSES

Section 223.0. Definitions

In this Article, unless a different meaning plainly is required:

(1) "deprive" means: (a) to withhold property of another permanently or for so extended a period as to appropriate a major portion of its economic value, or with intent to restore only upon payment of reward or other compensation; or (b) to dispose of the property so as to make it unlikely that the owner will recover it.

* * *

(4) "movable property" means property the location of which can be changed, including things growing on, affixed to, or found in land, and documents although the rights represented thereby have no physical location. "Immovable property" is all other property.

(5) "obtain" means: (a) in relation to property, to bring about a transfer or purported transfer of a legal interest in the property, whether to the obtainer or another; or (b) in relation to labor or service, to secure performance thereof.

(6) "property" means anything of value, including real estate, tangible and intangible personal property, contract rights, choses-in-action and other interests in or claims to wealth, admission or transportation tickets, captured or domestic animals, food and drink, electric or other power.

(7) "property of another" includes property in which any person other than the actor has an interest which the actor is not privileged to infringe, regardless of the fact that the actor also has an interest in the property * * *.

Section 223.1. Consolidation of Theft Offenses; Grading; Provisions Applicable to Theft Generally

(1) *Consolidation of Theft Offenses.* Conduct denominated theft in this Article constitutes a single offense embracing the separate offenses heretofore known as larceny, embezzlement, false pretense, extortion, blackmail, fraudulent conversion, receiving stolen property, and the like. * * *

(2) *Grading of Theft Offenses.*

(a) Theft constitutes a felony of the third degree if the amount involved exceeds $500, or if the property stolen is a firearm, automobile, or other motor-propelled vehicle, or in the case of theft by receiving stolen property, if the receiver is in the business of buying or selling stolen property.

(b) Theft not within the preceding paragraph constitutes a misdemeanor, except that if the property was not taken from the person or by threat, or in breach of a fiduciary obligation, and the actor proves by a preponderance of the evidence that the amount involved was less than $50, the offense constitutes a petty misdemeanor.

* * *

(3) *Claim of Right.* It is an affirmative defense to prosecution for theft that the actor:

(a) was unaware that the property or service was that of another; or

(b) acted under an honest claim of right to the property or service involved or that he had a right to acquire or dispose of it as he did; or

(c) took property exposed for sale, intending to purchase and pay for it promptly, or reasonably believing that the owner, if present, would have consented.

(4) *Theft from Spouse.* It is no defense that theft was from the actor's spouse, except that misappropriation of household and personal effects, or other property normally accessible to both spouses, is theft only if it occurs after the parties have ceased living together.

Section 223.2. Theft by Unlawful Taking or Disposition

(1) *Movable Property.* A person is guilty of theft if he takes, or exercises unlawful control over, movable property of another with purpose to deprive him thereof.

(2) *Immovable Property.* A person is guilty of theft if he unlawfully transfers immovable property of another or any interest therein with purpose to benefit himself or another not entitled thereto.

Section 223.3. Theft by Deception

A person is guilty of theft if he obtains property of another by deception. A person deceives if he purposely:

(a) creates or reinforces a false impression, including false impressions as to law, value, intention or other state of mind; but deception as to a person's intention to perform a promise shall not be inferred from the fact alone that he did not subsequently perform the promise; or

(b) prevents another from acquiring information which would affect his judgment of a transaction; or

(c) fails to correct a false impression which the deceiver previously created or reinforced, or which the deceiver knows to be influencing another to whom he stands in a fiduciary or confidential relationship; or

(d) fails to disclose a known lien, adverse claim or other legal impediment to the enjoyment of property which he transfers or encumbers in consideration for the property obtained, whether such impediment is or is not valid, or is or is not a matter of official record.

The term "deceive" does not, however, include falsity as to matters having no pecuniary significance, or puffing by statements unlikely to deceive ordinary persons in the group addressed.

Section 223.4. Theft by Extortion

A person is guilty of theft if he obtains property of another by threatening to:

(a) inflict bodily injury on anyone or commit any other criminal offense; or

(b) accuse anyone of a criminal offense; or

(c) expose any secret tending to subject any person to hatred, contempt or ridicule, or to impair his credit or business repute; or

(d) take or withhold action as an official, or cause an official to take or withhold action; or

(e) bring about or continue a strike, boycott or other collective unofficial action, if the property is not demanded or received for the benefit of the group in whose interest the actor purports to act; or

(f) testify or provide information or withhold testimony or information with respect to another's legal claim or defense; or

(g) inflict any other harm which would not benefit the actor.

It is an affirmative defense to prosecution based on paragraphs (b), (c) or (d) that the property obtained by threat of accusation, exposure, lawsuit or other invocation of official action was honestly claimed as restitution or indemnification for harm done in the circumstances to which such accusation, exposure, lawsuit or other official action relates, or as compensation for property or lawful services.

Section 223.5. Theft of Property Lost, Mislaid, or Delivered by Mistake

A person who comes into control of property of another that he knows to have been lost, mislaid, or delivered under a mistake as to the nature or amount of the property or the identity of the recipient is guilty of theft if, with purpose to deprive the owner thereof, he fails to take reasonable measures to restore the property to a person entitled to have it.

Section 223.6. Receiving Stolen Property

(1) *Receiving.* A person is guilty of theft if he receives, retains, or disposes of movable property of another knowing that it has been stolen, or believing that it has probably been stolen, unless the property is received, retained, or disposed with purpose to restore it to the owner. "Receiving" means acquiring possession, control or title, or lending on the security of the property.

* * *

Section 223.7. Theft of Services

(1) A person is guilty of theft if he obtains services which he knows are available only for compensation, by deception or threat, or by false token or other means to avoid payment for the service. "Services" includes labor, professional service, telephone or other public service, accommodation in hotels, restaurants or elsewhere, admission to exhibitions, use of vehicles or other movable property. Where compensation for service is ordinarily paid immediately upon the rendering of such service, as in the case of hotels and restaurants, refusal to pay or absconding without payment or offer to pay gives rise to a presumption that the service was obtained by deception as to intention to pay.

(2) A person commits theft if, having control over the disposition of services of others, to which he is not entitled, he diverts such services to his own benefit or to the benefit of another not entitled thereto.

LEE v. STATE

Supreme Court of Arkansas, 1978.
— Ark. —, 571 S.W.2d 603.

HOLT, Justice.

The trial court * * * found the appellant guilty of theft of property [consisting of four men's suits] and sentenced him to three years' imprisonment in the Department of Corrections. * * *

Viewing the testimony in the light most favorable to the state, evidence was adduced that appellant [and a companion entered a men's clothing store and that appellant], after saying to his companion, "everything is O.K.," removed a hook knife from his right rear pocket, cut the plastic cords attaching the four suits to the clothes rack, and removed them from the rack. He handed two of the suits to [his] companion and they started to leave the store with appellant carrying the other two which he handed to his companion before they exited the store. When appellant was apprehended outside the store, he had a hook knife in his right rear pocket. * * *

Appellant * * * asserts that the evidence was insufficient with respect to the actual theft of the property. He maintains that, in a theft from a store, asportation or concealment is a primary concern in determining whether a theft has been committed, since merchandise may be moved around the store without a theft occurring, even if the intent exists, if the merchandise is placed somewhere else in the store. [Therefore, appellant apparently argues, he merely removed the suits from the rack and handed them to his companion. If a theft was committed, it was committed only by the actions of his companion in removing the suits from the store. His own actions, however, did not constitute theft, he asserts.] Appellant misreads our statute on theft of property.

Ark.Stat.Ann. § 41–2203 (Repl.1977) provides that "[a] person commits theft of property if he: (a) knowingly takes or exercises unauthorized control over * * * the property of another person, with the purpose of depriving the owner thereof * * *." The comments to the statute make it plain that asportation and caption are not requisites of wrongful appropriation. Rather, they "are but circumstances to be considered along with all others relevant to the ultimate issue whether the behavior of the actor constituted a negation or usurpation of the owner's dominion." * * * The evidence is amply sufficient to show unauthorized control over the property with intent to deprive the store of its property.

NOTE

As *Lee* makes clear, modern theft statutes often ease the prosecution's task of showing that the defendant "took" the property by eliminating the specific requirements of caption and asportation. But in addition, the cases make clear that under many modern theft statutes the prosecution need not even show that the defendant was involved in the initial taking of the property. A defendant obtains or exerts control over property and therefore—if he has the requisite criminal intent—commits theft under many statutes if he takes possession of it after it has been taken from the victim. Commonwealth v. Adams, 479 Pa. 508, 388 A.2d 1046 (1978); People v. Nunn, 63 Ill.App.2d 465, 212 N.E.2d 342 (1965).

E. ROBBERY

Robbery is an offense against both the security of the person and of interests in property. It consists of the taking and asportation of personal property from the person or the presence of another against his will by means of violence or placing the other in fear of personal safety with the intent to permanently deprive him of his interest in the property. It was apparently the initial common law property offense, although it was defined somewhat more narrowly.

MODEL PENAL CODE *

(Proposed Official Draft, 1962).

Section 222.1. Robbery

(1) *Robbery Defined.* A person is guilty of robbery if, in the course of committing a theft, he:

(a) inflicts serious bodily injury upon another; or

(b) threatens another with or purposely puts him in fear of immediate serious bodily injury; or

(c) commits or threatens immediately to commit any felony of the first or second degree.

An act shall be deemed "in the course of committing a theft" if it occurs in an attempt to commit theft or in flight after the attempt or commission.

(2) *Grading.* Robbery is a felony of the second degree, except that it is a felony of the first degree if in the course of committing the theft the actor attempts to kill anyone, or purposely inflicts or attempts to inflict serious bodily injury.

COMMONWEALTH v. DAVIS

Appeals Court of Massachusetts, 1979.
79 Mass.App.Adv.Sh. 103, 385 N.E.2d 278.

HALE, Chief Justice.

The defendant was tried by a jury and convicted of unarmed robbery of seventeen dollars from the person of one Richard Lento. He has assigned as error the refusal of the judge to direct a verdict of not guilty on so much of the indictment as charged assault with intent to rob and robbery, on the ground that the Commonwealth's evidence disclosed, at most, larceny from the person.

The jury heard testimony from which it could have been found that Lento, his brother, and two friends had been walking together side by side through the Boston Common on the evening of August 12, 1977. While on a pathway near the bandstand, an area which is surrounded by a circular row of benches, they were approached from the rear by a group of four or five youths. The youths were talking in a "friendly fashion." The two groups "slowly merged together," with the youths forming a circle around Lento and his companions. The youths then separated Lento and his companions so that they were about eight to ten feet apart. One of Lento's companions, John Paquette, was outside the circle of benches, while the others were inside the circle, so that they formed the four corners of a square. There was a youth with each of Lento's companions. The defendant was with Lento.

The defendant leaned on Lento's back and pulled his wallet out of his left back pocket. Lento, upon feeling his wallet being removed, turned around, saw the defendant with his back turned toward him, and said that the defendant had taken his wallet. The defendant then turned around and handed the wallet back to Lento. Seventeen dollars which the wallet had contained were gone. Lento then observed another of the youths taking his friends' wallets. Lento testified that at the time of the incident [2] he felt "kind of afraid."

Lento and his companions then ran away and telephoned the police from Park Square. Shortly thereafter, two police officers arrived in a patrol car. They drove Lento and his companions through the Common, where the defendant was seen standing on the bandstand and was identified by Lento as the person who had stolen his money.

The defendant concedes that the Commonwealth presented sufficient evidence to support a guilty verdict of the lesser included offense of larceny from the person but argues that there was insufficient evidence to support a conviction of robbery. He contends that the evidence presented nothing more than a case of pickpocketing. The ordinary pickpocket is guilty of larceny from the person, rather than robbery, because there is neither violence nor intimidation involved in the perpetration of the theft. Perkins, Criminal Law 282 (2d ed. 1969). The force used to bring about the theft is only that amount of force needed to lift and remove the property and is not of the class of violence essential to robbery. Pickpocketing characteristically involves stealth and a lack of awareness of the taking by the victim. LaFave and Scott, Criminal Law § 94 (1972).

The Commonwealth argues that the rule of Commonwealth v. Jones, 362 Mass. 83, 283 N.E.2d 840 (1972), makes pickpocketing the crime of robbery whenever the victim has an awareness that the pickpocketing is taking place and that, as Lento was aware of the theft at the moment of its commission, the defendant was guilty as charged. We disagree. In the circumstances of a purse snatching, *Jones* held

2. Lento testified on direct examination that he felt "kind of afraid" at the time of the theft, on cross-examination that he first felt afraid after the theft, and on voir dire that he first felt fear when approached by the group of youths. However, the statement made at voir dire was not made before the jury.

that where the snatching or sudden taking of property from a victim is sufficient to produce awareness, there is sufficient evidence of force to permit a finding of robbery. *Jones* does not, however, stand for the proposition that awareness of the theft constitutes the essential difference between larceny and robbery. It is the "exertion of force, actual or constructive, [that] remains the principal distinguishing characteristic of the offence." Commonwealth v. Jones, supra, 362 Mass. at 86, 283 N.E.2d at 843. In Massachusetts prior to *Jones,* and in Kentucky, the jurisdiction from which the *Jones* rule was derived, cases of pickpocketing where the victim became aware of the taking have been treated as larceny from the person. We decline the Commonwealth's invitation to extend the *Jones* rule to include pickpocketing, even if inartfully performed.

However, upon considering the evidence in the light most favorable to the Commonwealth, we are of the opinion that in the circumstances of this case there was sufficient evidence for the jury to infer that the taking of Lento's money was brought about by "assault and putting in fear." The inferences drawn by the jury "need not be necessary or inescapable, as long as they are reasonable, possible, and not unwarranted because too remote from the ordinary course of events." There was evidence that Lento and his companions were followed, surrounded, and separated, that Lento did not resist the taking, and that he and his companions left the scene immediately after the thefts. That evidence warranted a finding by the jury that the defendant, and those acting with him, acted in a manner which would be reasonably expected to induce fear and that Lento's group acceded to their separation because of their apprehension of danger. They could also have found that Lento did not resist the taking of his wallet because of fear. Although there was a conflict in Lento's testimony before the jury on direct and cross-examination as to when he first felt afraid (see note 2, supra), whether his fear arose before the taking or afterwards was a question properly left for the determination of the jury.

Judgment affirmed.

NOTES AND QUESTIONS

1. Suppose in *Davis* the jurors believed that Lento did not feel afraid until after his wallet had been removed from his pocket. Could they still convict the defendant of robbery? The doubt reflected by the court's opinion illustrates the fact that there is substantial support for both sides of this issue. The general rule was stated in State v. Aldershof, 220 Kan. 798, 556 P.2d 371 (1976) as follows:

> For centuries the rule followed in England and later in the United States has been that in order for the defendant to be guilty of robbery it is essential that the prosecution prove that the defendant took the property by means of force or violence or by putting the victim in fear. * * * Furthermore, the general

> rule is that the violence or intimidation must precede or be concomitant or contemporaneous with the taking. Violence or intimidation by the thief subsequent to the taking will not render the act robbery.

556 P.2d at 373. In *Aldershof*, the defendant had taken the victim's purse from her lap as she sat in a tavern. She chased the defendant and managed to grab him by the back of the shirt in the parking lot outside the tavern. The defendant then struck the victim in the eye. Finding that the taking of the purse was complete when the defendant left the tavern with it in his control, the court held that the defendant's use of force to prevent the victim from regaining the purse did not change the theft into robbery. Other jurisdictions have somewhat relaxed the application if not the language of the rule. In People v. Anderson, 64 Cal.2d 633, 51 Cal.Rptr. 238, 414 P.2d 366 (1966), the defendant entered a pawnshop and asked to inspect some weapons. He was handed a rifle by the clerk and examined it. After stating that he would purchase the rifle, he asked for some shells. The clerk set a box of shells on the counter. As the clerk was totalling the price of the items, the defendant loaded the gun. When the clerk protested, the defendant threatened him with the rifle. Rejecting the defendant's argument that he had not threatened the victim until after the theft of the rifle and shells was complete, the California court stated:

> [I]f one who has stolen property from the person of another uses force or fear in removing * * * the property from the owner's immediate presence, as defendant did here, the crime of robbery has been committed.

414 P.2d at 369. Under some statutes, even less of a relationship between the taking and the force or threats is required. In Wilson v. State, 262 Ark. 339, 556 S.W.2d 657 (1977), a police officer observed defendant conceal a roast in his clothing and clear the check-out line of the store without paying for it. The officer approached the defendant, told him he was under arrest, and advised him that he would have to accompany the officer to the office in the store. On the way to this office, the defendant broke loose from the officer and a fight ensued in which the officer was injured. Under the applicable statute, a person commits robbery "if with the purpose of committing a theft or resisting apprehension immediately thereafter, he employs or threatens to immediately employ physical force upon another." Ark.Crim.Code § 41–2103. Affirming defendant's conviction for robbery, the court held that the force used against the officer was used to resist apprehension immediately after the theft within the meaning of the statute.

2. Robbery can be accomplished by threats only if the threats are of death or great bodily injury to the victim, a member of the victim's family or some other relative of the victim, or someone in the victim's presence. Threats to damage property will not suffice, with the exception of a threat to destroy a dwelling house. A threat to accuse the victim of the crime of sodomy has been held a sufficient threat to constitute robbery. See W. LaFave and A. Scott, Criminal Law 698–99 (1972).

3. If robbery is committed by threat, the threat must be of "immediate" harm. W. LaFave and A. Scott, Criminal Law 699 (1972). If the threatened harm is not sufficiently immediate, the offense committed is probably extortion. But courts have been willing to define "immediate" in a broad fashion. In People v. Woods, 41 N.Y.2d 279, 392 N.Y.S.2d 400, 360 N.E.2d 1082 (1977), the defendant attempted to persuade the victim to give him some money as part of a confidence game. When she balked, he "nudged" her on the elbow and told her that she had to give him $2,500 to insure that she would not tell anyone about the scheme and "for [her] own safety." She provided the money. Defendant was apprehended and convicted of robbery. This was affirmed on appeal. The appellate court found "ample evidence" from which a jury could conclude that defendant had used a threat of immediate harm to get the money.

4. Suppose the victim of a larceny or theft becomes fearful of immediate physical injury but a normal, reasonable person would not have entertained such fear. Is the crime now robbery? Courts have differed. Some hold that the threats must be such as to place a reasonable person in fear of immediate harm. Parnell v. State, 389 P.2d 370 (Okl.Crim.App. 1964). Others have held to the contrary, although they acknowledge that proof that the threat would not frighten a reasonable person would tend to show that the defendant did not intend to obtain the victim's property by means of the threat. Commonwealth v. Mays, 248 Pa.Super. 318, 375 A.2d 116 (1977). W. LaFave and A. Scott, Criminal Law 700 (1972), state the "correct" rule as being that it is only necessary to show that the victim was frightened.

5. Traditionally, the threats must have been the means by which the defendant obtained the property. If, therefore, the victim was not in fact placed in fear robbery was not committed. But some statutes have changed this. In Commonwealth v. Mays, 248 Pa.Super. 318, 375 A.2d 116 (1977), the defendant told the victim, an acquaintance, that "this is a stickup" and poked something in her ribs. Thinking that he was joking, she pushed him away. He then grabbed her purse and ran. Holding that the Pennsylvania statute required only threatening another with immediate bodily injury during the course of committing theft, the court affirmed defendant's conviction for robbery over his argument that the victim's lack of apprehension prevented robbery from taking place.

6. Robbery requires that the property be taken from the person or the "presence" of the victim. But courts have interpreted "presence" quite broadly. In State v. Atkins, 549 S.W.2d 927 (Mo.App.1977), defendant and a companion entered the house of a quadriplegic. One of the pair restrained the victim; the other went to a closet in another room and took money concealed there. After conviction for robbery, defendant appealed on the ground that the evidence failed to show that he had taken the property from the presence of the victim. "Property need not be taken from the immediate, physical presence of the victim in order to constitute robbery," the court commented. It cited, in support of this statement, State v. Hayes, 518 S.W.2d 40 (Mo.1975), in which the defendant had forced the victim into a jail cell and then took his automobile which was parked outside the building. A conviction for robbery was

upheld. In State v. Thompson, 37 N.C.App. 651, 247 S.E.2d 235 (1978), the court approved the following definition of presence:

> "Presence" * * * means a possession or control so immediate that violence or intimidation is essential to sunder it. A thing is in the presence of a person, with respect to robbery, which is so within his reach, inspection, observation, or control that he could, if not overcome by violence or prevented by fear, retain his possession of it.

247 S.E.2d at 241. This definition is widely accepted. See People v. Beebe, 70 Mich.App. 154, 245 N.W.2d 547 (1976).

STATE v. LEWIS

Court of Appeals of Arizona, 1978.
121 Ariz. 155, 589 P.2d 29.

HOWARD, Judge.

Appellant was convicted by a jury of one count of armed robbery * * *.

He claims on appeal that the trial court erred [in instructing the jury concerning his defense of lack of intent].

The victims in this case, Brent Ferrin and Terry Rustin, testified that they met appellant at their apartment complex three days prior to the crimes. Appellant discussed the possibility of their purchasing a camera and pocket calculator so he brought the items to their apartment for them to inspect. The camera was, according to Ferrin, a $20 Vivitar and the calculator cost $10 to $15 new. A price of between $20 and $30 for both was discussed. At first the victims said they were going to buy the items, but later told appellant that they did not want to because they did not have enough money. They offered them back to appellant but he insisted that they keep them and pay him when they got the money. The victims again told appellant that they did not want them even when appellant said he would take $5 or $10 for them. According to the victims appellant did not ask for return of these items.

The night before the crimes occurred, appellant went to the victims' apartment and told them that he had lost his keys and could not get into his apartment. He asked them if he could stay there and they reluctantly permitted him to sleep on the couch.

The next morning a visitor came to the apartment. Appellant told this visitor a false story in order to get him out of the apartment. He then went into the bedroom where the victims were standing, hit Ferrin on the head with a handgun and forced Ferrin and Rustin to lie on the floor. Appellant kept yelling that the victims were "jiving him" about his camera and calculator. He forced Ferrin to write him a check for $200 and then, at gunpoint had the victims drive him to a bank drive-in window where the check was cashed. Appellant took the money and had the victims drive him back to the apartment complex where appellant got out of the automobile and told the victims to keep driving. He also instructed them not to tell the police or either he or his brothers would "get" them.

The victims contacted the police who apprehended appellant at a friend's apartment in the complex. The police found the money in the bathtub. Appellant told the police in the presence of the victims, that he did not know them and denied any knowledge of the incident.

Appellant testified that the victims would not return the calculator and camera to him. When he found out that they intended to move, he asked them to give him $30 or $25 or his money. He stated that they had discussed a total price of between $75 or $100, but never did agree on a price for the items. He did not know how much they cost because his mother gave them to him but he had Ferrin write out the check for $200 because that was what they were worth to him. He stated that he told the police he did not know the victims because he was afraid.

Appellant's defense on the robbery charges was lack of animus furandi, intent to steal. In Arizona, a charge of robbery fails where the attempt is to collect a bona fide debt, since, to constitute that offense, there must be an animus furandi and this cannot exist if the person takes the property under a bona fide claim of right. * * * Since we are bound by the decisions of our Supreme Court we are constrained to follow the rule. We are not, however, precluded from criticizing it. In State v. Ortiz, 124 N.J.Super. 189, 305 A.2d 800 (1973), the court, in commenting on the majority rule, stated:

> "In our view, the proposition not only is lacking in sound reason and logic, but it is utterly incompatible with and has no place in an ordered and orderly society such as ours, which eschews self-help through violence. * * *" 305 A. 2d at 802.

The court in *Ortiz* also points out that in those jurisdictions which have had occasion to examine the question as a matter of first impression since 1937, all have rejected the so-called majority rule, with the exception of a single federal case decided by a divided three-judge court.

[In Edwards v. State, 49 Wis.2d 105, 181 N.W.2d 383 (1970) the court distinguished between cases in which the defendant repossesses specific personal property which he claims he owns and those in which money is taken under the claim it is owed because of a debt. In the first situation, the intent to steal may be lacking because the defendand believes he—and not the victim—owns the specific item taken. But this is not the case in the second situation:]

"The distinction between specific personal property and money in general is important. A debtor can owe another $150 but the $150 in the debtor's pocket is not the specific property of the creditor. One has the intention to steal when he takes money from another's possession against the possessor's consent even though he also intends to apply the stolen money to a debt. The efficacy of self-help by force to enforce a bona fide claim for money does not negate the intent to commit robbery. Can one break into a bank and take money so long as he does not take more than the balance in his savings or checking account? Under the majority rule the accused must make change to be sure he collects no more than the amount he believes is due him on the debt. A debt is a relationship and in respect to money seldom finds itself embedded in specific coins and currency of the realm. Consequently, taking money from a debtor by force to pay a debt is robbery. The creditor has no such right of appropriation and allocation." [181 N.W.2d at 387.]

The Oregon court in State v. Martin, 15 Or.App. 498, 516 P.2d 753 (1974) also quoted from Edwards v. State, supra, but went one step further and held that a creditor's intent to collect a debt from his debtor by force is not a defense to a charge or robbery under any circumstances. Were we at liberty to do so, we would follow the rule in Edwards v. State, supra.

In some states which apparently follow the majority rule, an exception has been created where the amount claimed to be owed was of an unliquidated nature. These cases are cited in State v. Austin, 60 Wash.2d 227, 373 P.2d 137 (1962). There the * * * appellate court held that the trial court did not err in refusing to give the instruction, stating:

> "* * * [T]he defendant's testimony, read in its entirety, makes it clear that the amount claimed was uncertain. Therefore, the taking in the instant case, even if it was for the purpose of securing an honestly claimed indebtedness, will support a robbery conviction. * * *" 373 P.2d at 140.

California followed this rule in People v. Poindexter, 255 Cal. App.2d 566, 63 Cal.Rptr. 332 (1967), a case involving an alleged tort claim. The court noted:

> "Clearly, it is one thing to entertain a bona-fide belief that the victim of a taking owes a sum certain to the taker, and quite another to help oneself to money in satisfaction of an unliquidated, questionable tort claim." 63 Cal.Rptr. at 334.

The testimony here clearly shows that the claim was unliquidated in nature. We therefore hold that the defense [of lack of intent] was not available to appellant. The instructions on the issue given by the trial court were therefore gratuitous and harmless.

NOTE

If the jury believed Lewis honestly thought he had a right to the money, could he be said to have intended to deprive Ferrin of *Ferrin's* money? Reconsider United States v. Richardson, page 198, supra.

F. EXTORTION

Extortion was a misdemeanor at common law consisting of the unlawful collection by an official of an unlawful fee under color of his office. Thus it was an offense against the administration of justice. But in modern codes extortion has often been expanded (sometimes under the label of blackmail) to include obtaining property by means of a threat not sufficient to constitute robbery, including threats to do future (i. e., not immediate) bodily injury, to injure property, to accuse the victim of a crime, or to reveal certain types of information concerning the victim.

The Model Penal Code would make extortion one form of theft. That form of theft covered in some jurisdictions by extortion is defined in Section 223.4, Theft by Extortion, reprinted at page 382, supra.

STATE v. HARRINGTON

Supreme Court of Vermont, 1969.
260 A.2d 692.

HOLDEN, Chief Justice. The respondent John B. Harrington has been tried and found guilty of the offense of threatening to accuse Armand Morin of Littleton, New Hampshire, of the crime of adultery. The indictment charges that the threat was maliciously made with the intent to extort $175,000 and to compel Morin to do an act against his will in violation of 13 V.S.A. § 1701.[a]

At the outset the respondent acknowledges that there is no serious conflict in the material evidence presented to the jury. The main effort of his appeal challenges the jurisdiction and the sufficiency of the evidence to sustain the conviction.

At the time of the alleged offense the respondent was engaged in the general practice of law in a firm with offices in Burlington, Vermont. Early in March, 1968, he was consulted by Mrs. Norma Morin, the wife of the alleged victim, Armand E. Morin. Mrs. Morin had separated from her husband because of his recent and severe

a. A person who maliciously threatens to accuse another of a crime or offense, or with an injury to his person or property, with intent to extort money or other pecuniary advantage, or with intent to compel the person so threatened to do an act against his will, shall be imprisoned in the state prison not more than two years or fined not more than $500.00.

physical abuse. Prior to their separation they owned and operated the Continental 93 Motel in Littleton, New Hampshire, where the Morins maintained a residential apartment. The respondent learned the marital estate of the parties had a net value of approximately $500,000. Mrs. Morin reported to the respondent that her husband had also been guilty of numerous marital infidelities with different women at the motel. Mrs. Morin also disclosed that she had been guilty of marital misconduct which apparently had been condoned.

During the first conference the respondent advised Mrs. Morin that, because of her residence in New Hampshire, she could not undertake divorce proceedings in Vermont for at least six months and for her to obtain a divorce in New Hampshire it would be necessary that she obtain counsel from that state. Mrs. Morin indicated she wished to retain Mr. Harrington to represent her.

On one of the subsequent conferences a friend of Mrs. Morin's, who accompanied her to the respondent's office, suggested that an effort should be made to procure corroborative evidence of Mr. Morin's marital misconduct. To this end, the floor plan of the motel was discussed and a diagram prepared. At this time a scheme was designed to procure the services of a girl who would visit the motel in an effort to obtain corroborative evidence of Morin's infidelity.

After some screening, a Mrs. Mazza, who had been suggested by the respondent, was selected to carry out the assignment. The respondent explained to Mrs. Mazza the purpose of her employment and the results she was expected to accomplish and provided her with a "cover story" to explain her registration and presence as a guest at the Continental 93 Motel. Warning Mrs. Mazza against enticement and entrapment, the respondent instructed the employee to be "receptive and available," but not aggressive. The agreement with Mrs. Mazza was that she would be paid one hundred dollars at the time she undertook the assignment and one hundred dollars when her mission was completed.

Mrs. Morin was without funds at the time. A contingent fee agreement was signed by Mrs. Morin and the firm of Harrington and Jackson, by the respondent. The agreement was dated March 5, 1968 and provided that in the event a satisfactory property settlement was obtained, the respondent's firm was to receive twelve and a half percent of the settlement, in addition to reimbursement for expenses advanced by counsel. Electronic listening and recording equipment was ordered and delivered by air.

On the afternoon of March 6 the respondent and two office associates traveled to St. Johnsbury in two vehicles. Mrs. Mazza continued on to Littleton unaccompanied. She registered on arrival at the Continental 93 Motel under the name of Jeanne Raeder. She called the respondent at St. Johnsbury from a public telephone and informed him of her room number and location. Mrs. Mazza later delivered the key to her room to the respondent to enable him to procure a duplicate. The respondent, representing that he was a book salesman, registered at the motel and procured a room directly above that occupied by Mrs. Mazza. He was accompanied by a junior associate and an investigator,—both employed by the respondent's law firm.

During the next day Mrs. Mazza attracted Mr. Morin's attention. The sequence of events which followed led to an invitation by Morin for her to join him at his apartment for a cocktail. Mrs. Mazza accepted. Later she suggested that they go to her room because Mr. Morin's young son was asleep in his quarters. Morin went to Mrs. Mazza's room about midnight. Soon after the appointed hour the respondent and his associates entered the room. With one or more cameras, several photographs were taken of Morin and Mrs. Mazza in bed and unclothed. Morin grabbed for one camera and broke it.

During the time of her stay at the motel Mrs. Mazza carried an electronic transmitter in her handbag. By means of this device, her conversations with Morin were monitored by the respondent and his associates.

The respondent and his companions checked out of the motel at about one in the morning. Before doing so, there was a brief confrontation with Morin. According to Morin's testimony, the respondent demanded $125,000. Morin testified—"at that time I made him an offer of $25,000 to return everything he had, and in a second breath I retracted the offer."

The following day the respondent conferred with Mrs. Morin and reported the events of the trip to New Hampshire. He asked Mrs. Morin to consider reconciliation over the weekend. On March 11, 1968, Mrs. Morin informed the respondent she decided it was too late for reconciliation. With this decision, the respondent dictated, in the presence of Mrs. Morin, a letter which was received in evidence as State's Exhibit 1. The letter was addressed to Armand Morin at Littleton, New Hampshire, and was placed in the United States mail at Burlington the same day.

The communication is designated personal and confidential. The following excerpts are taken from the full text:

> "—Basically, your wife desires a divorce, and if it can be equitably arranged, she would prefer that the divorce be as quiet and as undamaging as possible.
>
> This letter is being written in your wife's presence and has been completely authorized by your wife. The offer of settlement contained herein is made in the process of negotia-

> tion and is, of course, made without prejudice to your wife's rights.
>
> It is the writer's thinking that for the children's sake, for your sake, and for Mrs. Morin's sake, that neither the courts in New Hampshire nor in Vermont should become involved in this potentially explosive divorce. If a suitable 'stipulation or separation agreement' can be worked out, the writer would recommend a Mexican, Stipulation-Divorce. * * *
>
> Mrs. Morin is willing to give up the following:
>
> 1. All of her marital rights, including her rights to share in your estate.
>
> 2. All of her right, title, and interest, jointly or by reason of marital status, that she has in and to, any or all property of the marriage * * *. Furthermore, any such settlement would include the return to you of all tape recordings, all negatives, all photographs and copies of photographs that might in any way, bring discredit upon yourself. Finally, there would be an absolute undertaking on the part of your wife not to divulge any information of any kind or nature which might be embarrassing to you in your business life, your personal life, your financial life, [or] your life as it might be affected by the Internal Revenue Service, the United States Customs Service, or any other governmental agency.—"

The letter goes on to specify the terms of settlement required by Mrs. Morin, concerning custody of the minor child, her retention of an automobile and the disposition of certain designated personal effects. It further provides:

> "5. Mrs. Morin would waive all alimony upon receipt of One Hundred Seventy Five Thousand Dollars ($175,000)—."

The sum of $25,000 is specified to be paid at the signing of the separation agreement, with the balance due according to a schedule of payments over the period of eighteen months.

The letter continues:

> " * * * Unless the writer has heard from you on or before March 22, we will have no alternative but to withdraw the offer and bring immediate divorce proceedings in Grafton County. This will, of course, require the participation by the writer's correspondent attorneys in New Hampshire. If we were to proceed under New Hampshire laws, without any stipulation, it would be necessary to allege, in detail, all of the grounds that Mrs. Morin has in seeking the divorce. The writer is, at present, undecided as to advising Mrs. Morin whether or not to file for 'informer fees' with respect to the

> Internal Revenue Service and the United States Customs Service. In any event, we would file, alleging adultery, including affidavits, alleging extreme cruelty and beatings, and asking for a court order enjoining you from disposing of any property, including your stock interests, during the pendency of the proceeding.
>
> * * *
>
> With absolutely no other purpose than to prove to you that we have all of the proof necessary to prove adultery beyond a reasonable doubt, we are enclosing a photograph taken by one of my investigators on the early morning of March 8. The purpose of enclosing the photograph as previously stated, is simply to show you that cameras and equipment were in full operating order.—"

It was stipulated that the letter was received by Morin in Littleton, New Hampshire "in the due course of the mail."

Such is the evidence upon which the respondent was found guilty.

* * *

Turning to the other grounds advanced in the motion for acquittal, the respondent maintains his letter (State's Exhibit 1) does not constitute a threat to accuse Morin of the crime of adultery. He argues the implicit threats contained in the communication were "not to accuse of the CRIME of adultery but to bring an embarrassing, reputation-ruining divorce proceeding, in Mr. Morin's county of residence unless a stipulation could be negotiated." (Brief of Respondent-Appellant, p. 13.)

In dealing with a parallel contention in State v. Louanis, 79 Vt. 463, 467, 65 A. 532, 533, the Court answered the argument in an opinion by Chief Judge Rowell. "The statute is aimed at blackmailing, and a threat of any public accusation is as much within the reason of the statute as a threat of a formal complaint, and is much easier made, and may be quite as likely to accomplish its purpose. There is nothing in the statute that requires such a restricted meaning of the word 'accuse'; and to restrict it thus, would well nigh destroy the efficacy of the act."

The letter, marked "personal and confidential," makes a private accusation of adultery in support of a demand for a cash settlement. An incriminating photograph was enclosed for the avowed purpose of demonstrating "we have all of the proof necessary to prove adultery beyond a reasonable doubt." According to the writing itself, cost of refusal will be public exposure of incriminating conduct in the courts of New Hampshire where the event took place.

In further support of motion for acquittal, the respondent urges that the totality of the evidence does not exclude the inference that he acted merely as an attorney, attempting to secure a divorce for his client on the most favorable terms possible. This, of course, was the theory of the defense.

* * *

At the time of the writing, the respondent was undecided whether to advise his client to seek "informer fees." One of the advantages tendered to Morin for a "quiet" and "undamaging" divorce is an "absolute undertaking" on the part of the respondent's client not to inform against him in any way. The Internal Revenue Service, the United States Customs Service and other governmental agencies are suggested as being interested in such information. Quite clearly, these veiled threats exceeded the limits of the respondent's representation of his client in the divorce action. Although these matters were not specified in the indictment, they have a competent bearing on the question of intent. State v. Louanis, supra, 79 Vt. at 467, 65 A. 532.

Apart from this, the advancement of his client's claim to the marital property, however well founded, does not afford legal cause for the trial court to direct a verdict of acquittal in the background and context of his letter to Morin. A demand for settlement of a civil action, accompanied by a malicious threat to expose the wrongdoer's criminal conduct, if made with intent to extort payment, against his will, constitutes the crime alleged in the indictment.

The evidence at hand establishes beyond dispute the respondent's participation was done with preconceived design. The incriminating evidence which his letter threatens to expose was wilfully contrived and procured by a temptress hired for that purpose. These factors in the proof are sufficient to sustain a finding that the respondent acted maliciously and without just cause, within the meaning of our criminal statutes. State v. Muzzy, 87 Vt. 267, 269, 88 A. 895; Compare, State v. Sylvester, 112 Vt. 202, 206, 22 A.2d 505. The sum of the evidence supports the further inference that the act was done with intent to extort a substantial contingent fee to the respondent's personal advantage.

* * * The evidence of guilt is ample to support the verdict and the trial was free from errors in law.

Judgment affirmed.

NOTES

1. As the instant case demonstrates, modern extortion statutes are generally far broader in their coverage than the common law offense. Many statutes are broader than the Vermont statute applied in the instant case. Thus some cover threats to injure the victim's family or relatives and even threats to disclose disgraceful secrets or defects of the victim or his family or relatives. Others prohibit any threats to publish defamatory

materials or to injure the personal character or business reputation of the victim or others.

Most statutes—like the statute in the instant case—require only that a threat of a given nature be made with the specific intent indicated. Others, however, require that the property actually be obtained by means of these threats. The crime defined by these statutes is significantly broader than robbery for several reasons. First, the threat need not be of immediate harm to suffice for extortion, although it must for robbery. Second, the threatened harm that is sufficient for extortion is generally much broader than is necessary for robbery; see above. Third, robbery requires that the property be obtained from the person or presence of the victim; extortion has no such requirement.

A very similar statutory offense is that of blackmail. Under some statutory schemes a distinction between the two offenses is made on the basis that for extortion the accused must be a public official whereas blackmail involves private citizens.

2. What interest deserving protection is threatened by attempts to obtain money in exchange for a promise not to reveal the truth? Should the result be the same if the accused had not participated in the creation of the compromising situation? Is it extortion if law enforcement officials require a drug offender to "make" a certain number of cases for them in order to avoid prosecution?

VI. SPECIFIC OFFENSES: CRIMES AGAINST THE HABITATION

Two common law felonies—burglary and arson—were designed to protect the interest in the security of the habitation. Under modern criminal statutes, however, these two crimes, although generally retained, have often been expanded far beyond their original common law definitions.

A. BURGLARY

Common law burglary, as the discussion in the principal case indicates, was entry, by breaking, of the dwelling of another in the nighttime with the intent to commit a felony in the dwelling. But, as is also made clear in the principal case, modern statutes such as the Illinois statute applied in the case, have substantially modified this definition. "Breaking" is often not required, so any entry is sufficient. Structures covered include buildings other than residences and even such places as automobiles and enclosed storage yards. The requirement that entry occur in the nighttime is often eliminated, although burglary "in the nighttime" is frequently punishable by a more severe penalty than daytime burglary. Finally, the intent required is often expanded so that it is sufficient that the defendant intended to commit a felony or any theft (or larceny), whether that theft or larceny is felonious or not.

The principal case demonstrates the breadth in the modern law of burglary. While reading it, consider how the various issues discussed by the court would have been resolved if the common law definition of burglary were applicable. Consider also whether it is desirable to have the serious crime of burglary expanded so as to cover situations like that presented by the case.

Situations not giving rise to burglary are often covered by trespass statutes. The portions of the Model Penal Code presented in this section include the basic criminal trespass statute that supplements burglary.

PEOPLE v. DAVIS

Appellate Court of Illinois, 1977.
54 Ill.App.3d 517, 12 Ill.Dec. 362, 369 N.E.2d 1376.

MILLS, Justice:

* * *

The central issue to this appeal: what constitutes burglary in Illinois?

But first, some facts.

An information against Mr. Davis was filed charging him with the burglary of Consolidated Construction Co. in Champaign in that he knowingly and without authority "enter(ed) into part of" the building where its offices were located with the intent to commit a theft. At trial, Willie Gordon, Jr., owner and operator of Consolidated, stated that during the afternoon of May 4, 1976, he typed an estimate for a customer and left his offices at 3:20 p. m. to deliver it. The building had only one public entrance and he locked it when he left. He returned to his office at 4:05 p. m. and found the door open and his typewriter missing. Gordon left the building and, in a store two doors down, found John Lee Johnson. Johnson, who used part of the building for the Community Action Depot, was asked by Gordon if he took the typewriter. Johnson told Gordon he had unlocked the outside door about 3:55 p. m. and had left the building about ten minutes before Gordon's return. Gordon returned to the office, called the police and then went out to where 5 or 6 people were standing behind a nearby store. Gordon asked if any of them had seen anyone go into the office and get the typewriter or if any of them had taken it. Defendant was the only one of the group who replied, stating he "didn't know anything about the typewriter," and that he had not seen anyone go into the office and take the typewriter. Neither defendant nor the general public had authority to be in Consolidated's office or to take the typewriter.

Owen Fabert owns Trader's World Pawn Shop. About 4 p. m. on May 4, 1976, Fabert purchased a typewriter from defendant for $25. Defendant Davis' signature appeared on the bill of sale. Defendant was alone, didn't bargain over a price (Davis suggested $25) and the transaction took a very short time. Trader's World is two blocks from Consolidated's office. The typewriter was Consolidated's.

Defendant testified that he had been convicted of burglary in 1968 and 1972. He had been drinking alcohol all day on May 4 and about 4 p. m. he was near the train station when a man his height wearing sunglasses asked him to take a typewriter to a pawn shop. Of the $25 the man wanted for the typewriter, he would give defendant $7. Defendant made the transaction, received the $7 and purchased some whiskey. Defendant didn't know who the man was. Defendant stated he was never in Consolidated's office. * * *

The floorplan of the building is as follows: [editor's note: The sketch is part of the original opinion.]

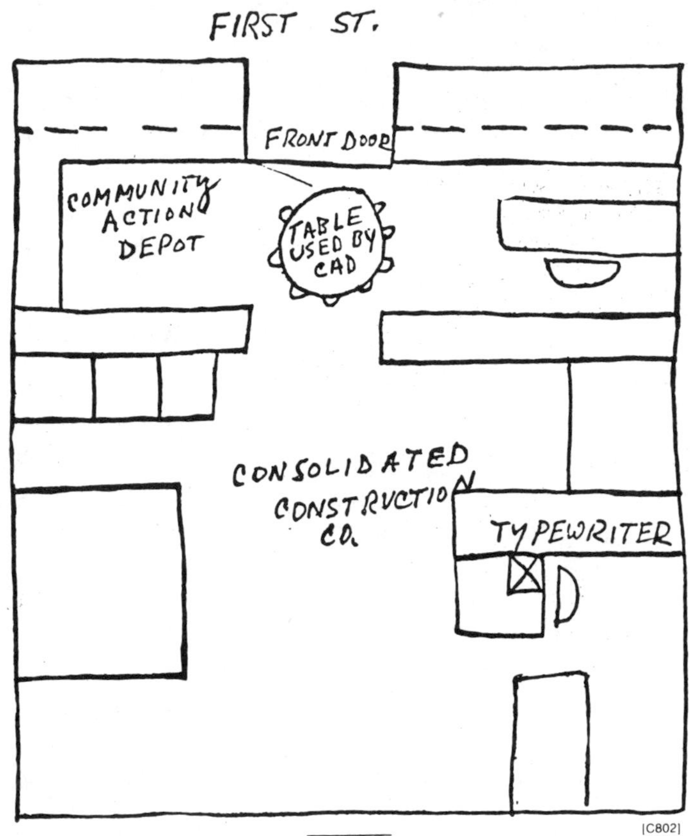

The connecting doorway to the area occupied by Consolidated Construction is somewhere between 5 and 15 feet wide. There is no door. Johnson and Terry Townsend, both of whom work in the front part of the building, have free access to Gordon's office. Gordon has seen members of the public come into the front part of the building. He never saw defendant with the typewriter. The front door showed no signs of forced entry.

Davis was found guilty by the jury and was sentenced to 6⅔ to 20 years' imprisonment. He * * * argues that the evidence adduced was insufficient to prove his entry into the building, his lack of authority, or his intent to commit theft. * * *

At common law, burglary was a crime against habitation. As described by the Committee Comments to our Criminal Code, the elements of burglary were "the breaking and entering of the dwelling house of another in the nighttime with the intent to commit a felony therein." The rather strict interpretation by those courts of the individual elements resulted not only from normal rules of penal construction, but also from the terminal sentence waiting for those convicted. Illinois' legislature has shaped what is now called "burglary" into a form unrecognizable to our common law ancestors. Gone is the element of "breaking", from which word such fine distinctions sprang. Gone too are the elements of "nighttime" and "dwelling house"; burglary is now a 24-hour crime which may be practiced upon a number of designated man-made cubicles. Section 19–1(a) of the Criminal Code now states:

> "A person commits burglary when without authority he knowingly enters or without authority remains within a building, housetrailer, watercraft, aircraft, motor vehicle as defined in The Illinois Vehicle Code, railroad car, or any part thereof, with intent to commit therein a felony or theft. This offense shall not include the offenses set out in Section 4–102 of The Illinois Vehicle Code." (Ill.Rev.Stat.1975, ch. 38, par. 19–1(a).)

The essence of the crime is *entry* into the designated areas with the requisite *intent*. Naturally, the State has the burden of proving the necessary intent at the time entry was made. Where a window has been broken or a door jimmied, intent is easily shown. However, since no breaking is now required, proof of an unforced entry by a person when there are no eyewitnesses can only be accomplished by circumstantial evidence and inferences drawn therefrom.

In this particular situation, clarity demands a discussion of what is *not* material to decide defendant's reasonable doubt issue. The use of force in entry has not been a necessary element of burglary in Illinois for some time. The "close" broken in the instant case was *not* the front door of the building; the "entry" occurred by passing through the doorway inside the building into Gordon's office area. Historically, Illinois courts have recognized that entry into certain separate areas of a building with the requisite intent could support a burglary charge. The statute implements this logic by providing entry into certain structures "or any part thereof" as an element of burglary. The charge and the State's arguments at trial in this case were directed to proof of burglary into a part of the building, namely Gordon's office area. Any discussion by the State or the defense regarding the front door is therefore immaterial to proof of burglary. The fact that Johnson left the door open merely provided a means of quicker entry to the front portion of the building.

The fact that the doorway contained no door is likewise immaterial. At common law, the burglary of any interior chamber had to be pursuant to some "breaking" thereof, directly requiring the existence of an interior barrier such as a hotel room door. Some recent authority indicates the requirement of an interior barrier (State v. Ortega (1974), 86 N.M. 350, 524 P.2d 522). However, the Illinois Supreme Court in People v. Blair (1972), 52 Ill.2d 371, 288 N.E.2d 443, found a car wash with an open entry and exit-way to be a "building" susceptible of being entered under the burglary statute. In People v. Shannon (1975), 28 Ill.App.3d 873, 329 N.E.2d 399, the court had no trouble finding an entry had occurred when defendant went through an open loading door. The key to the crime is entry into the prohibited space, not whether entry was made by turning a handle, cracking a lock, or walking through an open portal. In light of *Blair* and *Shannon,* logic demands that entry into a "part" of a building through an open doorway with the requisite intent is a prohibited act under our burglary statute.

"Authority" is likewise of little concern here for three reasons. First, Gordon testified that Davis and others had no authority to be in his office. No evidence before the jury or in any offers of proof showed that Johnson or Townsend had permission to allow others to use the office. Defendant's use of the public place rule to argue authority is inapposite. The rule states that authority to enter a business building, or other building open to the public, extends only to those who enter with a purpose consistent with the reason the building is open. Only the front part of the building was shown to be public in nature. Since the question revolves around intent upon entering the back section of the building, the rule does not apply. Even if the office area were public in nature, the entry which resulted in the typewriter being stolen was not consistent with the reason the office area was open, i. e., for Gordon to sell his construction services to customers. Lastly, entry of a protected area under the burglary statute with the intent to commit a theft implies the entry was without authority.

Therefore, we are left with entry and intent. Entry, and the manner thereof, as well as intent to commit a theft, may be inferred from the facts in evidence. Circumstantial evidence of burglary may arise from either evidence of entry or evidence of the criminal's later acts. For example, in the absence of inconsistent circumstances, proof of unlawful entry into a building which contains personal property that could be the subject of larceny gives rise to an inference that will sustain a burglary conviction. The inference, grounded in human experience is that the unlawful entry was not purposeless and indicates theft as the most likely purpose.

In addition, evidence of a defendant's subsequent acts may give rise to inferences sufficient to sustain a conviction. It is hornbook law that nothing need be taken in order to support a burglary conviction based on intent to commit a theft; however, inferences may arise from defendant's later possession of the fruits of his work. The fact that larceny or theft was actually committed is evidence that the earlier entry was accomplished with an intent to commit that offense. A defendant's participation in the crime is established circumstantially by his recent, exclusive and unexplained possession of the proceeds of the burglary which in itself gives rise to an inference of guilt which is sufficient to sustain a conviction. Even defendant Davis' trial and appellate counsel admitted that theft on defendant's part was strongly reflected in the record; trial counsel sought unsuccessfully to include a theft instruction for the jury. * * * [I]t was not improper for the jury to infer from the facts before them that Davis stole the typewriter, and that he entered Gordon's office area intending to commit theft.

NOTES

1. At common law, burglary requires that the thing entered be a "dwelling", i. e., a structure used by someone as a residence. It is not necessary that the resident be present at the time, and his temporary absence does not cause the structure to lose its character as a dwelling. But if no one has yet lived in the structure, it is not a dwelling, even if it was constructed for purposes of residence. And if the resident left with no intent to return, the structure is no longer a dwelling. As the instant case demonstrates, however, modern statutes have often expanded the crime of burglary to include entry into structures other than dwellings and even things other than structures.

The common law required the dwelling to be "of another". Since burglary was an offense against the dwelling, however, this does not require that ownership be in someone other than the defendant. All that is necessary is that the structure be used as a dwelling by another.

Entry constitutes burglary at common law only if it is by means of an opening created by a breaking. Breaking is actual or constructive. Actual breaking requires only some use of force; pushing open a door held shut by friction is sufficient. Constructive breaking occurs if entry is through the chimney or is accomplished by use of fraud, threats, or intimidation.

There must be entry for the burglary to be complete, but it is sufficient if any portion of the offender's body is inside the structure, even momentarily. It is also sufficient if a tool or inanimate object is inserted or otherwise placed in the structure, *if* it is placed in it for the purpose of accomplishing the crime that the offender intends. It is not sufficient if the instrument is inserted for purposes of gaining entry.

2. The court in the principal case discusses but finds inapplicable the so-called "public place" rule. The desirability of this rule has continued to divide the courts. As the discussion in the case indicates, the problem arises in jurisdictions where no breaking is required. Where premises are open to the public and the owner has therefore given general permission to enter, does one who enters with the intent of committing an offense on the premises commit burglary? Some courts say yes, reasoning that the permission given by the owner does not cover those who enter with the intent of committing a felony. E. g., State v. Adams, —— Nev. ——, 581 P.2d 868 (1978). Other courts, however, hold that if the defendant was given

permission to enter, the entry is not burglary even if the defendant had an undisclosed intention to commit an offense in the premises. E. g., Champlin v. State, 84 Wis.2d 621, 267 N.W.2d 295 (1978). But where the consent to entry is obtained by more direct deceit or fraud, the permission does not prevent the entry from constituting burglary. See State v. Ortiz, 92 N.M. 166, 584 P.2d 1306 (1978) (defendants gained entry by telling occupant that something was wrong with occupant's daughter and occupant should get hold of her daughter immediately).

3. Suppose two spouses are separated. One comes to the place where both spouses lived prior to their separation, and enters by breaking with the intent of assaulting the other spouse. Has the first spouse committed burglary? In Vazquez v. State, 350 So.2d 1094 (Fla.App.1977), the court held that where there was no final decree dissolving the marriage and no legal separation agreement, restraining order, or court decree limiting or ending the marital relationship, the entering spouse did not enter premises "of another" and thus was not guilty of burglary. Finding that no other jurisdiction had applied burglary to such domestic dispute situations, the court commented:

> We cannot conceive that the legislature intended to apply the burglary statute with its harsh criminal penalties to domestic disputes within the immediate family unit over the right to be on certain premises. Such disputes have been and should continue to be treated as purely civil matters to which the burglary statute is inapplicable.

350 So.2d at 1097.

MODEL PENAL CODE *

(Proposed Official Draft, 1962).

ARTICLE 221. BURGLARY AND OTHER CRIMINAL INTRUSION

Section 221.0. Definitions

In this Article, unless a different meaning plainly is required:

(1) "occupied structure" means any structure, vehicle or place adapted for overnight accommodation of persons, or for carrying on business therein, whether or not a person is actually present.

(2) "night" means the period between thirty minutes past sunset and thirty minutes before sunrise.

Section 221.1. Burglary

(1) *Burglary Defined.* A person is guilty of burglary if he enters a building or occupied structure, or separately secured or oc-

cupied portion thereof, with purpose to commit a crime therein, unless the premises are at the time open to the public or the actor is licensed or privileged to enter. It is an affirmative defense to prosecution for burglary that the building or structure was abandoned.

(2) *Grading.* Burglary is a felony of the second degree if it is perpetrated in the dwelling of another at night, or if, in the course of committing the offense, the actor:

(a) purposely, knowingly or recklessly inflicts or attempts to inflict bodily injury on anyone; or

(b) is armed with explosives or a deadly weapon.

Otherwise, burglary is a felony of the third degree. An act shall be deemed "in the course of committing" an offense if it occurs in an attempt to commit the offense or in flight after the attempt or commission.

Section 221.2. Criminal Trespass

(1) *Buildings and Occupied Structures.* A person commits an offense if, knowing that he is not licensed or privileged to do so, he enters or surreptitiously remains in any building or occupied structure, or separately secured or occupied portion thereof. An offense under this Subsection is a misdemeanor if it is committed in a dwelling at night. Otherwise it is a petty misdemeanor.

* * *

(3) *Defenses.* It is an affirmative defense to prosecution under this Section that:

(a) a building or occupied structure involved in an offense under Subsection (1) was abandoned; or

(b) the premises were at the time open to members of the public and the actor complied with all lawful conditions imposed on access to or remaining in the premises; or

(c) the actor reasonably believed that the owner of the premises, or other person empowered to license access thereto, would have licensed him to enter or remain.

B. ARSON

Arson at common law was the malicious burning of a dwelling (or some building used in connection with it) belonging to or occupied by another. Modern criminal codes often retain the offense in this general form. The major issues presented by arson law are: (1) What structures, buildings, or objects are covered? (2) What effect or damage must be done by the fire in order to complete the crime? and (3) What intent must the defendant have had? As the principal case in this section makes clear, modern statutes often modify the traditional common law definition of the offense. This is also demonstrated by the provision from the Model Penal Code.

LYNCH v. STATE

Court of Appeals of Indiana, 1977.
— Ind.App. —, 370 N.E.2d 401.

BUCHANAN, Judge.

Louis Lynch appeals his conviction of First Degree Arson * * *.

* * *

The evidence most favorable to the State reveals that in the early morning hours of June 18, 1975, a man identified as Lynch was seen throwing a burning object at the residence of Mr. and Mrs. Estel Barnett. Immediately after the object struck the house flames engulfed the side of the residence. The flames last for several minutes and then died out. The fire department was not called.

The Barnetts, who were awakened by a passing neighbor, investigated and discovered a bottle containing flammable liquid with a cotton or cloth wick protruding from the opening. A "burn trail" extended from the lawn approximately ten feet to the house. Damage to the building's aluminum siding consisted of blistering and discoloration of the paint. The amount of the damage was Ninety-one and 29/100 ($91.29) Dollars. No other part of the house was damaged.

Lynch was subsequently charged by information with the crime of First Degree Arson. * * *

* * *

The matter went to the jury and Lynch was convicted. This appeal followed.

* * *

* * * Lynch * * * argues that the verdict is not sustained by sufficient evidence of a "burning" of the house as no part of the house was actually consumed by fire.

* * *

The gist of Lynch's position is that he is not guilty of arson because "sets fire to" and "burns" as used in the First Degree Arson statute are synonymous, and no "burning" took place, i. e., the house was not consumed.

The statute, Ind.Code § 35–16–1–1 [10–301], provides:

> Arson in the First Degree.—Any person who willfully and maliciously *sets fire to or burns,* or causes the setting of fire to or the burning, or who aids, counsels or procures the setting of fire to or the burning of any dwelling house * * * shall be guilty of arson in the first degree, and, upon convic-

> tion thereof, shall be imprisoned in the state prison not less than five [5] years nor more than twenty [20] years, to which may be added a fine not to exceed two thousand dollars [$2,000]. (Emphasis added)

Observe that the drafter used the disjunctive word "or" in separating the phrase "sets fire to" from the word "burns".

* * *

If we construe "or" in its "plain, or ordinary and usual, sense" as we are bound to do, it separates two different things. "Sets fire to" and "burns" are not synonymous in this context. Thus the legislative intent is trumpeted in the first lines of the statute as heralding the assertion of different concepts strung out by a series of "ors" describing alternative (different) acts ("causes", "who aids", etc.).

Our search discloses no Indiana cases defining the two terms. Other jurisdictions have reached differing conclusions.

Traditionally the common law rigidly required an actual burning. The fire must be actually communicated to the object to such an extent as to have taken effect upon it.

Other jurisdictions have recognized the distinction between "sets fire to" and "burns" as two different concepts. To "set fire to" a structure is to "place fire upon", or "against" or to "put fire in connection with" it. It is possible to set fire to a structure which, by reason of the sudden extinction of the fire, will fail to change the charactristics of the structure. Nevertheless, it has been "set fire to".

* * *

Unlike Lynch, then, we cannot conclude that he is not guilty of first degree arson because there was no burning of the house. He set fire to the house by causing a flammable substance to burn thereon causing a scorching or blistering of the paint which was an integral part of the structure. The composition of the structure was changed. No more was necessary.

Thus the modern construction of statutory terms we are interpreting is that they are not synonymous, each having a separate, independent meaning, thereby eliminating any ambiguity.

The judgment is affirmed.

* * *

WHITE, Judge, dissenting:

* * *

Many jurisdictions hold that the statutory language "sets fire to or burns" is merely repetitive of the common law and thus requires an actual burning, i. e.

> "that the fire was actually communicated to the building itself to such an extent as to have taken effect on, and in some

> degree destroyed some portion of the fibrous part of the wood and lumber composing a part of it.
>
> "And this is true whether the material in question was actually in a blaze or merely charred, though a mere scorching, without any actual ignition of a portion of the building, would not be sufficient." State v. Schwartz (Del., 1932), 5 W.W.Harr. 418, 424, 166 A. 666, 668–669.

Other jurisdictions hold that the statutory language "sets fire to or burns" defines two different offenses, one being an actual burning and the other being a lesser act, such as to "put fire to" or to "place fire upon" or "against" or to "put fire in connection with." * * *

* * *

In still other jurisdictions the question is avoided by use of the phrase "set fire to with intent to burn". Such statutes clearly indicate that something less than a burning is required.

In view of the conflicting results reached in other jurisdictions it is obvious that the phrase "sets fire to" is ambiguous. The rule for construing a criminal statute containing such an ambiguity is that stated in Utley v. State (1972), 258 Ind. 443, 281 N.E.2d 888 * * *:

> * * * this Court must be guided by the well-settled rule of judicial construction that criminal statutes must be strictly construed against the State and in favor of the accused. Coleman v. State (1970), 253 Ind. 627, 256 N.E.2d 389. In practical effect this rule means that this Court, when faced with statutory language having two fairly well-settled meanings, will deem the Legislature to have intended the meaning which gives the narrowest range of applicability to the statute." (258 Ind. at 446, 281 N.E.2d at 890.)

Thus "sets fire to", as used in the first degree arson statute * * * should be construed as being synonymous with "burns", this being "the meaning which gives the statute the narrowest range of applicability."

* * *

NOTES

1. Common law arson required that the structure burned be the dwelling of another. This was defined as the same phrase was defined in burglary law.

2. As the instant case indicates, traditional arson does not require the destruction of the structure or even that extensive damage be done to it. Mere "charring"—some damage to the fiber of the material of the structure—is sufficient. But discoloration from heat or smoke—"scorching"—is not enough. Moreover, the damage must have been caused by fire. If a structure is destroyed by an explosion, this is not arson unless the explosion caused a fire which, in turn, burned the structure.

3. The traditional requirement is that the burning be "malicious." This was recently defined as follows:

> The requirement that defendant act "willfully and maliciously" does not signify that defendant must have *actual subjective* purpose that the acts he does intentionally shall produce either (1) a setting afire or burning of any structure * * * or (2) damage to or destruction of said structure. So long as (absent independent circumstances of justification, excuse or mitigation) defendant has actual subjective intention to do the act he does and does it in disregard of a conscious awareness that such conduct involves highly substantial risks that a structure . . . will be set afire, burned, or caused to be burned—notwithstanding that the defendant does not "intend" such consequences in the sense that he has no actual subjective purpose that his conduct produce them—defendant acts "willfully and maliciously."

State v. O'Farrell, 355 A.2d 396, 398 (Me.1976).

MODEL PENAL CODE *

(Proposed Official Draft, 1962).

Section 220.1. Arson and Related Offenses

(1) *Arson.* A person is guilty of arson, a felony of the second degree, if he starts a fire or causes an explosion with the purpose of:

(a) destroying a building or occupied structure of another; or

(b) destroying or damaging any property, whether his own or another's, to collect insurance for such loss. It shall be an affirmative defense to prosecution under this paragraph that the actor's conduct did not recklessly endanger any building or occupied structure of another or place any other person in danger of death or bodily injury.

(2) *Reckless Burning or Exploding.* A person commits a felony of the third degree if he purposely starts a fire or causes an explosion, whether on his own property or another's, and thereby recklessly:

(a) places another person in danger of death or bodily injury; or

(b) places a building or occupied structure of another in danger of damage or destruction.

* * *

(4) *Definitions.* "Occupied structure" includes a ship, trailer, sleeping car, airplane, or other vehicle, structure or place adapted for overnight accommodation of persons or for carrying on business

therein, whether or not a person is actually present. Property is that of another, for the purposes of this section, if anyone other than the actor has a possessory or proprietory interest therein. If a building or structure is divided into separately occupied units, any unit not occupied by the actor is an occupied structure of another.

VII. SPECIFIC OFFENSES: CRIMES AGAINST THE PERSON

A. ASSAULT AND BATTERY

Battery, a common law misdemeanor, consists of the application of force to the person of another. Injury is not required and even an offensive touching will suffice for the offense.

Assault, also a misdemeanor at common law, is in all jurisdictions committed if the defendant attempts to commit a battery. Thus the crime can, in this manner, be committed even if the victim is totally unaware of the situation, since no apprehension of harm is necessary for an attempted battery. As the principal case in this section illustrates, in many jurisdictions an alternative manner of committing assault is to cause the victim to experience a reasonable apprehension of immediate physical harm. This manner of committing assault, of course, requires that the victim be aware of the defendant's actions and experience fear of harm in response to them.

The Model Penal Code provisions contained in the section illustrate the trend to merge the two offenses into a single crime, usually labeled assault. These provisions are also typical of modern statutes distinguishing "simple" assaults and batteries from "aggravated" ones, which are punishable by a significantly more serious penalty.

STATE v. ROBERTS

Supreme Court of North Carolina, 1967.
270 N.C. 655, 155 S.E.2d 303.

Defendant was [convicted of assault upon a female, Debbie Pickett.]

The State presented evidence substantially as follows:

Mrs. Mary Stanford testified that she lived on Higby Street in Durham, and that her yard backed up to the I–85 By-pass. Mr. and Mrs. Harry Pickett lived next door, and their yards adjoined with a wire fence running along the back of both lots. On 6 May 1966 she was taking care of a neighbor's little boy and had sent him next door to play in the Pickett's back yard with Debbie Pickett, aged four. When she went out to call the little boy around lunch time, she saw the defendant "talking to the children, down at the lower end of the Pickett yard, the end that faces toward the bank of the By-pass. Debbie and the little boy that I was keeping were talking to James Roberts. I saw James Roberts take Debbie Pickett up in his arms and was talking to her. I could not understand what he was saying, but he took her up in his arms over the fence and was talking to her. I ran out into my back yard where I could get a better view and then he talked to her, and I hollered and told him to put her back across the fence. He didn't hardly look at me. He was looking at Debbie and was talking to her. He was holding her up in his arms. After I hollered at him another time and told him to put the child back across the fence, he put her across the fence and then came to my back yard." On cross-examination Mrs. Stanford testified that she did not see the defendant actually pick Debbie up. "I did not notice the manner in which he picked the child up; when I looked, he had Debbie up in his arms, and that was when I ran into my back yard where I could get a better view. I did not see the actual picking up; when I looked back he had her in his arms. I didn't see him reach across the fence. He just kept holding her in his arms. He didn't make any movement away from me, or any movement that I could see. He was talking to her."

Mrs. Stanford further testified that she asked defendant his name, and he told her. She then asked him what he was doing, and he told her it was none of her business and to go to h * * *, and then left.

* * *

BRANCH, Justice.

Defendant contends the court erred in refusing to grant his motion for nonsuit as to assault on a female.

There is no statutory definition of assault in North Carolina, and the crime of assault is governed by common law rules. * * *

This Court generally defines the common law offense of assault as "an overt act or an attempt, or the unequivocal appearance of an attempt, with force and violence, to do some immediate physical injury to the person of another, which show of force or menace of violence must be sufficient to put a person of reasonable firmness in fear of immediate bodily harm."

This common law rule places emphasis on the intent or state of mind of the person accused. The decisions of the Court have, in effect, brought forth another rule known as the "show of violence rule," which places the emphasis on the reasonable apprehension of the person assailed. The "show of violence rule" consists of a show of violence accompanied by reasonable apprehension of immediate bodily harm or injury on the part of the person assailed which causes him to engage in a course of conduct which he would not otherwise have followed. This rule has been extended to many cases of assault on a female. Thus, there are two rules under which a person may be prosecuted for assault in North Carolina.

Although assault has been defined by this Court many times, the extreme difficulty of applying the facts to the law was recognized in the case of State v. Hampton, 63 N.C. 13, when the Court stated: "It would seem that there ought to be no difficulty in determining whether any given state of facts amounts to an assault. But the behavior of men towards each other varies by such mere shades, that it is sometimes very difficult to characterize properly their acts and declarations." * * *

In answering the question presented, we must, of necessity, review the pertinent cases on assault.

In the case of State v. Hampton, supra, prosecutor was going down steps from a courtroom and defendant, being within striking distance, clenched his right hand and said: "I have a good mind to hit you," thereby causing prosecutor to take another stairway and direction. The Court held this to be an assault.

State v. Shipman, 81 N.C. 513, holds that where a defendant, using threatening language against prosecutor, advanced on him with knife in hand and prosecutor withdrew with the statement, "I shall have to go away," the defendant was properly convicted of an assault.

The case of State v. Williams, 186 N.C. 627, 120 S.E. 224, presents evidence that a 23-year old man on several occasions made indecent proposals to a 15-year old girl on public streets, causing her to flee in a direction other than her destination, and causing fear and anxiety on her part. The Court held this to be an assault.

The Court in the Per Curiam opinion of State v. Silver, 227 N.C. 352, 42 S.E.2d 208, held that in a prosecution for assault on a female, where the evidence tended to show that defendant had asked prosecutrix an improper question, unaccompanied by any show of violence, threat, or any display of force, defendant's motion for nonsuit should have been granted.

In the case of State v. Johnson, 264 N.C. 598, 142 S.E.2d 151, defendant's wife, after separation, came home to get some personal belongings. There was an argument and defendant came toward his wife with open knife in his hand. She told defendant to let her out and he immediately unlocked the door and complied. She threw lye on him and left. Holding the evidence insufficient to be submitted to the jury, the Court stated:

> " 'In order to constitute a criminal assault there must be an overt act or an attempt, or the unequivocal appearance of an attempt, with force and violence, to do some immediate physical injury to the person of another, which show of force or menace of violence must be sufficient to put a man of reasonable firmness in fear of immediate bodily harm.' 1 Strong: N.C. Index, Assault and Battery, § 4, p. 182 (Supp., p. 60)."

In State v. Ingram, 237 N.C. 197, 74 S.E.2d 532, the evidence tended to show that defendant drove his automobile along a public highway and "leered" at prosecutrix who was walking some distance away on a dirt road. She heard defendant's car stop as she was passing through a wooded area, and she ran about 215 feet until she was out of the woods. She then saw defendant walking fast about 70 feet away. Defendant stopped, and she continued to her destination. The Court held the evidence was insufficient to be submitted to the jury on the question of assault on a female * * *.

* * *

Again considering assault on a female, in State v. Gough, 257 N.C. 348, 126 S.E.2d 118, 95 A.L.R.2d 441, there was evidence that defendant, by false representations, induced two young girls to go with him in his automobile. He stopped the automobile in a wooded area in the nighttime, telling them if they would be nice to him and cooperate with him, they would not get hurt, and he would pay them nice. Whereupon, the girls jumped from the automobile and ran to a farm house where they asked for and received help. [The court held that] there was sufficient evidence of kidnapping, but that there was not sufficient evidence to submit the question of the lesser offense of assault on a female to the jury * * *.

* * *

The evidence in the instant case shows that witness saw defendant talking to the two children. She then saw the child in defendant's arms. Defendant made no movement to leave, nor did he offer any overt movement indicative of force or violence. Upon being twice told by the witness to put the child down, he placed her in the yard. There was no evidence that the child was frightened or suffered any fear or apprehension as a result of the acts of defendant, or that defendant molested or improperly held the child. It may have been that the sound of the child's voice created an abnormal sexual desire in the apparently disturbed mind of the defendant. On the other hand, he may have had the natural instinct that many normal men have to affectionately hold a child. It is, however, clear there was no threat of violence and no offer or attempt to injure. * * *

Considering the evidence most favorable to the State and giving the State the benefit of every reasonable intendment and inference to be drawn therefrom, as we must upon considering motion for nonsuit, but being mindful that to convict a person of a criminal offense there must be legal evidence of the commission of the offense charged, something more than is sufficient to raise a suspicion or conjecture, we hold that the trial court erred in denying defendant's motion for judgment of nonsuit.

Reversed.

NOTES

1. Spitting, at least in the victim's face, is sufficiently offensive to constitute battery. State v. Humphries, 21 Wash.App. 405, 586 P.2d 130 (1978).

2. A battery may be committed "indirectly," by administering poison or by causing a dog to bite the victim. J. A. T. v. State, 133 Ga.App. 922, 212 S.E.2d 879 (1975).

3. Some formulations of "attempted battery" assault impose a requirement that the defendant have the "present ability to carry out the attempt." But this is sometimes modified so as to require only an "*apparent* present ability" to carry out the intended battery. The difference is significant. Under the "present ability" requirement, a defendant who points an unloaded or nonfunctional gun at a victim is not guilty of assault because the condition of the weapon establishes that he lacks the ability to carry out his presumed intent to shoot the victim. But if only an apparent present ability is required, this defendant does commit assault, even if he knows the gun will not function, since from the victim's perspective the defendant has the apparent ability to shoot. If a jurisdiction defines assault as consisting only of an attempted battery but further provides that an apparent present ability to succeed is sufficient, the end result is probably very close to adopting a rule that provides that assault is committed by putting the victim in fear. See Anthony v. United States, 361 A.2d 202 (D.C.App.1976), holding that assault under District of Columbia law requires only the apparent ability to complete the attempt.

4. Under the "attempted battery" formulation of assault, an intent to complete the battery is essential. See Stoutmire v. State, 358 So.2d 508 (Ala.Crim.App.1978) (shooting at police officer's house and car is not assault, where evidence shows that defendants did not intend to hit any individual). A defendant who threatens to injure another is, therefore, not guilty of assault if he secretly intends not to carry out the threat, although one charged with assault may experience difficulty in convincing a judge or jury that such a secret reservation actually existed.

MODEL PENAL CODE *

(Proposed Official Draft, 1962).

Section 211.1. Assault

(1) *Simple Assault.* A person is guilty of assault if he:

(a) attempts to cause or purposely, knowingly or recklessly causes bodily injury to another; or

(b) negligently causes bodily injury to another with a deadly weapon; or

(c) attempts by physical menace to put another in fear of imminent serious bodily harm.

Simple assault is a misdemeanor unless committed in a fight or scuffle entered into by mutual consent, in which case it is a petty misdemeanor.

(2) *Aggravated Assault.* A person is guilty of aggravated assault if he:

(a) attempts to cause serious bodily injury to another, or causes such injury purposely, knowingly or recklessly under circumstances manifesting extreme indifference to the value of human life; or

(b) attempts to cause or purposely or knowingly causes bodily injury to another with a deadly weapon.

Aggravated assault under paragraph (a) is a felony of the second degree; aggravated assault under paragraph (b) is a felony of the third degree.

Section 211.2. Recklessly Endangering Another Person

A person commits a misdemeanor if he recklessly engages in conduct which places or may place another person in danger of death or serious bodily injury. Recklessness and danger shall be presumed where a person knowingly points a firearm at or in the direction of another, whether or not the actor believed the firearm to be loaded.

B. KIDNAPPING AND FALSE IMPRISONMENT

False imprisonment at common law was the unlawful confinement of another person. As the Model Penal Code provisions contained in this section illustrate, it is still frequently defined in the same way in modern criminal codes.

The common law misdemeanor of kidnapping consisted of the forcible abduction of another and transportation of the victim to another country. Modern statutes virtually always modify this offense and expand it beyond its limited common law definition. Generally, under modern statutes kidnapping is an aggravated form of false imprisonment. Thus kidnapping often consists of unlawful restraint of the victim involving some movement (or "asportation") of the victim, unlawful restraint in a "secret" place, or unlawful restraint for the purpose of holding the victim for ransom or to inflict harm upon the victim. Under these modern statutes, kidnapping is a serious felony with a heavy penalty attached to it.

As the principal case in this section illustrates, a major problem presented by kidnapping under modern statutes is determining whether kidnapping is committed when the victim is detained or moved during the commission of another crime, such as robbery or rape.

PEOPLE v. ADAMS

Court of Appeals of Michigan, 1971.
34 Mich.App. 540, 192 N.W.2d 19.

LEVIN, Judge. The defendant, Otis L. Adams, appeals his conviction of kidnapping.

Kidnapping is now a statutory, not a common-law crime. The relevant portion of our statute makes it unlawful to "wilfully, maliciously and without lawful authority * * * forcibly or secretly confine or imprison any other person within this state against his will." But every forcible confinement is not the capital offense of kidnapping.

Our kidnapping statute, like most, is so all-encompassing in its literal breadth that unless its operative effect is confined by objective standards it would be void for overbreadth.

Where a kidnapping statute does not in terms require a "carrying away" of the victim, an asportation requirement or, as a substitute, the elements of secrecy, has been judicially read into and made a part of the definition of the crime.

There are two basic kidnapping patterns. In one, the victim is seized and removed to another place; in the other, the victim is confined in the place where he is found. In the first, an asportation or movement of the victim is an essential element; in the second, movement is not an element, but secrecy of the confinement is required.

In this case the people do not charge the victim was secretly confined. The information charged the defendant Otis Adams with "forcibly confining and imprisoning" his victim—the word "secretly" in the statutory phrase "forcibly or secretly confine" was omitted when the charge was drawn.

To save the Michigan kidnapping statute, insofar as it applies to nonsecret confinements, from a declaration of unconstitutionality because of overbreadth we read it as requiring an asportation. A confinement (other than a secret confinement) without a movement of the victim is not kidnapping. And, for reasons which we will spell out, every movement of the victim of an assaultive crime incidental to the commission of that crime is not kidnapping; the asportation must have a significance independent of the assault in order to manifest the capital and separate offense of kidnapping.

In this case the victim, a prison official, was seized in Jackson State Prison by Adams and other inmates and moved from one part of the prison to another. The seizure and movement occurred in the presence of prison guards; the exact location of both the victim and of the defendant Adams was at all times known to prison guards who had the place cordoned off and surrounded by overwhelming armed force. It is not claimed that Adams ever intended to remove his victim from the prison or that he intended to attempt to effect an escape. This is not the usual hostage pattern, nor is it the usual kidnapping pattern.

I.

Facts

* * *

[In the course of a prison riot, Inspector Joseph Dembosky was seized by defendant Adams and other inmates and forced at knife point to the prison yard and ultimately to the prison hospital about 1500 feet from the place where he was originally seized. During the journey the inmates threatened the tower guards that Dembosky would be killed if they were fired upon. Dembosky and the other guards held captive were released unharmed after about five and one-half hours.]

The reprehensible nature of Adams' action does not alter our duty to determine whether the evidence against him is sufficient to support his conviction for kidnapping Inspector Dembosky.

II.

The statute and its overbreadth

* * *

What is immediately obvious about the language of our kidnapping statute is the extraordinary range of conduct it might proscribe.

In the phrase "forcible confinement or imprisonment," the word "imprisonment" is clearly a narrower term than "confinement"; every "imprisonment" would be a "confinement." The word "forcible" adds little, if anything, to the word "confine." "Confine," in the sense in which it is used in this statute, clearly speaks of an involuntary restraint of the liberty of the individual, which, of necessity, is brought about by the use of some force. Similarly, as to the words "against his will." If the confinement was voluntary, it would mean that the victim was confined although he was free to leave—an obvious contradiction of terms.

Since "confine" in this context strongly implies force of some kind, the offense is complete when the actor "wilfully, maliciously and without lawful authority" confines the victim. And, since in the ordinary case there is likely to be no question of lawful authority (and besides, lawful authority negatives "malice"), and since the wilfulness required by law does not enlarge the requirement of malice, *violation of the terms of the statute occurs whenever the actor "maliciously confines" any other person.*

"Malice, in its common acceptation, means ill will toward some person. In its legal sense, it applies to a wrongful act committed intentionally against that person, without legal justification or excuse."

Bonkowski v. Arlan's Department Store (1970), 383 Mich. 90, 99, 174 N.W.2d 765, 768.

* * *

Accordingly, freed of its tautology, the kidnapping statute, simply put, makes it kidnapping to *intentionally confine another person without legal justification or excuse.*

It will be observed that the statute makes no reference to the duration or circumstances of the confinement. Literally construed, the statute leads to absurd results. The trespasser who momentarily locks a caretaker in his cottage is placed on the same footing as the professional criminal who invade a home, seizes the occupants at gunpoint, transports them to a secret hideout, and holds them for ransom. The robber who orders his victim to stand motionless while his wallet is removed is guilty of the same crime as the robber who forces his victim to drive for miles to a deserted location, where he is terrorized and abandoned. A group of college students who invade a dean's office, wrongfully confining its occupants, commit the same offense as a gang of rapists who seize a woman and remove her from her family to a place of isolation.

Shopkeepers who wrongfully detain suspected shoplifters, cabdrivers who purposely deliver passengers to the wrong destinations, tavernkeepers who bar exits until bar bills have been paid, all may be subject to civil damage actions, but a sensible penology rebels at the classification of such acts as capital offenses.

As emphatically as these examples offend a rational penal code, they scarely embrace all the varieties of technically culpable, but scarcely menacing, conduct which violates a statutory ban on "intentional confinement" of any other person.

* * *

[The Court's discussion of the problems posed by statute under the void-for-vagueness doctrine (see section II.C.3. supra) is omitted. The Court concluded that a literal reading of the statute would expose perpetrators of virtually every crime against the person to capital sanctions in the discretion of prosecutors, judges and juries. To avoid such results and thereby preserve the statute the court turned to an analysis of its substance.]

III.

Substantive law of kidnapping

At common law, kidnapping required an asportation of the victim out of the country. Kidnapping was a misdemeanor, and was viewed merely as an aggravated form of false imprisonment; the aggravating factor was the removal of the victim from the sovereign's protection.

Kidnapping statutes in the United have abolished the requirement that a national or a regional boundary be breached.

Modification of the asportation element of the common-law crime was not the only American statutory departure from the common law. Public revulsion against the wave of carefully-planned and often brutal kidnappings for ransom of the 1920's and 1930's resulted in the imposition of heavy penalties,[23] including the death penalty, for kidnappers, and passage of the Federal Kidnapping Act, the so-called Lindbergh Law. It was in 1931 that Michigan imposed a maximum sentence of life imprisonment for kidnapping.

Another characteristic of kidnapping legislation has been its failure to distinguish between the crimes of kidnapping and false imprisonment. Michigan, along with most States, does not have a separate false imprisonment statute.

These matters aside, the principal question that has perplexed American courts in construing kidnapping legislation has been the degree of asportation required to transform an assault, robbery, or other crime into kidnapping. Torn between the common-law rule that a most significant asportation was required, and the obvious legislative intention to broaden the scope of the offense, the courts, virtually without exception, endorsed the idea that any asportation, however slight, was sufficient to constitute kidnapping.

Representative of this formulation were the opinions of the California Supreme Court in People v. Chessman (1951), 38 Cal.2d 166, 192, 238 P.2d 1001, 1017, and People v. Wein (1958), 50 Cal.2d 383, 399, 400, 326 P.2d 457, 466. In *Chessman,* the defendant forced his victim to move 22 feet to his automobile, where he sexually assaulted her. The Court held that, "It is the fact, not the distance, of forcible removal which constitutes kidnapping in this state." In *Wein,* the Court applied the *Chessman* standard to uphold the kidnapping conviction of a defendant who forced his victims to move from room to room in their own homes during a series of robberies and rapes. These holdings came under sharp criticism, but were accurate reflections of the state of the law until quite recently.

The first significant departure from the "any asportation" requirement came in another California case, Cotton v. Superior Court (1961), 56 Cal.2d 459, 464, 15 Cal.Rptr. 65, 68, 364 P.2d 241, 244. A

23. See Model Penal Code, Tentative Draft No. 11, comment p. 11, fn. 1: "Kidnapping (or some category of it) is punishable by life imprisonment or death in all States except Alaska (10 years), Connecticut (50 years), Minnesota (40 years), New Hampshire (25 years), and North Dakota (20 years). Where kidnapping is divided into degrees, even simple kidnapping is punishable by life imprisonment, in some States, and the maximum in other States is commonly 10–25 years."

* * *

Modern legislation, as an inducement to the felon to release his victim unharmed, reserves the capital offense of kidnapping for cases where the victim is not voluntarily released free of serious physical injury.

labor dispute led to the invasion of a farm worker's camp by union members. Several braceros were assaulted and dragged about the camp during the ensuing riot. The California Supreme Court ruled that the assailants could not be convicted of kidnapping, saying that "all 'asportation' in the instant case would appear to be only incidental to the assault and rioting." The Court declared that it should avoid "absurd consequences" in the application of the kidnapping laws; it warned that a literal reading of the California statute "could result in a rule that every assault could also be prosecuted for kidnapping." The Court ignored, it did not overrule, *Chessman* and *Wein*, but the significance of *Cotton* was not lost on the commentators.

A few years after *Cotton* was decided, the New York Court of Appeals articulated a new approach to the asportation requirement. In People v. Levy (1965), 15 N.Y.2d 159, 164, 256 N.Y.S.2d 793, 796, 204 N.E.2d 842, 844, the defendants accosted the victims, who had just arrived at their home in an automobile. One of the defendants took the wheel, and the victims, husband and wife, were driven about city streets for twenty minutes, covering twenty-seven blocks. During this journey the victims were robbed of money and jewelry.

The defendants were convicted by a jury of kidnapping under the New York statute, which provided that a person who "confines" another with intent to "cause him * * * to be confined" against his will is guilty of kidnapping. The Court of Appeals reversed. Central to the Court's holding was its concern that the broad statutory definition, "could literally overrun several other crimes, notably robbery and rape, and in some circumstances assault, since detention and sometimes confinement, against the will of the victim, frequently accompany these crimes * * * It is a common occurrence in robbery, for example, that the victim be confined briefly at gunpoint or bound and detained, or moved into and left in another room or place.

"It is unlikely that these restraints, sometimes accompanied by asportation, which are incidents to other crimes and have long been treated as integral parts of other crimes, were intended by the Legislature in framing its broad definition of kidnapping to constitute a separate crime of kidnapping, even though kidnapping might sometimes be spelled out literally from the statutory words." The Court overruled a contrary prior decision and held that the kidnapping statute was to be limited in its application "to 'kidnapping' in the conventional sense in which that term has now come to have acquired meaning."

Left unresolved in *Levy* was the precise degree of asportation necessary to constitute "kidnapping in the conventional sense." The opinion did, however, revive the requirement that some meaningful asportation must accompany the crime. In a subsequent case the Court of Appeals declared that "the direction of the criminal law has been to limit the scope of the kidnapping statute, with its very substantially more severe penal consequences, to true kidnapping situations and not to apply it to crimes which are essentially robbery, rape or assault and in which some confinement or asportation occurs as a subsidiary incident." People v. Lombardi (1967), 20 N.Y.2d 266, 270, 282 N.Y.S.2d 519, 521, 229 N.E.2d 206, 208. But, in a still more recent case, the Court held that "the more complicated nature of the asportation" pursued in the defendant's efforts to kill the victim, removed the case from the *Levy-Lombardi* rule.

The reasoning of the New York Court of Appeals was not accepted by other courts. Several jurisdictions expressly rejected the idea that a substantial asportation was necessary under broadly-worded kidnapping statutes.

In 1969, by a 6-to-1 decision the California Supreme Court overruled its prior constructions in the *Chessman-Wein* line of cases. People v. Daniels (1969), 71 Cal.2d 1119, 1139, 80 Cal.Rptr. 897, 910, 459 P.2d 225, 238, clearly repudiates the doctrine that any asportation of the victim is sufficient to constitute kidnapping. There the victims had been forced to move about in their apartments during the commission of crimes of robbery and rape. The Court declared:

> "We hold that the intent of the Legislature * * * was to exclude from [the statute's] reach not only 'standstill' robberies * * * but also those in which the movements of the victim are merely incidental to the commission of the robbery and do not substantially increase the risk of harm over and above that necessarily present in the crime of robbery itself."

* * *

Having reviewed the authorities in some detail, we approach decision.

IV.

The asportation requirement and the standard by which it is applied

We hold that, except in those relatively rare cases where the victim is intentionally locked in the place where he is found and there secretly isolated and confined, a reasonable construction of our kidnapping statute requires an asportation of the victim before the crime of kidnapping is complete. Still to be answered is the extent of the asportation required.

We believe that the history of kidnapping jurisprudence in this country demonstrates the futility of attempting to calculate the requisite asportation in terms of linear measurement. The harm sought to be prevented is not movement of the victim, but his removal from one place to another and attendant increased risks to the victim. The actual distance the victim is transported does not necessarily correspond with the invasion of his physical interest. An asportation of 50 feet may in some cases expose the victim to precisely those abuses which kidnapping statutes are designed to prevent; in other cases, an asportation of 500 feet may alter the victim's situation not at all.

We have concluded that under the kidnapping statute a movement of the victim does not constitute an asportation unless it has significance independent of the assault. And, unless the victim is removed from the environment where he is found, the consequences of the movement itself to the victim are not independently significant from the assault—the movement does not manifest the commission of a separate crime—and punishment for injury to the victim must be founded upon crimes other than kidnapping.

A comprehensive scheme for dealing with this offense rests within the province of the legislature, not the courts. The standard we apply today does, however, discriminate with some certainty between conduct which ought clearly to be punished under the kidnapping statute and conduct which falls within the scope of other crimes.[36]

V.

The standard applied to the facts of this case

To define "environment" restrictively, e. g., the mere geographic location of the victim, would be to return to the "any movement" concept. The relevant environment is the totality of the surroundings, animate and inanimate.

Applying these criteria to the assault on Inspector Dembosky, we conclude that Adams did not commit the crime of kidnapping. The movement of Inspector Dembosky did not remove him from the prison environment. As his duties customarily took him throughout the entire prison, it cannot be said that moving him from the confused threatening situation in 4-block to the fifth floor hospital was independently significant from the assault.

36. While, as Judge Gillis points out, this case does not involve movement of a victim incident to a robbery or rape, it does involve movement incident to a felonious assault which, too, is a separate crime.

Indeed, under Michigan law there is little reason to charge kidnapping where the movement is incidental to an armed robbery or a rape because both of those offenses are punishable by life sentences and in Michigan all sentences, with few exceptions, run concurrently. It is only where the other offense is punishable by a sentence less than life that there is likely to be an issue whether movement incidental to the commission of that offense constituted the separate crime of kidnapping.

Accordingly, the likelihood is that in Michigan kidnapping will be charged for a street assault most frequently where the assailant failed to consummate his objective, the prosecutorial purpose in charging kidnapping being to aggravate the penalty for the unsuccessful attempt. The degree of asportation that should be required to justify a kidnapping prosecution in such a case is beyond the scope of this opinion.

The purpose of the movement was neither to avoid detection nor to expose Inspector Dembosky to an increased risk of harm. He was moved to reduce the risk of escalation by providing a cooling-off period. When he was first assaulted the inspector asked, "Can't we talk about this?" And, when the group moved off, he suggested that they go to the prison gymnasium. Instead he was required to accompany the assailants to the fifth floor of the prison hospital. This case is not like a case of street assault where the victim is seized on a thoroughfare and pulled into a dark alley or into an automobile to prevent detection so that the assault can be completed in greater privacy; such a movement might have significance independent of the assault.

The evidence does not support a contention that the movement to the fifth floor of the hospital exposed the inspector to an increased risk of harm because it made his rescue more difficult. Adams and the other men were armed with knives. There is no evidence, no reason to suppose or infer that they were less likely to use their knives if a confrontation with rescuers had occurred at 4-block than at the fifth floor landing of the hospital. Might not the presence at 4-block of hundreds of milling men have made rescue there more difficult? Might not one of the three agitated, perhaps still intoxicated and narcotized, assailants reacted mortally on the spur of the moment to a taunting challenge from an unseen voice in the milling throng? Under the circumstances we are satisfied that the evidence does not support a finding that the movement had significance adverse to Inspector Dembosky independent of the continuing assault.[39]

The inspector was seized in Jackson Prison. It is an atypical place, an armed enclosure that no one can enter or leave without passing through guarded entranceways. Movement from one building to another in Jackson Prison, for purposes of the kidnapping statute, is not significantly different than movement from one room to another in a building, especially where, as here, the movement was under surveillance of armed guards who had the enclosure protected and

39. It is important in this case to make clear what we do not decide as well as what we hold so that our opinion is not misread.

The taking of a hostage may be the offense of kidnapping. In the hostage situation, if the victim is removed from the environment where he is found, the removal will generally have significance adverse to the victim independent of the assault and the offense of kidnapping will be completed upon his removal from the environment. Even if the victim is not so removed, if the actor intends to remove him from the environment where he is found and commits an overt act going beyond mere preparation, that would be attempted kidnapping. If the victim is seized with intent "to extort money or other valuable thing" or to hold the victim "to service against his will" that too *may* be kidnapping even though there has been no asportation * * *

Nor do we express any opinion as to when a seizure of a person on the street incidental to the commission or attempted commission of another offense (e. g., rape, robbery) becomes the separate offense of kidnapping. * * *

there was no intention on the part of Adams or the other felons themselves to leave or to remove Inspector Dembosky from the prison.

The movement of Inspector Dembosky did not make the apprehension of the felons less likely, nor did the movement make it less likely that the inspector would be released unharmed. It provided a cooling-off period—which Inspector Dembosky himself wisely sought. It provided time for these impetuous, desperate men to reflect and to draw back from worse folly.

Adams' conduct was highly dangerous and indefensible. The prison and prosecutorial authorities are understandably anxious to see that he is severely punished. Prison guards and officials like Inspector Dembosky mingle with frustrated, assaultive desperate men. An assault upon any of them is a serious breach of discipline; punishment should be clear, certain and severe.

Michigan, unlike other jurisdictions, does not have a specific statute making assault by a prisoner on a prison guard or official a crime carrying special penalties. In Michigan, assault upon a prison guard is treated no differently than assault outside of prison walls. The maximum penalties are relatively mild for the kind of aggravated conduct indulged in by Adams and his confederates. That is a good reason for the legislature to amend the penal code to provide adequate sanctions for an assault by a prisoner. It is not a reason for transforming, without legislative authorization, what under present law may be nothing more than a felonious assault, into an offense which carries with it a possible life sentence.

Criminal statutes, in contrast with the common law, may not be expanded to meet new problems beyond the contemplation of the legislature when the statute was enacted.[42]

Reversed.

42. * * *

The kidnapping statute is not a catchall, a means of aggravating the penalties —to fill in a gap in the law—so that penalties as severe as those that can be meted out for extortion, armed robbery and kidnapping can be imposed for "extortion" not involving threatened assault on a relative. We may not properly engraft an additional pattern and provide by judicial interpretation that any detention of a person for the purpose of extracting any advantage whatsoever is kidnapping even though there is no meaningful asportation and no secrecy, or that where "extortion" is involved the quality of the asportation required to establish kidnapping need not be of the kind required where extortion is not present * * *.

An asportation is the gist of the offense of kidnapping. If we sustain a conviction for kidnapping on evidence that the victim of the confinement has been held a "substantial" period of time and exposed to "serious" risk of harm even though there was not an asportation having significance independent of the assault, then most every assaultive crime can be the capital offense of kidnapping if the prosecutor so charges and a jury so finds.

* * *

J. H. GILLIS, Presiding Judge (dissenting).

Unlike my Colleagues, I am satisfied that there was sufficient evidence from which the jury could lawfully find defendant Adams guilty of kidnapping. Accordingly, I would affirm defendant's conviction.

In my view, the majority misapply the teachings of such cases as People v. Levy, People v. Lombardi and People v. Daniels. And, as a result, the majority reach what I consider to be an absurd result. This case is not one in which the restraint and forcible movement of Inspector Dembosky can be characterized solely as "incident[s] to other crimes and * * * integral parts of other crimes." People v. Levy, 15 N.Y.2d at 164–165, 256 N.Y.S.2d at 796, 204 N.E.2d at 844. This case does not involve movement of the victim incident to robbery (People v. Levy, supra; People v. Daniels, supra); nor does it involve asportation incident to rape (People v. Lombardi, supra; People v. Daniels, supra).

In People v. Miles (1969), 23 N.Y.2d 527, 539, 540, 297 N.Y.S.2d 913, 922, 245 N.E.2d 688, 694, 695, the New York Court of Appeals explained the *Levy-Lombardi* rationale as follows:

> "In the *Levy* and *Lombardi* cases, and especially in the *Levy* case, the restraint and asportation were parts of the crimes ultimately committed. The robbery and the rapes could not be committed in the forms planned without the limited asportations there involved. Indeed, in any robbery, there is a restraint of 'false imprisonment' and in every rape there is a similar restraint and often removal in some limited sense. It is this kind of factual merger with the ultimate crime of the preliminary, preparatory, or concurrent action that the rule is designed to recognize, and thus prevent unnatural elevation of the 'true' crime to be charged.
>
> * * *
>
> "Moreover, *the rule has no purpose of ignoring as independent crimes alternative or optional means used in committing another crime which, by the gravity and even horrendousness of the means used, constitute and should constitute a separately cognizable offense.*
>
> * * *
>
> "In short, the *Levy-Lombardi* rule was designed to prevent gross distortion of lesser crimes into a much more serious crime by excess of prosecutorial zeal. *It was not designed to merge 'true' kidnappings into other crimes merely because the kidnappings were used to accomplish ultimate crimes of lesser or equal or greater gravity."* (Emphasis supplied.)

Nothing in this record suggests to me an excess of prosecutorial zeal. Accordingly, the *Levy-Lombardi* rule is inapposite. In my view, Adams' conduct could lawfully be considered "true" kidnaping.

In People v. Congdon (1889), 77 Mich. 351, 354, 43 N.W. 986, the Michigan Supreme Court noted that the gist of the offense under the kidnaping statute is the involuntariness of the seizure. Similarly, the United States Supreme Court has stated that "the involuntariness of seizure and detention * * * is the very essence of the crime of kidnaping." Chatwin v. United States (1946), 326 U.S. 455, 464, 66 S.Ct. 233, 237, 90 L.Ed. 198, 203. On the facts as recited in the majority opinion, it clearly appears that the jury could find that Inspector Dembosky had been involuntarily seized.

Moreover, "the gravity and even horrendousness", People v. Miles, 23 N.Y.2d at 539, 297 N.Y.S.2d at 922, 245 N.E.2d at 694, of Adams' conduct serves to distinguish this case from mere false imprisonment. Inspector Dembosky was confined against his will for a substantial period of time. He was exposed to serious risk of harm. Thus, Inspector Dembrosky was subjected to the very abuses the kidnaping statute is intended to prevent. It follows that we should not, as a matter of law, refuse to characterize defendant Adams' conduct as kidnaping. At least, on this record, the jury should be permitted to so find.

I have discovered but two cases which factually resemble this case of *Adams*. In each, a prison guard was forcibly seized and held against his will within the prison by inmates. Jury convictions of kidnaping were affirmed in both cases on the law and the facts. The evidence was held sufficient to justify the verdicts. See State v. Randall (1960), 137 Mont. 534, 353 P.2d 1054, and State v. Frodsham (1961), 139 Mont. 222, 362 P.2d 413. See, also, People v. Shaw (1968), 11 Mich.App. 255, 160 N.W.2d 761. Such should be the result in this case.

Defendant's other contentions are without merit. His conviction should be affirmed.

NOTES

1. The California Supreme Court's requirement that the movement of the victim substantially increase the risk to the victim has been held to apply only to kidnapping to commit robberies. Kidnappings related to rapes and other crimes are so-called "simple" kidnappings under California law and the court has held that the asportation required for simple kidnapping does not demand that the movement increase the risk to the victim above what is necessarily involved in other crimes the defendant may be committing. People v. Stanworth, 11 Cal.3d 588, 114 Cal.Rptr. 250, 522 P.2d 1058 (1974).

2. Even if a court rejects the rather restrictive definition of asportation applied in the principal case, the requirement of asportation for kid-

napping may be a significant one. Although some courts continue to hold that any movement of the victim is sufficient, however short a distance may be involved, State v. Williams, 111 Ariz. 222, 526 P.2d 1244 (1974), others require more. The California Supreme Court, for example, has held that even for "simple" kidnapping under California law the movement of the victim must be "substantial in character" and not only "slight" or "trivial." The actual distance which the victim is moved is the only relevant consideration. Thus movement of rape victims fifteen or even 75 feet, within the same building, is not asportation. See People v. Caudillo, 21 Cal.3d 562, 146 Cal.Rptr. 859, 580 P.2d 274 (1978) (movement of rape victim unspecified distance from elevator to storage room and then to her apartment was not sufficient to constitute asportation required for simple kidnapping).

3. Kidnapping statutes sometimes require that the victim be "secretly confined." But this has not been read as requiring complete and total isolation of the victim. In State v. Weir, 506 S.W.2d 437, 440 (Mo.1974), the court explained:

> Secret confinement * * * does not require proof of total concealment and complete isolation whereby the victim is rendered invisible to the entire world. It is sufficient to show that the person kidnapped has been effectively confined against his will in such a manner that he is prevented from communicating his situation to others and accused's intention to keep the victim's predicament secret is made manifest.

In *Weir*, the defendant was held to have kept the victim "secretly confined" where he forced her to enter his automobile and then drove through some of Kansas City's busiest streets at midday while compelling her to remain in the car. The defendant finally drove on a country road to an open field where there were no houses. Although the victim could be seen by those passing by (and was in fact finally observed and rescued by passing police officers), the court upheld the defendant's conviction, reasoning that he violated the relevant statute "by preventing [the victim] from leaving the automobile and preventing her from waving or signalling to others for help or relief; transporting her from a heavily populated metropolitan center and secreting her by detaining her in an automobile in a field where there were no houses and intention to shield her from public view was manifest."

4. Under many statutes, kidnapping (and probably false imprisonment, as well) can be committed by deceit or fraud as well as by force or threats. The federal kidnapping statute covers victims who have been "inveigled" or "decoyed." 18 U.S.C.A. § 1201(a). A defendant who persuaded women to enter his vehicle and remain in it by falsely promising to drive them home or to a job interview kidnapped them within the meaning of the statute. United States v. Hoog, 504 F.2d 45 (8th Cir. 1974), cert. denied 420 U.S. 961, 95 S.Ct. 1349, 43 L.Ed.2d 437 (1975). A defendant who persuaded a fifteen year old youth to walk with him to a wooded area by falsely representing to the youth that there were squirrels in the area and the two of them would observe those squirrels was held to have "kidnapped" the youth within the meaning of a statute that did not define the offense further. The court explained:

> [I]n the last century this and other courts have progressively recognized that one's will may be coerced as effectively by fraud as by force. Accordingly, this Court has interpreted the common law definition of kidnapping to encompass not only the unlawful taking and carrying away of a person by force but also the unlawful taking and carrying away of a person by false and fraudulent representations amounting substantially to a coercion of the will. * * * [F]raud has become synonymous with force in the common law definition of kidnapping, and the equation of fraud with force has been accepted in the legal encyclopedias and approved in numerous jurisdictions.

State v. Murphy, 280 N.C. 1, 184 S.E.2d 845, 847 (1971).

MODEL PENAL CODE *

(Proposed Official Draft, 1962).

Section 212.1. Kidnapping

A person is guilty of kidnapping if he unlawfully removes another from his place of residence or business, or a substantial distance from the vicinity where he is found, or if he unlawfully confines another for a substantial period in a place of isolation, with any of the following purposes:

(a) to hold for ransom or reward, or as a shield or hostage; or

(b) to facilitate commission of any felony or flight thereafter; or

(c) to inflict bodily injury on or to terrorize the victim or another; or

(d) to interfere with the performance of any governmental or political function.

Kidnapping is a felony of the first degree unless the actor voluntarily releases the victim alive and in a safe place prior to trial, in which case it is a felony of the second degree. A removal or confinement is unlawful within the meaning of this Section if it is accomplished by force, threat or deception, or, in the case of a person who is under the age of 14 or incompetent, if it is accomplished without the consent of a parent, guardian or other person responsible for general supervision of his welfare.

Section 212.2. Felonious Restraint

A person commits a felony of the third degree if he knowingly:

(a) restrains another unlawfully in circumstances exposing him to risk of serious bodily injury; or

(b) holds another in a condition of involuntary servitude.

Section 212.3. False Imprisonment

A person commits a misdemeanor if he knowingly restrains another unlawfully so as to interfere substantially with his liberty.

C. RAPE AND RELATED SEX OFFENSES

Rape is unlawful sexual intercourse with a female without her effective consent. "Intercourse," for rape purposes, requires only some penetration:

> The penetration of the body of the victim need not be to any particular depth, so long as there is entry of the labia by the male organ. It may be partial and slight. * * * It is not necessary that penetration be proved by visual observation. It, like other facts, may be proved by circumstantial evidence.

Gardner v. State, 263 Ark. 739, 748, 569 S.W.2d 74, 78 (1978). No ejaculation or emission of sperm by the male is necessary. The intercourse is of course, without consent if it is accomplished by coercion or threats. Whether or not consent existed is often a difficult factual question and is explored in two cases in this section, State v. Studham and People v. Borak. The intent required for rape is discussed in Director of Public Prosecutions v. Morgan, reprinted at page 186, infra; this case should be reexamined for discussion in connection with this section.

Under some circumstances, consent given by the victim may be legally ineffective. This is the case where the victim is not competent because of mental abnormality to give consent or where the victim's age is such as to preclude an effective consent. This latter situation —often referred to as "statutory" rape—presents interesting problems of intent and is examined in another case in this section, State v. Guest.

In recent years, increased sensitivity to the role of women in society and the impact of the law and legal proceedings upon that role has called into question may aspects of the definition of rape and the manner in which rape cases are processed and prosecuted. See generally, Berger, Man's Trial, Woman's Tribulation: Rape Cases in the Courtroom, 77 Colum.L.Rev. 1 (1977). A number of these issues are raised in the following materials. Perhaps the most basic concerns the propriety of retaining rape as an offense, separate from—and punishable more severely than—other forms of assault or injury, whether sexually-related or not.

STATE v. STUDHAM

Supreme Court of Utah, 1977.
572 P.2d 700.

CROCKETT, Justice:

Defendant, Clyde Lloyd Studham, appeals from a jury conviction of rape. * * *

The prosecutrix, Janis ______, had lived with defendant in a meretricious relationship beginning in November, 1972. A son Chad ______ was born on September 14, 1973. The relationship between Janis and the defendant had terminated in December of 1974 and the defendant was under a court order not to annoy or visit her.

At approximately 4:00 a. m. on the morning of March 5, 1976, Janis was awakened at her apartment by a knocking and ringing of her doorbell. Defendant, who had been drinking, was at the door and he said he wanted to talk to her, but she refused to let him in. He kicked the door open and entered; and he remained in the apartment for about two hours, during which there was some kissing and amorous advances.

The prosecutrix testified that in his efforts to force sexual intercourse upon her the defendant threatened her, pinned her to the floor during a struggle, put his hand over her mouth so that she had difficulty breathing, and forced intercourse upon her against her will. She did not scream or attempt to run from her apartment, which she said was due to its futility and the fact that her young son was asleep in the adjoining room.

After the defendant left, she called her mother, who reported the incident to the police. Deputy Lester Newren of the Salt Lake County Sheriff's office came to investigate. Janis's only visible injuries were a bruised face and cut lip; and there were blood stains on her bathrobe. * * *

Defendant's argument that the evidence is not sufficient to prove his guilt beyond a reasonable doubt is: that it rests almost solely upon her own self-interested testimony; that it is inherently improbable and inconsistent because, though she claims force, and denies consent, she did not scream, or try to escape from the apartment even though during the time he was there she had opportunity to do so.

Most crimes are committed in such secrecy as can be effected; and that is particularly so of this type of offense. Therefore, the question of guilt or innocence often depends upon the weighing of the credibility of the victim against that of the accused. * * *

In regard to the failure of the victim to make an outcry, this is to be said: Whether an outcry was made, or should have been made, depends upon how practical and effective it might have been. It is evidence which may be received and it is one of the circumstances to be considered as bearing upon the critical issue of consent. But mere failure to make such an outcry does not render a conviction unsupportable.

The essential element in rape is the forcing of intercourse upon a woman "without her consent" and "against her will." It is sometimes said that those terms mean essentially the same thing, but this is not true because such an act might occur in circumstances which would be "without her consent" but which would not necessarily involve overcoming her will and her resistance, both of which must be proved. In that regard there has often been much preoccupation with and stress placed upon the matter of the physical confrontation between the accused and the victim; and it has sometimes been said that she "must resist to the utmost" or other expressions of that import. But that view no longer obtains. Even though it is necessary that the rape be against the victim's will, manifest by a determined effort on her part to resist, it is not necessary that it be shown that she engaged in any heroics which subjected her to great brutality or that she suffered or risked serious wounds or injuries.

What we think is a sounder view recognizes that the bruising and terrorizing of the senses and sensibilities can be just as real and just as wrong as the beating and bruising of the flesh; and that the law should afford a woman protection, not only from physical violence, but from having her feelings and sensibilities outraged by force or fear in violation of what she is entitled to regard and protect as the integrity of her person. Accordingly, in determining whether the victim's will and resistance were overcome, it is appropriate to consider that this may be accomplished by either physical force and violence, or by psychological or emotional stress imposed upon her, or by a combination of them. As to the degree of resistance required: The victim need do no more than her age and her strength of body and mind make it reasonable for her to do under the circumstances to resist. In this case there is a reasonable basis in the evidence upon which the jury could believe beyond a reasonable doubt that that test was met.

* * *

Affirmed.

PEOPLE v. BORAK

Appellate Court of Illinois, 1973.
13 Ill.App.3d 815, 301 N.E.2d 1.

SEIDENFELD, Justice:

Defendant, Walter J. Borak, was convicted in a bench trial of rape and deviate sexual assault, and was sentenced to 5 to 8 years on each charge, the sentences to run concurrently.

* * *

The prosecutrix, a married woman 18 years of age at the time of the acts in question, testified that defendant, a doctor, conducted gynecological examinations on her on two occasions. During the examinations, she laid on an examining table, unclothed from the waist down, with her hips at the end of the table and her feet in stirrups about a foot higher than the table and a foot out from it on either side. She had never before been examined internally.

She testified that during the first examination, conducted on September 22, 1970, defendant asked extremely personal questions about the details of her sexual relationship with her husband, and conducted intimate manipulations of her body for which he gave medical explanations. Defendant breathed heavily, but was not flushed. Defendant ceased his manipulations when she told him they were hurting her. After leaving, prosecutrix did not tell anyone what took place at this examination.

During the second examination, conducted two days after the first, defendant again asked personal questions and manipulated her body. Prosecutrix did not wear a brassiere to this examination. While manipulating his finger in her vagina, defendant asked, "Why don't you come?" "Why don't you come with your husband?" Prosecutrix noticed that he was breathing heavy and was flushed. She said she couldn't get off the table because he was standing right there, and she didn't ask him to let her up because she was scared and thought he was sexually stimulated. She closed her eyes, as instructed, and felt defendant's tongue on her vaginal area. She got up on her elbows, but laid back down and closed her eyes when defendant told her to in a voice that was not loud or soft, but "(k)ind of * * * commanding." About thirty seconds later, she felt his organ enter hers, at which time she sat up quickly and got dressed. After a brief conversation about what she owed defendant, she left. On arriving home, she related the incident to her husband, and the police were called.

Prosecutrix testified that she was not tied down or restricted while on the examining table, and could remove her feet from the stirrups. She also stated that defendant had no weapon and never threatened her or used force against her, and that she never cried out for help or used force against defendant.

Prosecutrix's husband testified that when his wife arrived home from the second examination she was crying and broken up, and that she told him what had occurred. He then called the police and her father.

* * *

Gertrude Borak, defendant's wife, testified for the defense that she was working in defendant's office during the prosecutrix's second examination and that she once entered the room and was seen by prosecutrix. She said after returning to her office, she did not hear voices coming from the examining room. She was not in the examining room while the examination was being conducted, and she did not see the prosecutrix leave.

* * *

* * * We conclude that prosecutrix's testimony, the credibility of which is for the trial court, and the corroboration provided by her prompt complaint are sufficient to establish that the acts complained of were committed.

The more difficult questions before us are whether the act of intercourse was performed "by force and against her will", as required to sustain a rape conviction (Ill.Rev.Stat.1969, ch. 38, par. 11–1(a)), and whether the act of deviate sexual conduct was "by force or threat of force", as required to constitute deviate sexual assault (Ill.Rev. Stat.1969, ch. 38, par. 11–3(a)). * * *

The general rules as to the degree of force required under our rape statute are stated in People v. Faulisi (1962) 25 Ill.2d 457, 461, 185 N.E.2d 211. It is stated that the degree of force exerted by the defendant and the amount of resistance on the part of the complaining witness are matters that depend on the facts of the particular case; that resistance is not necessary under circumstances where resistance would be futile and would endanger the life of the female as where the assailant is armed with a deadly weapon, and that proof of physical force is unnecessary if the prosecuting witness was paralyzed by fear or overcome by superior strength of her attacker; that it is, however, fundamental that there must be evidence to show that the act was committed by force and against the will of the female, and if she has the use of her faculties and physical powers, the evidence must show such resistance as will demonstrate that the act was against her will.

* * *

State v. Atkins (Mo.1926), 292 S.W. 422 is closely analogous here. There, during a vaginal examination, the woman closed her eyes and covered them with her arms because of embarrassment. She then felt the doctor's sex organ enter hers, whereupon she jumped out of the chair and pushed him away. The court agreed with defendant that no more physical force was employed by him than is necessarily incident to such an act when done with consent. It noted, however, that a previous Missouri case involving a sleeping woman had held that where the woman does not consent, no more force is required than the force incident to the act * * *.

* * *

* * * A requirement of actual force would, in cases of unexpected sexual attacks, relegate the state to a prosecution for the misdemeanor of battery. * * * We therefore conclude that in cases not involving children, "force" in the statutory sense, is present when

the victim is incapable of consenting to the sexual act involved because she has been given no opportunity to consent. Force is thus implied when the rape or deviate sexual acts proscribed by statute are accomplished under the pretext of medical treatment when the victim is surprised, and unaware of the intention involved.

In the case before us, even if the prosecutrix realized that defendant's questions were improper, this would not in itself indicate what was to follow. While defendant's appearance indicated to prosecutrix that he was sexually aroused, he had not performed any actions which she knew to be improper, and prosecutrix was not put on notice that defendant would perform an overt, deviate act upon her body. Defendant's act of deviate sexual conduct was, in the language of *Atkins* ((Mo.1926), 292 S.W. 422), "through surprise", with prosecutrix being "utterly unaware of his intention in that regard." Prosecutrix was therefore incapable of consenting to the act, and "statutory" force was present.

However, the contrary is true as to the act of intercourse. When defendant put his mouth on prosecutrix's organ, she became aware of his intentions, and nothing he did thereafter could come as a surprise. It then became her duty, under the previously stated general rules of force applicable to rape cases, to use resistance to prevent further acts. Yet she failed to object and followed defendant's instruction to lay back down and close her eyes. While prosecutrix points to her testimony that the instruction was given in a commanding voice, and that she was scared because of his appearance, the evidence does not show that she was restrained in any way, or that defendant used any actual force or threat of force upon her. We cannot conclude that prosecutrix was paralyzed by fear or overcome by defendant's superior strength. Her failure to resist when it was within her power to do so amounts to consent, and removes from the act an essential element of the crime of rape. We therefore reverse defendant's rape conviction.

* * *

The judgment of conviction for deviate sexual assault is affirmed. The judgment of conviction for rape is reversed.

NOTES

1. Suppose that in *Borak* the defendant had been able to accomplish the act of penetration by convincing the victim that he was inserting only a medical instrument into her vagina? Under accepted rape law, he would then have obtained her consent under fraud concerning the nature of the act (i. e., he deceived her in regard to whether the act was intercourse or not) and his action would have been rape. Courts are divided on whether rape is committed when the defendant deceives the victim into believing there is a marital relationship between them, as when the defendant persuades the victim to go through a ceremony representing that it creates a valid marriage. But other forms of fraud will not render consent ineffective and intercourse accomplished with consent induced by

such other forms of fraud or deception is not rape. Thus, for example, if the defendant in *Borak* had obtained the woman's consent through a false claim that intercourse with him was necessary as a form of medical therapy his action would not be rape since she was not deceived as to the nature of the act but only its purpose. See R. Perkins, Criminal Law 164–67 (2nd ed. 1969).

2. Appellate courts uphold rape convictions despite evidence that the complainant placed herself in a vulnerable position. People v. Reed, 57 Ill.App.3d 533, 15 Ill.Dec. 192, 373 N.E.2d 538 (1978) (complainant, a 19 year old art student, agreed to go with defendant to his apartment for a nude massage to "relieve tensions"); People v. Hunt, 72 Cal.App.3d 190, 139 Cal.Rptr. 675 (1977) (complainant, hitchhiking, accepted a ride from defendant who had three pictures of nude women attached to dashboard and represented he was a "porn" photographer). But trial court practice —and especially jury actions—may be significantly different. Convictions in cases like *Reed* and *Hunt* may, in other words, be difficult to obtain because juries are reluctant to convict rather than because conviction is inconsistent with any rule or requirement of law.

3. If a woman is, by reason of mental illness or retardation, unable to give effective consent, intercourse with her is rape regardless of any consent she may have given. Even women of very limited intelligence, however, are able to give a valid consent. As one court has summarized:

> It must be proved beyond a reasonable doubt that the prosecutrix was so idiotic as to be incapable of expressing any intelligent consent or dissent, or of expressing any judgment in the matter. The capacity to consent to intercourse presupposes the mental capability to form an intelligent opinion on the subject, with an understanding of the act, its nature, and its possible consequences.

Smith v. State, 345 So.2d 325, 327 (Ala.Crim.App.1976). This requires that the woman have an understanding of more than the physiological nature of the act of intercourse; she must also have "an appreciation of how it will be regarded in the framework of the societal environment and taboos" to which she will be exposed. People v. Easley, 42 N.Y.2d 50, 396 N.Y.S.2d 635, 364 N.E.2d 1328, 1332 (1977).

4. The traditional definition of rape requires that the male having intercourse with the female victim not be the husband of the victim. This has been defended on several grounds, each of which can legitimately be questioned. It is argued that a woman, by entering into marriage, has consented to intercourse with her husband at his demand. Permitting a wife to claim rape by her husband would encourage women involved in domestic disputes to bring fraudulent charges. And permitting the criminal law to intervene in domestic disputes would reduce the likelihood that the parties will reconcile. See Note, The Marital Rape Exception, 52 N.Y. U.L.Rev. 306 (1977). In a number of jurisdictions, this traditional rule has been modified. Some statutes permit conviction of a husband for rape of his wife if the two are living apart and have filed for divorce or have been separated by a judicial decree. New York, for example, permits conviction of the husband if the parties are living apart pursuant to a court order or judgment or under a written agreement which specifical-

ly provides that the husband will be guilty of rape if he compels the wife to engage in intercourse. N.Y.Penal Law § 130.00(4). Several jurisdictions have completely removed the marital exception, so that even a husband living with a wife can be convicted of rape. N.J.Stat.Ann. Ch. 95, § 2C:14–2; Ore.Rev.Stat. §§ 163.365, 163.375.

5. Some jurisdictions have permitted—and some have required—the trial judge in a rape case to give the jury the following instruction, based upon the writings of Sir Matthew Hale in the 1670's:

> A charge such as that made against the defendant in this case is one, which, generally speaking, is easily made, but difficult to disprove even though the defendant is innocent. Therefore, I charge you the law requires that you examine the testimony of [the victim] with caution.

But recent decisions have disapproved of this instruction. In People v. Rincon-Pineda, 14 Cal.3d 864, 123 Cal.Rptr. 119, 538 P.2d 247 (1975), the California Supreme Court reviewed studies and statistics and found the instruction unwarranted. The trauma of submitting to investigation, the fear of humiliation through publicity and trial, and concern that even a justified complaint will not be pursued disclose the "utter fallaciousness" of the assumption that rape charges are "easily made," the court concluded. Moreover, rape is not unique in often presenting a court or jury with a credibility contest between the alleged victim of a crime and the defendant; similar situations are presented by non-sexual assault cases, and narcotics cases. In addition, studies show that jurors scrutinize female complainants in rape cases "closely, and often harshly," and tend to acquit defendants clearly guilty of violent rape because of what jurors regard as suggestions of contributing behavior on the part of the victim. Consequently, the court concluded, there is no reason specially to instruct jurors to examine the testimony of rape complainants with care, and trial judges should never give the traditional cautionary instruction. Other courts have agreed. E. g., State v. Smoot, 99 Idaho 855, 590 P.2d 1001 (1978).

6. Traditionally, a majority of jurisdictions required corroboration of a rape victim's testimony to support a conviction for rape. These rules required that the prosecution introduce evidence other than the complainant's testimony tending to prove the defendant's guilt and therefore to "corroborate" her testimony. Perhaps the most difficult requirement for the state to meet was that of New York, New York Penal Law § 130.15, which required corroboration of the fact of sexual penetration, the absence of consent, and the identity of the accused as the assailant. See People v. Linzy, 31 N.Y.2d 99, 335 N.Y.S.2d 45, 286 N.E.2d 440 (1972). Under this statute, for example, it was held that evidence that the complainant promptly reported the crime, that the complainant was in a distraught emotional condition after the alleged assault, and proof of bruises on the complainant's body was not sufficient corroboration. People v. Watson, 45 N.Y.2d 867, 410 N.Y.S.2d 577, 382 N.E.2d 1352 (1978) (reversing a conviction obtained under the then-applicable statute). The New York provision was modified in 1972 and repealed completely in 1974. Other jurisdictions have or had somewhat more flexible provisions. The Virginia rule, for example, requires corroboration only if the com-

plainant's testimony "is inherently incredible, or so contrary to human experience or to usual human behavior as to render it unworthy of belief." Willis v. Commonwealth, 218 Va. 560, 238 S.E.2d 811 (1977). In the vast majority of cases arising under such rules no corroboration is required. But in *Willis*, the Virginia Supreme Court held that corroboration of the 65-year-old victim's testimony was necessary in light of (1) the victim's failure to report the attack for a month; (2) the victim's attempt to withdraw the charges after they had been filed; (3) contradictions between the victim's trial testimony and that given at a preliminary hearing concerning whether she had clothing on when she was taken upstairs before the attack, which of the two defendants raped her first, and whether the defendants wrestled with her before or after taking her upstairs. Where corroboration is required, it is usually not necessary that the corroborating evidence be as extensive as that demanded by pre-1974 New York law. The Nebraska rule, for example, requires only that the victim be "corroborated as to material facts and circumstances which tend to support her testimony as to the principal fact in issue." State v. Thompson, 198 Neb. 48, 251 N.W.2d 387 (1977). See Note, The Rape Corroboration Requirement: Repeal not Reform, 81 Yale L.J. 1365 (1972).

There is a definite trend among both courts and legislatures towards abolition of corroboration requirements. In addition to the New York legislation, see Arnold v. United States, 358 A.2d 335 (D.C.Ct.App.1976); United States v. Sheppard, 569 F.2d 114 (D.C.Cir. 1977). But the trend has not been without dissent. Judge Mack, dissenting in Arnold v. United States, supra, noted that the District of Columbia corroboration requirement was a flexible one and may even have permitted the introduction of evidence that was not otherwise admissible. In light of this, he argued that there could be no suggestion that the rule has actually been an impediment to conviction for rape in the jurisdiction. Without the corroboration requirement, he suggested, law enforcement officers may subject rape cases to even greater—and more embarrassing—scrutiny and complainants may be subjected to harsher cross examination at trial. He noted that other reforms have been suggested. One assumes that juries sometimes believe rape defendants guilty but refuse to convict because they believe convicted rapists receive unjustifiably harsh penalties. Thus reduction of the penalty for rape may ease the task of convicting guilty rape defendants. Another possibility is modification of the standard of proof. Until comprehensive reforms in rape law occur, he concludes, a liberally applied corroboration requirement is the best available protection for the innocent. 358 A.2d 349–52 (Mack, J., concurring in part and dissenting in part).

7. Efforts have been made to mitigate the harshness of administration of rape laws by enactment of so-called "Shield Statutes," which limit or prohibit inquiry into the complaining witness' prior sexual behavior. Some, such as the Kansas statute, require that the trial judge hold a closed hearing if the defense wishes to inquire concerning the complainant's prior sexual conduct. Only if the judge determines that specific sexual conduct is "relevant" to the issues in the case is inquiry to be permitted. Kan.Stat. Ann. 60–447a. Others, such as the Kentucky statute, also require the judge to find that the "probative value" of the evidence outweighs "its inflammatory or prejudicial nature." Kentucky Rev.Stat. § 510.145. Defendants have argued that these statutes prevent them from effectively

cross examining complaining witnesses and therefore violate the Sixth Amendment right to confront and cross examine prosecution witnesses. But the courts have tended to uphold the statutes. Interest of Nichols, 2 Kan.App.2d 431, 580 P.2d 1370 (1978); Smith v. Commonwealth, 566 S.W.2d 181 (Ky.App.1978). Under statutes such as these, when is evidence of prior sexual conduct relevant? Normally, prior sexual conduct of the woman with persons other than the defendant will not be regarded as relevant to the question of whether she consented to intercourse with the defendant. But the defendant may deny the act of intercourse and offer evidence that the woman had intercourse with other men to show an alternative source of physical evidence of intercourse, such as semen in the woman's vagina. In such circumstances, the evidence is likely to be admissible. Another important issue is the admissibility under these statutes of evidence concerning prior sexual contact between the defendant and the complaining witness. Suppose in a rape case the defendant acknowledges the act of intercourse but claims that the woman consented. He offers to prove (by cross examination of the woman) that he and the woman had sexual intercourse on prior occasions with her consent and this had involved "rough sex," with physical wrestling. He further argues that this is relevant to whether or not she consented on the occasion at issue and to whether or not he believed she consented. Should this evidence be found "relevant?" In Interest of Nichols, supra, the trial judge did not admit the evidence and on appeal this was held not to be error.

8. Some critics of present rape legislation argue that rape should be replaced by a "sex neutral" crime, that is, one which does not isolate vaginal penetration of a female victim by a male as a uniquely serious offense. See Ireland, Reform Rape Legislation: A New Standard of Sexual Responsibility, 49 U.Colo.L.Rev. 185 (1978). This is attempted by 1974 Michigan legislation which replaces rape with the crime of "criminal sexual conduct." Four degrees of criminal sexual conduct are distinguished:

1st degree: This consists of "sexual penetration," defined as sexual intercourse, cunnilingus, fellatio, anal intercourse, "or any other intrusion, however slight, of any part of a person's body or of any object into the genital or anal openings of another person's body." In addition, one of the following must have occurred: (1) the defendant must have been armed with a weapon; (2) force or coercion was used and the defendant was aided by another person; or (3) force or coercion was used and personal injury to the victim was caused. Mich.Stat. Ann. § 28.788(2).

2nd degree: This consists of "sexual contact," defined as the intentional touching of the victim's or actor's personal parts or the intentional touching of the clothing covering the immediate area of the victim's intimate parts, for purposes of sexual arousal or gratification. "Intimate parts" is defined as including the primary genital area, groin, inner thigh, buttock, or breast. In addition, one of the circumstances required for 1st degree criminal sexual conduct must have existed. Mich.Stat.Ann. § 28.788(3).

3rd degree: This consists of sexual penetration accomplished by force or coercion. Mich.Stat.Ann. § 28.788(4).

4th degree: This consists of sexual contact accomplished by force or coercion. Mich.Stat.Ann. § 28.788(5).

9. Recent cases have dealt with the extent to which rape or sexual assault suffices under a variety of statutes to enhance punishment for other offenses. In a leading case, People v. Caudillo, 21 Cal.3d 562, 146 Cal.Rptr. 859, 580 P.2d 274 (1978), the defendant forced his way into the victim's apartment, forcibly raped and sodomized her, and compelled her to orally copulate him. Under the California burglary statute, the penalty for burglary was substantially greater if the state proved that defendant inflicted "great bodily injury" upon an occupant of the premises. Although the court acknowledged that sexual attacks constitute serious crimes in their own right and generally cause substantial *psychological* and *emotional* distress to the victims, it held that the statute required *physical* injury to an occupant. Consequently, a showing that the defendant forcibly raped or otherwise sexually attacked the victim would not, in itself, suffice to permit the imposition of enhanced punishment. But other courts applying somewhat different statutory language, have arrived at different results. Thus a defendant who kidnapped a victim with intent to rape her was held to have committed the crime of kidnapping with intent "to inflict bodily injury." State v. Corn, 223 Kan. 583, 575 P.2d 1308 (1978). The same result was reached under a kidnapping statute requiring kidnapping with intent "to cause physical injury to the victim," where physical injury was defined as "impairment of physical condition or substantial pain." State v. Strickland, 36 Or.App. 119, 584 P.2d 310 (1978). And a kidnap victim who was raped was held not to have been released "unharmed" under a kidnapping statute which defined first degree kidnapping as a kidnapping in which the victim was not released unharmed. State v. Oakes, 373 A.2d 210 (Del.1977).

DIRECTOR OF PUBLIC PROSECUTIONS v. MORGAN

House of Lords, 1975.
1 All ER 347.

[Reprinted at page 186, infra.]

NOTE

Berger, Man's Trial, Woman's Tribulation: Rape Cases in the Courtroom, 77 Colum.L.Rev. 1, 61–62 (1977) notes that cases on the issue of intent (or mistake) concerning consent are sparse but concludes that the rule applicable in the United States is stricter than the rule applied in *Morgan*. In the United States, she asserts, an accused may escape liability only if he reasonably as well as honestly believed the woman was consenting to sexual relations.

STATE v. GUEST

Supreme Court of Alaska, 1978.
583 P.2d 836.

MATTHEWS, Justice.

The question presented in the State's petition for review is whether an honest and reasonable mistake of fact regarding a victim's age, may serve as a defense to a charge of statutory rape.

On April 7, 1977, the respondents, Moses Guest and Jacob Evan, were charged with the statutory rape of T.D.G., age fifteen, in violation of AS 11.15.120.[1] * * *

* * * Guest moved [and] the court ordered that it would instruct the jurors as follows:

> It is a defense to a charge of statutory rape that the defendant reasonably and in good faith believed that the female person was of the age of sixteen years or older even though, in fact, she was under the age of sixteen years. If from all the evidence you have a reasonable doubt as to the question whether defendant reasonably and in good faith believed that she was sixteen years of age or older, you must give the defendant the benefit of that doubt and find him not guilty.

The state brings a petition for review from that order.

Respondents concede that in most jurisdictions a reasonable mistake of age is not a defense to a charge of statutory rape.[2] Although the validity of this defense to a statutory rape charge has not been decided in Alaska, we were presented with a similar issue in Anderson v. State, 384 P.2d 669 (Alaska 1963) where the charge was contributing to the delinquency of a minor by a consensual act of sexual intercourse. We said that "[a]ppellant's belief that prosecutrix was over the age of eighteen, even though it may have some support, is no excuse" and "[p]ersons having illegal relations with children do so at their [own] peril." Id. at 671.

1. AS 11.15.120 provides in relevant part:

Rape. (a) a person who * * * (2) being 16 years of age or older, carnally knows and abuses a person under 16 years of age, is guilty of rape.

2. * * *

Several states, by statute, have recognized the defense. * * *

This point of view has also been adopted by the 1978 revisors of the Alaska Criminal Code. Alaska Criminal Code revision (effective 1980) provides:

11.41.445. (b) In a prosecution under secs. 410–440 of this chapter, whenever a provision of law defining an offense depends upon a victim's being under a certain age, it is an affirmative defense that, at the time of the alleged offense, the defendant reasonably believed the victim to be that age or older, unless the victim was under 13 years of age at the time of the alleged offense.

* * *

We recognized in Speidel v. State, 460 P.2d 77 (Alaska 1969), that consciousness of wrongdoing is an essential element of penal liability. "It is said to be a universal rule that an injury can amount to a crime only when inflicted by intention—that conduct cannot be criminal unless it is shown that one charged with criminal conduct had an awareness or consciousness of some wrongdoing." Id. at 78. In Alex v. State, 484 P.2d 677 (Alaska 1971), we reaffirmed this principle and noted the "necessity of basing serious crimes upon a general criminal intent as opposed to strict criminal liability which applies regardless of intention." We also observed that the goal of the requirement of criminal intent "is to avoid criminal liability for innocent or inadvertent conduct." Id. at 681. We held in both cases that it would be a deprivation of liberty without due process of law to convict a person of a serious crime without the requirement of criminal intent. Alex v. State, supra at 680–81; Speidel v. State, supra at 80.

Our opinion in *Speidel* stated that there are exceptions to the general requirement of criminal intent which are categorized as "public welfare" offenses. These exceptions are a rather narrow class of regulation, "caused primarily by the industrial revolution, out of which grew the necessity of imposing more stringent duties on those connected with particular industries, trades, properties, or activities that affect public health, safety or welfare." Speidel v. State, supra at 78. The penalties for the infraction of these strict liability offenses are usually relatively small and conviction of them carries no great opprobrium. Id. at 79. Statutory rape may not appropriately be categorized as a public welfare offense. It is a serious felony. If the offender is less than nineteen years of age, he may be imprisoned for up to twenty years. If he is nineteen years of age or older, he may be punished by imprisonment for any term of years.

We believe that the charge of statutory rape is legally unsupportable under the principles of *Speidel*, * * * unless a defense of reasonable mistake of age is allowed. To refuse such a defense would be to impose criminal liability without any criminal mental element. The defense of reasonable mistake of fact is generally allowed in criminal cases to permit the defendant to show that he lacked criminal intent. When that opportunity is foreclosed the result is strict criminal liability.

Although AS 11.15.120 is silent as to any requirement of intent, this is true of many felony statutes. The requirement of criminal intent is then commonly inferred. In fact, in such cases, where the particular statute is not a public welfare type of offense, either a requirement of criminal intent must be read into the statute or it must be found unconstitutional. Since statutes should be construed where possible to avoid unconstitutionality, it is necessary here to infer a requirement of criminal intent.

It has been urged in other jurisdictions that where an offender is aware he is committing an act of fornication he therefore has sufficient criminal intent to justify a conviction for statutory rape because what was done would have been unlawful under the facts as he thought them to be. We reject this view. While it is true that under such circumstances a mistake of fact does not serve as a complete defense, we believe that it should serve to reduce the offense to that which the offender would have been guilty of had he not been mistaken. Thus, if an accused had a reasonable belief that the person with whom he had sexual intercourse was sixteen years of age or older, he may not be convicted of statutory rape. If, however, he did not have a reasonable belief that the victim was eighteen years of age or older, he may still be criminally liable for contribution to the delinquency of a minor. It is significant that the Alaska Statutes do not proscribe fornication, and therefore, it may not be considered an offense of a lesser degree.

For the foregoing reasons, we hold that a charge of statutory rape is defensible where an honest and reasonable mistake of fact as to the victim's age is shown. Anderson v. State, supra, is overruled to the extent that its holding is inconsistent with the views expressed herein. The order of the superior court is affirmed.

Affirmed.

NOTES AND QUESTIONS

The position in *Guest* had earlier been adopted in People v. Hernandez, 61 Cal.2d 529, 39 Cal.Rptr. 361, 393 P.2d 673 (1964). However, other courts considering the same issue have rejected the Alaska and California Supreme Courts' conclusions. E. g., State v. Superior Court, 104 Ariz. 440, 454 P.2d 982 (1969); State v. Silva, 53 Haw. 232, 491 P.2d 1216 (1971); Eggleston v. State, 4 Md.App. 124, 241 A.2d 433 (1968); People v. Doyle, 16 Mich.App. 242, 167 N.W.2d 907 (1969) ("Current social and moral values make more realistic the California view that a reasonable and honest mistake of age is a valid defense to a charge of statutory rape * * * but this court is bound to follow the law presently in effect."); State v. Moore, 105 N.J.Super. 567, 253 A.2d 579 (1969); State v. Fulks, 83 S.D. 433, 160 N.W.2d 418 (1968). The cases seldom discuss any constitutional issues which might be raised by interpreting statutory rape statutes as to provide for no defense based upon mistake of age. Why might this be? But see Commonwealth v. Moore, 359 Mass. 509, 269 N.E.2d 636 (1971), in which the defendant was charged with "carnally knowing and abusing" a minor. The victim testified she had an identification card showing her age as eighteen and that she told the defendant she was that age. In addition, the victim had been convicted of prostitution and placed on probation; apparently the police officers, the lawyer representing her, the trial court judge, and the probation officer assumed she was eighteen. Nevertheless, the court held that no affirmative defense of mistake of age was available and that this "strict" liability did not deny the defendant due process of law.

MODEL PENAL CODE *

(Proposed Official Draft, 1962).

Section 213.1. Rape and Related Offenses

(1) *Rape.* A male who has sexual intercourse with a female not his wife is guilty of rape if:

(a) he compels her to submit by force or by threat of imminent death, serious bodily injury, extreme pain or kidnapping, to be inflicted on anyone; or

(b) he has substantially impaired her power to appraise or control her conduct by administering or employing without her knowledge drugs, intoxicants or other means for the purpose of preventing resistance; or

(c) the female is unconscious; or

(d) the female is less than 10 years old.

Rape is a felony of the second degree unless (i) in the course thereof the actor inflicts serious bodily injury upon anyone, or (ii) the victim was not a voluntary social companion of the actor upon the occasion of the crime and had not previously permitted him sexual liberties, in which cases the offense is a felony of the first degree. Sexual intercourse includes intercourse per os or per anum, with some penetration however slight; emission is not required.

(2) *Gross Sexual Imposition.* A male who has sexual intercourse with a female not his wife commits a felony of the third degree if:

(a) he compels her to submit by any threat that would prevent resistance by a woman of ordinary resolution; or

(b) he knows that she suffers from a mental disease or defect which renders her incapable of appraising the nature of her conduct; or

(c) he knows that she is unaware that a sexual act is being committed upon her or that she submits because she falsely supposes that he is her husband.

Section 213.3. Corruption of Minors and Seduction

(1) *Offense Defined.* A male who has sexual intercourse with a female not his wife, or any person who engages in deviate sexual intercourse or causes another to engage in deviate sexual intercourse, is guilty of an offense

(a) the other person is less than [16] years old and the actor is at least [4] years older than the other person; * *

* * *

(2) *Grading.* An offense under paragraph (a) of Subsection (1) is a felony of the third degree. * * *

Section 213.6 Provisions Generally Applicable to Article 213

(1) *Mistake as to Age.* Whenever in this Article the criminality of conduct depends on a child's being below the age of 10, it is no defense that the actor did not know the child's age, or reasonably believed the child to be older than 10. When criminality depends on the child's being below a critical age other than 10, it is a defense for the actor to prove that he reasonably believed the child to be above the critical age.

(2) *Spouse Relationships.* Whenever in this Article the definition of an offense excludes conduct with a spouse, the exclusion shall be deemed to extend to persons living as man and wife, regardless of the legal status of their relationship. The exclusion shall be inoperative as respects spouses living apart under a decree of judicial separation. Where the definition of an offense excludes conduct with a spouse or conduct by a woman, this shall not preclude conviction of a spouse or woman as accomplice in a sexual act which he or she causes another person, not within the exclusion, to perform.

* * *

(4) *Sexually Promiscuous Complainants.* It is a defense to prosecution under Section 213.3 * * * for the actor to prove by a preponderance of the evidence that the alleged victim had, prior to the time of the offense charged, engaged promiscuously in sexual relations with others.

(5) *Prompt Complaint.* No prosecution may be instituted or maintained under this Article unless the alleged offense was brought to the notice of public authority within [3] months of its occurrence or, where the alleged victim was less than [16] years old or otherwise incompetent to make complaint, within [3] months after a parent, guardian or other competent person specially interested in the victim learns of the offense.

(6) *Testimony of Complainants.* No person shall be convicted of any felony under this Article upon the uncorroborated testimony of the alleged victim. Corroboration may be circumstantial. In any prosecution before a jury for an offense under this Article, the jury shall be instructed to evaluate the testimony of a victim or complaining witness with special care in view of the emotional involvement of the witness and the difficulty of determining the truth with respect to alleged sexual activities carried out in private.

D. CRIMINAL HOMICIDE

The homicide offenses present an almost unique situation in the criminal law. All, of course, are based upon defendants' liability for the death of the victims. But the existence of several (or more) different crimes all based upon the fact of causing death reflects perception of a need to distinguish among killings according to varying degrees of culpability of the killer and perhaps according to the danger that the killer presents of future additional killings or assaultive criminal acts. In order to accomplish this, virtually all jurisdictions recognize several homicide offenses which differ from each other in terms of the state of mind required and to some extent by the presence of certain circumstances. While grading offenses according to culpability and dangerousness and doing this by carefully defining state of mind requirements and attendant mitigating circumstances is not unique to homicide, the perceived need to create so many different offenses constituting in effect graded degrees of criminal liability for the single "crime" of killing another person has made homicide law stand out as posing an especially difficult task for the law.

The need to distinguish among the homicide offenses may have been somewhat reduced by recently-imposed constitutional limits on capital punishment. The creation of a separate offense of first degree murder was motivated in large part by what was seen as the need to identify those killings for which death would be the appropriate and sometimes mandatory penalty. See McGautha v. California, 402 U.S. 183, 198, 91 S.Ct. 1454, 1462–63, 28 L.Ed.2d 711, 721 (1971). But it is now clear that the Eighth Amendment prohibition against cruel and unusual punishment prohibits a mandatory penalty of death for any particular homicide crime, Woodson v. North Carolina, 428 U.S. 280, 96 S.Ct. 2978, 49 L.Ed.2d 944 (1976), Roberts v. Louisiana, 428 U.S. 325, 96 S.Ct. 3001, 49 L.Ed.2d 974 (1976), and that the death penalty may be imposed only if the sentencing authority is permitted to consider a wide variety of possibly mitigating considerations relating to the offense and the offender, Lockett v. Ohio, 438 U.S. 586, 98 S.Ct. 2954, 57 L.Ed.2d 973 (1978). See the material at pages 36–45, infra. Thus there may be less need to use the definition of the homicide crimes to identify those killers deserving maximum harshness.

Although homicide law is to a large extent a matter of statute in most jurisdictions, many statutes retain to a greater or lesser extent the flavor and substance of common law distinctions. This section first presents several typical statutory schemes for grading criminal homicide. It then examines the traditional distinctions among murder, premeditated murder, voluntary manslaughter, and involuntary manslaughter. In examining the way in which the law has made these distinctions, consider how the cases would come out under different statutory schemes. Consider which method of distinguishing among the offenses best serves the purposes of the criminal law.

1. STATUTORY FORMULATIONS

MODEL PENAL CODE *

(Proposed Official Draft 1962).

ARTICLE 210. CRIMINAL HOMICIDE

Section 210.0. Definitions

In Articles 210–213, unless a different meaning plainly is required:

(1) "human being" means a person who has been born and is alive;

(2) "bodily injury" means physical pain, illness or any impairment of physical condition;

(3) "serious bodily injury" means bodily injury which creates a substantial risk of death or which causes serious, permanent disfigurement, or protracted loss or impairment of the function of any bodily member or organ;

(4) "deadly weapon" means any firearm, or other weapon, device, instrument, material or substance, whether animate or inanimate, which in the manner it is used or is intended to be used is known to be capable of producing death or serious bodily injury.

Section 210.1. Criminal Homicide

(1) A person is guilty of criminal homicide if he purposely, knowingly, recklessly or negligently causes the death of another human being.

(2) Criminal homicide is murder, manslaughter or negligent homicide.

Section 210.2. Murder

(1) Except as provided in Section 210.3(1)(b), criminal homicide constitutes murder when:

(a) it is committed purposely or knowingly; or

(b) it is committed recklessly under circumstances manifesting extreme indifference to the value of human life. Such recklessness and indifference are presumed if the actor is engaged or is an accomplice in the commission of, or an attempt to commit, or flight after committing or attempting to commit robbery, rape or deviate sexual intercourse by force or threat of force, arson, burglary, kidnapping or felonious escape.

(2) Murder is a felony of the first degree [but a person convicted of murder may be sentenced to death, as provided in Section 210.-6].

Section 210.3. Manslaughter

(1) Criminal homicide constitutes manslaughter when:

(a) it is committed recklessly; or

(b) a homicide which would otherwise be murder is committed under the influence of extreme mental or emotional disturbance for which there is reasonable explanation or excuse. The reasonableness of such explanation or excuse shall be determined from the viewpoint of a person in the actor's situation under the circumstances as he believes them to be.

(2) Manslaughter is a felony of the second degree.

Section 210.4. Negligent Homicide

(1) Criminal homicide constitutes negligent homicide when it is committed negligently.

(2) Negligent homicide is a felony of the third degree.

CALIFORNIA PENAL CODE

§ 187. Murder defined; death of fetus

(a) Murder is the unlawful killing of a human being, or a fetus, with malice aforethought.

(b) This section shall not apply to any person who commits an act which results in the death of a fetus if any of the following apply:

(1) The act complied with the Therapeutic Abortion Act * * *.

(2) The act was committed by a holder of a physician's and surgeon's certificate * * * in a case where, to a medical certainty, the result of a childbirth would be death of the mother of the fetus or where her death from childbirth, although not medically certain, would be substantially certain or more likely than not.

(3) The act was solicited, aided, abetted, or consented to by the mother of the fetus.

(4) Subdivision (b) shall not be construed to prohibit the prosecution of any person under any other provision of law.

§ 188. Malice, express malice, and implied malice defined

Malice Defined. Such malice may be express or implied. It is express when there is manifested a deliberate intention unlawfully to take away the life of a fellow creature. It is implied, when no considerable provocation appears, or when the circumstances attending the killing show an abandoned and malignant heart.

§ 189. Murder; degrees

All murder which is perpetrated by means of a destructive device or explosive, poison, lying in wait, torture, or by any other kind of willful, deliberate, and premeditated killing, or which is committed in the perpetration of, or attempt to perpetrate, arson, rape, robbery, burglary, mayhem, or any act punishable under Section 288 [prohibiting "any lewd or lascivious act * * * upon or with the body, or any part or member thereof, of a child under the age of fourteen years, with the intent of arousing, appealing to, or gratifying the lust or passions or sexual desires of such person or of such child * * * "], is murder of the first degree; and all other kinds of murders are of the second degree.

§ 190. Murder; punishment; discretion of jury

Every person guilty of murder in the first degree shall suffer death, confinement in state prison for life without possibility of parole, or confinement in state prison for life. * * * Every person guilty of murder in the second degree is punishable by imprisonment in the state prison for five, six, or seven years.

§ 192. Manslaughter; voluntary, involuntary, and in driving a vehicle defined; construction of section

Manslaughter is the unlawful killing of a human being, without malice. It is of three kinds:

1. Voluntary—upon a sudden quarrel or heat of passion.

2. Involuntary—in the commission of an unlawful act, not amounting to felony; or in the commission of a lawful act which might produce death, in an unlawful manner, or without due caution and circumspection; provided that this subdivision shall not apply to acts committed in the driving of a vehicle.

3. In the driving of a vehicle—

(a) In the commission of an unlawful act, not amounting to felony, with gross negligence; or in the commission of a lawful act which might produce death, in an unlawful manner, and with gross negligence.

(b) In the commission of an unlawful act, not amounting to felony, without gross negligence; or in the commission of a lawful act which might produce death, in an unlawful manner, but without gross negligence.

This section shall not be construed as making any homicide in the driving of a vehicle punishable which is not a proximate result of the commission of an unlawful act, not amounting to felony, or of the commission of a lawful act which might produce death, in an unlawful manner.

§ 193. Manslaughter; punishment

Manslaughter is punishable by imprisonment in the state prison for two, three or four years, except that a violation of subsection 3 of Section 192 of this code is punishable as follows: In the case of a violation of subdivision (a) of said subsection 3 the punishment shall be either by imprisonment in the county jail for not more than one year or in the state prison, and in such case the jury may recommend by their verdict that the punishment shall be by imprisonment in the county jail; in the case of a violation of subdivision (b) of said subsection 3, the punishment shall be by imprisonment in the county jail for not more than one year. In cases where, as authorized in this section, the jury recommends by their verdict that the punishment shall be by imprisonment in the county jail, the court shall not have authority to sentence the defendant to imprisonment in the state prison, but may nevertheless place the defendant on probation as provided in this code.

NOTES AND QUESTIONS

1. Those portions of California Penal Code § 187 that deal with killing a fetus are a reaction to Keeler v. Superior Court, 2 Cal.3d 619, 87 Cal. Rptr. 481, 470 P.2d 617 (1970), in which the defendant had been charged with murder on the basis of his actions in intentionally causing the death of a fetus that medical evidence established would have had a 75 to 96 percent chance of survival had it been prematurely born on the date of its death at the defendant's hands. Applying what it described as the common law rule which has long been accepted in the United States, the California Supreme Court held that only a child who has been born alive is a "human being" within the meaning of the statute defining murder as the unlawful killing of a human being. Was the reaction of the California legislature appropriate? If causing the death of a fetus should ordinarily be murder, why should there be an exception for situations in which the mother solicited or consented to the act? Is the matter at all affected by the United States Supreme Court decisions severely restricting the extent to which abortions may be prohibited? See Roe v. Wade, 410 U.S. 113, 93 S.Ct. 705, 35 L.Ed. 2d 147 (1973); Doe v. Bolton, 410 U.S. 179, 93 S.Ct. 739, 35 L.Ed.2d 201 (1973).

2. When does death occur for purposes of homicide analysis? Suppose the following situation: Defendant inflicts wound on victim. Victim's physician, after treating victim, decides that because victim's brain evidences no electrical activity victim is dead despite the fact that victim's heart and lungs are functioning because of respirator. Physician then removes victim from respirator and, as a result, victim's heart and lungs cease functioning. When did victim die or, to put the question in different

terms, did defendant "cause" death of victim or did physician? The traditional definition of death defined it in terms of cessation of heartbeat and respiration. But courts have indicated a willingness to accept a definition of death in terms of an absence of brain activity, i. e., "brain death." See Commonwealth v. Golston, 373 Mass. 249, 366 N.E.2d 744 (1977); People v. Saldana, 47 Cal.App.3d 954, 121 Cal.Rptr. 243 (1975). In a recent situation in Austin, Texas, however, an automobile accident victim was declared dead on the basis of a brain death analysis. The "body" was placed on an artificial life support system to permit the use of a kidney for a transplant. Twelve hours later, signs of life were noted and brain surgery was performed. Five days later, the victim was again declared dead. See Kaighin, Death Comes Second Time for Wreck Victim, Austin American Statesman, Oct. 3, 1978, p. B1. For general discussions, see Charron, Death: A Philosophical Perspective on the Legal Definition, 1975 Wash.U.L.Q. 979; Capron & Kass, A Statutory Definition of Standards for Determining Human Death: An Appraisal and a Proposal, 121 U.Pa.L.Rev. 87 (1972); Halley & Harvey, Medical vs Legal Definitions of Death, 204 J.A.M.A. 423 (1968).

2. THE STATE OF MIND REQUIRED FOR MURDER

Murder is the basic homicide offense and analysis of a criminal homicide situation will ordinarily begin with an inquiry into the possibility of the killing being murder. Unfortunately, the traditional definition of the crime leaves some uncertainty as to the state of mind required. Consider the following comments from People v. Morrin, 31 Mich.App. 301, 310–18, 187 N.W.2d 434, 438–43 (1971):

> A person who kills another is guilty of the crime of murder if the homicide is committed with malice aforethought. Malice aforethought is the intention to kill, actual or implied, under circumstances which do not constitute excuse or justification or mitigate the degree of the offense to manslaughter. The intent to kill may be implied where the actor actually intends to inflict great bodily harm or the natural tendency of his behavior is to cause death or great bodily harm. (The common-law felony-murder rule is an example of implied intent or implied malice aforethought.)
>
> Thus, as "malice aforethought" is now defined, a killing may be murder even though the actor harbored no hatred or ill will against the victim and even though he "acted on the spur of the moment." Whatever may be the philological origin of the words "malice aforethought," today "each word has a different significance in legal usage than in ordinary conversation."
>
> The nature of malice aforethought is the source of much of the confusion that attends the law of homicide. The cause of this confusion has been the evolution of malice aforethought from an independently significant element of

murder to a "term of art" whose significance is largely historical and procedural.

The precise roots of malice aforethought are uncertain. Common-law courts spoke of "malice prepense" as early as the 13th century. The requirement that malice aforethought be established in all murder prosecutions represented the common law's recognition that a rational legal system will punish certain homicides (for example, those that are intentional) while excusing others (accidental homicides, for example).

From the beginning malice aforethought was defined principally in functional terms. We know what it did; it both distinguished criminal from innocent homicide and murder from manslaughter. Yet what it was, the precise state of mind which it described, eluded symmetrical definition.

The common-law courts were faced with a difficult problem: malice aforethought was a requisite element of murder, but one so elusive that in many cases it resisted direct proof. Their solution was to create a presumption of malice. As early as the 16th century proof that the accused person killed the victim gave rise to a "presumption" that the act was done with malice aforethought. Once it was established that the accused killed the victim, the burden was upon the accused to prove circumstances of justification, excuse, or mitigation.

This rule, firmly rooted in English law, has taken hold in a great many American jurisdictions * * *.

The merits of the rule are that it relieves the prosecution from the necessity of proving the nonexistence of circumstances of excuse, justification, and mitigation—frequently an impossible burden—and instead allocates the burden of proving such circumstances to the defendant, who, arguably, has greater ability to do so than the prosecution.

* * *

There is also, however, a grave drawback to this presumptive device. This defect arises in connection with jury instructions, to instruct a jury that malice is presumed from the fact of killing is to invite confusion concerning the ultimate burden of proof in the trial. The prosecution must always prove the defendant guilty beyond a reasonable doubt; a rule of law that shifts the burden of proof with respect to "malice" tends to cloud the dimensions of the prosecution's ultimate burden.

It was this danger which led the House of Lords in 1935 to repudiate instructions that charged jurors that they are to presume malice from the mere fact of killing.[21] Speaking of the presumption of innocence as a "golden thread" running through the common law, the Court rejected a formulation that required the jurors to find a defendant guilty unless he discharged his burden of rebutting the presumption of malice.

The Court did not rule that malice must be proved by evidence independent of the killing itself. The fact of homicide still *permits* the jury to find malice aforethought. But it in no sense *compels* such a finding, even absent any evidence of excuse, justification or mitigation on the part of the defendant.

> "All that is meant is that if it is proved that the conscious act of the prisoner killed a man and nothing else appears in the case, there is evidence upon which the jury may, not must, find him guilty of murder." Woolmington v. The Director of Public Prosecutions, [1935] AC 462, 480.

But other authorities have undertaken the elusive task of defining with some precision the state of mind required by malice aforethought. The British Royal Commission on Capital Punishment concluded:

> "Malice aforethought" is simply a comprehensive name for a number of different mental attitudes which have been variously defined at different stages in the development of the law, the presence of any one of which in the accused has been held by the courts to render a homicide particularly heinous and therefore to make it murder. These states of mind have been variously expressed by various authorities, but the statement of the modern law most commonly cited as authoritative is that given in 1877 by Sir James Stephen in his *Digest of the Criminal Law:*[4]
>
> > "Malice aforethought means any one or more of the following states of mind preceding or co-existing with the act or omission by which death is caused, and it may exist where that act is unpremeditated.
> >
> > > *(a)* An intention to cause the death of, or grievous bodily harm to, any person, whether such person is the person actually killed or not;

21. Woolmington v. The Director of Public Prosecutions, [1935] A.C. 462, 472. * * *

4. 9th ed. (1950), Art. 264, pp. 211 ff.

(b) knowledge that the act which causes death will probably cause the death of, or grievous bodily harm to, some person, whether such person is the person actually killed or not, although such knowledge is accompanied by indifference whether death or grievous bodily harm is caused or not, or by a wish that it may not be caused;

(c) an intent to commit any felony whatever;

(d) an intent to oppose by force any officer of justice on his way to, in, or returning from the execution of the duty of arresting, keeping in custody, or imprisoning any person whom he is lawfully entitled to arrest, keep in custody, or imprison, or the duty of keeping the peace or dispersing an unlawful assembly, provided that the offender has notice that the person killed is such an officer so employed.

The expression 'officer of justice' in this clause includes every person who has a legal right to do any of the acts mentioned, whether he is an officer or a private person.

Notice may be given, either by words, by the production of a warrant or other legal authority, by the known official character of the person killed, or by the circumstances of the case."

Stephen himself, however, elsewhere expressed doubt whether *(c)* was not too widely stated * * *. As Stephen put it, "the loose term 'malice' was used, and then when a particular state of mind came under their notice the Judges called it 'malice' or not according to their view of the propriety of hanging particular people. That is, in two words, the history of the definition of murder".[6] There can be no doubt that the term now covers, and has for long covered, all the most heinous forms of homicide, as well as some cases—those of "constructive murder"—whose inclusion in the category of murder has often been criticised.

Thus the following propositions are commonly accepted [7]:

(i) It is murder if one person kills another with intent to do so, without provocation or on slight provocation, although there is no premeditation in the ordinary sense of the word.

6. Minutes of Evidence of the Royal Commission on Capital Punishment, 1866; Q. 2110.

7. Stephen's Digest, 9th ed., pp. 211–6 * * *.

(ii) It is murder if one person is killed by an act intended to kill another.

(iii) It is murder if a person is killed by an act intended to kill, although not intended to kill any particular individual, as if a man throws a bomb into a crowd of people.

(iv) It is murder if death results from an act which is intended to do no more than cause grievous bodily harm. An early example may be found in the case of *Grey,*[8] where a blacksmith, who had had words with an apprentice, struck him on the head with an iron bar and killed him. It was held that it "is all one as if he had run him through with a sword" and he was found guilty of murder.

(v) It is murder if one person kills another by an intentional act which he knows to be likely to kill or to cause grievous bodily harm, although he may not intend to kill or to cause grievous bodily harm and may either be recklessly indifferent as to results of his act or may even desire that no harm should be caused by it. Two examples may be given. A woman may be guilty of murder if she exposes a helpless infant in circumstances where there is not a reasonable expectation that it will be found and preserved by someone else.[9] A man was convicted of murder when he had killed a number of persons in the street by exploding a barrel of gunpowder against the wall of a prison, although his purpose was only to enable a prisoner to escape. Lord Cockburn, L.C.J., told the jury that such an act was murder, quite apart from the fact that it was committed in the prosecution of a felony.[10]

Royal Commission on Capital Punishment 1949–1953 Report, 27–28 (1953). The material that immediately follows explores two specific problems, the killing caused with awareness of a high risk of death and the killing caused with intent to do physical harm. Killings caused with an intent to commit a felony, i. e., felony murders, are considered separately later.

a. GROSS RECKLESSNESS

It is widely acknowledged that a killing is murder if it was caused, in the language of the Royal Commission "by an intentional act which [the killer] knows to be likely to kill or to cause grievous

8. R. v. Grey (1666) Kel. 64.

9. R. v. Walters (1841) C. & Mar. 164.

10. R. v. Desmond, Barrett and others, The Times, April 28, 1868.

bodily harm." Circumstances showing awareness of such a risk may show the "abandoned and malignant" heart required by statutory formulations such as the California Penal Code; see page —— supra. Thus juries may be instructed that implied malice is sufficient to make a killing murder and, in regard to the definition of implied malice:

> Implied malice is such as may be inferred from the circumstances of the killing, as for example * * * when an act [which] imports danger to another is done so recklessly or wantonly as to manifest depravity of mind in this and disregard for human life.

United States v. Dixon, 419 F.2d 288, 290 (D.C.Cir. 1969) (Leventhal, J., concurring). Probably the most important question is nature of the risk that must be involved in order to make the killing murder. This is the question posed by the following case.

COMMONWEALTH v. MALONE

Supreme Court of Pennsylvania, 1946.
354 Pa. 180, 47 A.2d 445.

MAXEY, Chief Justice. This is an appeal from the judgment and sentence under a conviction of murder in the second degree. William H. Long, age 13 years, was killed by a shot from a 32-caliber revolver held against his right side by the defendant, then aged 17 years. These youths were on friendly terms at the time of the homicide. The defendant and his mother while his father and brother were in the U. S. Armed Forces, were residing in Lancaster, Pa., with the family of William H. Long, whose son was the victim of the shooting.

On the evening of February 26th, 1945, when the defendant went to a moving picture theater, he carried in the pocket of his raincoat a revolver which he had obtained at the home of his uncle on the preceding day. In the afternoon preceding the shooting, the decedent procured a cartridge from his father's room and he and the defendant placed it in the revolver.

After leaving the theater, the defendant went to a dairy store and there met the decedent. Both youths sat in the rear of the store ten minutes, during which period the defendant took the gun out of his pocket and loaded the chamber to the right of the firing pin and then closed the gun. A few minutes later, both youths sat on stools in front of the lunch counter and ate some food. The defendant suggested to the decedent that they play "Russian Poker." Long replied: "I don't care; go ahead." The defendant then placed the revolver against the right side of Long and pulled the trigger three times. The third pull resulted in a fatal wound to Long. The latter jumped off the stool and cried: "Oh! Oh! Oh!" and Malone said:

"Did I hit you, Billy? Gee, Kid, I'm sorry." Long died from the wounds two days later.

The defendant testified that the gun chamber he loaded was the first one to the right of the firing chamber and that when he pulled the trigger he did not "expect to have the gun go off." He declared he had no intention of harming Long, who was his friend and companion. The defendant was indicted for murder, tried and found guilty of murder in the second degree and sentenced to a term in the penitentiary for a period not less than five years and not exceeding ten years. A new trial was refused and after sentence was imposed, an appeal was taken.

* * *

The killing of William H. Long by this defendant resulted from an act intentionally done by the latter, in reckless and wanton disregard of the consequences which were at least sixty per cent certain from his thrice attempted discharge of a gun known to contain one bullet and aimed at a vital part of Long's body. This killing was, therefore, murder, for malice in the sense of a wicked disposition is evidenced by the intentional doing of an uncalled-for act in callous disregard of its likely harmful effects on others. The fact that there was no motive for this homicide does not exculpate the accused. In a trial for murder proof of motive is always relevant but never necessary.

NOTES AND QUESTIONS

1. In Commonwealth v. Bowden, 456 Pa. 278, 309 A.2d 714 (1973), Saunders invited the defendant, Bowden, to share a bag of heroin with him. Bowden agreed, purchased half of Saunders' bag, and injected himself. Saunders, unable to properly inject himself, asked for Bowden's help. Bowden then injected heroin into Saunders, who died from an overdose. Is Bowden guilty of murder? The Pennsylvania Supreme Court held not, distinguishing Malone:

> Under the facts of the instant case, we do not believe the necessary element of malice can be implied from Bowden's act of injecting Saunders with the drug, heroin. Initially, although we recognize heroin is truly a dangerous drug, we also recognize that the injection of heroin into the body does not generally cause death. Unfortunately, there are thousands of individuals who use or abuse heroin daily. * * *
>
> Moreover * * *, Bowden knew Saunders was an addict and had used heroin with him for a period of time, he knew the deceased's tolerance to heroin and knew the quantity of heroin he injected into Saunders was his normal dosage, and he knew this dosage had never adversely affected Saunders before in the times he had used the drug. Moreover, the medical testimony established that the amount of heroin taken by Saunders would not normally cause death in an addict.

456 Pa. at 284–85, 309 A.2d at 718.

2. Consider the following facts from State v. Chalmers, 100 Ariz. 70, 411 P.2d 448 (1966):

> The defendant was driving his Chevrolet automobile at approximately 12:30 a. m. on April 24, 1963 in a northerly direction on Oracle Road * * *. Oracle Road is a two lane highway * * *.
>
> The Chevrolet car was traveling at a speed estimated between eighty and one hundred miles per hour. It passed several other cars moving in the same direction, and in order to do so crossed into the left or southbound lane. Two vehicles which were moving in a southerly direction were forced to leave the highway because the Chevrolet car was in the southbound lane. The first southbound vehicle was a pickup truck with a camper body, and the second was a * * * Sheriff's patrol car. The Chevrolet car swerved back into the right lane after forcing the patrol car off the road, and again into the left lane where it shortly thereafter collided with two vehicles moving in a southerly direction in the southbound or left lane.
>
> As a result of the collision two passengers in one of the cars involved in the collision were killed * * *.

Should the defendant's conviction for murder be upheld on appeal? The Arizona Supreme Court, characterizing the facts as showing at most gross negligence, held that the conviction must be reversed. Gross negligence is not such conduct "as appears to be contemplated when referring to 'an abandoned and malignant heart,' " the court concluded. The phrase, it commented, "seems to mean conduct by the use of a weapon or other appliance likely to produce death, and by the brutal and blood-thirsty use of such instrumentality."

b. INTENT TO DO PHYSICAL HARM

Malice can also be "implied," as the Royal Commission's Report makes clear, from an act "intended to do no more than cause grievous bodily harm." Why should this be so? Is it because of the difficulty of deciding, on the facts of particular cases, whether the defendant actually intended to kill or whether he simply intended to cause severe injury? Or is it because one who intends to inflict such injury upon another and does so (but unintentionally causes death) is as dangerous and as blameworthy as one who actually intended to cause death? Probably the major questions arising in the application of this aspect of homicide law are the kinds of injury that constitute "grievous bodily harm" and whether it is necessary that the defendant have actually intended the specific injuries that were caused and constitute the requisite harm. These issues are raised in the following case.

PEOPLE v. GEIGER

Court of Appeals of Michigan, 1968.
10 Mich.App. 339, 159 N.W.2d 383.

BURNS, Judge. Defendant appeals from a circuit court jury conviction of manslaughter.

Sometime after 11 p. m., May 6, 1965, defendant confronted his estranged wife, Sharon Geiger, in the parking lot of a bar in Prudenville, Michigan, as she was about to enter the bar with Joan Greening. Joan Greening testified that she and Mrs. Geiger had had only one drink at another bar prior to meeting the defendant, that Mrs. Geiger's health appeared normal and that she observed no black and blue marks or abrasions upon Mrs. Geiger that evening. Joan Greening further testified that she was told by the defendant to wait for Mrs. Geiger in the bar, but that she waited in the parking lot and observed the defendant talking to his wife and trying to force her into the car; he then "threw" her into the car and drove away.

State police officers who had interrogated the defendant after the alleged offense testified that defendant told them the couple drove to the Prudenville elementary school playing field. They argued and got out of the car. Defendant struck his wife "two or three times" with his open hand and pushed her to the ground in such a manner that she bumped her head against the car. When Mrs. Geiger failed to get up and appeared unconscious, defendant picked her up and placed her in his car. He then allegedly attempted to clean her after driving a short distance to a house trailer which the Geigers had rented until May 1, 1965.

Early in the morning on May 7, defendant left his wife in the trailer and drove to James Meigs' house where defendant had been residing while he and his wife were separated. Meigs was awakened around 3:15 a. m., at which time defendant persuaded Meigs to help move the automobile which Mrs. Geiger had driven to the bar. After taking the vehicle to Mrs. Geiger's parents' home, defendant finally replied to Meigs' inquiries as to what was going on; defendant stated that he might be "facing a murder rap."

Between 3:30 a. m. and 4:30 a. m., May 7, defendant aroused his employer, asked for $100 and was given $50 in order to get away for a few days.

Defendant apparently returned to the house trailer, placed his wife in the front seat of his car and put a blanket over her. He drove south for approximately 186 miles and at 7:30 a. m. or 8 a. m., stopped at the Addison Community Hospital, Addison, Michigan, where his wife was pronounced dead.

* * *

Defendant was charged with first-degree murder, but the jury was instructed only as to second-degree murder and manslaughter. Defendant contends that the instructions regarding second-degree murder should not have been submitted to the jury because there were no proofs showing malice.

Malice has been defined as "an intent to cause the very harm that results *or some harm of the same general nature, or an act done in wanton or wilful disregard of the plain and strong likelihood that some such harm will result.*" (Emphasis supplied.) People v. Hansen (1962) 368 Mich. 344, 350, 118 N.W.2d 422, 425. Consistent with this definition, it follows that an assault by blows without a weapon may, under certain circumstances, permit a jury to infer an intent to kill. Wellar v. People (1874), 30 Mich. 16; People v. Collins (1942), 303 Mich. 34, 5 N.W.2d 556; also, see 22 A.L.R.2d 854.

On pages 19 and 20 of 30 Mich. of the *Wellar* Case, supra, Justice Campbell said:

> "In determining whether a person who has killed another without meaning to kill him is guilty of murder or manslaughter, the nature and extent of the injury or wrong which was actually intended, must usually be of controlling importance.
>
> "It is not necessary in all cases that one held for murder must have intended to take the life of the person he slays by his wrongful act. It is not always necessary that he must have intended a personal injury to such person. But it is necessary that *the intent with which he acted shall be equivalent in legal character to a criminal purpose aimed against life.* Generally the intent must have been to commit either a specific felony, or at least an act involving all the wickedness of a felony. And if the intent be directly to produce a bodily injury, it must be such an injury as may be expected to involve serious consequences, either periling life or leading to great bodily harm. There is no rule recognized as authority which will allow a conviction of murder where a fatal result was not intended, *unless the injury intended was one of a very serious character which might naturally and commonly involve loss of life, or grievous mischief.*" (Emphasis supplied.)
>
> "The intent to kill must undoubtedly be established, as an inference of fact, to the satisfaction of the jury; but they may draw that inference, as they draw all other inferences, from any fact in evidence which, to their minds, fairly proves its existence. Intentions can only be proved by acts, as juries cannot look into the breast of the criminal. And where any act is knowingly committed which naturally and usually leads to certain consequences, a jury certainly has

the right, in the exercise of ordinary sagacity, to draw the inference that such results are intended." People v. Scott (1859) 6 Mich. 287, 296.

The question before this Court is: was there evidence from which a jury could infer defendant's alleged intent to produce great bodily injury with the attendant likelihood that death would result therefrom?

It was legally possible for the jury in this case to find that the nature and extent of Sharon Geiger's injuries were reflective of an intent equivalent to a criminal purpose aimed against life. This consideration standing alone would be insufficient to establish malice, but the extent and nature of the injuries is not set against a solitary backdrop. Defendant "forced" or "pushed" the deceased into his car shortly before he severely beat her. After the beating decedent's unconsciousness and general physical appearance, as revealed to the jury from photographs and the autopsy report, showed a need for medical attention. Notwithstanding this need, defendant failed to immediately take his wife to a local hospital; instead he waited approximately 6 to 8 hours, during which time he travelled over 180 miles. Although by no means conclusive, defendant's statement to James Meigs that he "might be facing a murder rap" would give a jury additional insight into defendant's intent. An inference of intent to kill could be drawn from these and other facts presented in this case.

3. FIRST DEGREE MURDER: THE PREMEDITATED KILLING

The common law crime of murder was not subdivided into degrees but American statutes have not infrequently created separate crimes of first degree murder and second degree murder. The California statute, see page 451, supra, is reasonably typical. These statutes often define first degree murder as those killings committed in the course of enumerated felonies and "premeditated" killings. Second degree murder consists of all killings that would be murder under the traditional definition of that term and which are not within the statutory definition of first degree murder. The issues presented by felony murder aspects of the statutory crime of first degree murder are not significantly different from those created by the general concept of felony murder and the material in the next section is therefore applicable to first degree felony murder as well as other felony murder. The concept of premeditation, however, is almost unique to the statutory crime of first degree murder and is therefore the subject of this separate section. In examining the material, consider several matters: How should premeditation be defined, as in instructions explaining it to a jury? What sort of evidence should be regarded as sufficient to uphold a verdict finding that a killing was the result of premeditation? In light of the answers to these questions, is it wise to separate out premeditated killings for the imposition of more severe penalties than are imposed for other murders?

STATE v. SNOWDEN

Supreme Court of Idaho, 1957.
79 Idaho 266, 313 P.2d 706.

McQUADE, Justice. This is an appeal by the defendant, who had entered a plea of guilty to an information charging him with the crime of murder in the first degree. At all times during the proceedings the defendant was represented by counsel. The district court, after hearing evidence to determine the degree of the crime and mitigating circumstances, if any, held the offense was murder in the first degree, and entered judgment sentencing the defendant to death.

The victim, Cora Lucyle Dean, was stabbed to death September 22, 1956, in Garden City, Idaho. The evidence showed the following sequence of events:

Defendant Snowden had been playing pool and drinking in a Boise pool room early in the evening. With a companion, one Carrier, he visited a club near Boise, then went to nearby Garden City. There the two men visited a number of bars, and defendant had several drinks. Their last stop was the HiHo Club.

Witnesses related that while defendant was in the HiHo Club he met and talked to Cora Lucyle Dean. The defendant himself said he hadn't been acquainted with Mrs. Dean prior to that time, but he had "seen her in a couple of the joints up town." He danced with Mrs. Dean while at the HiHo Club. Upon departing from the tavern, the two left together.

In statements to police officers, that were admitted in evidence, defendant Snowden said after they left the club Mrs. Dean wanted him to find a cab and take her back to Boise, and he refused because he didn't feel he should pay her fare. After some words, he related:

> "* * * she got mad at me so I got pretty hot and I don't know whether I back handed her there or not. And, we got calmed down and decided to walk across to the gas station and call a cab. * * *"

They crossed the street, and began arguing again. Defendant said:

> "* * * She swung and at the same time she kneed me again. I blew my top."

Defendant said he pushed the woman over beside a pickup truck which was standing near a business building. There he pulled his knife—a pocket knife with a two-inch blade—and cut her throat.

The body, which was found the next morning, was viciously and sadistically cut and mutilated. An autopsy surgeon testified the voice box had been cut, and that this would have prevented the victim from making any intelligible outcry. There were other wounds inflicted while she was still alive—one in her neck, one in her abdomen, two in the face, and two on the back of the neck. The second neck wound severed the spinal cord and caused death. There were other wounds all over her body, and her clothing had been cut away. The nipple of the right breast was missing. There was no evidence of a sexual attack on the victim; however, some of the lacerations were around the breasts and vagina of the deceased. A blood test showed Mrs. Dean was intoxicated at the time of her death.

Defendant took the dead woman's wallet. He hailed a passing motorist and rode back to Boise with him. There he went to a bowling alley and changed clothes. He dropped his knife into a sewer, and threw the wallet away. Then he went to his hotel and cleaned up again. He put the clothes he had worn that evening into a trash barrel.

After hearing the testimony of police officers and other witnesses, the trial court determined the killing was murder in the first degree and there were no circumstances in mitigation of the offense or of the punishment to be inflicted. The defendant was sentenced to death. This appeal is from that judgment.

* * *

The second assignment of error of the defendant is based upon the finding of the court that the defendant's acts in taking the life of Cora Lucyle Dean were willful, deliberate, and premeditated. I. C. § 18–4003 requires first degree homicide to be perpetrated by any kind of willful, deliberate, and premeditated killing * * * [.] The test to determine if the killing was willful, deliberate, and premeditated has been set out in State v. Shuff, 9 Idaho 115, 72 P. 664, 668, wherein the court stated:

> "* * * The unlawful killing must be accompanied with a deliberate and clear intent to take life, in order to constitute murder of the first degree. The intent to kill must be the result of deliberate premeditation. It must be formed upon the pre-existing reflection, and not upon a sudden heat of passion sufficient to preclude the idea of deliberation. * * *"

The court further stated in this case while approving an instruction:

> "* * * That instruction reads as follows, to wit: 'From these definitions the jury will see that any unlawful killing of a human being, with malice aforethought, is murder; but if nothing further characterizes the offense it is murder of the second degree. To constitute the higher of-

> fense there must be superadded, to the general definition above given, willfulness, deliberation, and premeditation. By willfulness is meant that it was of purpose, with the intent that, by the given act, the life of the party should be taken. It must be deliberate and premeditated. By this it is not meant that the killing must have been conceived or intended for any particular length of time. It is sufficient if it was done with reflection and conceived beforehand. And in this view, as I have said before, the deliberate purpose to kill and the killing may follow each other as rapidly as successive impulses or thoughts of the mind. It is enough that the party deliberate before the act—premeditate—the purpose to slay before he gave the fatal blow. But while the purpose, the intent, and its execution may follow thus rapidly upon each other, it is proper for the jury to take into consideration the shortness of such interval in considering whether such sudden and speedy execution may not be attributed to sudden passion and anger, rather than to deliberation and premeditation, which must characterize the higher offense. * * *."

The Supreme Court of Arizona held in the case of Macias v. State, 283 P. 711, 715:

> "* * * There need be no appreciable space of time between the intention to kill and the act of killing. They may be as instantaneous as successive thoughts of the mind. It is only necessary that the act of killing be preceded by a concurrence of will, deliberation, and premeditation on the part of the slayer, and, if such is the case, the killing is murder in the first degree * * *."

In the present case, the trial court had no other alternative than to find the defendant guilty of willful, deliberate, and premeditated killing with malice aforethought in view of the defendant's acts in deliberately opening up a pocket knife, next cutting the victim's throat, and then hacking and cutting until he had killed Cora Lucyle Dean and expended himself. The full purpose and design of defendant's conduct was to take the life of the deceased.

The fourth assignment of error is directed at the imposition of the penalty of death upon the defendant. * * * It is abuse of discretion we are dealing with, and in particular the alleged abuse of discretion in prescribing the punishment for murder in the first degree as committed by the defendant. To choose between the punishments of life imprisonment and death there must be some distinction between one homicide and another. This case exemplifies an abandoned and malignant heart and sadistic mind, bent upon taking human life. It is our considered conclusion, from all the facts and circumstances, the imposition of the death sentence was not an abuse of discretion by the trial court.

The judgment is affirmed.

NOTES AND QUESTIONS

1. As applied by the Idaho Supreme Court in *Snowden,* does the premeditation requirement serve as an effective device for identifying those killings that are significantly more serious or blameworthy than those that we want to label murder? Is the court correct in its statement that the trial court "had no other alternative" but to find premeditation on the facts presented? Isn't it arguable that at a minimum this case presents a situation in which a reasonable jury might go either way on the premeditation issue? Is the result here really the product of a careful application of the legal doctrine which the court says it is applying? Consider the possibility that the court found the killing to be so grossly offensive that, for reasons the court does not acknowledge or discuss, it merited the ultimate penalty. Having arrived at that conclusion, the court then significantly bent the concept of premeditation to permit it to uphold a conviction for first degree murder.

2. The California Supreme Court has attempted to devise a more structured analysis for determining whether a jury verdict finding premeditation is supported by the evidence. People v. Anderson, 70 Cal.2d 15, 73 Cal.Rptr. 550, 447 P.2d 942 (1968). It noted three categories of evidence tending to establish premeditation:

> (1) facts about how and what defendant did *prior* to the actual killing which show that the defendant was engaged in activity directed toward, and explicable as intended to result in, the killing—what may be characterized as "planning" activity; (2) facts about the defendant's *prior* relationship and/or conduct with the victim from which the jury could reasonably infer a "motive" to kill the victim, which inference of motive, together with facts of type (1) or (3), would in turn support an inference that the killing was the result of "a pre-existing reflection" and "careful thought and weighing of considerations" rather than "mere unconsidered or rash impulse hastily executed" * * *; (3) facts about the nature of the killing from which the jury could infer that the *manner* of killing was so particular and exacting that the defendant must have intentionally killed according to a "preconceived design" to take his victim's life in a particular way for a "reason" which the jury can reasonably infer from facts or type (1) or (2).

70 Cal.2d at 26–27, 73 Cal.Rptr. at 557, 447 P.2d at 949. A verdict of guilty of premeditated murder will be sustained, the court concluded, when the record contains evidence of all three kinds, when there is "extremely strong" evidence of type (1), or evidence of type (2) in conjunction with other evidence of either type (1) or (3). Is this analysis reasonable? Is it likely to accomplish its intended purpose?

3. Is premeditation, under any definition, an appropriate criterion with which to select those cases in which the maximum penalty—whatever it is—may be imposed? Consider the following:

The Significance of Deliberation and Impulse

Whether and to what extent homicidal behavior was preceded by deliberation is plainly of evidential value in determining what the actor knew and intended when he acted. The more extensive the deliberation, the more probable it is that at least the more palpable risks created by the homicidal act were clearly perceived, and at least its more immediate consequences intended. From this point of view, however, gradations in homicidal behavior from the purely impulsive to the completely deliberate bear directly upon the question whether the actor created the homicidal risk inadvertently or advertently and, if advertently, whether or not he intended to kill, and only indirectly upon his character. The difficult question is whether the impulsiveness or deliberateness of his behavior has direct and independent significance in relation to his character. Assuming that other factors indicative of his character, such as knowledge, intent and motive are the same, of what additional importance is it that his act was the product of or was preceded by more or less deliberation? It may be argued that the more carefully considered and the less impulsive the act is, the more it indicates basic perversion of the actor's conceptions of good and evil. But it is surely not self-evident that the man who acts on wrong principles is a more dangerous man than one who acts without considering what is good. There are, moreover, other objections to this view of the significance of deliberation. In the first place, it ignores that passion may influence deliberation as well as lead to action without deliberation, so that deliberate as well as impulsive action may be contrary to the actor's real notions of good and evil. In the second place, it does not embrace either deliberation about means rather than ends or acts which are preceded by but are not in accord with the results of deliberation. And yet it is extremely difficult in most cases to discover in what terms the actor deliberated or what was the relationship between deliberation and act. These objections are not avoided by stating the significance of deliberation in another way. Thus it may be said that reflection prior to action indicates that the actor lacks the sort of desires that will prevent such an act, since reflection is the opportunity to bring such desires into play, an opportunity which, by hypothesis, is not afforded by impulsive action; whereas action without reflection does not permit of that inference because if the actor had deliberated he might not have acted as he did. But in order to draw from these premises the conclusion that the man who acts deliberately is more dangerous than the man who acts impulsively, it must be asserted that the probability that the former's deliberations will result in wrong judgments is greater than the probability that the latter will not reflect before acting. This proposition also requires proof. The truth is, we think, that deliberation has no independent significance in relation to character and that the importance usually accorded it properly belongs to other factors

> which are its concomitants such, for example, as lapse of time, or to still other factors which it evidences, such as knowledge and intent. When the matter is viewed in that way, no difficulty is experienced in dealing with cases in which deliberation itself results in the intensification of passion, as it may when the enormity of an injury done the actor or the value of an end to be served by a homicidal act becomes apparent only after thought.

Wechsler and Michael, A Rationale of the Law of Homicide, 37 Colum.L. Rev. 701, 1261, 1282–84 (1937).

4. FELONY MURDER

As the Royal Commission's report indicates, there has been traditional acceptance of the rule that the intent to commit a felony suffices to make a killing murder, so that a killing caused by action undertaken with the intent to commit a felony constitutes the crime of murder. Statutory homicide schemes have been interpreted in light of this rule; the California Supreme Court has held, for example, that despite the absence of any provision in the California statutes (see pages 450–51, supra) for second degree felony murder, a killing caused during the commission of one of those felonies not enumerated in the statutory provision for first degree felony murder is second degree murder. People v. Phillips, 64 Cal.2d 574, 51 Cal.Rptr. 225, 414 P.2d 353 (1966).

The significance of the felony murder rule is increased when it is combined with the doctrine making all members of a conspiracy liable for the crimes committed by other members of the conspiracy, at least where those crimes are committed in furtherance of the conspiracy and are a foreseeable result of it. Combination of the two doctrines means, of course, that in jointly-committed felonies, all of the participants may be liable for the felony murder committed by one of their number. The impact of this is illustrated by People v. Friedman, 205 N.Y. 161, 98 N.E. 471 (1912), in which Friedman stood guard while Kuhn, his cofelon, entered a store to rob it. In a struggle, Kuhn killed the victim and Friedman was charged and convicted of felony murder. On appeal, the court held that the trial judge properly refused the following instruction requested by Friedman:

> If * * * the scope and plan of execution of [the] unlawful enterprise did not involve the use of force or violence which might result in the taking of human life, then the defendant is not responsible for the act of Kuhn in taking human life * * *.

Explaining, the court reasoned that the trial court had properly left to the jury the task of deciding whether the killing was a "natural and probable consequence" of the joint undertaking:

> If the natural and probable consequence of the common enterprise was the killing of Mr. Schuchart in case of resist-

> ance on his part, the defendant was liable for murder * * *, although he did not do the actual killing. The request assumes that, if the appellant did not fire the fatal shot, he could escape liability unless the conspiracy expressly contemplated the use of force or violence as might cause death. This is an erroneous view of the law. An express agreement by intending robbers not to kill in carrying out a plan of robbery would not save any of the conspirators from responsibility for a homicide by one of them in committing or attempting to commit the robbery, if such killing was the natural and probable result of the robbery or attempt to rob in such a contingency as actually occurred in this case.

205 N.Y. at 165–66, 98 N.E. at 473.

There has been a discernable but not universal trend towards limiting the felony murder doctrine and many of the issues presented by this section deal with the desirability and scope of possible limitations on the rule. The trend seems to be related to increasing skepticism as to the extent to which the felony murder rule in fact serves a legitimate function or at least as to whether it serves its function or functions at an acceptable cost. In evaluating the propriety of the rule itself as well as possible limitations upon it, it is important to identify the function which the rule is to serve and the extent to which possible limitations will or will not interfere with that function. One view concerning the function of the rule was stated by Chief Justice Traynor of the California Supreme Court in People v. Washington, 62 Cal.2d 777, 44 Cal.Rptr. 442, 402 P.2d 130 (1965):

> The purpose of the felony-murder rule is to deter felons from killing negligently or accidentally by holding them strictly responsible for killings they commit. * * *
>
> It is contended * * * that another purpose of the felony-murder rule is to prevent the commission of robberies [and other felonies]. Neither the common-law rationale of the rule nor the Penal Code supports this contention.

62 Cal.2d at 781, 44 Cal.Rptr. at 445, 402 P.2d at 133. But is Justice Traynor correct as a matter of logic and common experience? If it is reasonable to expect that the existence of the felony murder rule will cause persons who commit felonies to be careful in doing so, is it not also reasonable to expect that it will discourage some persons from committing felonies because they realize by committing a felony they run the risk of incurring liability for murder? In evaluating the issues raised in this section, consider whether it makes any difference whether the function of the rule is regarded as limited to encouraging felons to behave safely in the course of their felonious conduct or whether it also includes discouraging potential felons from engaging in felonious activity in the first place.

To what if any extent does the felony murder rule raise constitutional problems? In State v. Goodseal, 220 Kan. 487, 553 P.2d 279 (1976), the defendant attacked the rule as violative of the prohibition against cruel and unusual punishment and the rights to equal protection and due process. The court responded:

> The felony murder rule represents a long standing policy of this state. [Its rationale is] to furnish an added deterrent to the perpetration of felonies which, by their nature or attendant circumstances, create a foreseeable risk of death. "The legislature, acting in the exercise of the police power of the state, is empowered to enact measures in furtherance of the public welfare and safety, and its enactments in such areas are not to be judicially curtailed where they reasonably relate to the ends sought to be obtained. Classifications honestly designed to protect the public from evils which might otherwise arise are to be upheld unless they are unreasonable, arbitrary or oppressive.' * * * The felony murder rule, designed as it is to protect human life, represents sound public policy, is reasonably related to the end sought to be accomplished and is not constitutionally impermissible.

220 Kan. at 493–94, 553 P.2d at 286. Is this an appropriate result?

PEOPLE v. STAMP

California Court of Appeals, 1969.
2 Cal.App.3d 203, 82 Cal.Rptr. 598, cert. den.
400 U.S. 819, 91 S.Ct. 36, 27 L.Ed.2d 46.

COBEY, Associate Justice. These are appeals by Jonathan Earl Stamp, Michael John Koory and Billy Dean Lehman, following jury verdicts of guilty of robbery and murder, both in the first degree. Each man was given a life sentence on the murder charge together with the time prescribed by law on the robbery count.

Defendants appeal their conviction of the murder of Carl Honeyman who, suffering from a heart disease, died between 15 and 20 minutes after Koory and Stamp held up his business, the General Amusement Company, on October 26, 1965, at 10:45 a. m. Lehman, the driver of the getaway car, was apprehended a few minutes after the robbery; several weeks later Stamp was arrested in Ohio and Koory in Nebraska.

* * *

On this appeal appellants primarily rely upon their position that the felony-murder doctrine should not have been applied in this case due to the unforeseeability of Honeyman's death.

THE FACTS

Defendants Koory and Stamp, armed with a gun and a blackjack, entered the rear of the building housing the offices of General Amusement Company, ordered the employees they found there to go to the front of the premises, where the two secretaries were working. Stamp, the one with the gun, then went into the office of Carl Honeyman, the owner and manager. Thereupon Honeyman, looking very frightened and pale, emerged from the office in a "kind of hurry." He was apparently propelled by Stamp who had hold of him by an elbow.

The robbery victims were required to lie down on the floor while the robbers took the money and fled out the back door. As the robbers, who had been on the premises 10 to 15 minutes, were leaving, they told the victims to remain on the floor for five minutes so that no one would "get hurt."

Honeyman, who had been lying next to the counter, had to use it to steady himself in getting up off the floor. Still pale, he was short of breath, sucking air, and pounding and rubbing his chest. As he walked down the hall, in an unsteady manner, still breathing hard and rubbing his chest, he said he was having trouble "keeping the pounding down inside" and that his heart was "pumping too fast for him." A few minutes later, although still looking very upset, shaking, wiping his forehead and rubbing his chest, he was able to walk in a steady manner into an employee's office. When the police arrived, almost immediately thereafter, he told them he was not feeling very well and that he had a pain in his chest. About two minutes later, which was 15 to 20 minutes after the robbery had occurred, he collapsed on the floor. At 11:25 he was pronounced dead on arrival at the hospital. The coroner's report listed the immediate cause of death as heart attack.

The employees noted that during the hours before the robbery Honeyman had appeared to be in normal health and good spirits. The victim was an obese, sixty-year-old man, with a history of heart disease, who was under a great deal of pressure due to the intensely competitive nature of his business. Additionally, he did not take good care of his heart.

Three doctors, including the autopsy surgeon, Honeyman's physician, and a professor of cardiology from U.C.L.A., testified that although Honeyman had an advanced case of atherosclerosis, a progressive and ultimately fatal disease, there must have been some immediate upset to his system which precipitated the attack. It was their conclusion in response to a hypothetical question that but for the robbery there would have been no fatal seizure at that time. The fright induced by the robbery was too much of a shock to Honeyman's system. There was opposing expert testimony to the effect that it could not be said with reasonable medical certainty that fright could ever be fatal.

SUFFICIENCY OF THE EVIDENCE RE CAUSATION

* * *

A review of the facts as outlined above shows that there was substantial evidence of the robbery itself, that appellants were the robbers, and that but for the robbery the victim would not have experienced the fright which brought on the fatal heart attack.

APPLICATION OF THE FELONY-MURDER RULE

* * *

There is no requirement that the killing occur, "while committing" or "while engaged in" the felony, or that the killing be "a part of" the felony, other than that the few acts be a part of one continuous transaction. Thus the homicide need not have been committed "to perpetrate" the felony. There need be no technical inquiry as to whether there has been a completion or abandonment of or desistence from the robbery before the homicide itself was completed.

The doctrine is not limited to those deaths which are foreseeable. Rather a felon is held strictly liable for *all* killings committed by him or his accomplices in the course of the felony. As long as the homicide is the direct causal result of the robbery the felony-murder rule applies whether or not the death was a natural or probable consequence of the robbery. So long as a victim's predisposing physical condition, regardless of its cause, is not the *only* substantial factor bringing about his death, that condition, and the robber's ignorance of it, in no way destroys the robber's criminal responsibility for the death. So long as life is shortened as a result of the felonious act it does not matter that the victim might have died soon anyway. In this respect, the robber takes his victim as he finds him.

REX v. LUMLEY

Central Criminal Court, 1911.
22 Cox Crim.C. 635.

[Charles Lumley, a physician, was charged with the murder of Mabel Gorringe. The evidence tended to show that the defendant had performed an illegal abortion upon the victim, and that she had died as a result of this operation. The following is a portion of the trial court's instruction on the felony murder doctrine.]

AVORY, J. (in the course of his summing up) directed the jury as follows: If the evidence satisfies you beyond reasonable doubt that the prisoner did, in fact, either use an instrument or other means, for the purpose and with the intention of procuring abortion, and that death resulted from that act, then you must ask yourselves the further question: When he did the act, did he contemplate, or must he as a reasonable man have contemplated, that death was likely to result, or must he as a reasonable man have contemplated that grievous bodily harm was likely to result? If, in your opinion, he must as a reasonable man have contemplated either of those consequences, then your duty is to find him guilty of murder. If you are of the opinion, and are driven to the conclusion by the evidence, that he did the act which is charged against him, but that he had not at the time in contemplation, and would not as a reasonable man have contemplated, that either death or grievous bodily harm would result, but thought that by his own skill as a medical man he could perform this operation without any risk of either death or grievous bodily harm, then you would be justified in convicting him of manslaughter.

NOTES AND QUESTIONS

1. Although it is frequently said that a felon is not liable for murder if during the felony he causes a death in an unforeseeable manner because the felonious activity is not the "proximate cause" of the death, e. g., W. LaFave and A. Scott, Criminal Law 264 (1972), American case law support for this proposition is sparse. Most of the support is dicta in cases holding defendants liable for what is determined to have been a foreseeable death. E. g., State v. Glover, 330 Mo. 709, 50 S.W.2d 1049 (1932) (defendant who set fire to drug store to collect insurance liable for felony-murder of fireman killed fighting the blaze on the ground that he had reason to anticipate that members of the fire department would endanger themselves fighting the fire). See Ward v. State, 109 S.W.2d 207 (Tex.Crim.App.1937) in which the defendant caused fire to be set to a building; a person in an upper room was killed in the fire. "The testimony," concluded the court, "excludes the idea that the principals knew, or should have known, that any person was in the building at the time the arson was consummated." Defendant also denied any knowledge of this fact. He was charged with murder under a statute in the arson section of the penal code providing that "Where death is occasioned by any offense described in this * * * chapter the offender is guilty of murder." The conviction was upheld, although the court commented that in the absence of the statute it would have grave doubt that the defendant would be liable for murder "unless the death in question was the natural and reasonable consequence of [the] arson * * *." Should the existence of such a statute preclude application of a "proximate cause" requirement of foreseeability?

2. Perhaps the same result as is obtained by requiring foreseeability can be accomplished by requiring that the felony be a "dangerous" one. Some courts have rejected arguments that only dangerous felonies can give rise to felony murder. E. g., Baker v. State, 236 Ga. 754, 225 S.E.2d 269 (1976); State v. Chambers, 524 S.W.2d 826 (Mo.1975), cert. den. 423 U.S. 1058, 96 S.Ct. 794, 46 L.Ed.2d 694 (1976), conviction affirmed 554 S.W.2d 112 (Mo.1977). But most have accepted some sort of dangerousness requirement. The California Supreme Court, apparently reasoning that since felony murder is a "highly artificial concept" and therefore should be limited as much as possible, has required that the felony be one "inherently dangerous to human life." People v. Phillips, 64 Cal.2d 574, 51 Cal.Rptr. 225, 414 P.2d 353 (1966). Thus the court determines whether a felony is suffi-

ciently dangerous by looking at the elements of the crime in the abstract, not the manner in which it was committed on the facts of any particular case. Only in regard to such inherently dangerous felonies, the court has reasoned, is there sufficient probability that the potential felon will be deterred to justify applying the felony murder rule. People v. Henderson, 19 Cal.3d 86, 94, 137 Cal.Rptr. 1, 5, 560 P.2d 1180, 1183–84 (1977) (false imprisonment is not "inherently dangerous"). Other courts, however, have considered both the nature of the underlying felony in the abstract and the circumstances of its commission in the specific case in determining whether the felony is dangerous. E. g., State v. Goodseal, 220 Kan. 487, 553 P.2d 279 (1976). The difference in approach may, of course, have an impact upon how cases come out. Although the California Supreme Court has held that unlawful possession of a firearm by a convicted felon is not an "inherently dangerous" felony for purposes of its dangerousness requirement, People v. Satchell, 6 Cal.3d 28, 98 Cal.Rptr. 33, 489 P.2d 1361 (1971), the Kansas Supreme Court in Goodseal, supra, held that where a convicted felon pointed a firearm at another person and it allegedly accidentally discharged killing that person, the felony of unlawfully possessing a firearm after a felony conviction was sufficiently dangerous to bring the felony murder rule into play.

In deciding which approach leads to the most desirable outcomes, consider whether the felony murder rule should apply on the following facts:

> In the early morning hours (nighttime) of Sept. 5, 1972, [the defendant], accompanied by one Collins, drove his red Torino to a motor company's lot * * *. [Defendant] broke a window in a pickup truck belonging to the company, directed Collins to get into the truck and steer, hooked it by a log chain onto the Torino's rear bumper, and drove the Torino northward along the highway towing the truck "real fast and all over the road." * * * At some point during the asportation, the log chain became unhooked from both vehicles and the pickup truck traveled onto the wrong side of the highway and collided head-on with a southbound Valiant. All four occupants of the Valiant perished as a result of the crash.

Chambers v. State, 554 S.W.2d 112, 114 (Mo.1977).

STATE v. CANOLA

Supreme Court of New Jersey, 1977.
73 N.J. 206, 374 A.2d 20.

CONFORD, P. J. A. D., Temporarily Assigned.

Defendant, along with three confederates, was in the process of robbing a store when a victim of the robbery, attempting to resist the perpetration of the crime, fatally shot one of the co-felons. The sole issue for our resolution is whether, under N.J.S.A. 2A:113–1, defendant may be held liable for felony murder. * * *

The facts of this case * * * may be summarized as follows. The owner of a jewelry store and his employee, in an attempt to resist an armed robbery, engaged in a physical skirmish with one of the four robbers. A second conspirator, called upon for assistance, began shooting, and the store owner returned the gunfire. Both the owner and the felon, one Lloredo, were fatally shot in the exchange, the latter by the firearm of the owner.

Defendant and two others were indicted on two counts of murder, one count of robbery and one count of having been armed during the robbery. The murder counts were based on the deaths, respectively, of the robbery victim and the co-felon. After trial on the murder counts defendant was found guilty on both and was sentenced to concurrent terms of life imprisonment. * * * Conventional formulations of the felony murder rule would not seem to encompass liability in this case. * * * A recent study of the early formulations of the felony murder rule by such authorities as Lord Coke, Foster and Blackstone and of later ones by Judge Stephen and Justice Holmes concluded that they were concerned solely with situations where the felon or a confederate did the actual killing. Comment, 24 Rutgers L.Rev. 591, 600–601 (1970); and see Commonwealth v. Redline, 391 Pa. 486, 13 A.2d 472, 480 (Sup.Ct.1958). * * *

The precise issue in the present case is whether a broader concept than the foregoing—specifically, liability of a felon for the death of a co-felon effected by one resisting the felony—is required by the language of our statute applicable to the general area of felony murder. N.J.S.A. 2A:113–1. This reads:

> If any person, in committing or attempting to commit arson, burglary, kidnapping, rape, robbery, sodomy or any unlawful act against the peace of this state, of which the probable consequences may be bloodshed, kills another, *or if the death of anyone ensues from the committing or attempting to commit any such crime or act* * * * *then such person so killing is guilty of murder.* (emphasis added).

* * *

Before attempting, through analysis of the statutory language itself, a resolution of the contrasting views of the statute entertained below, it will be helpful to survey the progress of the pertinent law in the other American jurisdictions. * * *

It is clearly the majority view throughout the country that, at least in theory, the doctrine of felony murder does not extend to a killing, although growing out of the commission of the felony, if directly attributable to the act of one other than the defendant or those associated with him in the unlawful enterprise. * * * This rule is sometimes rationalized on the "agency" theory of felony murder.[2]

2. The classic statement of the theory is found in an early case applying it in a context pertinent to the case at bar, Commonwealth v. Campbell, 89 Mass. (7 Allen) 541, 544 (Sup.Jud.Ct. 1863), as follows:

> No person can be held guilty of homicide unless the act is either ac-

A contrary view, which would attach liability under the felony murder rule for *any* death proximately resulting from the unlawful activity—even the death of a co-felon—notwithstanding the killing was by one resisting the crime, does not seem to have the present allegiance of any court. See Johnson v. State, 386 P.2d 336 (Okl.Cr. App.1963); Miers v. State, 157 Tex.Cr.R. 572, 251 S.W.2d 404 (Cr. App.1952); and Hornbeck v. State, 77 So.2d 876 (Fla.Sup.Ct.1955), in all of which either an officer or other innocent person was killed.
* * *

At one time the proximate cause theory was espoused by the Pennsylvania Supreme Court, Commonwealth v. Moyer, 357 Pa. 181, 53 A.2d 736 (Sup.Ct.1947) (murder conviction for death of gas station attendant in exchange of gunfire during robbery, without proof that a felon fired fatal shot); Commonwealth v. Almeida, 362 Pa. 596, 68 A.2d 595 (Sup.Ct.1949); cert. den. 339 U.S. 924, 70 S.Ct. 614, 94 L.Ed. 1346, reh. den. 339 U.S. 950, 70 S.Ct. 798, 94 L.Ed. 1364, cert. den. 340 U.S. 867, 71 S.Ct. 83, 95 L.Ed. 633 (1950).[3] The reasoning of the *Almeida* decision, involving the killing of a policeman shot by other police attempting to apprehend robbers, was distinctly circumvented when the question later arose whether it should be applied to an effort to inculpate a defendant for the killing of his co-felon at the hands of the victim of the crime. Commonwealth v. Redline, 391 Pa. 486, 137 A.2d 472 (Sup.Ct.1958). The court there held against liability. Examining the common-law authorities relied upon by the *Almeida* majority, the *Redline* court concluded:

> As already indicated, *Almeida* was, itself, an extension of the felony-murder doctrine by judicial decision and is not to be extended in its application beyond facts such as those to which it was applied.

137 A.2d at 482. The court then held that *"in order to convict for felony-murder, the killing must have been done by the defendant or by an accomplice or confederate or by one acting in furtherance of the felonious undertaking."* 137 A.2d at 476 (emphasis in original). The court refused, however, actually to overrule the *Almeida* decision, thereby creating a distinction (although the opinion indicates it was a halfhearted one; 137 A.2d at 483) between the situation in which the victim was an innocent party and the killing therefore merely "excusable" and that in which the deceased was a felon and

tually or constructively his, and it cannot be his act in either sense unless committed by his own hand or by someone acting in concert with him or in furtherance of a common object or purpose.

3. Criticized in the leading commentary supporting adherence to the agency theory of felony murder, Morris, "The Felon's Responsibility For The Lethal Acts Of Others", 105 U.Pa.L.Rev. 50 (1956); in accord with such criticism, see also Ludwig, "Foreseeable Death In Felony Murder", 18 U.Pitt.L.Rev. 51 (1956); Comment, 71 Harv.L.Rev. 1565 (1958); Comment, 106 U.Pa.L. Rev. 1176 (1958).

the killing thus "justifiable".[4] Twelve years later the Pennsylvania court did overrule *Almeida* in a case involving Almeida's companion, Smith. (Commonwealth ex rel. Smith v. Myers, 438 Pa. 218, 261 A. 2d 550 (Sup.Ct.1970)). The court noted, inter alia, the harsh criticism leveled against the common-law felony rule, its doubtful deterrent effect, the failure of the cases cited in *Almeida* to support the conclusions reached therein, the inappropriateness of tort proximate-cause principles to homicide prosecution, and the "will-of-the-wisp" distinction drawn by the *Almeida* court between justifiable and excusable homicides. 261 A.2d at 553–558. It concluded, "beyond a shadow of a doubt * * * *Almeida* and *Thomas* [Commonwealth v. Thomas, 382 Pa. 639, 117 A.2d 204] constituted iberrations [sic] in the annals of Anglo-American adjudicature." Id. at 553.

* * *

To be distinguished from the situation before us here, and from the generality of the cases discussed above, are the so-called "shield" cases. The first of these were the companion cases of Taylor v. State, 41 Tex.Cr.R. 564, 55 S.W. 961 (Cr.App.1900) aff'd 63 S.W. 330 (Cr.App.1901), and Keaton v. State, 41 Tex.Cr.R. 621, 57 S.W. 1125 (Cr.App.1900). In attempting to escape after robbing a train, defendants thrust the brakeman in front of them as a shield, as a result of which he was fatally shot by law officers. The court had no difficulty in finding defendants guilty of murder. * * * In *Keaton,* the court said defendant would be responsible for the "reasonable, natural and probable result of his act" of placing deceased in danger of his life. 57 S.W. at 1129. The conduct of the defendants in cases such as these is said to reflect "express malice", justifying a murder conviction.

This review of the development in this country of the felony murder rule in relation to culpability for lethal acts of non-felons shows that, despite its early limitation to deadly acts of the felons themselves or their accomplices, the rule has undergone several transformations and can no longer be stated in terms of universal application. As one commentator noted, it appears from the reported cases that up until 1922 all cases in the general field denied liability; the period from 1922 to 1935 was one of vacillation; and cases from 1935 * * * to 1956 tended to impose liability on the grounds of proximate causation where the defendant knew that forceful resistance could be expected. *Morris,* supra, 105 U.Pa.L.Rev. at 57, note 40. But when the Pennsylvania court in *Redline,* supra, overruled its prior holding of liability, in apparent return to the original position of the common law, a number of other jurisdictions followed suit, and

4. Although * * * this distinction survives in a few jurisdictions, it has been criticized in principle, since, *inter alia,* the criminal immunity or liability of the third person killer is irrelevant to the criminal culpability of the accused felon. See Comment, 71 Harv.L.Rev. 1565, 1566 (1958). * * *

the trend since has been towards nonliability; see Annot., cit. supra (56 A.L.R.3d 237).

Reverting to our immediate task here, it is to determine whether our own statute necessarily mandates the proximate cause concept of felony murder * * *. [T]he view of the Appellate Division was that the "ensues clause" of N.J.S.A. 2A:113-1 must be deemed to have expanded the culpability of the felon to killings by others not confederated with him, if proximately related to the felonious enterprise, else the clause would be meaningless surplusage in the act. However, other plausible motivations for the ensues clause can be postulated consistent with a legislative intent to adhere to the traditional limitations of the felony murder doctrine.

Judge Handler, dissenting below, suggested that the purpose of the clause might have been to expand the class of victims of the felon's acts to cover all killings within the res gestae of the felony, even if they formerly would have been considered too distant to be connected therewith, so long as in furtherance of the felony. 135 N.J. Super. at 238, 343 A.2d 110. This view is also advanced by the Comment in Rutgers L.Rev., op. cit. supra (24 Rutgers L.Rev. at 606). It seems to us, moreover, that the ensues clause could well have been intended to ensure effectuation of either or both of the following concomitants of the traditional felony murder rule: (a) that accidental or fortuitous homicides "ensuing" from the felony were contemplated for inclusion, the purpose of the statutory language being to repel the inference of a requisite of intent to kill, normally associated with the unqualified word "kill" as used in the initial clause of the section; and (b) that liability extend to acts of or participation by the accomplice of the killer-felon, as well as those of the killer himself.

* * *

Finally, it is inescapable that the ensues clause is connected with the conclusion of the section, "then such person so killing is guilty of murder". This fortifies the view that even as to a death which "ensues" from the commission or attempt to commit the felony, liability for murder is intended to be restricted to the person "so killing", i. e., the felon or his agents, not third persons, conformably with the limitation of the Pennsylvania *Redline* doctrine.

* * *

With such background, and assuming the statute is facially susceptible of the interpretation here advocated by the State, it is appropriate to consider the public policy implications of the proposed doctrine as an extension of prior assumptions in this State as to the proper limitations of the felony murder rule.

Most modern progressive thought in criminal jurisprudence favors restriction rather than expansion of the felony murder rule. A leading text states: "The felony murder rule is somewhat in disfavor at the present time. The courts apply it when the law requires, but they do so grudgingly and tend to restrict its application where the circumstances permit." Perkins on Criminal Law (2d ed. 1969) 44. It has frequently been observed that although the rule was logical at its inception, when all felonies were punishable by death, its survival to modern times when other felonies are not thought to be as blameworthy as premeditated killings is discordant with rational and enlightened views of criminal culpability and liability. Id. at 44; Comments to A.L.I. Model Penal Code, Tentative Draft No. 9 (1959), Section 201.2, p. 37 * * *.

The final report of the New Jersey Criminal Law Revision Commission was, however, unwilling totally to reject the felony murder rule, concluding instead:

> It is true that we have no way of knowing how many of the homicides resulting in felony murder convictions were committed purposefully, knowingly or recklessly and how many were negligent or accidental. But it is our belief that this rule of law does lead some to refuse to assume a homicidal risk in committing other crimes. Vol. II Commentary, New Jersey Penal Code, p. 158.

The proposed New Jersey Penal Code * * * confines the rule to deaths caused by the felon or his co-felons "in the course of and in furtherance of [the felony]." New Jersey Penal Code § 2C:11–3 (Final Report 1971). This is standard "agency theory" formulation and would seem intended to exclude liability for acts of persons other than felons or co-felons though generally arising out of the criminal episode.

In view of all of the foregoing, it appears to us regressive to extend the application of the felony murder rule beyond its classic common-law limitation to acts by the felon and his accomplices, to lethal acts of third persons not in furtherance of the felonies scheme. The language of the statute does not compel it, and, as indicated above, is entirely compatible with the traditional limitations of the rule. Tort concepts of foreseeability and proximate cause have shallow relevance to culpability for murder in the first degree. Gradations of criminal liability should accord with degree of moral culpability for the actor's conduct. See the compelling thesis for rejection of the proximate cause theory of felony murder by Professor Morris in the article cited above, 105 U.Pa.L.Rev., esp. at 67–68.

It is our judgment that if the course of the law as understood and applied in this State for almost 200 years is to be altered so drastically, it should be by express legislative enactment.

The judgment of the Appellate Division is modified so as to strike the conviction and sentencing of defendant for murder of the co-felon Lloredo.

SULLIVAN, J. (concurring in result only).

The practical result of the majority holding is that even though some innocent person or a police officer be killed during the commission of an armed robbery, the felon would bear no criminal responsibility of any kind for that killing as long as it was not at the hand of the felon or a confederate. The legislative intent, as I see it, is otherwise.

The thrust of our felony murder statute, N.J.S.A. 2A:113–1, is to hold the criminal liable for any killing which ensues during the commission of a felony, even though the felon, or a confederate, did not commit the actual killing. The only exception I would recognize would be the death of a co-felon, which could be classified as a justifiable homicide and not within the purview of the statute.

The Legislature should act promptly to clarify the situation resulting from the majority opinion. If it does not extend the felony murder statute to encompass a killing during the commission of a felony not at the hand of the felon or confederate, it should, at least, provide that the felon be chargeable with manslaughter for such killing (in addition to liability for the felony).

I therefore concur in the result but only for the reason stated above.

HUGHES, C. J., dissenting.

I respectfully dissent from the opinion of the majority here, and would affirm the decision of the Appellate Division, 135 N.J.Super. 224, 343 A.2d 110, for the precise reasons stated in its majority opinion. I certainly believe that what was there referred to as the "ensues clause" can have no other logical or legislatively intended meaning than to extend criminal liability, in a causative sense, to death which ensues or is proximately caused by initiation and furtherance of the felony. This on the concept stated by the Appellate Division:

> The proximate cause theory, simply stated, is that when a felon sets in motion a chain of events which were or should have been within his contemplation when the motion was initiated, the felon, and those acting in concert with him, should be held responsible for any death which by direct and almost inevitable consequences results from the initial criminal act. [State v. Canola, 135 N.J.Super. 224, 235, 343 A.2d 110, 116 (1975)].

Resistance whether by victim or police, and even unintended or accidental deaths which occur in the confused res gestae of violent felony, can hardly be deemed outside the contemplation of the initiator of such criminal violence.

NOTES AND QUESTIONS

1. Might persons like Canola be guilty of murder because of the death of their cofelons on some theory other than felony murder? The California Supreme Court held in People v. Washington, 62 Cal.2d 777, 44 Cal. Rptr. 442, 402 P.2d 130 (1965) that the felony murder rule could not be invoked to hold one felon liable for the death of his cofelon occasioned by resistance to the underlying robbery by the victim. It noted, however:

> Defendants who initiate gun battles may also be found guilty of murder if their victims resist and kill. Under such circumstances, "the defendant for a base, anti-social motive and with wanton disregard for human life, does an act that involves a high degree of probability that it will result in death" * * *, and it is unnecessary to imply malice by invoking the felony-murder doctrine.

62 Cal.2d at 782, 44 Cal.Rptr. at 446, 402 P.2d at 134. This possibility was developed in Taylor v. Superior Court, 3 Cal.3d 578, 91 Cal.Rptr. 275, 477 P.2d 131 (1970) (Taylor I). Taylor waited outside a liquor store while his companions, Smith and Daniels, went in to rob it. Smith pointed a gun at the proprietors, Mr. and Mrs. West. According to the Wests' testimony, Daniels "chattered insanely," saying to Mr. West, "Put the money in the bag. * * * Don't move or I'll blow your head off. * * * Don't move or we'll have an execution right here." Mrs. West testified that Smith appeared "intent," "apprehensive," and as if "waiting for something to happen"; his apparent apprehension and nervousness were manifested by the manner in which he stared at Mr. West. As Smith and Daniels were forcing the Wests to lie on the floor, the Wests obtained weapons and shot at the robbers. Smith was fatally wounded. Taylor (and Daniels) were charged with murder. At a preliminary hearing the magistrate found probable cause to believe them guilty of murder. The magistrate's action was challenged by means of an application for a writ of prohibition. The California Supreme Court denied the writ, finding that evidence supported the magistrate's finding of probable cause. Noting that Taylor, as an accomplice to the robbery, would be vicariously responsible for any killing attributable to the intentional acts of his associates committed with "conscious disregard for life, and likely to cause death," the court concluded:

> [T]he evidence * * * discloses acts of provocation on the parts of Daniels and Smith from which the trier of fact could infer malice, including Daniels' coercive conduct towards Mr. West and his repeated threats of "execution," and Smith's intent and nervous apprehension as he held Mr. West at gunpoint. The foregoing conduct was sufficiently provocative of lethal resistance to lead a man of ordinary caution and prudence to conclude that Daniels and Smith "initiated" the gun battle, or that such conduct was done with conscious disregard for human life and with natural consequences dangerous to life.

3 Cal.3d at 584, 91 Cal.Rptr. at 279, 477 P.2d at 135. Prior to Taylor's trial on the merits of the charge, however, Daniels was tried; he was convicted of robbery but acquitted of murder. Taylor was nevertheless tried and con-

victed of both robbery and murder. On appeal, the conviction for murder was reversed on the ground that the state was collaterally estopped by Daniels' acquittal from obtaining Taylor's conviction for murder on the theory that Taylor was vicariously liable for a murder committed by Daniels. People v. Taylor, 12 Cal.3d 686, 117 Cal.Rptr. 70, 527 P.2d 622 (1974) (Taylor II).

If a defendant may be convicted under the *Washington-Taylor I* theory, is the offense first or second degree murder under the California statutory scheme (see page 450, supra)? In Pizano v. Superior Court, 21 Cal.3d 128, 145 Cal.Rptr. 524, 577 P.2d 659 (1978), the court made clear that a conviction of first degree murder would be permissible. The majority reasoned that Section 189 of the Penal Code made any murder "committed in the perpetration of, or attempt to perpetrate" the enumerated felonies first degree murder. This was held controlling, even though the theory on which the killing was murder was not first degree felony murder but rather "implied malice." 21 Cal.3d at 139, n. 4, 145 Cal.Rptr. at 530–31, n. 4, 577 P.2d at 665 n. 4. The dissenters would limit those killings raised to first degree murder by the language quoted above to felony murders based upon felonies enumerated in the statute. 21 Cal.3d at 142–43, 145 Cal.Rptr. at 533, 577 P.2d at 668.

Is the *Washington-Taylor I* theory significantly different from the felony murder rule rejected in *Washington*? In Sheriff, Clark County v. Hicks, 89 Nev. 78, 506 P.2d 766 (1973), the Nevada Supreme Court rejected the reasoning of *Taylor I*, relying in part upon the comment by the trial judge, "A rose, the felon[y] murder rule, is still a rose by any other name, vicarious liability." 89 Nev. at 82 n. 7, 506 P.2d at 768 n. 7.

The rule was somewhat limited in People v. Antick, 15 Cal.3d 79, 123 Cal.Rptr. 475, 539 P.2d 43 (1975). According to the prosecution's evidence, Antick and Bose had been involved in a burglary. When they were questioned by a police officer, Bose drew a gun and fired at the officer. The officer returned the fire, killing Bose. Antick was convicted of first degree murder, on the *Washington-Taylor I* theory; he did not personally participate in the gun battle and thus could not be found liable on the basis of his own acts. On appeal, the California Supreme Court reversed, reasoning that Antick could be vicariously liable under the *Washington-Taylor I* rule only if there was a cofelon who himself was—or could be—criminally responsible for the killing. Heavy reliance was placed on *Taylor II*. The court explained:

> In order to predicate defendant's guilt upon this theory, it is necessary to prove that Bose committed a murder * * *, in other words, that he caused the death of another human being [and] that he acted with malice. * * *
>
> It is well settled that Bose's conduct in initiating a shootout with police officers may establish the requisite malice. * * * However, Bose's malicious conduct did not result in the unlawful killing of another human being, but rather in Bose's own death. The only homicide which occurred was the justifiable killing of Bose by the police officer. Defendant's criminal liability certainly cannot be predicated upon the actions of the officer. As Bose could not be found guilty of murder in connection with his own

> death, it is impossible to base defendant's liability for this offense upon his vicarious responsibility for the crime of his accomplice.

15 Cal.3d at 90–91, 123 Cal.Rptr. at 482, 539 P.2d at 50.

2. As the court in *Canola* indicates, the "shield" cases can be resolved without reference to felony murder. But the felony aspect of these cases may nevertheless present problems. In Pizano v. Superior Court, 21 Cal.3d 128, 145 Cal.Rptr. 524, 577 P.2d 659 (1978), Pizano and Esquivel were interrupted by Cuna, a private citizen, during the robbery of Vaca. Pizano opened the door of the house and ran out, followed by Esquivel who forced Vaca at gunpoint to precede him. Without realizing Vaca was present, Cuna opened fire with his gun; Vaca was killed. Pizano was charged with murder and sought dismissal of the charge. He acknowledged that Esquivel's actions in using Vaca as a shield or hostage were acts from which malice could be implied. But he argued that it is necessary that the killing be attributable to those actions of the defendant which evidence the disregard for life from which malice is implied. Since Cuna opened fire without realizing that Esquivel was using Vaca as a shield, he urged, the killing of Vaca cannot be said to be attributable to the acts of the defendants from which malice is implied. Cuna fired solely to prevent the robbery, and a death caused by such action is insuffcient to create liability for murder. The California Supreme Court denied relief. For the killing to be murder, it reasoned, the use of the victim as a shield rather than the felony itself must have proximately caused the victim's death. Whether the shot was fired in response to the felony alone or in response to the defendants' malicious acts is not controlling, and on the facts of the case a trier of fact could properly conclude that Vaca's death was proximately caused by Esquivel's malicious conduct in using him as a shield.

STATE v. THOMPSON

Supreme Court of Washington, 1977.
88 Wash.2d 13, 558 P.2d 202.

DOLLIVER, Associate Justice.

This is an appeal from a conviction for murder in the second degree. * * *

Defendant was charged by an amended information with causing the death of Wayland Thompson while engaged in the commission of a felony, assault in the second degree. In the trial before a jury, defendant was found guilty of murder in the second degree. We affirm.

* * *

The state produced evidence that the defendant reported she shot her husband. There was additional evidence that there were three shots fired with a .38 caliber pistol. Testimony of the state's witnesses revealed that the defendant and her husband had been drinking on the evening of the shooting, that they had argued violently and that he had struck her. While the defendant claims that the shooting was done in self-defense, she apparently was disbelieved by the jury. In reviewing the record, we are satisfied that there was sufficient evidence to send the case to the jury and to support the verdict.

[A]ppellant urges that we overrule State v. Harris, 69 Wash.2d 928, 421 P.2d 662 (1966). * * *

In *Harris*, we held that, where the precedent felony in a felony murder is an assault and inherent in the homicide, the assault does not merge into the resulting homicide. Most states which have considerred the question have adopted the merger rule, resulting in a holding that only felonies independent of the homicide can support a felony murder conviction. State v. Mosley, 84 Wash.2d 608, 528 P.2d 986 (1974). Washington and Maine appear to be the only jurisdictions which have considered and rejected the merger rule. See Annot., 40 A.L.R.3d 1341 (1971). Both appellant and the courts of other jurisdictions consider this to be a matter of statutory interpretation rather than one of constitutional rights.

* * *

While it may be that the felony murder statute is harsh, and while it does relieve the prosecution from the burden of proving intent to commit murder, it is the law of this state. The legislature recently modified some parts of our criminal code, effective July 1, 1976. However, the statutory context in question here was left unchanged.

The rejection by this court of the merger rule has not been challenged by the legislature during the nearly 10 years since *Harris*, nor have any circumstances or compelling reasons been presented as to why we should overrule the views we expressed therein.

The judgment is affirmed.

UTTER, Associate Justice (dissenting).

The majority decision, by giving continuing approval to use of the doctrine of felony murder in instances where the sole felony providing the basis for implementation of the doctrine is the assault upon the victim which was the direct cause of death, leaves us in a position shared by virtually no other state. I am convinced that we are compelled by both the due process and equal protection clauses of the United States Constitution to abandon this isolated position and join with the vast majority of United States jurisdictions in holding the felony-murder rule applicable only to instances in which the underlying felony giving rise to the operation of the rule is independent in fact of the homicide.

* * *

The only act of the appellant relied upon to establish the felony necessary for conviction of murder in the second degree * * * was the shooting itself, which, standing alone, constitutes the crime of second-degree assault. RCW 9.11.020(4). The application of the felony-murder rule thus eliminated the necessity for proof by the state of the element of specific intent, which is the distinguishing aspect, in our statutory scheme, of murder in the second degree. Absent the proof of acts constituting an assault, the appellant could not have been found guilty of murder. In this situation it is apparent that the single act of shooting the victim can constitute one crime and one crime only. There exists no general malicious intent based upon proof of the commission of a separate felony which may be "transferred" from that crime to an independent homicide committed in the course thereof. The existence of such a separate intent is an analytical necessity to an inference of intent to kill. For this reason the felony-murder rule should not apply where the underlying felony sought to be used as a basis for the operation of the rule is an offense included in fact in the homicide itself. To hold otherwise constitutes, as Chief Justice Cardozo observed, "a futile attempt to split into unrelated parts an indivisible transaction." People v. Moran, 246 N.Y. 100, 104, 158 N.E. 35, 36 (1927).

This conclusion has been reached by every jurisdiction in this country, with the exception of the state of Washington, required to directly face the issue. The states have formulated their conclusions in slightly different ways. See, e. g., People v. Huther, 184 N.Y. 237, 77 N.E. 6 (1906) (where the only felony committed apart from the homicide itself is the assault upon the victim, the assault "merges" with the killing and does not provide a basis for operation of the felony-murder rule); State v. Fisher, 120 Kan. 226, 243 P. 291 (1926) (the felony must be so distinct as to not be an ingredient of the homicide). See also People v. Ireland, 70 Cal.2d 522, 75 Cal.Rptr. 188, 150 P.2d 580 (1969); State v. Branch, 244 Or. 97, 415 P.2d 766 (1966); State v. Essman, 98 Ariz. 228, 403 P.2d 540 (1965). * * *

* * *

The dissenters in *Harris* pointed out that the use of the rule approved by the majority would effectively convert into second-degree murder any crime properly viewed as manslaughter, because manslaughter itself is a felony, and that prevention of precisely such a result was the purpose of the New York court in adopting the felony-murder merger rule. (See State v. Harris, supra at 936–38, 421 P.2d 662, Hunter, J., dissenting).

I believe it clear that the underpinnings of the *Harris* dissent and the decisions of those courts adopting a merger rule, or its functional equivalent, are far more substantial than those recognized by the majority in *Harris*. Implicit in these holdings is a recognition that any statutory definition of murder, as a crime *malum in se*, must include an element of specific intent. A statutory formulation which eliminates the requirement of establishing this essential element is fundamentally defective and therefore violative of the defendant's right to substantive due process. * * *

The failure to limit the operation of the rule is equally violative of the Fourteenth Amendment right to equal protection of the laws. The net result of this court's decision in *Harris* is to vest in the prosecutor a degree of discretion which is prohibited by the principles enunciated by this court in a number of cases.

* * *

In this instance, on the basis of proof of precisely the same acts on the part of the defendant (i. e., the shooting of the decedent resulting in his unintended death), the prosecutor was free at his discretion to charge assault in the second degree, or manslaughter or murder in the second degree. The necessity to prove specific intent, the key element distinguishing manslaughter or murder in the second degree in our statutory system, is eliminated in these types of cases by use of the felony-murder rule. Thus the prosecutor could, by proving precisely the same facts, subject the defendant to substantially different penalties based upon varying proofs, depending upon his own judgment as to the appropriate charge. The broad discretion which results in this instance creates a possibility for unequal treatment under the law which cannot pass constitutional muster.

NOTE AND QUESTIONS

Under the merger rule, the assault by which a killing is accomplished cannot constitute the felony giving rise to felony murder because it "merges" into the homicide. But suppose the defendant entered the victim's residence with the intent of assaulting him and, under the law of the jurisdiction, this entry with the intent to commit felony assault, constituted burglary. Can the defendant now be convicted of murder on the theory that the burglary constituted a felony invoking the felony murder rule? In a jurisdiction such as California in which a killing committed in the perpetration of burglary is first degree murder (see page 451, supra), can the defendant be convicted of first degree murder? In People v. Wilson, 1 Cal.3d 431, 82 Cal.Rptr. 494, 462 P.2d 22 (1969), the California Supreme Court held that felony murder could not be based on burglary when "the entry would be nonfelonious but for the intent to commit the assault, and the assault is an integral part of the homicide and is included in fact in [the homicide]." In such situations, the court reasoned, like felony assault situations, potential killers are insufficiently likely to be deterred by the felony murder rule to justify its application. Other courts, however, have reached the opposite result. E. g., State v. Foy, 224 Kan. 558, 582 P.2d 281 (1978) (and cases cited therein). These courts appear to rely upon the assumption that an assault in the domicile is sufficiently more likely to result in a homicide than other assaults to justify applying the felony murder rule to killings preceded by felonious entry into the domicile with the intent to commit serious assault. E. g., People v. Miller, 32 N.Y.2d 157, 344 N.Y.S.2d 342, 297 N.E.2d 85 (1973).

STATE v. MAULDIN

Supreme Court of Kansas, 1974.
215 Kan. 956, 529 P.2d 124.

KAUL, Justice:

This is an appeal by the state * * * from an order dismissing a charge by information of felony murder * * *.

* * *

Our statute defining murder in the first degree reads as follows:

> "Murder in the first degree. Murder in the first degree is the killing of a human being committed maliciously, willfully, deliberately and with premeditation or committed in the perpetration or attempt to perpetrate any felony [K.S.A. 1973 Supp. 21–3401]."

* * *

The trial judge filed a well-reasoned memorandum decision setting forth the facts and thoroughly analyzing and discussing all of the issues and the cases from other jurisdictions cited by both parties. We believe the trial court's ruling was entirely correct. Therefore, we shall quote its memorandum decision in full:

"The defendant's motion to dismiss was argued to the court on March 22, 1974, and was taken under advisement. I have now reviewed the file and considered the briefs and arguments of counsel.

"The State contends that the evidence in this case will show that on the evening of November 27, 1974, Steve Cottrell and Gary McCallon purchased a quantity of heroin from the defendant Robert [Mauldin]. Thereafter, Steve and Gary went to Steve's apartment where Gary prepared and injected himself with a shot of the heroin. He subsequently died from an overdose. For the purpose of this motion, these facts must be accepted as true. The question presented, then, is whether the death of Gary McCallon under these circumstances was 'the killing of a human being. * * * committed in the perpetration. * * * of any felony', within the meaning of K.S.A. 21–3401.

"The question has not been decided in this state. There is precedent from other states, however, although it is not in accord. California holds that the sole act of selling or furnishing a dangerous drug to one who dies as a result of an overdose of such drug constitutes a felony-murder. (People vs Cine [Cline] [270 Cal.App.2d 328] 75 Cal.Repts. 459, Ct.Appeals 4th. Dist.1969). New York, Pennsylvania and Arizona hold to the contrary. (People vs Pickney [38 A. D.2d 217], 328 N.Y.Supp.2d 550–1972; State vs Dixon [109 Ariz. 441], 511 P.2d 623, Ariz.–1973; Commonwealth vs Bowden, 309 Atl. 2d 714, Pa.–1973).

"This difference results primarily from a difference of opinion as to what constitutes a homicide committed in the perpetration or attempt to perpetrate a felony. Our court has defined this to mean that there must be 'a direct causal relation between the commission of the felony and the homicide.' (State v. Moffit, 199 Kan. 514, l. c. 534 [431 P.2d 879]).

"The State relies rather strongly herein on the ruling in State vs Moffit. The facts in that case were that the defendant, a convicted felon, fired a pistol while assaulting two pedestrians and inadvertently killed a woman sitting on a motorcycle some distance down the street. The court held that the possession of a pistol, after conviction of a felony was a felony (K.S.A. 21–2611) and was inherently dangerous to human life, and that there was a direct causal relation between the commission of such felony and the homicide. It further held that it was no defense to the felony murder that the defendant did not intend to kill the victim.

"I have no quarrel with this reasoning. It is to be noted, however, that possession of a pistol by a convicted felon is a continuing offense. The court cited with approval from the case of People vs Ford, [60 Cal.2d 772], 388 P.2d 892 [36 Cal.Rptr. 620] Cal.–1964 in which what court speaking of such possession said:

" 'These later crimes are continuing ones, and were still in the process of being committed when the killing of the officer took place.'

"It should be further noted that even more directly related to the homicide than mere possession of the pistol was the fact that Moffit fired the pistol at two pedestrians in the perpetration of a felonious assault upon them. Thus direct causal relation was not dependent upon the concept of an illegal possession of a gun.

"In the case before me, the defendant's only connection with the homicide was that he sold a quantity of heroin to the deceased who some time later, voluntarily and out of the presence of the defendant, injected himself with an overdose and died as a result. This is not a case where the defendant injected the heroin into the deceased, or otherwise determined the amount of the dose, or assisted in administering the dosage, where different considerations are involved. (See: People vs Crusiani [Cruciani], [70 Misc.2d 528], 334 N.Y.S.2d 515–1972; People vs Poindexter, [51 Cal.2d 142], 330 P.2d 763, Cal. 1958).

"Under the State's theory, the time element, or other conduct subsequent to or preceding the sale, are not necessarily relevant if death results from use of the drug. It is felony-murder whether the victim injected himself a few hours later, as here, or a few days later, or whether the purchaser sold or furnished the drug to another who took the overdose. The result is the controlling factor.

"The objective of deterring the sale and use of heroin is, of course, very desirable, but an objective in itself does not justify a rule that is otherwise unsound. For example, there are many drugs other than heroin which are inherently dangerous if taken in excess. It is not only a felony to sell such drugs but to manufacture, prescribe, administer, deliver, distribute, dispense or compound these substances. (Uniform Controlled Substances Act, K.S.A. 65–4101 et. seq.) It is also becoming increasingly accepted that alcohol can be as addictive and inherently dangerous as many drugs. (K.S.A. 65–4001 et seq.; Time, April 22, 1974, Alcoholism). The State regulates the sale and use of many things other than drugs, liquor and firearms in the interest of the public welfare and safety. Any one of these transactions could conceivably be encompassed under the State's theory where death resulted from the use of a controlled item. Such a drastic extension of the felony-murder rule by judicial decree is unwarranted, in my opinion.

"What then, constitutes 'a direct causal relation' within the meaning of the felony-murder rule? It seems to me that something more is required beyond the fact the death sequentially followed the sale of the heroin. I have not found, nor has counsel cited, a ruling by our Supreme Court on this precise point, but it has been discussed elsewhere. (Commonwealth vs Root, [403 Pa. 571], 170 A.2d 310, Pa–1961; Commonwealth vs Redline, [391 Pa. 486], 137 A.2d 472, Pa–1958; People vs Scott, [29 Mich.App. 549], 185 N.W.2d 576, Mich.–1971; People vs Morris, [1 Ill.App.3d 566], 274 N.E.2d 898, Ill. –1971; Sheriff vs Hicks, 506 P.2d 766, Nev.–1973.

"These cases hold in principal that there must be a closer and more direct causal connection between criminal conduct and a homicide than is required by the tort concept of proximate cause, and that to convict of felony-murder it must be shown that the conduct causing the death was done while in the commission of a felony or in furtherance of the design to commit the felony. I believe State v. Moffit supports this view. In the case before me, the felony involved was the sale of heroin, and it was completed upon consummation of the sale.

"In conclusion, it is my opinion that the better reasoning supports the New York, Pennsylvania and Arizona cases. If the rule is to be broadened it should be done by the legislature.

"The defendant's motion to dismiss the charge of a felony murder in this case is, therefore, sustained effective 5 days from this date. Please present an approved journal entry for my signature."

On appeal the state reasserts the same contentions presented to the trial court and cites many of the cases discussed in the court's memorandum. We deem it unnecessary to reconsider matters fully covered by the trial court in its memorandum.

We would note that on the facts presented here the sole act of defendant was selling the heroin. The injection by the purchaser was out of the presence of defendant. In the California cases, cited by the state, the accused actively participated in administering the drugs as in People v. Poindexter, 51 Cal.2d 142, 330 P.2d 763, or at least was present while the purchaser consumed an overdose of narcotic tablets as in People v. Cline, 270 Cal.App.2d 328, 75 Cal.Rptr. 459, 32 A.L.R.3d 582.

* * *

Our statute explicitly requires that the killing be "committed in the perpetration or attempt to perpetrate any felony." Under the facts presented in the instant case the commission of the felony (the act of selling heroin) completely terminated when the seller and the purchaser parted company. As pointed out by the trial court, this is not a case such as State v. Moffitt, 199 Kan. 514, 431 P.2d 879, wherein the felony relied upon (possession of a pistol after conviction of a felony) was a continuing one.

* * *

The clear import of the language of the statute cannot be broadened so as to encompass felony murder upon the facts presented herein.

The judgment is affirmed.

NOTE AND QUESTIONS

In general, how long after the underlying felony has been "technically" completed does the felony last for purposes of the felony murder rule? There is widespread agreement that a killing caused during "immediate pursuit" of the felons and before they have reached even a place of temporary safety is still felony murder even though the felony was completed before death was caused. People v. Ford, 65 Cal.2d 41, 52 Cal.Rptr. 228, 416 P.2d 132 (1966). But some crimes are "continuing" in nature and it is at least arguable that they remain effective for felony murder purposes even after immediate pursuit has ended and the felons have reached a place of temporary safety. Consider the following facts from People v. Lopez, 16 Cal.App.3d 346, 93 Cal.Rptr. 885, vac. 6 Cal.3d 45, 98 Cal.Rptr. 44, 489 P.2d 1372 (1971): On Tuesday, Lopez and another prisoner, Galindo, escaped from a jail. They remained at large during Wednesday and Thursday, eating only wild berries. On several occasions they came close to apprehension; two high school students refused the escapees' request for help in obtaining food and clothing and officers searching a house near where the escapees were concealed failed to search the shed behind the house where they were hiding. On Friday morning, the two entered a house apparently to obtain food and clothing. During that entry, the occupants were assaulted and one died. Was this felony murder on the theory that the defendants were still engaged in the crime of escape or were at least still being pursued? The California courts found the felony murder rule not applicable on the ground that the crime of escape terminated once the escapees reached a place of temporary safety. The fact that a continuing search was being conducted for them did not prevent their situation from being one of at least temporary safety.

5. MANSLAUGHTER

The two manslaughter crimes—voluntary and involuntary manslaughter—are, as traditionally defined, significantly different offenses. Voluntary manslaughter is essentially a mitigated murder, i. e., a killing that would be murder except that the facts show *in addition* to the elements of murder certain mitigating circumstances. Involuntary manslaughter, on the other hand, consists of a killing that is not murder because the mental state required for murder did not exist. But the facts permit a finding of one of several "lesser" mental states that suffice for involuntary manslaughter. In addition to the problems posed by the definitions of the two offenses, consider the need to keep them separate. Section 210.3 of the Model Penal Code (see page 450, supra) abolishes the distinction between the two manslaughter offenses and creates a single crime of manslaughter. Is this desirable? Is there a need to keep them separate so that different penalty provisions can be assigned to them?

a. VOLUNTARY MANSLAUGHTER

Voluntary manslaughter is a mitigated killing that would otherwise be murder. As the principal case in this section makes clear, courts have tended to rigidly structure the analysis for determining whether the requisite mitigation exists. Consider the appropriate—and permissible—allocation of the burden of establishing mitigation or the absence of mitigation; reread the material at pages 17–22, supra. Consider also the desirability of limiting mitigation to "provocation" as defined in the principal case and in similar decisions. Compare Section 210.3(1)(b) of the Model Penal Code (page 450, supra). If it would be desirable to have greater flexibility than is provided by the traditional formulation of "provocation," does the proposed statutory provision contain it?

TRIPP v. STATE

Court of Special Appeals of Maryland, 1977.
36 Md.App. 459, 374 A.2d 384.

MOYLAN, Judge.

* * *

On October 12, 1974, the appellant went on a homicidal rampage at 1700 Guilford Avenue in Baltimore City with a .38 caliber revolver. He shot in the chest and killed 36-year-old Hazel Wilson, with whom he had been cohabiting over a two-year period until roughly one week before the killing. The appellant also shot seven-year-old James Wilson, son of Hazel Wilson, twice in the head, killing him. He also shot eleven-year-old Deborah Brewer, niece of Hazel Wilson, once in the head, killing her. He also shot 62-year-old Sarah Brewer, mother of Hazel Wilson, several times in the head and face, killing her. He also shot eleven-year-old Derak Wilson, son of Hazel Wilson, once in the face, seriously wounding him. There was no dispute as to the homicidal agency of the appellant—only as to his *mens rea* in two regards. The jury found the appellant to have been sane at the time of the attacks. The jury found the appellant guilty of four charges of murder in the first degree and of one charge of assault with intent to murder.

When Jury Instructions are Required

The first of the appellant's contentions which we shall discuss is his claim that Judge Levin committed prejudicial error by declining to instruct the jury on the subject of manslaughter. * * *

The appellant is * * * correct in his preliminary assertion of law that a trial judge is obliged to instruct the jury on every essential point of law supported by the evidence when requested to do so by either side.

The chink in the appellant's armor is the phrase "supported by the evidence." When instructing on the law of homicide, as when instructing on any other part of the law, it is not only required but it is, indeed, inappropriate to instruct upon a principle of law not suggested by the evidence in the case. * * *

* * *

In appellate brief and argument * * * the appellant has narrowed the focus of pertinent manslaughter relief. It is not involuntary manslaughter but voluntary manslaughter being urged by him. He narrows the focus further by claiming mitigation through hot-blooded response to legally adequate provocation. The suggested form of the legally adequate provocation is strangely blurred but seems to bear an at least impressionistic resemblance to that involving the sudden discovery of a spouse in an act of adultery. We will now turn to an examination of whether the evidence supports the necessary elements for extenuation of this variety.

The General Law as to Provocation

In Whitehead v. State, 9 Md.App. 7, 10–11, 262 A.2d 316, 319, Judge Orth set out fully the elements of provocation:

> "[T]here may be a homicide which would otherwise be murder which is reduced to manslaughter by circumstances of alleviation or mitigation. Such a case is where the circumstances surrounding the homicide establish that it was pro-

> voked. For the 'Rule of Provocation' to be invoked there are four requirements:
>
> (1) There must have been adequate provocation;
>
> (2) The killing must have been in the heat of passion;
>
> (3) It must have been a sudden heat of passion—that is, the killing must have followed the provocation before there had been a reasonable opportunity for the passion to cool;
>
> (4) There must have been a causal connection between the provocation, the passion, and the fatal act."

Against these bench marks, we will now measure the evidence at hand.

Extenuation Limited to the Killing of Provocateurs

Except for rare instances of "transferred intent," where one aims at A, misses and hits B by mistake, a defendant seeking to extenuate an intentional killing upon the theory that he killed in hot-blooded rage brought on by the provocative acts of his victim is limited to those killings where the victim is the provocateur. In the present case, Hazel Wilson was the only victim arguably in that category. In no event could the killings of Hazel Wilson's 62-year-old mother, her 11-year-old niece, her 7-year-old son nor the murderous wounding of her 11-year-old son be mitigated by even hot-blooded response to actions not of their doing. Even as the discussion moves forward in the case of Hazel Wilson, the other four convictions are factored out as objects of this contention. In this regard, LaFave and Scott, Criminal Law (1972), is unequivocal, at 582:

> "More difficult is the situation in which A, actually and reasonably provoked by B, in his passion strikes out at and kills C, known by A to be only an innocent bystander. The courts have quite consistently held that the killing of C does not qualify as manslaughter, apparently upon the assumption that a reasonable man would never be so greatly provoked as to strike out in blind anger at an innocent person."

* * *

Provocation in the Case of Hazel Wilson

The appellant is in deep trouble when it comes to the legal sufficiency of the evidence to establish the elements of provocation. There must, of course, be established all of the elements. We conclude that the appellant failed to establish at least three of the necessary four elements. Taking the evidence in the light most favorable to the appellant, with all inferences that fairly can be drawn therefrom, he may arguably have a jury issue with respect to the fourth element:

> "(4) There must have been a causal connection between the provocation, the passion, and the fatal act."

The story that emerges, from the testimony of the 11-year-old boy who lived and from the testimony of a neighboring minister who had but scant knowledge, is at best a surrealistic blur. It appeared that the appellant had been living with Hazel Wilson and her two sons for approximately two years, the last two months of which had been in the second-floor apartment at 1700 Guilford Avenue. When she would go out drinking or would make periodic visits to her former husband (or actual legal husband, for all we know), the appellant would be afflicted by fits of jealousy. He would beat Hazel Wilson. One week before the killings, the minister observed the appellant, gun in hand, dragging Hazel Wilson along. Six days before the murders, he came to the minister's church, where Hazel Wilson was then visiting, also with a gun in his hand. Events reached a critical impasse on the Tuesday, four days before the killings, when Hazel Wilson and her sons moved downstairs to the first-floor apartment and moved in with Hazel Wilson's mother. Arguments and efforts to get Hazel Wilson to return to the apartment with the appellant continued sporadically throughout the final week.

From this, it might fairly be inferred that the actions of Hazel Wilson 1) in going out and drinking, 2) in visiting periodically her husband (or ex-husband) and 3) in moving out of the second-floor apartment had provoked a passion in the appellant and that that passion was the effective cause of his decision to kill Hazel Wilson. This, however, is but one of four constituent elements, all of which must be present for legally recognizable provocation.

We turn our attention to the second necessary element:

"(2) The killing must have been in the heat of passion."

This is the subjective question of whether a particular defendant was actually in the heat of passion when he killed. (The objective, or reasonable man, question will constitute the next element to be considered.) All of the evidence in the case, clearly and decisively, indicated that the appellant was not in the heat of passion when he killed. At least a week had elapsed since the onset of domestic argument with Hazel Wilson. Four days had elapsed since she moved downstairs. Several hours before the killing, he utilized a ruse, directed toward Hazel Wilson's mother, in order to gain entrance to the downstairs apartment and particularly to the basement, where he manipulated in some fashion the lock to the basement door. After killing Hazel Wilson, he attempted to lure the other members of the family out of hiding in what inferentially appeared to be an effort to kill all witnesses to his first killing. The gun that he used was never recovered. He wore gloves at the time of the killing. He was seen by one witness in a West North Avenue grocery store less than an hour after the killing, blithely buying groceries. When he returned to the crime scene between one and one-half and two hours after the killings, he approached, with groceries in hand, feigning total ignorance of and surprise at the situation he there found.

Counterbalancing this evidence of actual, cool deliberation is not one shred of evidence indicating hot-blooded fury. In this case, the only available source of such evidence, the appellant himself, chose not to testify in this regard. * * *

The next element to be considered is the third:

> "(3) It must have been a sudden heat of passion—that is, the killing must have followed the provocation before there had been a reasonable opportunity for the passion to cool."

This element is the objective counterpart of the preceding one. We were there concerned with the subjective question of whether this particular killer was still in the throes of actual hot-blooded passion. We are here concerned with the objective test of whether there had been a sufficient cooling time for the passions of an average and reasonable man to abate. Deferring for the moment consideration of the inadequacy of the cause, the cause of the appellant's distress was jealousy. Eleven-year-old Derak Wilson testified that the appellant had argued with Hazel Wilson over the fact that "she go out and get drinks" and that "she be talking to somebody else" regularly over an unspecified but significant period of time. The neighboring minister had overheard quarrels between the appellant and Hazel Wilson over a period measured at least in weeks, if not over the course of the several months that they had been living on Guilford Avenue. A major flare-up of this domestic unrest had occurred at least one week before the killings. The situation had so deteriorated that Hazel Wilson moved out at least four days before the killings. We conclude that the evidence in this regard shows clearly and decisively that there was sufficient cooling time for the average and reasonable man to have his passions abate. * * *

* * * The law, in its wisdom, extenuates certain killings by lowering the degree of blameworthiness because it recognizes human fraility when one is in the clutches of blind and sudden fury. The long-smoldering grudge, by way of contrast, may be psychologically just as compelling a force as the sudden impulse but it, unlike the impulse, is a telltale characteristic of premeditation. The law extenuates certain killings not simply because they have been provoked but because there has also been the lack of time between the provoking cause and the impulsive response to think about the consequences or

the alternatives. In the case of the spontaneous explosion, reason has no opportunity to intervene; in the case of the "slow burn," it has. We demand that it intervene whenever it can. * * *

The absolutely foreclosing aspect, as we consider the availability of the defense of provocation, is our evaluation of the first essential element of that defense:

"(1) There must have been adequate provocation."

The appellant sets himself a difficult task in arguing now that the killing was the result of hot-blooded provocation; his trial position was that he was not the criminal agent at all, provoked or unprovoked. We are asked to speculate as to both the provoking act and the resultant state of provocation. We will, nevertheless, give the appellant the benefit in this regard of any inferences that may reasonably be drawn from the evidence.

We begin with the proposition that there must be not simply provocation in psychological fact, but one of certain fairly well-defined classes of provocation recognized as being adequate as a matter of law. Clark and Marshall, Law of Crimes (Sixth Wingersky Ed., 1958) describes the objective character of this test, at 621:

> "To reduce a homicide from murder to manslaughter, *the provocation must be adequate in law,* and to be so it must be so great as reasonably to excite passion and heat of blood. * * * Reasonableness is the test. The law contemplates the case of a reasonable man—an ordinarily reasonable man —and requires that the provocation be such as might naturally induce such a man, in the anger of the moment, to commit the deed." (Emphasis supplied)

* * *

The most that emerges from the scant and ambiguous evidence is a state of mind in the appellant of diffuse and undifferentiated jealousy. Derak Wilson, the victim's 11-year-old son, under examination by the appellant's attorney, could give, at most the following explanation for the appellant's state of mind:

> "Q. Which is it; she would go drinking first or drinking afterwards?
>
> A. Then—go drinking first.
>
> Q. Then they would have the arguments?
>
> A. Uh huh. Because when she go out and get drinks, then sometimes I think she be talking to somebody else."

Neither "going out and getting drinks" nor "talking to somebody else" remotely constitutes an act of legally recognized provocation. To begin with, they are acts of lawful behavior which, as Perkins

Criminal Law (Second Ed., 1969), points out, at 54, do not ordinarily * serve as triggers for legally sufficient provocation:

> "[T]he provocation is itself an *unlawful* act of another, since a lawful act, even if it involves physical violence, is not recognized by law as a mitigating circumstance."

The same holds true with respect to Hazel Wilson's act of moving out of the upstairs apartment, where she cohabitated with the appellant, and into her mother's apartment on the first floor of the same house. It is not unlawful to move out under any circumstances; even more so, it is not unlawful to move out to escape the appellant's fits of excessive jealousy and his physical beatings.

Nor does the third and final possible source of the appellant's passion constitute legally recognized provocation. This source was suggested by the testimony of the neighboring minister:

> "I said, 'Man, you seem to be an intelligent man. What is going on? Why you all fighting and carrying on that way? Well * * *' He said to me—tried to tell me something about her other husband, you know. Said that—this Hazel was getting some money from her first husband, and what have you. She will go by there and get it every weekend. I think that was the problem—that he was accusing her of her first husband."

For all which the evidence in this case reveals, Hazel Wilson's "other husband" was still her legal and, therefore, only husband.

Of the recognized varieties of action which constitute legally adequate provocation, the only one remotely suggested by the circumstances in this case is that of discovering a spouse in an act of adultery. As a necessary precondition for this type of provocation, there must be, at the very least, some significant sexual contact, if not literally intercourse itself. The law anciently required a spouse unexpectedly to discover the erring spouse *in flagrante delicto.* In its more modern and liberalized manifestations, it has been extended to situations where the spouse has suddenly been told of the other spouse's infidelity or has strong reason to believe that there has been such infidelity. Even in the liberalized forms, however, the indispensable predicate is sexual intercourse. * * * One cannot, as the appellant here apparently seeks to do, take a law which speaks exclusively of the unexpected discovery of one's legal spouse in an act of adultery and extrapolate from that a more general principle dealing with any act by any object of one's affection which gives rise to a state of jealousy.

* The hesitation to state the proposition in absolute terms is ours and not that of Professor Perkins.

Even more foreclosing than the innocuous nature of the acts, however, is the legally uncountenanced status of the actors. Even where the provocative act is the direct, unexpected and visual discovery of sexual intercourse in progress, the defense is still only available to the "cuckold" who is a lawful spouse. LaFave and Scott, Criminal Law, speaks to this very point, at 576:

> "The rule of mitigation does not, however, extend beyond the marital relationship so as to include engaged persons, divorced couples and unmarried lovers—as where a man is enraged at the discovery of his mistress in the sexual embrace of another man."

Rex v. Palmer, [1913] 2 K.B. 29 (defense not available where defendant discovered financée in an act of intercourse with another); Rex v. Greening, [1913] 3 K.B. 846, 23 Cox Crim.Cas. 601 (defense not available where defendant and unfaithful companion had been living together as man and wife); People v. Pecora, 107 Ill.App.2d 283, 246 N.E.2d 865 (1969) (defendant's ex-wife told him she had been intimate with other men: held, not adequate provocation even if he "had not psychologically disengaged himself from the marital relationship since the divorce"); People v. McDonald, 63 Ill.App.2d 475, 212 N.E. 2d 299 (1965) (where defendant had lived with the woman he killed for some 25 years, the court ruled it would not apply the "exculpatory features of *crime passionel* to the killings of a mistress, regardless of the duration of the relationship").

Each of the four elements is a *sine qua non* for a defense of mitigation based upon hot-blooded response to legally adequate provocation. The evidence was palpably insufficient with respect to at least three of the elements, all of which would be necessary to generate a genuine jury issue. * * *

* * * In this case, no such detour was indicated by the evidence. Under the circumstances, Judge Levin had no more cause to expound upon the law of manslaughter than to expound upon the Rule in Shelley's Case.

* * *

Judgments Affirmed * * *.

NOTES AND QUESTIONS

1. Perhaps the major limitation upon those provoking acts that will reduce a killing to voluntary manslaughter has been the rule that "mere words" cannot be adequate provocation. In State v. Benson, 183 N.C. 795, 111 S.E. 869 (1922) the court held:

> The legal provocation which will reduce murder in the second degree to manslaughter must be more than words; as language, however abusive, neither excuses nor mitigates the killing, and the law

> does not recognize circumstances as a legal provocation which in themselves do not amount to an actual or threatened assault.

183 N.C. at 799, 111 S.E. at 871. This position was recently reaffirmed by the same court. State v. Watson, 287 N.C. 147, 214 S.E.2d 85 (1975). Is this a realistic position? In State v. Watson, supra, the white decedent had called the black defendant a "nigger" and "a black mother f– – – – –." Is it appropriate for the law to take the position that even words of this sort cannot reduce a killing from murder to manslaughter? Despite the implications of the language of the court in *Benson,* courts are split on whether an unsuccessful attempt to commit a battery, i. e., a criminal assault, can be adequate provocation and there is authority for the proposition that a light blow is not adequate provocation although courts are agreed that a violent painful blow will constitute provocation within the meaning of voluntary manslaughter. W. LaFave & A. Scott, Criminal Law 574–75 (1972).

2. What impact must the provocation have had upon the defendant's mental processes to reduce a killing to voluntary manslaughter? In State v. Davis, 50 S.C. 405, 27 S.E. 905 (1897), the defendant objected to an instruction that told the jury they must find that as a result of the provocation the defendant "had an uncontrollable impulse, and he was so inflamed with passion that he hardly knew that he was doing." After an extensive review of the authorities, the appellate court affirmed, explaining:

> "[T]he sudden heat and passion, upon sufficient legal provocation," * * * while it need not dethrone reason entirely, or shut out knowledge and volition, must be such as would naturally disturb the sway of reason and render the mind of an ordinary person incapable of cool reflection, and produce what, according to human experience, may be called an "uncontrollable impulse to do violence."

50 S.C. at 423–24, 27 S.E. at 911. Is this a reasonable definition of the requisite impact? A desirable one?

3. In determining whether provocation would have the requisite effect upon a reasonable person, to what extent should the reasonable person be assumed to have characteristics of the defendant? English courts traditionally refused to attribute any of the defendant's characteristics to the reasonable person. See the review of the cases in The Queen v. McGregor, [1962] N.Z.L.R. 1069. In Bedder's case [1954] 1 W.L.R. 1119, [1954] 2 All E.R. 801, the defendant, who was apparently impotent, killed a prostitute who jeered and hit him when he tried unsuccessfully to have intercourse with her. The House of Lords rejected the defendant's argument that the provocation should be evaluated according to its likely impact upon a reasonable impotent man. The decision was based in part upon what the lords saw as the impossibility of giving the reasonable person some but not all of the defendant's characteristics; to attribute all of the defendant's characteristics to the reasonable person would, the lords felt, destroy the objective nature of the standard. Compare the New Zealand Crimes Act 1961, § 169(2)(a), which directs the evaluation of offered provocation according to its impact upon "a person having the power of self-control of an ordinary person, but otherwise having the characteristics of the offender." See generally, Milligan, Provocation and the Subjective Test, 1967 N.Z.L.J. 19.

In 1978, however, the House of Lords reversed its position. D.D.P. v. Camplin, [1978] 2 All E.R. 168 involved a 15-year-old youth who had killed an older man after the man had sexually molested the youth and then mocked him. The trial judge instructed the jury that they should consider the adequacy of the victim's provocation according to the impact that it would have upon a reasonable adult. Relying heavily upon the Homicide Act of 1957 (which prohibited trial judges from determining that provocation was inadequate "as a matter of law"), the House determined that the jury should not have been directed to ignore the fact that the defendant was only 15 in determining whether the provocation was adequate. A contrary position, it was reasoned, would amount to almost the same as holding such provocation inadequate as a matter of law, a procedure clearly disallowed by the Act. Generalizing, Lord Diplock concluded:

> [A] proper direction to a jury * * * would * * * explain to them that the reasonable man referred to in the question is a person having the power of self-control to be expected of an ordinary person of the sex and age of the accused, but in other respects sharing such of the accused's characteristics as they think would affect the gravity of the provocation to him, and that the question is not merely whether such a person would in like circumstances be provoked to lose his self-control but also would react to the provocation as the accused did.

Id. at 175. The case is discussed in Wells, The Death Penalty for Provocation?, 1978 Crim.L.R. 662 (1978).

What would be the result in such cases under § 210.3 of the Model Penal Code? (See page 450, supra.) The comment to that section explained it as follows:

> Though it is difficult to state a middle ground between a standard which ignores all individual peculiarities and one which makes emotional distress decisive regardless of the nature of its cause, we think that such a statement is essential. For surely if the actor had just suffered a traumatic injury, if he were blind or were distraught with grief, if he were experiencing an unanticipated reaction to a therapeutic drug, it would be deemed atrocious to appraise his crime for purposes of sentence without reference to any of these matters. They are material because they bear upon the inference as to the actor's character that it is fair to draw upon the basis of his act. * * *
>
> We submit that the formulation in the [section] affords sufficient flexibility to differentiate between those special factors in the actor's situation which should be ignored. * * * The question in the end will be whether the actor's loss of self-control can be understood in terms that arouse sympathy enough to call for mitigation.

Model Penal Code § 210.3, comment (Tent. Draft No. 9, 1959). Does § 210.3 do what the authors of the comment say it does?

4. The cases frequently speak of "mutual combat" as adequate provocation to reduce a killing from murder to manslaughter. Mutual combat

arises where the victim and the defendant intend to fight and are ready to do so, and the defendant acts in the "heat of blood" engendered by the situation. It is not necessary that blows have actually been struck for mutual combat to exist, but if any blows have been struck it is not material which participant struck the first blow or that the deceased may have struck no blows at all. See Whitehead v. State, 9 Md.App. 7, 262 A.2d 316 (1970). But see also United States v. Hardin, 443 F.2d 735, 738 n. 6 (D.C.Cir. 1970): "[M]utual combat alone is not a true alternative ground for mitigating a murder to manslaughter; it is merely one of the circumstances from which the jury could find adequate provocation." If this is accurate, under what circumstances should mutual combat constitute adequate provocation? The court in Whitehead v. State, supra, noted that in that case "the [trial] court did not find that an unfair advantage was taken by appellant at the outset of the combat or that at the commencement of the contest they did not start on equal terms." Is this relevant? controlling?

5. In contrast to the approach taken by the court in *Tripp*, other courts have used voluntary manslaughter as a means of providing substantial although informal flexibility in homicide law. In Commonwealth v. Butcher, 451 Pa. 359, 304 A.2d 150 (1973), for example, the defendant had been charged with murder but convicted of voluntary manslaughter. He attacked the conviction on the ground that the evidence did not support the verdict. In upholding the conviction, the Pennsylvania Supreme Court explained:

> [T]his court has consistently held that a jury may in a murder prosecution return a verdict of voluntary manslaughter even where there is no evidence of passion or provocation. * * * The symmetry of the law at time must give way to the policy sought to be effectuated. Thus, even though the jury was moved by mitigating factors not recognized by the law in determining that the lesser of the two charges should be found, we will not disturb their determination.

451 Pa. at 364–65, 304 A.2d at 153. Is this a desirable approach? If so, is a defendant in a murder prosecution entitled to have voluntary manslaughter submitted to the jury as a possible verdict even if the evidence contains no basis for such a verdict?

b. INVOLUNTARY MANSLAUGHTER

Unlike voluntary manslaughter, involuntary manslaughter as traditionally defined is not a mitigated murder. Rather, it consists primarily of killings caused during the commission of unlawful acts not sufficient to make the killing murder and killings with "criminal negligence." There is considerable diversity concerning the unlawful acts that do or should suffice to make a killing involuntary manslaughter. There is also considerable uncertainty regarding the meaning of the "criminal negligence" that will make a killing involuntary manslaughter under the alternative route contained in traditional definitions of the offense. After considering the desirable resolution of these problems, consider the alternative formulation of the offense contained in Section 210.3(1)(a) of the Model Penal Code (page 450, supra). Consider also the wisdom of a separate offense of negligent homicide; see Section 210.4 of the Model Penal Code (page 450, supra).

(1) NEGLIGENT OMISSION

COMMONWEALTH v. WELANSKY

Supreme Judicial Court of Massachusetts, 1944.
316 Mass. 383, 55 N.E.2d 902.

LUMMUS, Justice. On November 28, 1942, and for about nine years before that day, a corporation named New Cocoanut Grove, Inc., maintained and operated a "night club" in Boston, having an entrance at 17 Piedmont Street, for the furnishing to the public for compensation of food, drink and entertainment, consisting of orchestra and band music, singing and dancing. It employed about eighty persons. The corporation, its officers and employees, and its business, were completely dominated by the defendant Barnett Welansky, who is called in this opinion simply the defendant, since his codefendants were acquitted by the jury. He owned, and held in his own name or in the names of others, all the capital stock. He leased some of the land on which the corporate business was carried on, and owned the rest, although title was held for him by his sister. He was entitled to, and took, all the profits. Internally, the corporation was operated without regard to corporate forms, as though the business were that of the defendant as an individual. It was not shown that responsibility for the number or condition of safety exits had been delegated by the defendant to any employee or other person.

The defendant was accustomed to spend his evenings at the night club, inspecting the premises and superintending the business. On November 16, 1942, he became suddenly ill, and was carried to a hospital, where he was in bed for three weeks and remained until discharged on December 11, 1942. During his stay at the hospital, although employees visited him there, he did not concern himself with the night club, because, as he testified, he "knew it would be all right" and that "the same system * * * [he] had would continue" during his absence. There is no evidence of any act, omission or condition at the night club on November 28, 1942 (apart from the lighting of a match hereinafter described), that was not within the usual and regular practice during the time before the defendant was taken ill when he was at the night club nearly every evening. While the defendant was at the hospital, his brother James Welansky and an employee named Jacob Goldfine, who were made codefendants, assumed some of the defendant's duties at the night club, but made no change in methods. * * *

A little after ten o'clock on the evening of Saturday, November 28, 1942, the night club was well filled with a crowd of patrons. It was during the busiest season of the year. An important football game in the afternoon had attracted many visitors to Boston. Witnesses were rightly permitted to testify that the dance floor had from eighty to one hundred persons on it, and that it was "very crowded." Witnesses were rightly permitted to give their estimates, derived from their observations, of the number of patrons in various parts of the night club. Upon the evidence it could have been found that at that time there were from two hundred fifty to four hundred persons in the Melody Lounge, from four hundred to five hundred in the main dining room and the Caricature Bar, and two hundred fifty in the Cocktail Lounge. Yet it could have been found that the crowd was no larger than it had been on other Saturday evenings before the defendant was taken ill, and that there had been larger crowds at earlier times. There were about seventy tables in the dining room, each seating from two to eight persons. There was testimony that all but two were taken. Many persons were standing in various rooms. The defendant testified that the reasonable capacity of the night club, exclusive of the new Cocktail Lounge, was six hundred fifty patrons. He never saw the new Cocktail Lounge with the furniture installed, but it was planned to accommodate from one hundred to one hundred twenty-five patrons.

A bartender in the Melody Lounge noticed that an electric light bulb which was in or near the cocoanut husks of an artificial palm tree in the corner had been turned off and that the corner was dark. He directed a sixteen year old bar boy who was waiting on customers at the tables to cause the bulb to be lighted. A soldier sitting with other persons near the light told the bar boy to leave it unlighted. But the bar boy got a stool, lighted a match in order to see the bulb, turned the bulb in its socket, and thus lighted it. The bar boy blew the match out, and started to walk away. Apparently the flame of the match had ignited the palm tree and that had speedily ignited the low cloth ceiling near it, for both flamed up almost instantly. The fire spread with great rapidity across the upper part of the room, causing much heat. The crowd in the Melody Lounge rushed up the stairs, but the fire preceded them. People got on fire while on the stairway. The fire spread with great speed across the foyer and into the Caricature Bar and the main dining room, and thence into the Cocktail Lounge. Soon after the fire started the lights in the night club went out. The smoke had a peculiar odor. The crowd were panic stricken, and rushed and pushed in every direction through the night club, screaming, and overturning tables and chairs in their attempts to escape.

The door at the head of the Melody Lounge stairway was not opened until firemen broke it down from outside with an axe and found it locked by a key lock, so that the panic bar could not operate.

Two dead bodies were found close to it, and a pile of bodies about seven feet from it. The door in the vestibule of the office did not become open, and was barred by the clothing rack. The revolving door soon jammed, but was burst out by the pressure of the crowd. The head waiter and another waiter tried to get open the panic doors from the main dining room to Shawmut Street, and succeeded after some difficulty. The other two doors to Shawmut Street were locked, and were opened by force from outside by firemen and others. Some patrons escaped through them, but many dead bodies were piled up inside them. A considerable number of patrons escaped through the Broadway door, but many died just inside that door. Some employees, and a great number of patrons died in the fire. Others were taken out of the building with fatal burns and injuries from smoke, and died within a few days.

* * *

The defendant, his brother James Welansky, and Jacob Goldfine, were indicted for manslaughter in sixteen counts of an indictment * * *[.] Voluntarily the Commonwealth filed specifications as to those counts, by which it specified among other things that the alleged misconduct of the defendant consisted in causing or permitting or failing reasonably to prevent defective wiring, the installation of inflammable decorations, the absence of fire doors, the absence of "proper means of egress properly maintained" and "sufficient proper" exits, and overcrowding.

The defendant was found guilty * * *[.] He was sentenced to imprisonment in the State prison upon each count for a term of not less than twelve years and not more than fifteen years, the first day of said term to be in solitary confinement and the residue at hard labor * * *, the sentences to run concurrently.

The Commonwealth disclaimed any contention that the defendant intentionally killed or injured the persons named in the indictments as victims. It based its case on involuntary manslaughter through wanton or reckless conduct. The judge instructed the jury correctly with respect to the nature of such conduct.

Usually wanton or reckless conduct consists of an affirmative act, like driving an automobile or discharging a firearm, in disregard of probable harmful consequences to another. But where as in the present case there is a duty of care for the safety of business visitors invited to premises which the defendant controls, wanton or reckless conduct may consist of intentional failure to take such care in disregard of the probable harmful consequences to them or of their right to care. * * *

To define wanton or reckless conduct so as to distinguish it clearly from negligence and gross negligence is not easy. * * * Sometimes the word "wilful" is prefaced to the words "wanton" and "reckless" in expressing the concept. That only blurs it. Wilful means intentional. In the phrase "wilful, wanton or reckless conduct," if "wilful" modifies "conduct" it introduces something different from wanton or reckless conduct, even though the legal result is the same. Wilfully causing harm is a wrong, but a different wrong from wantonly or recklessly causing harm. If "wilful" modifies "wanton or reckless conduct" its use is accurate. What must be intended is the conduct, not the resulting harm. * * * The words "wanton" and "reckless" are practically synonymous in this connection, although the word "wanton" may contain a suggestion of arrogance or insolence or heartlessness that is lacking in the word "reckless." But intentional conduct to which either word applies is followed by the same legal consequences as though both words applied.

The standard of wanton or reckless conduct is at once subjective and objective * * *[.] Knowing facts that would cause a reasonable man to know the danger is equivalent to knowing the danger. * * * The judge charged the jury correctly when he said, "To constitute wanton or reckless conduct, as distinguished from mere negligence, grave danger to others must have been apparent and the defendant must have chosen to run the risk rather than alter his conduct so as to avoid the act or omission which caused the harm. If the grave danger was in fact realized by the defendant, his subsequent voluntary act or omission which caused the harm amounts to wanton or reckless conduct, no matter whether the ordinary man would have realized the gravity of the danger or not. But even if a particular defendant is so stupid [or] so heedless * * * that in fact he did not realize the grave danger, he cannot escape the imputation of wanton or reckless conduct in his dangerous act or omission, if an ordinary normal man under the same circumstances would have realized the gravity of the danger. A man may be reckless within the meaning of the law although he himself thought he was careful."

The essence of wanton or reckless conduct is intentional conduct, by way either of commission or of omission where there is a duty to act, which conduct involves a high degree of likelihood that substantial harm will result to another. Wanton or reckless conduct amounts to what has been variously described as indifference to or disregard of probable consequences to that other * * * or the rights of that other. * * * But we are not prepared to give unqualified approval to a further statement found in some of our reported decisions, for example in Query v. Howe, 273 Mass. 92, 96, 172 N.E. 887, that to constitute wanton or reckless conduct, disregard of the rights of another must be as complete or utter as though such rights did not exist. If taken literally, that statement would permit a trifling regard for the rights of another to exonerate a defendant from the criminal consequences of flagrant wrongdoing.

The words "wanton" and "reckless" are thus not merely rhetorical or vituperative expressions used instead of negligent or grossly negligent. They express a difference in the degree of risk and in the voluntary taking of risk so marked, as compared with negligence, as to amount substantially and in the eyes of the law to a difference in kind. * * * For many years this court has been careful to preserve the distinction between negligence and gross negligence, on the one hand, and wanton or reckless conduct on the other. * * *

Notwithstanding language used commonly in earlier cases, and occasionally in later ones,[3] it is now clear in this Commonwealth that at common law conduct does not become criminal until it passes the borders of negligence and gross negligence and enters into the domain of wanton or reckless conduct. There is in Massachusetts at common law no such thing as "criminal negligence." * * *

If by wanton or reckless conduct bodily injury is caused to another, the person guilty of such conduct is guilty of assault and battery. * * * And since manslaughter is simply a battery that causes death * * *, if death results he is guilty of manslaughter. * * *

To convict the defendant of manslaughter, the Commonwealth was not required to prove that he caused the fire by some wanton or reckless conduct. Fire in a place of public resort is an ever present danger. It was enough to prove that death resulted from his wanton or reckless disregard of the safety of patrons in the event of fire from any cause.

* * *

Judgments affirmed.

NOTES

1. For discussions of the English law, see Turpin, Mens Rea in Manslaughter, 1962 Cambridge L.J. 200; Walker, Mens Rea in Manslaughter, 117 New L.J. 950 (1967). Canadian law is emphasized in O'Hearn, Criminal Negligence: An Analysis in Depth, 7 Crim.L.Q. 27 (1964), 7 Crim.L.Q. 407 (1965). The development of American manslaughter law is dealt with in Coldiron, Historical Development of Manslaughter, 38 Ky.L.J. 527 (1950).

2. Another category of killings that are sometimes regarded as manslaughter are the so-called "imperfect defense" cases. These involve situations in which the defendants have killed in reliance upon beliefs that for some reason—often their unreasonableness—fall short of establishing a defense. In Sanchez v. People, 172 Colo. 168, 470 P.2d 857 (1970), for example, there was evidence that the defendant killed the victim in the belief

3. In early cases what is now known as wanton or reckless conduct was variously described as wilful negligence, wanton negligence, gross negligence, and culpable negligence * * *. So in criminal cases what was necessary to make conduct criminal was often so described. The expression "criminal negligence" was often used. But it seems that what we now know as wanton or reckless conduct was in fact required. The terminology, not the law, is what has changed. * * *

In other jurisdictions a variety of similar expressions has been used in describing conduct that will create criminal liability. But in many of them the substantial equivalent of wanton or reckless conduct is required. * * *

that the fatal assault was necessary in self defense. The evidence further suggested, however, that the defendant had used more force than could have been justified in the situation by the right of self defense. Given the state of the evidence, the appellate court found reversible error in the trial court's failure to instruct the jury on involuntary manslaughter. If death was caused by a lawful act—the defendant's actions in self defense—which became unlawful because of the manner in which they were committed—with excessive force—then the defendant would be guilty only of involuntary manslaughter. Somewhat similar is Wentworth v. State, 29 Md.App. 110, 349 A.2d 421 (1975), in which the defendant, at gunpoint, participated in a murder. She claimed coercion or duress but failed because of the rule that duress is not a defense to an intentional killing. On appeal, however, the Court of Special Appeals held that the defendant was entitled to go to the jury on the theory that her near-duress situation, even if it did not constitute a defense, was sufficiently mitigating to establish the absence of malice aforethought and thus reduce the killing from murder to manslaughter.

Should the "imperfect defense" cases be voluntary or involuntary manslaughter? W. LaFave & A. Scott, Criminal Law 584 n. 7 (1972) observe that often the killings are generally described as manslaughter without any modifying adjectives. These authors conclude, without explanation, that voluntary manslaughter would be the proper classification; *Wentworth*, supra, suggests that this position can be defended on the ground that the imperfect defense—even though not meeting the requirements for "adequate provocation"—nevertheless establishes the absence of malice aforethought in a manner similar to that of provocation. But in at least many cases, liability seems to be imposed for negligence, i. e., the defendant has negligently acted on the basis of an unreasonable perception of a risk or has used force beyond that which a reasonable person would believe is justified by the situation. In such cases, is it not conceptually sounder to regard the offense as involuntary manslaughter on a criminal negligence theory?

(2) THE "UNLAWFUL ACT" DOCTRINE

STATE v. GIBSON

Court of Special Appeals of Maryland, 1968.
4 Md.App. 236, 242 A.2d 575, affirmed 254 Md. 399, 254 A.2d 691.

MURPHY, Chief Judge. A six-count indictment was returned against appellee Gibson by the Grand Jury of Baltimore County as a result of the death on September 10, 1966 of Diane Grempler by reason of appellee's alleged illegal and improper operation of a motor vehicle. Each of the first three counts of the indictment charged that appellee "did feloniously kill and slay" the deceased as a direct result of his commission of certain statutory misdemeanors, viz., that he operated his motor vehicle in violation of the motor vehicle laws of Maryland, Maryland Code (1967 Repl.Vol.) Article 66½, and more specifically:

1. *As to the first count*—that appellee, in violation of Sections 233 and 242, did fail to stop his motor vehicle in obedience to

a stop sign and grant the right of way to a vehicle traveling on a paved highway.

2. *As to the second count*—that appellee, in violation of Section 209, recklessly operated his motor vehicle upon a public highway.

3. *As to the third count*—that appellee, in violation of Section 206, operated his motor vehicle under the influence of intoxicating liquors.

The fourth count of the indictment charged that appellee "did feloniously kill and slay" the deceased as a direct result of his commission of a misdemeanor, *viz.,* that he violated the provisions of Section 19.2 of the Baltimore County Code in that he bought, consumed, and possessed an alcoholic beverage on a public highway, he then being a minor.

Each of the first four counts of the indictment expressly characterized the offenses therein charged as constituting a "common law misdemeanor—manslaughter."

The fifth count of the indictment charged that appellee, while operating a motor vehicle "unlawfully in a grossly negligent manner" caused the death of the decedent. This count of the indictment was expressly based upon Section 388 of Article 27 of the Maryland Code (1967 Repl.Vol.), which provides, in pertinent part, as follows:

> "Every person causing the death of another as the result of the driving, operation or control of an automobile, motor vehicle, motorboat, locomotive, engine, car, streetcar, train or other vehicle in a grossly negligent manner, shall be guilty of a misdemeanor to be known as 'manslaughter by automobile, motor vehicle, motorboat, locomotive, engine, car, streetcar, train or other vehicle,' and the person so convicted shall be sentenced to jail or the house of correction for not more than three years, or be fined not more than $1,000.-00 or be both fined and imprisoned. * * * "

* * *

On June 28, 1967, Judge W. Albert Menchine in the Circuit Court for Baltimore County, granted appellee's motion to dismiss [the first four counts of the indictment] stating in a brief opinion accompanying his order that under the common law, a showing of gross negligence was the main requirement for conviction of involuntary manslaughter; and that as none of the four counts alleged either an intention or purpose to harm in the operation of a motor vehicle, or the existence of gross negligence, such counts were not legally sufficient to charge a common law offense. The State has appealed from that order.

The State contends that involuntary manslaughter at common law consisted of an unintentional killing while doing some unlawful act not amounting to a felony, nor naturally tending to cause death or great bodily harm, or in negligently doing some act lawful in itself. More particularly, it differentiates the two classes of involuntary manslaughter by characterizing the first class as comprising all those cases wherein the defendant has caused the death of another as a direct and proximate result of doing an unlawful act not amounting to a felony, i. e., a misdemeanor (misdemeanor-manslaughter). As to this category of involuntary manslaughter, the State urges that the existence of negligence is not an element of the offense; that the doing of an unlawful act, which is *malum in se* or which if *malum prohibitum,*[a] was in violation of a statute provided to prevent injury to the person, constitutes involuntary manslaughter irrespective of the existence of negligence. The State identifies the second distinct class of involuntary manslaughter as comprising those cases where the defendant, while doing a lawful act in a grossly negligent manner, kills.

It is the State's position that the common law misdemeanor-manslaughter rule is applicable in Maryland and has not been revised, amended or repealed by the manslaughter by automobile statute (Section 388), which it contends applies only to a case where the defendant is charged with an unintentional killing in the course of doing a lawful act in an unlawful manner, i. e., driving a motor vehicle in a grossly negligent manner. It is upon this premise that the State maintains that the first four counts of the indictment properly charged the offense of common law manslaughter in that the appellee operated his vehicle in violation of the law in the four particulars set forth in counts one through four of the indictment; that the first three of these are *mala in se*, but even if *mala prohibita*, they were violations of statutes calculated to prevent injury to the person.

The appellee, on the other hand, urges that the common law crime of involuntary manslaughter where homicide was the unintentional result of an automobile accident has been repealed by Section 388, and that all cases involving the unintentional killing of a person by an automobile can only be prosecuted under the manslaughter by automobile statute; and that in such prosecutions the State carries the burden of proving gross negligence in order to obtain a conviction.

Manslaughter is a common law offense and a felony in Maryland; it may be voluntary or involuntary, depending upon the requisite intent, and since the crime is not defined by statute, it is afforded its common law meaning in this State. * * * By Section 387 of Article 27 of the Maryland Code, manslaughter, whether voluntary or

a. These terms are commonly employed to distinguish crimes into two classes: mala in se, which are inherently wrong, usually involving danger to life or limb and having criminal intent as an element; and mala prohibita, which are wrong only because so pronounced by statute.

involuntary, is punishable by a term of imprisonment not exceeding ten years. The crime of manslaughter by automobile created by Section 388 is a separate statutory misdemeanor, unknown to the common law, and is punishable under the statute by a designated fine and/or imprisonment in jail or the house of correction for a term not to exceed three years.

Involuntary manslaughter at common law has been generally defined as the killing of another unintentionally and without malice (1) in doing some unlawful act not amounting to a felony, or (2) in negligently doing some act lawful in itself, or (3) by the negligent omission to perform a legal duty. * * *

It is well settled in this State that where a charge of involuntary manslaughter is predicated on negligently doing some act lawful in itself, or by negligently failing to perform a legal duty (the second and third classes of involuntary manslaughter above delineated), the negligence necessary to support a conviction must be gross or criminal, *viz.*, such as manifests a wanton or reckless disregard of human life. * * * It is equally well settled that the Legislature, in enacting Section 388, making it a misdemeanor to cause the death of another as a result of operating an automobile "in a grossly negligent manner," intended to adopt this same standard of gross negligence (a wanton or reckless disregard of human life) as the minimum requirement to support a conviction for this statutory offense. * * *

It is likewise clear that the Maryland cases have generally recognized that a charge of involuntary manslaughter at common law could in some circumstances at least be based on the doing of an unlawful act. * * * [The cases] * * * seemingly share a common thread—that where a prosecution for involuntary manslaughter is based on the commission of an unlawful act causing death, the act must itself be dangerous to life. * * *

It is against this background that we examine whether the first four counts of the indictment returned against the appellee—which are expressly bottomed upon the applicability of the so called misdemeanor-manslaughter rule (an unintended homicide committed in the course of doing an unlawful act, i. e., committing a misdemeanor)—properly charge an existing offense in this State, when considered in light of the provisions of Section 388 and of the legislative intention in enacting that statute.

We note at the outset that the manner of operating a motor vehicle is commonly regulated in detail by statute or ordinance and that it is an unlawful act in itself to drive a vehicle in violation of such laws. It is not, however, a generally accepted rule that the fact alone that the operator of an automobile was violating the motor vehicle laws when his car struck and killed a person renders him, without more, guilty of involuntary manslaughter at common law. The authorities are divided on the question, some holding, as in State v.

Hupf, 9 Terry 254, 101 A.2d 355 (Del.), that where a person violates a traffic statute which proximately results in the death of another, he is guilty of involuntary manslaughter, without regard to whether the violation was *malum prohibitum* or *malum in se*, and irrespective of whether there was any proof that the motorist's conduct evidenced a wanton or reckless disregard for the lives and safety of others. Other authorities support the view as articulated in State v. Strobel, 130 Mont. 442, 304 P.2d 606, that such violations of law proximately resulting in the death of another, whether the violation was *malum in se*, or *malum prohibitum*, do not constitute involuntary manslaughter, unless the element of criminal negligence is also present. Still other authorities distinguish between unlawful acts *mala prohibita* and *mala in se*, and conclude in effect, that where the violation was merely *malum prohibitum*, no criminal homicide results, unless the violation was dangerous to life and constituted a reckless disregard for the safety of others; but that where the unlawful act underlying death was *malum in se* the violator would be guilty of involuntary manslaughter, even though the unlawful act was not calculated to cause death. * * *

While [the] cases might be construed to place Maryland among those authorities which hold that an unintentional killing committed in the course of doing some non-felonious unlawful act dangerous to life or *malum in se*, constitutes involuntary manslaughter at common law, irrespective of the existence of criminal negligence, we are persuaded that if such was ever the law of this State, it no longer has any application to those cases where the homicide results unintentionally from the operation of a motor vehicle—it being our view that such cases can only be prosecuted under Section 388.

There is no legislative history to which we may turn to ascertain the exact reach of Section 388, or of the effect of that statute upon the common law felony of involuntary manslaughter. We think it plain, however, that when Section 388 was enacted by Chapter 414 of the Acts of 1941, there then existed much confusion and little enlightenment among the authorities with respect to which of the several theories underlying application of the misdemeanor-manslaughter rule was the correct one. Quite clearly, where such unintentional homicides proximately resulted from driving an automobile in violation of laws designed to regulate and control the operation of motor vehicles in the interest of public safety there was an overlapping and blurring between and among the different theories of criminal responsibility, since in most instances such a violation constituted not only an unlawful act, but one dangerous to the lives and safety of others and such as manifested a wanton and reckless disregard of human life. We believe that the Legislature in enacting Section 388 to punish persons who cause the death of another "as the result of the driving, operation or control of an automobile * * * in a grossly negligent manner," intended to treat all unintended homicides thereby resulting in the same way, without regard to whether the homicide occurred in the course of doing a lawful or an unlawful act, or whether such act was *malum in se* or merely *malum prohibitum*. To otherwise conclude would be to attribute an intention to the Legislature to permit the prosecution of offenders either for the felony of common law manslaughter, with its ten-year penalty, or for the statutory misdemeanor of manslaughter by automobile, with its three-year penalty, even though, where the prosecution is based upon gross negligence, the proof necessary to justify a conviction in either case would be precisely the same (a wanton or reckless disregard of human life). A similarly incongruous result would follow from attributing an intention to the Legislature to permit a felony conviction and ten-year sentence upon simple proof that the accidental homicide occurred in the commission of an unlawful act (a misdemeanor), while requiring a greater degree of proof under the statute to support a conviction for a lesser grade of homicide, a misdemeanor punishable by a maximum of three years imprisonment. In construing statutes, results that are unreasonable or inconsistent with common sense should be avoided, whenever possible. We conclude, therefore, that in enacting Section 388, the Legislature intended to deal with an entire subject matter—unintended homicides resulting from the operation of a motor vehicle—and that the common law crime of involuntary manslaughter, when based on homicides so occurring, is in conflict with the statute and must yield to it to the extent of the inconsistency. * * *

Order affirmed.

VIII. DEFENSES NOT DIRECTLY RELATED TO THE BASIC REQUIREMENTS FOR LIABILITY

To a large extent, the definition of specific criminal offenses and the requirement that the prosecution prove each element of the crime charged serves to define who should be subject to criminal liability. But it is clear that the definitions of the various crimes do not and perhaps cannot be the sole vehicle for defining the scope of criminal liability. The so-called defenses to criminal liability also play an important role in this process. These defenses are the subject of the present chapter.

The doctrines with which this chapter is concerned can be distinguished from those covered in Section III.B.5. by the fact that the present matters are not logically and directly related to the elements of the crime charged. One court recently commented:

> Properly speaking, the description Defense in a criminal case should be reserved for matters in the nature of confession and avoidance where the accused asserts and proves facts in addition to those directly involved in proof or disproof of the ultimate facts alleged in the charge.

Wilson v. State, 284 So.2d 24, 26 (Fla.App.1973), rev'd on other grounds 294 So.2d 327 (Fla.1974). Evidence concerning an alibi, for example, does not go to establishing a defense in the sense in which that word is used by this court; such evidence simply contradicts the proof of the prosecution that tends to show that the defendant committed the acts constituting the crime. A defendant who has produced evidence of an alibi is generally entitled to have the jury instructed that he does not have the burden of establishing an alibi and that if the whole evidence, including that tending to show alibi, leaves the jury with a reasonable doubt of the defendant's guilt, he should be acquitted. State v. Hunt, 283 N.C. 617, 197 S.E.2d 513 (1973).

The definition of "defense" offered in *Wilson* is misleading, however, insofar as it suggests that an inherent characteristic of a defense is placement of the burden of proof on the matter upon the defendant. Since defenses are not directly related to elements of the crime charged, of course, they need not be negated in the prosecution's pleading. Sometimes the defendant must not only raise defensive matters but must also carry the burden of proof. In other instances, however, local law imposes upon the defendant only the burden of raising the matter by some evidence showing that the defense is an issue in the case. When the matter is so raised by a defendant, the prosecution then has the burden of negating the existence of the defense by proof beyond a reasonable doubt.

Traditionally, distinctions have been drawn between doctrines that involve "justification" and those that involve "excuse." The former, under this division, establish that despite the fact that the prosecution has fulfilled its burden of proof the act committed by the defendant was not in fact a wrongful one. The latter, on the other hand, concede the wrongfulness of the action but establish that the defendant is nevertheless not accountable for it. See G. Fletcher, Rethinking Criminal Law 759 (1978). Although there were formerly important differences in result between establishment of an excuse and of a justification, these no longer exist. J. Miller, Handbook of Criminal Law 255 (1934). But the distinction may still be of value in conceptualizing the impact of the various doctrines considered in this material.

In regard to each area of concern in this Chapter, it is important to consider whether the development of a separate defensive doctrine is necessary or desirable. In some cases at least, it is arguable that the underlying problem—insofar as there is one—can best be accommodated by permitting the defendant to challenge the adequacy of the prosecution's proof of the elements of the crime charged, especially the intent necessary for guilt. If a separate defensive doctrine is appropriate, it is necessary to consider the extent to which it should be specified in narrowly drawn rules applicable to particular fact situations. In resolving this, it is necessary to consider the need to provide a vehicle for preventing or minimizing conviction of nonblameworthy or nondangerous persons. But consideration must also be given to the danger that broad defensive doctrines may be misused by defendants who can falsely persuade judges and juries who may use the flexibility of broad defensive doctrines to acquit defendants who should be convicted.

As with other areas of criminal law, it is necessary to consider the extent to which federal and state constitutional considerations limit the flexibility available to courts and legislatures in regard to defensive doctrines. In each area here, it is necessary to consider whether constitutional doctrines require that a defense be made available to defendants and what if any limitations constitutional doctrines impose upon any such defense as is made available. To some extent, constitutional considerations may define the outer parameter within which policy choices may be made on the legislative or judicial level.

A. NECESSITY, DURESS, AND JUSTIFICATION GENERALLY

The doctrine of "necessity" has been most widely discussed in regard to situations in which a human life was taken in order to prevent the death of others. One leading case, United States v. Holmes, 26 F.Cas. 360 (No. 15,383) (C.C.E.D.Pa.1842) involved an American vessel which struck an iceberg in April, 1842. Nine crew members and thirty-two passengers got into the ship's longboat commanded by the first mate. Twenty-four hours after the ship had sunk, the weather worsened and the longboat appeared about to sink. The mate commanded that some of the passengers be thrown overboard, although he directed his crew not to part man and wife and not to throw over any women. Fourteen men and two women went overboard and perished; the women may have jumped into the sea after their brother was ejected from the boat. After daylight the next morning, two men who had hidden themselves were discovered and thrown into the sea. At no point had the passengers been consulted concerning these events. All passengers and crew members aboard the longboat were saved the next day when the boat was sighted by another ship. One of the crew members was indicted and tried for manslaughter. The trial judge instructed the jury as follows:

> Where * * * a case does arise, embraced by [the] "law of necessity," the penal laws pass over such case in silence * * *. For example, suppose that two persons who owe no duty to one another that is not mutual, should by accident, not attributable to either, be placed in a situation where both cannot survive. Neither * * * would * * * commit a crime in saving his own life in a struggle for the only means of safety * * *.
>
> But * * * the slayer must be under no obligation to make his own safety secondary to the safety of others * * *. [On shipboard, officers and sailers have a duty to protect passengers.] Should [an] emergency become so extreme as to call for the sacrifice of life, there can be no reason why the law does not remain the same. The passenger, not being bound either to labour or to incur the risk of life, cannot be bound to sacrifice his existence to preserve the sailor's. The captain, indeed, and a sufficient number of seamen to navigate the boat, must be preserved; for, except these abide in this ship, all will perish. But if there be more seamen than are necessary to manage the boat, the supernumerary sailors have no right, for their safety, to sacrifice the passengers * * *.
>
> But, in addition, if the source of the danger have been obvious, and destruction ascertained to be certainly about to arrive, although at a future time, there should be consultation, and some mode of selection fixed, by which those in equal relations may have equal chance for their life * * *. [T]he selection is [to be] by lot.

26 Fed.Cas. at 366–67. The defendant was convicted and sentenced to six months at hard labor and a fine of $20. After the president refused a pardon, the penalty was remitted.

In July of 1884, three English seamen—Dudley, Stephens, and Brooks—and a seventeen year old youth were forced to abandon an English yacht in an open boat. After twenty days, eight without any food at all, Stephens and Dudley killed the youth over the objections of Brooks. All three fed upon the youth's body and were rescued four days later. Dudley and Stephens were charged with murder. The jury found the basic facts of the case as stated above but disclaimed an ability to determine whether the acts constituted murder. On referral to the court, the facts were held to constitute murder. Regina v. Dudley and Stephens, 14 Q.B.D. 273 (1884). The court explained:

> [T]he temptation to the act which existed here was not what the law has ever called necessity. Nor is this to be regretted. Though law and morality are not the same, and many things may be immoral which are not necessarily illegal, yet the absolute divorce of law from morality would be of fatal consequence; and such divorce would follow if the temptation to murder in this case were to be held by law an absolute defense of it. It is not so. To preserve one's life is generally speaking a duty, but it may be the plainest and highest duty to sacrifice it * * *. It is not needful to point out the awful dangers of admitting the principle which has been contended for. Who is to be the judge of this sort of necessity? By what measure is the comparative value of lives to be measured? Is it to be strength, or intellect, or what? * * * We are often compelled to set up standards we cannot reach ourselves, and to lay down rules which we could not ourselves satisfy. But a man has no right to declare temptation to be an excuse, though he might himself have yielded to it, nor allow compassion for the criminal to change or weaken in any manner the legal definition of the crime.

14 Q.B.D. at 287–88. The defendants were sentenced to death but this was later commuted by the Crown to six months' imprisonment.

As the following case demonstrates, the doctrine of necessity is closely related to and sometimes indistinguishable from the doctrine of duress, which deals with wrongful pressure by another person to engage in criminal activity. The traditional law of duress was recently summarized as follows:

> "At common law the defense of duress was recognized only when the alleged coercion involved a use or threat of harm which is 'present, imminent and pending' and 'of such a

nature as to induce a well-grounded apprehension of death or serious bodily harm if the act is not done.' * * *

It was commonly said that duress does not excuse the killing of an innocent person even if the accused acted in response to immediate threats. * * * Aside from this exception, however, duress was permitted as a defense to prosecution for a range of serious offenses [including treason, kidnapping, and arson]. * * *

To excuse a crime, the threatened injury must induce 'such a fear as a man of ordinary fortitude and courage might justly yield to.' Although there are scattered suggestions in early cases that only a fear of death meets this test, an apprehension of immediate serious bodily harm has been considered sufficient to excuse capitulation to threats. Thus, the courts have assumed as a matter of law that neither threats of slight injury nor threats of destruction of property are coercive enough to overcome the will of a person of ordinary courage. A 'generalized fear of retaliation' by an accomplice, unrelated to any specific threat, is also insufficient.

More commonly, the defense of duress has not been allowed because of the lack of immediate danger to the threatened person. When the alleged source of coercion is a threat of 'future' harm, courts have generally found that the defendant had a duty to escape from the control of the threatening person or to seek assistance from law enforcement authorities.

* * * [H]owever, there is no requirement that the threatened person be the accused. Although not explicitly resolved by the early cases, recent decisions have assumed that concern for the well-being of another, particularly a near relative, can support a defense of duress if the other requirements are satisfied."

State v. Toscano, 74 N.J. 421, 378 A.2d 755, 760–62 (1977).

MODEL PENAL CODE *

(Proposed Official Draft 1962).

Section 2.09. Duress

(1) It is an affirmative defense that the actor engaged in the conduct charged to constitute an offense because he was coerced to do so by the use of, or a threat to use, unlawful force against his person or the person of another, which a person of reasonable firmness in his situation would have been unable to resist.

(2) The defense provided by this Section is unavailable if the actor recklessly placed himself in a situation in which it was probable that he would be subjected to duress. The defense is also unavailable if he was negligent in placing himself in such a situation, whenever negligence suffices to establish culpability for the offense charged.

(3) It is not a defense that a woman acted on the command of her husband, unless she acted under such coercion as would establish a defense under this Section. [The presumption that a woman, acting in the presence of her husband, is coerced is abolished.]

(4) When the conduct of the actor would otherwise be justifiable under Section 3.02, this Section does not preclude such defense.

Section 3.02. Justification Generally: Choice of Evils

(1) Conduct which the actor believes to be necessary to avoid a harm or evil to himself or to another is justifiable, provided that:

(a) the harm or evil sought to be avoided by such conduct is greater than that sought to be prevented by the law defining the offense charged; and

(b) neither the Code nor other law defining the offense provides exceptions or defenses dealing with the specific situation involved; and

(c) a legislative purpose to exclude the justification claimed does not otherwise plainly appear.

(2) When the actor was reckless or negligent in bringing about the situation requiring a choice of harms or evils or in appraising the necessity for his conduct, the justification afforded by this Section is unavailable in a prosecution for any offense for which recklessness or negligence, as the case may be, suffices to establish culpability.

PEOPLE v. UNGER

Supreme Court of Illinois, 1977.
66 Ill.3d 333, 5 Ill.Dec. 848, 362 N.E.2d 319.

RYAN, Justice.

Defendant, Francis Unger, was charged with the crime of escape (Ill.Rev.Stat.1971, ch. 108, par. 121), and was convicted following a jury trial before the circuit court of Will County. * * *

At the time of the present offense, the defendant was confined at the Illinois State Penitentiary in Joliet, Illinois. Defendant was serving a one- to three-year term as a consequence of a conviction for auto theft in Ogle County. Defendant began serving this sentence in December of 1971. On February 23, 1972, the defendant was transferred to the prison's minimum security, honor farm. It is undisputed that on March 7, 1972, the defendant walked off the honor farm. Defendant was apprehended two days later in a motel room in St. Charles, Illinois.

At trial, defendant testified that prior to his transfer to the honor farm he had been threatened by a fellow inmate. This inmate allegedly brandished a six-inch knife in an attempt to force defendant to engage in homosexual activities. Defendant was 22 years old and weighed approximately 155 pounds. He testified that he did not report the incident to the proper authorities due to fear of retaliation. Defendant also testified that he is not a particularly good fighter.

Defendant stated that after his transfer to the honor farm he was assaulted and sexually molested by three inmates, and he named the assailants at trial. The attack allegedly occurred on March 2, 1972, and from that date until his escape defendant received additional threats from inmates he did not know. On March 7, 1972, the date of the escape, defendant testified that he received a call on an institution telephone. Defendant testified that the caller, whose voice he did not recognize, threatened him with death because the caller had heard that defendant had reported the assault to prison authorities. Defendant said that he left the honor farm to save his life and that he planned to return once he found someone who could help him. None of these incidents were reported to the prison officials. As mentioned, defendant was apprehended two days later still dressed in his prison clothes.

The State introduced prior statements made by the defendant which cast some doubt on his true reasons for leaving the prison farm. In these statements, defendant indicated that he was motivated by a desire for publicity concerning the sentence on his original conviction, which he deemed to be unfair, as well as fear of physical abuse and death.

* * *

* * * The following instruction (People's Instruction No. 9) was given by the trial court over defendant's objection.

> "The reasons, if any, given for the alleged escape are immaterial and not to be considered by you as in any way justifying or excusing, if there were in fact such reasons."

* * * Two instructions which were tendered by defendant but refused by the trial court are also germane to this appeal. Defendant's instructions Nos. 1 and 3 were predicated upon the affirmative defenses of compulsion and necessity. Defendant's instructions Nos. 1 and 3 read as follows:

> "It is a defense to the charge made against the Defendant that he left the Honor Farm of the Illinois State Penitentiary by reason of necessity if the accused was without blame in occasioning or developing the situation and reasonably be-

lieved such conduct was necessary to avoid a public or private injury greater than the injury which might reasonably result from his own conduct."

"It is a defense to the charge made against the Defendant that he acted under the compulsion of threat or menace of the imminent infliction of death or great bodily harm, if he reasonably believed death or great bodily harm would be inflicted upon him if he did not perform the conduct with which he is charged."

The principal issue in the present appeal is whether it was error for the court to instruct the jury that it must disregard the reasons given for defendant's escape and to conversely refuse to instruct the jury on the statutory defenses of compulsion and necessity. * * *

Both the People and the defendant are entitled to appropriate instructions which present their theories of the case to the jury when and if such theories are supported by the evidence. * * *

Proper resolution of this appeal requires some preliminary remarks concerning the law of compulsion and necessity as applied to prison escape situations. Traditionally, the courts have been reluctant to permit the defenses of compulsion and necessity to be relied upon by escapees. This reluctance appears to have been primarily grounded upon considerations of public policy. Several recent decisions, however, have recognized the applicability of the compulsion and necessity defenses to prison escapes. In People v. Harmon (1974), 53 Mich.App. 482, 220 N.W.2d 212, the defense of duress was held to apply in a case where the defendant alleged that he escaped in order to avoid repeated homosexual attacks from fellow inmates. In People v. Lovercamp (1974), 43 Cal.App.3d 823, 118 Cal.Rptr. 110, a limited defense of necessity was held to be available to two defendants whose escapes were allegedly motivated by fear of homosexual attacks.

As illustrated by *Harmon* and *Lovercamp,* different courts have reached similar results in escape cases involving sexual abuse, though the question was analyzed under different defense theories. A certain degree of confusion has resulted from the recurring practice on the part of the courts to use the terms "compulsion" (duress) and "necessity" interchangeably, though the defenses are theoretically distinct. Note, Duress—Defense to Escape, 3 Am.J.Crim.L. 331, 332 (1975).) It has been suggested that the major distinction between the two defenses is that the source of the coercive power in cases of compulsion is from human beings, whereas in situations of necessity the pressure on the defendant arises from the forces of nature. (LaFave and Scott, Handbook on Criminal Law 381 (1972).) Also, * * * the defense of compulsion generally requires an impending, imminent threat of great bodily harm together with a demand that the person perform the specific criminal act for which he is eventually charged. Additionally, where the defense of compulsion is successfully asserted the coercing party is guilty of the crime. LaFave and Scott, Handbook on Criminal Law 380 (1972).

It is readily discernible that prison escapes induced by fear of homosexual assaults and accompanying physical reprisals do not conveniently fit within the traditional ambits of either the compulsion or the necessity defense. However, it has been suggested that such cases could best be analyzed in terms of necessity. (LaFave and Scott, Handbook on Criminal Law 381–82 n. 2 (1972).) One commentator has stated that the relevant consideration should be whether the defendant chose the lesser of two evils, in which case the defense of necessity would apply, or whether he was unable to exercise a free choice at all, in which event compulsion would be the appropriate defense. Gardner, The Defense of Necessity and the Right to Escape from Prison—A Step Towards Incarceration Free From Sexual Assault, 49 S.Cal.L.Rev. 110, 133 (1975).

In our view, the defense of necessity, as defined by our statute is the appropriate defense in the present case. In a very real sense, the defendant here was not deprived of his free will by the threat of imminent physical harm which, according to the Committee Comments, appears to be the intended interpretation of the defense of compulsion as set out in section 7–11 of the Criminal Code. Rather, if defendant's testimony is believed, he was forced to choose between two admitted evils by the situation which arose from actual and threatened homosexual assaults and fears of reprisal. Though the defense of compulsion would be applicable in the unlikely event that a prisoner was coerced by the threat of imminent physical harm to perform the specific act of escape, no such situation is involved in the present appeal. We, therefore, turn to a consideration of whether the evidence presented by the defendant justified the giving of an instruction on the defense of necessity.

The defendant's testimony was clearly sufficient to raise the affirmative defense of necessity. That defense is defined by statute (Ill.Rev.Stat.1971, ch. 38, par. 7–13):

> "Conduct which would otherwise be an offense is justifiable by reason of necessity if the accused was without blame in occasioning or developing the situation and reasonably believed such conduct was necessary to avoid a public or private injury greater than the injury which might reasonably result from his own conduct."

Defendant testified that he was subjected to threats of forced homosexual activity and that, on one occasion, the threatened abuse was carried out. He also testified that he was physically incapable of defending himself and that he feared greater harm would result from a report to the authorities. Defendant further testified that just prior to his escape he was told that he was going to be killed, and that he therefore fled the honor farm in order to save his life. Though the State's evidence cast a doubt upon the defendant's motives for escape and upon the reasonableness of defendant's assertion that such conduct was necessary, the defendant was entitled to have the jury consider the defense on the basis of his testimony. It is clear that defendant introduced some evidence to support the defense of necessity. As previously mentioned, that is sufficient to justify the giving of an appropriate instruction.

The State, however, would have us apply a more stringent test to prison escape situations. The State refers to the *Lovercamp* decision, where only a limited necessity defense was recognized. In *Lovercamp*, it was held that the defense of necessity need be submitted to the jury only where five conditions had been met. Those conditions are:

> "(1) The prisoner is faced with a specific threat of death, forcible sexual attack or substantial bodily injury in the immediate future;
>
> (2) There is no time for a complaint to the authorities or there exists a history of futile complaints which make any result from such complaints illusory;
>
> (3) There is no time or opportunity to resort to the courts;
>
> (4) There is no evidence of force or violence used towards prison personnel or other 'innocent' persons in the escape; and
>
> (5) The prisoner immediately reports to the proper authorities when he has attained a position of safety from the immediate threat." 43 Cal.App. 823, 831–32, 118 Cal.Rptr. 110, 115.

The State correctly points out that the defendant never informed the authorities of his situation and failed to report immediately after securing a position of safety. Therefore, it is contended that, under the authority of *Lovercamp*, defendant is not entitled to a necessity instruction. We agree with the State and with the court in *Lovercamp* that the above conditions are relevant factors to be used in assessing claims of necessity. We cannot say, however, that the existence of each condition is, as a matter of law, necessary to establish a meritorious necessity defense.

The preconditions set forth in *Lovercamp* are, in our view, matters which go to the weight and credibility of the defendant's testimony. The rule is well settled that a court will not weigh the evidence where the question is whether an instruction is justified. The absence of one or more of the elements listed in *Lovercamp* would not necessarily mandate a finding that the defendant could not assert the defense of necessity.

By way of example, in the present case defendant did not report to the authorities immediately after securing his safety. In fact, defendant never voluntarily turned himself in to the proper officials. However, defendant testified that he intended to return to the prison upon obtaining legal advice from an attorney and claimed that he was attempting to get money from friends to pay for such counsel. Regardless of our opinion as to the believability of defendant's tale, this testimony, if accepted by the jury, would have negated any negative inference which would arise from defendant's failure to report to proper authorities after the escape. The absence of one of the *Lovercamp* preconditions does not alone disprove the claim of necessity and should not, therefore, automatically preclude an instruction on the defense. We therefore reject the contention that the availability of the necessity defense be expressly conditioned upon the elements set forth in *Lovercamp*.

In conclusion, we hold that under the facts and circumstances of the present case the defendant was entitled to submit his defense of necessity to the jury. It was, therefore, reversible error to give People's Instruction No. 9 to the jury and to refuse to give an appropriate instruction defining the defense of necessity, such as the instruction tendered by the defendant. In light of our disposition of this appeal, we need not consider contentions raised by defendant as to the propriety of his sentence.

Therefore the judgment of the appellate court is affirmed, and the cause is remanded to the circuit court of Will County for further proceedings in accordance with the views expressed herein.

Affirmed and remanded.

UNDERWOOD, Justice, dissenting:

My disagreement with my colleagues stems from an uneasy feeling that their unconditional recognition of necessity as a defense to the charge of escape carries with it the seeds of future troubles. Unless narrowly circumscribed, the availability of that defense could encourage potential escapees, disrupt prison discipline, and could even result in injury to prison guards, police or private citizens. * * *

Lovercamp * * * imposed well-defined conditions which must be met before a defendant is entitled to have the defense of necessity submitted to the jury * * *.

I am not totally insensitive to the sometimes brutal and unwholesome problems faced by prison inmates, and the frequency of sexually motivated assaults. Prisoner complaints to unconcerned or understaffed prison administrations may produce little real help to a prisoner or may actually increase the hazard from fellow inmates of whose conduct complaint has been made. Consequently, and until adequate prison personnel and facilities are realities, I agree that a necessity defense should be recognized. The interests of society are better served, however, if the use of that defense in prison-escape cases is confined within well-defined boundaries such as those in *Lovercamp.* In that form it will be available, but with limitations precluding its wholesale use.

It is undisputed that defendant here did not meet those conditions. He did not complain to the authorities on this occasion even though, following an earlier threat and demand by a fellow inmate that defendant submit to homosexual activity, defendant had requested and been granted a transfer to the minimum security honor farm. Nor did he immediately report to the authorities when he had reached a place of safety. Rather, he stole a truck some nine hours after his escape, drove to Chicago, and later drove to St. Charles, using the telephone to call friends in Canada. This conduct, coupled with his admitted intent to leave in order to gain publicity for what he considered an unfair sentence, severely strain the credibility of his testimony regarding his intention to return to the prison.

Since defendant's conduct does not comply with conditions such as those in *Lovercamp* which, in my judgment, should be required before a necessity defense may be considered by a jury, I believe the trial court did not err in its instructions.

NOTES

1. Compare the following provision that appeared in the Proposed Federal Criminal Code (Final Draft, 1971):

§ 610. Duress

(1) *Affirmative Defense.* In a prosecution for any offense it is an affirmative defense that the actor engaged in the proscribed conduct because he was compelled to do so by threat of imminent death or serious bodily injury to himself or another. In a prosecution for an offense which does not constitute a felony, it is an affirmative defense that the actor engaged in the proscribed conduct because he was compelled to do so by force or threat of force. Compulsion within the meaning of this section exists only if the force, threat or circumstances are such as would render a person of reasonable firmness incapable of resisting the pressure.

2. No provision for "justification generally" or "necessity" appeared in the Proposed Federal Criminal Code. § 608 of the Study Draft, which was not included in the final version, provided as follows:

§ 608. Conduct Which Avoids Greater Harm

Conduct is justified if it is necessary and appropriate to avoid harm clearly greater than the harm which might result from such conduct and the situation developed through no fault of the actor. The necessity and justifiability of such conduct may not rest upon considerations pertaining only to the morality and advisability of the penal statute defining the offense, either in its general application or with respect to its application to a particular class of cases arising thereunder.

3. The duress standard provided in Section 2.09 of the Model Penal Code, page 518, supra, is substantially different from the traditional common law standard. The duress need not consist of threats of death or serious bodily harm. Moreover, there is no need for a preliminary determination by the trial judge that the threats posed a danger of "present, imminent and impending" harm before the jury is instructed to consider whether the facts raise the defense of duress. One court approving the Model Penal Code approach noted that under the Code duress would exist if the threats were such that a normal member of the community, of the defendant's size, strength, age, and health, would be unable to resist them. Among the factors bearing on the matter are the immediacy of the threatened harm, the seriousness of it, the possible opportunities for escape or help, and the identities of the persons threatened. In addition, the seriousness of the crime which the threatening person wants the defendant to commit is relevant; the more serious the crime, the more "serious" the threats must be before they suffice to establish a duress defense. State v. Toscano, 74 N.J. 421, 378 A.2d 755 (1977). In *Toscano*, the defendant had participated in efforts to defraud an insurance company by submitting false reports. He testified he had participated because of threats by another participant. The most direct threat, made while the threatening person sounded "vicious" and "desperate," was as follows:

> Remember, you just moved into a place that has a very dark entrance and you leave there with your wife. * * * You and your wife are going to jump at shadows when you leave that dark entrance.

The court held that this testimony would not raise the defense of duress under the traditional common law standard. But under the Model Penal Code standard, adopted by the court, it was sufficient to require that the jury be instructed to acquit the defendant if it found that a normal member of the community would have responded to these threats by committing the crime which the defendant committed.

4. Some courts and statutes make the duress defense unavailable if the defendant has intentionally or recklessly placed himself in a position in which it is likely that he would be subject to duress. See Section 2.09(2) of the Model Penal Code. In People v. Bailey, — Colo.App. —, 590 P.2d 508 (1978), defendants charged with narcotics sales claimed that the conduct of undercover law enforcement officers posing as "big time gangsters" constituted duress. Some of this conduct was discussion of noncooperating persons the officers had allegedly "eliminated." Assuming that the officers' conduct was otherwise sufficient to constitute duress, the court held the defense unavailable to the defendants because by entering into the drug sale transactions they had at least recklessly placed themselves in a situation where it was foreseeable that such coercion would be imposed upon them.

B. DEFENSE OF PERSONS, PROPERTY AND RELATED MATTERS

Legal doctrines relating to the use of force in defense of oneself, others, or property reflect a balancing between the obvious human instinct to meet physical aggression with counterforce, and the desirability, in a civilized society, of encouraging the resolution of disputes through peaceful means. Although questions may be raised as to the efficacy of the criminal law as a guide for the conduct of persons faced with aggression by other persons, the degree to which their reactions comport with the standards of our society is obviously relevant to their culpability for harm caused in such circumstances. As the following materials indicate, these doctrines reflect a sliding scale of justification. In essence, force will be justified when it is employed by one who is without fault, and does not exceed what reasonably appears necessary to protect the defendant, or another, or property, from the imminent use of unlawful force by another. No greater force than seems reasonably necessary will be permitted; one cannot respond to an offer of non-deadly force with deadly force. Nor, given the relative weights assigned by our society to persons and property, may deadly force be employed merely to recapture property unlawfully taken. The elaboration of these and other fundamental rules is the subject of this chapter. In studying these materials, bear in mind that in practice there is a high probability that more than one of these defenses may be available in any particular case. For example, the use of force to defend another is likely to also involve the defense of self or the prevention of crime (see section VIII.D., infra).

MODEL PENAL CODE*

(Proposed Official Draft 1962).

Section 3.04. Use of Force in Self-Protection

(1) *Use of Force Justifiable for Protection of the Person.* Subject to the provisions of this Section and of Section 3.09, the use of force upon or toward another person is justifiable when the actor believes that such force is immediately necessary for the purpose of protecting himself against the use of unlawful force by such other person on the present occasion.

(2) *Limitations on Justifying Necessity for Use of Force.*

(a) The use of force is not justifiable under this Section:

(i) to resist an arrest which the actor knows is being made by a peace officer, although the arrest is unlawful; or

(ii) to resist force used by the occupier or possessor of property or by another person on his behalf, where the actor knows that the person using the force is doing so under a claim of right to protect the property, except that this limitation shall not apply if:

(1) the actor is a public officer acting in the performance of his duties or a person lawfully assisting him therein or a person making or assisting in a lawful arrest; or

(2) the actor has been unlawfully dispossessed of the property and is making a re-entry or recaption justified by Section 3.06; or

(3) the actor believes that such force is necessary to protect himself against death or serious bodily harm.

(b) The use of deadly force is not justifiable under this Section unless the actor believes that such force is necessary to protect himself against death, serious bodily harm, kidnapping or sexual intercourse compelled by force or threat; nor is it justifiable if:

(i) the actor, with the purpose of causing death or serious bodily harm, provoked the use of force against himself in the same encounter; or

(ii) the actor knows that he can avoid the necessity of using such force with complete safety by retreating or by surrendering possession of a thing to a person asserting a claim of right thereto or by complying with a demand that he abstain from any action which he has no duty to take, except that:

(1) the actor is not obliged to retreat from his dwelling or place of work, unless he was the initial aggressor or is assailed in his place of work by another person whose place of work the actor knows it to be; and

(2) a public officer justified in using force in the performance of his duties or a person justified in using force in his assistance or a person justified in using force in making an arrest or preventing an escape is not obliged to desist from efforts to perform such duty, effect such arrest or prevent such escape because of resistance or threatened resistance by or on behalf of the person against whom such action is directed.

(c) Except as required by paragraphs (a) and (b) of this Subsection, a person employing protective force may estimate the necessity thereof under the circumstances as he believes them to be when the force is used, without retreating, surrendering possession, doing any other act which he has no legal duty to do or abstaining from any lawful action.

(3) *Use of Confinement as Protective Force.* The justification afforded by this Section extends to the use of confinement as protective force only if the actor takes all reasonable measures to terminate the confinement as soon as he knows that he safely can, unless the person confined has been arrested on a charge of crime.

Section 3.05. Use of Force for the Protection of Other Persons

(1) Subject to the provisions of this Section and of Section 3.09, the use of force upon or toward the person of another is justifiable to protect a third person when:

(a) the actor would be justified under Section 3.04 in using such force to protect himself against the injury he believes to be threatened to the person whom he seeks to protect; and

(b) under the circumstances as the actor believes them to be, the person whom he seeks to protect would be justified in using such protective force; and

(c) the actor believes that his intervention is necessary for the protection of such other person.

(2) Notwithstanding Subsection (1) of this Section:

(a) when the actor would be obliged under Section 3.04 to retreat, to surrender the possession of a thing or to comply with a demand before using force in self-protection, he is not obliged to do so before using force for the protection of another person, unless he knows that he can thereby secure the complete safety of such other person; and

(b) when the person whom the actor seeks to protect would be obliged under Section 3.04 to retreat, to surrender the possession of a thing or to comply with a demand if he knew that he could obtain complete safety by so doing, the actor is obliged to try to cause him to do so before using force in his protection if the actor knows that he can obtain complete safety in that way; and

(c) neither the actor nor the person whom he seeks to protect is obliged to retreat when in the other's dwelling or place of work to any greater extent than in his own.

Section 3.06. Use of Force for the Protection of Property

(1) *Use of Force Justifiable for Protection of Property.* Subject to the provisions of this Section and of Section 3.09, the use of force

upon or toward the person of another is justifiable when the actor believes that such force is immediately necessary:

(a) to prevent or terminate an unlawful entry or other trespass upon land or a trespass against or the unlawful carrying away of tangible, movable property, provided that such land or movable property is, or is believed by the actor to be, in his possession or in the possession of another person for whose protection he acts; or

(b) to effect an entry or re-entry upon land or to retake tangible movable property, provided that the actor believes that he or the person by whose authority he acts or a person from whom he or such other person derives title was unlawfully dispossessed of such land or movable property and is entitled to possession, and provided, further, that:

(i) the force is used immediately or on fresh pursuit after such dispossession; or

(ii) the actor believes that the person against whom he uses force has no claim of right to the possession of the property and, in the case of land, the circumstances, as the actor believes them to be, are of such urgency that it would be an exceptional hardship to postpone the entry or re-entry until a court order is obtained.

(2) *Meaning of Possession.* For the purposes of Subsection (1) of this Section:

(a) a person who has parted with the custody of property to another who refuses to restore it to him is no longer in possession, unless the property is movable and was and still is located on land in his possession;

(b) a person who has been dispossessed of land does not regain possession thereof merely by setting foot thereon;

(c) a person who has a license to use or occupy real property is deemed to be in possession thereof except against the licensor acting under claim of right.

(3) *Limitations on Justifiable Use of Force.*

(a) *Request to Desist.* The use of force is justifiable under this Section only if the actor first requests the person against whom such force is used to desist from his interference with the property, unless the actor believes that:

(i) such request would be useless; or

(ii) it would be dangerous to himself or another person to make the request; or

(iii) substantial harm will be done to the physical condition of the property which is sought to be protected before the request can effectively be made.

(b) *Exclusion of Trespasser.* The use of force to prevent or terminate a trespass is not justifiable under this Section if the actor knows that the exclusion of the trespasser will expose him to substantial danger of serious bodily harm.

(c) *Resistance of Lawful Re-entry or Recaption.* The use of force to prevent an entry or re-entry upon land or the recaption of movable property is not justifiable under this Section, although the actor believes that such re-entry or recaption is unlawful, if:

(i) the re-entry or recaption is made by or on behalf of a person who was actually dispossessed of the property; and

(ii) it is otherwise justifiable under paragraph (1)(b) of this Section.

(d) *Use of Deadly Force.* The use of deadly force is not justifiable under this Section unless the actor believes that:

(i) the person against whom the force is used is attempting to dispossess him of his dwelling otherwise than under a claim of right to its possession; or

(ii) the person against whom the force is used is attempting to commit or consummate arson, burglary, robbery or other felonious theft or property destruction and either:

(1) has employed or threatened deadly force against or in the presence of the actor; or

(2) the use of force other than deadly force to prevent the commission or the consummation of the crime would expose the actor or another in his presence to substantial danger of serious bodily harm.

(4) *Use of Confinement as Protective Force.* The justification afforded by this Section extends to the use of confinement as protective force only if the actor takes all reasonable measures to terminate the confinement as soon as he allows that he can do so with safety to the property, unless the person confined has been arrested on a charge of crime.

(5) *Use of Device to Protect Property.* The justification afforded by this Section extends to the use of a device for the purpose of protecting property only if:

(a) the device is not designed to cause or known to create a substantial risk of causing death or serious bodily harm; and

(b) the use of the particular device to protect the property from entry or trespass is reasonable under the circumstances, as the actor believes them to be; and

(c) the device is one customarily used for such a purpose or reasonable care is taken to make known to probable intruders the fact that it is used.

(6) *Use of Force to Pass Wrongful Obstructor.* The use of force to pass a person whom the actor believes to be purposely or knowingly and unjustifiably obstructing the actor from going to a place to which he may lawfully go is justifiable, provided that:

(a) the actor believes that the person against whom he uses force has no claim of right to obstruct the actor; and

(b) the actor is not being obstructed from entry or movement on land which he knows to be in the possession or custody of the person obstructing him, or in the possession or custody of another person by whose authority the obstructor acts, unless the circumstances, as the actor believes them to be, are of such urgency that it would not be resonable to postpone the entry or movement on such land until a court order is obtained; and

(c) the force used is not greater than would be justifiable if the person obstructing the actor were using force against him to prevent his passage.

Section 3.09. Mistake of Law as to Unlawfulness of Force or Legality of Arrest; Reckless or Negligent Use of Otherwise Justifiable Force; Reckless or Negligent Injury or Risk of Injury to Innocent Persons

(1) The justification afforded by Sections 3.04 to 3.07, inclusive, is unavailable when

(a) the actor's belief in the unlawfulness of the force or conduct against which he employs protective force or his belief in the lawfulness of an arrest which he endeavors to effect by force is erroneous; and

(b) his error is due to ignorance or mistake as to the provisions of the Code, any other provision of the criminal law or the law governing the legality of an arrest or search.

(2) When the actor believes that the use of force upon or toward the person of another is necessary for any of the purposes for which such belief would establish a justification under Sections 3.03 to 3.08 but the actor is reckless or negligent in having such belief or in acquiring or failing to acquire any knowledge or belief which is material to the justifiability of his use of force, the justification afforded by those Sections is unavailable in a prosecution for an offense for which

recklessness or negligence, as the case may be, suffices to establish culpability.

(3) When the actor is justified under Sections 3.03 to 3.08 in using force upon or toward the person of another but he recklessly or negligently injures or creates a risk of injury to innocent persons, the justification afforded by those Sections is unavailable in a prosecution for such recklessness or negligence towards innocent persons.

Section 3.11. Definitions

In this Article, unless a different meaning plainly is required:

(1) "unlawful force" means force, including confinement, which is employed without the consent of the person against whom it is directed and the employment of which constitutes an offense or actionable tort or would constitute such offense or tort except for a defense (such as the absence of intent, negligence, or mental capacity; duress; youth; or diplomatic status) not amounting to a privilege to use the force. Assent constitutes consent, within the meaning of this Section, whether or not it otherwise is legally effective, except assent to the infliction of death or serious bodily harm.

(2) "deadly force" means force which the actor uses with the purpose of causing or which he knows to create a substantial risk of causing death or serious bodily harm. Purposely firing a firearm in the direction of another person or at a vehicle in which another person is believed to be constitutes deadly force. A threat to cause death or serious bodily harm, by the production of a weapon or otherwise, so long as the actor's purpose is limited to creating an apprehension that he will use deadly force if necessary, does not constitute deadly force;

(3) "dwelling" means any building or structure, though movable or temporary, or a portion thereof, which is for the time being the actor's home or place of lodging.

1. SELF DEFENSE

The right of self defense is the most obvious and basic of the doctrines embodied in the Model Penal Code provision set out above. Indeed, all other defense doctrines may be considered to be derived from self defense. Yet this right is not unlimited in scope. Application of the basic principle justifying the use of such force as is necessary to repel the imminent use of unlawful force by another is complicated by a number of issues developed in the following materials. These include such questions as the degree to which, if at all, the reasonableness of the defendant's response to the situation is to be measured by his subjective characteristics, or by the behavior of the hypothetical ordinary and reasonable person. Can the use of deadly force ever be justified if its use might have been avoided by the defendant's retreat from the aggressor's offer of violence? What should be the effect of the defendant's status as the initial aggressor in a conflict in which the defendant later found it necessary to use force in self defense?

UNITED STATES v. PETERSON

United States Court of Appeals for the District of Columbia, 1973.
483 F.2d 1222.

Spottswood W. ROBINSON, III, Circuit Judge:

Indicted for second-degree murder, and convicted by a jury of manslaughter as a lesser included offense, Bennie L. Peterson * * * contends * * * that the evidence was legally insufficient to establish his guilt of manslaughter, and that in consequence the judge erred in denying his motion for a judgment of acquittal. He [also] complains * * * that the judge twice erred in the instructions given the jury in relation to his claim that the homicide was committed in self-defense. One error alleged was an instruction that the jury might consider whether Peterson was the aggressor in the altercation that immediately foreran the homicide. The other was an instruction that a failure by Peterson to retreat, if he could have done so without jeopardizing his safety, might be considered as a circumstance bearing on the question whether he was justified in using the amount of force which he did. After careful study of these arguments in light of the trial record, we affirm Peterson's conviction.

The events immediately preceding the homicide are not seriously in dispute. The version presented by the Government's evidence follows. Charles Keitt, the deceased, and two friends drove in Keitt's car to the alley in the rear of Peterson's house to remove the windshield wipers from the latter's wrecked car. While Keitt was doing so, Peterson came out of the house into the back yard to protest. After a verbal exchange, Peterson went back into the house, obtained a pistol, and returned to the yard. In the meantime, Keitt had reseated himself in his car, and he and his companions were about to leave.

Upon his reappearance in the yard, Peterson paused briefly to load the pistol. "If you move," he shouted to Keitt, "I will shoot." He walked to a point in the yard slightly inside a gate in the rear fence and, pistol in hand, said, "If you come in here I will kill you." Keitt alighted from his car, took a few steps toward Peterson and exclaimed, "What the hell do you think you are going to do with that? Keitt then made an about-face, walked back to his car and got a lug wrench. With the wrench in a raised position, Keitt advanced toward Peterson, who stood with the pistol pointed toward him. Peterson warned Keitt not to "take another step" and, when Keitt continued onward shot him in the face from a distance of about ten feet. Death was apparently instantaneous. Shortly thereafter, Peterson left home and was apprehended 20-odd blocks away.

This description of the fatal episode was furnished at Peterson's trial by four witnesses for the Government. Peterson did not testify or offer any evidence, but the Government introduced a statement which he had given the police after his arrest, in which he related a somewhat different version. Keitt had removed objects from his car before, and on the day of the shoooting he had told Keitt not to do so. After the initial verbal altercation, Keitt went to his car for the lug wrench, so he, Peterson, went into his house for his pistol. When Keitt was about ten feet away, he pointed the pistol "away of his right shoulder;" adding that Keitt was running toward him, Peterson said he "got scared and fired the gun. He ran right into the bullet." "I did not mean to shoot him," Peterson insisted, "I just wanted to scare him."

* * *

Self-defense, as a doctrine legally exonerating the taking of human life, is as viable now as it was in Blackstone's time, and in the case before us the doctrine is invoked in its purest form.[37] But "[t]he law of self-defense is a law of necessity;" the right of self-defense arises only when the necessity begins, and equally ends with the necessity; and never must the necessity be greater than when the force employed defensively is deadly.[40] The "necessity must bear all semblance of reality, and appear to admit of no other alternative, before taking life will be justifiable as excusable." Hinged on the exigencies of self-preservation, the doctrine of homicidal self-defense emerges from the body of the criminal law as a limited though important exception to legal outlawry of the arena of self-help in the settlement of potentially fatal personal conflicts.

So it is that necessity is the pervasive theme of the well defined conditions which the law imposes on the right to kill or maim in self-defense. There must have been a threat, actual or apparent, of the use of deadly force against the defender. The threat must have been unlawful and immediate. The defender must have believed that he was in imminent peril of death or serious bodily harm, and that his response was necessary to save himself therefrom. These beliefs must not only have been honestly entertained, but also objectively

37. While any unlawful aggression against one's person, habitation or property may justify such reasonable nondeadly force as may be necessary to repel, in this opinion we address specifically, and only, the right of self-defense—defense of the person—as it relates to the use of force of a deadly character.

40. When we speak of deadly force, we refer to force capable of inflicting death or serious bodily harm.

reasonable in light of the surrounding circumstances. It is clear that no less than a concurrence of these elements will suffice.

Here the parties' opposing contentions focus on the roles of two further considerations. One is the provoking of the confrontation by the defender. The other is the defendant's failure to utilize a safe route for retreat from the confrontation. The essential inquiry, in final analysis, is whether and to what extent the rule of necessity may translate these considerations into additional factors in the equation. To these questions, in the context of the specific issues raised, we now proceed.

The trial judge's charge authorized the jury, as it might be persuaded, to convict Peterson of second-degree murder or manslaughter, or to acquit by reason of self-defense. On the latter phase of the case, the judge instructed that with evidence of self-defense present, the Government bore the burden of proving beyond a reasonable doubt that Peterson did not act in self-defense; and that if the jury had a reasonable doubt as to whether Peterson acted in self-defense, the verdict must be not guilty. The judge further instructed that the circumstances under which Peterson acted, however, must have been such as to produce a reasonable belief that Keitt was then about to kill him or do him serious bodily harm, and that deadly force was necessary to repel him. In determining whether Peterson used excessive force in defending himself, the judge said, the jury could consider all of the circumstances under which he acted.

These features of the charge met Peterson's approval, and we are not summoned to pass on them. There were, however, two other aspects of the charge to which Peterson objected, and which are now the subject of vigorous controversy. The first of Peterson's complaints centers upon an instruction that the right to use deadly force in self-defense is not ordinarily available to one who provokes a conflict or is the aggressor in it. Mere words, the judge explained, do not constitute provocation or aggression; and if Peterson precipitated the altercation but thereafter withdrew from it in good faith and so informed Keitt by words or acts, he was justified in using deadly force to save himself from imminent danger or death or grave bodily harm. And, the judge added, even if Keitt was the aggressor and Peterson was justified in defending himself, he was not entitled to use any greater force than he had reasonable ground to believe and actually believed to be necessary for that purpose. Peterson contends that there was no evidence that he either caused or contributed to the conflict, and that the instructions on that topic could only mislead the jury.

It has long been accepted that one cannot support a claim of self-defense by a self-generated necessity to kill. The right of homicidal self-defense is granted only to those free from fault in the difficulty; it is denied to slayers who incite the fatal attack, encourage the fatal quarrel or otherwise promote the necessitous occasion for taking life. The fact that the deceased struck the first blow, fired the first shot or made the first menacing gesture does not legalize the self-defense claim if in fact the claimant was the actual provoker. In sum, one who is the aggressor in a conflict culminating in death cannot invoke the necessities of self-preservation. Only in the event that he communicates to his adversary his intent to withdraw and in good faith attempts to do so is he restored to his right of self-defense.

This body of doctrine traces its origin to the fundamental principle that a killing in self-defense is excusable only as a matter of genuine necessity. Quite obviously, a defensive killing is unnecessary if the occasion for it could have been averted, and the roots of that consideration run deep with us. A half-century ago, in Laney v. United States,[53] this court declared

> that, before a person can avail himself of the plea of self-defense against the charge of homicide, he must do everthing in his power, consistent with his safety, to avoid the danger and avoid the necessity of taking life. If one has reason to believe that he will be attacked, in a manner which threatens him with bodily injury, he must avoid the attack if it is possible to do so, and the right of self-defense does not arise until he has done everything in his power to prevent its necessity.[54]

And over the many years since *Laney,* the court has kept faith with its precept.

In the case at bar, the trial judge's charge fully comported with these governing principles. The remaining question, then, is whether there was evidence to make them applicable to the case. A recapitulation of the proofs shows beyond peradventure that there was.

It was not until Peterson fetched his pistol and returned to his back yard that his confrontation with Keitt took on a deadly cast. Prior to his trip into the house for the gun, there was, by the Government's evidence, no threat, no display of weapons, no combat. There was an exchange of verbal aspersions and a misdemeanor against Peterson's property was in progress but, at this juncture, nothing more. Even if Peterson's post-arrest version of the initial encounter were accepted—his claim that Keitt went for the lug wrench before he armed himself—the events which followed bore heavily on the question as to who the real aggressor was.

The evidence is uncontradicted that when Peterson reappeared in the yard with his pistol,[61] Keitt was about to depart the scene.

53. 54 App.D.C. 56, 294 F. 412 (1923).

54. Id. at 58, 294 F. at 414.

61. One may deliberately arm himself for purposes of self-defense against a pernicious assault which he has good reason to expect. * * * On the

Richard Hilliard testified that after the first argument, Keitt reentered his car and said "Let's go." This statement was verified by Ricky Gray, who testified that Keitt "got in the car and * * * they were getting ready to go;" he, too, heard Keitt give the direction to start the car. The uncontroverted fact that Keitt was leaving shows plainly that so far as he was concerned the confrontation was ended. It demonstrates just as plainly that even if he had previously been the aggressor, he no longer was.

Not so with Peterson, however, as the undisputed evidence made clear. Emerging from the house with the pistol, he paused in the yard to load it, and to command Keitt not to move. He then walked through the yard to the rear gate and, displaying his pistol, dared Keitt to come in, and threatened to kill him if he did. While there appears to be no fixed rule on the subject, the cases hold, and we agree, that an affirmative unlawful act reasonably calculated to produce an affray foreboding injurious or fatal consequences is an aggression which, unless renounced, nullifies the right of homicidal self-defense. We cannot escape the abiding conviction that the jury could readily find Peterson's challenge to be a transgression of that character.

* * *

The second aspect of the trial judge's charge as to which Peterson asserts error concerned the undisputed fact that at no time did Peterson endeavor to retreat from Keitt's approach with the lug wrench. The judge instructed the jury that if Peterson had reasonable grounds to believe and did believe that he was in imminent danger of death or serious injury, and that deadly force was necessary to repel the danger, he was required neither to retreat nor to consider whether he could safely retreat. Rather, said the judge, Peterson was entitled to stand his ground and use such force as was reasonably necessary under the circumstances to save his life and his person from pernicious bodily harm. But, the judge continued, if Peterson could have safely retreated but did not do so, that failure was a circumstance which the jury might consider, together with all others, in determining whether he went further in repelling the danger, real or apparent, than he was justified in going.

Peterson contends that this imputation of an obligation to retreat was error, even if he could safely have done so. He points out that at the time of the shooting he was standing in his own yard, and argues he was under no duty to move. We are persuaded to the conclusion that in the circumstances presented here, the trial judge did not err in giving the instruction challenged.

Within the common law of self-defense there developed the rule of "retreat to the wall," which ordinarily forbade the use of deadly

other hand, the true significance of the fact of arming can be determined only in the context of the surrounding circumstances. * * *

force by one to whom an avenue for safe retreat was open. This doctrine was but an application of the requirement of strict necessity to excuse the taking of human life, and was designed to insure the existence of that necessity. Even the innocent victim of a vicious assault had to elect a safe retreat, if available, rather than resort to defensive force which might kill or seriously injure.

In a majority of American jurisdictions, contrarily to the common law rule, one may stand his ground and use deadly force whenever it seems reasonably necessary to save himself. While the law of the District of Columbia on this point is not entirely clear, it seems allied with the strong minority adhering to the common law. In 1856, the District of Columbia Criminal Court ruled that a participant in an affray "must endeavor to retreat, * * * that is, he is obliged to retreat, if he can safely."[80] The court added that "[a] man may, to be sure, decline a combat when there is no existing or apparent danger, but the retreat to which the law binds him is that which is the consequence."[81] In a much later era this court, adverting to necessity as the soul of homicidal self-defense,[82] declared that "no necessity for killing an assailant can exist, so long as there is a safe way open to escape the conflict."[83] Moreover, the common law rule of strict necessity pervades the District concept of pernicious self-defense, and we cannot ignore the inherent inconsistency of an absolute no-retreat rule. Until such time as the District law on the subject may become more definitive, we accept these precedents as ample indication that the doctrine of retreat persists.

That is not to say that the retreat rule is without exceptions. Even at common law it was recognized that it was not completely suited to all situations. Today it is the more so that its precept must be adjusted to modern conditions nonexistent during the early development of the common law of self-defense.[86] One restriction on its operation comes to the fore when the circumstances apparently fore-

80. United States v. Herbert, 26 Fed. Cas. 287, p. 289, No. 15,354a (D.C. Crim.Ct.1856). There a waiter was slain by a guest during an altercation concerning the service.

81. Id. at 290.

82. Laney v. United States, supra note 53, 54 App.D.C. at 58, 294 F.2d at 414. * * *

83. Id.

86. "We are aware of the wide diversity of opinion as to the duty to retreat, but this difference arises from the circumstances of the particular case under consideration, rather than from any difference of conception as to the rule itself. Time, place, and conditions may create a situation which would clearly justify a modification of the rule. For example, the common-law rule, which required the assailed to retreat to the wall, had its origin before the general introduction of firearms. If a person is threatened with death or great bodily harm by an assailant, armed with a modern rifle, in open space, away from safety, it would be ridiculous to require him to retreat. Indeed, to retreat would be to invite almost certain death." Laney v. United States, supra note 53, 54 App.D.C. at 58–59, 294 F. at 414–415.

close a withdrawal with safety. The doctrine of retreat was never intended to enhance the risk to the innocent; its proper application has never required a faultless victim to increase his assailant's safety at the expense of his own. On the contrary, he could stand his ground and use deadly force otherwise appropriate if the alternative were perilous, or if to him it reasonably appeared to be. A slight variant of the same consideration is the principle that there is no duty to retreat from an assault producing an imminent danger of death or grievous bodily harm. "Detached reflection cannot be demanded in the presence of an uplifted knife," nor is it "a condition of immunity that one in that situation should pause to consider whether a reasonable man might not think it possible to fly with safety or to disable his assailant rather than to kill him."

The trial judge's charge to the jury incorporated each of these limitations on the retreat rule. Peterson, however, invokes another —the so-called "castle" doctrine. It is well settled that one who through no fault of his own is attacked in his home is under no duty to retreat therefrom. The oft-repeated expression that "a man's home is his castle" reflected the belief in olden days that there were few if any safer sanctuaries than the home. The "castle" exception, moreover, has been extended by some courts to encompass the occupant's presence within the curtilage outside his dwelling. Peterson reminds us that when he shot to halt Keitt's advance, he was standing in his yard and so, he argues, he had no duty to endeavor to retreat.

Despite the practically universal acceptance of the "castle" doctrine in American jurisdictions wherein the point has been raised, its status in the District of Columbia has never been squarely decided. But whatever the fate of the doctrine in the District law of the future, it is clear that in absolute form it was inapplicable here. The right of self-defense, we have said, cannot be claimed by the aggressor in an affray so long as he retains that unmitigated role. It logically follows that any rule of no-retreat which may protect an innocent victim of the affray would, like other incidents of a forfeited right of self-defense, be unavailable to the party who provokes or stimulates the conflict. Accordingly, the law is well settled that the "castle" doctrine can be invoked only by one who is without fault in bringing the conflict on. That, we think is the critical consideration here.

We need not repeat our previous discussion of Peterson's contribution to the altercation which culminated in Keitt's death. It suffices to point out that by no interpretation of the evidence could it be said that Peterson was blameless in the affair. And while, of course, it was for the jury to assess the degree of fault, the evidence well nigh dictated the conclusion that it was substantial.

The only reference in the trial judge's charge intimating an affirmative duty to retreat was the instruction that a failure to do so, when it could have been done safely, was a factor in the totality of the circumstances which the jury might consider in determining whether the force which he employed was excessive. We cannot believe that any jury was at all likely to view Peterson's conduct as irreproachable. We conclude that for one who, like Peterson, was hardly entitled to fall back on the "castle" doctrine of no retreat, that instruction cannot be just cause for complaint.

* * *

The judgment of conviction appealed from is accordingly

Affirmed.

NOTES AND QUESTIONS

1. In a jurisdiction which requires retreat except in one's own dwelling house, what constitutes the dwelling house? Must one on one's own front porch retreat? See State v. Bonano, 59 N.J. 515, 284 A.2d 345 (1971) (no, because porch or similar appurtenance is within the concept of being one's dwelling house). Must one accosted in the common hallway or stairway of one's apartment house retreat? See Commonwealth v. Daniels, 451 Pa. 163, 301 A.2d 841 (1973) (assuming, over vigorous dissent, that such a person need not retreat into his own apartment). Must one attacked in one's place of business retreat? See Commonwealth v. Johnston, 483 Pa. 485, 263 A.2d 376 (1970) (no, because courts have generally held that a person has the same right to defend his office or place of business against intrusion that he has to defend his dwelling). If a jurisdiction does not extend the right to stand one's ground to business premises as a general matter, should a private security guard hired to preserve order be required to retreat? See People v. Johnson, 75 Mich.App. 337, 254 N.W.2d 667 (1977) (no retreat is necessary, because to require such a security guard to flee to a place of safety when confronted by a deadly attack "is to disregard the possibility that such a withdrawal might permit an aggressor to vent his anger on those patrons remaining").

2. Should the standard for self defense require that the defendant's belief in the necessity for the use of force be reasonable? Are there constitutional considerations that bear upon the question? In State v. Goodseal, 186 Neb. 359, 183 N.W.2d 258 (1971), the court considered a statute (since repealed) that provided:

> No person in this state shall be placed in legal jeopardy of any kind whatsoever for protecting, by any means necessary, himself, his family, or his real or personal property, or when coming to the aid of another who is in imminent danger of or the victim of aggravated assault, armed robbery, holdup, rape, murder, or any other heinous crime.

As read by the court, the statute permitted one entitled to use force to use any force desired, "even beyond all reason." This, the court reasoned, delegated to the person later claiming self defense the power to determine the punishment to be imposed upon the aggressor. As a result, the statute was an unconstitutional attempt by the legislature to delegate powers placed exclusively with the legislature by the state constitution. What, if anything, is wrong with the court's analysis?

3. Should a citizen be permitted to use force in self defense against what he perceives to be an unlawful arrest? In Miller v. State, 462 P.2d 421, 426–27 (Alaska 1969) the court addressed the issue:

> The weight of authoritative precedent supports a right to repel an unlawful arrest with force. * * * This was the rule at common law. It was based upon the proposition that everyone should be privileged to use reasonable force to prevent an unlawful invasion of his physical integrity and personal liberty.
>
> But certain imperfections in the functioning of the rule have brought about changes in some jurisdictions. A new principle of right conduct has been espoused. It is argued that if a peace officer is making an illegal arrest but is not using force, the remedy of the citizen should be that of suing the officer for false arrest, not resistance with force. The legality of a peaceful arrest may frequently be a close question. It is a question more properly determined by courts than by the participants in what may be a highly emotional situation. Because officers will normally overcome resistance with necessary force, the danger of escalating violence between the officer and the arrestee is great. What begins as an illegal misdemeanor arrest may culminate in serious bodily harm or death.
>
> The control of man's destructive and aggressive impulses is one of the great unsolved problems of our society. Our rules of law should discourage the unnecessary use of physical force between man and man. Any rule which promotes rather than inhibits violence should be re-examined. Along with increased sensitivity to the rights of the criminally accused there should be a corresponding awareness of our need to develop rules which facilitate decent and peaceful behavior by all.
>
> The common law rule was developed in a time when self-help was a more necessary remedy to resist intrusions upon one's freedom.
>
>> "[It] was developed largely during a period when most arrests were made by private citizens, when bail for felonies was usually unattainable, and when years might pass before the royal judges arrived for a jail delivery. Further, conditions in English jails were then such that a prisoner had an excellent chance of dying of disease before trial." Warner, "The Uniform Arrest Act," 28 Va.L.Rev. 315 (1942).
>>
>> Section 5 of the Uniform Arrest Act provides:
>>
>> "If a person has reasonable ground to believe he is being arrested by a peace officer, it is his duty to refrain from using force or any weapon in resisting arrest regardless of whether or not there is a legal basis for the arrest."

> That provision, or its equivalent, has been enacted as statutory law in California, Rhode Island, New Hampshire, and Delaware. * * *
>
> To us the question is whether any amount of force should be permitted to be used by one unlawfully but peaceably arrested. We feel that the legality of a peaceful arrest should be determined by courts of law and not through a trial by battle in the streets. It is not too much to ask that one believing himself unlawfully arrested should submit to the officer and thereafter seek his legal remedies in court. Such a rule helps to relieve the threat of physical harm to officers who in good faith but mistakenly perform an arrest, as well as to minimize harm to innocent bystanders. The old common law rule has little utility to recommend it under our conditions of life today. We hold that a private citizen may not use force to resist peaceful arrest by one he knows or has good reason to believe is an authorized peace officer performing his duties, regardless of whether the arrest is illegal in the circumstances of the occasion.

For similar conclusions, see State v. Richardson, 95 Idaho 446, 511 P.2d 263 (1973); State v. Koonce, 89 N.J.Super. 169, 214 A.2d 428 (1965).

But suppose that an arrestee believes that the arresting officer is using excessive force to make the arrest? Should the arrestee have the right to use force to resist this perceived excessive force by the officer? In State v. Mulvihill, 57 N.J. 151, 270 A.2d 277 (1970) the court accepted the proposition that a citizen must submit to even an unlawful arrest by a police officer. It continued:

> If, in effectuating the arrest or the temporary detention, the officer employs excessive and unnecessary force, the citizen may respond or counter with the use of reasonable force to protect himself, and if in so doing the officer is injured no criminal offense has been committed. * * *
>
> There is sound reason for a difference in the rights and duties of the citizen in the two situations. Despite his duty to submit quietly without physical resistance to an arrest made by an officer acting in the course of his duty, even though the arrest is illegal, his right to freedom from unreasonable seizure and confinement can be protected, restored and vindicated through legal processes. However, the rule permitting reasonable resistance to excessive force of the officer, whether the arrest is lawful or unlawful, is designed to protect a person's bodily integrity and health and so permits resort to self-defense. Simply stated, the law recognizes that liberty can be restored through legal processes but life or limb cannot be repaired in a courtroom. And so it holds that the reason for outlawing resistance to an unlawful arrest and requiring disputes over its legality to be resolved in the courts has no controlling application on the right to resist an officer's excessive force.
>
> Two qualifications on the citizen's right to defend against and to repel an officer's excessive force must be noticed. He cannot use greater force in protecting himself against the officer's unlaw-

> ful force than reasonably appears to be necessary. If he employs such greater force, then he becomes the aggressor and forfeits the right to claim self-defense to a charge of assault and battery on the officer. See Restatement, Torts 2d, § 70, p. 118 (1965). Furthermore, if he knows that if he desists from his physically defensive measures and submits to arrest the officer's unlawfully excessive force would cease, the arrestee must desist or lose his privilege of self-defense.
>
> It has been suggested that the latter qualification is not reasonable because it would require a citizen being subjected to excessive force or attack and defending against it to make a split second determination, amounting to a gamble, as to whether if he terminates his defensive measures, he will suffer further beyond arrest. But application of the rule does not require such action as should follow opportunity for detached reflection. It merely commands that the citizen's conduct be reasonable in the light of all the circumstances apparent to him at the moment. And thus it is a counter-protective measure for the original aggressor officer. Administration of the rule should be no more difficult than those dealing with the duty of an assaulted person to retreat to avoid the attack or the duty not to continue the affray after the original aggressor ceases the assault; once the danger is past, the original victim cannot continue measures that were originally defensive.

57 N.J. at 156–58, 270 A.2d at 279–80.

2. DEFENSE OF OTHERS

The extent to which a person should be free to use force in defense of another has been the subject of considerable debate. The instinct to defend oneself from violence may be so powerful that the law must recognize it and seek to limit it in only minor ways. But perhaps this is not the case where another person, particularly a stranger, is threatened. Should intervention in such situations be discouraged? In some American jurisdictions, a person's use of force must, to be justified, not only seem reasonably necessary to prevent unlawful harm to the third person, but must also have been such as the person defended might himself have lawfully enployed. If the person aided, in other words, actually had no legal right to defend himself, another person who comes to his aid will have no defense to a criminal charge based upon his actions, even if it reasonably appeared that the person aided was legally entitled to defend himself. Intervention in disputes among others will presumably be discouraged by such a rule.

The right to defend others might also be limited by extending it only to persons who defend others to whom they are closely related. Perhaps where a stranger is the subject of an attack, a bystander can be expected to restrain his instinct to intervene. But should the law seek to discourage citizens from coming to the aid of anyone who appears to be the victim of an unlawful attack? There may be a significant need to discourage the escalation of disputes. But is there not also an important need to provide assistance to the victims of unlawful attacks?

COMMONWEALTH v. MARTIN

Supreme Judicial Court of Massachusetts, 1976.
369 Mass. 640, 341 N.E.2d 885.

KAPLAN, Justice.

The defendant Daniel R. Martin appeals, * * * from his multiple convictions * * * arising from a clash between inmates and guards at Massachusetts Correctional Institution at Concord on October 15, 1972. The issue on appeal is whether the trial judge committed error in failing to instruct the jury with respect to the defendant's claimed justification or defense, namely, that the acts of which he was accused were part of an attempt on his part to come to the aid of a fellow inmate and friend, Gene Tremblay (tried and convicted together with the defendant), who was being unlawfully beaten by prison guards. * * *

According to the prosecution's case, a struggle erupted between two correction officers and two inmates as the inmates were being escorted from a second-floor segregation unit down to a first-floor area for showers and exercise. One of the inmates, Tremblay, fought with an officer near the stairwell and the officer fell or was shoved down the stairs, with Tremblay following him down. The fallen officer yelled to officers on the first floor for help, and one of them, John Quealey, restrained Tremblay, while others went to summon aid. Officer Quealey held Tremblay by the hair while pushing him toward and into an open cell on the first floor. According to the prosecution's proof, Tremblay was held in the cell but not beaten; no clubs or other weapons were used by the officers in the affray although it appeared that clubs were kept in a nearby desk.

Meantime the second inmate involved in the fight on the second floor had taken the cell keys from the other officer and released other inmates of the segregation unit. Several of the inmates, including the defendant, ran down the stairs and met officers who had arrived to give help. In the melee, Officer Quealey was stabbed a number of times in the chest and once on the arm. Officer Quealey testified that as he was struggling with an inmate, he saw the defendant strike at him three times, and he saw a knife in the defendant's hand as the defendant stepped back. Other officers testified that they saw an attack by the defendant on Officer Quealey, or saw the defendant with a knife immediately after the attack (the testimony was not entirely consistent). There was further testimony that the defendant struck Frederick Taylor, a correction officer, with his fist and threatened him with a knife, saying "Back off, or I will give it to you, too."

The defendant took the stand to give his version of the facts. He was corroborated in part by the codefendant Tremblay. Because the defendant's view was obstructed by a partition between the rows of cells on either side of the second floor, he had not been able to see the fight there and did not know who had started it. When his cell was opened, he walked to the end of the partition but, seeing blood on the floor and hearing sounds of a struggle on the stairs, he started back to his cell. He then heard Tremblay calling for help and surmised that Tremblay was in grave danger. The defendant raced down the stairs and saw Officer Quealey and two other officers striking Tremblay with clubs and a metal mop handle as he lay on the floor of an open cell. Tremblay had his arms over his head and was trying to fend off the blows. He was yelling for help. The defendant struck several officers, including Officers Quealey and Taylor, with his fists in his effort to pull the officers off Tremblay. The defendant denied that he had a knife at this time; he did not stab Officer Quealey or threaten Officer Taylor with a knife. He testified that he first saw the knife on the floor where another inmate had dropped it after the stabbing of Officer Quealey.

The violence ended when assistant deputy superintendent Nicholas Genakos ordered the officers to withdraw while he and Jon Cooke, a social worker, negotiated with the inmates. During the negotiation Cooke saw the defendant with a knife and, when Genakos asked for it, the defendant said, "We'll see how this goes." The defendant testified that he made the statement and that he did have a knife, but only for a short interval when Cooke saw it. A search by the state police after the inmates had returned peaceably to their cells failed to turn up a knife.

* * *

The judge instructed the jury with respect to self-defense and even related these instructions to the question whether the defendant was privileged to use a dangerous weapon to protect himself from attack by Officer Quealey. But he gave the jury no instructions on the subject of the privileged use of force to protect another. This failure seems to have been due to the judge's belief that the claimed justification was not recognized in the law of Massachusetts.

* * *

The defendant made due request in writing for jury instructions on the subject. His request was submitted the day before the judge charged the jury. The main requested instruction (No. 9) was a quotation from the relevant statute law of Illinois as reproduced in the case of People v. Johnson, 4 Ill.App.3d 249, 251, 280 N.E.2d 764 (1972): "A person is justified in the use of force against another when and to the extent that he reasonably believes that such conduct is necessary to defend himself or another against such other's imminent use of unlawful force. * * * " Smith-Hurd Ill.Ann.Stat. c. 38, § 7–1(1972). * * *

We hold that a justification corresponding roughly to that quoted from the Illinois statute is recognized by the law of the Commonwealth. Of course the justification may exist although it is not found in so many words in our statute law: it may be read into the definition of a statutory offense or considered a common-law adjunct to, or qualification of, the offense. This is easily accepted and understood as to the more commonplace justification of self-defense. [I]t is hardly conceivable that the law of the Commonwealth, or, indeed, of any jurisdiction, should mark as criminal those who intervene forcibly to protect others; for the law to do so would aggravate the fears which lead to the alienation of people from one another * * *. To the fear of "involvement" and of injury to oneself if one answered a call for help would be added the fear of possible criminal prosecution.

It becomes necessary to sketch the conditions justifying the use of intervening protective force. The essence is this: An actor is justified in using force against another to protect a third person when (a) a reasonable person in the actor's position would believe his intervention to be necessary for the protection of the third person, and (b) in the circumstances as that reasonable person would believe them to be, the third person would be justified in using such force to protect himself. The reasonableness of the belief may depend in part on the relationships among the persons involved (a matter to which we return below). The actor's justification is lost if he uses excessive force, e. g., aggressive or deadly force unwarranted for the protective purpose.

Of course, the subject cannot be exhausted in a paragraph. Without subscribing in advance to all the relevant provisions of the Model Penal Code of the American Law Institute, we recommend it for study. Accelerated by that Code, the trend, which is exemplified by legislation adopted in many States, has been to interweave closely the justification of defense of a third person with self-defense; to eliminate some earlier authority restricting the justification of third-person defense to situations where the third person is seen retrospectively to have been entitled to use force in his own defense (regardless of the belief, which might be mistaken, of the "reasonable person" at the time); and to remove earlier artificial or factitious restrictions of the justification, e. g., restrictions to protection of spouse, child, parent, master, or servant.

One such possible factitious restriction was rejected, we think correctly, in United States v. Grimes, 413 F.2d 1376 (7th Cir. 1969), a case resembling the present. The defendant Grimes, an inmate of the Federal penitentiary in Marion, Illinois, seeing (as he claimed) a fellow inmate, Reid, being beaten by prison guards with metal flashlights, ran to Reid's aid and struck one of the guards. Grimes was indicted and convicted of assault upon an employee of a United States Correctional institution (18 U.S.C.A. §§ 111, 1114 [1970]). On appeal, it was held that the trial judge erred in refusing a jury instruction regarding justified use of force to protect a third person. The court spoke as follows to the point that, while the justification might be suitable generally, it should be rejected in the prison context because of its effect on institutional discipline: "We perceive no serious threat to prison discipline from a defense which merely protects inmates from unauthorized physical abuse by overzealous officials. Our decision in no way limits the power of prison officials to restrain or subdue unruly inmates, to carry out all reasonable orders necessary for the maintenance of prison discipline, or to cope with attempted assaults or escapes by prison inmates. See A.L.I. Model Penal Code §§ 3.07, 3.08 (Proposed Official Draft 1962). The Government's concern that recognition of this limited defense will emasculate Section 111 is belied by the fact that since 1905, when this statute was originally enacted, this is apparently the first such case." Id. at 1379.

We agree with the court in the *Grimes* case that the justification of defense of a third person does not necessarily stop short at the prison gates. But the fact that an episode occurs in prison may have considerable significance. So the question of the reasonableness of a belief that an inmate would be justified in using force against a prison guard, thus justifying intervening protective force, is conditioned by the fact that the guard, by the nature of his job, is himself privileged to apply force to inmates when necessary to preserve order in the institution. Therefore the guard's mere taking an inmate into custody or holding him in custody would not be a proper occasion for intervening force. This may have an important bearing on the present case in the event of retrial.

Judgments reversed.

Verdicts set aside.

NOTES AND QUESTIONS

1. In Commonwealth v. Monico, 373 Mass. 298, 366 N.E.2d 1241 (1977), the trial judge instructed the jury that the right to use force in defense of others was limited to defending persons related to the defendant by consanguinity or affinity, unless the force used upon the third person "almost" amounts to deadly force. On appeal, this was held to be error under *Martin*. But the error was held to be harmless, since on the facts of the case the defendant was not entitled to any instruction on defense of others. The defendant himself testified that he assaulted a police officer at the scene of a disturbance after he observed the officer shove his girlfriend. "[T]he defense of others does not authorize resort to punitive force," the court held, and noted that even under the defendant's version of the facts

his assault upon the police officer was not made until the officer had already completed the harm done to defendant's girlfriend. Thus the defendant's facts raised no more than a use of punitive or "merely retaliatory" force, not covered by the defense recognized in *Martin*. What might be said in favor of limiting the privilege to situations in which the defendant came to the aid of another person with whom he had a close relationship?

2. In People v. Young, 11 N.Y.2d 274, 229 N.Y.S.2d 1, 183 N.E.2d 319 (1962), defendant had come upon two middle-aged men struggling with an eighteen year old youth on the street. He intervened on behalf of the youth, injuring one of the men. It ultimately turned out the men were police officers making a valid arrest and the youth was improperly resisting them. But even the testifying officer acknowledged that the defendant had no way of knowing that the men were officers or that they were making an arrest. The defendant was convicted of assault. On appeal, the intermediate appellate court reversed on the ground that defendant was entitled to the defense of defense of others if it reasonably appeared that the youth had the right to use force in his own defense. In support of its position, the majority quoted from the comments to the Model Penal Code, Tentative Draft No. 8, 1958, at page 32:

> [I]t may perhaps be said that the potentiality for deterring the actor from the use of force is greater where he is protecting a stranger than where he is protecting himself or a loved one, because in the former case the interest protected is of relatively less importance to him; moreover the potential incidence of mistake in estimating fault or the need for action on his part is increased where the defendant is protecting a stranger, because in such circumstances he is less likely to know which party to the quarrel is in the right. These arguments may be said to lead to the conclusion that, in order to minimize the area for error or mistake, the defendant should act at his peril when he is protecting a stranger. This emasculates the privilege of protection of much of its content, introducing a liability without fault which is indefensible in principle. The cautious potential actor who knows the law will, in the vast majority of cases, refrain from acting at all. The result may well be that an innocent person is injured without receiving assistance from bystanders. It seems far preferable, therefore, to predicate the justification upon the actor's belief, safeguarding if thought necessary against abuse of the privilege by the imposition of a requirement of proper care in evolving the belief.

The dissenters stressed the identity of the victims as police officers:

> It would be a dangerous precedent for courts to announce that plain-clothes police officers attempting lawful arrests over wrongful resistance are subject to violent interference by strangers ignorant of the facts, who may attack the officers with impunity so long as their ignorance forms a reasonable basis for a snap judgment of the situation unfavorable to the officers. * * * It is more desirable * * * that in such cases the intervening citizen be held to act at his peril when he assaults a stranger, who unknown to him is a police officer legally performing his duty.

12 A.D.2d 262, 271, 210 N.Y.S.2d 358, 367. On further appeal, the New York Court of Appeals reversed the intermediate appellate court and reinstated the defendant's conviction. Espousing what it described as the majority rule that one who goes to the aid of a third person does so at his own peril, the court reasoned that the alternative "would not be conducive to an orderly society." The decision is critically examined in 63 Colum.L.Rev. 160 (1963) and 111 U.Pa.L.Rev. 506 (1963). It was apparently "reversed" by the New York legislature. See N.Y.Penal Law § 35.15 (McKinney 1975) (one may use force to defend another person "from what he reasonably believes to be the use or imminent use of unlawful physical force" by a third person).

3. DEFENSE OF PROPERTY

Where an attacker threatens only the safety or possession of property, there is agreement that the right to use defensive force should be more limited than where human safety is threatened. This is reflected in several limitations upon the general rule that one is entitled to use force that reasonably appears necessary to protect property from unlawful interference. Force may be used only to prevent an interference with the property or in "hot pursuit" of one who has taken it; force may not be otherwise used to regain property improperly taken by another person. Nor, as a general rule, is force permissible to end or avoid an interference with the enjoyment of property if a non-forcible request would suffice. Deadly force may never be used to protect property. But efforts to interfere with property in an unlawful fashion are often accompanied by conduct giving rise to a right in the possessor of the property to defend himself. If deadly force is justified by the right of self defense (or any other doctrine), it may, of course, be used.

These same principles apply to defense of realty and dwellings. Nondeadly force may be used to prevent unlawful entries or trespasses. Moreover, deadly force may, under certain circumstances, be used to resist efforts to enter a dwelling. The inhabitant must, of course, reasonably believe that deadly force is necessary to prevent the entry, i. e., that nondeadly force would not suffice.

STATE v. RULLIS

Superior Court of New Jersey Appellate Division, 1963.
79 N.J.Super. 221, 191 A.2d 197.

The opinion of the court was delivered by FREUND, J. A. D.

Defendant appeals from a County Court judgment of conviction, after a trial *de novo* without a jury, "for assault and battery * * *." This judgment affirmed the conviction entered in the municipal court of the Township of Hillside, N. J.

The essential facts of the case are as follows. Defendant described his trade as "a memorialist. We deal in monuments for the deceased families." He is the owner of the property at 1200 North Broad Street, Hillside, where he displays monuments. The property of the complaining witness Herbert F. Jacobi, a retail florist, is adjacent, at 1202–14 North Broad Street. On or near the boundary between these properties, defendant had erected granite posts connected with iron bars or pipes that served as a fence between the two properties.

At approximately 9 A.M. on November 1, 1960 Jacobi and two assistants were removing the granite posts by "breaking them down with a hand crane" and "a sledge hammer." When defendant arrived at his place of business, he saw Jacobi destroying the fence and demanded that the destruction be halted. Jacobi refused, claiming that the granite posts were on his property. Defendant continued to protest that he owned the property upon which the posts were resting. He asked a passing patrolman, Arthur Issler of the Hillside police force, to intervene. Issler testified that he "told him [defendant] that he wouldn't stop him [Jacobi], because the fence posts to me looked like they were well in his [Jacobi's] property, and that he [defendant] consult his lawyer." Defendant rejected this advice to settle his differences peacefully and continued to argue with Jacobi, saying that "he was going to stop Mr. Jacobi himself."

Patrolman Issler testified that in the course of this argument defendant walked onto Jacobi's property, "grabbed his [Jacobi's] clothing and reached down to a bar, and lifted it from the ground." Karl Kohl, one of the workmen assisting Jacobi, testified that defendant "put his hand around the pipe, and the pipe wouldn't move. He let it go. He came up and pushed Mr. Jacobi." Jacobi testified that defendant "struck me on the upper part of the arm" and "with his right hand he [defendant] grabbed me, and then with his left hand he started to pick up an iron post, an iron railing." Jacobi feared that defendant would strike him with the pipe. Consequently, Jacobi "started backing up" and eventually "got away from him." All three witnesses on behalf of the State testified that defendant called Jacobi "a son of a bitch."

* * *

[D]efendant argues that this use of force was privileged because it was employed in the protection of his property.

Preliminarily, in determining the merits of this defense, we note that defendant claims the monuments were personalty and within his possession. We cannot agree with this characterization. "At any particular instant of time every piece of property in the world is either real or personal." 1 Reeves, Real Property, § 9, p. 10 (1909). Certain types of property, other than fixtures, are sometimes realty and sometimes personalty, depending upon the circumstances in which they are found. Thus, fences are "ordinarily a part of the real property to which they are attached." Reeves, supra, § 45, p. 53. * * *

Applying these principles to the present case, we find that the granite posts and rails forming a fence were attached to the soil with every indication that their annexation was of a permanent character. The posts were, consequently, part of the disputed realty.

During the trial before the County Court, defendant repeatedly attempted to demonstrate his ownership of the disputed land and the fence. Although the trial judge took some evidence concerning the boundary in order to determine the nature of the dispute and to ascertain the proper penalty, he expressly declined to decide the question of title in this criminal action. For example, during the course of the trial the judge stated:

> "You cannot resolve a title, in my view by a fist fight or pipe fight, or even an argument. * * * once there is a disputed ownership there are Courts to settle it; assault and battery is not the solution. We simply can't live on that solution. * * * I am not concerned, and I cannot be concerned with the soundness or the accuracy of the defendant's view as to who owned the property."

Under the circumstances, the trial judge properly rejected the defense of protection of property and refused to decide the question of title. Even assuming defendant could establish his title to the disputed land, he was not in actual possession of the premises on the morning of the altercation. As noted, Jacobi and his assistants were on the disputed property removing the posts and pipes when defendant arrived.

Although the question has apparently never been decided in New Jersey, we note that the authorities and cases from other jurisdictions suggest that, in order to justify an assault, the possession of the property—in the present instance land—must be actual and not merely constructive. 6 C.J.S. Assault and Battery § 94, p. 951 (1937). The author of the annotation, "Right to use force to obtain possession of real property to which one is entitled," 141 A.L.R. 250, 276 (1942), concluded as follows:

> "The cases involving criminal liability for assault committed in regaining possession of land by one entitled thereto are not numerous, but are harmonious in holding that the owner of real property with a right to possession has no right to resort to force in attempting to gain such possession from one wrongfully withholding it."

For instance in a case factually similar to the present prosecution, the Circuit Court of Appeals affirmed the trial court's refusal to take testimony concerning title to land. Hickey v. United States, 168 F. 536 (9 Cir. 1909). There, defendant struck an individual named Powell with a revolver while attempting forcefully to eject Powell and his associates from a mining claim of which they were in possession. Hickey maintained in his defense to the resultant prosecution for assault and battery that he owned the mining claim and that his previous application to the district attorney for assistance had been denied. In rejecting these contentions, the Circuit Court stated:

> "There was manifestly a dispute between the parties about the right of possession as it respects the claim, and the defendant had no right to attempt to settle that dispute by undertaking to eject Powell and his men by physical force, after they had refused to vacate the premises, when so ordered. Even if the defendant were the owner, with a perfect title, he had no legal right to oust trespassers in that way. The law provides peaceable methods for obtaining possession where wrongfully denied, and a resort to force and violence without pursuing the due course of law is seldom excused." (at p. 537)

The court deplored defendant's taking the law into his own hands in these terms:

> "There is no warrant of law for such a course of action. It would lead to riot and bloodshed, and make every man the judge of his own property rights and the executioner of his own judgments. A person has a right to defend his domicile or habitation against the intrusion of others, and to apply ample force to remove any such found therein. Long v. People, 102 Ill. 331. And he may prevent trespass upon his lands by force sufficient to repel the same; but, being himself dispossessed, he has no right to recover possession by force and by a breach of the peace. Sampson v. Henry, 11 Pick. (Mass.) 379, 387. The law applicable here is pertinent ly stated by Pollock, J., in State v. Bradbury, 67 Kan. 808, 809, 74 Pac. 231, 232. He says:
>
> > 'While one rightfully in possession of property may defend his possession against an attack, and while one lawfully entitled to the possession of real property may, if he can, enter and take peaceable possession, yet, no matter what lawful right to possession one out of the actual possession of real property may have, he will not be justified in making a forcible entry and committing a breach of the peace in ejecting by force an actual occupant.'
>
> It is clear, from the record, that Powell and his men were in possession, and were working there. While the de-

> fendant, if in possession, might have kept them out by force, yet, finding them in possession, though trespassers, he could not use force to oust them, because the law provides a more peaceable way for doing it." (at p. 538)

The judgment of conviction was affirmed. Similarly, in the instant case defendant cannot be exonerated because he claimed to own the disputed realty or because he sought unsuccessfully to have law enforcement authorities intervene on his behalf.

* * *

Defendant relies upon State v. Ruta, 112 N.J.L. 271, 169 A. 628 (E. & A. 1934), for the proposition that "a defendant clearly has the right to assert the defense of personalty whether ownership or right to possession of the chattel be in dispute or not." We find Ruta to be factually inapposite. There, the defendant was still in possession of an automobile when he assaulted one McQuaid who was attempting to repossess the automobile under an alleged conditional sales contract. In the instant case, as we have already emphasized, defendant was not in possession of the fence posts at the time he committed the offense upon Jacobi. Even assuming that the posts and pipes were personalty, the applicable principles are those previously enunciated in regard to realty, and were succinctly summarized in Lockland v. State, 73 S.W. 1054, 45 Tex.Cr.R. 87 (Tex.Ct.Crim.App.1903):

> "The law accords one in possession of property the right to protect such possession; but the possession must be actual, and not merely constructive; and when one has parted with the possession of personal property he may not regain it by such means as result in homicide or assault."

From our review of the testimony and the applicable principles of law, we are satisfied that the conviction of defendant for assault and battery was proper.

NOTES AND QUESTIONS

1. Would Rullis have been permitted to use force against Jacobi and his assistants if Rullis had come upon them immediately after they had walked up to the posts? Force is generally regarded as permissible if it is used immediately after the dispossession or in "hot pursuit" of the dispossessor:

> If force is allowed to defend possession, it is only a small extension to allow similar force to be used to regain possession immediately after its loss. * * * Moreover, it is an ancient principle of the common law, commended by common sense, that when property is retaken on fresh pursuit it is deemed to be taken at the beginning of the pursuit. The retaking is not any the less immediate because the fresh pursuit turns out to be a protracted chase.

Model Penal Code § 3.06, Comment, at 44 (Tent. Draft No. 8, 1958).

2. If Rullis had been justified in using force to protect the posts, how much force could he have used? Could he have shot Jacobi? Could he have pointed a gun at Jacobi? Could he have threatened to use a gun against Jacobi? In State v. Murphy, 7 Wash.App. 505, 500 P.2d 1276 (1972), the defendant armed himself with a pistol and confronted trespassers on his property with the gun in his hand dropped at his side. In finding no right to engage in such behavior to eject trespassers, the court explained:

> Mr. Murphy's action in arming himself with a revolver was well calculated to excite apprehension of great bodily harm in the minds of the two persons who, he believed, were harassing his business interests. * * * There is a recklessness—a wanton disregard of humanity and social duty—in the threatened use of deadly force to repel what at most could be considered a petty inconvenience, which is essentially wicked and which the law abhors. The law forbids such a menacing of human life for so trivial a cause.

7 Wash.App. at 515, 500 P.2d at 1283.

3. To what extent does—or should—a person have a right to use greater force than would otherwise be available because the confrontation takes place in the person's residence? Although there is widespread recognition in the cases that a doctrine of "defense of habitation" exists, there is substantial disagreement on its scope. Some authorities, especially older ones, suggest that the doctrine gives an occupant the right even to kill to prevent an entry into the residence:

> In Ohio it is the law that where one is assaulted in his home, or the home itself is attacked, he may use such means as are necessary to repel the assailant from the house, or to prevent his forcible entry, or material injury to his home, even to the taking of life. But a homicide in such a case would not be justifiable unless the slayer, in the careful and proper use of his faculties, in good faith believes, and has reasonable grounds to believe, that the killing is necessary to repel the assailant or prevent his forcible entry.

State v. Reid, 3 Ohio App.2d 215, 221, 32 O.O.2d 316, 210 N.E.2d 142, 147 (1965). But the effect of this is diminished by the requirement that the entry justifying a killing be "by force." This has traditionally meant that the trespass must be such as would amount to a breach of the peace; entering premises after being warned not to do so but without force would not make the trespass such a breach of the peace. Carroll v. State, 23 Ala. 28 (1853).

The more modern statement of the doctrine limits the right to kill in defense of the dwelling to situations in which the resident has a reasonable apprehension that the trespasser intends felonious or serious injury to the occupants:

> When a trespasser enters upon a man's premises, makes an assault upon his dwelling, and attempts to force an entrance into his house in a manner such as would lead a reasonably prudent

> man to believe that the intruder intends to commit a felony or to inflict some serious personal injury upon the inmates, a lawful occupant of the dwelling may legally prevent the entry, even by the taking of the life of the intruder.

State v. Miller, 267 N.C. 409, 411, 148 S.E.2d 279, 281 (1966). What does this add to the right to use force to defend oneself, other persons, and property? If the jurisdiction is one in which retreat is necessary before deadly force is used, the doctrine of defense of habitation dispenses with the requirement of retreat. Law v. State, 21 Md.App. 13, 318 A.2d 859 (1974). In addition, however, it appears to authorize the use of force against one believed to pose a threat to oneself or others before the danger becomes as immediate as is required by the doctrines of defense of self or others:

> [O]ne may [in defense of his habitation] resist with force an unlawful entry by one whose purpose is to assault or to do violence to him, to the extent of taking the aggressor's life, even though the circumstances may not be such as to justify a belief that there was actual peril of life or great bodily harm.

People v. Givens, 26 Ill.2d 371, 375, 186 N.E.2d 225, 227 (1962). See also State v. Gray, 162 N.C. 608, 614, 77 S.E. 833, 834 (1913) (householder need not wait until assailant is upon him but may open his door and shoot). Thus the doctrine arguably permits one to use force before such force would be permitted by the other doctrines.

C. ENTRAPMENT

The defense of entrapment has given rise to a great deal of discussion concerning the appropriate role a defense to crime should play in this area. Much of the debate has acknowledged the desirability of a defense of entrapment but has concerned the most appropriate formulation of that defense. The leading case supporting the traditional "subjective" formulation of the entrapment defense is Sorrells v. United States, 287 U.S. 435, 53 S.Ct. 210, 77 L.Ed. 413 (1932). Sorrells had been approached during Prohibition by an undercover agent who had been a member of Sorrell's military unit during World War I. At several points during their discussion of war experiences, the agent asked if Sorrells could get him some liquor. Sorrells demurred to the first two requests but after the third left and returned with some liquor. He was arrested and tried for possession and sale of the liquor. The trial court refused to either direct a verdict for the defendant on entrapment grounds or to instruct the jury on entrapment. The Supreme Court reversed. Formulating the issue before the Court, Chief Justice Hughes noted:

> It is well settled that the fact that officers or employees of the government merely afford opportunities or facilities for the commission of the offense does not defeat the prosecution. Artifice and stratagem may be employed to catch those engaged in criminal enterprises. * * * A different

> question is presented when the criminal design originates with the officials of the government, and they implant in the mind of an innocent person the disposition to commit the alleged offense and induce its commission in order that they may prosecute.

287 U.S. at 441–42. Acknowledging the existence of a defense in such situations, he continued:

> "[G]eneral terms descriptive of a class of persons made subject to a criminal statute may and should be limited, where the literal application of the statute would lead to extreme or absurd results, and where the legislative purpose gathered from the whole act would be satisfied by a more limited interpretation."
>
> We think that this established principle of construction is applicable here. We are unable to conclude that it was the intention of the Congress in enacting this statute that its processes of detention and enforcement should be abused by the instigation by government officials of an act on the part of persons otherwise innocent in order to lure them to its commission and to punish them. We are not forced by the letter to do violence to the spirit of the statute.

287 U.S. at 447–48. Turning to the government's contention that defendants such as Sorrells should not be permitted to raise entrapment upon a plea of not guilty where no plea in bar was made, the Court concluded that the conceptual basis for the defense permitted it to be raised by a simple plea of not guilty:

> The government [assumes] * * * that the accused is not denying his guilt but is setting up special facts in bar upon which he relies regardless of his guilt or innocence of the crime charged. This * * * is a misconception. The defense is available, not in the view that the accused though guilty may go free, but that the government cannot be permitted to contend that he is guilty of a crime where the government officials are the instigators of his conduct. The federal courts in sustaining the defense in such circumstances have proceeded in the view that the defendant is not guilty.

287 U.S. at 452. The trial court erred, the majority concluded, in failing to submit the issue of entrapment to the jury.

Subsequent discussions have focused to a large extent upon the comparative value of the "subjective" formulation accepted in *Sorrells* as compared with an "objective" standard such as is contained in the Model Penal Code provision set out below.

MODEL PENAL CODE *

(Proposed Official Draft 1962).

Section 2.13. Entrapment

(1) A public law enforcement official or a person acting in cooperation with such an official perpetrates an entrapment if for the purpose of obtaining evidence of the commission of an offense, he induces or encourages another person to engage in conduct constituting such offense by either:

(a) making knowingly false representations designed to induce the belief that such conduct is not prohibited; or

(b) employing methods of persuasion or inducement which create a substantial risk that such an offense will be committed by persons other than those who are ready to commit it.

(2) Except as provided in Subsection (3) of this Section, a person prosecuted for an offense shall be acquitted if he proves by a preponderance of evidence that his conduct occurred in response to an entrapment. The issue of entrapment shall be tried by the Court in the absence of the jury.

(3) The defense afforded by this Section is unavailable when causing or threatening bodily injury is an element of the offense charged and the prosecution is based on conduct causing or threatening such injury to a person other than the person perpetrating the entrapment.

SHERMAN v. UNITED STATES

United States Supreme Court, 1958.
356 U.S. 369, 78 S.Ct. 819, 2 L.Ed.2d 848.

Mr. Chief Justice WARREN delivered the opinion of the Court.

The issue before us is whether petitioner's conviction should be set aside on the ground that as a matter of law the defense of entrapment was established. Petitioner was convicted under an indictment charging three sales of narcotics in violation of 21 U.S.C. § 174, 21 U.S.C.A. § 174. A previous conviction had been reversed on account of improper instructions as to the issue of entrapment. 2 Cir., 200 F.2d 880. In the second trial, as in the first, petitioner's defense was a claim of entrapment: an agent of the Federal Government induced him to take part in illegal transactions when otherwise he would not have done so.

In late August 1951, Kalchinian, a government informer, first met petitioner at a doctor's office where apparently both were being treated to be cured of narcotics addiction. Several accidental meetings followed, either at the doctor's office or at the pharmacy where both filled their prescriptions from the doctor. From mere greetings, conversation progressed to a discussion of mutual experiences and problems, including their attempts to overcome addiction to narcotics. Finally Kalchinian asked petitioner if he knew of a good source of narcotics. He asked petitioner to supply him with a source because he was not responding to treatment. From the first, petitioner tried to avoid the issue. Not until after a number of repetitions of the request, predicated on Kalchinian's presumed suffering, did petitioner finally acquiesce. Several times thereafter he obtained a quantity of narcotics which he shared with Kalchinian. Each time petitioner told Kalchinian that the total cost of narcotics he obtained was twenty-five dollars and that Kalchinian owed him fifteen dollars. The informer thus bore the cost of his share of the narcotics plus the taxi and other expenses necessary to obtain the drug. After several such sales Kalchinian informed agents of the Bureau of Narcotics that he had another seller for them. On three occasions during November 1951, government agents observed petitioner give narcotics to Kalchinian in return for money supplied by the Government.

At the trial the factual issue was whether the informer had convinced an otherwise unwilling person to commit a criminal act or whether petitioner was already predisposed to commit the act and exhibited only the natural hesitancy of one acquainted with the narcotics trade. The issue of entrapment went to the jury, and a conviction resulted. Petitioner was sentenced to imprisonment for ten years. The Court of Appeals for the Second Circuit affirmed. 240 F.2d 949. We granted certiorari. 353 U.S. 935, 77 S.Ct. 812, 1 L.Ed.2d 758.

In Sorrells v. United States, 287 U.S. 435, 53 S.Ct. 210, 77 L.Ed. 413, this Court firmly recognized the defense of entrapment in the federal courts. The intervening years have in no way detracted from the principles underlying that decision. The function of law enforcement is the prevention of crime and the apprehension of criminals. Manifestly, that function does not include the manufacturing of crime. Criminal activity is such that stealth and strategy are necessary weapons in the arsenal of the police officer. However, "A different question is presented when the criminal design originates with the officials of the government, and they implant in the mind of an innocent person the disposition to commit the alleged offense and induce its commission in order that they may prosecute." 287 U.S. at page 442, 53 S.Ct. at page 212. Then stealth and strategy become as objectionable police methods as the coerced confession and the unlawful search. Congress could not have intended that its statutes were to be enforced by tempting innocent persons into violations.

However, the fact that government agents "merely afford opportunities or facilities for the commission of the offense does not" constitute entrapment. Entrapment occurs only when the criminal conduct was "the product of the *creative* activity" of law-enforcement officials. (Emphasis supplied.) See 287 U.S. at pages 441, 451, 53 S. Ct. at pages 212, 216. To determine whether entrapment has been established, a line must be drawn between the trap for the unwary innocent and the trap for the unwary criminal. The principles by which the courts are to make this determination were outlined in Sorrells. On the one hand, at trial the accused may examine the conduct of the government agent; and on the other hand, the accused will be subjected to an "appropriate and searching inquiry into his own conduct and predisposition" as bearing on his claim of innocence. See 287 U.S. at page 451, 53 S.Ct. at page 216.

We conclude from the evidence that entrapment was established as a matter of law. In so holding, we are not choosing between conflicting witnesses, nor judging credibility. Aside from recalling Kalchinian, who was the Government's witness, the defense called no witnesses. We reach our conclusion from the undisputed testimony of the prosecution's witnesses.

It is patently clear that petitioner was induced by Kalchinian. The informer himself testified that, believing petitioner to be undergoing a cure for narcotics addiction, he nonetheless sought to persuade petitioner to obtain for him a source of narcotics. In Kalchinian's own words we are told of the accidental, yet recurring, meetings, the ensuing conversations concerning mutual experiences in regard to narcotics addiction, and then of Kalchinian's resort to sympathy. One request was not enough, for Kalchinian tells us that additional ones were necessary to overcome, first, petitioner's refusal, then his evasiveness, and then his hesitancy in order to achieve capitulation. Kalchinian not only procured a source of narcotics but apparently also induced petitioner to return to the habit. Finally, assured of a catch, Kalchinian informed the authorities so that they could close the net. The Government cannot disown Kalchinian and insist it is not responsible for his actions. Although he was not being paid, Kalchinian was an active government informer who had but recently been the instigator of at least two other prosecutions.[2] Undoubtedly the impetus

2. "Q. And it was your [Kalchinian's] job, was it not, while you were working with these agents to go out and try and induce somebody to sell you narcotics, isn't that true?

* * *

"A. No, it wasn't my job at all to do anything of the kind.

"Q. Do you remember this question [asked at the first trial]— * * * 'Q. And it was your job while working with these agents to go out and try and induce a person to sell narcotics to you, isn't that correct? A. I would say yes to that.' Do you remember that?

"A. If that is what I said, let it stand just that way.

* * *

"Q. So when you testify now that it was not your job you are not telling the truth?

for such achievements was the fact that in 1951 Kalchinian was himself under criminal charges for illegally selling narcotics and had not yet been sentenced.[3] It makes no difference that the sales for which petitioner was convicted occurred after a series of sales. They were not independent acts subsequent to the inducement but part of a course of conduct which was the product of the inducement. In his testimony the federal agent in charge of the case admitted that he never bothered to question Kalchinian about the way he had made contact with petitioner. The Government cannot make such use of an informer and then claim disassociation through ignorance.

The Government sought to overcome the defense of entrapment by claiming that petitioner evinced a "ready compliance" to accede to Kalchinian's request. Aside from a record of past convictions, which we discuss in the following paragraph, the Government's case is unsupported. There is no evidence that petitioner himself was in the trade. When his apartment was searched after arrest, no narcotics were found. There is no significant evidence that petitioner even made a profit on any sale to Kalchinian. The Government's characterization of petitioner's hesitancy to Kalchinian's request as the natural wariness of the criminal cannot fill the evidentiary void.

The Government's additional evidence in the second trial to show that petitioner was ready and willing to sell narcotics should the opportunity present itself was petitioner's record of two past narcotics convictions. In 1942 petitioner was convicted of illegally selling narcotics; in 1946 he was convicted of illegally possessing them. However, a nine-year-old sales conviction and a five-year-old possession conviction are insufficient to prove petitioner had a readiness to sell narcotics at the time Kalchinian approached him, particularly when we must assume from the record he was trying to overcome the narcotics habit at the time.

The case at bar illustrates an evil which the defense of entrapment is designed to overcome. The government informer entices someone attempting to avoid narcotics not only into carrying out an illegal sale but also into returning to the habit of use. Selecting the proper time, the informer then tells the government agent. The setup is accepted by the agent without even a question as to the manner

"A. I mean by job that nobody hired me for that. That is what I inferred, otherwise I meant the same thing in my answer to your question." R. 100.

3. "Q. But you had made a promise, an agreement, though, to cooperate with the Federal Burea of Narcotics before you received a suspended sentence from the court?

"A. [Kalchinian]. I had promised to cooperate in 1951.

"Q. And that was before your sentence?

"A. Yes, that was before my sentence." R. 99.

Kalchinian received a suspended sentence in 1952 after a statement by the United States Attorney to the Judge that he had been cooperative with the Government. R. 89, 98.

in which the informer encountered the seller. Thus the Government plays on the weaknesses of an innocent party and beguiles him into committing crimes which he otherwise would not have attempted. Law enforcement does not require methods such as this.

It has been suggested that in overturning this conviction we should reassess the doctrine of entrapment according to principles announced in the separate opinion of Mr. Justice Roberts in Sorrells v. United States, 287 U.S. 435, 453, 53 S.Ct. 210, 217, 77 L.Ed. 413. To do so would be to decide the case on grounds rejected by the majority in Sorrells and, so far as the record shows, not raised here or below by the parties before us. We do not ordinarily decide issues not presented by the parties and there is good reason not to vary that practice in this case.

At least two important issues of law enforcement and trial procedure would have to be decided without the benefit of argument by the parties, one party being the Government. Mr. Justice Roberts asserted that although the defendant could claim that the Government had induced him to commit the crime, the Government could not reply by showing that the defendant's criminal conduct was due to his own readiness and not to the persuasion of government agents. The handicap thus placed on the prosecution is obvious.[7] Furthermore, it was the position of Mr. Justice Roberts that the factual issue of entrapment—now limited to the question of what the government agents did—should be decided by the judge, not the jury. Not only was this rejected by the Court in Sorrells, but where the issue has been presented to them, the Courts of Appeals have since Sorrells unanimously concluded that unless it can be decided as a matter of law, the issue of whether a defendant has been entrapped is for the jury as part of its function of determining the guilt or innocence of the accused.

To dispose of this case on the ground suggested would entail both overruling a leading decision of this Court and brushing aside the possibility that we would be creating more problems than we would supposedly be solving.

The judgment of the Court of Appeals is reversed and the case is remanded to the District Court with instructions to dismiss the indictment.

Reversed and remanded.

Mr. Justice FRANKFURTER, whom Mr. Justice DOUGLAS, Mr. Justice HARLAN, and Mr. Justice BRENNAN join, concurring in the result.

7. In the first appeal of this case Judge Learned Hand stated: "Indeed, it would seem probable that, if there were no reply [to the claim of inducement], it would be impossible ever to secure convictions of any offences which consist of transactions that are carried on in secret." United States v. Sherman, 2 Cir., 200 F.2d 880, 882.

Although agreeing with the Court that the undisputed facts show entrapment as a matter of law, I reach this result by a route different from the Court's.

The first case in which a federal court clearly recognized and sustained a claim of entrapment by government officers as a defense to an indictment was, apparently, Woo Wai v. United States, 9 Cir., 223 F. 412. Yet the basis of this defense, affording guidance for its application in particular circumstances, is as much in doubt today as it as when the defense was first recognized over forty years ago, although entrapment has been the decisive issue in many prosecutions. The lower courts have continued gropingly to express the feeling of outrage at conduct of law enforcers that brought recognition of the defense in the first instance, but without the formulated basis in reason that it is the first duty of courts to construct for justifying and guiding emotion and instinct.

Today's opinion does not promote this judicial desideratum, and fails to give the doctrine of entrapment the solid foundation that the decisions of the lower courts and criticism of learned writers have clearly shown is needed. Instead it accepts without re-examination the theory espoused in Sorrells v. United States, 287 U.S. 435, 53 S. Ct. 210, 77 L.Ed. 413, over strong protest by Mr. Justice Roberts, speaking for Brandeis and Stone, JJ., as well as himself. The fact that since the Sorrells case the lower courts have either ignored its theory and continued to rest decision on the narrow facts of each case, or have failed after penetrating effort to define a satisfactory generalization, see, e. g., United States v. Becker, 2 Cir., 62 F.2d 1007 (L. Hand, J.), is proof that the prevailing theory of the Sorrells case ought not to be deemed the last word. In a matter of this kind the Court should not rest on the first attempt at an explanation for what sound instinct counsels. It should not forego re-examination to achieve clarity of thought, because confused and inadequate analysis is too apt gradually to lead to a course of decisions that diverges from the true ends to be pursued.

It is surely sheer fiction to suggest that a conviction cannot be had when a defendant has been entrappped by government officers or informers because "Congress could not have intended that its statutes were to be enforced by tempting innocent persons into violations." In these cases raising claims of entrapment, the only legislative intention that can with any show of reason be extracted from the statute is the intention to make criminal precisely the conduct in which the defendant has engaged. That conduct includes all the elements necessary to constitute criminality. Without compulsion and "knowingly," where that is requisite, the defendant has violated the statutory command. If he is to be relieved from the usual punitive consequences, it is on no account because he is innocent of the offense described. In these circumstances, conduct is not less criminal because the result of temptation, whether the tempter is a private person or a government agent or informer.

The courts refuse to convict an entrapped defendant, not because his conduct falls outside the proscription of the statute, but because, even if his guilt be admitted, the methods employed on behalf of the Government to bring about conviction cannot be countenanced. As Mr. Justice Holmes said in Olmstead v. United States, 277 U.S. 438, 470, 48 S.Ct. 564, 575, 72 L.Ed. 944 (dissenting), in another connection, "It is desirable that criminals should be detected, and to that end that all available evidence should be used. It also is desirable that the government should not itself foster and pay for other crimes, when they are the means by which the evidence is to be obtained. * * * [F]or my part I think it a less evil that some criminals should escape than that the government should play an ignoble part." Insofar as they are used as instrumentalities in the administration of criminal justice, the federal courts have an obligation to set their face against enforcement of the law by lawless means or means that violate rationally vindicated standards of justice, and to refuse to sustain such methods by effectuating them. They do this in the exercise of a recognized jurisdiction to formulate and apply "proper standards for the enforcement of the federal criminal law in the federal courts," McNabb v. United States, 318 U.S. 332, 341, 63 S.Ct. 608, 613, 87 L.Ed. 819, an obligation that goes beyond the conviction of the particular defendant before the court. Public confidence in the fair and honorable administration of justice, upon which ultimately depends the rule of law, is the transcending value at stake.

The formulation of these standards does not in any way conflict with the statute the defendant has violated, or involve the initiation of a judicial policy disregarding or qualifying that framed by Congress. A false choice is put when it is said that either the defendant's conduct does not fall within the statute or he must be convicted. The statute is wholly directed to defining and prohibiting the substantive offense concerned and expresses no purpose, either permissive or prohibitory, regarding the police conduct that will be tolerated in the detection of crime. A statute prohibiting the sale of narcotics is as silent on the question of entrapment as it is on the admissibility of illegally obtained evidence. It is enacted, however, on the basis of certain presuppositions concerning the established legal order and the role of the courts within that system in formulating standards for the administration of criminal justice when Congress itself has not specifically legislated to that end. Specific statutes are to be fitted into an antecedent legal system.

It might be thought that it is largely an academic question whether the court's finding a bar to conviction derives from the statute or from a supervisory jurisdiction over the administration of criminal justice; under either theory substantially the same considerations will determine whether the defense of entrapment is sustained. But to look to a statute for guidance in the application of a policy not remotely within the contemplation of Congress at the time of its enactment is to distort analysis. It is to run the risk, furthermore, that the court will shirk the responsibility that is necessarily in its keeping, if Congress is truly silent, to accommodate the dangers of overzealous law enforcement and civilized methods adequate to counter the ingenuity of modern criminals. The reasons that actually underlie the defense of entrapment can too easily be lost sight of in the pursuit of a wholly fictitious congressional intent.

The crucial question, not easy of answer, to which the court must direct itself is whether the police conduct revealed in the particular case falls below standards, to which common feelings respond, for the proper use of governmental power. For answer it is wholly irrelevant to ask if the "intention" to commit the crime originated with the defendant or government officers, or if the criminal conduct was the product of "the creative activity" of law-enforcement officials. Yet in the present case the Court repeats and purports to apply these unrevealing tests. Of course in every case of this kind the intention that the particular crime be committed originates with the police, and without their inducement the crime would not have occurred. But it is perfectly clear from such decisions as the decoy letter cases in this Court, e. g., Grimm v. United States, 156 U.S. 604, 15 S.Ct. 470, 39 L.Ed. 550, where the police in effect simply furnished the opportunity for the commission of the crime, that this is not enough to enable the defendant to escape conviction.

The intention referred to, therefore, must be a general intention or predisposition to commit, whenever the opportunity should arise, crimes of the kind solicited, and in proof of such a predisposition evidence has often been admitted to show the defendant's reputation, criminal activities, and prior disposition. The danger of prejudice in such a situation, particularly if the issue of entrapment must be submitted to the jury and disposed of by a general verdict of guilty or innocent, is evident. The defendant must either forego the claim of entrapment or run the substantial risk that, in spite of instructions, the jury will allow a criminal record or bad reputation to weigh in its determination of guilt of the specific offense of which he stands charged. Furthermore, a test that looks to the character and predisposition of the defendant rather than the conduct of the police loses sight of the underlying reason for the defense of entrapment. No matter what the defendant's past record and present inclinations to criminality, or the depths to which he has sunk in the estimation of society, certain police conduct to ensnare him into further crime is not to be tolerated by an advanced society. And in the present case it is clear that the Court in fact reverses the conviction because of the conduct of the informer Kalchinian, and not because the Government has failed to draw a convincing picture of petitioner's past criminal conduct. Permissible police activity does not vary according to the particular defendant concerned; surely if two suspects have been solicited at the same time in the same manner, one should not go to jail simply because he has been convicted before and is said to have a criminal disposition. No more does it vary according to the suspicions, reasonable or unreasonable, of the police concerning the defendant's activities. Appeals to sympathy, friendship, the possibility of exorbitant gain, and so forth, can no more be tolerated when directed against a past offender than against an ordinary law-abiding citizen. A contrary view runs afoul of fundamental principles of equality under law, and would espouse the notion that when dealing with the criminal classes anything goes. The possibility that no matter what his past crimes and general disposition the defendant might not have committed the particular crime unless confronted with inordinate inducements, must not be ignored. Past crimes do not forever outlaw the criminal and open him to police practices, aimed at securing his repeated conviction, from which the ordinary citizen is protected. The whole ameliorative hopes of modern penology and prison administration strongly counsel against such a view.

This does not mean that the police may not act so as to detect those engaged in criminal conduct and ready and willing to commit further crimes should the occasion arise. Such indeed is their obligation. It does mean that in holding out inducements they should act in such a manner as is likely to induce to the commission of crime only these persons and not others who would normally avoid crime and through self-struggle resist ordinary temptations. This test shifts attention from the record and predisposition of the particular defendant to the conduct of the police and the likelihood, objectively considered, that it would entrap only those ready and willing to commit crime. It is as objective a test as the subject matter permits, and will give guidance in regulating police conduct that is lacking when the reasonableness of police suspicions must be judged or the criminal disposition of the defendant retrospectively appraised. It draws directly on the fundamental intuition that led in the first instance to the outlawing of "entrapment" as a prosecutorial instrument. The power of government is abused and directed to an end for which it was not constituted when employed to promote rather than detect crime and to bring about the downfall to those who, left to themselves, might well have obeyed the law. Human nature is weak enough and sufficiently beset by temptations without government adding to them and generating crime.

What police conduct is to be condemned, because likely to induce those not otherwise ready and willing to commit crime, must be picked out from case to case as new situations arise involving different crimes and new methods of detection. The Sorrells case involved persistent solicitation in the face of obvious reluctance, and appeals to sentiments aroused by reminiscences of experiences as companions in arms in the World War. Particularly reprehensible in the present case was the use of repeated requests to overcome petitioner's hesitancy, coupled with appeals to sympathy based on mutual experiences with narcotics addiction. Evidence of the setting in which the inducement took place is of course highly relevant in judging its likely effect, and the court should also consider the nature of the crime involved, its secrecy and difficulty of detection, and the manner in which the particular criminal business is usually carried on.

As Mr. Justice Roberts convincingly urged in the Sorrells case, such a judgment, aimed at blocking off areas of impermissible police conduct, is appropriate for the court and not the jury. "The protection of its own functions and the preservation of the purity of its own temple belongs only to the court. It is the province of the court and of the court alone to protect itself and the government from such prostitution of the criminal law. The violation of the principles of justice by the entrapment of the unwary into crime should be dealt with the court no matter by whom or at what stage of the proceedings the facts are brought to its attention." 287 U.S. at page 457, 53 S.Ct. at page 218 (separate opinion). Equally important is the consideration that a jury verdict, although it may settle the issue of entrapment in the particular case, cannot give significant guidance for official conduct for the future. Only the court, through the gradual evolution of explicit standards in accumulated precedents, can do this with the degree of certainty that the wise administration of criminal justice demands.

UNITED STATES v. RUSSELL

United States Supreme Court, 1973.
411 U.S. 423, 93 S.Ct. 1637, 36 L.Ed.2d 366.

Mr. Justice REHNQUIST delivered the opinion of the Court.

Respondent Richard Russell was charged in three counts of a five count indictment returned against him and codefendants John and Patrick Connolly. After a jury trial in the District Court, in which his sole defense was entrapment, respondent was convicted on all three counts of having unlawfully manufactured and processed methamphetamine ("speed") and of having unlawfully sold and delivered that drug in violation of 21 U.S.C.A. §§ 331(q)(1), (2), 360a(a), (b) (Supp. V, 1964). He was sentenced to concurrent terms of two years in prison for each offense, the terms to be suspended on the condition that he spend six months in prison and be placed on probation for the following three years. On appeal the United States Court of Appeals for the Ninth Circuit, one judge dissenting, reversed the conviction solely for the reason that an undercover agent supplied an essential chemical for manufacturing the methamphetamine which formed the basis of respondent's conviction. The court concluded that as a matter of law "a defense to a criminal charge may be founded upon an intolerable degree of governmental participation in the criminal enterprise." United States v. Russell, 459 F.2d 671, 673 (CA9 1972). We granted certiorari, 409 U.S. 911 (1972), and now reverse that judgment.

There is little dispute concerning the essential facts in this case. On December 7, 1969, Joe Shapiro, an undercover agent for the Federal Bureau of Narcotics and Dangerous Drugs, went to respondent's home on Whidbey Island in the State of Washington where he met with respondent and his two codefendants, John and Patrick Connolly. Shapiro's assignment was to locate a laboratory where it was believed that methamphetamine was being manufactured illicitly. He told the respondent and the Connollys that he represented an organization in the Pacific Northwest that was interested in controlling the manufacture and distribution of methamphetamine. He then made an offer to supply the defendants with the chemical phenyl-2-propanone, an essential ingredient in the manufacture of methamphetamine, in return for one-half of the drug produced. This offer was made on the condition that Agent Shapiro be shown a sample of the drug which they were making and the laboratory where it was being produced.

During the conversation Patrick Connolly revealed that he had been making the drug since May 1969 and since then had produced three pounds of it.[2] John Connolly gave the agent a bag containing a quantity of methamphetamine that he represented as being from "the last batch that we made." Shortly thereafter, Shapiro and Patrick Connolly left respondent's house to view the laboratory which was located in the Connolly house on Whidbey Island. At the house Shapiro observed an empty bottle bearing the chemical label phenyl-2-propanone.

By prearrangement Shapiro returned to the Connolly house on December 9, 1969, to supply 100 grams of propanone and observe the chemical reaction. When he arrived he observed Patrick Connolly and the respondent cutting up pieces of aluminum foil and placing them in a large flask. There was testimony that some of the foil pieces accidentally fell on the floor and were picked up by the respondent and Shapiro and put into the flask.[3] Thereafter Patrick Connolly added all of the necessary chemicals, including the propanone brought by Shapiro, to make two batches of methamphetamine. The manufacturing process having been completed the following morning,

2. At trial Patrick Connolly admitted making this statement to Agent Shapiro but asserted that the statement was not true.

3. Agent Shapiro did not otherwise participate in the manufacture of the drug or direct any of the work.

Shapiro was given one-half of the drug and respondent kept the remainder. Shapiro offered to buy, and the respondent agreed to sell, part of the remainder for $60.

About a month later Shapiro returned to the Connolly house and met with Patrick Connolly to ask if he was still interested in their "business arrangement." Connolly replied that he was interested but that he had recently obtained two additional bottles of phenyl-2-propanone and would not be finished with them for a couple of days. He provided some additional methamphetamine to Shapiro at that time. Three days later Shapiro returned to the Connolly house with a search warrant and, among other items, seized an empty 500-gram bottle of propanone and a 100-gram bottle, not the one he had provided, that was partially filled with the chemical.

There was testimony at the trial of respondent and Patrick Connolly that phenyl-2-propanone was generally difficult to obtain. At the request of the Bureau of Narcotics and Dangerous Drugs, some chemical supply firms had voluntarily ceased selling the chemical.

At the close of the evidence, and after receiving the District Judge's standard entrapment instruction, the jury found the respondent guilty on all counts charged. On appeal the respondent conceded that the jury could have found him predisposed to commit the offenses, 459 F.2d at 672, but argued that on the facts presented there was entrapment as a matter of law. The Court of Appeals agreed, although it did not find the District Court had misconstrued or misapplied the traditional standards governing the entrapment defense. Rather, the court in effect expanded the traditional notion of entrapment, which focuses on the predisposition of the defendant, to mandate dismissal of a criminal prosecution whenever the court determines that there has been "an intolerable degree of governmental participation in the criminal enterprise." In this case the court decided that the conduct of the agent in supplying a scarce ingredient essential for the manufacture of a controlled substance established that defense.

This new defense was held to rest on either of two alternative theories. One theory is based on two lower court decisions which have found entrapment, regardless of predisposition, whenever the government supplies contraband to the defendants. United States v. Bueno, 447 F.2d 903 (C.A.5 1971); United States v. Chisum, 312 F. Supp. 1307 (C.D.Cal.1970). The second theory, a nonentrapment rationale, is based on a recent Ninth Circuit decision that reversed a conviction because a government investigator was so enmeshed in the criminal activity that the prosecution of the defendants was held to be repugnant to the American criminal justice system. Greene v. United States, 454 F.2d 783 (C.A.9 1971). The court below held that these two rationales constitute the same defense, and that only the label distinguishes them. In any event, it held that "[b]oth theories are premised on fundamental concepts of due process and evince the reluctance of the judiciary to countenance 'overzealous law enforcement.'" 459 F.2d, at 674, quoting Sherman v. United States, 356 U.S. 369, 381 (1958). (Frankfurter, J., concurring).

* * *

In the instant case respondent asks us to reconsider the theory of the entrapment defense as it is set forth in the majority opinions in *Sorrells* and *Sherman*. His principal contention is that the defense should rest on constitutional grounds. He argues that the level of Shapiro's involvement in the manufacture of the methamphetamine was so high that a criminal prosecution for the drug's manufacture violates the fundamental principles of due process. The respondent contends that the same factors that led this Court to apply the exclusionary rule to illegal searches and seizures, Weeks v. United States, 232 U.S. 383 (1914); Mapp v. Ohio, 367 U.S. 643 (1961), and confessions, Miranda v. Arizona, 384 U.S. 436 (1966), should be considered here. But he would have the Court go further in deterring undesirable official conduct by requiring that any prosecution be barred absolutely because of the police involvement in criminal activity. The analogy is imperfect in any event, for the principal reason behind the adoption of the exclusionary rule was the government's "failure to observe its own laws." Mapp v. Ohio, supra, 367 U.S., at 659. Unlike the situations giving rise to the holdings in *Mapp* and *Miranda*, the government's conduct here violated no independent constitutional right of the respondent. Nor did Shapiro violate any federal statute or rule or commit any crime in infiltrating the respondent's drug enterprise.

Respondent would overcome this basic weakness in his analogy to the exclusionary rule cases by having the Court adopt a rigid constitutional rule that would preclude any prosecution when it is shown that the criminal product would not have been possible had not an undercover agent "supplied an indispensable means to the commission of the crime that could not have been obtained otherwise, through legal or illegal channels." * * *

The record discloses that although the propanone was difficult to obtain it was by no means impossible. The defendants admitted making the drug both before and after those batches made with the propanone supplied by Shapiro. Shapiro testified that he saw an empty bottle labeled phenyl-2-propanone on his first visit to the laboratory on December 7, 1969. And when the laboratory was searched pursuant to a search warrant on January 10, 1970, two additional bottles labeled phenyl-2-propanone were seized. Thus, the facts in the record amply demonstrate that the propanone used in the illicit manufacture of methamphetamine not only *could* have been obtained without the intervention of Shapiro but was in fact obtained by these defendants.

While we may some day be presented with a situation in which the conduct of law enforcement agents is so outrageous that due process principles would absolutely bar the government from invoking judicial processes to obtain a conviction, cf. Rochin v. California, 342 U.S. 165 (1952), the instant case is distinctly not of that breed. Shapiro's contribution of propanone to the criminal enterprise already in process was scarcely objectionable. The chemical is by itself a harmless substance and its possession is legal. While the government may have been seeking to make it more difficult for drug rings, such as that of which respondent was a member, to obtain the chemical, the evidence described above shows that it nonetheless was obtainable. The law enforcement conduct here stops far short of violating that "fundamental fairness, shocking to the universal sense of justice," mandated by the Due Process Clause of the Fifth Amendment. Kinsella v. United States ex rel. Singleton, 361 U.S. 234, 246 (1960).

The illicit manufacture of drugs is not a sporadic, isolated criminal incident, but a continuing, though illegal, business enterprise. In order to obtain convictions for illegally manufacturing drugs, the gathering of evidence of past unlawful conduct frequently proves to be an all but impossible task. Thus in drug-related offenses law enforcement personnel have turned to one of the only practicable means of detection: the infiltration of drug rings and a limited participation in their unlawful present practices. Such infiltration is a recognized and permissible means of apprehension; if that be so, then the supply of some item of value that the drug ring requires must, as a general rule, also be permissible. For an agent will not be taken into the confidence of the illegal entrepreneurs unless he has something of value to offer them. Law enforcement tactics such as this can hardly be said to violate "fundamental fairness" or "shocking to the universal sense of justice," *Kinsella*, supra.

Respondent also urges as an alternative to his constitutional argument, that * * * the views of Justices Roberts and Frankfurter, concurring in *Sorrells* and *Sherman*, respectively, which make the essential element of the defense turn on the type and degree of governmental conduct, be adopted as the law.

We decline to overrule these cases. *Sorrells* is a precedent of long standing that has already been once reexamined in *Sherman* and implicitly there reaffirmed. Since the defense is not of a constitutional dimension, Congress may address itself to the question and adopt any substantive definition of the defense that it may find desirable.

* * *

* * * [I]t [does not] seem particularly desirable for the law to grant complete immunity from prosecution to one who himself

planned to commit a crime, and then committed it, simply because government undercover agents subjected him to inducements which might have seduced a hypothetical individual who was not so predisposed. We are content to leave the matter where it was left by the Court in *Sherman* * * *[.]

Several decisions of the United States district courts and courts of appeals have undoubtedly gone beyond this Court's opinions in *Sorrells* and *Sherman* in order to bar prosecutions because of what they thought to be for want of a better term "overzealous law enforcement." But the defense of entrapment enunciated in those opinions was not intended to give the federal judiciary a "chancellor's foot" veto over law enforcement practices of which it did not approve. The execution of the federal laws under our Constitution is confided primarily to the Executive Branch of the Government, subject to applicable constitutional and statutory limitations and to judicially fashioned rules to enforce those limitations. We think that the decision of the Court of Appeals in this case quite unnecessarily introduces an unmanageably subjective standard which is contrary to the holdings of this Court in *Sorrells* and *Sherman*.

Those cases establish that entrapment is a relatively limited defense. It is rooted not in any authority of the Judicial Branch to dismiss prosecutions for what it feels to have been "overzealous law enforcement," but instead in the notion that Congress could not have intended criminal punishment for a defendant who has committed all the elements of a prescribed offense, but who was induced to commit them by the government.

* * * It is only when the government's deception actually implants the criminal design in the mind of the defendant that the defense of entrapment comes into play.

Respondent's concession in the Court of Appeals that the jury finding as to predisposition was supported by the evidence is, therefore, fatal to his claim of entrapment. He was an active participant in an illegal drug manufacturing enterprise which began before the government agent appeared on the scene, and continued after the government agent had left the scene. He was, in the words of *Sherman*, supra, not an "unwary innocent" but an "unwary criminal." The Court of Appeals was wrong, we believe, when it sought to broaden the principle laid down in *Sorrells* and *Sherman*. Its judgment is therefore

Reversed.

[The dissenting opinion of Mr. Justice Douglas, with Mr. Justice Brennan concurring, is omitted.]

Mr. Justice STEWART, with whom Mr. Justice BRENNAN and Mr. Justice MARSHALL join, dissenting.

* * *

In my view [the] objective approach to entrapment advanced by the concurring opinions in *Sorrells* and *Sherman* is the only one truly consistent with the underlying rationale of the defense.

In the case before us, I think that the District Court erred in submitting the issue of entrapment to the jury, with instructions to acquit only if it had a reasonable doubt as to the respondent's predisposition to committing the crime. Since, under the objective test of entrapment, predisposition is irrelevant and the issue is to be decided by the trial judge, the Court of Appeals, I believe, would have been justified in reversing the conviction on this basis alone. But since the appellate court did not remand for consideration of the issue by the District Judge under an objective standard, but rather found entrapment as a matter of law and directed that the indictment be dismissed, we must reach the merits of the respondent's entrapment defense.

Since, in my view, it does not matter whether the respondent was predisposed to commit the offense of which he was convicted, the focus must be, rather, on the conduct of the undercover government agent. What the agent did here was to meet with a group of suspected producers of methamphetamine, including the respondent; to request the drug; to offer to supply the chemical phenyl-2-propanone in exchange for one-half of the methamphetamine to be manufactured therewith; and, when that offer was accepted, to provide the needed chemical ingredient, and to purchase some of the drug from the respondent.

It is undisputed that phenyl-2-propanone is an essential ingredient in the manufacture of methamphetamine; that it is not used for any other purpose; and that, while its sale is not illegal, it is difficult to obtain, because a manufacturer's license is needed to purchase it, and because many suppliers, at the request of the Federal Bureau of Narcotics and Dangerous Drugs, do not sell it at all. It is also undisputed that the methamphetamine which the respondent was prosecuted for manufacturing and selling was all produced on December 10, 1969, and that all the phenyl-2-propanone used in the manufacture of that batch of the drug was provided by the government agent. In these circumstances, the agent's undertaking to supply this ingredient to the respondent, thus making it possible for the Government to prosecute him for manufacturing an illicit drug with it, was, I think, precisely the type of governmental conduct that the entrapment defense is meant to prevent.

Although the Court of Appeals found that the phenyl-2-propanone could not have been obtained without the agent's intervention

—that "there could not have been the manufacture, delivery, or sale of the illicit drug had it not been for the Government's supply of one of the essential ingredients," 459 F.2d 671, 672—the Court today rejects this finding as contradicted by the facts revealed at trial. The record, as the Court states, discloses that one of the respondent's accomplices, though not the respondent himself, had obtained phenyl-2-propanone from independent sources both before and after receiving the agent's supply, and had used it in the production of methamphetamine. This demonstrates, it is said, that the chemical was obtainable other than through the government agent; and hence the agent's furnishing it for the production of the methamphetamine involved in this prosecution did no more than afford an opportunity for its production to one ready and willing to produce it. Thus, the argument seems to be, there was no entrapment here, any more than there would have been if the agent had furnished common table salt, had that been necessary to the drug's production.

It cannot be doubted that if phenyl-2-propanone had been wholly unobtainable from other sources, the agent's undercover offer to supply it to the respondent in return for part of the illicit methamphetamine produced therewith—an offer initiated and carried out by the agent for the purpose of prosecuting the respondent for producing methamphetamine—would be precisely the type of governmental conduct that constitutes entrapment under any definition. For the agent's conduct in that situation would make possible the commission of an otherwise totally impossible crime, and, I should suppose, would thus be a textbook example of instigating the commission of a criminal offense in order to prosecute someone for committing it.

But assuming in this case that the phenyl-2-propanone was obtainable through independent sources, the fact remains that that used for the particular batch of methamphetamine involved in all three counts of the indictment with which the respondent was charged—i. e., that produced on December 10, 1969—was supplied by the Government. This essential ingredient was indisputably difficult to obtain, and yet that used in committing the offenses of which the respondent was convicted was offered to the respondent by the government agent, on the agent's own initiative, and was readily supplied to the respondent in needed amounts. If the chemical was so easily available elsewhere, then why did not the agent simply wait until the respondent had himself obtained the ingredients and produced the drug, and then buy it from him? The very fact that the agent felt it incumbent upon him to offer to supply phenyl-2-propanone in return for the drug casts considerable doubt on the theory that the chemical could easily have been procured without the agent's intervention, and that therefore the agent merely afforded an opportunity for the commission of a criminal offense.

In this case, the chemical ingredient was available only to licensed persons, and the Government itself had requested suppliers not to sell that ingredient even to people with a license. Yet the government agent readily offered and supplied that ingredient to an unlicensed person and asked him to make a certain illegal drug with it. The Government then prosecuted that person for making the drug produced *with the very ingredient* which its agent had so helpfully supplied. This strikes me as the very pattern of conduct that should be held to constitute entrapment as a matter of law.

It is the Government's duty to prevent crime, not to promote it. Here, the Government's agent asked that the illegal drug be produced for him, solved his quarry's practical problems with the assurance that he could provide the one essential ingredient that was difficult to obtain, furnished that element as he had promised, and bought the finished product from the respondent—all so that the respondent could be prosecuted for producing and selling the very drug for which the agent had asked and for which he had provided the necessary component. Under the objective approach that I would follow, this respondent was entrapped, regardless of his predisposition or "innocence."

In the words of Mr. Justice ROBERTS:

> "The applicable principle is that courts must be closed to the trial of a crime instigated by the government's own agents. No other issue, no comparison of equities as between the guilty official and the guilty defendant, has any place in the enforcement of this overruling principle of public policy." Sorrells v. United States, supra, at 459.

I would affirm the judgment of the Court of Appeals.

NOTES AND QUESTIONS

1. In Hampton v. United States, 425 U.S. 484, 96 S.Ct. 1646, 48 L.Ed. 2d 113 (1976), Hampton testified that a federal informant had provided the heroin which Hampton was charged with selling and had initially suggested selling it. The trial court refused to instruct the jury that Hampton should be acquitted if the jury found that the heroin had been supplied to Hampton by a government informer. Hampton was convicted and he appealed. The Supreme Court affirmed. Justice Rehnquist, in the plurality opinion, held that Hampton's predisposition rendered entrapment unavailable to him and even if his testimony were accurate none of his federal constitutional rights had been violated. Justice Powell, joined by Justice Blackmun, con-

curred but indicated an unwillingness to join some of Justice Rehnquist's language rejecting the likelihood that outrageous police behavior in such situations might offend due process. Justice Brennan, joined by Justices Stewart and Marshall, dissented on the ground that either due process or federal entrapment doctrine should bar conviction where the subject of the charge is the sale of contraband provided to the defendant by a government agent.

2. In State v. Sainz, 84 N.M. 259, 261, 501 P.2d 1247, 1249 (Ct.App. 1972), the New Mexico Court of Appeals adopted the following formulation of the entrapment defense:

> When the state's participation in the criminal enterprise reaches the point where it can be said that except for the conduct of the state a crime would probably not have been committed or because the conduct is such that it is likely to induce those to commit a crime who would normally avoid crime, *or, if the conduct is such that if allowed to continue would shake the public's confidence in the fair and honorable administration of justice,* this then becomes entrapment as a matter of law. (emphasis supplied).

The court further noted agreement with the proposition that as the state's participation in a criminal enterprise increases, the importance of the defendant's predisposition and intent decreases. Id. Does this standard—especially the emphasized portion—go beyond the Model Penal Code formulation? Does it appear to use the entrapment defense to promote interests other than the prevention of criminal acts that would not occur except for government activity? Sainz was overruled by the New Mexico Supreme Court in State v. Fiechter, 89 N.M. 74, 547 P.2d 557 (1976). See State v. Paiz, 91 N.M. 5, 569 P.2d 415 (Ct.App.1977) (state supreme court urged to review *Fiechter's* overruling of *Sainz*).

3. Consider the following proposal made by the American Civil Liberties Union in its Report of its testimony before the Senate Subcommittee on Criminal Law and Procedure on the Final Report of the National Commission on Reform of the Federal Criminal Laws 37–38 (March 21, 1972):

> **§ 702. Entrapment**
>
> (1) *Defense.* It is a defense that the defendant was entrapped into committing the offense.
>
> (2) *Entrapment Defined.* Entrapment occurs (i) when a law enforcement agent induces the commission of an offense, using persuasion or other means likely to cause normally law abiding persons to commit the offense; or (ii) when the criminal design originates with a law enforcement agent and he implants in the mind of an innocent person the disposition to commit an offense and induce its commission in order that the government may prosecute; or (iii) when the law enforcement agent induces the criminal act without reasonable suspicion [probable cause] that the person being solicited to commit an offense or with whom an illegal transaction is initiated is engaged in or prepared to engage in such

offense or transaction. Conduct merely affording a person an opportunity to commit an offense does not constitute entrapment.

(3) The defense afforded by this section may be raised under a plea of not guilty. The defendant shall be entitled to have the issue of entrapment decided by the court and to have the fact that the defense has been raised and evidence introduced in support thereof kept from the attention of the jury. Evidence of the defendant's past criminal conduct is inadmissible on the entrapment issue.

(4) *Law Enforcement Agent Defined.* In this section "law enforcement agent" includes personnel of state and local law enforcement agencies as well as of the United States, and any person cooperating with such an agency.

4. It is often held that a defendant may not deny commission of the crime charged and also assert entrapment. This rule may even be applied to require that a defendant take the stand and admit commission of the acts constituting the crime before entrapment will be regarded as having been raised. See State v. Montano, 117 Ariz. 145, 571 P.2d 291 (1977). Although there is no general prohibition against criminal defendants asserting inconsistent matters, the special rule applied to entrapment cases is defended on the ground that denial of the acts constituting the crime and assertion of entrapment is *too* inconsistent to be acceptable. See United States v. Greenfield, 554 F.2d 179, 182 (5th Cir. 1977). Can it be argued that there is a reasonable basis for requiring that a defendant who wishes to put entrapment (and therefore his own predisposition) into issue take the witness stand and subject himself to questioning concerning the issues made relevant by his claim of entrapment?

D. LAW ENFORCEMENT AND RELATED MATTERS

The most frequent application of the "defense" of law enforcement involves the use of force to make an arrest. Traditionally, a peace officer or a private person aiding an officer may use force to effect the arrest or prevent the escape of one reasonably believed to have committed an offense. Only nondeadly force may be used if the suspected offense is only a misdemeanor but deadly force may be used if the subject is reasonably believed to have committed a felony. The principal case in this subsection, Mattis v. Schnarr, poses the question of whether a more limited right to use deadly force is appropriate and perhaps constitutionally necessary. *Mattis* is not a criminal prosecution but rather is a civil action for damages, based on the allegation that the officers exceeded their legal right in using force and thereby exposed themselves to criminal liability. If the officers did exceed their right to use force to effect an arrest, however, they would be subject to criminal charges for their activity as well as to civil damages.

MATTIS v. SCHNARR

United States Court of Appeals for the Eighth Circuit, 1976.
547 F.2d 1007.

HEANEY, Circuit Judge, with whom LAY, BRIGHT and ROSS, Circuit Judges, concur.

This appeal concerns the constitutionality of Missouri statutes [1] which permit law enforcement officers to use deadly force to effect the arrest of a person who has committed a felony if the person has been notified that he or she is under arrest and if the force used is restricted to that reasonably necessary to effect the arrest.[2] We hold the statutes unconstitutional as applied to arrests in which an officer uses deadly force against a fleeing felon who has not used deadly force in the commission of the felony and whom the officer does not reasonably believe will use deadly force against the officer or others if not immediately apprehended.

The challenge to the constitutionality of the Missouri statutes arose out of the killing of Michael Mattis by Robert Marek, a police officer.

Michael Mattis, age eighteen, and Thomas Rolf, age seventeen, were discovered in the office of a golf driving range at approximately 1:20 A.M. by police officer, Richard Schnarr. Shortly thereafter, the two boys left the office by climbing out through the back window. Schnarr shouted at the boys to halt. They ran in different directions. Schnarr then shouted, "Halt or I'll shoot" two times. When the boys failed to stop, he fired one shot into the air and one shot at Rolf. Meanwhile, Officer Robert Marek, who had arrived on the scene, ran to intercept the boys. He collided with Mattis as he came around the corner of the building. Both fell to the pavement. Marek grabbed Mattis by the leg. Mattis broke away. Marek ran after

1. *Justifiable Homicide*

Homicide shall be deemed justifiable when committed by any person in either of the following cases:

* * *

(3) When necessarily committed in attempting by lawful ways and means to apprehend any person for any felony committed, or in lawfully * * * keeping or preserving the peace.

V.A.M.S. § 559.040.

Rights of officer in making arrests

If, after notice of the intention to arrest the defendant, he either flee or forcibly resist, the officer may use all necessary means to effect the arrest.

V.A.M.S. § 544.190.

2. "Deadly force" is not defined in either of the challenged statutes. We use the term in this opinion as it is used in the Model Penal Code § 3.11(2) (1962) [reprinted at page 533, supra] * * *. *See also* Comment, *Deadly Force to Arrest: Triggering Constitutional Review*, 11 Harv.Civ.Rights-Civ.Lib.L.Rev. 361, 363 (1976) [hereinafter cited as Comment, 11 Harv.Civ.Rights-Civ.Lib.L.Rev. 361]:

[D]eadly force is such force as under normal circumstances poses a high risk of death or serious injury to its human target, regardless of whether or not death, serious injury or any harm actually results in a given case.

him. Marek was losing ground. He shouted, "Stop or I'll shoot." Mattis did not stop. Marek, believing it was necessary to take further action to prevent Mattis's escape, fired one shot in the direction of Mattis and killed him. Both officers believed that the use of their guns was reasonably necessary to effect an arrest and was authorized by valid Missouri statutes.

Robert Dean Mattis, the father of Michael, brought an action against the officers and the City of Olivette under 42 U.S.C.A. §§ 1983 and 1988, V.A.M.S. § 537.080, 28 U.S.C.A. §§ 1343(4), 2201 and 2202, and the Constitution of the United States, Amendments XIV, VIII and IX. It is alleged in the complaint that the officers, acting under color of law, deprived Michael Mattis of his life without due process of law, deprived him of equal protection of the laws in violation of the Fourteenth Amendment to the Constitution, and inflicted a cruel and unusual punishment on him in violation of the Fourteenth, Eighth and Ninth Amendments of the Constitution. The court was asked to declare V.A.M.S. §§ 559.040 and 544.190 unconstitutional * * *. The State of Missouri filed an answer admitting that Michael Mattis was shot and killed by Officer Marek while Mattis was attempting to escape from an arrest sought to be made on suspicion of burglary, a felony under Missouri law. The answer also asserted that V.A.M.S. §§ 559.040 and 544.190, as construed by the Supreme Court of Missouri to authorize the use of deadly force by police officers if reasonably necessary to prevent a felon but not a misdemeanant from escaping, are constitutional.

The District Court entered a judgment upholding the constitutionality of the statutes. * * * Mattis v. Schnarr, 404 F.Supp. 643, 646–647 (E.D.Mo.1975).

* * *

This appeal followed.

We emphasize initially that no claim is made that the statutes are unconstitutional insofar as they permit police officers to use deadly force where reasonably necessary to effect the arrest of a fleeing felon who has used or has threatened to use deadly force in the commission of the felony for which he or she is being apprehended or insofar as they permit such force to be used to apprehend a fleeing felon whom the officers reasonably believe will use deadly force against the arresting officers or others if he or she is not immediately apprehended. The claim is the narrower one that the statutes are unconstitutional as applied to fleeing felons suspected of a nonviolent felony whom the officers do not reasonably believe will use deadly force against the officers or others.

We also emphasize that we are not concerned in this case with whether the force used was that reasonably necessary to effect the immediate arrest of the fleeing Michael Mattis. It was necessary if

Michael was to be apprehended at that time. The question is, rather, whether deadly force could constitutionally be used to effect the arrest of this fleeing eighteen-year-old burglar who threatened no one's life during the commission of the burglary and posed no threat to the apprehending officers or others.

With the issue thus defined, we turn to a brief discussion of common and statutory law, scholarly opinion and present police practice with respect to the use of deadly force.

At common law, deadly force could be used by a law enforcement officer if necessary to effect the arrest of a felony suspect but not of a suspected misdemeanant.[7] While the rule has been severely criticized by legal scholars, most jurisdictions governed by common law have continued to adhere to the distinction. * * *

At least twenty-four states, including five in this Circuit—Arkansas, Iowa, Minnesota, Missouri, South Dakota—codify the common law and provide that deadly force may be used to arrest any felony suspect. Seven states depart from the common law by specifying the felonies for which deadly force may be used to arrest or by stating that only "forcible felonies" justify the use of deadly force. North Dakota permits a law enforcement officer to use deadly force if that force is necessary to effect an arrest of a person who has committed or attempted to commit a felony "involving violence, or is attempting to escape by the use of a deadly weapon, or has otherwise indicated that he is likely to endanger human life or to inflict serious bodily injury unless apprehended without delay." N.D.Cent.Code § 12.1–05–07(2)(d) (1975). Another seven states, including Nebraska of this Circuit, have adopted the Model Penal Code approach, which permits the use of deadly force only when the crime for which the arrest is made involves conduct including use or threatened use of deadly force or when there is a substantial risk that the person to be arrested will cause death or serious bodily harm if his apprehension is delayed.[12]

7. This rule reflected the social and legal context of felonies in 15th century England and 18th century America. Since all felonies—murder, rape, manslaughter, robbery, sodomy, mayhem, burglary, arson, prison break, and larceny—were punished by death, the use of deadly force was seen as merely accelerating the penal process, albeit without providing a trial. "It made little difference if the suspected felon were killed in the process of capture, since, in the eyes of the law, he had already forfeited his life by committing the felony." It was also assumed that a suspected felon facing death upon capture was more desperate than a misdemeanant and that greater force was required for his apprehension. Finally, because there was no network of police forces a felon eluding his initial pursuers would probably escape ultimate arrest.

12. § 3.07 Use of Force in Law Enforcement

(1) *Use of Force Justifiable to Effect an Arrest.* * * * [T]he use of force upon or towards the person of another is justified when the actor is making * * * an arrest and the actor believes that such force is immediately necessary to effect a lawful arrest.

The President's Commission on Law Enforcement and Administration of Justice, the National Commission on Reform of Federal Criminal Laws, and legal scholars whose writings span the last five decades generally support a rule which would limit the use of deadly force by police officers to those circumstances where the use of force is essential to the protection of human life and bodily security, or where violence was used in committing the felony.

The reasons advanced by the President's Commission are particularly important. The Commission found, through its studies, that

> [p]olice use of firearms to apprehend suspects often strains community relations or even results in serious disturbances. * * *
>
> When studied objectively and unemotionally, particular uses of firearms by police officers are often unwarranted.
>
> * * *
>
> It is essential that all departments formulate written firearms policies which clearly limit their use to situations of strong and compelling need. * * *
>
> 1. Deadly force should be restricted to the apprehension of perpetrators who, in the course of their crime threatened the use of deadly force, or if the officer believes there is a substantial risk that the person whose arrest is sought will cause death or serious bodily harm if this apprehension is delayed. The use of firearms should be flatly prohibited in the apprehension of misdemeanants, since the value of human life far outweighs the gravity of a misdemeanor.
>
> * * *
>
> 5. Officers should be allowed to use any necessary force, including deadly force, to protect themselves or other persons from death or serious injury. In such cases, it is immaterial whether the attacker has committed a serious felony, a misdemeanor, or any crime at all.

(2) *Limitations on the Use of Force.*

* * *

(b) The use of deadly force is not justified under this Section unless:

(i) the arrest is for a felony; and

(ii) the person effecting the arrest is authorized to act as a peace officer or is assisting a person whom he believes to be authorized to act as a peace officer; and

(iii) the actor believes that the force employed creates no substantial risk of injury to innocent persons; and

(iv) the actor believes that:

(1) the crime for which the arrest is made involved conduct including the use or threatened use of deadly force; or

(2) there is a substantial risk that the person to be arrested will cause death or serious bodily harm if his apprehension is delayed. * * *

The President's Commission on Law Enforcement and Administration of Justice, Task Force Report: The Police, 189, 190 (1967) (footnote omitted).

More recent studies indicate that an important factor in increasing community tensions is that there is often a disproportionate use of deadly force against non-white suspects.[15]

* * *

However, it is not for this Court to decide whether the Missouri statutes are wise or not. The sole question before this Court is whether the statutes are unconstitutional. We hold they are.

We are concerned with the right of an individual to life, expressly recognized in the due process clauses of the Fifth and Fourteenth Amendments to the United States Constitution, which respectively ordain:

> No person shall * * * be deprived of life, liberty, or property, without due process of law[.]

U.S.Const. Amend. V; and

> nor shall any State deprive any person of life, liberty, or property, without due process of law[.]

U.S.Const. Amend. XIV.

Clearly, the right to life is "fundamental," and has often been so recognized in the equal protection and due process contexts.

* * *

If we were to read the due process clause literally, we would have to conclude that life could never be taken without a trial. Such a literal reading would fail to recognize the interests of the state in protecting the lives and safety of its citizens.

The District Court properly recognized that the situations in which the state can take a life, without according a trial to the individual whose life is taken, are to be determined by balancing the in-

15. The Metropolitan Applied Research Center, Inc., conducted a study, in 1974, which showed that of 248 persons killed by the New York City Police from 1970 through 1973, seventy-three percent were black or Puerto Rican and under thirty years of age.

A similar study conducted of the Chicago Police Department, entitled The Police and Their Use of Fatal Force, concluded:

> Blacks were more than six times as likely to die at the hands of police as were whites during the period surveyed.
>
> [I]ndividuals under 25 remained twice as likely to die at the hands of the police as those over 25.

Id. at 27.

From 1950 through 1960, the death rate for blacks at the hands of police was nine times higher than that for whites in Akron, Chicago, Kansas City, Miami, Buffalo, Philadelphia, Boston and Milwaukee. Robin, Justifiable Homicide By Police Officers, 54 J. of Crim.L., Criminology and Police Science 225, 229 (1963). In any given year, an Akron police officer was forty-five times more likely to kill a fleeing felon than a Boston police officer. Id.

terests of society in guaranteeing the right to life of an individual against the interest of society in insuring public safety. It went on to hold that the task of determining how the balance should be struck was exclusively within the province of the legislature. It is with the latter statement that we disagree. The legislature has an important role to play in the balancing process, but the court has the ultimate responsibility to determine whether the balance struck is a constitutional one.

Because we deal with a fundamental right, the Missouri statutes can be sustained only if they protect a compelling state interest and are "narrowly drawn to express only the legitimate state interests at stake." Roe v. Wade [410 U.S. 113, 155, 93 S.Ct. 705, 728, 35 L.Ed. 2d 147 (1973)]. The state, in this case, must demonstrate the existence of an interest equivalent to, or greater than, the right to life to justify the use of deadly force against fleeing felons. No such demonstration has been made here. Rather, the statute creates a conclusive presumption that all fleeing felons pose a danger to the bodily security of the arresting officers and of the general public. The presumption is incorrect in its application to the facts of this case and has not otherwise been shown to be factually based. We find nothing in this record, in the briefs of the parties or of the Attorney General, in scholarly literature, in the reports of distinguished study commissions, or in the experience of the nation's law enforcement agencies, to support the contention of the state that statutes as broad as these deter crime, insure public safety or protect life. Felonies are infinite in their complexity, ranging from the violent to the victimless. The police officer cannot be constitutionally vested with the power and authority to kill any and all escaping felons, including the thief who steals an ear of corn, as well as one who kills and ravishes at will. For the reasons we have outlined, the officer is required to use a reasonable and informed professional judgment, remaining constantly aware that death is the ultimate weapon of last resort, to be employed only in situations presenting the gravest threat to either the officer or the public at large. Thus, we have no alternative but to find V.A.M.S. §§ 559.040 and 544.190 unconstitutional in that they permit police officers to use deadly force to apprehend a fleeing felon who has used no violence in the commission of the felony and who does not threaten the lives of either the arresting officers or others.

It is not for this Court to write new statutes for the State of Missouri. We can only say that the statutes would be constitutional if carefully drawn to limit the use of deadly force by law enforcement officers in the apprehension of fleeing felons to situations where the officer has a warrant or probable cause to arrest the felon where the felon could not be otherwise apprehended and where the felon had used deadly force in the commission of the felony, or the officer reasonably believed the felon would use deadly force against the officer or others if not immediately apprehended.

GIBSON, Chief Judge, dissenting, joined by STEPHENSON and HENLEY, Circuit Judges.

* * *

* * * I find no justification for the majority's deviation from the approach taken by all other courts faced with this issue. Judicial self-restraint may not be relaxed by the simple expedient of labelling clear questions of public policy as questions of constitutional law. Most issues of public policy have constitutional implications, but they are not thereby automatically removed from the legislative province and placed in the hands of the courts.

An examination of the history of the American Law Institute's experience in attempting to modify the common law rule on the use of deadly force to effect arrest also supports the conclusion that the issue at stake in the present case is one of public policy appropriate for the legislature, not the judiciary. In 1934 the ALI, in its First Restatement of Torts, modified the common law principle permitting the use of deadly force to effect the arrest of a felon. Restatement (First) of Torts § 131 (1934). This modification was abandoned in 1948, however, and the common law rule was readopted. The 1966 Appendix to the Second Restatement of Torts justifies this abandonment on the grounds that the modification contained in § 131 had, from its inception, lacked any support other than dicta and argument by analogy. Moreover, in 1966, no case could be found which had cited § 131 or had been in accord with it.

Significantly, however, the ALI's abandonment of proposed modifications of the common law rule on the use of deadly force was limited to the Restatement. In drafting the Model Penal Code, the ALI did not hesitate to propose that the common law rule be legislatively modified. According to the majority opinion, * * * at least seven states have now chosen to legislatively adopt Model Penal Code § 3.07 on the use of deadly force in effecting an arrest. It is ironic that the majority, which cites the Model Penal Code extensively and clearly relies on Model Penal Code § 3.07 in suggesting what sort of statute it would consider proper, ignores the fact that the ALI drafted the Model Penal Code as a proposal of legislative, not judicial, modification of the common law. The majority would now judicially legislate it.

* * *

Indeed, the sensitivity of this issue is easily blurred by a single-minded focus on the seemingly absolute right of an individual to life. An individual's right to life is, however, beset with many obstacles, limitations and contradictions. Life is not permanent; it is subject to obliteration by accidents, inadvertence and by the hazards of everyday living. There is no constitutional right to commit felonious offenses and to escape the consequences of those offenses. There is no constitutional right to flee from officers lawfully exercising their authority in apprehending fleeing felons.

To measure the constitutionality of the Missouri statutes here, the individual's right must be weighed against the interests of the state. Rather than identifying the state interests involved here, however, the majority simply concludes that the state has failed to show an interest equivalent to the right to life. Thus, the majority balances a specific individual right to life against amorphous, unidentified state interests and, not surprisingly, finds the right to life to be weightier. I believe that the state's interests must be identified before a proper constitutional balancing can be made. These interests include effective law enforcement, the apprehension of criminals, the prevention of crime and the protection of members of the general populace, who, like fleeing felons, also possess a right to life.

Furthermore, I consider the majority's proposed modification of the common law rule a remarkably impractical means of balancing the interests and rights at stake. [The majority's proposed standard] * * * presupposes that law enforcement officers are endowed not only with foresight, but also with that most characteristic judicial vision, hindsight. The majority does not suggest how law enforcement officers are to make the on-the-spot constitutional analysis called for by its proposal and still react quickly enough to meet the exigencies of an emergency situation. How can a police officer ever know, reasonably or otherwise, whether the felon will use force against others if not immediately apprehended? It is clearly the prerogative of the state legislature to decide whether such restrictions on the use of force are consonant with public policy.

Ultimately it seems that we have at conflict the interest of the state in effectively bringing felony suspects to answer charges against them and the interest of the felony suspect in being brought to submission, if at all, with the greatest degree of protection of his safety. I think it is not our duty, upon the legislative facts before us, to balance those conflicting interests and if it is, I cannot agree that on balance the choice made by the legislature of Missouri is an impermissible one. The state is not required to adopt a policy which might encourage the fleet of foot and the foolhardy felon or to reject a policy of apprehending suspects by use of all reasonable force.

For the foregoing reasons I am unable to join in the majority opinion.

NOTES AND QUESTIONS

1. On further appeal by the State of Missouri to the United States Supreme Court, the Court refused to consider the merits of the Court of Appeals' ruling that the Missouri statute is unconstitutional. Noting that

no award of damages or other present right would be affected by a ruling on the statute's validity, the Court found that the case did not present a "case or controversy." The judgment of the Court of Appeals was therefore vacated and the case was remanded to the District Court with instructions to dismiss the complaint. Ashcroft v. Mattis, 431 U.S. 171, 97 S.Ct. 1739, 52 L.Ed.2d 219 (1977).

2. Suppose that Michael Mattis had been shot by a private citizen rather than a police officer. Under what circumstances should the private citizen be privileged to use force to effectuate a "citizen's arrest?" The traditional rules governing the validity of citizens' arrests and the use of force to make those arrests was summarized in United States v. Hillsman, 522 F.2d 454, 460–61 (7th Cir. 1974), cert. denied 423 U.S. 1035, 96 S.Ct. 570, 46 L.Ed.2d 410 (1975):

> Indiana follows the general common law rule that "a private citizen has the right to arrest one who has committed a felony in his presence, and may even arrest one he reasonably believes to have committed a felony, so long as the felony was in fact committed." * * * Where a felony of violence has been committed, moreover, a private citizen may use reasonable force, including deadly force, to prevent the felon's escape from the scene. * * *
>
> The private citizen's right to make an arrest, however, is limited by the fact that he, unlike a police officer, acts at his peril. A police officer has the right to arrest without a warrant where he reasonably believes that a felony has been committed and that the person arrested is guilty, even if, in fact, no felony has occurred. A private citizen, on the other hand, is privileged to make an arrest only when he has reasonable grounds for believing in the guilt of the person arrested and a felony has *in fact* been committed.

Several courts have imposed even greater limitations upon the right of private citizens to use force in the arrest situation. In Commonwealth v. Chermansky, 430 Pa. 170, 173–74, 242 A.2d 237, 240 (1968), the court explained:

> The common law principle that a killing necessary to prevent the escape of a felon developed at a time when the distinction between felony and misdemeanor was very different than it is today. Statutory expansion of the class of felonies has made the common law rule manifestly inadequate for modern law. Hence, the need for a change or limitation in the rule is indicated. We therefore hold that from this date forward the use of deadly force by a private person in order to prevent the escape of one who has committed a felony * * * is justified only if the felony committed is treason, murder, voluntary manslaughter, mayhem, arson, robbery, common law rape, common law burglary, kidnapping, assault with intent to murder, rape or rob, or a felony which normally causes or threatens death or great bodily harm.

See also Commonwealth v. Klein, 372 Mass. 823, 363 N.E.2d 1313 (1977), adopting § 3.07 of the Model Penal Code (reprinted at page 580, supra) as the standard for determining the right of a private person to use force to effect an arrest. In *Chermansky,* the court carefully preserved prior law requiring proof that one of the felonies in fact was committed and that the person injured or killed committed it. Both courts also were persuaded that the defendants before them should not be held to have had knowledge of the "possible criminality" of their use of force to effect an arrest and consequently directed that the new and limited standards be applied only to actions taken after the decision of the appellate court.

What justification is there for providing private persons with a lesser privilege to use force for arrest purposes than is extended to a police officer? In *Klein*, the court stressed the need to set limits "against the dangers of uncontrolled vigilantism and anarchistic actions" and "particularily against the danger of death or injury of innocent persons at the hands of untrained volunteers using firearms." 372 Mass. at —, 363 N.E.2d at 1317–18. Does this need—or others—justify the disparity created by the caselaw? Does it justify continuing to hold that a private citizen acts "at his peril?"

3. Some discussions appear to recognize a separate defense of prevention of an offense:

> A homicide commited to prevent a felony which is being attempted by force or surprise can, depending on the circumstances, be justifiable or legally excusable homicide. However, there must be a necessity for the killing and it must be committed under a bona fide and reasonable belief by the defendant that a felony is in process of commission. In Commonwealth v. Russogulo, 263 Pa. 93, 106 A. 180 (1919), the Court said * * *: "The general rule of law is: 'A bona fide belief by the defendant that a felony is in the process of commission, which can only be averted by the death of the supposed felon, makes the killing excusable homicide; though, if such belief be negligently adopted by the defendant, then the killing is manslaughter'; Wharton on Homicide, par. 533."

Commonwealth v. Harris, 444 Pa. 515, 518, 281 A.2d 879, 881 (1971). In light of the other doctrines discussed in this chapter, would a defense of this sort add anything of significance to a person's right to use force? If the defense applies only where the "victim" was reasonably believed to have been in the process of committing a felony "by force or surprise," can it be invoked by one who reasonably believes another is in the process of burglarizing his residence? See Commonwealth v. Harris, supra (no).

4. To what extent does a police officer or one cooperating with law enforcement officers have a privilege to engage in criminal conduct pursuant to other law enforcement activities? The caselaw is minimal. See Lilly v. West Virginia, 29 F.2d 61 (4th Cir. 1928), holding that a prohibition agent engaged in the pursuit of a suspect was not subject to a city's speed ordinance as long as he acted in good faith and "with the prudence, care, and caution that an ordinarily prudent person would have exercised under the circumstances". Is this a reasonable and complete statement of the standard for determining the scope of the privilege of law enforcement personnel? May an undercover officer attempting to infiltrate a criminal organization engage in the use of drugs to dispel the suspicions of members of the organization? May he sell or transfer drugs? May he engage in theft or robbery for the same purpose? Does it make any difference what offenses are under investigation?

E. CONSENT OR FORGIVENESS BY THE VICTIM

A fundamental premise of the criminal law is that crimes are offenses against the state and not the "victim." Thus, in contrast to the law of torts which deals with recoveries of damages by one private person for injury caused by another, the criminal law has not looked favorably upon the proposition that the perpetrator of a crime should be excused because the "victim" consented to the injury before the fact or agreed, after the fact, to accept financial compensation in lieu of pursuing criminal charges. As a practical matter, these issues seldom arise. The absence of an enthusiastic or at least willing victim to serve as a complaining witness makes detection and prosecution of such offenses extremely unlikely.

MODEL PENAL CODE*

(Proposed Official Draft 1962).

Section 2.11. Consent

(1) *In General.* The consent of the victim to conduct charged to constitute an offense or to the result thereof is a defense if such consent negatives an element of the offense or precludes the infliction of the harm or evil sought to be prevented by the law defining the offense.

(2) *Consent to Bodily Harm.* When conduct is charged to constitute an offense because it causes or threatens bodily harm, consent to such conduct or to the infliction of such harm is a defense if:

(a) the bodily harm consented to or threatened by the conduct consented to is not serious; or

(b) the conduct and the harm are reasonably foreseeable hazards of joint participation in a lawful athletic contest or competitive sport; or

(c) the consent establishes a justification for the conduct under Article 3 of the Code.

(3) *Ineffective Consent.* Unless otherwise provided by the Code or by the law defining the offense, assent does not constitute consent if:

(a) it is given by a person who is legally incompetent to authorize the conduct charged to constitute the offense; or

(b) it is given by a person who by reason of youth, mental disease or defect or intoxication is manifestly unable or known by the actor to be unable to make a reasonable judgment as to the nature or harmfulness of the conduct charged to constitute the offense; or

(c) it is given by a person whose improvident consent is sought to be prevented by the law defining the offense; or

(d) it is induced by force, duress or deception of a kind sought to be prevented by the law defining the offense.

STATE v. BROWN

Superior Court of New Jersey, Law Division, 1976.
143 N.J.Super. 571, 364 A.2d 27.

BACHMAN, J. S. C.

Pursuant to R. 2:5–1, this opinion is to serve as amplification of this court's ruling on the issue of consent of the victim to the alleged atrocious assault and battery (N.J.S.A. 2A:90–1).

Specifically, defendant contends that he is not guilty of the alleged atrocious assault and battery because he and Mrs. Brown, the victim, had an understanding to the effect that if she consumed any alcoholic beverages (and/or became intoxicated), he would punish her by physically assaulting her. The testimony revealed that the victim was an alcoholic. On the day of the alleged crime she indulged in some spirits, apparently to Mr. Brown's dissatisfaction. As per their agreement, defendant sought to punish Mrs. Brown by severely beating her with his hands and other objects.

* * *

Some courts have allowed the defense of consent in civil suits, while denying it in criminal prosecutions for battery (e. g., Wright v. Starr, 42 Nev. 441, 179 P. 877 (Sup.Ct.1919)). According to these courts, there are two different interests at stake. While criminal law is designed to protect the interests of society as a whole, the civil law is concerned with enforcing the rights of each individual within the society. So, while the consent of the victim may relieve defendant of liability in tort, this same consent has been held irrelevant in a criminal prosecution, where there is more at stake than a victim's rights. Love, "Criminal Law: Consent as a Defense to Criminal Battery—The Problem of Athletic Contests," 28 Okla.L.Rev. 840 (1975).

Because of the dearth of authority in New Jersey, it will be useful to examine the manner in which other jurisdictions have resolved the issue of consent to criminal assaults. Several of these courts have ruled on the issue of consent in criminal assault cases that did not have sexual overtones but did involve actual batteries. These courts have almost invariably taken the position that since the offense in question involved a breach of the public peace as well as an invasion of the victim's physical security, the victim's consent would not be recognized as a defense, especially where the battery is a substantial or severe one. * * *

This was the governing law in Vermont as far back as 1884, where the court in State v. Burnham, 56 Vt. 445, 48 Am.Rep. 801 (Sup.Ct.1884), held that defendant's consent to engage in assaultive conduct (sparring and boxing) constituting a breach of the peace was not determinative of the quality of the same in regard to guilt or innocence. The consent to acts prohibited by law (i. e., street boxing) does not give character to their acts and prevent their becoming a breach of the peace.

* * *

The reasoning and public interest that is of concern and served by this rule is that of peace, health and good order. An individual or victim cannot consent to a wrong that is committed against the public peace. The state, not the victim, punishes a person for fighting or inflicting assaults. As astutely noted in Wright v. Starr, supra, the court, citing with approval 1 *Cooley,* Torts, 283, "There are three parties involved in criminal assaults, one being the state, which for its own good does not suffer the others to deal on a basis of contract with the public." It has been stated, and perhaps rightly so, that the only true consent to a criminal act is that of the community. Hughes, "Criminal Law—Defense of Consent—Test to be Applied," 33 Can.B.Rev. 88, 92 (1955).

This is so because these acts (the physical assaults by defendant upon Mrs. Brown), even if done in private, have an impingement (whether direct or indirect) upon the community at large in that the very doing of them may tend to encourage their repetition and so to undermine public morals.

State v. Fransua, 85 N.M. 173, 510 P.2d 106, 58 A.L.R.3d 656 (App.Ct.1973), bears further illustration and support for this court's holding, as it is a classic and recent case of an invitation and consent to an aggravated assault. There, as the result of an argument the victim, in compliance with defendant's wishes, produced a loaded pistol, laid it within defendant's reach and said: there's the gun, if you want to shoot me go ahead. The defendant picked up the pistol and shot the victim, wounding him seriously. In response to defendant's argument of consent on the part of the victim, the court wisely opined,

> We cannot agree. It is generally conceded that a state enacts criminal statutes making certain violent acts crimes for at least two reasons: One reason is to protect the persons of its citizens; the second, however, is to prevent a breach of the peace [citing] State v. Seal, 76 N.M. 461, 415 P.2d 845 (1966). While we entertain little sympathy for either the victim's absurd actions or the defendant's equally unjustified

> act of pulling the trigger, we will not permit the defense of consent to be raised in such cases. Whether the victims of crimes have so little regard for their own safety as to request injury, the public has a stronger and overriding interest in preventing and prohibiting acts such as these. [510 P.2d at 107]

* * *

There are a few situations in which the consent of the victim (actual or implied) is a defense. These situations usually involve ordinary physical contact or blows incident to sports such as football, boxing, or wrestling. People v. Samuels, 250 Cal.App.2d 501, 58 Cal. Rptr. 439 (D.Ct.App.1967), cert. den. *sub nom.* Samuels v. California, 390 U.S. 1024, 88 S.Ct. 1404, 20 L.Ed.2d 281. But this is expected and understood by the participants. The state cannot later be heard to charge a participant with criminal assault upon another participant if the injury complained of resulted from activity that is reasonably within the rules and purview of the sports activity.

However this is not to be confused with sports activities that are not sanctioned by the state. Thus, street fighting which is disorderly and mischievous on many obvious grounds (even if for a purse and consented to), and encounters of that kind which tend to and have the specific objective of causing bodily harm, serve no useful purpose, but rather tend to breach the peace and thus are unlawful. Commonwealth v. Collberg, 119 Mass. 350 (Sup.Jud.Ct.1876); Willey v. Carpenter, 64 Vt. 212, 23 A. 630 (Sup.Ct.1892). No one is justified in striking another, except it be in self defense, and similarly whenever two persons go out to strike each other and do so, each is guilty of an assault. It is no matter who strikes the first blow, for the law proscribes such striking.

As stated by this court in its ruling and by the court in People v. Samuels, supra, it is a matter of common knowledge that a normal person in full possession of his or her mental faculties does not freely and seriously consent to the use upon his or herself of force likely to produce great bodily harm. Those persons that do freely consent to such force and bodily injury no doubt require the enforcement of the very laws that were enacted to protect them and other humans. A general principle of law is that a person cannot contract out of protective legislation passed for his other benefit. Day v. Davies, 2 K.B. 74 (C.A. 1938). "If an act be prohibited, it cannot be the subject of a valid contract." The laws of this State and others that have dealt with the question are simply and unequivocally clear that the defense of consent cannot be available to a defendant charged with any type of physical assault that causes appreciable injury. See also, Commonwealth v. Farrell, 322 Mass. 606, 78 N.E.2d 697 (Sup.Jud.Ct.1948); People v. Lenti, 44 Misc.2d 118, 253 N.Y.S.2d 9 (Co.Ct.1964). If the law were otherwise, it would not be conducive to a peaceful, orderly and healthy society.

* * *

State v. Beck [19 S.Car.L. 363 (1833)] however, cannot be squared with the authority herein. It represents a very minority view that is not followed today. There a conviction for assault and battery was reversed, the court saying that while under some circumstances a license to beat another would be [void], this would only be where the person receiving the license entertained a hostile disposition toward the other, and that defendant had no "evil disposition" toward the victim but acted at the victim's own earnest request to save him from what he considered a greater evil.

This view and reasoning cannot be sustained as it is no longer held by courts in the United States. It not only is the only case this court could find with such anachronistic reasoning and twisted logic, but it is also the oldest case (excepting *Wright's Case,* [(Leicester Assizes 1604), reported Beale, Cases on Criminal Law (3 ed. 1915), 209]), on the question of consent to physical assaults. Commonwealth v. Collberg, supra, decided some 40 years after Beck, expressly disagrees with its holding. And by necessary implication the other cases cited herein likewise disagree. "Evil or hostile disposition" is not an element of atrocious assault and battery or plain assault. The only necessary mens rea is intent, the existence of which is not contested in this case.

* * *

This court concludes that, as a matter of law, no one has the right to beat another even though that person may ask for it. Assault and battery cannot be consented to by a victim, for the State makes it unlawful and is not a party to any such agreement between the victim and perpetrator. To allow an otherwise criminal act to go unpunished because of the victim's consent would not only threaten the security of our society but also might tend to detract from the force of the moral principles underlying the criminal law.

NOTES AND QUESTIONS

1. On appeal in the instant case, the trial judge was affirmed. State v. Brown, 154 N.J.Super. 511, 381 A.2d 1231 (1977). Noting that the crime of which the defendant was convicted was a "high misdemeanor," the court found no necessity to decide whether consent of the victim might be a defense to less serious charges, such as simple assault and battery. Should consent be a defense in such a situation?

2. People v. Samuels, 250 Cal.App.2d 501, 58 Cal.Rptr. 439 (1967), cert. den. 390 U.S. 1024, 88 S.Ct. 1404, 20 L.Ed.2d 281 (1968) involved a defendant who allegedly beat the victim during the filming of a sadomasochistic movie. Should consent be a defense in this situation? Should the

availability of such a defense turn upon whether the film is obscene or otherewise legally impermissible?

3. Statutes in some states authorize the "compromise" of certain offenses. Ariz.Rev.Stat. § 13—3981, for example, provides as follows:

§ 13–3981. Compromise of misdemeanors; effect of order of dismissal; exceptions and limitations

A. When a defendant is accused of a misdemeanor or petty offense for which the person injured by the act constituting the offense has a remedy by a civil action, the offense may be compromised as provided in this section, except:

1. When the offense is committed by or upon any officer of justice while in the execution of the duties of his office.

2. When the offense is committed riotously.

3. When the offense is committed with intent to commit a felony.

B. If the party injured appears before the court in which the action is pending at any time before trial, and acknowledges that he has received satisfaction for the injury, the court may, on payment of the costs incurred, order the prosecution dismissed, and the defendant discharged. The reasons for the order shall be set forth and entered of record on the minutes and the order shall be a bar to another prosecution for the same offense.

C. No public offense shall be compromised or the prosecution or punishment upon a compromise dismissed or stayed except as provided by law.

The statute and its history are discussed in State v. Garoutte, 95 Ariz. 234, 388 P.2d 809 (1964). Are such statutes wise? If so, what offenses should be subject to compromise? 1978 legislation removed manslaughter in the driving of a vehicle from those offenses that could not be compromised under the Arizona statute. Ariz.Session Laws 1978, ch. 201, § 248. Was this a sound decision?

F. DOMESTIC AUTHORITY AND RELATED SITUATIONS

As the preceding materials make clear, the usual rule in our society is that one may not employ force against another in the absence of a necessity to prevent the other's use of unlawful force against the actor or another, or to prevent the other's unlawful interference with property rights, or to effect the lawful arrest of the other person. If force is used upon another to compel or encourage that person to behave "appropriately" or to refrain from undesirable (but noncriminal) conduct, that force is itself criminal, i. e., there is no defense available to a criminal charge based on its use. An exception to this rule has, however, been recognized for persons in certain special relationships with each other. Most important, parents have been regarded as possessing the right to inflict reasonable corporal punishment upon their children. This authority has often been extended to others who stand in a parent-like relationship to a child, such as school teachers. Another group recognized as having similar authority consists of those who, like prison supervisors, have special duties to maintain institutional discipline. As is suggested by the principal case in this subsection, the exercise of this authority, at least by non-parents, has come under sharper scrutiny in recent years.

MODEL PENAL CODE *

(Proposed Official Draft 1962).

Section 3.08. Use of Force by Persons with Special Responsibility for Care, Discipline or Safety of Others

The use of force upon or toward the person of another is justifiable if:

(1) the actor is the parent or guardian or other person similarly responsible for the general care and supervision of a minor or a person acting at the request of such parent, guardian or other responsible person and:

(a) the force is used for the purpose of safeguarding or promoting the welfare of the minor, including the prevention or punishment of his misconduct; and

(b) the force used is not designed to cause or known to create a substantial risk of causing death, serious bodily harm, disfigurement, extreme pain or mental distress or gross degradation; or

(2) the actor is a teacher or a person otherwise entrusted with the care or supervision for a special purpose of a minor and:

(a) the actor believes that the force used is necessary to further such special purpose, including the maintenance of reasonable discipline in a school, class or other group, and that the use of such force is consistent with the welfare of the minor; and

(b) the degree of force, if it had been used by the parent or guardian of the minor, would not be unjustifiable under Subsection (1) (b) of this Section; or

(3) the actor is the guardian or other person similarly responsible for the general care and supervision of an incompetent person; and:

(a) the force is used for the purpose of safeguarding or promoting the welfare of the incompetent person, including the prevention of his misconduct, or, when such incompetent person is in a hospital or other institution for his care and custody, for the maintenance of reasonable discipline in such institution; and

(b) the force used is not designed to cause or known to create a substantial risk of causing death, serious bodily harm, disfigurement, extreme or unnecessary pain, mental distress, or humiliation; or

(4) the actor is a doctor or other therapist or a person assisting him at his direction, and:

(a) the force is used for the purpose of administering a recognized form of treatment which the actor believes to be adapted to promoting the physical or mental health of the patient; and

(b) the treatment is administered with the consent of the patient or, if the patient is a minor or an incompetent person, with the consent of his parent or guardian or other person legally competent to consent in his behalf, or the treatment is administered in an emergency when the actor believes that no one competent to consent can be consulted and that a reasonable person, wishing to safeguard the welfare of the patient, would consent; or

(5) the actor is a warden or other authorized official of a correctional institution, and:

(a) he believes that the force used is necessary for the purpose of enforcing the lawful rules or procedures of the institution, unless his belief in the lawfulness of the rule or procedure sought to be enforced is erroneous and his error is due to ignorance or mistake as to the provisions of the Code, any other provision of the criminal law or the law governing the administration of the institution; and

(b) the nature or degree of force used is not forbidden by Article 303 or 304 [dealing with discipline in jail and prison] of the Code; and

(c) if deadly force is used, its use is otherwise justifiable under this Article; or

(6) the actor is a person responsible for the safety of a vessel or an aircraft or a person acting at his direction, and

(a) he believes that the force used is necessary to prevent interference with the operation of the vessel or aircraft or obstruction of the execution of a lawful order, unless his belief in the lawfulness of the order is erroneous and his error is due to ignorance or mistake as to the law defining his authority; and

(b) if deadly force is used, its use is otherwise justifiable under this Article; or

(7) the actor is a person who is authorized or required by law to maintain order or decorum in a vehicle, train or other carrier or in a place where others are assembled, and:

(a) he believes that the force used is necessary for such purpose; and

(b) the force used is not designed to cause or known to create a substantial risk of causing death, bodily harm, or extreme mental distress.

PEOPLE v. BALL

Appellate Court of Illinois, 1973.
15 Ill.App.3d 143, 303 N.E.2d 516.

JONES, Justice:

Defendant appeals his conviction in a bench trial of the crime of battery in violation of ch. 38, sec. 12–3, Ill.Rev.Stat.1971. The penalty imposed was a fine of $100 and costs. The case presents the question of the proper test to be applied in determining whether a schoolteacher has exceeded the legally permissible limits in administering corporal punishment.

At the time of the incident in question the defendant was a schoolteacher, aged 54, with 23 years teaching experience, the last 7 as a sixth grade teacher in the Henry Robb School in Belleville, the site of the occurrence in question.

The prosecuting witness was a student of defendant, age 11. On the day in question the defendant's class was practicing unison exercises for an approaching school festival. The boy disrupted the practice by talking, facing in a direction opposite that of the rest of the class and doing "jumping jacks." He was directed by defendant to go to a bench alongside the schoolhouse and remain seated there until he was directed otherwise by defendant. Shortly thereafter the boy left the bench and commenced talking to a friend of his who had approached. The defendant thereupon decided that disciplinary action was necessary. He took the boy into the school and got another teacher as an observer. In the hallway of the school, outside the classroom of the observing teacher, the defendant had the boy bend down with his hands on his knees and he then struck him 10 times on the buttocks with a wooden paddle about 20 inches long, one-fourth inch thick and three inches wide. Following the paddling the defendant took the boy to the classroom and in a conversation explained why the punishment was administered and why it would help the boy.

The defendant stated, and the teacher-observer confirmed, that he was not angry, had not lost his temper and remained calm and rational throughout. The boy admitted that he was wrong and deserving of punishment.

The paddling occurred at approximately 2:30 in the afternoon. When school dismissed at 3:15 the boy walked to his home and reported the paddling to his parents. His father took him to the police station and then to the home of their family doctor where they were directed to the emergency room of a local hospital. There the boy was treated by a doctor who applied a surface anesthesia and gauze bandage. The condition as described by the doctor was that the boy had severe burn-type bruises of both buttocks, the right side being worse than the left. The skin temperature was hot to the touch, there was marked discoloration and redness requiring treatment. There may have been minute abrasions in the bruised area but the main effect was one of swelling, redness, heat and a thickening of the area above the surface surrounding the skin. The redness and swelling disappeared in due course with no after effects, except that the mother testified that the boy had some lingering emotional problems stemming from the paddling. We note at this point that defendant has conceded that bodily injury was inflicted.

A written judgment order was entered in which the court merely found defendant guilty as charged. However, in his remarks delivered from the bench the court stated that a teacher is a substitute parent and "may administer just and reasonable punishment, switch or paddle accepted." The court further stated that there was no indication the defendant lost his temper and the discipline was tendered in an orderly manner. The court concluded that defendant administered punishment more severe even than a parent had the right to administer, and that the events and their results indicated that the punishment was more than a spanking, it was a beating. The court also stated that it was not his purpose to take the right to discipline away from the teacher but to insure the student that discipline will be "just and reasonable."

* * *

Defendant next argues that under an applicable statute and the governing case law he was acting within legally prescribed limits and the corporal punishment therefore was administered with legal justification and his conviction cannot stand. The concern of this argument is that in determining whether defendant's actions were "just and reasonable" the trial court applied an erroneous test to the evidence to determine criminal liability. With this we must agree.

Art. 24, sec. 24 of the Illinois School Code of 1961 (Ill.Rev.Stat. 1971, ch. 122, art. 24, sec. 24) provides:

> "Teachers and other certificated educational employees shall maintain discipline in the schools. In all matters relating to

> the discipline in and conduct of the schools and the school children, they stand in the relation of parents and guardians to the pupils. This relationship shall extend to all activities connected with the school program and may be exercised at any time for the safety and supervision of the pupils in the absence of their parents or guardians."

It is defendant's position that under the foregoing statute he was acting in the place of the boy's parents in administering the paddling and that under the rule established by the applicable Illinois cases the paddling he administered did not go beyond permissible limits. We are referred to three Illinois cases concerned with the administration of corporal punishment by schoolteachers, Fox v. People, 1899, 84 Ill. App. 270; Drake v. Thomas, 1941, 310 Ill.App. 57, 33 N.E.2d 889, and City of Macomb v. Gould, 1969, 104 Ill.App.2d 361, 244 N.E.2d 634. The rule of the *Fox* and *Drake* cases is concisely stated as the governing law in the *Gould* case as follows:

> "He (a teacher) may not wantonly or maliciously inflict corporal punishment and may be guilty of battery if he does so. Whether he has done so may be inferred from the unreasonableness of the method adopted or the force employed under the circumstances. This presents a question of fact requiring reference to the evidence."

It thus becomes apparent that when the trial court, in delivering his findings from the bench, stated that a teacher may administer "just and reasonable" punishment and that the purpose of his ruling was to insure that student discipline will be "just and reasonable," he was applying criteria other than that adopted by the above cases. Those cases prohibit a teacher from wantonly or maliciously inflicting corporal punishment or from acting out of malice.

The People suggest in their brief that the rule of "reasonableness" be adopted and followed and they cite authorities to show that the "reasonable" rule is followed in a clear majority of States. However, we see no reason to abandon the established Illinois rule. We deem it sufficient to protect the teachers in the discharge of their statutory duty to maintain discipline and also sufficient to protect pupils from abuse by teachers overzealous in their belief that "to spare the rod is to spoil the child."

In our view the trial court erred in considering whether the evidence showed the corporal punishment was "just and reasonable." Properly it should be determined whether the teacher was actuated by malice, or inflicted the punishment wantonly. For an error in judgment although the punishment is unnecessarily excessive, if it is not of a nature to cause lasting injury, and he acts in good faith, the teacher is not liable. (Fox v. People.)

Accordingly we remand the case to the trial court for reconsideration of the evidence and a determination of guilt under the proper rule. * * *

Reversed and remanded with directions.

George J. MORAN, Justice (dissenting):

* * *

More important than the facts of this case is the question of which standard to apply in determining whether a teacher's corporal punishment of a student constitutes battery. Two divergent standards have been applied in this country, which I shall refer to as the "reasonableness" and the "malice" tests.

The reasonableness test is clearly the rule in the majority of American courts. Its philosophical basis is that the right or privilege of a parent or teacher to discipline a child is grounded not in the adult's liberty of action, but in the child's welfare. Therefore, this discipline must not exceed what is reasonable and moderate under the circumstances, considering the age, sex, physical and mental condition of the child, the nature of his offense and his apparent motive, and whether the punishment is disproportionate to the offense, unnecessarily degrading, or likely to cause serious or permanent harm. If the punishment is unreasonable the adult is criminally liable.

The minority "malice" rule is that a parent or teacher in punishing a child acts in a judicial or quasi-judicial capacity and is not criminally liable for an assault because of an error in judgment or because the punishment was disproportionate to the offense, but is liable only if the punishment either results in permanent injury or was inflicted with malice, either express or implied. This view is grounded more in a desire to protect the adult from liability for otherwise criminal actions than in a desire to protect children from excessive punishment and in my opinion is so concerned with the adult's "right" to punish that it overlooks the reason for the "right", which is the welfare of the child. This outmoded concept was criticized by the Supreme Court of Indiana in Cooper v. McJunkin, 4 Ind. 290, as long ago as 1853:

> "The public seem to cling to the despotism in the government of schools which has been discarded everywhere else. * * * The husband can no longer moderately chastise his wife; nor * * * the master his servant or apprentice. Even the degrading cruelties of the naval service have been arrested. Why the person of the schoolboy * * * should be less sacred in the eye of the law than that of the apprentice or the sailor, is not easily explained." (4 Ind. at 291–293.)

Fortunately, most modern decisions (except the present one) have turned away from the "malice" test. According to Annot., "Criminal Liability for excessive or improper punishment inflicted on child by parent, teacher, or one in loco parentis," 89 A.L.R.2d 396, only two American cases since 1905 have applied the "malice" test to teachers. Furthermore, even among the older cases applying the "malice" test almost all allow malice to be inferred, usually from excessive punishment * * *.

Although the majority opinion sees "no reasons to abandon the established Illinois rule," analysis shows that the rule—if indeed it is the rule—has a very weak foundation. * * * I would clarify any ambiguity left by the language of [the Illinois caselaw] by expressly adopting the better-reasoned reasonableness test.

NOTES AND QUESTIONS

1. On further appeal in the instant case, the Illinois Supreme Court reversed and ordered the judgment of the trial court affirmed. People v. Ball, 58 Ill.2d 36, 317 N.E.2d 54 (1974). The rule that would give teachers greater latitude in disciplining a child than is given the child's parents, concluded the court, "constitutes an anomaly for which there is no sound basis." 58 Ill.2d at 39–40, 317 N.E.2d at 56.

2. May a teacher administer corporal punishment to a child if the child's parents oppose such action? Perhaps the answer to this depends upon whether a teacher is exercising an independent privilege or whether, in the alternative, this is merely a delegation of the parents' privilege. A leading case, State v. Mizner, 45 Iowa 248 (1876), involved punishment inflicted upon a student who was over the age of eighteen and who therefore could not have been physically punished by her parents. Finding that the teacher was nevertheless privileged to use reasonable force to chastise the student, the court rejected the argument that the right of a teacher to inflict corporal punishment is "correlative simply with the right of a parent." To hold otherwise, the court continued, "might destroy the authority of the teacher and be utterly subversive of good order." 45 Iowa at 250–51.

G. "DEFENSES" AND OTHER DOCTRINES RELATED TO MENTAL ILLNESS

Perhaps the most perplexing problem of substantive criminal law has been the task of accommodating some offenders' psychological abnormality in the decision as to whether—or to what extent—to hold persons criminally responsible for their conduct. This section explores two possible vehicles for this task. The first is the traditional defense of insanity. The second is the "doctrine" [a] of dimin-

a. Given the existence of a mens rea requirement and the general rule that evidence relevant to issues in the case is admissible, a question might be raised as to why a special "doctrine" is necessary to justify the admission of such evidence. Perhaps the question might be better put as whether there

ished capacity, under which a defendant's psychological abnormality is considered in determining whether the defendant had the state of mind required by the crime charged.

Both of these doctrines need to be distinguished from another issue often presented in criminal litigation which also involves an inquiry into defendants' mental condition. It is a violation of due process as well as the procedural requirements of virtually all states to place on trial a defendant who is incompetent to stand trial. Pate v. Robinson, 383 U.S. 375, 86 S.Ct. 836, 15 L.Ed.2d 815 (1966). There is widespread agreement that a defendant is incompetent within the meaning of this rule if, because of psychological abnormality, he lacks present ability to consult with his lawyer with a reasonable degree of understanding or if he lacks a reasonable as well as factual understanding of the proceedings. Dusky v. United States, 362 U.S. 402, 80 S.Ct. 788, 4 L.Ed.2d 824 (1960). The competency inquiry, then, focuses upon defendants' mental condition at the time of trial; the questions concerning responsibility considered in this section are concerned with defendants' mental condition at the time of the commission of the acts constituting the alleged offense. There is a far more fundamental difference between the doctrines, however. Incompetency to stand trial is not a "defense" in the sense that it addresses the merits of the charges pending against the accused. Rather, it is simply a bar to trial of the defendant and therefore to disposition of the charges. If, after a determination of incompetency, a defendant is restored to a condition in which he no longer suffers from disabilities rendering him incompetent, he may at that point be tried upon the still pending charges. Both insanity and diminished capacity, on the other hand, are defensive doctrines. If they are successfully asserted by a defendant, the charges are permanently disposed of and there is no danger of a subsequent retrial and conviction.

In discussing the matters covered in this section, it is important to begin with a consideration of what objectives the law is or ought to be pursuing by means of the doctrines at issue. Among those policy objectives which might be considered proper ones are the following:

> 1. *Exculpation of the Nonblameworthy.* Insofar as criminal liability involves a judgment of ethical reprehensibility, it is desirable to have doctrines that prevent the conviction of those who are not in fact blameworthy despite their conduct. Not only does exculpation avoid what some argue is the stigmatization resulting from criminal convic-

is or should be a special rule barring the admissibility of evidence tending to show that the defendant was psychologically abnormal and therefore lacked the intent required by the crime charged. See generally the discussion at pages 514–15, supra.

tion, but it also may prevent the infliction of punishment containing at least an element of retribution.

2. *Channeling Offenders into Appropriate Systems.* To some extent, the insanity defense serves not only to prevent criminal liability but also to channel a defendant who asserts it into the mental health system. This may be seen as desirable for several reasons. It is arguable that it implements society's interest in preventing further offenses by the defendant. Admission to the mental health system may result in an offender being provided with "treatment" that is more appropriate to his needs than any therapy available in the correctional system. Moreover, such action may provide society with the means of retaining the defendant as long as he presents a danger. A defendant sentenced under criminal provisions must usually be released at the expiration of the sentence no matter how dangerous he is believed to be at that time; one committed to psychiatric facilities following exculpation under the doctrines discussed here may sometimes be retained until—and if—it is determined that he no longer poses a danger to society. Further, it is argued that society's interests in protection are accomplished at less cost to offenders, since treatment in the mental health system is less stigmatizing and less disabling in other ways. It may, for example, have less effect upon offenders' employment opportunities.

3. *Reinforcement of General Notions of Responsibility.* Some argue that the concept of criminal irresponsibility and its litigation in occasional cases tends to reinforce the sense of responsibility held by most members of the community. By the process of attempting to identify exceptional cases in which defendants will be regarded as irresponsible, the community reaffirms its belief in the general rule of responsibility and this process of reaffirmance itself tends to cause members of the community to act in a responsible way.

4. *Avoidance of Misuse of Exculpatory Doctrines.* In addition to the general objectives outlined above, it seems clear that there is a strong and legitimate interest in avoiding the misuse of any exculpatory doctrines that might be adopted. For example, an exculpatory rule that might in theory be justifiable on the ground that it would excuse persons who are not in fact blameworthy might be subject to the objection that in practice so many blameworthy defendants would be able to falsely claim the benefits of the rule that the costs of the rule would exceed its benefits. Closely related to this is the danger that a rule might pose questions that, in the context of individual cases, are either impossible

of resolution or are so expensive and timeconsuming to resolve that society cannot afford to have the judicial system spend time on efforts to administer them. Some formulations of the insanity defense or the diminished responsibility rule might be subject to such objections.

1. THE DEFENSE OF INSANITY

Traditionally, discussions of the insanity defense have focused upon the appropriate standard to be used for determining which defendants to exculpate on the ground of insanity. Recently, however, there has been more serious discussion of proposals to abolish the defense entirely. Some proposals would establish a diminished capacity rule and rely upon that doctrine to serve whatever functions traditionally served by the insanity defense remain appropriate ones. Others would postpone any inquiry into a defendant's psychological abnormality until the sentencing stage. Despite these proposals, however, the appropriate standard for evaluating defendants' claims of insanity remains an important issue.

Any discussion of insanity must begin with Daniel M'Naghten's Case, 10 Cl. & F. 200, 8 Eng.Rep. 718 (1843), which is the basis for the traditional standard. M'Naghten, in an apparent effort to kill Sir Edward Peel, shot and killed Edward Drummond, Sir Peel's private secretary. At the trial, defense testimony tended to show that the defendant experienced delusions that others were pursuing him and wanted to kill him and that he fired the fatal shot believing that this would bring him peace from his persecution. The jury acquitted. Public outcry was so great that the matter was taken up in the House of Lords and the judges gave an opinion on the question of the nature and extent of unsoundness of mind excusing the commission of a crime of the sort involved. Lord Chief Justice Tindal delivered the opinion, in which all but one of the judges concurred:

> Your Lordships are pleased to inquire of us * * * "What are the proper questions to be submitted to the jury, where a person alleged to be afflicted with insane delusion respecting one or more particular subjects or persons, is charged with the commission of a crime (murder, for example), and insanity is set up as a defense?" And * * * "In what terms ought the question to be left to the jury as to the prisoner's state of mind at the time when the act was committed?" And as these two questions appear to us to be more conveniently answered together, we have to submit our opinion to be, that the jurors ought to be told in all cases that every man is to be presumed to be sane, and to possess a sufficient degree of reason to be responsible for his crimes, until the contrary be proved to their satisfaction; and that

to establish a defence on the ground of insanity, it must be clearly proved that, at the time of the committing of the act, the party accused was labouring under such a defect of reason, from disease of the mind, as not to know the nature and quality of the act he was doing; or, if he did know it, that he did not know he was doing what was wrong. The mode of putting the latter part of the question to the jury on these occasions has generally been, whether the accused at the time of doing the act knew the difference between right and wrong: which mode, though rarely, if ever, leading to any mistake with the jury, is not, as we conceive, so accurate when put generally and in the abstract, as when put with reference to the party's knowledge of right and wrong in respect to the very act with which he is charged. If the question were to be put as to the knowledge of the accused solely and exclusively with reference to the law of the land, it might tend to confound the jury, by inducing them to believe that an actual knowledge of the law of the land was essential in order to lead to a conviction; whereas the law is administered upon the principle that every one must be taken conclusively to know it, without proof that he does know it. If the accused was conscious that the act was one which he ought not to do, and if that act was at the same time contrary to the law of the land, he is punishable; and the usual course therefore has been to leave the question to the jury, whether the party accused had a sufficient degree of reason to know that he was doing an act that was wrong; and this course we think is correct, accompanied with such observations and explanations as the circumstances of each particular case may require.

The [next] question which your Lordships have proposed to us is this:—"If a person under an insane delusion as to existing facts, commits an offence in consequence thereof, is he thereby excused?" To which question the answer must of course depend on the nature of the delusion: but [assuming] that he labours under [a] partial delusion only, and is not in other respects insane, we think he must be considered in the same situation as to responsibility as if the facts with respect to which the delusion exists were real. For example, if under the influence of his delusion he supposes another man to be in the act of attempting to take away his life, and he kills that man, as he supposes, in self-defence, he would be exempt from punishment. If his delusion was that the deceased had inflicted a serious injury to his character and fortune, and he killed him in revenge for such supposed injury, he would be liable to punishment.

As most courts have read the so-called M'Naghten Rule derived from this opinion, the only impairments that are relevant to the defense of insanity are those of the defendant's reasoning ability, i. e., his cognition. Thus an abnormality that has no effect upon a defendant's thinking processes or reasoning but does impair his ability to control his conduct, i. e., his volition, is irrelevant. This position came under bitter attack by mental health professionals, who argued that it was based upon an unrealistic and unscientific conception of human behavior.[b] Judge David Bazelon summarized the opposition to the M'Naghten Rule in Durham v. United States, 214 F.2d 862, 870–71 (D.C.Cir. 1954):

> Medico-legal writers in large numbers * * * present convincing evidence that the right-and-wrong test is 'based on an entirely obsolete and misleading conception of the nature of insanity. The science of psychiatry now recognizes that a man is an integrated personality and that reason, which is only one element in that personality, is not the sole determinant of his conduct. The right-wrong test, which considers knowledge or reason alone, is therefore not an adequate guide to mental responsibility for criminal behavior.

In response to such criticism of the M'Naghten Rule, a number of American jurisdictions have abandoned it.[c] Others have supplemented it with the "irresistible impulse" doctrine, under which a defendant is entitled to exculpation if his impairment was such that he met the M'Naghten Rule or if he was caused to commit the crime by an insane impulse. See Parsons v. State, 81 Ala. 577, 2 So. 854 (1887), finding error in the trial judge's refusal to instruct jury that the defendants were not guilty if they were "moved to action by an insane impulse controlling their will or their judgment." These formulations

b. Concern has also been expressed that courts applying *M'Naghten* will exclude testimony concerning the defendant's mental condition that would be useful in an evaluation of the defendant's blameworthiness. Although this would be the result of a careful scrutiny of evidence offered by the defendant under the *M'Naghten* Rules, A. Goldstein, The Insanity Defense 53–56 (1967) reports that this is not a problem in actual practice. Testimony that would establish a valid defense only under other formulations of the defense is admitted freely in *M'Naghten* jurisdictions, he reports, and consequently "there is virtually no support in law for the view that *M'Naghten* is responsible for inhibiting the flow of testimony on the insanity issue." But see Grissom v. State, 237 So.2d 57 (Fla.App.1970), finding no error in the exclusion of offered psychiatric testimony because "it would have presented as exculpatory a mental attitude of the defendant not adequate for defense under the *McNaughten* Rule."

c. Perhaps the most significant of recent abandonments of the *M'Naghten* Rule is that of the California Supreme Court, which had followed the rule since 1864. People v. Coffman, 24 Cal. 230 (1864). In People v. Drew, 22 Cal.3d 333, 149 Cal.Rptr. 275, 583 P.2d 1318 (1978), the court rejected the *M'Naghten* Rule and adopted the American Law Institute's formulation of the defense, reprinted at page —, infra.

of the defense, although they permitted exculpation on the basis of volitional as well as cognitional impairments, were criticized on the ground that they suggested that only "sudden, momentary or spontaneous inclinations" to commit the unlawful acts would excuse defendants and therefore failed to accommodate illnesses that were slow in developing but nevertheless destroyed a person's ability to exercise control over his actions. See Durham v. United States, 214 F.2d 862, 873–74 (D.C.Cir. 1954). Some formulations of the rule, however, arguably avoid this problem. In State v. Noble, 142 Mont. 284, 384 P.2d 504, 508 (1963), for example, the jury was instructed as follows:

> [I]f the defendant had not sufficient reason to be able to judge of the consequences of his act, or was so far deprived of volition or self-control by the overwhelming violence of mental disease that he was not capable of voluntary action and therefore not able to choose the right and avoid the wrong, he was not responsible for any act committed while in this condition.

A minority of courts have reached much the same result by interpreting the M'Naghten Rule in a manner that emphasizes impairments of the defendant's knowledge of the "nature and quality" of his actions as distinguished from his knowledge that what he was doing was wrong. The Wisconsin Supreme Court, considering the case of a defendant convicted of murder, reasoned as follows:

> Suppose that one vaguely realizes that particular conduct is forbidden, but lacks real insight into the conduct. He may be furtive about such conduct, but not really be able to make a normal moral judgment about it. * * * Although defendant Esser realized very soon after the fatal shot, first that it would be advisable to hide the victim's body, and later that he should report his act to the police, even referring to it as "murder," yet the expert testimony tends to create a reasonable doubt that he could appreciate and evaluate his act at the time he did it. Although Esser's conduct after the shooting suggests a knowledge that his act had been wrong and therefore that he could distinguish right from wrong, the expert testimony describing his mental illness tends to show that at the time of the killing he did not understand the nature and quality of his acts and therefore could not distinguish right from wrong with respect to them.

State v. Esser, 16 Wis.2d 567, 598–99, 115 N.W.2d 505, 521–22 (1962). This approach has been criticized on the ground that the practical burden of stretching the M'Naghten Rule in this fashion rests unfairly upon medical witnesses who must be prepared to accept and defend a definition of the legal standard that may not be consistent with the definition of the legal standard given it by counsel and the court. See Royal Commission on Capital Punishment 1949–53 Report, 103–04 (1953).

But this trend towards broadening the insanity defense beyond the consideration of cognitive impairments has not been without objection. Professor Herbert Wechsler, for example, has noted what he characterizes as "impressive arguments" against broadening the insanity standard further than is provided for in the M'Naghten Rules:

> The purpose of the penal law is to express a formal social condemnation of forbidden conduct, buttressed by sanctions calculated to prevent it—not alone by incapacitating and so far as possible correcting the offending individual, but also by their impact on the general imagination, i. e., through the medium of general deterrence. Considerations of equality and of effectiveness conspire to demand that sanctions which are threatened generally be applied with generality upon conviction—not that the sentence disregard differences in circumstances or in individuals but that the sentence be imposed within the framework of such formal condemnation and conviction. Responsibility criteria define a broad exception. The theory of the exception is that it is futile thus to threaten and condemn persons who through no fault of their own are wholly beyond the range of influence of threatened sanctions of this kind. So long as there is any chance that the preventive influence may operate, it is essential to maintain the threat. If it is not maintained, the influence of the entire system is diminished upon those who have the requisite capacity, albeit that they sometimes may offend.
>
> On this analysis, the category of the irresponsible must be defined in extreme terms. The problem is to differentiate between the wholly non-deterrable and persons who are more or less susceptible to influence by law. The category must be so extreme that to the ordinary man, burdened by passion and beset by large temptations, the exculpation of the irresponsibles bespeaks no weakness in the law. He does not identify himself and them; they are a world apart. This will be found to be the case in every instance where *M'Naghten* operates; with tight administration that distinguishes with care between the irresistible and unresisted impulse, it is the case under this test as well, though doubts about the possibility of such administration surely have their point. Beyond such extreme incapacities, however, the exception cannot go. This, to be sure, is not poetic justice. It is public justice, which in the interest of the common good prescribes a standard all must strive to satisfy who

> can, those whose nature or nurture leads them to conform with difficulty no less than those who find compliance easy. Only so can the general effort be required and maintained. If finer distinctions are in order, let them be weighed with other factors that have bearing on the nature of the sentence and the mitigations that at that point may be made.

Wechsler, The Criteria of Criminal Responsibility, 22 U.Chi.L.Rev. 367, 374–75 (1955). Those tests that permit consideration of volition or control were criticised in a draft of a proposed Senate Judiciary Committee report:

> Functionally, there is much appeal in * * * a criterion [which permits consideration of lack of power to avoid criminal conduct]. If one conceives the major purpose of the insanity defense to be the exclusion of the non-deterrables from criminal responsibility, a control test seems designed to meet that objective. Furthermore, notions of retributive punishment seem particularly inappropriate with respect to one powerless to do otherwise than he did. And treatment and incapacitation can be accomplished in a mental hospital, as well as in a prison. * * *
>
> A powerful criticism of the control tests, however, is that they tend to exculpate some persons who should be adjudged guilty. * * *
>
> A related difficulty with a control test is associated with a determinism which seems dominant in the thinking of many expert witnesses. Modern psychiatry has tended to view man as controlled by antecedent hereditary and environmental factors. * * *
>
> Such a view is consistent with a conclusion that *all* criminal conduct is evidence of lack of power to conform behavior to the requirements of law. The control tests and volitional standards thus acutely raise the problem of what is *meant* by lack of power to avoid conduct or to conform to the requirement of law which leads to the most fundamental objection to the control tests—their lack of determinate meaning. The Royal Commission on Capital Punishment stated:
>
> > Most lawyers have consistently maintained that the concept of an "irresistible" or "uncontrollable" impulse is a dangerous one, since it is impracticable to distinguish between those impulses which are the product of mental disease and those which are the product of ordinary passion, or, where mental disease exists, between impulses that may be genuinely irresistible and those which are merely not resisted.

> [Royal Commission on Capital Punishment 1949—53, Report 80 (1953).] * * * To be sure, there are situations in which there would be substantial agreement that freedom of choice was absent * * *. They pose no challenge for a volitional insanity defense. Beyond this core type of situation, however, one can expect little agreement as to the meaning of a volitional standard. * * *
>
> The indeterminacy problem of control tests is not sufficiently mitigated by the requirement of mental disease or defect. The disease or defect requirement is present in all of the statements of insanity defenses * * *. It is almost never defined, however. Primary reliance is conveniently placed on expert testimony, apparently because it is widely assumed, first, that there is a medical consensus on the meaning of these terms, and second, that this meaning is relevant to the legal purposes at hand. Neither assumption is entirely accurate.

Staff of Senate Comm. on the Judiciary, 93d Cong., 2d Sess., Report on Criminal Justice Codification, Revision and Reform Act of 1974 102–04 (Comm. Print 1974).

Two final developments in the law of criminal insanity need to be considered. One is the so-called Durham Rule, adopted in Durham v. United States, 214 F.2d 862 (D.C.Cir. 1954). This was abandoned by the same court in Brawner v. United States, reprinted in this section, and is discussed in that opinion. The other is the American Law Institute's formulation of the insanity defense in Section 4.01 of the Model Penal Code; the tentative draft formulations and the final language of the section are reprinted in this section. As the Brawner decision illustrates, the clear trend among both courts and legislatures has been toward adoption of the Model Penal Code's formulation.

In evaluating the material in this section, consider the need for an insanity defense. Insofar as a need for such a defense exists, should it permit consideration of volitional as well as cognitive impairments? If insanity depends upon volitional impairments, is it practical to expect that judges and juries will be able to determine whether defendants were in fact so impaired as to make conviction inappropriate? After examining the next section dealing with diminished capacity, consider whether an insanity defense is still necessary or desirable in a jurisdiction which adopts diminished capacity.

Consider also whether evaluating a defendant's insanity claim under the M'Naghten Rules raises a viable constitutional issue. In Leland v. Oregon, 343 U.S. 790, 72 S.Ct. 1002, 96 L.Ed. 1302 (1952), the Supreme Court rejected the argument that legislative adoption of "the 'right and wrong' test of legal insanity in preference to the 'irresistible impulse' test" violated due process of law:

> Knowledge of right and wrong is the exclusive test of criminal responsibility in a majority of American jurisdictions. The science of psychiatry has made tremendous strides since the "right and wrong" test was laid down in M'Naghten's Case, but the progress of science has not reached a point where its learning would compel us to require the states to eliminate the right and wrong test from their criminal law. Moreover, choice of a test of legal insanity involves not only scientific knowledge but questions of basic policy as to the extent to which that knowledge should determine criminal responsibility. The whole problem has evoked wide disagreement among those who have studied it. In these circumstances it is clear that adoption of the irresistible impulse test is not "implicit in the concept of ordered liberty."

343 U.S. at 800–01. Would the Court reach the same result today? Should it?

MODEL PENAL CODE *

(Tent. Draft No. 4, 1955).

Article 4. Responsibility

Section 4.01. Mental Disease or Defect Excluding Responsibility

(1) A person is not responsible for criminal conduct if at the time of such conduct as a result of mental disease or defect he lacks substantial capacity either to appreciate the criminality of his conduct or to conform his conduct to the requirements of law.

(2) The terms "mental disease or defect" do not include an abnormality manifested only by repeated criminal or otherwise antisocial conduct.

* * *

Alternative formulations of paragraph (1).

(a) A person is not responsible for criminal conduct if at the time of such conduct as a result of mental disease or defect his capacity either to appreciate the criminality of his conduct or to conform his conduct to the requirements of law is so substantially impaired that he cannot justly be held responsible.

(b) A person is not responsible for criminal conduct if at the time of such conduct as a result of mental disease or defect he lacks substantial capacity to appreciate the criminality of his conduct or is in such state that the prospect of conviction and punishment cannot constitute a significant restraining influence upon him.

Comment

* * *

The draft accepts the view that any effort to exclude the nondeterrables from strictly penal sanctions must take account of the impairment of volitional capacity no less than of impairment of cognition; and that this result should be achieved directly in the formulation of the test, rather than left to mitigation in the application of *M'Naghten*. It also accepts the criticism of the "irresistible impulse" formulation as inept in so far as it may be impliedly restricted to sudden, spontaneous acts as distinguished from insane propulsions that are accompanied by brooding or reflection.

Both the main formulation recommended and alternative (a) deem the proper question on this branch of the inquiry to be whether the defendant was without capacity to conform his conduct to the requirements of law. * * * The application of the principle will call, of course, for a distinction between incapacity, upon the one hand, and mere indisposition on the other. Such a distinction is inevitable in the application of a standard addressed to impairment of volition. We believe that the distinction can be made.

Alternative (b) states the issue differently. Instead of asking whether the defendant had capacity to conform his conduct to the requirements of law, it asks whether, in consequence of mental disease or defect, the threat of punishment could not exercise a significant restraining influence upon him. To some extent, of course, these are the same inquiries. To the extent that they diverge, the latter asks a narrower and harder question, involving the assessment of capacity to respond to a single influence, the threat of punishment. Both Dr. Guttmacher and Dr. Overholser considered the assessment of responsiveness to this one influence too difficult for psychiatric judgment. Hence, though the issue framed by the alternative may well be thought to state the question that is most precisely relevant for legal purposes, the Reporter and the Council deemed the inquiry impolitic upon this ground. In so far as non-deterrability is the determination that is sought, it must be reached by probing general capacity to conform to the requirements of law. The validity of this conclusion is submitted, however, to the judgment of the Institute.

4. One further problem must be faced. In addressing itself to impairment of the cognitive capacity, *M'Naghten* demands that impairment be complete: the actor must *not* know. So, too, the irresistible impulse criterion presupposes a complete impairment of capacity for self-control. The extremity of these conceptions is, we think, the point that poses largest difficulty to psychiatrists when called upon to aid in their administration. The schizophrenic, for example, is disoriented from reality; the disorientation is extreme; but it is rarely total. Most psychotics will respond to a command of

someone in authority within the mental hospital; they thus have some capacity to conform to a norm. But this is very different from the question whether they have the capacity to conform to requirements that are not thus immediately symbolized by an attendant or policeman at the elbow. Nothing makes the inquiry into responsibility more unreal for the psychiatrist than limitation of the issue to some ultimate extreme of total incapacity, when clinical experience reveals only a graded scale with marks along the way. * * *

We think this difficulty can and must be met. The law must recognize that when there is no black and white it must content itself with different shades of gray. The draft, accordingly, does not demand *complete* impairment of capacity. It asks instead for *substantial* impairment. This is all, we think, that candid witnesses, called on to infer the nature of the situation at a time that they did not observe, can ever confidently say, even when they know that a disorder was extreme.

If substantial impairment of capacity is to suffice, there remains the question whether this alone should be the test or whether the criterion should state the principle that measures how substantial it must be. To identify the degree of impairment with precision is, of course, impossible both verbally and logically. The recommended formulation is content to rest upon the term "substantial" to support the weight of judgment; if capacity is greatly impaired, that presumably should be sufficient. Alternative (a) proposes to submit the issue squarely to the jury's sense of justice, asking expressly whether the capacity of the defendant "was so substantially impaired that he can not justly be held responsible." Some members of the Council deemed it unwise to present questions of justice to the jury, preferring a submission that in form, at least, confines the inquiry to fact. The proponents of the alternative contend that since the jury normally will feel that it is only just to exculpate if the disorder was extreme, that otherwise conviction is demanded, it is safer to invoke the jury's sense of justice than to rest entirely on the single word "substantial", imputing no specific measure of degree. The issue is an important one and it is submitted for consideration by the Institute.

* * *

Paragraph (2) of section 4.01 is designed to exclude from the concept of "mental disease or defect" the case of so-called "psychopathic personality." The reason for the exclusion is that, as the Royal Commission put it, psychopathy "is a statistical abnormality; that is to say, the psychopath differs from a normal person only quantitatively or in degree, not qualitatively; and the diagnosis of psychopathic personality does not carry with it any explanation of the causes of the abnormality." While it may not be feasible to formulate a definition of "disease", there is much to be said for excluding a condition that is manifested only by the behavior phenomena that must, by hypothesis, be the result of disease for irresponsibility to be established. Although British psychiatrists have agreed, on the whole, that psychopathy should not be called "disease", there is considerable difference of opinion on the point in the United States. Yet it does not seem useful to contemplate the litigation of what is essentially a matter of terminology; nor is it right to have the legal result rest upon the resolution of a dispute of this kind.

MODEL PENAL CODE *

(Proposed Official Draft, 1962).

Section 4.01. Mental Disease or Defect Excluding Responsibility

(1) A person is not responsible for criminal conduct if at the time of such conduct as a result of mental disease or defect he lacks substantial capacity either to appreciate the criminality [wrongfulness] of his conduct or to conform his conduct to the requirements of law.

(2) As used in this Article, the terms "mental disease or defect" do not include an abnormality manifested only by repeated criminal or otherwise anti-social conduct.

UNITED STATES v. POLLARD

United States District Court for the Eastern District of Michigan, 1959.
171 F.Supp. 474, set aside 282 F.2d 450, mandate clarified 285 F.2d 81.

LEVIN, District Judge. The defendant, Marmion Pollard, having waived indictment, the Government instituted this prosecution on a three-count information charging him, under Section 2113(d), Title 18 U.S.C.A., with the attempted robbery of the Chene-Medbury Branch of the Bank of the Commonwealth and the 24th-Michigan Branch of the Detroit Bank & Trust Company on May 21, 1958, and the attempted robbery on June 3, 1958, of the Woodrow Wilson-Davison Branch of the Bank of the Commonwealth. These banks, members of the Federal Reserve System and insured by the Federal Deposit Insurance Corporation, are located in Detroit, Michigan.

On arraignment, the accused pleaded guilty before another judge of this Court. Subsequently, upon advice of counsel, he moved to set aside the guilty plea on the ground that he was insane at the time he committed the acts upon which the prosecution was based. The Court, with the acquiescence of the Government, permitted the defendant to withdraw his guilty plea, and a plea of not guilty was entered. The case was then assigned to me for trial.

Prior to trial, I was advised that a psychiatric report of a psychiatrist retained by the defendant indicated that the defendant was, at the time of the offenses, suffering from a diseased mind which produced an irresistible impulse to commit the criminal acts. Subsequently, a report was submitted to the Government by each of two psychiatrists who had examined the defendant at its request. These reports, which were made available to me, agreed with the conclusion of the defendant's psychiatrist. It then appeared to me that it would be in the interest of justice to secure a psychiatric evaluation of defendant's state of mind based upon more extensive study. I was particularly desirous of having such a study made inasmuch as the psychiatric reports submitted to me were based on interviews that did not exceed a maximum of two hours with each of the three psychiatrists. I, thereupon, on October 10, 1958, entered an order that the defendant be sent to the United States Medical Center at Springfield, Missouri. After a study of thirty days, the Medical Center submitted a report which was introduced in evidence. The gist of the report may be set out as follows:

> During the period under inquiry, "a dissociative state may have existed and that his [defendant's] actions may not have been consciously motivated.
>
> "It is, therefore, our opinion that during the period in question, Pollard, while intellectually capable of knowing right from wrong, may have been governed by unconscious drives which made it impossible for him to adhere to the right.
>
> "* * * We readily acknowledge our inability either to marshal sufficient objective facts or formulate a completely satisfactory theory on which to base a solid opinion as to subject's responsibility during the period in question." [1]

The defendant elected to be tried by the Court without a jury. During the trial, the following facts appeared:

The defendant is an intelligent, twenty-nine year old man. In 1949, he married and, during the next four years, three sons and a daughter were born of this marriage. He was apparently a well-adjusted, happy, family man. In 1952, he became a member of the Police Department of the City of Detroit and continued to work as a policeman until he was apprehended for the acts for which he is now

1. Not only is this report, in the light most favorable to the defendant, inconclusive but in part is based upon facts which were not substantiated during the trial. The personal and social history section of the report states that after his wife's death "it was noted by his supervisors that he [defendant] became less efficient, less interested, more withdrawn and a noticeably less effective policeman". However, the police department records introduced in evidence reveal that the defendant's police work covering the period of inquiry, if anything, was more effective than his service prior to the death of his wife.

being prosecuted. In April, 1956, his wife and infant daughter were brutally killed in an unprovoked attack by a drunken neighbor.

On May 21, 1958, one day before he remarried, at about 11:00 A.M., defendant entered the 24th-Michigan Branch of the Detroit Bank & Trust Company. He paused for a few moments to look over the bank and then proceeded to an enclosure in which a bank official was at work. He told the official, whom he believed to be the manager, that he wanted to open a savings account. He then walked through a swinging gate into the enclosure, sat down at the desk, pulled out a gun and pointed it at the official. He ordered the official to call a teller. When the teller arrived, the defendant handed a brown paper grocery bag to him and told him to fill it with money. While it was being filled, defendant kept the bank official covered. The teller filled the bag with money as ordered and turned it over to the defendant. Thereupon, defendant ordered the bank official to accompany him to the exit. As both the defendant and bank official approached the exit, the official suddenly wrapped his arms around the defendant, who then dropped the bag and fled from the bank and escaped.

About 4:00 P.M., on the same day, he entered the Chene-Medbury Branch of the Bank of the Commonwealth and walked to a railing behind which a bank employee was sitting. He pointed his gun at the man and told him to sit quietly. The employee, however, did not obey this order but instead raised an alarm, whereupon the defendant ran from the bank and again escaped.

After the defendant was apprehended by the Detroit Police under circumstances which I shall later relate, he admitted to agents of the Federal Bureau of Investigation that after his abortive attempts to rob the two banks, he decided to rob a third bank and actually proceeded on the same day to an unnamed bank he had selected but decided not to make the attempt when he discovered that the bank was "too wide open"—had too much window area so that the possibility of apprehension was enhanced.

On June 3, at about 3:00 P.M., the defendant entered the Woodrow Wilson-Davison Branch of the Bank of the Commonwealth and went directly to an enclosure behind which a male and female employee were sitting at desks facing each other. Defendant held his gun under a jacket which he carried over his right arm. He ordered the woman employee to come out from behind the railing. In doing so, she grasped the edge of her desk. Defendant, in the belief that she may have pushed an alarm button, decided to leave but ordered the woman to accompany him out of the bank. When they reached the street, he told her to walk ahead of him, but not to attract attention. Defendant noticed a police car approaching the bank and waited until it passed him, then ran across an empty lot to his car and again escaped.

On June 11, 1958, he attempted to hold up a grocery market. He was thwarted in the attempt when the proprietor screamed and, becoming frightened, the defendant fled. In so doing, he abandoned his automobile in back of the market where he had parked it during the holdup attempt. Routinely, this car was placed under surveillance and later when the defendant, dressed in his Detroit Police Officer's uniform, attempted to get in it, he was arrested by detectives of the Detroit Police Force.

After his apprehension, the defendant confessed to eleven other robberies, or attempted robberies.

The three psychiatrists who submitted the written reports, all qualified and respected members of their profession, testified that in their opinion the defendant, at the time he committed the criminal acts, knew the difference between right and wrong and knew that the acts he committed were wrong but was suffering from a "traumatic neurosis" or "dissociative reaction", characterized by moods of depression and severe feelings of guilt, induced by the traumatic effect of the death of his wife and child and his belief that he was responsible for their deaths because by his absence from home he left them exposed to the actions of the crazed, drunken neighbor. They further stated that he had an unconscious desire to be punished by society to expiate these guilt feelings and that the governing power of his mind was so destroyed or impaired that he was unable to resist the commission of the criminal acts. In their opinion, however, the defendant was not then, nor is he now, psychotic or committable to a mental institution.

Three of defendant's fellow police officers, called as defense witnesses, testified that during the period in which the defendant committed the criminal acts he had a tendency to be late for work; that at times he was despondent; and that he occasionally seemed to be lost in thought and did not promptly respond to questions directed to him. One of the officers testified that on one occasion, he repeatedly beat the steering wheel of the police car in which they were riding, while at the same time reiterating the name of his murdered wife. However, none of them found his conduct or moods to be of such consequence that they believed it necessary to report the defendant to a superior officer.

Defendant's present wife, who impressed me as an intelligent person, testified that on two occasions defendant suddenly, and for no reason apparent to her, lapsed into crying spells and that he talked to her once or twice about committing suicide. She also testified that during one such period of depression he pointed a gun at himself; that she became frightened and called the police; that the police came, relieved him of his gun, and took him to the precinct police station; and that after his release he appeared jovial and acted as if nothing had happened. Defendant's brother-in-law stated that the defendant had always been a very happy person but that he became noticeably despondent after the death of his wife and child and expressed a desire to commit suicide because he now no longer had a reason for living.

A police lieutenant of the Detroit Police Department testified that the defendant's police work, during the period with which we are now concerned, as evidenced by his efficiency rating and his written duty reports, was, if anything, more effective than his service prior to the death of his wife.

Counsel for defendant contends that since all the medical testimony was to the effect that the defendant was suffering from an irresistible impulse at the time of the commission of the offenses, this Court must accept this uncontroverted expert testimony and find him not guilty by reason of insanity.

* * *

I have great respect for the profession of psychiatry. Vast areas of information have been made available through its efforts. I have found much comfort in having the assistance of psychiatrists in the disposition of many cases on sentence. Yet, there are compelling reasons for not blindly following the opinions of experts on controlling issues of fact. Expert testimony performs a valuable function in explaining complex and specialized data to the untutored lay mind. When the experts have made available their knowledge to aid the jury or the Court in reaching a conclusion, their function is completed. The opinions and judgments or inferences of experts, even when unanimous and uncontroverted, are not necessarily conclusive on the trier of the facts and may be disregarded when, in the light of the facts adduced, such judgments, opinions or inferences do not appear valid. The jury, in determining the probative effect to be given to expert testimony, is not to disregard its own experience and knowledge and its collective conscience. It follows that this is also true of the judge sitting without a jury.

The psychiatrists, as I hereinbefore related, testified that the defendant suffered from severe feelings of depression and guilt; and that in their opinion he had an irresistible impulse to commit criminal acts, an unconscious desire to be apprehended and punished; and that he geared his behavior to the accomplishment of this end. However, his entire pattern of conduct during the period of his criminal activities militates against this conclusion. His conscious desire not to be apprehended and punished was demonstrably greater than his unconscious desire to the contrary. After his apprehension, despite searching interrogation for over five hours by Detroit Police Officers and by agents of the Federal Bureau of Investigation, he denied any participation in criminal conduct of any kind. It was only after he was positively identified by bank personnel that he finally admitted that he did attempt to perpetrate the bank robberies. I asked one of the psychiatrists to explain this apparent inconsistency. In answer to my question, he stated that although the defendant had an unconscious desire to be apprehended and punished, when the possibility of apprehension became direct and immediate, the more dominating desire for self-preservation asserted itself. This explanation may have merit if applied to individual acts. However, the validity of a theory that attempts to explain the behavior of a person must be determined in light of that person's entire behavioral pattern and not with reference to isolated acts which are extracted from that pattern. The defendant's pattern of behavior of May 21, 1958, discloses that the desire for self-preservation was not fleeting and momentary but continuing, consistent and dominant. What, then, becomes of the theory of irresistible impulse? Looking to the events of that day, I am asked to believe, first, that the defendant, acting pursuant to an irresistible impulse, selected a bank site to rob, entered the bank to accomplish that end, purposely failed in the attempt and when the end he sought, apprehension, was in view, escaped because of the dominance, at the moment of ultimate accomplishment, of the stronger drive for self-preservation. I must then believe that when the defendant knew he was apparently free from detection, his compulsive state reasserted itself and that he again went through the steps of planning, abortive attempt and escape. And if I acquiesce in this theory, what other psychiatric theory explains his subsequent conduct—his plan to rob a third unnamed bank and the rejection of that plan because of his subjective belief that the possibility of apprehension would be too great? If the theory remains the same, then it appears that in the latter case, the fear of apprehension and punishment tipped "the scales enough to make resistible an impulse otherwise irresistible." Guttmacher and Weihofen, Psychiatry and the Law, 413. It is a logical inference that, in reality, the other robbery attempts were made as the result of impulses that the defendant did not choose voluntarily to resist because, to him, the possibility of success outweighed the likelihood of detection which is in essence a motivation for all criminal conduct. The impulse being resistible, the defendant is accountable for his criminal conduct.

Psychiatrists admit that the line between irresistible impulse and acts which are the result of impulses not resisted is not easy to trace. Guttmacher and Weihofen, Psychiatry and the Law. To the extent that the line may be traced, the distinguishing motivation of the action, whether the act is performed to satisfy an intrinsic need or is the result of extrinsic provocation, is a determining factor. Admittedly, motivations may be mixed. However, all the facts have clearly established that defendant's criminal activity was planned to satisfy an extrinsic need by a reasoned but anti-social method. The defendant had financial problems of varying degrees of intensity throughout his life. He had financial difficulties during his first marriage. He was now embarking upon a second marriage. He was about to undertake the responsibility of supporting not only a wife and himself, but also four children, three of them the product of his first marriage. In statements given to agents of the Federal Bureau of Investigation admitting his criminal activity, he stated: "Inasmuch as I was about to marry my second wife, I decided that I would not lead the same type of financially insecure life that I led with my first wife. I needed about $5,000 in order to buy a house. My only purpose in deciding to rob a bank was to obtain $5,000 and if I obtained the money, I did not intend to continue robbing." Defendant's entire pattern of conduct was consistent with this expressed motivation.

Life does not always proceed on an even keel. Periods of depression, feelings of guilt and inadequacy are experienced by many of us. Defendant was a devoted husband and loving father. His feelings of despondency and depression induced by the brutal killing of his wife and infant daughter were not unnatural. How else the defendant should have reacted to his tragic loss I am not told. His conduct throughout this crucial period did not cause any concern among his colleagues. All stated unequivocally that in their opinion he was sane. Significant also is the fact that his present wife married him on May 22, 1958, after a year of courtship. It is a permissible inference that defendant's conduct relative to his mental condition, as related by her, did not suggest to her that the defendant was insane.

I am satisfied beyond a reasonable doubt that the defendant committed the acts for which he is now charged and that when he committed them he was legally sane.

I, therefore, adjudge the defendant guilty of the three counts of the information.

NOTES AND QUESTIONS

1. On appeal, the trial judge's decision was reversed. In view of the "unanimous testimony of the government's medical experts * * * and appellant's expert witnesses" and the testimony of the lay witnesses, the presumption of sanity was overcome and the government failed to sustain its burden of proving sanity under the federal rule. Pollard v. United States, 282 F.2d 450, mandate clarified, 285 F.2d 81 (6th Cir. 1960).

2. Under a recently-enacted Michigan statute, a defendant who asserts the defense of insanity may be found "guilty but mentally ill:"

768.36 Guilty but mentally ill, finding by jury, plea of guilty but mentally ill, sentence probation

Sec. 36. (1) If the defendant asserts a defense of insanity * * * the defendant may be found "guilty but mentally ill" if, after trial, the trier of fact finds all of the following beyond a reasonable doubt:

(a) That the defendant is guilty of an offense.

(b) That the defendant was mentally ill at the time of the commission of that offense.

(c) That the defendant was not legally insane at the time of the commission of that offense.

A defendant who is found "guilty but mentally ill" may be sentenced to any punishment that could be imposed upon a defendant who is convicted of the same offense. If the defendant is sentenced to imprisonment, he is to be specially evaluated and any treatment necessary is to be provided, including transfer to a hospital run by the Department of Mental Health. In the event that the parole board considers the defendant for parole, the Board is directed by statute to obtain information from the facility administering treatment to the defendant. In the event that probation is imposed as a penalty—and if treatment is recommended after an evaluation of the defendant by the Center for Forensic Psychiatry—such treatment is to be made a condition of probation. Is such an alternative to the verdict of "not guilty by reason of insanity" a desirable one? Why, or why not?

UNITED STATES v. BRAWNER

United States Court of Appeals, District of Columbia Circuit, 1972.
471 F.2d 969.

LEVENTHAL, Circuit Judge:

The principal issues raised on this appeal from a conviction for second degree murder and carrying a dangerous weapon relate to appellant's defense of insanity. After the case was argued to a division of the court, the court *sua sponte* ordered rehearing en banc. We identified our intention to reconsider the appropriate standard for the insanity defense * * *.

* * *

[A] *Prior Developments of the Insanity Defense in this Jurisdiction*

History looms large in obtaining a sound perspective for a subject like this one. But the cases are numerous. And since our current mission is to illuminate the present, rather than to linger over the past, it suffices for our purposes to review a handful of our opinions on the insanity defense.

The landmark opinion was written by Judge Bazelon in Durham v. United States, 94 U.S.App.D.C. 228, 214 F.2d 862 (1954). Prior to *Durham* the law of the District of Columbia was established by United States v. Lee, 15 D.C. (4 Mackey) 489, 496 (1886) and Smith v. United States, 59 App.D.C. 144, 36 F.2d 548 (1929), which, taken together, stated a traditional test of insanity, in terms of right and wrong and irresistible impulse. *Durham* adopted the "product rule," pioneered in State v. Pike, 49 N.H. 399, 402 (1869–70), and exculpated from criminal responsibility those whose forbidden acts were the product of a mental disease or defect.

Few cases have evoked as much comment as *Durham*. It has sparked widespread interest in the legal-judicial community and focused attention on the profound problems involved in defining legal responsibility in case of mental illness. It has been hailed as a guide to the difficult and problem-laden intersection of law and psychiatry, ethics and science. It has been scored as an unwarranted loophole through which the cunning criminal might escape from the penalty of the law. We view it more modestly, as the court's effort, designed in the immemorial manner of the case method that has built the common law, to alleviate two serious problems with the previous rule.

The first of these was a problem of language which raised an important symbolic issue in the law. We felt that the language of the old right-wrong/irresistible impulse rule for insanity was antiquated, no longer reflecting the community's judgment as to who ought to be held criminally liable for socially destructive acts. We considered the rule as restated to have more fruitful, accurate and considered reflection of the sensibilities of the community as revised and expanded in the light of continued study of abnormal human behavior.

The second vexing problem that *Durham* was designed to reach related to the concern of the psychiatrists called as expert witnesses for their special knowledge of the problem of insanity, who often and typically felt that they were obliged to reach outside of their professional expertise when they were asked, under the traditional insanity rule established in 1843 by *M'Naghten's* Case, whether the defendant knew right from wrong. They further felt that the narrowness of the traditional test, which framed the issue of responsibility solely in terms of cognitive impairment, made it impossible to convey to the judge and jury the full range of information material to an assessment of defendant's responsibility.

* * *

A difficulty arose under the *Durham* rule in application. The rule was devised to facilitate the giving of testimony by medical experts in the context of a legal rule, with the jury called upon to reach a composite conclusion that had medical, legal and moral components. However the pristine statement of the *Durham* rule opened the door to "trial by label." *Durham* did distinguish between "disease," as used "in the sense of a condition which is considered capable of either improving or deteriorating," and "defect," as referring to a condition not capable of such change "and which may be either congenital or the result of injury, or the residual effect of a physical or mental disease." 94 U.S.App.D.C. at 241, 214 F.2d at 875. But the court failed to explicate what abnormality of mind was an essential ingredient of these concepts. In the absence of a definition of "mental disease or defect," medical experts attached to them the meanings which would naturally occur to them—medical meanings—and gave testimony accordingly. The problem was dramatically highlighted by the weekend flip flop case, In re Rosenfield, 157 F.Supp. 18 (D.D.C.1957).

The petitioner was described as a sociopath. A St. Elizabeths psychiatrist testified that a person with a sociopathic personality was not suffering from a mental disease. That was Friday afternoon. On Monday morning, through a policy change at St. Elizabeths Hospital, it was determined as an administrative matter that the state of a psychopathic or sociopathic personality did constitute a mental disease.

The concern that medical terminology not control legal outcomes culminated in McDonald v. United States, 114 U.S.App.D.C. 120, 312 F.2d 847, 851 (en banc, 1962), where this court recognized that the term, mental disease or defect, has various meanings, depending upon how and why it is used, and by whom. Mental disease means one thing to a physician bent on treatment, but something different, if somewhat overlapping, to a court of law. We provided a legal definition of mental disease or defect, and held that it included "any abnormal condition of the mind which substantially affects mental or emotional processes and substantially impairs behavior controls." (312 F.2d at 851). "Thus the jury would consider testimony concerning the development, adaptation and functioning of these processes and controls." Id.

While the *McDonald* standard of mental disease was not without an attribute of circularity, it was useful in the administration of justice because it made plain that clinical and legal definitions of mental disease were distinct, and it helped the jury to sort out its complex task and to focus on the matters given it to decide.

The *Durham* rule also required explication along other lines, notably the resolution of the ambiguity inherent in the formulation concerning actions that were the "product" of mental illness. It was supplemented in Carter v. United States, 102 U.S.App.D.C. 227 at 234, 235, 252 F.2d 608 at 615–616 (1957):

> The simple fact that a person has a mental disease or defect is not enough to relieve him of responsibility for a crime. There must be a relationship between the disease and the criminal act; and the relationship must be such as to justify a reasonable inference that the act would not have been committed if the person had not been suffering from the disease.

Thus *Carter* clarified that the mental illness must not merely have entered into the production of the act, but must have played a necessary role. *Carter* identified the "product" element of the rule with the "but for" variety of causation.

The pivotal "product" term continued to present problems, principally that it put expert testimony on a faulty footing. Assuming that a mental disease, in the legal sense, had been established, the fate of the defendant came to be determined by what came to be referred to by the legal jargon of "productivity." On the other hand, it was obviously sensible if not imperative that the experts having pertinent knowledge should speak to the crucial question whether the mental abnormality involved is one associated with aberrant behavior. But since "productivity" was so decisive a factor in the decisional equation, a ruling permitting experts to testify expressly in language of "product" raised in a different context the concern lest the ultimate issue be in fact turned over to the experts rather than retained for the jurors representing the community.

* * *

It was in this context that the court came to the decision in Washington v. United States, 129 U.S.App.D.C. 29, 390 F.2d 444 (1967), which forbade experts from testifying as to productivity altogether. Chief Judge Bazelon's opinion illuminates the basis of the ruling, as one intended "to help the psychiatrists understand their role in court, and thus eliminate a fundamental cause of unsatisfactory expert testimony," namely, the tendency of the expert to use "concepts [which] can become slogans, hiding facts and representing nothing more than the witness's own conclusion about the defendant's criminal responsibility." (at 41, 390 F.2d at 456).

* * *

[B] *Comments Concerning Reason for Adoption of ALI Rule and Scope of Rule as Adopted By This Court*

[The court announced its decision to adopt the ALI Rule and turned to the reasons for this decision.]

1. *Need to depart from "product" formulation and undue dominance by experts.*

A principal reason for our decision to depart from the *Durham* rule is the undesirable characteristic, surviving even the *McDonald* modification, of undue dominance by the experts giving testimony. * * * The difficulty is rooted in the circumstance that there is no generally accepted understanding, either in the jury or the community it represents, of the concept requiring that the crime be the "product" of the mental disease.

* * *

The doctrine of criminal responsibility is such that there can be no doubt "of the complicated nature of the decision to be made—intertwining moral, legal, and medical judgments," see King v. United States, 125 U.S.App.D.C. 318, 324, 372 F.2d 383, 389 (1967) and *Durham* * * *. Hence, as *King* and other opinions have noted, jury decisions have been accorded unusual deference even when they have found responsibility in the face of a powerful record, with medical evidence uncontradicted, pointing toward exculpation. The "moral" elements of the decision are not defined exclusively by religious considerations but by the totality of underlying conceptions of ethics and justice shared by the community, as expressed by its jury surrogate. The essential feature of a jury "lies in the interposition between the accused and his accuser of the commonsense judgment of a group of laymen, and in the community participation and shared responsibility that results from that group's determination of guilt or innocence." Williams v. Florida, 399 U.S. 78, 100, 90 S.Ct. 1893, 1906, 26 L.Ed.2d 446 (1970).

The expert witnesses—psychiatrists and psychologists—are called to adduce relevant information concerning what may for convenience be referred to as the "medical" component of the responsibility issue. But the difficulty—as emphasized in *Washington*—is that the medical expert comes, by testimony given in terms of a non-medical construct ("product"), to express conclusions that in essence embody ethical and legal conclusions. There is, indeed, irony in a situation under which the *Durham* rule, which was adopted in large part to permit experts to testify in their own terms concerning matters within their domain which the jury should know, resulted in testimony by the experts in terms not their own to reflect unexpressed judgments in a domain that is properly not theirs but the jury's. The irony is heightened when the jurymen, instructed under the esoteric "product" standard, are influenced significantly by "product" testimony of expert witnesses really reflecting ethical and legal judgments rather than a conclusion within the witnesses' particular expertise.

It is easier to identify and spotlight the irony than to eradicate the mischief. The objective of *Durham* is still sound—to put before the jury the information that is within the expert's domain, to aid the jury in making a broad and comprehensive judgment. But when the instructions and appellate decisions define the "product" inquiry as the ultimate issue, it is like stopping the tides to try to halt the emergence of this term in the language of those with a central role in the trial—the lawyers who naturally seek to present testimony that will influence the jury who will be charged under the ultimate "product" standard, and the expert witnesses who have an awareness, gained from forensic psychiatry and related disciplines, of the ultimate "product" standard that dominates the proceeding.

The experts have meaningful information to impart, not only on the existence of mental illness or not, but also on its relationship to the incident charged as an offense. In the interest of justice this valued information should be available, and should not be lost or blocked by requirements that unnaturally restrict communication between the experts and the jury. The more we have pondered the problem the more convinced we have become that the sound solution lies not in further shaping of the *Durham* "product" approach in more refined molds, but in adopting the ALI's formulation as the linchpin of our jurisprudence.

The ALI's formulation retains the core requirement of a meaningful relationship between the mental illness and the incident charged. The language in the ALI rule is sufficiently in the common ken that its use in the courtroom, or in preparation for trial, permits a reasonable three-way communication—between (a) the law-trained, judges and lawyers; (b) the experts and (c) the jurymen—without insisting on a vocabulary that is either stilted or stultified, or conducive to a testimonial mystique permitting expert dominance and encroachment on the jury's function. There is no indication in the available literature that any such untoward development has attended the reasonably widespread adoption of the ALI rule in the Federal courts and a substantial number of state courts.

* * *

2. *Consideration and rejection of other suggestions*

a. *Proposal to abolish insanity defense*

A number of proposals in the journals recommend that the insanity defense be abolished altogether. This is advocated in the amicus brief of the National District Attorneys Association as both desirable and lawful. The amicus brief of American Psychiatric Association concludes it would be desirable, with appropriate safeguards, but would require a constitutional amendment. That a constitutional amendment would be required is also the conclusion of others, generally in opposition to the proposal.

This proposal has been put forward by responsible judges for consideration, with the objective of reserving psychiatric overview for the phase of the criminal process concerned with disposition of the person determined to have been the actor. However, we are convinced that the proposal cannot properly be imposed by judicial fiat.

The courts have emphasized over the centuries that "free will" is the postulate of responsibility under our jurisprudence. 4 Blackstone's Commentaries 27. The concept of "belief in freedom of the human will and a consequent ability and duty of the normal individual to choose between good and evil" is a core concept that is "universal and persistent in mature systems of law." Morissette v. United States, 342 U.S. 246, 250, 72 S.Ct. 240, 243, 96 L.Ed. 288 (1952). Criminal responsibility is assessed when through "free will" a man elects to do evil. * * *

The concept of lack of "free will" is both the root of origin of the insanity defense and the line of its growth. This cherished principle is not undercut by difficulties, or differences of view, as to how best to express the free will concept in the light of the expansion of medical knowledge. We do not concur in the view of the National District Attorneys Association that the insanity defense should be abandoned judicially, either because it is at too great a variance with popular conceptions of guilt or fails "to show proper respect for the personality of the criminal [who] is liable to resent pathology more than punishment."

These concepts may be measured along with other ingredients in a legislative re-examination of settled doctrines of criminal responsibility, root, stock and branch. Such a reassessment, one that seeks to probe and appraise the society's processes and values, is for the legislative branch, assuming no constitutional bar. * * *

b. *Proposal for defense if mental disease impairs capacity to such an extent that the defendant cannot "justly be held responsible."*

We have also pondered the suggestion that the jury be instructed that the defendant lacks criminal responsibility if the jury finds that the defendant's mental disease impairs his capacity or controls to such an extent that he cannot "justly be held responsible."

This was the view of a British commission, adapted and proposed in 1955 by Professor Wechsler, the distinguished Reporter for the ALI's Model Penal Code, and sustained by some, albeit a minority, of the members of the ALI's Council. * * *

However, there is a substantial concern that an instruction overtly cast in terms of "justice" cannot feasibly be restricted to the ambit of what may properly be taken into account but will splash with unconfinable and malign consequences. The Government cautions that "explicit appeals to 'justice' will result in litigation of extraneous issues and will encourage improper arguments to the jury phrased solely in terms of 'sympathy' and 'prejudice.' "

Nor is this solely a prosecutor's concern.

* * *

The amicus submission of the Public Defender Service argues that it would be beneficial to focus the jury's attention on the moral and legal questions intertwined in the insanity defense. It expresses concern, however, over a blameworthiness instruction without more, saying (Br. 19) "it may well be that the 'average' American condemns the mentally ill." * * *

We are impressed by the observation of Professor Abraham S. Goldstein, one of the most careful students of the problem:

> [The] overly general standard may place too great a burden upon the jury. If the law provides no standard, members of the jury are placed in the difficult position of having to find a man responsible for no other reason than their personal feeling about him. Whether the psyches of individual jurors are strong enough to make that decision, or whether the "law" should put that obligation on them, is open to serious question. It is far easier for them to perform the role assigned to them by legislature and courts if they know—or are able to rationalize—that their verdicts are "required" by law.[28]

* * *

28. A. Goldstein, The Insanity Defense 81–82 (1967).

* * * There is wisdom in the view that a jury generally understands well enough that an instruction composed in flexible terms gives it sufficient latitude so that, without disregarding the instruction, it can provide that application of the instruction which harmonizes with its sense of justice. The ALI rule generally communicates that meaning.

Taking all these considerations into account we conclude that the ALI rule as announced is not productive of injustice, and we decline to proclaim the broad "justly responsible" standard.

* * *

3. *ALI rule is contemplated as improving the process of adjudication, not as affecting number of insanity acquittals*

* * *

We have no way of forecasting what will be the effect on verdicts, of juries or judges, from the reduction in influence of expert testimony on "productivity" that reflects judgments outside the domain of expertise. Whatever its effect, we are confident that the rule adopted today provides a sounder relationship in terms of the giving, comprehension and application of expert testimony. Our objective is not to steer the jury's verdict but to enhance its deliberation.[35]

4. *Elements of the ALI rule adopted by this court*

Though it provides a general uniformity, the ALI rule leaves room for variations. * * *

[a] *At the time of the conduct*

Under the ALI rule the issue is not whether defendant is so disoriented or void of controls that he is never able to conform to external demands, but whether he had that capacity at the time of the conduct. The question is not properly put in terms of whether he would have capacity to conform in some untypical restraining situation—as with an attendant or policeman at his elbow. The issue is whether he was able to conform in the unstructured condition of life in an open society, and whether the result of his abnormal mental condition was a lack of substantial internal controls. * * *

[b] *Capacity to appreciate wrongfulness of his conduct*

As to the option of terminology noted in the ALI code, we adopt the formulation that exculpates a defendant whose mental condition is such that he lacks substantial capacity to appreciate the wrongful-

35. We do not share the cynical view that treats the instruction as devoid of consequence. In a study of the reactions of more than a thousand jurors to two experimental trials involving a defense of insanity, it was found that juries deliberated significantly longer when instructed under *Durham* than under *M'Naghten*. Yet this did not undercut consensus; there was no significant difference in the percentages of hung juries. R. Simon, The Jury and the Defense of Insanity 213 *ff.* (1967).

ness of his conduct. We prefer this on pragmatic grounds to "appreciate the criminality of his conduct" since the resulting jury instruction is more like that conventionally given to and applied by the jury. While such an instruction is of course subject to the objection that it lacks complete precision, it serves the objective of calling on the jury to provide a community judgment on a combination of factors. And since the possibility of analytical differences between the two formulations is insubstantial in fact in view of the control capacity test, we are usefully guided by the pragmatic considerations pertinent to jury instructions.[40]

* * *

[c] *Broad presentation to the jury*

Our adoption of the ALI rule does not depart from the doctrines this court has built up over the past twenty years to assure a broad presentation to the jury concerning the condition of defendant's mind and its consequences. Thus we adhere to our rulings admitting expert testimony of psychologists, as well as psychiatrists, and to our many decisions contemplating that expert testimony on this subject will be accompanied by presentation of the facts and premises underlying the opinions and conclusions of the experts, and that the Government and defense may present, in Judge Blackmun's words, "all possibly relevant evidence" bearing on cognition, volition and capacity. We agree with the amicus submission of the National District Attorneys Association that the law cannot "distinguish between physiological, emotional, social and cultural sources of the impairment"—assuming, of course, requisite testimony establishing exculpation under the pertinent standard—and all such causes may be both referred to by the expert and considered by the trier of fact.

40. * * *

When the question arose as to whether "wrong" means moral or legal wrong, the American courts split. One group, following *M'Naghten*, held the offender sane if he knew the act was prohibited by law. A second group, following the lead of Judge Cardozo in People v. Schmidt, 216 N.Y. 324, 110 N.E. 945, 948–950 (1915) ruled that, e. g., the defense was available to a defendant who knew the killing was legally wrong but thought it morally right because he was so ordered by God. The issue is discussed and authorities collected in A. Goldstein, The Insanity Defense, and notes thereto. In Sauer v. United States, 241 F.2d 640, 649 (9th Cir. 1957), Judge Barnes summed up the practicalities: "[The] practice has been to state merely the word 'wrong' and leave the decision for the jury. While not entirely condonable, such practice is explained in large measure by an awareness that the jury will eventually exercise a moral judgment as to the sanity of the accused."

This issue rarely arose under *M'Naghten*, and its substantiality was reduced if not removed by the control capacity test, since anyone under a delusion as to God's mandate would presumably lack substantial capacity to conform his conduct to the requirements of the law.

We are not informed of any case where a mental illness left a person with capacity to appreciate wrongfulness but not a capacity to appreciate criminality. If such a case ever arises, supported by credible evidence, the court can then consider its correct disposition more meaningfully, in the light of a concrete record.

Breadth of input under the insanity defense is not to be confused with breadth of the doctrines establishing the defense. As the National District Attorneys Association brief points out, the latitude for salient evidence of e. g., social and cultural factors pertinent to an abnormal condition of the mind significantly affecting capacity and controls, does not mean that such factors may be taken as establishing a separate defense for persons whose mental condition is such that blame can be imposed. We have rejected a broad "injustice" approach that would have opened the door to expositions of e. g., cultural deprivation, unrelated to any abnormal condition of the mind.

We have recognized that "Many criminologists point out that even normal human behavior is influenced by such factors as training, environment, poverty and the like, which may limit the understanding and options of the individual." King v. United States, supra, 125 U.S.App.D.C. at 323, 372 F.2d at 388. Determinists may contend that every man's fate is ultimately sealed by his genes and environment, over which he has no control. Our jurisprudence, however, while not oblivious to deterministic components, ultimately rests on a premise of freedom of will. This is not to be viewed as an exercise in philosophic discourse, but as a governmental fusion of ethics and necessity, which takes into account that a system of rewards and punishments is itself part of the environment that influences and shapes human conduct. Our recognition of an insanity defense for those who lack the essential, threshold free will possessed by those in the normal range is not to be twisted, directly or indirectly, into a device for exculpation of those without an abnormal condition of the mind.

Finally, we have not accepted suggestions to adopt a rule that disentangles the insanity defense from a medical model, and announces a standard exculpating anyone whose capacity for control is insubstantial, for whatever cause or reason. There may be logic in these submissions, but we are not sufficiently certain of the nature, range and implications of the conduct involved to attempt an all-embracing unified field theory. The applicable rule can be discerned as the cases arise in regard to other conditions—somnambulism or other automatisms; blackouts due, e. g. to overdose of insulin; drug addiction. Whether these somatic conditions should be governed by a rule comparable to that herein set forth for mental disease would require, at a minimum, a judicial determination, which takes medical opinion into account, finding convincing evidence of an ascertainable condition characterized by "a broad consensus that free will does not exist." Salzman v. United States, 131 U.S.App.D.C. 393, 400, 405 F.2d 358, 365 (1968) (concurring opinion of Judge Wright).

[C.] *Issue of Causality Testimony*

We are urged to reverse appellant's conviction on the ground that the trial court erred in allowing Government experts to testify in terms of "causality" [in violation of] * * * Washington v. United States, 129 U.S.App.D.C. 29, 390 F.2d 444 (1967) * * *. We think the expert testimony in this case adequately and lucidly ventilated the issues, there was no use of the term "product," and we see no sign of overreaching.

* * *

The goal of avoiding undue dominance of the jury by expert testimony does not require ostrich disregard of the key issue of causality. That issue, however, is focused more meaningfully, for both expert and jury, by asking whether the mental disease or defect resulted in lack of substantial capacity to control the behavior in question (or appreciate its wrongfulness). * * * The rule contemplating expert testimony as to the existence and consequence of a mental disease or defect is not to be construed as permission to testify solely in terms of expert conclusions. * * *

[W]e do not retain *Washington* insofar as it reflects the product rule, and we permit testimony by the expert, and cross-examination, on the causal relationship between the mental disease and the existence of substantial capacity for control (and knowledge) at the time of the act. * * *

* * *

The case is remanded for further consideration by the District Court in accordance with this opinion.

So ordered.

BAZELON, Chief Judge, concurring in part and dissenting in part:

We are unanimous in our decision today to abandon the formulation of criminal responsibility adopted eighteen years ago in Durham v. United States, 94 U.S.App.D.C. 228, 214 F.2d 862 (1954). * * * As described in Judge Leventhal's scholarly opinion, the ALI test may make possible an improvement in the adjudication of the responsibility issue. But on the whole I fear that the change made by the Court today is primarily one of form rather than of substance.

* * *

In my view, the ALI test of criminal responsibility, with or without the *McDonald* side bar, cannot remedy the problems in the administration of the defense which have come to light as a result of our efforts to implement the *Durham-McDonald* rule. * * * Nothing in the Court's opinion today suggests a departure from our long-standing view that * * * the evaluation of the defendant's impairment in light of community standards of blameworthiness is the very essence of the jury's role. * * *

Against this background it is clear that *Durham* focused the jury's attention on the wrong question—on the relationship between the act and the impairment rather than on the blameworthiness of the defendant's action measured by prevailing community standards. If the ALI test is indeed an improvement, it is not because it focuses attention on the *right* question, but only because it makes the *wrong* question so obscure that jurors may abandon the effort to answer it literally.

Instead of asking the jury whether the act was caused by the impairment, our new test asks the jury to wrestle with such unfamiliar, if not incomprehensible, concepts as the capacity to appreciate the wrongfulness of one's action, and the capacity to conform one's conduct to the requirements of law. The best hope for our new test is that jurors will regularly conclude that no one—including the experts—can provide a meaningful answer to the questions posed by the ALI test. And in their search for some semblance of an intelligible standard, they may be forced to consider whether it would be just to hold the defendant responsible for his action. By that indirect approach our new test may lead juries to disregard (or at least depreciate) the conclusory testimony of the experts, and to make the "intertwining moral, legal, and medical judgments" on which the resolution of the responsibility question properly depends. * * *

Our instruction to the jury should provide that a defendant is not responsible *if at the time of his unlawful conduct his mental or emotional processes or behavior controls were impaired to such an extent that he cannot justly be held responsible for his act.* This test would ask the psychiatrist a single question: what is the nature of the impairment of the defendant's mental and emotional processes and behavior controls? It would leave for the jury the question whether that impairment is sufficient to relieve the defendant of responsibility for the particular act charged.

The purpose of this proposed instruction is to focus the jury's attention on the legal and moral aspects of criminal responsibility, and to make clear why the determination of responsibility is entrusted to the jury and not the expert witnesses. * * *

In a distressing number of recent cases this Court has been asked to consider questions unrelated to the substantive test of responsibility, but which have, as a practical matter, far greater impact on the operation of the defense than the language of the rule. The Court's decision to abandon *Durham-McDonald* in favor of ALI–*McDonald* does nothing to obsolete these questions or the Court's responses to them. If our paramount goal is an improvement of the process of adjudication of the responsibility issue, our attention should be focused on these questions rather than on the ultimate definition of the test. Obviously, these questions cannot all be resolved by one opinion. But the Court's approach to the disposition of this case offers some indication of the manner in which these questions will be handled in the future.

1. The one consistent note in the Court's analysis of our experience under *Durham* is the objection to domination by the experts accomplished through the productivity requirement. We attempted to deal with that problem in Washington v. United States by barring conclusory, expert testimony on the issue of productivity. Virtually all of the expert witnesses at Brawner's trial agreed that he was suffering from an abnormal condition of the mind. The issue in dispute was productivity—the ultimate issue for the jury. And the transcript is riddled with conclusory, expert testimony on that issue. It is hard to imagine a case which could make a stronger appeal for enforcement of the *Washington* rule.

* * *

The Court's unwillingness to reverse Brawner's conviction on this ground makes clear that this Court and the trial courts no longer have any weapons to combat the problem of conclusory testimony and the resulting domination by experts.

* * *

2. * * * As a practical matter, the defendant often has very great difficulty obtaining adequate expert assistance to gather the information necessary for the presentation of a significant defense. * * *

With limited access to expert psychiatric assistance, indigent defendants normally rely on the government to provide an adequate psychiatric examination at the hospital to which the defendant is committed for observation. In a large number of cases the government's experts are called to testify on behalf of the defense, and their testimony has often proved inadequate. * * *

The practical burden on the defendant is greatly enhanced by the ease with which defense testimony can often be torn to pieces on cross-examination. Where a psychiatrist testifying for the government asserts that the defendant did not suffer from any abnormal condition which could impair his mental processes or behavior controls, defense counsel must have considerable expertise in psychiatry to pick out the weak points in the analysis. Yet "very few attorneys, if any, possess the requisite expertise, and we have no automatic procedure for enabling them to consult with psychiatric experts in the preparation and conduct of the defense." United States v. Leazer, 148 U.S.App.D.C. 356 at 363, 460 F.2d 864 at 871 (Jan. 19, 1972), (Bazelon, C. J., concurring). Even where the defendant has obvious symptoms of mental disorder, defense counsel is frequently helpless to rebut the suggestion by government psychiatrists that the defendant is malingering. If he produces testimony from a private psychiatrist that the defendant is not a malingerer, he is almost sure to find that the government and its expert witnesses will disparage that testimony on the grounds that it was based on an insufficient period of observation.

The defendant might be able to cope with these obstacles to the successful use of the defense if we were willing to set aside jury verdicts unsupported by the evidence. In fact, we have been extremely reluctant to overturn a jury verdict even in the face of substantial evidence that the defendant's act was the product of a condition which impaired his mental or emotional processes and behavior controls.

NOTES AND QUESTIONS

1. Following *Brawner*, the District of Columbia Court of Appeals announced that the decision in *Brawner* was not binding upon that court in light of the Court Reorganization Act, Pub.L. No. 91–358 (July 29, 1970). In Bethea v. United States, 365 A.2d 64 (D.C.Ct.App.1976), the District of Columbia Court of Appeals addressed for itself the question of whether the *Durham* rule should be abandoned. It decided to abandon the rule and to adopt the Model Penal Code formulation of the insanity defense.

2. Should the fact that a defendant has been diagnosed as a "psychopath" or a "sociopath" preclude successful assertion of the insanity defense? See § 4.01(2) of the Model Penal Code and the comments to that section, reprinted at pages 610–13), supra. In Bethea v. United States, 365 A.2d 64 (D.C.Ct.App.1976), the court adopted the language of § 4.01(2) but did not read it as precluding a defendant diagnosed as a psychopath from asserting the insanity defense. Rather, the court read the section as requiring only "that there be some demonstrable dimension to the alleged impairment [offered as establishing insanity] beyond the simple fact of criminal behavior." The court thereby left open the opportunity for a defendant to convice a jury that his impairment, despite the fact that it has been diagnosed "only" as psychopathic behavior, so deprived him of control over his conduct as to constitute insanity. But expert testimony offered in support of such a claim must "provide the trier with more than a bare conclusion resting on the single 'symptom' of a pattern of antisocial conduct." 365 A.2d at 81.

3. Most jurisdictions make provisions for persons acquitted by reason of insanity to be channeled into the mental health system. There is generally a procedural requirement that an acquittal because of insanity be reflected in the verdict. Model Penal Code § 4.03(3); Tex.Code Crim.Procedure, art. 46.03(1)(b). The return of a verdict of "not guilty by reason of insanity" often triggers further proceedings which may result in the acquitted defendant's commitment to the mental health system. But procedures for automatic and indefinite commitment to psychiatric facilities simply upon the fact of acquittal have been attacked on equal protection grounds. These challenges have asserted that such procedures violate equal protection because they create a significant and constitutionally-offensive difference between the manner in which criminal defendants are "committed" and the procedure for "civil" commitment of mentally ill persons who have not been acquitted of a criminal offense by reason of insanity. There is widespread agreement that equal protection is not offended if acquitted defendants are automatically detained for a brief period in order to evaluate them and determine whether they meet applicable standards for mental health commitment. But a number of courts have held that equal protection is violated "where there is substantial difference in either the commitment or release

of persons accused or convicted of a crime on one hand and those who are not so accused or convicted on the other." State v. Clemons, 110 Ariz. 79, 84, 515 P.2d 324, 329 (1973). See also, Bolton v. Harris, 395 F.2d 642 (D. C.Cir.1968). In *Clemons*, the court held invalid a procedure that required an acquitted defendant seeking release from hospitalization to convince a jury (or the court, if a waiver of jury trial was accepted) that he was no longer mentally ill while a person civilly committed can be released when the superintendent of the hospital determines further treatment is unnecessary. But some courts are willing to tolerate certain differentiation between the procedure for detaining acquitted defendants and that for civil commitment:

> An individual who has committed an act of violence, and has thus demonstrated his dangerousness, and who has successfully asserted an insanity defense, may quite properly be treated somewhat differently than from other individuals who, although they may in fact be potentially dangerous as a result of mental problems, have not yet so vehemently demonstrated their dangerousness by violent antisocial behavior.

People ex rel. Henig v. Commissioner, 43 N.Y.2d 334, 338, 401 N.Y.S.2d 462, 465, 372 N.E.2d 304, 306 (1977). The court consequently upheld a procedure that provided for mandatory commitment without a hearing of defendants found not guilty by reason of insanity, where defendants were authorized to seek a hearing at any time to challenge the validity of the detention. The same court in a companion case held that at such a hearing, the burden can be placed upon the acquitted defendant to show by a preponderance of the evidence that he may be released without danger to himself or others. Lublin v. Central Islip Psychiatric Center, 43 N.Y.2d 341, 401 N.Y. S.2d 466, 372 N.E.2d 307 (1977). If persons whose civil commitment are sought must be proved to meet the standard for commitment, does the New York rule concerning the burden of proof upon acquitted defendants deny them equal protection? See generally, Note, Commitment of Persons Acquitted by Reason of Insanity: The Example of the District of Columbia, 74 Colum.L.Rev. 733 (1974).

4. A recent study by the New York Department of Mental Hygiene calls into question the assumption that—in New York, at least—offenders acquitted by reason of insanity are most effectively and efficiently "treated" in the mental health system. Placing such persons in the mental health system "is detrimental not only to the hospitals, but also to the other patients, the individuals themselves and * * * to the aims and needs of society at large." Wright, Problems in Administering the Insanity Defense, in The Insanity Defense in New York 107, 117 (N.Y.Dep't of Mental Hygiene, 1978). By the time the defendants are well enough to be tried (and acquitted), they are usually not sick enough to require treatment in a psychiatric hospital, the report concludes. Yet legal requirements demand that they be retained in custody; this requires significant staff efforts that would otherwise be devoted to treatment of other patients. The requirement of custody also prohibits what are likely to be the most effective forms of treatment, i. e., increasing responsibility, gradual reintegration into the community, vocational training, and similar measures. Wright, supra. On the other hand, the report asserts that New York has developed

the capacity to ensure treatment of mentally disturbed offenders in correctional programs. Wright, Mental Health Services in Correctional Settings, in The Insanity Defense in New York 119 (N.Y.Dep't of Mental Hygiene, 1978).

But probably the "greatest problem" in administering the post-acquittal process, the report indicates, is the task of determining whether acquitted defendants committed to the mental health system are no longer "dangerous" and can therefore be discharged:

> Cocozza and Steadman [The Failure of Psychiatric Predictions of Dangerousness: Clear and Convincing Evidence, 29 Rutgers L.Rev. 1034 (1976)] have repeatedly and convincingly documented that there are no empirical data on which to base a valid prediction of future behavior. No matter how careful the procedures, observations, and tests used by facility staff to arrive at the opinion that an individual can be released without peril * * * the fact of the matter is that the opinion can never be more than guesswork dressed up in the false cloth of reassuring pseudo-science.

Wright, Problems in Administering the Insanity Defense, supra, at 116.

5. What would be gained—and lost—if evidence of psychological abnormality was regarded as totally irrelevant to guilt or innocence but was used in sentencing to determine what should be done with or to the convicted offender? This has been proposed by a number of persons, generally those disillusioned with the operation of the insanity defense. E. g., Weintraub, Criminal Responsibility: Psychiatry Alone Cannot Determine It, 49 A.B.A.J. 1975 (1963). For a general discussion, see Shwedel and Roether, The Disposition Hearing: An Alternative to the Insanity Defense, 49 J.Urban L. 711 (1972).

2. DIMINISHED CAPACITY AND RELATED MATTERS

The doctrine frequently referred to as "diminished capacity" [c] can be stated with deceptive simplicity. Section 4.02(1) of the Model Penal Code (P.O.D.1962), for example, states it as follows:

> Evidence that the defendant suffered from a mental disease or defect is admissible whenever it is relevant to prove that the defendant did or did not have a state of mind which is an element of the offense.

Despite the simplicity of the rule and its apparent logical relationship to the requirement of criminal intent, courts are divided on whether

c. The doctrine is apparently called diminished *capacity* because expert testimony utilized pursuant to it is often in the form of an assertion that because of a mental illness or other abnormality, the defendant lacked the capacity or ability to form the state of mind required for the offense. From such testimony, of course, the trier of fact is urged to infer that the defendant did not in fact have the intent required. There seems no reason, however, why expert testimony could not directly address the question of whether the defendant in fact had the intent at issue. An expert might even testify that, in his opinion, although the defendant had the capacity to form the intent required in fact he did not do so.

evidence of psychological abnormality is admissible on the question of state of mind. Those jurisdictions which reject the so-called diminished capacity rule regard expert testimony and other evidence tending to show that the defendant was psychologically impaired at the time of the crime as limited to establishing a defense of insanity. Even if such evidence is admitted on insanity, these jurisdictions hold that the trier of fact should not consider the evidence as bearing upon whether the defendant had the state of mind required by the crime charged if they find the evidence insufficient to establish the defense of insanity under the standard applicable in the jurisdiction. See generally, Annot., 22 A.L.R.3d 1228 (1968).

In evaluating the issue, it is important to consider the reasons why such evidence is urged as admissible and what policy objectives are sought to be implemented by admitting the evidence. Some analyses urge that admissibility is dictated by the logical application of the state of mind requirement. In United States v. Brawner, 471 F.2d 969 (D.C.Cir. 1972), for example, the court noted that voluntary intoxication was admissible to prove lack of intent. It then continued:

> Neither logic nor justice can tolerate a jurisprudence that defines the elements of an offense as requiring a mental state such that one defendant can properly argue that his voluntary drunkenness removed his capacity to form the specific intent but another defendant is inhibited from a submission of his contention that an abnormal mental condition, for which he was in no way responsible, negated his capacity to form a particular specific intent, even though the condition did not exonerate him from all criminal responsibility.

471 F.2d at 999. This argument appears to assume that implementation of the diminished capacity rule would serve the same policy objectives as are served by the requirement of criminal intent. The "logical relevance" argument of *Brawner* was rejected in Bethea v. United States, 365 A.2d 64 (D.C.Ct.App.1976). Recognizing that evidence of mental disease or defect is, "in the abstract," as relevant to the issue of intent as intoxication, the court nevertheless noted the "unique position" of the defense of insanity in the framework of criminal responsibility. 365 A.2d at 86. It then continued:

> It is true, of course, that the existence of the required state of mind is to be determined subjectively in the sense that the issue must be resolved according to the particular circumstances of a given case. However, this fact may not be allowed to obscure the critical difference between the legal concepts of mens rea and insanity. * * * The former refers to the existence in fact of a "guilty mind"; insanity, on the other hand, connotes a presumption that a particular in-

dividual lacks the capacity to possess such a state of mind. It is upon this distinction that the "logic" of the diminished capacity doctrine flounders.

The concept of mens rea involves what is ultimately the fiction of determining the actual thoughts or mental processes of the accused. * * * It is obvious that a certain resolution of this issue is beyond the ken of scientist and laymen alike. Only by inference can the existence of intent —or the differentiation between its forms, such as general or specific—be determined. * * * The law presumes that all individuals are capable of the mental processes which bear the jurisprudential label "mens rea"; that is, the law presumes sanity. Moreover, for the sake of administrative efficiency and in recognition of fundamental principles of egalitarian fairness, our legal system further presumes that each person is equally capable of the same forms and degrees of intent. * * * The concept of insanity is simply a device the law employs to define the outer limits of that segment of the general population to whom these presumptions concerning the capacity for criminal intent shall not be applied. The line between the sane and the insane for the purposes of criminal adjudication is not drawn because for one group the actual existence of the necessary mental state (or lack thereof) can be determined with any greater certainty, but rather because those whom the law declares insane are demonstrably so abberational in their psychiatric characteristics that we choose to make the assumption that they are incapable of possessing the specified state of mind. Within the range of individuals who are not "insane," the law does not recognize the readily demonstrable fact that as between individual criminal defendants the nature and development of their mental capabilities may vary greatly. * * *

We recognize that there are exceptions to the basic principle that all individuals are presumed to have a similar capacity for mens rea. The rule that evidence of intoxication may be employed to demonstrate the absence of specific intent [is one such exception] * * *. The * * * analogy [asserted in *Brawner*] is flawed, however, by the fact that there are significant evidentiary distinctions between psychiatric abnormality and the recognized incapacitating circumstances. Unlike the notion of partial or relative insanity, conditions such as intoxication, medication, epilepsy, infancy, or senility are, in varying degrees, susceptible to quantification or objective demonstration and to lay understanding.

Id. at 87–88. Noting the widespread dispute as to the validity and reliability of psychiatric testimony and the danger that insufficient procedures existed for protecting the community against defendants who might secure complete acquittal under a diminished capacity rule, the court concluded:

> [T]he potential impact of concepts such as diminished capacity * * * is of a scope and magnitude which precludes their proper adoption by an expedient modification of the rules of evidence. If such principles are to be incorporated into our law of criminal responsibility, the change should lie within the province of the legislature.

Id. at 92.

Other proponents of the diminished capacity doctrine clearly see it as serving broader—or at least different—functions than the general mens rea requirement. Discussion of the proposals of such proponents of the doctrine requires consideration of other factors. Some have urged the rule as a substitute for the insanity defense. S. 1, 94th Cong., 1st Sess. (1975), for example, provided:

> **§ 522. Insanity**
>
> It is a defense to a prosecution under any federal statute that the defendant, as a result of mental disease or defect, lacked the state of mind required as an element of the offense charged. Mental disease or defect does not otherwise constitute a defense.

One discussion of the bill suggests that the proposal was a reaction to what were perceived as overwhelming problems in the administration of the traditional insanity defenses. The discussion describes the provision as "quite simple" and urges that this simplicity, when compared to existing insanity law, is a major virtue. Staff of Senate Comm. on the Judiciary, 93d Cong., 2d Sess., Report on Criminal Justice Codification, Revision, and Reform Act of 1974, 107 (Comm. Print 1974). The proposal is defended in that discussion and in Robinson, Consultant's Report on Criminal Responsibility—Mental Illness: Section 503, in I Working Papers of the National Commission on Reform of Federal Criminal Laws 229 (1970). It is critically discussed in Wales, An Analysis of the Proposal to "Abolish" the Insanity Defense in S. 1: Squeezing a Lemon, 124 U.Pa.L.Rev. 687 (1976).

A third approach to diminished capacity regards the doctrine as a vehicle for mitigating the severity of the offenses for which offenders are convicted on the basis of those considerations which reduce the blameworthiness of human conduct.[d] This view is often based on

d. Insofar as it accomplishes this purpose, the diminished capacity doctrine may also be said to supplement a narrow standard for insanity. See People v. Henderson, 60 Cal.2d 482, 490, 35 Cal.Rptr. 77, 82, 386 P.2d 677, 682

the proposition that the insanity defense unfortunately poses courts with an "all or nothing" decision—either defendants must be found "completely responsible" and convicted of the offenses charged or they must be found totally irresponsible and completely excused through acquittals by reason of insanity. Some proponents of the diminished capacity doctrine offer it as a means of permitting courts to acknowledge the "partial" or "reduced" culpability or capacity of some defendants by convicting them of an offense less serious than the most serious offense indicated by their conduct taken alone. See Arenella, The Diminished Capacity and Diminished Responsibility Defenses: Two Children of a Doomed Marriage, 77 Colum.L.Rev. 827 (1977). Dix, Psychological Abnormality as a Factor in Grading Criminal Liability: Diminished Capacity, Diminished Responsibility, and the Like, 62 J.Crim.L., Crim. & P.S. 313 (1971) suggests that implementation of this approach may involve significant problems. First, he argues that the pattern of criminal statutes in many jurisdictions may not lend themselves to such an approach. In some cases, a defendant who is found not to be guilty of a serious offense because of the absence of intent may—as a logical matter—nevertheless be guilty of a lesser included offense which requires only an intent not disproved under diminished capacity. But in other situations this may not be true. Where it is not true, the structure of the statutes does not provide a vehicle for "mitigating" an offender's crime by convicting him only of a lesser included offense. Id. at 322. Second, he suggests that the doctrine will not provide a means of considering all of those characteristics of offenders that do and should bear upon culpability. The states of mind required for criminal liability are limited to matters of cognition, i. e., the offenders' conscious awareness and thought processes. Evidence of impaired volition, which is clearly important to culpability, would not—as a logical matter—tend to disprove the existence of criminal intent and therefore would not be relevant under a careful application of diminished capacity. Consequently, the doctrine would not be as effective a device for mitigating liability as its proponents urge. Id. at 325–26.

To what—if any—extent is the decision on whether to adopt the diminished capacity doctrine affected by federal constitutional principles? A number of decisions have found a due process right to have evidence of psychological abnormality considered as bearing upon mens rea. In Hughes v. Mathews, 440 F.Supp. 1272 (E.D.Wis. 1977), a defendant convicted of first degree murder in a Wisconsin state court sought federal habeas corpus relief. At his trial, he had offered psychiatric testimony that he had an abnormal mental condition which prevented him from forming the intent to kill his victim; first degree murder under Wisconsin law requires proof of intent to

(1963), in which Justice Traynor described the "purpose and effect" of the diminished capacity rule as being "to ameliorate the law governing criminal responsibility prescribed by the *M'Naughton* rule."

kill. The evidence was excluded by the trial court and the defendant was convicted. The federal District Court found that the conviction violated due process and the requirement that the state prove guilt beyond a reasonable doubt:

> The prosecution might not be able to prove that a defendant acted with specific intent to kill if the defendant could introduce proof to establish that he did not possess the capacity to form such intent. The jury instruction on presumed intent erects a presumption that the defendant *intended* the natural and probable consequences of his acts. Since all defendants in Wisconsin who are determined to be legally sane are prohibited from rebutting this presumed capacity to form an intent to kill, the presumption becomes conclusive. This relieves the state of its responsibility to prove one of the crucial facts necessary for a first degree murder conviction. I hold that this procedure inescapably comes into conflict with In re Winship [397 U.S. 358, 90 S. Ct. 1068, 25 L.Ed.2d 368 (1970), holding that due process demands the prosecution prove each element of the crime charged beyond a reasonable doubt].

440 F.Supp. at 1275. Several courts have also held that bifurcated trial procedures (in which the jury determines guilt or innocence and only if the defendant is first found guilty considers a possible insanity defense) violate due process if defendants are not permitted at the first stage of the trial to introduce evidence of mental abnormality tending to disprove the existence of the mens rea required for the crime charged. State v. Shaw, 106 Ariz. 103, 471 P.2d 715 (1970); State ex rel. Boyd v. Green, 355 So.2d 789 (Fla.1978); Sanchez v. State, 567 P.2d 270 (Wyo.1977). Is the issue more complex than the analysis of the District Court in *Hughes* assumes?

STATE v. SIKORA

Supreme Court of New Jersey, 1965.
44 N.J. 453, 210 A.2d 193.

FRANCIS, J. [Defendant shot and killed Douglas Hooey in a tavern on January 15, 1962. Following a fight between the two, defendant returned to his apartment, got a gun, and returned to the tavern where he shot Hooey. At his apartment, police found a note saying, "The first bullet is for Doug and the second is for Stella Miller." Stella Miller was defendant's former girlfriend. He was tried and convicted of first degree premeditated murder.]

The error asserted in this Court as requiring reversal of the conviction had its origin in one hypothetical question put by defense counsel to Dr. Noel C. Galen, a psychiatrist produced on behalf of the defendant.

Dr. Galen specializes in psychiatry and psychoanalysis. He received his M.D. degree in 1949. In addition to postgraduate work in neurology and psychiatry, he had three years of training as a psychoanalyst. This last training, he said, dealt with psychodynamics on a very detailed and sophisticated level. It taught him that people are a product of their own life history, their own genetic patterns, and that they all react differently under the stresses of their daily lives. As a result of his study and experience, he believes that mental disturbance and disorder, as distinguished from objective disease, are merely gradients, that people range from being essentially normal, perceiving the world substantially in its normal appearance, all the way to marked distortion of the thinking mechanism, and between the two extremes is a rather jagged line which is prone to and open to many variations. * * * Mental illness or disorder in this context is a relative term as he sees it; it is a disorganization of the personality which causes a person to react in a specific way to a specific kind of stress in a way characteristic for him.

* * *

The idea seems to be that every deed, no matter how quickly executed, is never fully the result of the apparent immediate cause, and must be judged according to the probable unconscious motivations of an individual with the actor's lifelong history. Therefore, if in the opinion of the psychodynamically oriented psychiatrist, the deed, when evaluated against a background of the individual's life history, was probably produced by unconscious rather than conscious motivations, there was no *mens rea*, no criminal intent, and therefore no criminal guilt. In his view the conduct must be considered as having been conditioned by internal and external forces quite beyond the actor's control.

[At trial, defense counsel asked Dr. Galen whether, given the facts of the case, in Dr. Galen's opinion the defendant was capable of premeditating a murder. The prosecution's objection was sustained; the following represents what Dr. Galen would have testified if he had been permitted to answer.]

According to Dr. Galen, tensions had been building up in Sikora, particularly since his female friend rejected him. When he was humiliated in the tavern by the remarks about her availability for other men because she had broken with him, and then physically beaten by Hooey and his companions, the tensions mounted to the point where they represented a situation in life with which he felt unable to cope. So he began to act in an automatic way; the manner in which a person with his personality inadequacy would characteristically act. He responded to the stress in the way which inevitably would be his way of dealing with that kind of stress. He reacted automatically in the fashion of Dr. Galen's physician friend when he was cut off by another motorist. His successive actions, walking home from the tavern, reporting the assault upon him to the police, deciding against a criminal complaint, obtaining his gun from its place of concealment in the apartment, putting the extra bullets in his pocket, writing the note that the first bullet was for Doug and the second for Stella Miller, contemplating suicide, test-firing the gun, rejecting the idea of suicide, reloading the gun on the stairway of his apartment while thinking about Hooey and the beating in the tavern, walking to the tavern to "talk" to Hooey, deciding to use the alley entrance in an effort to draw Hooey out that way, and putting four bullets into Hooey after backing some distance from the tavern while warning him not to come closer and advising him he was "liable" to find out the gun would fire if he came closer, and then walking to the Miller woman's apartment still carrying the gun and searching for her, all showed strong elements of automatism. The beating administered by Hooey in the tavern precipitated the disorganization of his personality to the extent that from then on he probably "acted in at least a semi-automatic way, and probably an automatic way."

The doctor went on to say that from the defendant's course of conduct it could be seen that he was acting in an automatic way "rather than being totally aware of his environment, and the situation * * *." Although the state was not completely an automatic one there were "strong elements of automatism" present. He was not "fully conscious of his activities" and not "completely aware" of what he was doing. The stress to which he had been subjected had distorted his personality mechanism. His personality disorder, the kind of man life had made him, when subjected to that stress prevented him from "seeing reality, or premeditating or forming a rational opinion of what is going on in his life." He had been confronted with a situation and reacted with conduct which was his characteristic way of dealing with the particular kind of stress. * * *

In short the doctor opined that the circumstances to which Sikora had been subjected imposed on his personality disorder a stress that impaired or removed his ability consciously to premeditate or weigh a design to kill. The tension was so great that he could handle it only by an automatic reaction motivated by the predetermined influence of his unconscious. Plainly the doctor meant that Sikora's response was not a voluntary exercise of his free will. The stress was such as to distort his mechanisms. During the various actions Sikora took leading up to the killing, which so clearly indicate conception, deliberation and execution of a plan to kill, he was thinking but the thinking was automatic; it was simply subconscious thinking or reaction; it was not conscious thinking. The doctor said Sikora's anxieties at the time were of such a nature that conceivably, his reaction in that automatic way and the commission of the homicide, actually prevented a further disorganization of his personality. The killing, said the doctor, was "a rational murder" but "everything this man did was irrational," and engaged in when he could not conceive the design to kill. * * *

The question now presented is whether psychiatric evidence of the nature described is admissible in first degree murder cases on the issue of premeditation. Defendant argues that it should have been received at the trial on that issue.

In [State v.] Di Paolo [, 34 N.J. 279, 168 A.2d 401, cert. denied, 368 U.S. 880, 82 S.Ct. 130 (1961)] the Chief Justice said that evidence of "any defect, deficiency, trait, condition, or illness which rationally bears upon the question" whether the defendant did in fact premeditate is admissible at a first degree murder trial. But he indicated also that if such evidence was unreliable or too speculative or incompetent when tested by concepts established in law for the determination of criminal responsibility, it should not be received on the issue of guilt or innocence. That is the situation here. * * *

Criminal responsibility must be judged at the level of the conscious. If a person thinks, plans and executes the plan at that level, the criminality of his act cannot be denied, wholly or partially, because, although he did not realize it, his conscious was influenced to think, to plan and to execute the plan by unconscious influences which were the product of his genes and his lifelong environment. So in the present case, criminal guilt cannot be denied or confined to second degree murder (when the killing was a "rational murder" and the product of thought and action), because Sikora was unaware that his decisions and conduct were mechanistically directed by unconscious influences bound to result from the tensions to which he was subjected at the time. If the law were to accept such a medical doctrine as a basis for a finding of second rather than first degree murder, the legal doctrine of *mens rea* would all but disappear from the law. Applying Dr. Galen's theory to crimes requiring specific intent to commit, such as robbery, larceny, rape, etc., it is difficult to imagine an individual who perpetrated the deed as having the mental capacity in the criminal law sense to conceive the intent to commit it. Criminal responsibility, as society now knows it, would vanish from the scene, and some other basis for dealing with the offender would have to be found. At bottom, this would appear to be the ultimate aim of the psychodynamic psychiatrists.

WEINTRAUB, C. J. (concurring). * * *

It seems clear to me that the psychiatric view expounded by Dr. Galen is simply irreconcilable with the basic thesis of our criminal law, for while the law requires proof of an evil-meaning mind, this psychiatric thesis denies there is any such thing. To grant a role in our existing structure to the theme that the conscious is just the innocent puppet of a nonculpable unconscious is to make a mishmash of the criminal law, permitting—indeed requiring—each trier of the facts to choose between the automaton thesis and the law's existing concept of criminal accountability. It would be absurd to decide criminal blameworthiness upon a psychiatric thesis which can find no basis for personal blame. So long as we adhere to criminal blameworthiness, *mens rea* must be sought and decided at the level of conscious behavior.

NOTES AND QUESTIONS

1. It is often said that diminished capacity can only be asserted in a prosecution for a crime which involves specific intent. People v. Gauze, 15 Cal.3d 709, 125 Cal.Rptr. 773, 542 P.2d 1365 (1975) (assault with a deadly weapon is a general intent crime and therefore diminished capacity cannot be asserted); People v. Nance, 25 Cal.App.3d 925, 102 Cal.Rptr. 266 (1972) (arson is only general intent crime and diminished capacity not available). How might such a limitation on the doctrine be defended? In Bethea v. United States, 365 A.2d 64 (D.C.Ct.App.1976) the court commented:

> We are not satisfied that the rule [of diminished capacity] could be confined [to the trial of offenses involving specific intent] * * * easily. Assuming the competency of experts to testify as to an accused's capacity for specific intent, we see no logical bar to their observations as to the possible existence or lack of malice or general intent. Moreover, it does not appear to us that the balance between the evidentiary value of medical testimony and its potential for improper impact upon the trier of fact would vary sufficiently as between the various degrees of mens rea to warrant such an artificial distinction.

365 A.2d at 90. See generally, Comment, Rethinking the Specific-General Intent Doctrine in California Criminal Law, 63 Cal.L.Rev. 1352 (1975).

2. If the doctrine of diminished capacity should result in the acquittal of a defendant, do adequate procedures exist for protecting society from him? Procedures for commitment following a verdict of "not guilty by reason of insanity" would not, of course, be applicable. In United States v. Brawner, 471 F.2d 969 (D.C.Cir. 1972), the court argued that procedures for "civil" commitment of dangerous mentally ill persons were available for use against persons acquitted under a diminished capacity rule. Id. at 1001–02. But the soundness of this was questioned in Bethea v. United States, 365 A.2d 64 (D.C.Ct.App.1976). The court noted that in civil commitment proceedings the burden of proof is upon the petitioner to establish the dangerousness of the proposed patient beyond a reasonable doubt, while a defendant acquitted by reason of insanity can gain release only by medical authorization or establishing at a hearing that a preponderance of the evidence shows he is no longer dangerous. Id. at 92.

3. If it is desirable to provide a means of reducing the harshness of conviction for those defendants who are so impaired as to be less culpable than normal offenders, could this be done more effectively than through diminished capacity? The English Homicide Act, 5 & 6 Eliz. II, ch. 11, § 2 establishes for homicide cases what has come to be known as diminished responsibility. Under this doctrine, a defendant shown guilty of murder is to be convicted only of manslaughter if the defense shows that at the time of

the killing the defendant "was suffering from such abnormality of mind * * * as substantially impaired his mental responsibility for acts and omissions in * * * the killing." Administration of the provision is examined in Wootton, Diminished Responsibility: A Layman's View, 76 L.Q. Rev. 224 (1960). Consider the advisability of the following hypothetical statute:

§ ——. Diminished Responsibility of Offender

1. An offender shall be regarded as being of diminished responsibility if the trier of fact finds that at the time of the offense his psychological condition was such that he should not be regarded as fully responsible for his actions.

2. In any case in which the trier of fact finds that the defendant was of diminished responsibility, the sentencing judge must consider this as a mitigating factor in imposing sentence. A less severe penalty should be imposed in such cases as compared to the penalty that would have been imposed had no such finding been made. In no case in which such a finding has been made may the sentence imposed exceed, in minimum or maximum terms, two-thirds of the minimum and maximum that are generally authorized for the offense.

*

INDEX

References are to Pages

References are to Pages

†